GW01376946

COLETTE OF CORBIE
(1381-1447)
LEARNING AND HOLINESS

ELISABETH LOPEZ

TRANSLATED BY JOANNA WALLER

EDITED BY ELISE SAGGAU, O.S.F.

This work constitutes the reworked edition of a dissertation prepared for a doctoral degree in history at the Univeristy of Jean Moulin-Lyon III under the title of *Sainte Colette: Aspects culturels d'une forme de sainteté à la fin du Moyen Age.*

© Centre Européen de Recherches sur les Congrégations
et Ordres Religieux (C.E.R.C.O.R.)
Université de Saint-Etienne, 1994

I.S.N.N. 1242-8043
I.S.B.N. 2-86272-049-6
C.E.R.C.O.R.
Travaux et Recherches V

Published in cooperation with the Association de Soutien au
C.E.R.C.O.R.
Publications of the Université de Saint-Etienne
1994

COLETTE OF CORBIE
(1381-1447)
LEARNING AND HOLINESS

© Franciscan Institute Publications
The Franciscan Institute
St. Bonaventure University
St. Bonaventure, NY
2011

ISBN: 1-57659-217-0
978-1-57659-217-5

Cover design by Mark Sullivan
Cover image by Lorenzetti (1329) used with permission of
The National Gallery, UK

Library of Congress Control Number: 2010938754

Printed in the United States of America
BookMasters, Inc.
Ashland, Ohio

TABLE OF CONTENTS

Abbreviations	viii
Acknowledgements	ix
Preface	xi
Introduction	xvii

PART ONE – SAINT COLETTE
ACCORDING TO THE FIRST BIOGRAPHIES AND THE FIRST WITNESSES

CHAPTER 1 – CHILDHOOD AND ADOLESCENCE — 1

The Authors and Their Works	3
Review of Texts on Childhood	7
The Parents and Colette as a Child	11
The Narrative Technique	16

CHAPTER 2 – VOCATION AND SECLUSION — 27

Seeking Religious Life	27
Awareness of Mission	39
The Saint before the Heavenly Court	40
The Consequences of the Vision	43

CHAPTER 3 – THE JOURNEY TO NICE AND THE VISIT TO THE POPE — 47

Accounts of the Journey	47
The Interview with the Pope	49
Official Documents and Hagiographical Interpretation	53

CHAPTER 4 – COLETTE'S PERSONALITY AND HER PIETY — 61

Colette's Personality	62
Prayer	68
Devotions	86

Chapter 5 – Marvels, Extraordinary Events, and Spirituality 97

The Marvelous 97
The Extraordinary 100
Spirituality 102

Chapter 6 – Colette's Virtues 109

Religious Virtues and Vows 109
Antithetical Structure 111
Materiality of Signs and Spiritualization
  of the Physical 119
The Function of Suffering 124

Chapter 7 – Eternity in Time 129

Reality Emerges 129
Colette Confronts Eternity: The Story Restored 140

Chapter 8 – The First Enquiries for Canonization 149

Testimony of the "Old People of Corbie" 150
Katherine Rufiné's Letter 153
The "Memoir of Hesdin" 156

Part Two – Colette's Writings and Contemporary Works

Chapter 1 – The Letters 165

Presentation 165
The Purpose of the Letters 168

Chapter 2 – The Themes of the Letters 175

Relationships with People outside the Order 175
Relations with Religious Brothers and Sisters in Her
  Congregation 188
The Inner life and the Representation
  of Spiritual Realities 205

Chapter 3 – The Heritage — 212

The Origins of the Rule of Saint Clare — 212
Some Aspects of the Rule — 216
    Daily life at San Damiano — 217
    Interpersonal Relationships at San Damiano — 222
    Relationships Outside the Monastery — 231

Chapter 4 – The Constitutions of Saint Colette — 235

Structure — 236
Analysis — 239
The Internal Operation of the Community — 240
    Enclosure and Relations with the Outside World — 254
    Relationships with the Order and the Church — 260

Chapter 5 – Colette's Other Writings — 267

The *Sentiments*: Key Ideas — 267
The *Regulations* — 272
The *Counsels*, *Little Regulations*, and *Intentions* — 277
The *Testament* or Colettine Fruitfulness — 289

Part Three – Colette and Her Times: What Became of the Reform?

Chapter 1 – Witnesses of Colette — 303

Relationship with the World — 303
    The House of Bourbon — 303
    Other Houses and the Cities — 310
Relations with the Church — 317
Relations with the Franciscan Order — 320

Chapter 2 – The Reform Movement — 337

Legislative Texts of the Observant Friars — 344
The Writings of Brother Henry de Baume — 355
The Text and the References — 360
Interpersonal Relations and Those with the Sisters — 368
The Moral and Spiritual Picture of the Friar Minor — 370
Works Intended for Lay People — 372

Chapter 3 – The Italian Clarisses of the Fifteenth Century — 383

General Features of the Reform — 385
The Main Centers — 385
   The Issue of Poverty for Italian Clarisses — 388
The Nuns — 393
Two Writers of a "Spiritual Treatise"
   and a Biography — 402
   Saint Catherine of Bologna — 402
   The *Specchio di Illuminazione* by Sister Illuminata
   Bembo — 420
   Blessed Battista Varani — 423

Chapter 4 – Imitating the Model of Holiness — 431

Extension of the Colettine Reform — 431
   Foundations in New Provinces — 431
   Reform in Regions already Influenced by Colette — 434
   Foundations in Spain — 438
   Reformed Monasteries — 440
The Struggle with the Observants — 442
The Colettine Clarisses — 451
   Contemporaries — 451
   The Second Generation: — 455
Reformed, Non-Colettine Clarisses (Except in Italy) — 459

Chapter 5 – Monastery Life or Living the Heritage — 465

Monasteries and Society — 465
The Regular Life — 478

Chapter 6 – Hagiography and History: The Canonization Process — 487

Fifteenth and Sixteenth Centuries — 487
The Seventeenth Century — 490
The Canonization Process — 498

CHAPTER 7 – THE COLETTINES IN MODERN TIMES AND TODAY   507

    The Nineteenth Century   508
    The Twentieth Century   517

CONCLUSION   533

APPENDICES   539

    Synoptic Table: Colette and Her Times   540
    Table of Foundations by Saint Colette   554
    Table of Foundations Made before 1520   555
    Map of Foundations   556
    Map of Journeys of Colette (1406-1420)   557
    Map of Journeys of Colette (1421-1447)   558
    Map of Distribution of Colettines
        in Fifteenth Century   559

Glossary   561
Bibliography   565
Index of Names   599
Index of Places   611

* The maps on pages 556-59 were drawn by André Ponsonnet, cartographer at the University Jean Monnet-Saint-Etienne.

Initials and Abbreviations

A.I.A.	Archivio Ibero Americano
An. Franc.	Analecta Franciscana
A.F.H.	Archivum Franciscanum Historicum
An. Min.	Annales Minorum of Wadding
A.A.SS.	Acta Sanctorum
Bibl. Sanc.	Bibliotheca Sanctorum
Bull. Franc.	Bullarium Franciscanum
Coll. Franc.	Collectanea Franciscana
D.H.G.E.	Dictionnaire d'Histoire et de Géographie Ecclésiastiques
D.S.	Dictionnaire de Spiritualité
F.F.	(La) France Franciscaine
Rg Ben.	Rule of Saint Benedict
Rg Cl.	Rule of Saint Clare
1 Rg Fr.	First Rule of Saint Francis
2 Rg Fr.	Second Rule of Saint Francis
R.H.E.F.	Revue d'Histoire de l'Eglise de France
R.H.F.	Revue d'Histoire franciscaine
SC	Collection of Christian Sources

Acknowledgements

A chain of fortunate circumstances, too long to describe here, led to my interest in Saint Colette, as well as in medieval hagiography in general and its cultural implications. This has taken the form of a doctoral thesis.

I would never have succeeded in this enterprise, no matter how keen I was to devote study to this great fifteenth-century figure, without the constant support and consideration of Professor René Fédou, thanks to whom this work was completed. I also depended greatly on the frequently stimulating advice and valuable insights of Professor André Vauchez.

I would also like to thank those who, whether known or unknown, assisted me with so many different resources, such as:

- microfilms from the archives of the monastery of Amiens held in Poligny (these microfilms were produced, thanks to Professor Vauchez, by a team from CNRS-IRHT);
- documents supplied or loaned by the brothers and sisters responsible for the archives of the Order in Paris, Lyon, Le Puy, etc;
- the generally accessible archives of the Poor Clare communities that particularly helped me or made me welcome, such as Besançon, Gand, etc;
- information provided by other researchers whom I met personally or with whom I corresponded;
- microfilms loaned from the Besançon municipal library (to the staff of which I am particularly grateful for the time they were able to give me);
- unfailing help from my friends throughout these sometimes arduous years.

I owe a particular debt of gratitude to Marie-Colette Roussey, Françoise-Marie Loin, and Jacques Fontana who, day after day, whether close at hand or far away, gave me their time and their knowledge to help me successfully complete this research.

PREFACE

Although Saint Colette (1381-1447) founded or reformed seventeen Poor Clare monasteries in France, Burgundy, and Savoy in the first half of the fifteenth century and was canonized in 1807, she has attracted more attention from story-tellers than from historians, with the exception of one learned Franciscan, Ubald of Alençon, who, at the beginning of the twentieth century, wrote a number of publications about her life and work. More recently, some studies have concentrated on particular aspects of her influence. Hence the considerable interest of this work, undertaken with both sensitivity and insight by Elisabeth Lopez in order to shed light on this important figure. Saint Colette seems truly to have fascinated those around her during her lifetime, and her influence has endured to the present day through the so-called Colettine Poor Clares.

It is not, however, a simple undertaking to discover the true face of Colette and the precise historical role she played. Except for the *Constitutions*, about fifteen letters covering very specific subjects, and a *Testament* (the authenticity of which is still disputed), she left few writings. As the author of this book neatly puts it, the reformer of the Order of St. Clare is "a woman who claims nothing for herself," preferring action to speech. It is not even certain that she knew how to write. But, after her death, others wrote about her, particularly the authors of the two oldest *Lives* – her confessor Pierre de Vaux and Sister Perrine – who left first-hand accounts.[1] Scholars need to find out how to interpret or, more precisely, decode these.

It is this task that, unlike her predecessors, Lopez has begun, without following to the letter the cryptic language of the hagiographical texts. Historians today recognize how important these documents are, but they are also aware of the dangers of searching within them for a true reflection of the lived experience. The actual intention of their authors was to ensure that a personality (known for its merits and eventually its miracles) conformed to a certain model of sanctity honored by the Church at a particular period in history. In her outstanding first part, the author shows very clearly how this bias led Colette's hagiographers to remove from their biographies almost every concrete reference to her work as a reformer, as well as to the sometimes very turbulent ecclesial and political context in which she lived. The image thus drawn is of a sanctity that travels through the world while remaining above it and detached from it.

This critical approach to the hagiographical sources ultimately brings us back to the fundamental questions that historians and contemporary readers must ask. Who was the real Colette? And what is her relationship to the conventional portrait left to us by her biographers? In this respect, the *Constitutions* play a vital role as a collection of customized rules that she developed for the monasteries she reformed. Lopez provides a wise commentary on these.

The status of the Order of St. Clare in France at the beginning of the fifteenth century was unsatisfactory. There were few communities, and those there were had adopted the "Urbanist" rule at the end of the thirteenth century (named after Pope Urban IV who promulgated it). This authorized them to own property. The crises of the fourteenth century and the ravages of the Hundred Years War had caused considerable destruction, and convent life, where it survived, was often noted for its laxity. The value of the current work is that it allows us to enter into the spirit, rather than the concrete

---

[1] Elisabeth Lopez prepared a new edition of the life of St. Colette by Pierre de Vaux, published by CERCOR in 1994.

processes (later to be investigated more thoroughly), of a reforming movement at the very heart of the world of women religious. After a long period of uncertainty over her vocation (first joining a Benedictine community, then becoming an anchorite and Franciscan tertiary), Colette finally decided to enter the Order of St Clare and restore it by main force.

In this respect, her situation is doubly significant. First of all, from the point of view of the history of the female condition, religious or otherwise, the Poor Clares were at that time the only female order not legally dependent on a male order. Secondly, Colette was the first woman to reform a cloistered congregation of women religious. She did this by vigorously restoring the original *Rule* written by Saint Clare herself, which had never been properly applied after her death. Colette's methods appear very different from those of the founder, and even more so from those of St. Francis, whom she claimed, on several occasions, to be following.

Colette was a saint for a time of trials and crises, clearly believing more in the influence of structures and strict observance than in that of charity. In a way that was more Benedictine than Franciscan, she considerably strengthened the powers of the abbess within the monastery, ensuring firm control of the community, but lacking any indulgence for human weakness.

Similarly, Colette's attachment to poverty is demonstrated primarily through a search for a strict, personal asceticism. Even though the friars' quest for alms for the convent was not ruled out, basic resources were ensured by generous donations from the rich and powerful – which explains the princely, or at least aristocratic, origins of almost all her foundations. Her aim was to make the female monastery a perfect society, strengthening the demands of the enclosed religious life (imposing, in fact, an unprecedented vow of enclosure on the sisters). It was as if she wanted to thwart a society that was moving further and further away, in terms of actual behavior, from the Christian values it pretended to observe.

The concept of religious life and of sanctity that emerges from the early texts is distinctly sacrificial. Colette and her sisters intended to bring salvation to the world around them, but not through opening themselves up to its problems and miseries. (There is no mention in her letters of the Great Schism that was then tearing Christianity apart!) Rather, they meant to take upon themselves the punishment merited by the people and their leaders for their immorality. This faith in the redemptive value of suffering and the effectiveness of communal prayer in wiping away the multitude of sins committed by the human race has left its mark upon the life of her order to the present day. Lopez questions whether a spirituality designed to suit the needs and aspirations of a given period and that endures by virtue of the provisions of a rule can remain valid for a very different civilization and culture without a critical re-evaluation of the charism from which it originates. Despite taking us a long way from the Middle Ages, these considerations on the durability of a spiritual model and its repercussions are among the factors that make this scientific and committed work so interesting.

In the final analysis, the meticulous study carried out by Lopez leads to an issue that would benefit from a broader comparative perspective – the reforming and regenerative function of woman in society and in the Church in the second half of the fourteenth century and throughout the fifteenth. There are plenty of outstanding figures: Saint Bridget of Sweden (d. 1373), Saint Catherine of Siena (d. 1430), Joan of Arc (d. 1431), and Colette herself (d. 1447). All fall easily into this framework to the extent that a pious legend – with no basis in history – has the final two (Joan and Colette) meeting and giving each other mutual support.

As for Colette, we still need to probe more deeply into her personal life. Certainly, the oldest of the hagiographical traditions has cast a shadow over the man who was her main inspiration: the "Burgundian" Franciscan (his family originated from Franche-Comté), Henry de Baume. We know little of their spiritual friendship, particularly as he died before her, but his influence on Colette and on her movement is indisputable. Was she a charismatic, inspired figure for him, through whose influence he was able to implement his plan to reform the Franciscan family? Or was he simply a discreet counselor, who, without a decisive role in the development of her project, enabled this exceptional woman to obtain more easily the backing of the ecclesiastical authorities and the support of some of the influential aristocratic families – starting with the Dukes of Burgundy? With no sources to draw on, the question remains unanswered.

We cannot but be aware, also, in reading this book, of the part played by a number of influential ladies – from Blanche of Geneva to Louise of Savoy – in the success of the Colettine reform. We notice, at the same time, that Charles VII never managed to overcome the resistance of the friars at Corbie, who were reluctant to see the Poor Clares established in the birthplace of the saint.

We note, as well, the fierce energy with which Colette sought to keep her movement out of the control of the Observant Franciscans, whose aims were, nonetheless, similar to her own. Undoubtedly this was because, in Italy, the Observants subjected the Poor Clare monasteries that they reformed to the authority of male visitators. Until the end, Colette successfully fought to retain the autonomy of her congregation and even sought to draw in her wake religious brothers who took the name of Colettins. In this respect, she acted like Saint Bridget who, some decades earlier, had founded the Order of St. Savior (approved by Pope Urban V in 1370). These monasteries, governed by abbesses, brought together a majority of religious sisters in complex arrangements with a group of religious brothers. In both cases, it seemed as if the superiority of the woman over the man in the spiritual domain showed that a reform movement or a new foundation had to have a daughter of Eve at its head. At the end of the Middle Ages, would woman become the hypostatic image of the divine? It is a question at least worth asking.

These few lines cannot possibly summarize a work of this size nor even cover all its themes. We simply intend to give a taste of its richness. It will not provide a detailed study of the stages and methods of the Colettine reform nor a thorough analysis of the political and religious forces that sustained it. This would require another book, which the author of this one is the best qualified to write. But it was important – and Lopez has achieved this here – to remove the figure of Colette from the embellishments and distortions that the hagiographic tradition has imposed on her, not for the sake of iconoclasm, but to define better her true greatness as well as her limitations. We must not forget that the very difficult period in which she lived was marked by a widespread crisis in institutions and authorities. This created a vacuum that, in fact, offered certain women from the elite in society an opportunity to make their voices heard.

André Vauchez
Member of the Institut Universitaire de France

INTRODUCTION

The first *Vitae* were written in the fifteenth century by two followers of Saint Colette – Brother Pierre de Vaux, her confessor and first biographer, and Sister Perrine, the reforming abbess's companion in several convents. Since that time, her legend has been enriched with numerous embellishments, attributable to the cultural and religious preoccupations of later editors. Historical discipline gradually developed, forcing authors to use documentary sources. Nevertheless, the focus of the work remained hagiographic, aiming to celebrate the saint's heroic virtues, her qualities as a miracle-worker and the extraordinary nature of her life.

As the values of society developed and moved away from Christianity (particularly from the eighteenth century onwards), the hagiography about Colette became repetitive. The main elements relating to her life, already fixed by the fifteenth century, provided more a necessary narrative framework than a meaningful system susceptible to emulation and imitation.[1]

However, from the end of the 1880s, a series of historical studies and publications began to appear. These witnessed to the interest of historians in Colette's life and work and demonstrated the vigor of her influence on the numerous Colettine foundations of the nineteenth and twentieth centuries.[2]

---

[1] A. Vauchez, "L'hagiographie entre la critique historique et la dynamique narrative," *La Vie Spirituelle* (1989): 251 ff.

[2] These texts, especially the most complete of them, the *Vita* of Pierre de Vaux, were distributed very quickly. Worth mentioning, in particular, is the fine illuminated manuscript made (after 1468) for Margaret of York, wife of Charles the Bold, and the two copies found in the library of Philippe the Good. M. Sommé, "Sainte Colette de Corbie et la réforme franciscaine,"

At the same time, accounts of Colette's life multiplied. These were of mixed worth, some being merely more or less satisfactory compilations of earlier works. Joseph Goulven's contribution (1952) is worth mentioning because it attempts to reconcile history and hagiography and to produce a twentieth-century picture of the Colettine branch of the order. Hagiography remains fundamental, however. Daniel-Rops notes rather maliciously in his preface: "It begins just like a chapter of the *Golden Legend*."

In the end, the figure of Colette remains obscure, partly because of the cultural values of her biographers. There is no doubt that the "difficult times" (as the period between 1340 and 1460 is often called) left their mark on attitudes. It is from this era that the prayer, *A fame, peste et bello, libera nos Domine,* dates.

In 1378, the deposition of Urban VI gave rise to religious upheavals, adding to existing economic and political problems. The Great Western Schism that followed lasted until 1417 when the Council of Constance elected Martin V. The confusion of those years undermined papal authority.

National church authorities, often supported by political power, sometimes tried to take advantage of the situation, with the popes distributing ecclesiastical preferments in order to gain loyalty. Moreover, kings and princes more easily gained control of the Church by styling themselves defenders of reform, expressing their intention to combat the incompetence of clerics. These latter were divided into higher clergy (reserved to the nobility) and lower clergy (often characterized by ignorance and lack of discipline). The situation was made worse by tensions between secular and regular clergy, who quarreled about offices in the University and in the Church and about parish rights.

Within religious orders, various currents also came into conflict. For example, the Franciscan Order was in ferment, spontaneously reacting to the decadence of religious life, and this despite the generally mediocre nature of its members.

Horizons marins — itinéraires spirituels (V^e—XVIIIe siècles), I, *Mentalités et sociétés* (Paris, 1987): 255-64, note 58.

Separate movements originated in Italy, France and Spain, but had no shared links and were not always coordinated or supported by the popes.

Before and during the time of Colette, the Franciscan Observance reform movement, born in Italy, significantly influenced the Order as a whole and enclosed religious women in particular. The "four pillars" of this movement were Saint Bernardine of Siena (1380-1444), Albert of Sarteano (1385-?), Saint John of Capistrano (1386-1456) and Saint James of the Marches (1394-1476), the last two contributing to reform in Eastern Europe. Colette was to meet John of Capistrano and play her own part in these attempts at renewal.

Tensions within the Church and religious orders were manifested in attitudes and cultures. Ways of thinking contrasted with pious practices. We can see a dual current flowing here. Visionary women, such as Bridget of Sweden (1302-1373) and Catherine of Siena (1347-1380) were quick to question the papacy and to denounce abuses. They created an intense spiritual life in their own spheres of influence. To a certain extent Colette shared in this type of sanctity. Some thirteenth and fourteenth-century spiritual masters were at the heart of a renewal movement that became widespread in Europe in the fifteenth century. The Rheno-Flemish mystics (Master Eckhart 1260-1327), Tauler 1290-1361, Blessed Henri Suso 1295-1365 and Ruysbroek 1293-1381) explored paths for the soul's union with God and asserted the primacy of the heart over the intellect.

Those initiating the *Devotio Moderna*, as well as the "Brethren of the Common Life," also contributed to this renewal. They stressed the soul's search for God by attachment to his will and self-renunciation. Turning away from the speculative mysticism of the scholastic era, these spiritual teachers brought a practical mysticism within reach of the laity. They expressed it in simple, moral maxims, such as those contained in the *Imitation of Christ* (which appeared around 1400).

The early humanists represented a more intellectual strand. They proposed to purify the Church through rational reflection on faith and discipline. Thus, influenced by the nominalism of the English Franciscan, William of Ockham[3] (1298?-1349) on the one hand and by Rheno-Flemish mysticism on the other, a gap opened up between faith and reason.

The moral and religious climate was also marked by the "presence" of death. Wars and epidemics shortened life expectancy. Anxiety about personal salvation became acute. Young men in charge of society reacted against the depression of the old. There was a swing between the instinct for pleasure, dissolution, greed, violence and the cheapening of human life and an exacerbated religious sensitivity consisting of bloody penances, spectacular repentances and devotion to the Passion. (This was the time of the "flagellants," who traveled around Europe begging God for mercy.) The Mass was seen more as a memorial of Calvary than as a work of grace. Devotion to the Holy Face, to the Five Wounds and to the Holy Blood expressed a theology articulated particularly around the redeeming sacrifice of Christ and the suffering aspect of the incarnation.

This book, then, attempts to locate Colette of Corbie, her type of sanctity and her role as a reformer within her sociocultural environment. It examines how the portrait of this Picardy nun, born into a typical era of Western civilization, developed after her death. Finally, it explores how the reform continued after the time of crisis had ended and after the urgent situations that gave rise to it had disappeared.

---

[3] Nominalism: philosophical doctrine denying the reality of "universals," that is, types and species. It also denies any possibility in reason of knowing God, unintelligible and free, and separates the domain of the divine, where reason does not enter, from that of earthly phenomena, susceptible to understanding.

Part One

Saint Colette according to the First Biographies and the First Witnesses

CHAPTER 1

CHILDHOOD AND ADOLESCENCE

This study will begin with an examination of the two *Vitae* of Saint Colette because they are the most authoritative documents available. Of these, one was written by a Colettine Franciscan, Pierre de Vaux, around 1447, and the other by a Colettine Poor Clare, Sister Perrine, around 1477. Both authors were contemporaries of Colette and witnesses of her life.

The hagiographical genre of literature, highly developed at this period of the Middle Ages, followed very different rules from those of history. A hagiography is not written to tell a life story in chronological order of its events described in their objective order of importance. It rather seeks to describe the sanctity of persons, the intangible yet undeniable "aura" that shines through their actions and gestures and is revealed as much in the details of daily life as in the major points of their existence. Sanctity is a phenomenon that is both divine and human and is therefore difficult, even impossible, to describe in words. To use a comment by Michel de Certeau, sanctity is "an intuition of the absolute in a singular mode."[1] It is ineffable by its very nature.

The writer of hagiography is not interested in persons and events as a whole. Rather, the hagiographer arranges

---

[1] M. de Certeau, "Historicités mystiques," in *Revue des Sciences Religieuses,* 73 (1988): 349.

material according to a particular purpose: to describe the work of God in the life of a subject.

Criteria for sanctity have changed over the centuries, as have the ways in which the Church describes them. The influence of culture on writers of hagiography and on the audiences addressed cannot be ignored in the attempt to cause the saint to shine out as a model. In this respect, hagiography is a valuable measure of changing attitudes.

In his account of holiness in the West,[2] André Vauchez describes the gradual change in hagiography, especially in investigations for the purposes of the canonization process. It had developed from a catalogue of miracles (or at least of extraordinary demonstrations of the power of the saint) to a commendation of the saint's virtues.

By the time Pierre de Vaux wrote his Life of Colette, this change was complete: holiness had become a "purely spiritual concept, unconnected to temporal realities and the values of the surrounding society." This ever sharper distinction between the profane and the holy is also part of the history of attitudes.[3]

In addition to its method, then, hagiography has its own criterion: moral truth. Hence, facts may be arranged or even invented to make the spiritual reality clearer. The formulae, the images and the scenes are means to express one particular virtue: holiness. Historians in later centuries accuse hagiographers of lying. But they are simply using the tools available to express sanctity, the only virtue in which they are interested.

Hagiographical language therefore has to be decoded, stripped of its literary coating as far as possible to extract the kernel of a saint's real life. In doing this, we will, however, also release a great deal of information about the authors' thoughts, particularly about their representation of sanctity and their concepts of the human being and of life. A *Vita* does

---

[2] A. Vauchez, *La sainteté en Occident aux derniers siècles du Moyen Age d'après les procès de canonisation et les documents hagiographiques* (Rome: Diffusion de Boccard, 1981).

[3] Vauchez, *La sainteté,* 628.

not give us the face of the saint as a series of flash photographs, nor even witness statements about the person's life; it is more of an illustrative analysis.

Identifying an author's contribution and literary construct of the facts, comparing these with other sources (written by the saint or from other documents), and considering the various descriptions given of the same saint, provide us with analytical guidelines. We can use these to make our own contribution to the study of the representation of holiness, a factor in the development of attitudes and religious feelings.

THE AUTHORS AND THEIR WORKS

The Authors

Pierre de Vaux is normally known as Pierre de Rains. We know little about him. It is not even certain that he came from Rheims. The only certain fact is that he was a follower of Saint Colette; but we cannot be sure when he made her acquaintance.

He was a spiritual son of the saint, her confessor and confidant. He was with her until she died. As an active and competent disciple, he was entrusted with making a journey to Rome on business relating to the reform,[4] of which he was a staunch proponent, as witnessed by his letter to the people of Amiens supporting a foundation in the city. As a Colettine devoted to the reformer, a convinced admirer of her holiness, he revered her as a son does his mother.

Pierre de Vaux is representative of more than just himself. He speaks for a whole group of followers, enthused by the memory of Colette. Pierre de Vaux was the "pillar and support" of all Colette's daughters, responsible for sustaining their fervor and unity. He is the spiritual heir to Saint Colette's reform at a time when her originality and particu-

---

[4] P. de Vaux, *Vita*, Ubald D'Alençon, "Introduction," XXIX.

lar character could easily have been absorbed by the main trend of the Observance.

The life of Saint Colette by Pierre de Vaux is more than just the witness of a follower. It demonstrates her sanctity, which urgently needed official recognition so that it could glorify the reform movement as a whole. Strangely, Pierre de Vaux says nothing of this need in his *Vita*. In the fifteenth century, sanctity was demonstrated through virtues, not actions.

Pierre de Vaux wrote immediately after the death of Colette at the request of the "Reverend Father Minister" (no doubt the general minister), clearly for the informative process. One could only hope that canonization would follow fairly quickly, as it had done for Saint Clare (1255) or for Saint Bernardino of Siena (1450). The *Vita* was therefore an official work produced for the Order with the intention of determining the elements of Colette's sanctity and arranged by a literate cleric who knew the criteria of the period.

Perrine is better known. She is the daughter of Alard de la Roche et de Baume, brother of Henry de Baume. Her father welcomed Colette to his château after the meeting at Nice in 1406. This château thus became the first haven and the cradle of the reform. Perrine was born in 1408 during or just after Colette's visit. Entering a reformed Poor Clare convent at a very young age, she followed in the footsteps of her sister Mahaut, who joined Colette in 1408.

Perrine lived for nearly thirty years with Saint Colette in seven different convents.[5] She is, therefore, a direct witness of Colette's life, someone who also listened to Colette's account of her memories. Perrine herself wrote, or rather dictated, her own memoirs to Father François des Maretz, the confessor of the Poor Clares at Hesdin, more than twenty years after Pierre de Vaux, probably in 1471. By then the *Vita* of Pierre de Vaux was already well known and existed in numerous copies.

---

[5] D'Alençon, "Introduction," XXXIV and following for the location of the château de la Baume. D'Alençon locates it in Burgundy (Baume-les-Dames, Doubs).

Her account is obviously reliant on his. No doubt she was too shy to produce an original work. It was entirely natural in the context of the times that Perrine should take refuge behind the authority of the priest, P. de Vaux. It does not appear that she was a prominent figure. Except for a period as novice mistress, she does not seem to have taken significant responsibility in the communities where she lived. She confirms what P. de Vaux says and never explicitly contradicts him. Her silences, however, can also be eloquent.

The *Vitae* of P. de Vaux and Perrine are extremely valuable. Supplemented by the writings of the saint herself and by other contemporary documents, they help us understand a spiritual current that still persists within the great Franciscan family. As the earliest and most complete sources, their influence on the picture of the reformer's holiness is most enduring.

The Structure of the Works

Pierre de Vaux calls his writing a "short extract" or "reconstruction" (§3), professing the "littleness" of his understanding and of his memory in rendering an account of the "greatness" of Saint Colette's life. He describes the content of the twenty chapters forming the work. We have grouped these according to their chronology and the topics covered.

1)	–Childhood or the birth of a mission.
2),3),4)	–The virtue of humility, the virtue of obedience to which belongs observance of God's commandments and of feasts days.
	The start of the religious life considered from the point of view of the virtues.
5),6),7)	–The great vision of the state of the country, the Church and the order that results in departure from the hermitage. The meeting at Nice and the beginning of the reform.
8), 9)	–Virtues of poverty and chastity.
10),11),12)	–Prayer; devotion to the Passion and the Eucharist.

13),14) –Colette, austere towards herself and humane towards others; her sufferings.
15),16),17),18)–Her gift of prophecy; persecutions, special graces, patience.
19) –Her death.
20) –Miracles accomplished in her lifetime.

Perrine's text, a witness statement and less elaborate account, is basically in the form of a sequence of sections describing memories. In fact she follows the same plan as that of Pierre de Vaux, without bothering to reproduce chapters and titles. It is interesting to compare the two texts, not so much for their similarities as for their differences, the importance and value of which should be appreciated.

At first sight, the texts follow a chronological sequence, beginning with infancy and ending with death. A section is added on miracles, common in hagiography, and more specifically in the *Vitae* of Francis and Clare.[6] However, Saint Bonaventure, in the *Legenda minor*, states the need for seven testimonies; and Celano,[7] in the *Vita of Saint Clare*, states unambiguously that the life is more important than miracles, which simply condescend to popular need.[8] He follows this with directives from the papacy.[9] There is no trace, in Pierre de Vaux, of any such reservations or clarifications.

The relative importance given to the subject's childhood is a common feature of *Vitae* in the fourteenth and fifteenth centuries.[10] And from the point in the narrative at which

---

[6] T. de Celano, "Vita prima," § 127-50, 105-14, in *Saint François d'Assise, Documents: Ecrits et première biographies*, rassemblés et présentés par les PP. Théophile Desbonnets et Damien Vorreux, ofm; deuxième édition revue et augmentée (Paris: Ed. Franciscaines, 1981). This *Vita* devotes some paragraphs to the miracles *post mortem*. Pierre de Vaux gives four, according to a now traditional plan; the small number is because of the date of publication, only shortly after Colette's death. Perrine also reports these.

[7] T. de Celano, "Vita secunda," in *Saint François d'Assise, Documents*.

[8] T. de Celano, "Vita," in *Sainte Claire d'Assise, Documents*, rassemblés, présentés et traduits par Damien Vorreux ofm (Paris: Ed. Franciscaines, 1983), 69.

[9] Vauchez, *La sainteté*, 589 ff.

[10] Vauchez, *La sainteté*, 593-94.

Colette leaves her hermitage, biography in the modern sense is of little interest to either of her hagiographers. Pierre de Vaux's table of contents shows this. It consists of a list of virtues. He focuses more on Colette's canonization than on a study of her life and work.

It is only incidentally, then, that these authors provide biographical information. Since the sections on her infancy and youth are fairly brief and are the only parts that generally follow a chronological sequence, we will pay special attention to them. This will allow us to define more closely the function of the narrative in these two authors.

Review of Texts on Childhood

Summary table

PIERRE DE VAUX	PERRINE
Chapter I: How she came to know God, and the graces he gave to her father and mother.	§1: According to Colette herself, her knowledge of God emerged at the age of four. She avoided children's games, had an oratory at home, and loved solitude. Perrine observed this later.
§4: Knowledge of God. There are two references in the passage: St. Augustine (quotation) and Saint John the Baptist. Its fruit: solitude in an oratory at home. §5: Allusion to Colette's love of the cloister, rooted in her early experience of solitude and withdrawal in the parental home. She avoided children's games.	§2: By the testimony of Colette and brother Henri to Perrine, she hid under the bed to avoid invitations to go out with her friends. According to brother Henri, Pierre de Rains and Pierre de Lyon, Colette's conversation "at a young age" ... "appeared to be more heavenly than earthly or human," ... "it is a new treasure of grace and virtue sent from God and given to the world."

§6: She is physically small and still young, but already "her conversation appeared to be more heavenly than earthly, more angelic than human." Her senses were in no way "open or given up to external things." ... "All her thoughts, her words or her joys were made in purity and faithfulness to conscience."	§3: By the testimony of Colette, as told to brother Henri before a "good older woman" to whom she said she owed "many spiritual goods": – as a child, as far as she could, she mortified her body "with plain, limited nourishment." – she slept on a hard bed. – one of her neighbors, Adam Mangnier, a leading citizen of Corbie, took her to matins at the monastery during the night; to avoid these nightly excursions, her father made her an oratory at home.
§7: Everyone believed her to be a new treasure from heaven. Further reference to John the Baptist: as he was the forerunner of the first coming of Christ, she was sent "before the second coming for creatures, to exhort and admonish them to dispose their hearts to submit more surely to the strict judgment of God at the second coming."	§4: A personal memory of Perrine: childhood memories directly from Colette: – Colette calls herself "a poor, ugly creature." – as a young girl, she was "sad and mournful" when she became aware of her beauty; she prayed to the Lord to take away her rosy complexion.

§8: A physical portrait as a manifestation of her spiritual and moral qualities. §9: Her parents marveled at their child, thanked God, believed that she would lead "such a life that by means of her and through her meritorious works, they would obtain the grace of God." Moreover she "showed" them "fine lessons" and gave them "wonderful exhortations." §10: Thanks to Colette, her father helped people angry with each other to be reconciled and helped repentant prostitutes. He provided the latter with one of his houses and provided for their needs. Her mother went to confession and communion at least once a week.	§5: Personal memory from Perrine, received directly from Colette: "Her parents were happy with her holiness and good works." –they allowed her to pray as the Lord inspired her. –through her they hoped to have the love of our Lord, and "obtain remission of their sins." She gave them "fine lessons." –her father was gentle and peaceful: he brought harmony to all in conflict. –he gave shelter to prostitutes who repented thanks to Colette's admonitions. –her mother frequently carried out penances and went to confession "at least" once a week.
§11: Her father was mocked because his daughter was so small. One day, Colette made a pilgrimage "to a church of some saints." There she recalled the event and asked the Lord to make her grow taller. This came about. She saw it as an encouragement to give "good and salutary lessons" to "good girls and worthy women."	§6: The father on his deathbed placed Colette under the protection of the priest in Corbie. On her father's death, she sought religious life, although the priest wanted her to marry.

The remainder of the work contains the following details: §20, §17: She fed lepers.	§7: Personal memory of Perrine: –Colette said that she was born of an elderly mother: around 60 years "of age passed according to her natural span of life."
§49, §50: She gave her own meals or food from her home to the needy and to young children.	This section gives a list of facts relating to childhood and youth. The period as a recluse and the search prior to that for a way of life will be treated as part of the entrance to adult life.
§62, §67: Her mother remarried, which Colette deplored "for religious reasons."	Other matters relating to childhood are given elsewhere in the text:
§88, §94: The mother's devotion to the Passion. Every day from a young age, Colette saw her say "pious prayers of the passion, pleading and groaning. She piteously bemoaned the beatings and torments our Savior suffered for love of us and prayed in great sadness of heart. She preferred the little maiden to hear all the sorrowful words that she said in her heart so that throughout her whole life she should remember and recall them."	§23, p. 219: She gave everything to the poor after the death of her parents. §34, p. 220: On the way to school, she gave her own snack to the poor. §38, p. 230: The mother's devotion to the Passion made an impression on the child.

THE PARENTS AND COLETTE AS A CHILD

It seems that Colette's family belonged to the comfortable middle class. Her father owned several houses and made one available to people whom he sheltered and fed. He provided his daughter with an oratory in his "hostel" or town house. The child slept in a feather bed. A neighbor and friend, Adam Mangnier, was a "leading citizen of Corbie" (Perrine §3).[11] Food was plentiful and varied. As a child, Colette gave her food to the poor: "bread, eggs, cheese, butter or other, better things ..." (P. de Vaux § 50).

Her parents let her be and encouraged her piety. It is of interest to note that she was (according to P. de Vaux §9) an only child. Her mother was sixty years old when Colette was born (Perrine §7). The parents both led "good and honest lives," "in awe and fear of God." Her father, gentle and peaceful by nature, offered to reconcile people who were quarrelling and provided shelter and nourishment to repentant prostitutes. Her mother went to confession and communion at least once a week (Pierre de Vaux §10). She had tremendous devotion to Christ's Passion, on which she meditated, weeping profusely, every day.[12]

As regards the child, she avoided games suitable to her age, say these writers, and even hid under the bed to escape her friends (Perrine §2). She mortified herself and ate "plain food and little of it." She gave her school snack to the poor and, Pierre de Vaux adds, she cared for lepers (§17).

She once went to matins with the Benedictines, helped by her friend Adam Mangnier. In order to prevent such nightly excursions, her father made her an oratory. We can see that, psychologically, she was headstrong and disobeyed her fa-

---

[11] The references to each author are quoted as they appear.

[12] Devotion to the Passion was a well-known feature of the Middle Ages, especially the fifteenth century. As a child, Gerson was deeply impressed by his father, standing with his back to the wall and his arms spread out like a cross, saying to him: "My son, this is how the God who created and saved you was crucified and died." (Quoted by M. Mollat in E. Perroy, J. Auboyer, C. Cahen, G. Duby, M. Mollat, *Le Moyen-Age*, v. III, *Histoire générale des civilisations* [Paris: PUF, 1955], 440.)

ther's wishes in going to matins. He made her sleep in a "high chamber," but the child had Adam collect her. He "made a way and brought her down through a window" (Perrine §3).

Similarly, she ignored her mother, who forbade her to sleep on "straw or leaves." Later on, when her father died, she became the godchild of the parish priest of Corbie and made him too yield to her. He wanted her to marry, but she wanted to become a nun. She took the opportunity of a grand dinner given by her guardian to repeat her request for this. As he refused, speaking harshly to her, the guests rose to the young girl's defense. The priest then gave way (Perrine §12). Note how clever and determined Colette was.

She seems to have had religious formation from "her mistress" (§3), as Perrine says. The term indicates a woman responsible for a beguinage during the Middle Ages.[13]

Colette told Perrine that, since childhood, she had been impressed by her mother's devotion to the Passion (§38), a point also made by Pierre de Vaux, without giving its source.

Morally speaking, she dominated her parents, who, according to our authors, hoped to obtain mercy for their sins through her virtues.[14]

Physically, Colette was pretty, with a rosy complexion, which she successfully lost through praying for its removal. But despite her pallor, say the authors, she remained beautiful, to her great disappointment. This attitude echoes the scorn for the body that had been common among saints since the thirteenth century. Pierre de Vaux adds that she was small in stature, but miraculously grew tall (§11). Her demeanor and her conversation were "angelic."

This survey leads us to some observations. The family environment was very fervent and hence favored the dawning of a religious vocation. It was not an isolated case in France in the fifteenth century, as Delaruelle demonstrates in a

---

[13] M. Pacaut, *Les ordres monastiques et religieux au Moyen Age* (Paris, 1970), 168.

[14] P. Contamine, *La vie quotidienne pendant la guerre de Cent ans en France et en Angleterre* (Paris, 1976), 191.

study of popular piety.[15] Colette attended matins and other offices, thus receiving some religious and cultural formation, although Latin remained inaccessible to her. She was nourished by the liturgy and went to school; that is, she enjoyed the teaching given by the monks at the abbey.[16]

Neither of the biographers mentions the causes of the wars during this troubled period of France's history. It is as if the country's situation and that of its people had no effect on the environment.[17] We must try to understand the reasons for this silence and see if the remainder of the work confirms it.

While Perrine observes that Colette as a child gave her snack to poor children on the way to school, Pierre de Vaux adds "to the needy and to lepers," specifying that she even gave away food from the house: eggs, butter, cheese, etc.

In the first case, we have a fairly common example of a generous child; in the second, we have an exceptional case. Care of "lepers" in the Middle Ages was a heroic work of the greatest charity, as lepers were outcasts from the human

---

[15] E. Delaruelle, *La piété populaire au Moyen Age* (Turin, 1976).

[16] Benedictine abbeys provided two types of education: the school itself for young monks and those considering joining and "little schools" open to children living around the abbey. These gave a rudimentary education, particularly to boys. It may also be noted that, as we can confirm from comments in the manuscripts of the *Lettres*, Pierre de Vaux and Perrine record that Colette read the psalter. Comparison may be drawn with Joan of Arc, who belonged to a more culturally disadvantaged social stratum and lived in the country. But the difference between a town-dweller and a country dweller was not huge. The basic educational principles, mainly religious, were the same – Joan talks about the part her "father and mother" played in her upbringing as regards her "belief" and also by the priest. Joan was illiterate and could barely write her name. As Delaruelle has shown for Joan of Arc, Colette too was a success story for evangelisation of the medieval people, benefiting from the abbey, the cultural and economic center of the community. She demonstrates the fervour of the laity, desiring to lead a good Christian life nourished by meditation on the passion of Christ, which was a widespread devotion among the ordinary people, especially since Francis of Assisi.

[17] Corbie experienced upheavals as a result of the divisions between Burgundy and France. Cf. Dom Grenier, *Histoire de la ville et du comté de Corbie des origines à 1400* (Paris, 1910), 494 and following.

community. This gesture inevitably recalls that of the young Francis, embracing the leper and giving his food to the poor.

Perrine gives her source: Colette herself passed on this memory. Pierre de Vaux gives no source. The structure of his work – the childhood, the list of virtues, the miracles – clearly reflects that of the *Vitae* of Thomas of Celano and of Saint Bonaventure.[18] We might assume that Pierre de Vaux implicitly draws a portrait to parallel that of Francis. He adds a hyperbole, as further analysis will confirm. While Francis met the lepers when he had reached manhood, Colette went to them while still a child. Hence her sanctity appeared earlier and more distinctly.

P. de Vaux does not follow Celano's portrayal of the childhood and youth of Francis, where it appears that the young man was something of a bon vivant in danger of moving away from God. Celano worked from a different perspective. Criteria of holiness change. The theme of conversion had been important in the thirteenth century, but by the fourteenth and fifteenth centuries, it had been replaced with the idea of divine choice.[19] This subject fits very well therefore into the schema that came to prevail at that time.

Pierre de Vaux also describes the miracle of Colette's growth. Her father was the butt of malicious comments because of his daughter's small stature. On a pilgrimage to a church, the child prayed to the Lord to make her grow. The prayer was granted at once. This encouraged Colette to give religious instruction to other young girls and to ladies.

Once again, the sources for these accounts are not given. One of the two events is unusual; the other is miraculous. The physical body is a sign of what is moral and spiritual. Thus her beautiful body and face revealed Colette's inner, spiritual beauty. The "miracle" of her change of size may be seen as a sign of her maturity, her spiritual "growth." In a way, it gave her "permission" to teach women older than herself.

Pierre de Vaux emphasizes the marvelous in his account. For example, he depicts Colette's social position as being very

---

[18] P. De Vaux, *Vita*, U. D'Alençon, "Introduction," XXX.
[19] Vauchez, *La sainteté*, 590 ff.

comfortable. In fact, her father was only the abbey carpenter. The family's financial situation would not actually have been as the author suggests (owning several houses). The alms distributed to the poor (§50) are similar to those given by Clare, the child of a rich and noble family: "Spontaneously she opened her hand to the poor, using her wealth to relieve the misery of many," observes Thomas of Celano, borrowing from the book of Proverbs (31:20).

Pierre de Vaux thus uses particular elements to indicate a comfortable position in society, where early saintliness, marked by divine interventions, could blossom. Comparing the elements chosen by P. de Vaux with those used by Perrine reveals contradictions between the two. These are seen mainly in the relationship between parents and child and in the spiritual portrait given of Colette.

For Pierre de Vaux (§9), the child's sanctity reflects back on her parents. According to Perrine (and curiously enough, P. de Vaux also says this), Colette herself states that her mother's example deeply influenced her. The mother's frequent confession and communion certainly count for a great deal in the child's own piety along with her love of solitary prayer.

Her pious and gentle parents did remain vigilant of her. However, Pierre de Vaux erases from his account all factors that would tend to enhance the parents and demonstrate the little girl's dependence on them (cf. §3 Perrine). He avoids mentioning Colette's double disobedience (attending matins and sleeping on the ground). Although he says she slipped away, he notes that "she knew in her heart" her friends were going to come (§5). By not mentioning that she hid under the bed to avoid her playmates (Perrine §1), he avoids having to make her behavior seem ordinary. Not giving his sources makes it easier for him to filter the facts and invent others (the miracle of her size). Indirectly, Perrine (§2) confirms this:

> Similarly, I heard it said to my brother called Henry and to brother Pierre de Rains and to brother Pierre

de Lyon that, at this young age, the speech of our glorious mother and sister Colette appeared to be more heavenly than earthly or human. All was composed and ordered, and in her behavior no frivolity or vanity was to be seen. All her thoughts, words and deeds were pure and unsullied, intended only to please God.

Narrative Technique

None of the three brothers knew Colette in her young age. They first met her when she was already a recluse and deduced her youthful qualities from the impression of saintliness she gave as an adult. The vocabulary used is commonplace in *Vitae*, especially that of Clare.

When we compare Perrine's text to the corresponding material from P. de Vaux (§6), we can see that she copies him, with very few differences. Perrine is then indebted to the brothers. She transcribes what she "has heard said." Her source is all the more interesting in that one of the witnesses she mentions is, in fact, the author of the first biography of the saint. He invented a childhood for Colette and established a context for her hagiography. This account was first passed on orally by the brothers to the sisters in convents founded by the reformer herself.

Pierre de Vaux's *Legenda*, composed by order of the general minister, puts down in writing various oral "traditions" conveyed particularly by the brothers of the Colettine reform. They incorporated personal memories of Colette where it suited their purpose and removed others (that Perrine preserved) in favor of inventions that better met their needs.

Pierre de Vaux's narrative technique, clearly seen in his first three chapters, is typical of his handling of facts. References are either explicit or implicit.

The Bible:

Chap. 1 (§4) is the first in the biographical narration giving a reference to John the Baptist. Luke 1 and 7 (§7) refer to John the Baptist in the desert, his penitence and austerity.

Chap. 2 (§15) makes reference to "our Savior Jesus Christ" who "comforted poor sinners."

Chap. 3 (§18) makes reference to the apostles who obeyed the call of Christ and to St. Andrew who heard the call three times.

The Early Fathers:

Chap. 1 (§4) refers to Saint Augustine, Soliloquium, L.I, Chap. 1. Pat. Lat., XL, col 863 on knowledge of God.

Chap. 2 (§12) refers to Saint Augustine on humility: Pat. Lat., XXXVIII, col 441 and to Saint Bernard on humility: Trans. of *Statu virtutis*, Part. I. Pat. Lat., CLXXXIV, col 793.

Chap. 3 (§18) refers to "the ancient Fathers" on obedience.

Saint Francis:

Already noted, devotion to the lepers.[20]

Saint Clare:

Generosity, prayer, solitude, physical penance. We should note that these characteristics are common in the descriptions of sanctity as applied to childhood.[21]

---

[20] T. De Celano, "Vita prima" 17, 203-04; 103, 281-82; "Vita secunda" 9, 328-29.

[21] T. De Celano, "Vita," *Saint Clare of Assisi, Documents*, 32.

Placed at the head of a paragraph or chapter, a quote is given a priori of the analysis or account of the facts. For example, the reference to John the Baptist acts as a basis for comparison. Knowledge of God drew John to the desert and to solitude. Similarly, "she deliberately sought solitude for herself."

According to the value system used by Pierre de Vaux, the reference to John lifts Colette out of ordinary nature and places her higher on the human scale. At the same time, she is presented as a second precursor. (§7).

Key notions, such as knowledge of God, humility and obedience, are expressed in a clerical, technical vocabulary. The terms are abstract and undefined. It is assumed that readers will understand their meaning, that they share a reference system. Pierre de Vaux, writing at the request of the general minister, seems spontaneously to address fellow clerics or at least a class of fairly educated people who share his own value system; hence the frequency of statements given as premises.

Note, however, that the expression, "knowledge of God," attributed to Colette as a child and important here because this is a spiritual biography, does require defining. Pierre de Vaux asserts that four-year-old children do not have this "naturally or concretely." Colette's "knowledge of God" was "more by divine and supernatural grace than by human or natural means." The use of the technical vocabulary of spiritual language contrasts natural with supernatural and human with divine. The author completes his comparison with John the Baptist by using a negative contrast with ordinary children who follow the natural course of development.

Recall how, in paragraph 6, another set of antitheses follows the same plan: "Her speech appeared more heavenly than earthly, angelic rather than human."

Stylistic devices and processes complete the reference system. The comparison with John the Precursor is an example of hyperbole. The most commonly used expressions demonstrate related processes: sometimes a comparative of superiority is combined with antithesis. A few brief examples suffice:

(§8) "The grace of God and the virtuous life, so strong and fervent in such a young girl" (but strong and fervent with the desire for God).
"She was young in years but old in her ways and honest speech and in her mortifications."
(§9) "Her parents saw that their only daughter had begun "a life of great excellence and perfection."
(§8) "A very beautiful and pleasant girl."
(§7) Hyperbole: many fervent people thought "that it might be a new treasure of grace and virtue that God, for certain reasons of which they were ignorant, had newly given to the world."

A semantic field making reference to an exceptional feature:

(§9) "A special grace that God had made for them [the parents] to have given such a noble treasure."
(§8) God gave her "abundance of grace and virtues within, so it pleased him to endow her with graces externally."

Expressions covering all qualitative and temporal matters:

(§5) Her virtuous state "was not only for her childhood but for her whole life."
(§6) "In all her behavior, no frivolity or vanity could be seen."
Chap. 2 (§12) "Marvelously pure and unsullied in her conscience."

An adverb used about miracles, expressing how quickly they followed upon Colette's prayers, evidence of her "effectiveness" with God.

(§8) Her beauty was an affliction to her, and she asked God "if he willed, to take it from her ... and forthwith her rosy coloring was taken away completely."

(§11) Colette prayed to God about her small stature, and "as soon as her prayer ended she found she had grown."

From the portrait of her childhood, then, the basic elements of the typology of sainthood were established.

Stylistic devices, technical, clerical vocabulary, the frequency of a particular type of overall process are the linguistic means for translating basic representations of sanctity as it appears in Pierre de Vaux. Its excellence is inseparable from its counterpart: *contemptus mundi* (contempt for the world). In monastic circles, this was a constant theme throughout the Middle Ages, and gradually it came to dominate the preaching directed at all Christian people.

This theme emerges in many places. In paragraph four, the comparison with John the Baptist includes one of its components. The precursor's departure for the desert results not from a call of the Spirit but from a desire to flee the world (by which is meant sin). Similarly, the "glorious handmaid of the Lord began to flee the affected and unworthy things of youth and childhood and to scorn the world and its worldly vanities and pleasures." This explains the lack of chronology in the work and even the confusion of biographical elements. In paragraph five, for example, Pierre de Vaux moves from describing the child Colette's desire to remain "in a secret hiding place" to asserting her wish not to leave the cloister; and, when she did leave it, instead of being "ashamed and shy" as she had been in her childhood, she was "ashamed and an outsider in worldly society" (§4).

In his *Vita of Saint Clare*, Thomas de Celano wrote (§4): "[She] gradually prepared for her future enclosed life" and further on: "She considered that the changing appearance of worldly beauty was to be condemned: her anointing by the Spirit had taught her to scorn what is not scorned here." Celano carefully handles a spiritual development where P. de Vaux sees a starting point.

The aspect of predestination in the life of a saint was a given during the period from the thirteenth to the fifteenth centuries. Flight was demonstrated by the search for "certain secret places, such as beneath a bed or elsewhere until they had all departed." We understand the tendency to present fairly ordinary facts by changing their meaning. Embedded in a particular form of speech, a fact can become a sign of a religious attitude, of a separation from the world.

The old monastic theme takes over religious discourse. The misfortunes of the era strengthen the pessimism of the priests, who provide moral discourse about a world that seems to be coming apart. This assumes a concept of sanctity that features one of the elements we have been considering: flight from a sinful world. P. de Vaux asserts that Colette, being a child, cannot seek the desert. The monastic cell and, prior to that, a place hidden from others within the parental home had to replace it.

This fleeing the world is precisely counter to the movement of the Incarnation in which God comes to live among human beings. A saint is profoundly alone. When Colette addresses others, including her parents, it is to give them "fine exhortations" (§9), so that God should be "understood, feared and loved" by all (§6). In such "good and salutary lessons," she asks everyone to "flee from worldly pleasure, to hate the delights of the flesh, to abominate corporeal delectation" (§11). The spiritual world and the human world are separated. It is impossible to save the human world except by fleeing from it and converting it from outside. In this, the old doctrine of Manichaeism reappears, which opposes body and spirit, God and humanity, and confuses the various meanings of the Johannine term "world."

A saint seems human only by appearance (§7). The salvation he or she brings is duplicated by a "millenarianism" typical of the period. God's judgment is nigh because of "enormous sins." God is angry; the Virgin has scarcely been able to hold back the arm of her Son; the time has come for punishment, but not for the second coming of Christ. In this scenario, a saint must rescue as many converted sinners as possible. Once they are redeemed, they will escape the dies irae. This critical period precedes a thousand years of earthly peace before the final judgment. The imminent end of the world is a typical theme of preaching at this time. We see it in Vincent Ferrier, who met Colette at Besançon.[22] Such themes are taken literally and pushed to the extreme.

The physical, real world is, then, only a sign of the invisible. The spiritual world, on the other hand, is filled with materiality. Everything that happens is as if each component in the picture of the world, a world of appearances and of evil, has a precise counterpart in the invisible world, the spiritual essence of which is in fact very material.

A saint, "preordained" (§12) by God, is set apart from childhood. This very "special" humanity (a common expression) seems to be free from original sin. While not explicity stated, all the elements of a saint's human nature promote its exceptional quality to an extreme degree. This exceptionality is not the result of a gradual transformation by grace, but is a basic factor, almost from the womb. Thus the idea of time is absent in the development of sanctity and human personality. The childhood period does not interest Pierre de Vaux as a beginning. Rather it is a proof of predestination.

The biography cannot be considered in temporal terms. This may be one of the fundamental reasons for the misconceptions about chronology in stories of the lives of the saints. No doubt this device was long used in a type of writing that was at the same time literary and "historical," since texts of this kind became accounts of real facts. But the same device appears in a different narrative framework, e.g. in the *Golden Legend*, rightly considered to be a basic model for medieval hagiography. The marvelous and the timeless abound in stories of long ago saints, where only some main events, often a description of the end of the life, are told. For more recent saints, however, such as Saint Louis or Saint Thomas Aquinas,[23] the narrative structure, though brief, follows the chronology; and the marvelous, given less space, allows room

---

[22] P. Fagès, *Histoire de saint Vincent Ferrier*, I (Paris, 1901).
[23] J. de Voragine, *La Légende Dorée* (Paris, 1920), 323-28.

for an account of historical facts. The same applies to the *Vitae* of Francis and Clare of Assisi.

Pierre de Vaux brings this sense of timelessness into his treatment of Colette, as was the general practice of the time.[24] By contrast, Illuminata Bembo, biographer and companion of Catherine of Bologna, places Catherine in her socio-cultural setting. It is true that the nun is of noble birth; nevertheless her roots are clearly indicated.[25]

In summary, this chapter devoted mainly to Colette's childhood gives us little information about the early period of her life. However, in the way it represents sanctity, it provides some important information, as we have just shown. This enables us to define more clearly the concept of sanctity and how it functioned in Church and society at that time.

Another point should be made about this. As is common in hagiography, Pierre de Vaux does not dwell on the prophetic function of the precursor, other than to proclaim the advent of the Messiah. In this context, it becomes millenarianism.[26]

Comparison with the Precursor might naturally encourage the biographer to exploit this avenue. However, he does not do it in the first chapter. The rest of the work might confirm this initial observation or not. In any event, we need to investigate the content of the prophetic function and its meaning as it is touched on in this initial chapter.

Perrine's account combines direct and indirect witness. (Sections 1 to 5 correspond with Chapter 1 in Pierre de Vaux). Preference is given to procedures for testing information:

> ... I have seen and also I have heard and experienced many times the holy, honorable life and conversation ...

---

[24] Vauchez, *La sainteté,* general conclusion, 625 ff.
[25] I. Bembo, *Specchio di Illuminazione, vita di Santa Catarina da Bologna*, 1787, Edizione divulgata a cure delle clarisse del Corpus Domini da Ferrare, collana serafica, I (Ferrare, 1975).
[26] A. Vauchez, "Les pouvoirs informels dans l'Église aux derniers siècles du Moyen-Age: visionnaires, prophètes et mystiques," *Mélanges de l'École Française de Rome – Moyen Age et temps modernes*, v. 96, (1984), 281-92.

(§1) First of all, I, sister Perrine as named above ... bear witness that I have heard our glorious mother and sister Collette herself say ...

Perrine herself guarantees points made by Pierre de Vaux (§4 and §5): the desire for solitude and the flight from childish games. Perrine adds:

and this she said, in her amiable way, to my late brother Henry, and I myself heard her say it.

and she mentions some childhood memories:

Similarly, I heard it said that our glorious mother spoke in conversation with a good old woman there present, with whom she had formed many close spiritual bonds and whom she called her mistress. (§3)

About her physical appearance, Perrine wrote (§4):

I saw her living as if at the age of (X) XIX to XXX I believe.

Every paragraph begins with the formula "I heard it said," but within the paragraph, the testimony is from others who reported facts about Colette (paragraph two, for example).

From what we have seen, it seems that Perrine's witness does not, a priori, constitute a narrative. The facts reported operate as presuppositions about proofs of sanctity. For the outline of the facts, she follows Pierre de Vaux, but she adds others, as we have seen.

Colette seems to have had informal conversations in the parlor with the brothers, in which she recalled memories of childhood. She also shared these in the presence of her "mistress" and of Perrine, as well as of other sisters no doubt.

Through Perrine, we get a glimpse of a Colette who was not in the least austere, but cheerful ("she said, in her amiable way"). This Colette recalls her childhood games for example and remembers her faithful tenderness for this "old woman," her "mistress," along with people who had been friends since childhood, like Adam Mangnier. The atmosphere thus evoked of her childhood is much warmer. The saint may be seen to arouse affection.

We must pay attention to the part played by friars minor in the witness given by Perrine. They provide evidence about the life of Colette, about her childhood conversations, about her bearing and her purity of conscience. Perrine receives their witness. In her text it has the same standing as that of Colette herself, although we can see one essential difference. The friars forged the legend of Colette's life, and the first ones to hear it were Colette's sisters.

It may be assumed that Colette grew up in an atmosphere that was both warm and encouraging. A kind of aura must have surrounded her, favorable to a particular viewpoint that embellished and turned the facts of her life into "marvels."

It may be noted that in the explicit reference system underlying the account of her childhood, Francis and Clare are strangely absent. No doubt, their first biographers had little interest in this period of life. We see a certain development in the biographical genre, since childhood does come to play a part, although somewhat limited and subordinate, in the idea of sanctity. The childhood period is seen, however, as a vital factor in understanding the adult.

The implicit reference to Francis on the subject of charity towards lepers and the passing allusion to Clare's childhood indicate that the reference system is not ignorant of the founders. However, these references are not seen as particularly important factors in a hagiographical type of biography.

The explicit reference system is different: that of John the Baptist and the Fathers of the Church. We will see later on that Francis plays a part. However, when we consider the form this takes, we must recognize that with reference to the higher types of sanctity, to archetypes (since these are located at the beginnings of Christianity), Colette is basically situated at the highest level of the hierarchy of the saints. Hence she is equal to Francis and Clare.

We should also note that directly linking her with the founding saints suggests that she herself is a founder. We may remember Pierre de Vaux's insistence, repeated obligingly by Perrine, that she is "a new treasure of grace and virtues, sent by God into the world" (§2, Perrine). Her parents simply bring her to birth and wait for their salvation by her merits. It is God's choice to create her *ex nihilo* in the order of grace. In this sense, Pierre de Vaux is firmly established in the hagiographical tradition of the fifteenth century.[27]

---

[27] Vauchez, *La sainteté*, conclusion of III, 615 and following, and general conclusion, 623 ff.

CHAPTER 2

Vocation and Seclusion

Seeking Religious Life

In her youth, Colette passed through a period of uncertainty.

> She fervently desired to serve some good and devout religious women. So, in order to fulfill this desire, while still dressed in secular clothing, she humbly went to present herself at a monastery of religious ladies, where she expected to be able to live before God according to her holy wish. But our Lord, who had predestined her for a state of greater perfection, forthwith showed her that it was not his pleasure that she should reside at this monastery and made her leave there very hastily, not to return (P. de Vaux, §12).

A little further on, the author adds:

> ... she voluntarily and solemnly promised and vowed the three counsels (obedience, poverty, and chastity) with perpetual enclosure and took the third order of my Lord Saint Francis; and in a cell situated near a church where she could hear the holy masses and receive the holy sacrament, she had herself enclosed and shut in (§19).

On his deathbed, Colette's father entrusted his daughter to the parish priest of Corbie. Perrine comments:

> I heard tell from our glorious mother that she had gone to a monastery of Ladies of the order of Saint Benedict ... (Perrine, §6).

However, this attempt was not conclusive. The priest wanted

> oftentimes to have her married off ... but she would never consent, wishing always to serve our Lord in some place of devotion. This did not accord with his wishes ... (§6).

> Still in secular clothing, she went humbly to present herself at the monastery of the religious ladies of Saint Clare at Pont-Saint-Maxence, a monastery she believed would meet her holy desires ... (§7).

> ... I heard tell from our glorious mother that being still in the world, she desired above all things to be a religious; but she did not find a place where she could rest according to her spirit (§12).

Pierre de Vaux devotes a few lines to her search for the religious life and then moves directly on to the three vows she took as a member of the third order. Section 19 seems to assume that she had been a tertiary before becoming a recluse. He gives no details about the first monastery. As the Lord "made her leave hastily," it would seem she did not stay there long, although the duration is not given – a few weeks? a few months? We do not know why she departed, but there was a supernatural reason: the Lord "predestined her" to "a state of greater perfection." The description given of the facts seems to show that it was she who decided to join the third order, just as she decided to become a recluse.

Pierre de Vaux affirms that, just after her initial negative attempts, Colette felt herself chosen by Saint Francis to reform the three orders. She rejected this idea, but decided to visit the pope and ask him to instigate the reform. She herself would serve in a reformed monastery. This would seem to indicate that, even before she entered the life of a recluse, Colette already knew what her mission would be. A more careful study of chapters two and three, however, shows that the chronology is reversed: her seclusion is dealt with in section 21 of chapter three.

Perrine, while following Pierre de Vaux's plan as she does for the childhood account, gives more information and more precise detail than he does. For example, Colette tried the religious life not in one monastery but in two. It may be assumed that her guardian, the parish priest of Corbie, was responsible for presenting her. However it would seem that this initial attempt followed a period of discernment. "After that (the death of her father) she often enquired where she could serve God according to her spirit." And she tells Perrine the name of the first monastery.

After this first fruitless attempt, and as the priest wished "oftentimes" to marry her off, Colette continued to seek "some place of devotion." The next section gives the name of the second monastery, this time the Poor Clares; but "our Lord inspired her that she must not stay there, and thus she returned, without ever going back, as she tells us." Where Pierre de Vaux gives a metaphysical reason (God has "preordained" her to a higher perfection), Perrine gives Colette's own explanation ("as she tells us"). Although such an explanation may seem inadequate to an historian, it at least has the merit of remaining within the scope of simple experience. Section 12 repeats a fact already noted twice before – the difficulty of finding a religious way of life. Perrine specifies that this disclosure comes from Colette herself.

Comparing texts from the two biographers shows that Pierre de Vaux does not mention facts that might indicate a series of experimental attempts resulting in failures. In addition, he does not describe any external influences. Colette always took the initiative, even when choosing the third order. She was in charge of her life because God himself was directing her. Perrine, on the other hand, suggests how difficult it was for her to find her religious vocation, describes her hesitation and other influences (e.g., the parish priest of Corbie).

We complete these few observations by considering where they are inserted into the account. We have seen how significant this is for Pierre de Vaux.

Section 12 in Perrine corresponds to section 1, chapter 2, entitled "Of her deep humility." The chronological account is now abandoned, even though there might still be some useful elements. The search for a monastery where she could be a "servant" is a proof of her humility. This attitude can be compared only to that of Jesus himself, but "our Lord wanted her to be in a state of even greater perfection." In other words, humility is a source of error. Her difficulty in discovering her rather illusive religious vocation was no failure therefore. Pierre de Vaux emphasizes that she felt herself invested with a mission.

The facts are reported in chapter 3, entitled: "Of obedience, and how she was called to the evangelical state." By the way he presents the story, Pierre de Vaux suggests that Colette's call came in stages of which she was aware before they took place. Like Saint Andrew, she was called three times:

> The first was when he gave her this grace in her childhood [that of knowing God]; the second was becoming familiar with him, achieved by calling her to the counsels of the Holy Gospel [the third order]; and the third was when he gave her a clear sign that he wished her to commit herself to the evangelical state (a religious in the second order).

Seclusion

Pierre de Vaux gives some details:

... and in a cell located near a church where she could hear the holy masses and receive the holy sacrament of the altar, in a very small and poor habitation, she had herself enclosed and shut up (§19).

And in order the better and appropriately to implement this, God provided her with a religious adviser from the order of my Lord Saint Francis, a man of good and honest life, prudent and with great knowledge, observer of the rule, ... who with great and very solemn mystery put her into this seclusion where she was and for a long time gave her great assistance and much comfort (§20).

In this seclusion she remained III years and in this space very virtuously she profited and brought forth fruit for herself and for other creatures ... (§21).

Perrine writes (§12): "I heard it said from our glorious mother..." that she

... found no place where she wanted to be. But a notable and good father, a friar minor of the convent of Saint Francis in Hesdin, to whom she made her confession and who gave her many good teachings and counsels from our Lord, put it before her that she should become a recluse in order to serve our Lord well, which was very pleasing to her and to which her spirit was much inclined ..." (§12).

and also:

In a short time the said priest had a small cell built for her, as comfortable as he could, where she could hear all the divine offices, see our Lord in holy masses, and receive the very precious body of our Lord. And when this said cell was completed, the good father, friar Jehan Pinet, gave a very fine sermon on contempt for

Paulette L'Hermite-Leclercq[2] emphasizes the negative reasons for women choosing the life of a recluse in greater numbers than men at the end of the Middle Ages. For poor women, the monastic dowry was a handicap, and the life of an anchorite gave status and affirmed a dignity recognized by all. The biographers state that Colette's humility led her to ask to be received as a laywoman at the royal abbey of Moncel. Without denying this interpretation, one wonders if financial reasons contributed to this choice. Colette, an orphan of lowly social position, probably did not have the money required to enter the monastery as a nun. Pierre de Vaux states that she gave all her goods to the poor. The legacy of a carpenter could not have constituted a substantial fortune.

Other negative reasons include fear of rape, of misery, of humiliation, and of forced marriage. (The latter recalls the plans of the parish priest of Corbie to arrange a marriage for his unwilling ward.) Alongside genuine anchorite vocations, there were numerous women for whom the "cell" represented a way of escaping social constraints. Paradoxically, the recluse, the enclosed woman, could be spiritually and morally free.

The fifteenth century saw a gradual decline in the reclusive life, which became the preserve of women because of the negative reasons already mentioned. Colette is the best known and most celebrated of the true reclusive vocation, which, in her case, remained interior to her mission as a reformer.

The period Colette spent as a recluse, during which she was aware of her mission as a reformer, has a precise meaning for Pierre de Vaux. As a stage in her personal development, it is considered from the point of view of God or as a completed action. From this a posteriori reading, the biographer discovers signs of the work of Providence in the life of the saint. The account cannot, consequently, be seen as an attempt to grasp reality in all its dynamism and its evolution. Bringing

---

[2] P. L'Hermite-Leclercq, "Reclus dans le Sud-Ouest de la France," *La femme dans la vie religieuse du Languedoc (XIIIe-XIVe siècles)* (Toulouse, 1988), Cahiers de Fanjeaux, n° 23.

together historical facts does not in itself produce "meaning." Rather, meaning is a given that allows understanding and the choice of facts perceived as important. From this perspective, chronology and the identification of human causes in the growth of holiness are unimportant in themselves. They contribute only as examples of virtues demonstrating Colette's humility and obedience.

The meeting with the Franciscan friar seems to come later (§20 in the text), after the decision to enter the enclosure:

> She had herself enclosed and shut away. And in order the better and appropriately to implement this, God provided her with ...

The religious is an observant friar, though Pierre de Vaux, records neither his name nor that of his friary. This man presides, however, over the rite of committal to the anchorage. Pierre de Vaux comments here that before that day, "he had given her much assistance and comfort."

Do we need to assume that it was this friar who advised her to become a recluse? The text does not say so, and the analysis of the facts given indicates that Colette is always seen as taking the initiative.

Perrine, on the other hand, gives more precise information. She says it was Colette's confessor, a friar minor from Hesdin, who suggested to her that seclusion could be a solution to her search, since she "found nowhere she wanted to be."

The parish priest of Corbie also played a fairly significant part. Colette needed his permission, in fact, since she was his ward. Pierre de Vaux ignores his existence. The scene described by Perrine ("I heard our glorious mother say") indicates the young girl's strategy for persuading the priest. A few sentences demonstrate his irritation with a ward who wants neither marriage nor a religious life in accordance with the available options. Once the decision was made, however, the priest concerned himself with providing a recluse's cell that was "as comfortable as possible."

Note that Pierre de Vaux does not mention the costs incurred by the priest in building the cell, nor does he mention the existence of a Benedictine abbess. Does not this silence on the part of Pierre de Vaux show his intention to disregard any possible Benedictine influence on Colette, although it was fairly significant, beginning in childhood and continuing until she became a recluse? Up to this point, Colette's life had been governed by the Benedictine monastic liturgy. Knowing of the struggles for influence between the mendicant orders and the old monastic orders, this silence from Pierre de Vaux does not seem so innocent.

Our biographer's method confirms this: he supresses certain facts with particular intent. What he omits is as revealing as what he includes. This is true in regard to his conception of holiness as well as to his understanding of contemporary trends in the Church. Studies show that the phenomenon of the recluse was fairly widespread at this period; every town or village felt honored to have its "own" recluse.

According to Perrine, it would appear that Colette's joining the third order came at the same time as she entered the cell. We have some clues as to the ceremonial procedure used.

When Pierre de Vaux comments that the Franciscan friar "placed her in her cell," Perrine specifies:

> Thus the said priest and his venerable convent, the said good father and several notable persons, put her in the said enclosure. Thus have I heard it said.

She was about eighteen years old, reports Perrine, according to the sisters to whose care Colette gave herself up. She would stay there four years, according to Pierre de Vaux.

While Pierre de Vaux deliberately ignores Colette's relationship with the parish priest of Corbie and the secular clergy, he does include, as we have seen, her relationship with the "observant" Franciscans. This should be noted as a factor when assessing her later relations with the first order. The biographer remarks that the Franciscan friar gave her "many and good teachings, which she held in special remembrance for the rest of her life."

The homily given during the enclosure ceremony was on "contempt" for the world (§13). Pierre de Vaux adds that the friar had a vision in which God revealed to him how Colette was called to "strip away unworthy things" and to "repair seemly things." This vision suggests that the friar's role was limited: he was the chance instrument of a pre-existing mission.

Perrine says nothing about this vision. She does, on the other hand, corroborate Pierre de Vaux as regards Colette's foreknowledge of the death of Father Pinet in Hesdin. This was a testimony received not from Colette herself, however, but from brother Henry, sister Agnès, and the famous "mistress." From the latter, Perrine also has it that the deceased priest came to visit Colette once a year. But while Pierre de Vaux stresses the joy that this occasioned, Perrine notes a reproachful comment: "Colette, Colette, where is the fervor of your seclusion now ...?"

Can we see in this an indication of some uneasiness on the part of Colette about the intensity of her spiritual life and some nostalgia for the period spent in seclusion? Perhaps studying her relations with her sisters and her idea of community life in general will provide something of an answer.

Her daily life was marked by penitential mortifications, listed by Pierre de Vaux. Perrine mentions only an "iron chain with a cross, hanging on her breast, which caused her great pain to wear" (§13). This detail does not come from Colette but from sister Agnès de Vaux and the "mistress." The reformer was perhaps discreet about the penances she practiced in seclusion. According to Pierre de Vaux, these aimed to extingush and mortify "all concupiscent vices and wicked inclinations" in order to render body and senses obedient to the spirit of God. The penitent becomes eager to respond to the movements of the Spirit. The biographer, however, describes in detail the young girl's precocious knowledge of

God, her speech and behavior more "celestial" than "human," her superior virtues making her like John the Baptist.

We detect here an example of the limited nature of Pierre de Vaux's categories of thought. He is using the preacher's commonplaces, the moralist's reflex, which, according to the ascetic tradition, despises the body. Curiously, the fairly standard medieval idea of participating in the sufferings of Christ through such mortifications is not apparent. Distrust of the "carnal" dominates.

Relations with the outside world were not entirely suspended during the period of seclusion. Perrine notes, as regards the news of the death of Father Pinet: "She spoke to some devout women, who remained near her place of seclusion." These "devout women" no doubt included this "mistress." The word "remained" seems to indicate that their presence was more than occasional; there was an affectionate entourage. The silence of seclusion was not absolute. Despite the exceptional conditions that constituted her life as a recluse, Colette was able to live in a psychologically balanced way.

Recluses were integrated into the life of the village or town.[3] Perrine's short observations indicate integration into daily life and human activity, without the added dimension of extreme and somewhat dramatic heroism as cultivated by Pierre de Vaux. To Colette's other works, he adds exhortation and teaching, which she had practiced, he says, since adolescence. A dichotomy separates the world of shadows in which sinners are immersed from the world of God and the saints to which Colette belongs. She tries to draw "poor weak" humans from these "transient things," from vanity and "affliction of spirit."

Perrine does not mention Colette's carrying out such work during her time of seclusion. However, she does follow Pierre de Vaux in describing Colette's zeal for obeying and

---

[3] E. Delaruelle, E. R. Labande, P. Ourliac, *L'Eglise au temps du Grand Schisme et de la crise conciliaire*, t. XIV, vol. 2, dans *Histoire de l'Eglise depuis les origines jusqu'à nos jours*, fondée par A. Fliche et V. Martin, (Paris, 1962), 829, note 48.

ensuring obedience to God's commandments, this section being inserted immediately after the account of her life during seclusion.

One must assume that, here again, Perrine can give no direct witness. As with her physical penances, Colette must also have been discreet about her spiritual activity. Its existence may reasonably be assumed, but there is no evidence for the breadth of detail given by Pierre de Vaux.

AWARENESS OF MISSION

The Vision

It is in chapter five that Pierre de Vaux describes Colette's coming to awarenes of her mission, which resulted in her decision to journey to Nice.

Perrine devotes one section to it (§17). The "astonishing vision" was of "all the states of the church and of the worldly arm." She heard the account of this vision at Poligny from the lips of father Henry de Baume, who told it to the sisters, doubtless in a parlor conversation. Brother François Claret said that Colette had seized hold of an iron bar and could not let it go.

The content of the vision mainly concerned the "faults and offenses made against God, ... and consequently the horrible pains and terrible punishments of each person," without going into further detail. Fear seized Colette, who for eight days dreaded falling into such torments.

Perrine practically repeats the terms used by Pierre de Vaux, in the same way as she does in the chapter on the childhood of Colette. But, because the account has been given to her by someone else, she refrains from expanding on it.

The Franciscan friar's account of the vision stretches to a whole section, with a better-constructed text, more dramatic and marked by movement towards a dénouement. It gives the impression of greater detail because the pains and punishments are shown as a consequence, and the final emphasis in the sentence falls on the last word "punished." The account is then taken up again, after an interval, repeating the words "horrible pains and tormenting grief." The construction allows us to think that Colette had this hallucination constantly before her eyes, hence the dramatic effect, and explains why she attempted to hold onto the bar as a support in her vertigo once the vision was over. The bar is found "suddenly." The more that stylistic effects are missing in Perrine, detracting from the power of her story, the more she tends to quote the "inventors" of these scenes. Without intending to, Perrine makes the text as she has it from Pierre de Vaux sound commonplace. Thus the reader can more easily detect the elements the latter uses in building his story.

Pierre de Vaux also notes that the vision leaves an ineradicable impression "throughout her whole life" – a device already met in the account of her childhood. It shows the author's desire to present the episode as decisive in the saint's life. The enduring result is prayer. Where Perrine notes that she has "heard said" that the reformer asked that three *ave marias* be recited at the end of the office, Pierre de Vaux states that sadness and sorrow resulted in prayers at various times during the day and the night – a dramatic effect here again.

THE SAINT BEFORE THE HEAVENLY COURT

Saint Francis asked Colette to reform the three orders. In Perrine's account, two sentences relate the fact that she aimed not only to reform herself but also the friars Pierre de Rains, Henry de Baume, and François Claret. Jehan Toursiau even claimed that Christ himself appeared to her in person.

Colette, said to be the founder of the reform, is strangely silent about such a significant event. It might reasonably be assumed that, given the importance of the episode in her life, her loyal companion of more than thirty years would have remembered it. It is the friars, however, who are the source of this fact, along with other supernatural events recounted by Perrine.

Pierre de Vaux is not as succinct as the Clarisse. The scene moves from earth to heaven as cause to effect: the state of society and of the Church in this "frightening" vision requires a "correction" which "will be made by the reformed orders that Saint Francis established." One thinks of those paintings in which both heaven and earth are simultaneously represented, most perfectly expressed at a later date by El Greco.[4] The scene refers to a vision described in Wadding for the year 1216.[5]

---

[4] Cf. Chapter VII of this work, note 11.

[5] Luke Wadding, *An. Min.*, I, Year 1216, 253. *Vidit enim Christum vice ingenti succensum, ob intolerande hominum flagita, a Patris dextera exurrexisse ... uno eorum superbos, altero alvaros, tertio libidinosos deleret; Virginum vero Principem, ac Coeli Reginam ejus venerabilem Genitricem, ad illius genua procumbentam sese illi opposuisse, ac rogasse, ne genus humanum tanta clade afficeret: habere se, per quos emendari hominum flagitia possent. Matris precibus ac verbis motum, cui nihil petenti negare potest, substitisse ac petiisse, ubinam essent per quos fieri, ea quae diceret, possent? Tunc humani generis tutalam ac servatricem hinc Dominicum Praedicatorum, inde Franciscum Minoritarum Institutores, ac Principes ostendisse, ac dixisse: Hi sunt, Fili, per quos quassa in terris, et collapsa pietas instaurabitur, ac restituetur. Delnitum pollicitatione Matris Filium continuisse paratem ad feriendum manum, ac sententiam mutasse et jacula deposuisse. Quo quidem divono spectaculo Vir sanctus fiduciae plenus, ac minime ambigens voti se compotem futurum, dum ex Templo egrederetur obvium habuit, quem non neverat ante, nec viderat uncuam, beatum Franciscum, quem, ut socium sibi a Deo ad instaurandam Ecclesiam traditum, injetis collo branchiis pie admodum et cum ingenti laetitia cimplexus est. Tum, quae vidisset et audisset illi omnia narravit, et addidit: stemus simul, et nullus praevalebit contra nos; inter quos mutua, et incredibilis deinceps caritas fuit. Quae quidem, tanquam a beato Dominico visa divus postea Franciscus Praedicatoribus narravit* ["She saw the risen Christ himself, at the right hand of the Father, aflame with an immense fire, because of the unbearable, shameful deeds of man ... he destroyed one of those who are proud, another who was greedy, a third lustful; this revered mother, the true Virgin, noble lady and Queen of Heaven, stationed herself before him, kneeling in supplication, for truly the human race was afflicted by so much misery: that through them, the unbearable faults of men might be corrected.

She stood beside the Mother, who is moved by prayers and words, and who can deny no request, and entreated, "Where are they for whom these things might be done, as it has been said?"

Then, pointing to Dominic of the Preachers on one side, and on the other, Francis the Founder of the Friars Minor, and the noble ladies, the

Francis, in turn, under circumstances of equal seriousness, solemnly presents Colette and asks of her the "reformation of his orders, and consequently the correction of the faltering poor." We saw previously that Pierre de Vaux seems to place her outside the tradition of the order in terms of her relationship with it. This episode does not give the lie to this hypothesis, but rather corrects it: Colette, whom Francis presents to Christ before the heavenly court, becomes a kind of female *alter ego* with a mission that is very similar to Francis's own in a previous age. The difference lies not in the quality of her sanctity but in the nature of the mission – Francis is the founder, Colette the reformer.

In the reference system that contributes to the integration of great saints into the Church's gallery, Clare, though the founder of the women's order, is missing. Perhaps for the friar minor writing about Colette after her death, she is seen more as a Franciscan than as a Clarisse. Is this view not the result of the writer's concept of her sanctity and the evaluation of her work? The general analysis should provide answers to this.

One variant on the vision is given in the evidence of Sister Élisabeth de Bavière.[6] Saint Clare appears in this version. The source of the vision is also attributed to a friar, Henry de Baume. Francis and Clare ask Colette to reform their order. John the Baptist and Mary Magdalene claim her for the "contemplative and solitary life." The Virgin Mary speaks out in favor of the Franciscan order. Is the presence of these latter

---

protector and preserver of the human race said: "O Son, here are those for whom ruined piety on earth was restored and reinstated."

The Son promised his Mother that he would continue to hold in his hand, that he would change hearts and cause arms to be abandoned. Indeed, on beholding this divine sight, the holy Man, full of faith, was seized with great joy, and firm belief, made this vow, as he went forth from the Temple, through which Blessed Francis had restored the surrendered Church, dutifully shouldering the task. At that time, she who saw and heard all this, told of it and added: We stood fast, together, and nothing prevailed against us: among us all, there was mutual and extraordinary love. Francis thereafter related this blessed vision to the preachers, just as if it were from Blessed Dominic himself].

[6] *Mémoire d'Hesdin*, Archives d'Amiens, n° 11, liasse 23.

two saints here a distant echo of Colette's attraction to the eremitical life?

From another point of view, Élisabeth de Bavière's version includes the presence of two women missing in Pierre de Vaux's account – Mary Magdalene and particularly Clare, whose name occurs twice. Here it is Mary and not Christ who decides. Pierre de Vaux has practically eliminated all female presence. Mary plays only an auxiliary role. Reform is a matter for men, which is why Colette must be raised to the highest level. She must not have a female equivalent. The two versions also show that we are dealing with a literary model that is certainly inspired by the text quoted by Wadding for the event in 1216 when Francis and Dominic were chosen by Christ to bring the Gospel to a sinful world.

The Consequences of the Vision

> I heard our glorious mother say that she was thus constrained in her spirit to come forth from her seclusion to do good … (Perrine, §17).

The words telling of supernatural events come from the witness of Franciscan friars. Perrine, for her part, seems to portray an inner conviction in terms of a pathway or a process of discernment. Colette was afraid of being the victim of illusion and went to "all devout people" to ask them for "counsel and advice."

Pierre de Vaux is not unaware of the event, but the evidence seems to him insufficient. First of all, he does not recognize this "spiritual constraint," which assumes a work of intelligence alone illuminated by prayer. What is more, the counsel and advice of devout persons, although positive, did not help Colette make decisions. It was extraordinary events that forced her to consent. Made dumb like Zachary for three days, and blind, she recovered the use of speech and sight when she consented. The theme of resistance to a greater calling with the loss of one of the senses is a feature of hagiographical literature. And as if this were not enough, Colette had a vision of a great tree with golden fruit protecting other smaller trees.

Despite communing with heaven and because of her humility, Colette still felt hesitant in accepting such a great responsibility. It is then that she wrote an "account," a "memorandum," about her experiences. Perrine does not at first mention it, although later on, at the time of the visit to the pope, she notes its existence. The perception differs here as well: Pierre de Vaux, after the set of three miracles, describes it almost as divine revelation: "He gave her clear understanding of all things ..." Perrine describes it simply as a memorandum of what Colette proposed asking of the pope, without referring to any extraordinary circumstances around its composition.

Similarly, "the Lord" sent her, in a "short time" "all manner of people," including Henry de Baume. Everything happened as if by magic. Though Pierre de Vaux mentions "many contradictions and much opposition," it is only to stress that they "could not be overcome in such a short time." Divine intervention was needed: "at once all obstacles were removed and set aside." From Perrine, we discover that these obstacles came from "the priest of the said place of Corbie": he did not "wish to give his consent."

In Pierre de Vaux, the dramatic and marvelous setting of the incidents replaces an analysis of the causes of the mission. Perrine draws on this account, but reduces it to its component parts, removing any sense of a literary creation, no doubt because she believed herself incapable of such efforts.

Implicitly recognizing the clerical culture and her own limitations and constantly concerned about identifying the sources of her knowledge, Perrine throws into sharp relief the presuppositions of Pierre de Vaux's account, allowing us to draw closer to the essential kernel of the true story. She tells us nothing of Colette's secret inner quest or of her uncertainties, no doubt because she knows nothing of them herself and also because she values the confidences of the reformer, gained mostly through the commentaries of the friars, who seem to be the true creators of the legend. However, in the simple account of her own memories, even while relying on the friar's plan, Perrine manages to outline a possible way into the real Colette, stripped of all the marvels.

This narrow path is all the more precious because the topics and images developed by Pierre de Vaux are key to the representation of Colette's holiness.

It must be borne in mind that a saint is a providential being, charismatic, "predestined." He or she is "celestial." Religious orders are given the task of compensating for and correcting the chaos and sinfulness of the world. Reform has a religious and a social function. Sinners must be led to repentance and, above all, divine punishment must be averted. At a theological level, we have a concept of God as an avenger, more Old Testament than New. In this context, the reference to John the Baptist at the cusp between the two Testaments makes sense.

Religious brothers and sisters are seen in a way as elite troops, responsible for stopping divine wrath. Baptism is evidently not enough. Society, despite being Christian in name, is a place of perdition.

No details are given, however, on the political or even the religious situation at the time of Colette (political divisions, schism in the Church). The biographer only alludes to them, no doubt because, at the time of writing, these divisions had been partly overcome. Consecrated women had a part to play, certainly prophetic, but strictly within a religious context and within an order. We do know that there were numerous female figures, contemporary with Colette or before her time, who were able to or desired to play a role at political or church levels. As visionaries, they questioned the highest in society and even popes. They played a part in the quarrel known as the Great Schism.

Pierre de Vaux would have been able to situate Colette in this movement. But clearly, in his view, her activity is more "spiritual" once she becomes aware of the mission. The mystical life seems detached from historical, political, social, and religious reality, even while Colette's actions are focused on reform of the sisters.

Comparing Colette with Joan of Arc might seem obvious to us, and later biographers have tried to do this. Pierre de Vaux's silence on this subject might indicate a deep-seated trauma – the prophetess, the woman who mixed in politics, died at the stake. Pierre de Vaux's writings certainly date from 1447 and Joan of Arc seems to have been rehabilitated at a much later date. The woman who had visions and heard voices, who took action in her own time, was condemned by the clergy. It seemed opportune to avoid such dangerous paths with Colette and rather to stress "orison and prayer" as the essential work of consecrated women. Her sanctity found its equivalent only in Francis of Assisi and other great figures from the origins of Christianity and not in Clare, whose order she was to reform.[7]

---

[7] Nonetheless, in 1446 it was possible to compare Joan of Arc restoring the Kingdom to the Virgin Mary restoring the "human condition," cf. R. Fédou, "Jeanne d'Arc vue de Lyon," *Horizons marins-Itinéraires spirituels*, 1: *Mentalités et Sociétés*, 43-54.

CHAPTER 3

THE JOURNEY TO NICE AND THE VISIT TO THE POPE

ACCOUNTS OF THE JOURNEY

The decision to go and see the pope followed acceptance of the mission. According to chapter II of Pierre de Vaux, while the recluse felt herself under obligation to Saint Francis, she considered an appeal to the pope to be a simple call to the reform in which she herself wished only to be a "servant." She would live "near the reformed monastery." Pierre de Vaux appears to be unaware that she does not need the pope's permission to be a servant. He is concerned only with her humility, which is the subject of his chapter.

God continues to act directly on people and events. As if in a play, there are forces that oppose the good will of God and of Colette. But God is the stronger. All the difficulties that "human means alone could not have removed in so short a time" disappear abruptly. In this struggle between Good and Evil, Colette, at the start of her mission, is given powerful help from those sent by God – a sign that the cause she championed was divine. The Baronne de Brisay, along with the pope, faced with the wild behavior of the ambassadress, interpreted it as tangible evidence of the action of God.[1] The interest of the modern reader is held by the social origins of

---

[1] P. De Vaux, §36. She is persecuted by "hell's enemy": "he caused her to show disordered behavior and unseemly mien, so that right and honest

the characters. These are the nobles whom Pierre de Vaux, elsewhere so meager in detail, identifies by their titles. The clergy come first with brother Henry de Baume at the head of the list.

The material preparations for the visit to Nice and the journey there are funded by Madame de Brisay, "diplomatically" thanks to the ambassadress who is getting ready for the meeting. There is a paradox here between the "marvelous" character of the story as it is told and the practical realism that governed the meeting with the pope. The narrative reconstructs reality to emphasize the *deus ex machina* and the one God has chosen, Colette. While highlighting characters from a Manichean world, the drama accommodates the obligation to honor the noble families who helped bring the mission about. It is no accident that, once more, Pierre de Vaux does not mention the name of the person stirring up "opposition," namely, the parish priest of Corbie (Perrine §18).

At another level, his text raises the issue of the part played by noble families in the Colettine reform. It is not of secondary importance that they are present from the very start of the mission. What are the social categories described in the biographies? What does Pierre de Vaux actually mean when he talks of the sinful world? There are many other aspects to be considered in the thematic study and in that of the work of the reform.

As usual, Perrine writes without any concerns of this kind. She does observe that God was the instigator of Madame de Brisay's arrival in Corbie, but in this context, it is a pious comment arising from faith in God as the source of all things. Pierre de Vaux, on the other hand, writes that he "gave no acknowledgement of her [Colette] and of her holy life and of her holy desire ..."

As for the ambassadress's madness, this story again comes from a Franciscan: brother Henry told of its germination on the "vine" among the Clarisses at Poligny. Anoth-

---

people did not dare to approach her, since she stripped herself completely naked."

er Poor Clare, Agnès de Vaux, a relative of Pierre, also told the story. She must have been one of the small inner circle around the founder, a majority of whom were men. It should be noted that, in Perrine, this episode seems to be included just for its own sake, since there is no mention that the pope saw it as a sign from heaven.

Perrine does not speak of the journey itself. She remembers nothing of significance. But Pierre de Vaux observes that to all who saw her "it seemed that an angel had descended from heaven." Held by filaments of power radiating from above, Colette, while traveling among people, yet remained apart, as if in another nature. Her behavior and conversation revealed it. She preached and seemed in ecstasy. She appeared to float above the ground as she walked and thus traveled long distances in a very short space of time.

THE INTERVIEW WITH THE POPE

Extraordinary Signs

Colette's meeting with the pope is accompanied by extraordinary signs:

- The first is the madness of the ambassadress, already mentioned (cf. note 1 of this chapter).
- The second is the pope's collapse at the moment he saw Colette (§37): "a thing greatly to be wondered at." "And just as he fell, God gave him clear knowledge of who she was, and what she was asking, through which he was greatly comforted."
- The third is the plague, which removed Colette's opponents from among the cardinals in the pope's entourage.
- The fourth may be associated with the other three, even though it is not a direct sign of the divine origin of the mission. The pope seems to have a kind of premonition about his own end. After appointing Colette reverend mother and abbess, he declares: "Now may it please God

to make me worthy to seek and search out bread for the life of this young woman."

Just as the first and third signs are of the same kind, the second and fourth resemble each other, both having the pope as subject. Perrine does not mention the second and states that Brother Henry told her about the fourth, having seen it with his own eyes. There is no way of ascertaining the authenticity of this evidence. It can be said, however, that the pope's prophetic words carry a different meaning in Pierre de Vaux than in Perrine because of the context. Perrine does not record the pope's fall or the plague, thus undeniably removing from the scene its dramatic and extraordinary character. Consequently, in her version, the pope's words can be understood in a more banal way, almost as if he is overcome by humility, perhaps sighing at the burden of his responsibilities.

In Pierre de Vaux's account, the pope's statement closes the interview just as the fall opens it. The plague lies between the two. The meaning is fundamentally changed. The symbolism of the pope's falling as he is faced with Colette's holiness gives his words the value of a prediction about his own end. This raises an interesting question. Pierre de Vaux seems to want to give a veiled hint about the pope's much debated character. He will spend his final days enclosed and alone at Péñiscola rather than ending the schism by abdicating. Colette, holy and knowing the future, speaks to this important man. France certainly was under obedience to Benedict XIII, but the biographer, by using the symbolism of the fall, hints at his own embarrassment over the unhappy situation in the Church. Thus he seems also embarrassed to have to say that Colette spoke to Benedict XIII. Perrine, when talking about the papal city, writes "Romme" instead of Nice. This lapse demonstrates the way memory can play tricks when one is alluding to an event traumatic to a Christian conscience.

The Content of the Meeting

Both biographers describe the meeting, and Perrine credits Colette herself as the source of the reported recollection.

As usual, Pierre de Vaux stresses direct divine intervention, indicating that Colette wrote the "scroll" because, during her seclusion, God "manifested to her [some things] that were necessary to her" and everything was written so accurately that, in reading it, the Pope was: "fully aware of the whole matter and everything he needed to know for the whole religion." Perrine, on the other hand, understands the "scroll" to be simply a kind of memo in which Colette noted "what she understood was required."

Colette submits her request in two parts. Pierre de Vaux and Perrine have the same general original information – the Clarisse follows the Franciscan's text closely yet without elaborating on the nature of the two orders (note the lack of reference to the third order). Colette primarily wants to enter the second order, but she is also seeking "the correction and reform of the orders which Saint Francis instituted."

It is essential to note Perrine's statement, that she heard of the second request "from my good father, brother Henry," not from Colette. The pope's entourage are opposed to it because she appears to be too "young and tender" to face such an "austere, hard and difficult" life. The scene recalls the interview of the young Francis with Pope Innocent III. Again a parallel is drawn with the figure of the great founder without any reference to Saint Clare, who, according to Pierre de Vaux, followed only the rule established by Francis. Clare wrote her rule in 1253, long after Francis's death in 1226.

As we have seen, according to Pierre de Vaux, the episode of the plague influences the pope to give a positive response, causing him to reflect on "the marvelous works of God demonstrated every day." According to Perrine reflecting Henry, a cardinal's speech convinced Benedict XIII. But where Pierre de Vaux states that "he granted her the ii requests," Perrine says only that she "was received into the holy religious life of Saint Clare" and that she "was professed in this order." Pierre de Vaux adds: "… afterwards he blessed her and made her mother and abbess of all the religious women who will commit themselves to the reform of this order."

It should be noted that, at this point, Perrine is reporting nothing at all from her own recollections. The remainder of the facts she reports come from brother Henry: the Pope's invitation to visit his country, the prophecy of his decease, Colette's astonishment at being made abbess, her wish to renounce it, the gift of a breviary. Pierre de Vaux, so forthcoming about the pope's attentions to Colette, says nothing about Colette receiving a breviary that day.[2] Careful study of this breviary shows that it dates from after 1420 (the death of Jeanne de Maillé is mentioned in the list of saints). It belonged to the House of Savoy, probably to Amadeus VIII (the future Felix V), who could have given it to Colette.

A comparison of the two texts and results of the study on Colette's childhood raise doubts about the authenticity of several facts reported by Pierre de Vaux. The most notable of these is the reform of the two orders plus its consequences and Colette being made mother and abbess. The fact that Perrine reports the first, after the account of brother Henry, and omits the latter tends to impose an interpretation different from that of Pierre de Vaux. Colette's request involves a return to the way of life intended by the founder. According to Pierre de Vaux, it makes Colette the obvious candidate to bring about an ultimately successful conclusion.

Pierre de Vaux's text as a whole mixes marvelous events with historical facts. Perrine casts doubt on his account and gives some certainty that we are dealing with a scenario that the Franciscan constructed using all the elements needed to claim Colette as a prophetess and an unusual type of saint against whom no force could prevail.

As the Franciscan describes it, Colette's request for reform of the two orders is exorbitant, presenting Colette herself in the role of reformer, certain of her mission. The pope

---

[2] Some people nowadays dispute the assertion that Benedict XIII owned the breviary. This may perhaps be further evidence of the creation of a legend by the brothers. The breviary, which is presently in the monastery at Besançon, would bear the faded arms of the House of Savoy. The sanctoral list, which notes five or six Franciscan saints, may indicate that the breviary belonged to the order.

becomes nothing more than an instrument to carry out the divine will as expressed by this young prophetess and visionary.

The dramatic construction of the episode reveals a typology reminiscent of another famous scene that the biographer may have known: Joan of Arc's meeting with the "gracious dauphin," Charles. While there are differences, both are petitioners, both are young, both are girls with an unusual mission revealed through extraordinary channels. The authority figure is a dignitary (king or pope) who recognizes God's messenger by means of "signs." In the case of Colette, of course, the field of action is strictly religious, concerned only with the life of a religious order.

Pierre de Vaux's construction avoids any politico-religious aspects, namely, the end of the schism that Colette could have requested, as did her forerunner Catherine of Siena. André Vauchez clearly describes the vitality of a whole female prophetic movement that influenced decisions made by the Catholic hierarchy at the end of the fourteenth and beginning of the fifteenth centuries.[3] The *Vita* of Colette dates from after this female prophetic movement, and biographers of the seventeenth and eighteenth centuries tried to give her a political and religious dimension. Pierre de Vaux, however, distances himself from this approach.

It could be said therefore that his *Vita* marks a return to the kind of female biography that exclusively addresses religious issues. Circumstances, of course, could have influenced both his choices and his silences.

OFFICIAL DOCUMENTS AND HAGIOGRAPHICAL INTERPRETATION

Volume VII of the *Bullarium Franciscanum* contains the papal bulls of Benedict XIII. N° 1004 from the twelfth year of his pontificate is a copy of a bull dated April 29, 1406, writ-

---

[3] A. Vauchez, "Jeanne d'Arc et le prophétisme féminin aux XIVe et XVe siècles," *Les laïcs au Moyen Age* (Paris, 1987), 277-86.

ten in Savona and addressed to Colette Bellecte (alias Boilette) *mulieri reclusae in loco de Corbie Ambianem* [a woman recluse in Corbie Amiens]. It explicitly mentions some petitions ("*petitionibus tuis*") and the pope's agreement to grant

> *facultatem fundandi ... unum monasterium monialium inclusarum ordini*s *s. Clarae per Innocentium IV papam approbati pro te et certis virginibus, cupientibus sub voto altissimae paupertatis virtutum. Domino famulari, in alique parte Ambianen, Parisien, seu Noviomen, dioec.*[4]

The authorization to leave the hermitage dates from August 1, 1406. It is issued by Jean de Boissy, bishop of Amiens, authorizing Colette to enter the Benedictine order or the order of St. Clare.[5]

When Colette left the cell, she had in her hand the bull of April 1406, giving her authority to found a monastery with the privilege of observing the strictest poverty. This was therefore a return to the primitive ideal of the Damianites, since the privilege of the strict vow of poverty was granted by Innocent IV to the monastery of San Damiano and to a few others that requested it.[6] We may wonder if the famous "scroll" did not simply contain the official text already giving her what she had asked for, i.e., "reform" through the creation of a single monastery for poor ladies.

According to the documents, we seem to be dealing with a personal initiative, certainly supported by some Franciscans of the Observance, for founding a reformed monastery. Father

---

[4] *Bull. Franc.*, VII, n° 1004 ff., 342. "... powers of founding ... a monastery of enclosed nuns of the order of St. Clare approved by Pope Innocent IV for you and certain virgins, desiring of virtue under the strictest vow of poverty. To be servants of the Lord, in any part of Amiens, Paris or Noyen dioceses."

[5] U. D'Alençon, "Lettres inédites de Guillaume de Casal ...," *Études Franciscaines*, vol. 19 (1908).

[6] Florence and Prague, in particular. Cf. Clarisse de Nice, *Regard sur l'histoire des clarisses*, v. II, *pro manuscripto* (Paray-le-Monial, 1981), 100 and 108.

Pinet was from a reformed house. Brother Henry de Baume, according to a letter from Colette's companion Katherine Rufiné, was from the friary of Mirebeau in Poitou, which experienced a reform movement around 1388 but which broke up at the beginning of the fifteenth century. There were three branches of reformed friars: the French, Burgundian Franccomtoise and Italian.[7] Because of his birthplace, Henry de Baume very probably belonged to the Burgundian group.[8]

At this point, it seems that Father Pinet, who was having problems in his own monastery, entrusted Colette to Henry. According to Katherine Rufiné, a pilgrimage to Jerusalem, real or assumed, which he had planned before getting to know Colette, revealed serious problems with his brothers.[9] The Franciscan movement was divided over the issue of obedience to the general ministers. Did some of the friars wish to propose a female reform, as there had been in Italy? One might think so, as attempts at reform arose everywhere in one monastery or another. Two sisters of Benedict XIII, both Clarisses, tried to implement a reform in Spain.[10] Hence the Pope's invitation to Colette to visit his own country (Pierre de Vaux §40). He was therefore aware of reform among the Clarisses and was ready to support many such initiatives happening in the Church at this difficult time.

At the outset, the wishes of Colette and the brothers advising her were completely normal in a religious context, and the authorization given in April 1406 to found a monastery was by no means unusual. Why, then, should she travel to Nice after obtaining this bull? The three bulls from October

---

[7] U. D'Alençon, "Lettres inédites de Guillaume de Casal ..."
[8] U. D'Alençon, *Les Vies de Sainte Colette...*, "Introduction," XXXIV to XLIII.
[9] Cf. below, first part, chap. VIII, "Letter from K. Rufiné."
[10] H. Lippens, "Henry de Baume, coopérateur de sainte Colette. Recherche sur sa vie et publication de ses statuts inédits," *Sacris Erudiri*, I (Bruges, 1948), 239. Lippens adds that two years before Colette's visit to the pope, he gave Father Bartolini, general minister, in return for the obedience of Avignon, extraordinary powers "to reintroduce rigor and discipline to the order of Clarisses."

1406, written during her stay in Nice, provide some of the answers.

As regards bull N° 1013,[11] it should be noted that Colette is no longer called *"mulieri reclusae"* but *"moniali ord. S. Clarae"* [nun of the order of St. Clare].[12] The title of abbess is not given her officially in this or in the other bulls. This term does not appear until the bull of June 1, 1412,[13] which speaks of the abbess of the monastery, but without explicitly mentioning Colette. As was often the case, the founder, who may be a lay woman (or man), does not necessarily become abbess, but may appoint her.

The dioceses chosen for the new foundation are the same as those mentioned in April 1406: Paris, Amiens and Noyon. But this text is more precise as regards the possibility of accepting nuns from other monasteries and persons from the third order. Recluses from other places may, with or without permission from their superiors, join this monastery. Colette would not have found many lay companions ready to adopt this way of life, so she would have needed to recruit from among women already committed to religious life but not satisfied with their situations. This did not in fact happen, but the formula used is typical of this type of bull, which is not tailored especially for Colette. The monastery would have a superior who would receive the profession of the nuns and who would have the authority to dismiss or change the friars minor who served them.

Bull n° 1014 of October 15, 1406 authorizes the foundation at Hesdin.[14] Bull n° 1015 of October 24, 1406 allows Colette to have two brothers with her to help in founding the monastery.[15] Bulls n° 1013 and 1014, in addition to confirming the privilege of extreme poverty, also include the detail that it was actually Benedict XIII who received and person-

---

[11] *Bull. Franc.*, VII, 345.
[12] We should note that the Church considers the second order as being the "order of St. Clare," and not of St. Francis.
[13] *Bull. Franc.*, VII, n° 1105, 377.
[14] *Bull. Franc.*, VII, 346.
[15] *Bull. Franc.*, 347.

ally accepted Colette's profession, *hodie* [today]. But the title of abbess and, *a fortiori*, of reformer, was not given to her any more than she was given the responsibility to reform the first order, despite the tenacious legends.

Therefore, the bull of April 1406, given during the time she was still a recluse, did not fully satisfy Colette, although it did authorize her to found a monastery. In October, she received permission to enter the order as a professed religious and to receive religious from other places and orders. She did not have the title of abbess, but being professed with permission to found, she could become the abbess without being explicitly named so by the pope. It therefore seems that it was indeed she who asked to be professed at once in order to avoid having to spend time in the novitiate and consequently be able to take up her position as head of the monastery.

What did she have in mind at this time? A reform of the order? Whatever it was, the documents seem to indicate that she was expecting a return to the rule of Saint Clare, thus joining a general reform movement together with the brothers around her. At the time the pope granted her the foundation, no one could have predicted the outcome. It should be noted that Benedict XIII was not risking much by issuing these bulls in April and October 1406. If the monastery failed, the consequences would be very limited and would not cause upheaval in the order. If the monastery flourished and further foundations were made, he would be seen as the initiator of the movement. In 1406, Benedict XIII's position was already in jeopardy, and countries obedient to him, including France, were pressing him to end the schism by withdrawing.[16] It was to the pope's advantage, therefore, to be seen as-

---

[16] France withdrew its obedience between 1398 and May 1403, when it was restored. But France tended to revoke this decision because of the excessive taxation demanded by Benedict XIII. An initial edict on this was promulgated on September 11, 1406, followed by another on February 18, 1407 on the freedoms of the Church in France, forming a partial withdrawal. Cf. E. Delaruelle, E. R. Labande, P. Ourliac, *L'Église au temps du Grand Schism et de la crise conciliaire*, v. XIV/1 of *Histoire de l'Eglise depuis les origines jusqu'à nos jours*, ed. A. Fliche and V. Martin (Paris, 1962), 92-125.

sisting the reform of a religious order at a time when Christian people felt the need for reform in the Church's head and in its members. It goes without saying that for Colette to be clothed in the habit and become a professed sister meant significant success for her and boded well for the future.

It seems as though nothing was left to chance. Everything pointed to brother Henry de Baume. His noble origins gave him useful contacts and his spiritual orientation led him to create an "observant" monastery for women. It is unlikely that Colette, coming from a fairly modest background and still young and living as a recluse, could have been the initiator of a project requiring such precise application and with such a bold vision of the future.

At the very start of what would eventually become the reform, Colette seemed to be a rather youthful, consecrated woman, directed by the Franciscans. They no doubt believed her to be capable of attempting a return to a stricter, contemplative life because of her human and spiritual qualities.

Colette was no doubt aware of the political situation, as well as that of the Church and the order, through brother Henry and, first of all, through Father Pinet. The latter would have suggested that she try a form of religious life in keeping with Clare's ideal, which would meet her personal need for a demanding life with a radical commitment to the service of the divided Church.

Was Colette's astonishment at being appointed abbess authentic? Undoubtedly not. It is unlikely that the pope gave her this title. Nevertheless, being a vowed religious and enjoying the confidence of brother Henry, the post of abbess of this future monastery would go to her. If she felt, historically-speaking, some real astonishment as a result of a kind of misunderstanding between herself and the pope, this would demonstrate that she was not the originator of the initiative. At the moment, she was under the influence of someone whose guidance she was following.

The documents give us an appreciation of the way in which Pierre de Vaux reconstructs the facts. He reduces the role of Henry de Baume, which we can guess at through Perrine, almost to nothing. He eliminates some of the historical elements from his explanation and uses supernatural intervention as sufficient cause. The behavior of the characters is viewed from a psychological angle: Colette's reaction to the announcement of her appointment as abbess, the pope's reaction to her and his behavior after the profession.

By the time Pierre de Vaux was writing this, the story had already unfolded. He knew the premises, the phases and what would become of those involved. He reconstructed a special moment when something was just beginning, but he did it knowing the future outcome, which for him was already past. The "truth" that he gives to his readers is not historical in the modern sense of the word; it is psychological. He sees in the pope who received this young girl's profession the future Pedro de Luna, dethroned and obstinate. In brother Henry, who was present and active in those early days, he saw the man who would devote himself to the work and remain in the shadow of the little Picardy maiden, who, at the time of writing, was ready for canonization. So Pierre de Vaux told his tale from this perspective. At the heart of his portayal, when Colette received the habit, she already bore within herself the untiring reformer and the great abbess of a new branch of the Order of St. Clare.

Pierre de Vaux reconstructed the truth he knew with the materials at his disposal. What we see as an account of the marvelous was for him and his contemporaries only a way of speaking that revealed God's actions to believers. Problems having to do with the freedom of the individual do not arise with him. Neither is he concerned with the idea of development of personality nor with complex sets of influences at play in the visit to the pope or the beginnings of maturity. In recounting the abbess's work, the chronological markers disappear as if the marvelous and the supernatural, always present from her childhood, were all that could truly demonstrate a sanctity fulfilled.

CHAPTER 4

COLETTE'S PERSONALITY AND HER PIETY

After the visit to the pope and the beginning of her mission, the chronological record ceases and gives way to a portrayal of Colette. Thus, following the schema of Pierre de Vaux's work, chapters V, VI and VII describe Colette's personality and virtues and the importance of the supernatural in her religious life. What portrait of sanctity does the author depict? How far does Perrine match this or deviate from it?

The selection of facts and the way they are presented give an idea of the concept of sainthood in the fifteenth century, one commonly held by the clergy. Our inquiry will provide information in a number of areas relating to what one might call "the chronology of daily life," i.e., life in Church and society, life in the convents, various social types, etc. Is there, perhaps, in spite of everything, some historical truth within a hagiography written in this period?

An historical sense of the account can be found only in the deathbed episode, a connecting point between history and hagiography. The text is nearly identical in the two *Vitae*, and seems to indicate a notion of time that is rather surprising for this kind of hagiographical work.

Colette's Personality

Physical Appearance

Pierre de Vaux describes Colette as an exceptional creature, who bears in her body signs of a way of being unique in the world. Remember the miracle of her height. It is no accident that Perrine places less emphasis on physical details. The physical description given by P. de Vaux forms an integral part of the portrait of the saint. Since she is out of the ordinary, she must have exceptional physical traits.

Colette is, therefore, beautiful, amiable and attractive (§8). Her coloring is a sign of her moral beauty; her deportment is pleasing (§6). "Her manners [were] in no way studied nor abandoned to anything that could injure conscience" (§64). She was so pure that she never awakened the slightest feelings of concupiscence in anyone. On this point, Pierre de Vaux seems a bit hesitant or somewhat contradictory. Later on (§78) he will say that a nobleman, during a conversation with Colette, was not listening to her words but indulging himself in unseemly thoughts about her. Perceiving this, the saint reproached him. This rather forced element in the story is used to prove Colette's "infused knowledge," an example of how she could read souls. There is a whole series of such examples, covering a variety of areas in which the saint exercises her sagacity.[1] She is "so bright and beautiful" she

---

[1] A statement about "Joan of Arc during the rehabilitation process" provides a strikingly similar example from Jean d'Aulon, whom Charles VII appointed to watch over "la Pucelle" and serve as her steward and who gave evidence to the rehabilitation process (the interrogation took place in Lyon in 1456). He reported with admiration "the excellent life and honest conversation at each and every stage from this very devout creature" and particularly the respect she inspired in everyone who came near her, not least himself. "Although she was a beautiful young girl, well-developed ... never through any sight or touch he had of the young girl was his body moved to any base desire ...," R. Fédou, "Jeanne d'Arc vue de Lyon," in *Horizons marins-Itinéraires spirituels*, (Ve-XVIIIe siècles), I, *Mentalités et sociétés* (Paris, 1987), 51 (with reference to the whole passage); see, too, J. Quicherat, *Procès de condamnation et de réhabilitation de Jeanne d'Arc*, IV (Paris, 1947), 206.

seems to have "the flesh of a child" (§57). Similarly, "there are never any unpleasant odors" from her body (§62). The water in which she washes her hands remains "clear and clean" for seven years (§62). In this way, God wishes to demonstrate her purity and clarity.

Fecal matter came from her "with no bad smell" (§61) and "as fine and clean as when it entered her body." The body did not perform its digestive functions. This is a good example of how some facts presented by the Franciscan – and not used by Perrine – belong to a particular genre and are not describing a physical reality. The writer uses them as signs of the spiritual world to which they refer. The spiritual is a way of deciphering the physical world.

Perrine points out, though without so much emphasis, Colette's physical but "holy" beauty, which demonstrates the presence of God in the being entrusted with a mission. This is particularly true when the reformer chants the divine office: "during the divine office her face was bright and dazzling"; "I dared not look at her" (§29, also 62a).

Sanctity and physical frailty are intrinsically combined. Perrine observes that Colette "was very feeble, weak" (§27). She had trouble with her eyes. Perrine adds that she had her feet washed when they were "burning" (§56). Her teeth too burned her "with great pain which she bore." When she came out of her raptures, she had to plunge her hands and feet into cold water (§43). These concrete details, not mentioned by P. de Vaux, seem to indicate circulatory problems and the efforts to soothe them by natural means. Perrine's wide experience gives her an insight into the real life of the "glorious mother," thus providing a better understanding.

Pierre de Vaux and Perrine both report that Colette is ill while traveling, as, for example, on the return from Nice. This makes the scale of her undertaking all the more remarkable. P. de Vaux does not fail to stress this on many occasions. Her physical suffering is out of the ordinary. It is proof of her sanctity and will therefore be considered when we come to deal with her work. Suffering is not something Colette simply submits to. It is desired and sent expressly by God.

Her Psychological and Moral Nature

The portrait arises from the needs of the story, hence the problems in detecting what is authentic. Perrine may be used as a benchmark, but not consistently and absolutely, as our study of the childhood and youth of Colette has shown.

Colette must have practiced a level of hygiene unusual at the time. Without making of it a spiritual matter, Perrine comments that Colette made sure her water had been boiled before drinking it (§62). So it may well be authentic.

At a cultural level, apart from what we know about her attendance at the abbey's "children's schools," it seems that Colette spoke a number of dialects (Perrine §32). During one journey, she and her companions entered a "foreign region," where they met combatants. She spoke to them "sweetly and kindly, and no sooner did they hear her voice than their cruelty softened to love and charity." She was like the "glorious apostles, [who] understood all languages." Elsewhere, it is said that she understood Latin and German and "other languages" (P. de Vaux §176).

As far as her character was concerned, she could be described as both courageous and fearful. "Fearful as a woman of religion," states Pierre de Vaux (§76). The description is of a particular concept of the nun against the background of the protective enclosure. In Colette's case, however, this idea is not entirely relevant since she traveled so much in order to establish her foundations. Its purpose is to show that she traveled only out of necessity, that she took no pleasure in it (she was sick) and feared the hazards of such journeys, a real concern in such troubled times. It is worth noting that there is no mention of her being afraid because of a lack of safety or that it was dangerous for a woman to travel. The criterion is different – she is "fearful as a woman of religion," indicating that the political context is not considered particularly important.

She was also afraid of ghosts, and there were many. This is another feature that it is hard to appreciate nowadays. The appearances of Father Pinet she found comforting, but the ghost of the parish priest from Corbie (Perrine §48) frightened her. She seemed to believe that he was not in heaven, because he made "a very great noise of clanking, like chains." These apparitions continued for seven years. It is suggested that the problems that the priest caused for Colette resulted in divine punishment for him – "a great noise and clanking, which greatly frightened her and the other sisters as well who also heard the noise" (Perrine §55). Different kinds of incidents are mixed together, so it is impossible to discern the personality of Colette without giving due consideration to the supernatural, so tightly intertwined are the worlds of the visible and invisible, the physical and the transcendent.

She is brave in the face of danger during her journeys. Once, when she, her sisters, brothers and their friends were attacked, "she made her brothers and friends leave and go away, and remained with her sisters, prepared and ready to die alone."

Traveling was, in fact, an adventure requiring passage through territories occupied by warring parties, and there was a risk of being charged with spying. Colette was never alone; brothers and laymen, often armed, accompanied her.[2]

---

[2] Cf., for example, the safe-conduct provided by the Duke of Burgundy: sister Colette, going from Burgundy to Amiens. Gand, March 15, 1443 (Copy D. Grenier): "Philippe by the grace of God, Duke of Burgundy.... As the devout and religious person, our well-beloved in God, Sister Colette, of the order of Saint Francis, has explained to us that, in order to populate the new convent she has recently established, built and constructed in our city of Amiens, to institute there her rule and observance, to remain and live there in poverty, and night and day apply herself to offering prayer and praises, and to the divine service, and to celebrate other matters of her said rule and observance she wishes and intends to leave our region of Burgundy where she presently resides, and go to our said city of Amiens and elsewhere in our lands and domains and beyond, to others of her houses and convents, and for this purpose to take with her in her company a number of religious brothers and sisters of this observance whom she has with her in our above-mentioned lands of Burgundy, we order and command and strictly enjoin you our subjects, we beg those of my lord the King and we require all others, that the said sister Colette and forty people in her company, regular or secular, should be allowed, suffered and given leave to come and go .... Given in our city of Gand on the fifteenth day of March, the year of grace one thousand four hundred and forty three. By my Lord the Duke, M. Renberch," quoted by U. D'Alençon, "Lettres inédites

In the example mentioned above, the presence of her entourage serves to highlight the devotion and courage of Colette, who remains alone to face the brigands. The entourage acts as a foil to her.

Pierre de Vaux does not see fear and bravery as contradictory. From his standpoint, these are two "qualities" playing out on two different registers, depending on the virtue to be demonstrated.

In another area, Colette demonstrates charity to everyone, yet excludes from her convents women who have been married. The important factor is not the authenticity of the vocation, but rather the state of virginity, showing its value in Colette's eyes. In the same vein arises her "friendship" with John the Evangelist, a virgin, and her hardened attitude towards her mother. The biographers record that Colette would have preferred to have had a mother who had only been married once, rather than be born of a woman who had remarried.

At the level of her nervousness, tears, cries and anguish seem to demonstrate behavior associated with ecstasy or mystical phenomena. It does not accord well with the self-control needed to deal with hazardous situations.

In brief then:

She is beautiful	and not desirable.
She is beautiful but	she suffers physically, she has lost her radiance.
She is humble, self-effacing;	she is bold, enterprising in her journeys, cultured.
She is fearful, timid;	she is courageous.
She is anxious, nervous;	she is self-controlled, understands situations, mocks at obstacles.

de Guillaume de Casal …", 34-35 (Archives of the convent of Amiens, presently in the monastery of Poligny).

She worries about hygiene, washes, etc suffers with her eyes;	her body is practically incorruptible; she doesn't "function" like other people.
	she excludes those who are not virgins from her order;
She is charity itself;	she is unfeeling towards her own mother.

In the eyes of P. de Vaux, therefore, a saint is able to live in profoundly different and psychologically impossible states. A kind of totality is being sketched out here describing a being who encompasses all human potential.

In the face of human brokenness, a saintly person is seen to be out of the ordinary, of another nature. Perhaps this is the resurgence of an old tradition that views the "mad" person, someone outside the norm, as an inversion of the divine. Dostoevsky's "The Idiot" is a literary example of how this tradition has persisted in the Orthodox Church. It has almost disappeared in the West, replaced perhaps in seventeenth-century France with the model of the balanced "honest man," who eschews extremes. The eighteenth century confirmed this new type of human being, only more secularized. The "vagabond" Benoît Labre presents an interesting break with this rational European endeavor to overcome folly, irrationality and the inversion of the divine. At a sociological level, the adventurer, the "picaro," shows how disruptive types still persist even though established civilization tries to eliminate uncontrollable elements.

In the fifteenth century, a time of upheaval and turmoil, the end of civilization, all options were still open. The humanist in search of a new type of human being rubbed shoulders with the madman in Christ, the holy-hero, the unconventional.

Her Spiritual Personality

Like her moral and physical personality, her spiritual personality was exceptional, all the more so as it was the driving force for Colette's work. It can be deduced, in fact, from her mode of being, from the way she acted. This is why the saint's different ways of operating must be studied separately. For the time being, it is enough to sketch in the main themes of her personality. The biographer's presentation technique is simply to describe external events without, in general, attempting to analyse the interior life.

This fixes the book firmly in the hagiographical genre. It is not a precursor to the theoretical works on the mystical life that will appear in the next century and seems to disregard completely the contemporary movement towards introspective mysticism in the Rhineland.

Colette's spiritual world is described as including ecstasies and communication with supernatural beings such as angels and demons, saints (in a series of apparitions) and the dead. Her nervous system is overwhelmed, particularly at the time of the elevation of the host. She prophesies, cures, teaches, suffers and prays. Like her moral personality, her spiritual personality encompasses all facets and manifestations of the spiritual life. Pierre de Vaux follows the template developed by the Curia that tends to see the entire life as one continuous miracle.[3] The visions were certainly reported in the fifteenth century after the emergence of the phenomenon of mystical sanctity. Later we will look at how Pierre de Vaux deals with these basic data.

Prayer

Chapter X of Pierre de Vaux is devoted mainly to a description of prayer. Its title explains its intentions: "Of the sacrifice of holy orisons, and how these orisons were accept-

---

[3] A. Vauchez, *La sainteté en Occident d'après les procès de canonisation et les documents hagiographiques* (Rome, 1981), 592 and 608.

able to God and profitable for his creatures." The definition of the term "orison" is revealed gradually throughout the chapter. Prayer has two main features: it must be "acceptable to God" and "profitable to his creatures." It is worth noting the "apostolic" dimension of prayer – it is intercessory. The chapter includes a description of the "effects" of prayer. It is devoted to direct, tangible, immediate action. In fact, paragraphs 84 to 93a (twelve out of twenty-four paragraphs; there are two with [a] sections) describe miracles obtained through Colette's prayer:

- She obtains moral or spiritual conversions.
- Armed men or nobles change their behavior, from being aggressive or dishonest to being Christian and charitable (P. de Vaux §77 to §81).
- The high point is either the protection of a castle or the deliverance of a town from besieging troops.
- A father agrees to give his daughter to Colette after initially refusing to allow her to join the monastery (P. de Vaux §92).
- A religious sister confesses her "grave sins" (Perrine §35); (P. de Vaux §86/87).
- She obtains physical or mental cures (Perrine §40/41) (P. de Vaux §93a).
- She revives dead children (Perrine §40).
- She acts on the elements: the water in the well at the monastery of Poligny.
- During her lifetime, people prayed to her when fording a river or in order to reach a difficult place, to cure a horse or to find a lost object.

Earlier paragraphs also include, among other things, accounts of miracles. These will be considered later when the miracles are listed and examined in detail.

Few texts analyze mental prayer. This is enlightening as regards Pierre de Vaux's views. He sees prayer as a kind of tribute offered to God that must be made under certain conditions (which we will look at later). The quality of prayer is measured by its consequences. These show whether God approves of it, making the effects of prayer evidence of the degree of sanctity of the person concerned.

The renewal begun by Colette and the friars, according to this hagiographical testimony, was not rooted in the order's mystical tradition. We recall the works of Saint Bonaventure – *The Soul's Journey into God* and *The Triple Way*. In summary, these works trace the path of the soul to union with God according to classical mysticism, the germ of which is contained in Francis of Assisi: "... purified, illuminated and inflamed with the fire of the Holy Spirit," as he wrote. We find here the so-called purgative, illuminative and unitive ways.

Historians of spirituality note the impoverishment of the fifteenth century. In this respect, the major orders, including that of the Friars Minor, had somewhat lost contact with their origins. Some of their members however borrowed and adapted elements from Rheno-Flemish spirituality. It seems Pierre de Vaux did not belong to the section of the order that subscribed to this movement.[4]

Supernatural Manifestations

Perrine has nothing original to add; she only specifies the sources as far as possible when speaking of manifestations or the effects of prayer. In many cases, she was able to be present, since the prayer often took place inside the monastery; but she reproduces the Franciscan's text word for word in places.

For example, Perrine omits the miracles that Pierre de Vaux puts in his chapter X:

- the lamb at matins,
- the plague in a convent,
- the sister missing from office for eight years,
- episodes during journeys: four in all, according to P. de Vaux (they have this in common, that Colette is injured,

---

[4] Dom. J. Leclercq, P. Vandenbroucke and L. Bouyer, *La Spiritualité du Moyen Age* (Paris, 1961), 53 and following.

is at risk of violence or of being killed in the last journey; she is not threatened directly however),
- the fire in the oratory where Colette prays,
- the collapse of a sister who saw Colette radiant,
- the sun blazing from her mouth.

Perrine omits particular details given by Pierre de Vaux. She does briefly mention the levitation incident, but suppresses the vision of Saint Anne with her offspring collecting the prayers of the saints to help Colette in her work. Perrine adds

- that the abbess of Seurre saw a rose in Colette's mouth,
- that the sisters at Besançon saw angels hold a cover over her bed.

Perrine notes the origin of the testimony given:

- Brother Henry told

    –how the miraculous chanting was heard, which persuaded Colette and himself to sing the divine office,
    –with Brother Claret, of the "vexations" of the enemy of hell when Colette recited the psalms,
    –of several encounters with demons,
    –of the vision of Vincent Ferrier, who saw Colette praying for sinners before God,
    –of the vision of the dismembered child, representing Jesus killed by the sins of humanity.

- The sisters told:

    –of the abbess of Seurre: the rose,
    –of the sisters at Besançon: the angels,
    –of Sister Agnès de Vaux: the levitation.

Perrine repeats almost exactly the text of Pierre de Vaux in other sections, especially those on prayer, litanies, masses, the time of mental or spoken prayer, the meeting with armed men in foreign countries. Perrine claims to have been with Colette.

In the second part of Chapter X, there are two sections that Pierre de Vaux and Perrine have in common:

Perrine (§35) = P. de Vaux (§87)
Perrine (§36) = P. de Vaux (§89)

We stop comparing the two texts at Perrine's section 45. From section 42 onward, Perrine gives examples of Colette's raptures, which may be considered as being associated with her prayer since they arise from it.

Pierre de Vaux finishes up by reporting cases in which lay people pray to Colette (§90/91/93), receive the effects of her powerful prayer (§92, §88) or ask her directly to pray for a sick person (§93a).

Perrine, for her part, tells of the raptures (§37/38-42a to 45), stresses Colette's devotion to the Passion (§38), to holy places (§39), to the cross and to the sign of the cross with miracles (§40/41), to Christ's body (§42). The arrangement of the paragraphs shows that her account does not follow the same order as that of Pierre de Vaux, who reserves two chapters for the devotions, one of which is solely concerned with the sacrament of the altar.

Perrine omits the sections on the laity, no doubt because she had little contact with them. Her examples are mainly taken from religious life. As regards the journeys, she mentions those in which she took part. She gives the names of witnesses who are religious – brother Henry, brother Pierre de Lendresse (for the one hundred stillborn children revived), Colette's niece, sisters. On rare occasions, Perrine gives her own testimony (§41/42/42a, §36, §38): accounts of Colette's own words (§33), the levitation.

She seems to consider that prayer includes the raptures as well as the devotions, the desire for martyrdom in the Holy Land, the miracles Colette performs when her name is invoked (the water at Poligny, the overturned wagon, dead children restored to life).

The sections matching the two parts of Pierre de Vaux's chapter X linger less on details. It may be concluded from this that Perrine implicitly disclaims or shows herself reticent on the subject of extraordinary phenomena; she reports only a few of them. The quality of the text as a whole is modified. In her thematic plan, she follows that of the Franciscan without seeming to understand it very well, since she adds other elements, mixing them up. The very "literary" quality of Pierre de Vaux's text and his demonstrative narration seem to leave her unmoved. She must have considered herself unqualified to replicate this style. She is, however, always careful to report only what she has seen or heard, which allows her to develop an interesting new approach to the materials used.

The friars play an ever more important part in these stories. While Colette seems to have been very discreet about the extraordinary phenomena, the friars, on the other hand, pass the latest "news" of the "glorious mother" from one house to another, thus contributing to the creation of the legend. Nor were the sisters left out in this extraordinary setting. Colette's religious entourage seems to have been very attentive to her person, to her behavior. She was constantly watched.

Orison

"Orison" too is a characteristic of prayer. The text of Pierre de Vaux includes several definitions that supplement each other (§69, with a reference to Saint Augustine):

> *Orison* [prayer] is [the] refuge of the holy soul, soothes the good angel, torments the enemy, to God gives acceptable service from perfect religion, all glory and praise, certain hope, and incorrupt holiness.

In heaven it is not just God's presence that matters. The syntax of the sentence aligns angels and demons together with God in its definition of prayer. It indicates the concept of the search for God. The center is shifted as against that of Saint Bonaventure's plan in which the soul is on a purposeful quest, gradually rising towards union with God. Prayer has not yet attained what it will be for the Spanish mystics: desolation or consolation of the soul with purification in the "dark nights" that recreate the spiritual being. Nor is it like that of the contemporary mystics of the Rhine area. Theirs involves a search for God within the self, giving passionate attention to the work of transformation of the soul as it comes into contact with the divine.

However, section 82 gives conditions for prayer that show how the long and rich tradition of the great "pray-ers" has its influence:

> She gathered and set out all these sensual and corporeal forces and natural, powerful, spiritual virtues in order to think more perfectly on God and pray fervently and affectionately to him. And thus her spirit was so ardently and closely joined to him that she was as if entirely ravished and enslaved by him; nor did she see or notice anything else.

This demonstrates the emptying of the mind and the recollection of the faculties – necessary conditions for prayer – as well as the orientation of the soul towards God, seeking to unite itself with him, forgetting external things. The term "affectionately" is interesting: Francis of Assisi himself preferred the prayer of the heart, "affective" prayer. It is characteristic of prayer in Franciscan spirituality, unlike other more intellectual schools.

The above-mentioned passage helps to clarify comments made about sections 69 and 84. Teaching on prayer in convents no doubt followed the basic traditional plan developed since the early centuries of Christianity. It was enhanced by the contribution of successive generations, mainly monks and theologians. Other elements can also be detected: the concerns of the contemporary Church and the spiritual ambience. The fifteenth century was a time of deep divisions in society, upheaval and desire for reform of the Church. The fact that prayer should always be prayer of intercession on behalf of the "weak" and directed towards a heaven peopled with angels and demons reveals fairly well the anguish people experienced when facing the question of eternal salvation. Prayer takes on the daily problems people face, but at the risk of obscuring its essential purpose, which is the search for God. This makes prayer into a means of obtaining specific outcomes, an effective way of finding remedies for life's misfortunes.

Types of Prayer

The issue is one of mental prayer and spoken prayer (§69 and §81). The term "orison" used in the text covers the two most common types of prayer. It does not have the very precise, technical meaning it would come to have for Teresa of Avila, which carefully distinguishes "orison," or prayer of the heart itself, from spoken and mental prayer.

The divine office is considered "orison" and must therefore be located in spoken prayer. In paragraph 69, the first example appears after the definition of the "sacrifice of holy orison" – it is the duty by which God is "diligently and devoutly served." This service must be "pleasing and agreeable to God" or "pleasant and acceptable" (§70). The office is chanted, which at that time was not always so. Section 71 tells an interesting story of the hesitation shown by the reformer herself and Henry de Baume on this matter. It should be recalled that the rule of Saint Clare, as clearly indicated here, prescribes that the office "will be recited not chanted" (Rg III, 1 – Perrine quotes the text of the Rule in §28). The two religious pray that God will reveal to them how the office should be said (§71):

> ... suddenly in their midst was heard a very pleasant, melodious voice, which seemed angelic rather than anything else.

Immediately, seeing in this an answer to their prayer, they "commanded and ruled that, from then on, the office should always be said and done like this."

There is an important point to note in this passage, which we will consider when we come to Colette's work. She does not hesitate to change a fairly significant point in the Rule, since it concerns the divine office. Colette adds a further requirement to the nuns' obligation to pray the divine office:

> the divine office of *pater noster* which the lay sisters[5] must say, and the hours of the cross, and double vigils every month of at least IX lessons and the others with III" (§73).

In addition, "she was singularly devout in saying the psalter and the VII psalms with the litanies." These were certainly litanies of the saints. In addition, the "signacles" of the pater nosters she held very dear, and day and night she carried them with her, saying them countless and numberless times. We might see in these "very dear signacles," a forerunner of the rosary.

The text gives very little information about mental prayer. It may be that at "certain moments the *paters* could be said mentally." Section 81 might indicate this. It would mean there was a kind of alternating between spoken prayer and mental prayer, while the content remained the same. "She ceased to pray aloud to God and began to pray mentally once more."

The general condition for prayer, however, remains valid whatever the type:

> ... sparing nothing, she set out and abandoned herself to do him pleasing and acceptable service ... (§70).

---

[5] The "lay sisters" are those who do not recite the divine office. In the beginning, this discrimination did not exist. Clare distinguished only between the sisters who could read and those who were illiterate, but both had the same rights. For the latter, she replaced the office with a particular number of Paters. In practice, the Paters were recited by the lay sisters, of whom many were illiterate. They performed the hardest physical work. Colette seems to have removed this distinction between "choir sisters" and "lay sisters" and restored a single category of sisters, as Clare intended, but the so-called "extern" sisters, who did not enter the enclosure, were assimilated to the lay sisters. They enjoyed none of the rights of the nuns.

Prayer impregnated her whole life, all her actions (§67):

> The main occupation of the little handmaid of the Lord, throughout her whole life, was to give God praise, honor and prayer.

The three words used to characterize prayer indicate the divine office (praise), reverence for God (honor through service to the Creator) and intercession for the "weak" (prayer).

According to the concrete guidance given for spoken and mental prayer, Colette would have constantly kept her spirit at prayer, as described by Pierre de Vaux and Perrine, since after the office, she would recite *paters* and litanies. This kind of prayer seems to disregard what spiritual directors describe as the plunge into the center of the soul, where words are abandoned and nothing remains but silent adoration. But Colette would seem to have experienced the traditional stages of prayer. Pierre de Vaux emphasizes that "she was so ardently and firmly joined to him [God], it was as if she were wholly ravished and enslaved by him, nor did she see or notice anything else" (§82).

The rapture described by Perrine on several occasions would, therefore, in fact be this mystical state in which the soul remains as if absorbed by contemplation of the presence of God. It should be noted that this passage comes in a description of "mental prayer." The imprecision of terms makes analysis of Colette's prayer difficult. In Pierre de Vaux, as we have seen, there are insufficient tools to carry out such a technical study of prayer. While he could have found these analytical tools in Saint Bonaventure, he seems to have had available only commonly held ideas.

For Colette, such privileged states of being seem to have lasted for long periods of time:

> For a space of VI hours and sometimes for X or XII, she remained in this state, knowing nothing of what was said or done. And when she returned to herself,

she believed that she had been there only for a short space (Perrine §32).

This loss of a sense of time is classic. Theologians see it as an experience "of eternity."

Such states are incompatible with spoken or mental prayer, and describing them is intended to indicate total involvement. Colette experienced constantly all the states of prayer. This is a clear sign of sanctity.

The length of time spent in prayer reduces the time available for sleep. Where Perrine notes simply that Colette had little sleep (§32), the Franciscan has no hesitation in saying that she often slept only one hour in eight days (§82). However, Perrine also says that "it was as if she did not sleep at all" (§50).

The Circumstances of the Prayer

If time is taken up entirely by prayer, it does not mean that individual moments are of an indifferent character. Circumstances influence the kind of prayer, the rhythm of the divine office governing the monastic day (P. de Vaux §70).

In section 27, Perrine qualifies this: "Her entire pleasure was to attend it [office] as frequently as possible, so much did she delight in giving our Lord her time and her effort." This qualification is important, allowing a proper appreciation of what the two biographers are saying in these sections. Her physical ailments sometimes prevented her from attending the office. Pierre de Vaux emphasizes that "when it pleased God to take from her, for a short time, the pains from which she suffered, she went there ..." Elsewhere, he says that God made her suffer "at all times of her life" and especially at the time of great liturgical feasts.

Perrine's testimony is of particular importance because she shared Colette's life, even if she does not here use the explicit formula "thus did I see it." While Colette did not attend divine office regularly, sickness was not the only reason. The other, which the Franciscan does not include, is that of "time." Perrine alludes to the various occupations of an abbess and reformer, including journeys made for foundations or visits to the convents, (noted elsewhere by Pierre de Vaux, §78 and §81, and Perrine, §41/42a and §37). Colette prayed with great intensity during these journeys, to the point of falling into rapture: "In particular, I once held her enraptured on my knee when traveling through the fields in a wagon" (§42).

Colette prayed especially before undertaking these journeys, during which she and her companions had to face great danger because of the wars (§76-78):

> ... and in order to assure their security and safety, before she left the house each day, it was her practice to hear the holy mass of the III kings. And as soon as she had set out, she began to say the litanies devoutly, and by the grace of God and by the merits of all the saints named in the litany, all the perils that were sometimes so great as to be life-threatening she safely avoided and escaped.

She also made the sisters who accompanied her pray (§78), the formula always being a "holy litany." This constant inclusion of "orison" with all types of prayer should be noted. The dimension of sisterhood is also present. She made the sisters pray, and first of all required that, especially before celebrating the office, sisterly charity should be restored if it had been damaged, referring to the words of the gospel (§69). The Franciscan note is clearly sounded. Prayer retains to a great extent the fraternal character beloved of Francis and Clare of Assisi. Colette also prays to meet the needs of others, intercession being extremely important as we have seen in this chapter.

The devil is integrally involved, it may be said, in the circumstances of prayer. The traditional, underlying notion is that the devil tends to prevent the believer from achieving union with God or from interceding for his or her brothers and sisters. In the *Vita* of Celano, Clare sees an apparition of the devil, who mocks her tears during her prayers. A retort by the saint puts him to flight. The function of this is to authenticate the seriousness of prayer. She is destroying the devil's work. It is therefore in his interests to prevent her.

> Of all the orisons where the enemy caused her more vexation and hindrance, it was most commonly when she was saying the psalter. Several times, when she said (it) by night, he would come to blow out and extinguish her candle or her lamp.

She relit the lamp; he put it out again. The merry-go-round continued until the devil spilt the oil from the lamp on the book. She believed it to be damaged, but there was no damage at all (§74). At other times, demons came in pairs:

> Two most cruel and terrible enemies appeared to her in horrible, frightful forms, one on one side of her and one on the other, to frighten her and to cause so much hindrance that she could not present her orisons to God as she was accustomed to do (P. de Vaux §75).

Comparing the function of the demon in the prayer of Clare to that of Colette throws light on the very idea of prayer. In the first case,[6] the example given is almost comical – the demon tells Clare that she will lose her sight and that her brain will be forced out through her nose with the effort of her tears. But this has a didactic purpose. "No one is blind who sees God," answers Clare. In the second case, the story is frankly anecdotal. The example of spilling oil from the lamp onto the book verges on the marvelous. The anecdote then becomes evidence for prayer.

Another example corroborates this assessment:

> Several times, when she was preparing particularly to go to matins in the choir where it was held, several

---

[6] Celano, *Vita, Sainte Claire d'Assise, Documents,* rassemblés, présentés et traduits par Damien Vorreux, OFM (Paris: Ed. Franciscaines, 1983), 46.

of the sisters saw a very beautiful, pleasant lamb that accompanied her (P. de Vaux §70).

Perrine does not mention this episode.

The element of marvel makes up for the lack of analysis of Colette's interior life. "Miracles" replace speech and reflection. They become a symbolic language, signs of reality.

The Places

Liturgical prayer takes place in the choir; the sung office, however, is not exclusively the province of professed religious. Henry de Baume and Colette prayed to God that he would "teach them how to say the office to his honor and for the edification of the people" (P. de Vaux §71). In case nuns in a convent should be afflicted with epidemics, the office would still be sung by the able-bodied (P. de Vaux §72). Perrine describes only the episode of the sung office (§21). An ecclesial dimension was preserved to a certain extent by the presence of the Christian "people," but they did not take part in the office, they only "heard it." The divine office was still reserved to the nuns.

Colette provided an oratory in every convent she founded: "... her oratories (*oratoirs*) where she normally went each day, where she heard the holy masses and received the blessed sacrament ..." (§49). Perrine repeats the same phrase in section 23, using the plural form "*oratorez.*" The expression is not unique (P. de Vaux, chapters XI and XII, §96, §107). Lay people wished "to be in the oratory, where mass was celebrated before her ..." (§110). Perrine also testifies to this (§50 and §45).

Was the mass celebrated in her oratory additional to the conventual mass? Pierre de Vaux and Perrine cite, as justification for Colette's being most often in her oratory, her desire not to be seen in ecstasy even for the Eucharist. Francis of Assisi asked his brother priests to join together in one celebration of the Eucharist, the locus of charity. Colette seems unaware of this essential feature of the Eucharist, preferring to be in "private and secret."

It is true that solitary prayer is a Franciscan characteristic, and Francis himself retreated for long periods to hermitages. But he wanted to be accompanied by a brother who would remain at some distance from him.[7] Celano notes in the *Vita* of Clare that she prayed for long periods. It seems she would remain in the choir when her sisters left to rest (XII, 19 and 20). The note that "she brought burning words from the fire on the altar of the Lord ..." shows that she did indeed stay in adoration before the Blessed Sacrament in the choir.

A private oratory in a monastery of Clarisses is surprising. Nothing in the life and the writings of Clare or Francis justifies such a practice. This seems to be a personal decision by Colette, one that does not comply with the spirit and custom of the order before her time. One might legitimately believe that she retained the mark of her experience as a recluse. Other factors arising in the course of the study may confirm or qualify this assessment.

For the time being, we may draw an initial conclusion. While she did not attend divine office regularly (even for legitimate reasons) and remained for many hours in her oratory, including during the daytime (Perrine §50), it may be asserted that she did not always have to be present to her community. There were also many journeys and long periods when she stayed in different monasteries. She seems to have had a solitary temperament, with hermit-like tendencies. It is nowhere indicated that she considered this way of life as being possible for other sisters. In practice, it seems she was allowed a kind of special status, by which she would have been both with her sisters and apart. Her reclusive character, in any case, destroys the outlandish idea sometimes proposed that it was somehow vital to her sanity to leave her seclusion.[8]

---

[7] "Fioretti," VII, *Saint François d'Assise, Documents: Ecrits et première biographies*, rassemblés et présentés par les PP. Théophile Desbonnets et Damien Vorreux, OFM, deuxième édition (Paris: Ed. Franciscaines, 1981), 1076.

[8] J. Doyon, *La Recluse* (Paris, 1984), 319.

The Effects of Prayer on Colette

She prayed so well that during the office, she seemed to see "clearly and perfectly the presence of the sovereign King." The expression on her face changed:

> And thus her precious face appeared so bright and resplendent that the sisters could see nothing of that face, because of the brightness and light (P. de Vaux §72).

Perrine confirms:

> She chanted so fervently that it seemed she was visibly before God; and at this divine office she had a bright, resplendent face. I did not dare look at her, and I heard the same said by several sisters after the divine office when they spoke about it (§29).

Pierre de Vaux draws from an oral tradition in the formation of which Colette's sisters play their part. There is an inescapable parallel to be drawn with Celano's *Vita*: this characteristic always forms part of the typology of holiness. The sisters, in the teaching they received from the brothers, were no doubt nourished by these proofs of holiness, which to a great extent conditioned their attitude. It is very difficult to distinguish objective from subjective reality. But it is certain that any human group a priori imposes its own particular perspectives. This is all the more true in the case of closed environments where the members are nourished almost exclusively from the same sources.

The radiance of the face is incompatible with an attitude of fear, since prayer opens the praying person to God. Now, in chapter II, the biographer writes that when Colette had to preside at a chapter or at the refectory (not substantially different from the choir, since wherever the community meets, God is present), "she had such great doubt and fear that it seemed as if she had visible before her eyes her sovereign judge" (§17). An explanation may be found in the fact that this passage belongs to the chapter on humility. The particular point of view governs how the fact is presented.

The office also has a pacifying influence on the reformer:

> ... and sometimes, if she was desolate for any just cause before the office, forthwith as she entered she was completely comforted and pacified (P. de Vaux §72).

The *signacle* has a similar effect:

> Several times, so troubled by the grievous pains and sufferings that she bore that she did not know where she was, no sooner had she touched the pater noster *signacle* than she returned to herself and recognized where she was (§73).

Perrine also notes the effect of the *signacles* (§30) and the pacifying effect of the office (§27), to which Colette completely abandoned herself: "and it caused such great courage in her that she could be heard above all the others." Pierre de Vaux adds:

> At the beginning of her reformation, as she was at divine office, a number of persons several times heard her voice, by the grace of God, from a great distance (§70).

It was in prayer that she knew of "horrible sins and offences" that caused "in her heart for a long time after a great sorrow and excessive suffering" (P. de Vaux §84). Perrine, too, says that intercessory prayer provoked such states in her:

> ... often she would pass several nights with little or no rest, since she occupied herself in tears, groaning and weeping and uttering devout prayers begging mercy of our Lord (end of §32).

One is reminded of Clare's tears (*Vita,* XII, 19):

> Very often during her prayer, she prostrated herself in tears, her face to the earth, raining kisses on the ground. It seemed that she wanted to hold her Jesus in her arms, wetting his feet with her tears and covering them with kisses.

The meaning Celano attributes to the tears is not, however, reflected in Pierre de Vaux. From the time of the Desert Fathers, the first monastics, the "gift of tears" is a constant theme. Saint Francis had eye maladies from crying and groaning over Christ's Passion. A painting shows him wiping his diseased eyes. In the spirituality of the Fathers, the gift of tears is a stage in the spiritual life[9] in which the heart opens to contrition and to mercy. It does not last, and it precedes a more important stage in which the liberated being enters into the very joy of God. In the text we are examining, tears are linked to prayers of intercession for poor "weak" creatures, and thus they accompany this type of prayer throughout life.

Of course the most striking point to note is the lack of reference to Scripture, especially to the New Testament. Christ taught about prayer, he prayed himself, and he recommended that his followers pray to God the Father. He promised those who received his word that God would be present in them. He scorned formulaic and repetitive prayers: "Do not babble like the pagans."

In our texts, the amount and seriousness of sins call for a corresponding amount of prayer. Hence the importance of the quantitative concept for formulaic prayers, some of which seem more appropriate than others, such as litanies, etc.[10] There is a genuine risk of monasteries becoming mere dispensaries of prayer, delivering fixed quantities of spoken

---

[9] O. Clément, *Sources, les mystiques chrétiens des origines,* 146.

[10] "The piety of this period, even among the best of people, became a matter of arithmetic," F. Rapp, *L'Église et la vie religieuse en Occident à la fin du Moyen Age* (Paris: PUF, 1980) 161.

prayers. On the other hand, lay people, believing that their inferior status prevents their having access to the divine, pray to living saints rather than to God. Immediate efficacy is an essential factor, most frequently relating to material things: physical cures, resurrections, mental healings. Spiritual healing is not ignored, but does not lead to intimacy with the God who is Love. Prayer may also be a kind of recipe for obtaining resources for daily life: horses restored to health, lost items found, etc.

The vagueness of the term *orison*, applying both to the office and to private prayers, also witnesses to an impoverishment of thinking and of spiritual experience. It effectively enhances the value of external signs, such as tears, moans, and the physical appearance of the person who prays.

One wonders if the absence of scriptural roots goes hand in hand with disregard for the great patristic tradition (only one quotation from Augustine) and with using extraordinary phenomena as evidence that prayer is authentic and acceptable to God, that only a true saint could accomplish it.

There are, nonetheless, some signs of a tradition: recollecting the soul's faculties in order to enter into prayer, a certain ecclesial and fraternal dimension, and finally, concern for solidarity with contemporary human beings.

DEVOTIONS

Devotion to Christ is characterized above all by devotion to the Passion, to the Cross and to the Eucharist.

Devotion to the Passion

Pierre de Vaux spends sections 94 to 98 of chapter XI on devotion to the passion of Christ; Perrine sections 38 and 45. As we have seen, this devotion originated in childhood.[11] Meditating on the Passion evoked physical reactions in the

---

[11] After 1350, the role of parents and childhood in the life of the saints was enhanced, cf. A. Vauchez, *La sainteté en Occident* ..., 593 ff.

mother "often in tears and groaning, bemoaning the injuries and torments of grief he suffered for us." The Passion is experienced particularly in feelings, being perceived first of all as physical torture. The believer identifies with Christ through a kind of imitation. This is the phenomenon experienced by Colette:

> When she recalled and remembered the excessive suffering of the passion of our Lord, and the bitter painful sufferings that he endured for such a long time...

and also

> One could not sufficiently recount or tell of the abundance of tears and piteous weeping and groaning she made and experienced during holy week as I saw in the convent at Besançon (Perrine, §38, same quotation §45).

Pierre de Vaux has the same account, but emphasizes even more her tears and meditations on

> the opprobrium, injuries, beatings and the very horrible and very shameful death that he chose so peacefully and sweetly to suffer and to bear for love of us (§94).

In doing this he modifies the impression that true *orison* is solely the preserve of religious. In the previous chapter, when lay people pray, it is actually to invoke Colette rather than address God directly. The mother's devotions provide invaluable testimony to the prayer of the laity. Colette's initiation into a way of prayer, practised throughout her life, did not come to her from the monastic environment (abbey of Corbie) but from her family life. This assumes deep-rooted piety in Christian people. It is marked by compassionate sensitivity certainly conveyed by preachers, mainly Franciscan, and modelled on monastic devotions.

The difference between Colette and her mother comes from their situations – the mother does not cease to work while she prays, but Colette frequently retires to her oratory. The former does not seem to choose a particular time to pray. Colette, however, according to her biographers, gives due importance to the symbolism of the liturgical seasons (the three holy days without eating), the time of day (matins or midday according to Pierre de Vaux, from six hours after matins to six hours after midday), or the days of the week (Fridays).

Time at prayer brings about raptures, ecstasies and visions, and her features change:

> ... in such meditation she suffered torments so great that the sisters meeting her outside the chapel and looking her in the face saw that she seemed to have been beaten as with sticks (Perrine §38).

Pierre de Vaux is even more forthcoming about raptures and visions and more categorical:

> She was estranged from the use of all these senses, without feeling anything from without (§94);

> Christ appears to her to "demonstrate" in both form and manner how "he had been crucified, and he manifested to her how there was no part of him that had not ... suffered" (§95).

Fixation on physical suffering gives rise to the kind of visualization common since the thirteenth century and accentuated during the fourteenth and fifteenth centuries. In the *Lives* of Francis we find elements that he was able to use, as well as in certain passages from the *Letters* of Clare to Agnes of Prague or in the prayer known as the "Five Wounds," also attributed to Clare. For Francis and Clare, reflection on the Passion is only one factor in their prayer. Here it is a major element, given all the more emphasis since it is not qualified by devotion to the birth of Christ, as it is for Francis at Greccio, nor to the risen and glorified Christ as in Clare, nor indeed by the trinitarian approach to the mystery of God taken by both the saints of Assisi. The Passion, with its overwhelmingly sorrowful character, becomes an essential part of Colette's prayer and devotions.

This is very clear through the examples given in the Franciscan's biography – the vision of the crucified Christ and the pains felt by Colette. His terminology consists of words such as "suffering," "sorrowful passion," "pains, sufferings and torments," "bitter and sorrowful pains," "great torments." These are repeated numerous times in the five sections. Colette's sufferings extend to a real, though invisible, stigmatization: Christ's sufferings "were experientially renewed and imprinted on her heart and her body." Strangely, these pains are compared to those of a woman in labor (P. de Vaux §95).

Perrine says nothing of the stigmata. Colette is not known in the order as a stigmatic. This fact seems to be pure invention on the part of the Franciscan, evidently thinking of the illustrious model of Francis of Assisi. Pierre de Vaux favors the spectacular features – tears and cries are signs of spiritual suffering. Spiritual realities are constantly perceived through physical realities.

Devotion to the Cross

The sign of the cross is an effective remedy. Making it on a sick person produces a cure (Perrine §41). In section 40, Perrine recalls that Colette cured children with the sign of the cross. Pierre de Vaux, in chapter XI, goes into more detail on this type of cure associating it with devotion to the Passion. Of the ten miracles described, six are cures (§99/99a, 95b, 102, 103, 104). The others cover human activities – fording a river (§100), a "bug-ridden" wine changed into one of good quality (§105) and a broken object repaired (§106).

Initially, the sign of the cross recalls the power of the Redeemer who allowed himself to be crucified. From the well-known hymn, *O crux Ave spes unica,* in the liturgy, to the legend of the cross appearing to Constantine in a dream and giving him victory ("by this sign shall you be victorious"), the emblem was deeply significant at a theological level. In the lives of the saints, it tends to demonstrate their sanctity: "... God by his merits wished to manifest many miracles by this sign." (P. de Vaux §98).

In the presence of the pope, Clare made the sign of the cross over the bread, where it was deeply imprinted. In our story, it remains an efficacious sign of Colette's holiness, producing physical or mental cures in demonic situations (the sister who had for years used unseemly speech "as a wild boar might" §102). The meaning is degraded when it becomes a magical sign for repairing or finding an object.

The hagiographical process culminates in the episode of the cross sent from heaven (§98) (which can still be found in the monastery at Besançon). Pierre de Vaux connects Colette's devotion to the "true cross on which our piteous Savior was crucified" to her devotion to the Passion. Perrine omits such detail, but this section follows one in which she reports Colette's wish to die in the Holy Land (a desire shared by Clare). Colette, according to the Franciscan, longs for a relic of the cross,

> and she was not disappointed in her desire, because a beautiful little cross in fine gold was sent to her from heaven, in which a tiny portion of the holy cross itself was contained (Perrine §40).

Then comes the testimony of "several [who] affirm that this little cross had not been made or forged by human hands." According to Perrine: "Good father Henry told us that our Lord had sent it from heaven to our glorious mother." And a degraded theological meaning follows: "I saw it, and when she signed it over us, it thundered, as a remedy for the fear of thunderstorms." The cross from heaven becomes a kind of amulet. Pierre de Vaux avoids such clumsiness and maintains the relationship with devotion to the true cross, allowing him to move on to "reverence for the sign of the cross."

Devotion to the Eucharist

Chapter XIII of Pierre de Vaux covers devotion to the Eucharist (§107 to §113 inclusive). Perrine spends relatively little time on this (§42 and part of §42a, with a short mention in §32 – the mass of the three kings said before traveling – and §62/62a).

Pierre de Vaux distinguishes the mass from the reception of the Eucharist. The term "blessed sacrament" is linked to the consecration during mass. The frequency of her attendance is noted:

> The holy mass ... at some proper place where she was, she had celebrated for her every day, with great devotion and abundant tears (P. de Vaux §107).

Confession often preceded the mass "... for more devout hearing." Perrine specifies (§42a): "For a whole year, she received it every day" (daily communion was exceptional at the time).

When traveling with her sisters, she attended mass celebrated in public churches. But she preferred mass in private, as we have seen, that is, in her personal oratory (P. de Vaux §107; Perrine §62).

Colette uses communion for moral support:

> In her affairs, which were oftentimes great, obscure and difficult, her recourse and refuge was the blessed sacrament of the altar, or before journeys, a special mass was celebrated (P. de Vaux §112).

As with prayer, communion involved physical behavior. The elevation was a moment of great emotion (Perrine §62) as was that of communion, manifested by tears and groans.

> In a loud voice she claimed herself to be unspeakably low, soiled and filthy, abominable and unworthy to live and reside and converse with poor sinners, because of the offences she said she had committed against the

divine majesty and goodness, from which she had such great sadness, sorrow and displeasure that it seemed her heart should break with her unrelieved weeping (P. de Vaux §111).

Her raptures were frequent (Perrine §62a). The feelings described by Pierre de Vaux are no doubt those to be expected from a saint, since in the corresponding passage, Perrine uses a solemn, legal formula, showing she is following a predetermined pattern:

> Firstly I, sister Perrine de la Roche et de Basme named above, aged lxiij years, witness to the glorious handmaid of our Lord, sister Colette, as said above, how devoutly and in great and excessive fear she received the very worthy and precious body of our Lord. I heard several times the great cries and groans she made, as if, through the great devotion she had to the said precious body of our Lord, her bones were cracking (§42).[12]

Communion became a means for God to apply pressure when Colette appeared recalcitrant or reticent. Both biographers recount the following episode (P. de Vaux §112 and Perrine §62), but the latter adds: "I heard it said to brother Henri, to Father de Raims and to brother François Claret ..." According to them, the species did not melt in her mouth until she had agreed to God's plan. When she was hesitant, she went to her confessor to ask advice and then returned to the Mass. "As soon as her consent had been given, the species were used" (P. de Vaux §112). These episodes doubtless took place in her oratory, since the sisters were not present.

The secondhand story is important and very often supports the testimony. It relates to material, dramatic events,

---

[12] The importance given to the sacraments, the marvels during the Eucharist, with the intensity of the mystics belong to the typology of sanctity in the fourteenth and fifteenth centuries. Cf. A. Vauchez, *La sainteté en Occident* ..., 596-97.

in which sight plays a significant part. When Colette is seen groaning, one concludes that she has seen Christ (P. de Vaux §108); the religious and lay people want to see her at such times (P. de Vaux §110; Perrine §62). She accepts only those "most spiritual, or very familiar to her." The others "conceal themselves in secret places near the oratory to hear in secret the weeping and bitter complaints that she makes before our Lord" (P. de Vaux §110). She complains about this because she senses the presence of strangers.

The situation is ambiguous. Colette accepts some people, knowing their wishes. Others, who conceal themselves, can do so only with the complicity of her entourage. The solitude of the oratory is entirely relative. Devotion to the Eucharist brings out particular features, and a sense of the spectacular assures that there are always witnesses present who interpret these external manifestations. In this enclosed world, Colette is continually being watched by others who can so easily become spies.

Devotion to the Saints

Just as the people are devoted to Colette, she is devoted to saints in general and loves to recite litanies. She has her favorites: Saint John the Evangelist and Saint Anne (later on we will see her reasons relating to the virtues). These saints come to her aid. Saint Anne obtains the approval of other saints for her. Francis and Clare are not, however, objects of devotion exactly. They pray to God to entrust her with reform of the order.

She ensures that feast days and solemnities are observed. Her biographer sees this as evidence of her holiness. (Around the same time, theologians such as Pierre d'Ailly[13] are protesting at the increasing number of feast days.) Colette did not want people to work on these days, and miracles come to reinforce her arguments.

---

[13] J. Huizinga, *Le déclin du Moyen Age* (Paris, 1932), 183.

Conclusion

A study of devotions confirms the conclusions reached about prayer. The classic features of the fifteenth century are all here: devotion to the Passion and to the Eucharist and elements of Franciscan spirituality centered on the dual nature of Christ, divine and human. Devotion to the Eucharist, while not absent in the founders of the order, is affirmed here by Pierre de Vaux as very important. It is clearly established in fourteenth and especially fifteenth century spirituality. Along with the *Devotio Moderna,* this trend culminates in the *Imitation of Christ,* two chapters of which are devoted to the Eucharist.

This spirituality actually moves away from the mystical towards a solid piety that encourages a virtuous life. We have seen that Pierre de Vaux does not really attempt to analyze Colette's interior life and thus distances himself from Franciscan mysticism. It would appear that, as F. Rapp comments,[14] the Colettine reform, like reforms in various other orders, adopts and adapts the spirituality of the *Devotio Moderna* rather than attempting to return to the origins of its own spirituality.

The methods used by Pierre de Vaux and followed by Perrine show some lacunae, some loss of meaning. Emphasis is put on the physical sufferings of Christ, and the faith of the believer is tested by imitation. This runs the risk of morbid excitement of feeling and imagination. The gaze of the Christian, remaining fixed on the wounds and injuries of Christ, also tries to find similar sufferings in the saint. The saint, then, welcomes the sufferings of the Passion in his or her own body. The Eucharist is often understood from this perspective.

At a narrative level, Colette's biographer uses existing material as it had been carried from convent to convent by the sisters and especially by the Franciscan brothers, for whom any phenomenon has a "spiritual" significance. The real is

---

[14] F. Rapp, *L'Église et la vie religieuse en Occident,* 248.

saturated with the supernatural, which in turn is contaminated by the material; and the closed world of the convents spreads this spiritual state to the laity. On the other hand, the lay people also demonstrate their fondness for extraordinary phenomena. A deep ambiguity in meaning arises and all action and reflection is Christianized. Spirituality risks deteriorating and becoming, in some way, a magical religion. Colette, as seen through this perspective by witnesses and biographers, is difficult for us to access. Here and there, we can detect signs of her resistance to the infatuation she provoked. Thus, while she seems to have perceived the dangers herself, she does not in any way jeopardize the general method for evaluating holiness, no doubt because she had no way herself of analyzing such widely recognized criteria.

CHAPTER 5

MARVELS, EXTRAORDINARY EVENTS AND SPIRITUALITY

As a measure of the quality of the spiritual life, as well perhaps as revealing a particular attitude, the marvelous is especially important to Pierre de Vaux.

THE MARVELOUS

Colette's miracles reveal both the authentic nature of her virtues and the power of her prayer. It is outside the scope of this study to judge the veracity of these accounts, but we can consider the features within them that are undoubtedly real. The most numerous occurring during Colette's own lifetime were those that she performed herself. These are of particular interest as they cover a wide range of activities. The least common were those involving physical healing. Some seem to have been cases of epilepsy.

During her journeys of foundation, Colette's prayerful intervention in a context of war averted physical and verbal attacks (P. de Vaux §77).

Miracles relevant to morality and spirituality were rather numerous. Some of the people healed were suffering from "melancholia," in the classic sense of that word. In particular, these were nuns who refused to attend office or join in community activities. Colette drew on her gifts of persuasion and suggestion. The invalid, recovering confidence, returned to the office and proclaimed herself cured (P. de Vaux §102, 103, §73).

Colette pressed the idea, particularly to religious brothers and sisters, that their eternal salvation was endangered. The subject's confession was a response to Colette's prayer. The confession might have to be repeated if the sick person did not do it "properly." Colette would know if "great sins" still remained (P. de Vaux §128), and she would send the person back until a state of grace was fully restored. There were two possible outcomes: the subject might die, but receive eternal salvation, or else the subject might be cured, the physical cure becoming a tangible sign of spiritual healing.

If Colette arrived too late, and the sick had already died, she would revive them to make a confession. Then they would die again. This happened in one of her convents to a religious sister who was in the state of mortal sin, writes Pierre de Vaux (§206).

On two occasions, Colette confessed on behalf of the recalcitrant subject, since she had foreknowledge of the sins. The sinner then, benefitting from the spiritual effects of the confession, was morally healed and made his own confession (§208).

Towns and family groups were saved or protected. The enemy did not besiege a town where Colette was staying, the soldiers simply turning back at some distance without attacking (§212). Her prayers even stopped a battle between two groups (P. de Vaux §139). Families that gave Colette shelter were protected. The protection was manifested by a vision of angels who ascended and descended from the castle, somewhat reminiscent of the vision of Arezzo.[1]

The great biblical vision of the ladder of Jacob, prophet of the Messiah, which Jesus himself repeated, is here reduced

---

[1] The vision of Arezzo: demons above the town chased away by the prayers of Saint Francis. Cf. Bonaventure, *Legenda Major*, VI-VII in *Saint François d'Assise, Documents, Ecrits et première biographies*, rassemblés et présentés par les PP. Théophile Desbonnets et Damien Vorreux, OFM; deuxième édition (Paris: Ed. Franciscaines, 1981).

to a commonplace, used to indicate the temporary protection of one family (and incidentally confirming how hagiographical literature waters down Biblical symbolism).

Colette also intervened with regard to food and drink, which she multiplies. Reference to the multiplication of the loaves in the Gospel, for example, is fundamental, yet without any obvious spiritual significance. Wine or oil could be drawn from a container as needed, but the liquid never dried up. Guests felt they had eaten a very tasty dish (P. de Vaux §116-117). The miracle, in this case, had more to do with powers of suggestion than the materialization or multiplication of food.

Some miracles during her lifetime might have been indirect, performed by simply invoking her name in prayer, commending the person concerned to her even at a distance. They applied to lost and found objects and to physical and spiritual cures.

The saint therefore has spiritual, social and even domestic usefulness and is seen as a protector and healer, making life easier. People feel the need for an intermediary between themselves and a dimly understood and frightening reality. This, at least, is how Pierre de Vaux describes Colette's role as a thaumaturge.

At another level, the miraculous criteria in his description are vague enough to allow facts that permit rational explanation to qualify as miracles. Two good examples are the water at Poligny and the cloth whose length appeared to have changed.

> –The workers at Poligny could not find any water. After praying, Colette told them where to look. They dug there and water gushed forth. What Pierre de Vaux describes as a miracle might be seen as a happy coincidence, no more. The miraculous nature of the incident is not entirely obvious.

> –A lay brother could not manage to cut out a habit from a piece of cloth. Colette advised him to leave the

work and go and pray. (A good psychological touch: when work is causing too much stress, leave it for a while and, for a religious, find renewed strength in prayer.) When he came back, Colette helped him cut out the habit. We might think that she was better able than he to lay out the material and that he worked better as a result.

Once more, the real has been contaminated by the supernatural. The saint, as a "heavenly" being, controls spiritual realities and things.

THE EXTRAORDINARY

These are the freely performed actions of supernatural forces or beings. They do not always come from Colette, but they follow "in her wake."

"Heavenly" Beings

"Heavenly" beasts: a pure white lamb accompanied Colette, appearing and disappearing with no apparent reason. Chased by the whole community, the animal could not be caught, and for several moments Colette and the lamb became invisible. The lamb followed the saint constantly (P. de Vaux §60), even attending the Eucharist and kneeling at the elevation of the host. A dove also came into her oratory.

Besides animals, which had both a decorative and symbolic function representing Colette's supernatural purity, there were also demons as a permanent opposing force. They appeared as hideous, black, grimacing monsters (P. de Vaux §154). Even more than the "heavenly" beasts, they were ever-present in Colette's world. They might be perceived as the reverse of a coin, as dark counterparts to the "heavenly" animals.

Colette never had to deal with temptations of a solely internal and spiritual kind. There are no signs of doubt in her attitude to her mission or spiritual agonies of the kind experienced by Francis of Assisi when he wondered what would become of his order in future.

Angels, counterparts to the demons, were the luminous daytime faces, supernatural beings who intervened in Colette's life. (Remember those who ascended and descended above the castle as a sign of protection.) They also held a cloth above the reformer, a point that has no function in the story, but is only an ornamental detail (Perrine §33, P. de Vaux §88).

"Heavenly" beings include a man dressed all in white (P. de Vaux §53), a beautiful young girl (only in Pierre de Vaux) who, on Colette's return from Nice, healed her by kissing her on the mouth (brother Henry decided she must have been the Virgin Mary, Perrine §63b). This is a curious detail: is it a reference to the "mystical kiss" dear to the medieval tradition? This is highly possible if the episode is compared with the legend of the knight who becomes a leper and is then healed by a kiss on the mouth by Christ himself.[2] This category of apparitions may also include ghosts, comforting or frightening depending on whether they were going to heaven or to purgatory.

Things

These elements are those that did not result from any intervention of Colette, but which, rather, she receives or sees. A white rope descends from the sky. The mystical ring and the cross are signs, one of spiritual marriage and the other of the fulfillment of Colette's "holy desire" to have a relic of the true cross.

The physicality of the signs arises from the need to visualize spiritual realities. It is interesting to note Colette's fear of losing her sight (for reading the office and seeing the Eucharist) while being so totally abandoned to the divine will.

The senses of sight or taste are frequently used to affirm the concrete reality of the fact reported. There is a wealth

---

[2] G. Flaubert covered this theme in his story "The Legend of Saint Julian the Hospitaller," one of *The Three Tales*.

of linguistic expressions used for delicious bread (P. de Vaux §54), for food (§116), for a vision of Christ (§108 and 121).

Psychologically, affectivity takes the lead. Emotional sensitivity resulting from a perception of the real is triggered by sight as well as by hearing (for example, the "heavenly" voices that choose the office to be sung) and by touching (the "heavenly" beasts that the nuns want to seize). To a lesser extent the sense of smell also plays a role.

In this exclusively "celestial" domain (including demonology), there are nonetheless what might be called "fracture zones." The incriminating features are not radically different by nature, but would seem to point to the presence of other elements less easily identified by the system used. These might include the shameful folly of Colette in her ambassadorial position before the Pope, the dual role reversal of this purest of recluses; the strange kiss on the mouth given by the female apparition, who only afterwards is identified as the Virgin; the inverted scatology (the saint's feces have a pleasant smell).[3]

A study of the spirituality aspect shows also that the emotional sensitivity springs from religious feeling.

Spirituality

Instead of analyzing the saint's spirituality, Pierre de Vaux describes the psychological effects of her inner states. The dominant emotions were horror and fear, felt both by Colette herself and by her occasional or permanent circle.

---

[3] This type of thing also happens surprisingly with Clare – an event having a symbolic meaning while the example has little significance from a spiritual point of view. In a dream, Clare sucks the milk from Francis's breast, signifying her filial relationship to him whom his brothers called *pro mater* [like a mother]; cf. "Canonization process," Testimonies: 3-29, 179; 4-16, 184; 6-13, 190; 7-10, 193 in *Sainte Claire d'Assise, Documents*, rassemblés, présentés et traduits par Damien Vorreux, O.F.M. (Paris: Ed. Franciscaines, 1983).

Dominant Feelings

Horror or fear was caused by demonic visions and by visions of ghosts clanking their chains. The sisters who heard these noises had the same feelings.

The vision of the dismembered child, calmly displayed by the Virgin, was to help Colette understand how much Christ is offended by sinners (P. de Vaux §84). The world of good and the world of evil use the same means of arousing horror. The psychological and affective reactions resulting from the shock to the nervous system replace meditation or inner knowledge.

In her prayers or visions, Colette responded with abundant tears, cries, groans, or terror. This relationship of fear towards God was also found in those around Colette. They did not dare to address God directly; hence the saint's function as "intermediary" between them and a formidable God, whose activity is ever-present in daily life. The saint, while endowed with extraordinary powers and capable of benevolent action, was also feared because of these same uncommon powers. Colette's gift of reading hearts or knowing from a distance the secret actions of those in her entourage were perceived as something frightening. A certain religious who was told what he had done during one of his journeys was so frightened that he never did it again, even when Colette was not there (P. de Vaux §136, Perrine §67). The same happened with a repeated confession: the penitent found himself detected by Colette's insight into his soul and the quality of his disclosures to the priest.

Some of Colette's opponents were removed or punished by physical death. At the interview with Benedict XIII in Nice, the cardinals who hesitated to approve her mission were struck down by plague (P. de Vaux §39). During the reform, Colette's "enemies" were either converted to her viewpoint or punished by death (P. de Vaux §115 and 116).

Those suffering from physical illness, especially religious brothers or sisters, were often cured after going to confession because their sufferings were perceived to be punishment for sin.

Much of Colette's dominance over her own circle and over people in general came from her ability to detect sin and evil in them. In the presence of her perfect purity, each felt his or her own sin and hence feared discovery and felt terror when it happened.

In such a world, each person was exposed to the gaze of others. The difference with Colette is that she had something of God's own gaze in her. She was not lacking in mercy: her compassion for sinners was constantly stressed (Perrine §50, §77, §32).

This does, however, involve a sharing of roles. While God was the judge, Colette had the task of naming and revealing the sin. She herself did not "sit at the table of sinners." A comparison might be made with Thérèse of Lisieux and how she perceived herself at the end of her life. In both the fifteenth and twentieth centuries, the saint, like Christ, was seen as taking on the sins of the world. The Carmelite experienced a real, spiritual participation in the sinful state, while never making the slightest value judgment.

It must be firmly borne in mind that, for Colette, according to her biographer, this participation was not so much through her inner state (as it would have been for Thérèse up to the dark night of faith), but in her physical and moral sufferings, such as terror. In other words, in experiencing the Passion of Christ, the fifteenth century focuses on the scourging, the drops of blood, the bearing of the cross, and the crucifixion itself as torture, but has nothing to say about the despairing cry from Psalm 21 repeated by Christ: "*Eloï, Eloï lama sabachtani.*"

Colette, according to Pierre de Vaux, did not experience spiritually the mystery of redemption. In this way, she differs fundamentally from Francis of Assisi. His prayer at Alverna ("Let me experience as far as possible the suffering and love you felt in your Passion"), to which the answer was the stigmata, was directed to spiritual conformity with Christ in terms of the ascent of the soul to God. Colette, on the other hand, already a kind of saint at her birth, was sent by God as a final attempt to avoid the ultimate catastrophy for this corrupt and sinful age, the only possible consequence of the sinfulness of the world. The same old thread of millenarianism runs through the story, and Pierre de Vaux makes reference to it from the chapter on her childhood onwards.

Colette might be seen as providing a way of turning punishment aside. God sent her "pains and sufferings," particularly physical sufferings. She underwent them with patience and gentleness. Thus, in the view of her biographer, she imitated Christ, who saved us from the *dies irae*. The abundant sufferings sent to her or promised by the Sovereign Judge reduced or removed altogether the punishments intended for others, often winning them over to a good life. The final disaster was thus averted as the number of sins was reduced.

There seems no eschatological expectation in the correct sense of the term. The establishment of the coming Kingdom at the end of History is not mentioned directly. The text places Colette in the time of struggle between Good and Evil, the outcome of which seems uncertain. This concept of God and God's relationship with humanity implies a negative attitude to the world.

The Negative Attitude

Christian society belongs to the sinful world under threat of chastisement. The monasteries represent islands of peace and salvation where "poor sinners," wishing to escape their state, take refuge. All earthly realities are described in negative terms, first among them the body itself, seat of "carnal desires" and "filthy thoughts." The only way to escape this is to remain a virgin and thus be able to approach the "celestial" world and its values.

The world of animals and objects is also part of this scheme. It is divided into pure and impure, a dichotomy reminiscent of that in the Old Testament. White is a sign of purity. Some animals are pure, others impure. We are in the presence of a kind of traditional "discourse" required by this genre of biography. It has an "ornamental" rather than a descriptive value.

The theology underlying the virtues and vows gives a better indication. We have already seen that their description demonstrates a "materialist" concept. Chastity of the heart and chastity of love, for example, are unknown. In section 57, Saint Paul's hymn to love is rewritten as a hymn to physical chastity, primarily conceived as virginity.

Humility extends even to the refusal of grace (§13/14). Spiritual meaning is also weakened by changing the meaning of expressions such as "infused knowledge" or "prophecy and knowledge." When applied to Colette, these terms simply mean that she could read into things. She knew when someone had died; she once foretold the coming of the anti-pope Felix V (P. de Vaux §169). She may also have had a "revelation" of the state of the Church, the Order, and France during her seclusion in Corbie and later that of her mission. Whatever the truth, it should be noted that Pierre de Vaux seems not to know the meaning of "knowledge of God" or "infused knowledge." In the traditional spiritual vocabulary, these terms always mean the human spirit's penetration into the mystery of God.

A number of points arise from this study of the marvelous and of spirituality.

Some aspects of the great traditions of the Church and of the Franciscan Order are lost by uprooting them from their biblical origins. It is striking how few quotations or allusions there are to Holy Scripture, giving an archaic concept of God. This reflects some Old Testament attitudes, but ignores the God of mercy, slow to anger, whom Israel already knew well.

This basic fact has several consequences. First of all, we see the importance of formalism in behavior, even in spiritual realities. If it is a question of appeasing a vengeful God, the laity simply seek intercessors, and prayer is reserved for an elite group of experts. Saintliness is built on a particular concept of the imitation of Jesus Christ – the dominant features of a saint's life are physical suffering and lack of joy.

It is like this from start to finish. As scapegoats, bearing sin and evil to expiate human fault, saints might exorcise the pain of their contemporaries faced with crises and wars. The sufferings of saints, lived through patiently, could save all from horror.

The life of a saint would then be cathartic as in a drama. A decadent mindset with no control over reality might try, through a system of signs, to exorcise the pain and distress of human beings. The process is more "poetry" than science.

The interpenetration of the visible and invisible, materializing the spiritual and spiritualizing the physical, together with the loss of theological meaning and scriptural rootedness, marks the end-point of a particular spiritual line of thought. Without the nourishment of a living theology, the reflection deteriorates into a technique for approaching the phenomenon of sanctity. Studying the virtues allows us to discern these more precisely.

CHAPTER 6

COLETTE'S VIRTUES

VIRTUES AND RELIGIOUS VOWS

The virtues refer to the three traditional vows of poverty, chastity and obedience. They also hide others such as humility, patience in trials, and austerity of life. In Pierre de Vaux, the virtues of obedience, poverty, and chastity frame the biographical passages from the period of seclusion to the start of the reform. The relationship between these virtues and the religious vows is also given great emphasis. The other virtues are described after devotion and prayer as attributes resulting from a consecrated life.

Comparing this list with that made by Francis of Assisi in the *Salutation of the Virtues*,[1] we see some differences.

---

[1] Cf. *Francis of Assisi: Early Documents,* ed. Regis J. Armstrong, O.F.M.Cap., J. A. Wayne Hellmann, O.F.M.Conv., William J. Short, O.F.M., Vol. I (New York: New City Press, 1999), 164-65.
SALUTATION OF THE VIRTUES

1. Hail, Queen Wisdom! May the Lord protect You, with Your Sister, holy pure Simplicity!

2. Lady holy Poverty, may the Lord protect You, with Your sister, holy Humility!

3. Lady holy charity, may the Lord protect You, with Your sister, holy Obedience.

4. Most holy Virtues, may the Lord protect all of You, from Whom you come and proceed.

5. There is surely no one in the whole world who can possess any one of You without dying first.

This text focuses on poverty, obedience, and charity, whereas wisdom and simplicity are greeted first in the Salutation and the virtues are paired: wisdom with simplicity, poverty with humility, charity with obedience This process gives them an intrinsically spiritual dimension, strengthened further by the affirmation, in verse 5, of the need to die to the self. Each therefore applies to a particular part of human and spiritual activity. This authentic text was copied and recopied throughout the fourteenth century. Did Pierre de Vaux and the Order in general know it? The question is worth asking since any reform is basically a return to the origins. For us this text is a standard against which we can evaluate the direction and quality of the rediscovery of topics that were important to Francis of Assisi.

Perrine does not follow the Franciscan's plan very closely. She develops few of the examples of Colette's poverty (§23/24/25), repeating some of those given by Pierre de Vaux and adding to those from childhood. For example, when traveling, Colette dared not raise her eyes in spacious rooms to the lofty ceilings; she ensured religious habits were appropriately poor; she loved the fine prayerbooks used for the service of God, but did not hesitate to give them away; noble men

---

6. Whoever possesses one and does not offend the others possesses all.

7. Whoever offends one does not possess any and offends all.

8. And each one confounds vice and sin.

9. Holy Wisdom confounds Satan and all his cunning.

10. Pure holy Simplicity confounds all the wisdom of this world and the wisdom of the body.

11. Holy Poverty confounds the desire for riches, greed, and the cares of this world.

12. Holy Humility confounds pride, all people who are in the world and all that is in the world.

13. Holy Charity confounds every diabolical and carnal temptation and every carnal fear.

14. Holy Obedience confounds every corporal and carnal wish, binds its mortified body to obedience of the Spirit and obedience to one's brother, so that it is subject and submissive to everyone in the world, not only to people but to every beast and wild animal as well that they may do whatever they want with it insofar as it has been given to them from above by the Lord.

and women gave her gold, which she never used for herself. One might add the episode of the habit made by a lay brother at Hesdin (§51). Perrine "testifies" to Colette's austerity and penitence. Part of section 77 is given over to "grievous pains" and persecutions.

Perrine does not spend as much time on the virtues as Pierre de Vaux, and she omits the miracle of the young man dressed all in white carrying "a fine large bag full of good white bread" (§53) and several other miracles dealing with food and drink (§54/55). She is silent about the virtues of obedience, "chastity and virginity" followed by theoretical developments and miracles.

Did Perrine actually understand Pierre de Vaux's plan? It seems not. Why such major omissions? She might have felt that chastity and virginity were delicate or even taboo subjects for a religious sister to discuss, reserved only for "learned men."

We will therefore consider Pierre de Vaux's text in particular. Since it is better constructed, it is more revealing of both intentions and a system of thought.

The various virtues allow three different approaches:

- They evoke an antithetical structure.
- They refer to the materiality of signs and spiritualization of the physical world.
- They reveal a negative approach and a loss of theological meaning, detected in the function of suffering.

ANTITHETICAL STRUCTURE

There is a sharp distinction made throughout, as noted in the section on childhood and youth, between the world of the saint and the world of others. In her physical body, as well as in her human and spiritual activities, Colette represents the "other," demonstrated by contrast.

A similar procedure is also used. She brings a virtue to absolute perfection to the point of being out of the ordinary, and other people expect to benefit from her exercise of this virtue. Pierre de Vaux is directly in line with the tradition of fourteenth- and fifteenth-century *Vitae* as they developed through directives issued by the popes.[2] These various techniques can be seen in different settings.

The State of Perfection

Colette's virginity is itself a sign of perfection. Married people, by their state of life, cannot attain perfection because of the disorders and carnal thoughts intrinsic to marriage. From childhood, Colette chose to associate only with virgins in order to avoid "all talk of the affairs of the state of marriage, in which sometimes [there are] many impurities, which she found very displeasing to hear."

This system was taken to extremes. Colette had a horror of marriage. She could, however, resign herself to its necessity in order to perpetuate the race as long as there was no second marriage. Her remarried mother told her "gently":

> Daughter, you would not be, if I had not remarried. To which response she replied: God who was all-powerful would have made me be the daughter of one of our neighbors who had only been married once (P. de Vaux §67).

The Franciscan sees this as reflecting a highly virtuous attitude, disregarding the lack of tact it implies. (Perrine does not include this episode, though we might expect her to, judging by the importance of childhood memories in her text.) However, such an attitude seems to be inconsistent with what Colette has to say about her parents, her mother in particular, to whom she owed, for example, her devotion to the

---

[2] Cf. A. Vauchez, *La sainteté en Occident aux derniers siècles du Moyen-Age d'après les procès de canonisation et les documents hagiographiques* (Rome, 1981), 605 ff. The writer observes that as regards the definition of holiness, "the Curia remains faithful to models inspired by the most traditional hagiograpical literature." Virtue must be heroic and activity ultra-human.

Passion. For the Franciscan, virtuous deeds are demonstrations, each one treated separately without connecting it to others in the biography. This approach tends to demonstrate that an adult life marked by consecration to religious life and holiness is of interest because it reveals virtues rather than because it is a continuous human experience.

The Saint Anne episode, following §67, is a repeat of the story about Colette's mother, but in the context of "the world above." Colette does not like her mother because she was "several times married" (P. de Vaux §68). In a vision, however, Colette saw the numerous "progeny" of Saint Anne, who

> revealed how, despite her having been married several times, nonetheless the whole church militant and triumphant of her most noble progeny greatly honored and revered her.[3]

Perrine understandably does not describe the vision since she does not herself choose to repeat Colette's comment on her mother's remarriage. This reinforces the impression that, in the mind of Pierre de Vaux, the two episodes are linked. Colette, who was convinced by the vision, from then on had a great devotion to Saint Anne, as confirmed by Perrine (§43). Through the excellence of their holiness, Anne's children and grandchildren "redeemed" the successive marriages of the mother of the Virgin. Colette's mother's second marriage was implicitly "saved" by her daughter's holiness. This again reflects the idea that her parents were saved through the merits of their daughter.[4]

---

[3] Saint Anne's eldest daughter is Mary "holding by the hand her very dear son; ... the second was Mary James with her four children: James the Less, Saint Simon, Saint Jude and Joseph the Just. The III daughter was Saint Mary Salome with her two children: Saint James the Great and Saint John the Evangelist" (§68).

[4] The text mentioned, *Vieillards de Corbie,* does not mention this remarriage at all. A. Vauchez, *La sainteté en Occident*, 593, notes that the miraculous birth of the saint in an elderly household may indicate an adoption.

The examples given partially resolve the opposition between the virginal state and the married state (a second marriage can occur only after widowhood) through the holiness of the children alone. Intrinsically, however, the married state brings "many impurities" (§65).

The State of Innocence

For Colette, a "state of innocence" follows, which causes her to flee

> ... for all the times of her life ... all vices and all sins. And especially she had a great horror and abomination of sins of the flesh against which she guarded the bodily senses, which are the doors to the heart, and closed them so firmly that never since she had knowledge of God did vain delight or pleasure of the flesh reach her (P. de Vaux §57).

In detaching her still further from human nature, Pierre de Vaux does not hesitate to use a comparison:

> ... If it is permitted to say it, after the glorious virgin Mary, she was one of the purest and freshest bodily creatures of the feminine sex that ever there was in all the world (§ 57).

This is the most extreme hyperbole. Childhood connotes innocence. The contrast with "great rational creatures" is here reinforced.

Pierre de Vaux sees the innocence of childhood when contrasting Colette with adults in general:

> Little, innocent children, with the graces they have, for they are pure and clear of conscience and without sin and willingly see each other and are familiar together (P. de Vaux §58).

But when he has to prove Colette's exceptional childhood, he does see her as a sinner (P. de Vaux §4 already quoted). The process is identical but applied in different terms, according to the needs of the demonstration.

Once an adult, she sought out the children from whom she had fled as a child herself:

> The little handmaid of our Lord, because of the conformity or similarity she had with little children in their pure, clean bodies and consciences, saw them very willingly and became familiar with them, talking to them sweetly and joyfully (§58).

The significance of childhood changes, depending on whether it is contrasted with or compared to Colette. There are two consequences of this: the state of innocence makes her "like little children ... marvelously fearful and doubtful" (§58), always coupled with its explicit contrast: "She was fearful and doubtful towards great and important creatures" (§59).

Concupiscence is frustrated by her innocence:

> And what is more, several who, before they visited her, were inflamed with carnal concupiscence were afterward cooled by the sight of her purity and blessed presence (§63).

The State of Patient Suffering

Unique in her purity, this creature was also unique in her suffering, lived out with exceptional patience. The contrast with others plays with registers of time, place, and intensity:

> A thing very piteous was that, in the places and the times when creatures take their rest and comfort, in those places of bed where all manner of people take their rest, both healthy and sick, never took she any rest; for despite longing to be in her bed after the

pains she sometimes bore by day, she however could never have any rest (§122).

This stylistic form is once again pushed to its limits:

> Just as on Sundays and feastdays and solemnities, when all manner of people of religion and devotion in church and society took their rest, if not spiritually at least bodily, she, on those days, bore greater and incomparably worse pain than on other ferial days. And the greater the feastday and solemnity, so much greater was the agony of her pain ... (§122).

These two long quotes show how the biographer insists on how different Colette's way of life was from that of others, using the registers of rest, joy, places, and times to indicate the differences.

The liturgical feast means suffering: this is sanctity. Perrine repeats Pierre de Vaux's words, with the assertion: "I have seen," but a few lines later she writes:

> ... and in the same way, I have heard them say and also I have heard Brother Pierre de Rains and brother Franchois Claret recall that the greater was the feast and solemnity the greater the grief and evil she bore (§63a).

Perrine also specifically mentions Christmas, Easter, and Pentecost, repeating the reference to the brothers. She confirms that Colette suffered patiently and that the pains "seemed sweet to her," although she herself may sometimes have complained of them and noted the coincidence with the feastdays. It seems that the brothers drew out the notion, "suffering feast," together with this inversely proportional comparison. The Franciscan's biography confirms this interpretation, following from gathered recollections of the sisters.

The virtue of patience in the face of excessive suffering puts the finishing touches to the saint's exceptional character.

> So many and such infirmities and maladies, so many dreadful pains and physical and spiritual agonies, so many horrible sufferings and cruel torments, for her whole life, joyously and patiently she wished to suffer and to bear for love. It is an indescribable and incredible thing and she never showed any sign of disturbance or impatience (P. de Vaux §185).

Her patience is all the more remarkable when it is friends or family members who cause her sufferings. The antithetical process recurs here:

> She loves. / She is not loved.
> She does good. / She suffers persecution.

The subject of the persecuted just person, alone against all others, is also hinted at:

> The enemy ... caused her to be persecuted by those privy to her, and by strangers, by clerics and by the rich and the nobles (P. de Vaux §186).

Then come examples of her troubles, including the time she was accused of being a usurer, a woman rich in gold and silver (§189).

Perrine emphasizes her patience in suffering, but says nothing of persecution by her friends. She mentions the part played by the brothers:

> Her good father confessors knew and were truly familiar with these pains and troubles (§63a).[5]

---

[5] A. Vauchez emphasizes the importance of the confessor in the biographies of the saints, *La sainteté en Occident*, 119.

Colette's possible confidences are replaced by a collection of demonstrations and proofs:

> To the glorious holy martyrs who are in paradise God has given great grace and happy result; they have been roasted, burned, taken down, skinned and quartered and killed, etc. (§63a).

Colette, through the intensity and variety of her sufferings, has suffered more than all of them.

The function of antithesis is revealed from the first few lines:

> Whoever might wish to consider the sobriety and sparseness of her eating would find that she lived more by divine than human means. Who could naturally fast for XI days and XI nights without eating and without drinking? (§114).

The heroic virtue required of a saint becomes a sort of record to be broken. But conversely, Colette is liberal to others. (Is this a memory of an episode in Clare's life, who washed and kissed the feet of the mendicant sisters?)

> To the brothers "who have the administration of the convents" or to the friars who beg, "all sweetly and charitably she gave them to drink, filling the vessel to the very brim" (§116).

Several examples of her generosity follow, all relating to food or drink.

MATERIALITY OF SIGNS AND SPIRITUALIZATION OF THE PHYSICAL

Since the same process applies to all the virtues under consideration, it would be tedious to cover them all; so we will simply look at a broad sample.

Poverty

This applies to clothing, bedding, newly-built convents, the habits of the reformed religious, attitudes toward money, books (particularly breviaries), and to the poor.

The habit:

> She had nothing ... to cover her poor body except just one patched habit and a simple short coat without fur or lining, and a thin cloak. This habit could never be completely new (§47).

On a bitterly cold day, the sisters lined her habit on the sly, but Colette noticed and refused to wear it. Here is a clear reference to Francis. The various biographers stressed the Poverello's vigilance in avoiding anything unnecessary in the habit.

This initial description immediately follows the definition of poverty given by Francis: "The friars conform to the life of Jesus Christ and that of the apostles and, through this, they are supereminent and different from all other orders."

While poverty is founded on imitation of Jesus Christ, the examples given are of a material kind. For Francis, poverty is frequently combined with obedience as the renunciation of the will and submission to "any human creature" through the love of God.[6] Colette's biographer does not stress the link

---

[6] Cf. *Saint François d'Assise, Documents: Ecrits et première biographies*, rassemblés et présentés par les PP. Théophile Desbonnets et Damien Vorreux, ofm; deuxième édition revue et augmentée (Paris: Ed. Franciscaines, 1981). Saint Bonaventure, *Legenda Major*, VII, *FA:ED* 2, 577-85.

between the two virtues. Each is seen separately with a set of examples.

The bed and the constructions:

—The bed:

A small amount of straw, covered with a single, poor coverlet, and a sack filled with the same straw was the couch for her rest, although she never rested there (P. de Vaux §48).

—Construction of her oratories:

She wanted them to be humble, poor and small [...] in some ... it was impossible for her to rise or stand straight, and they seemed more than otherwise like huts or small sheds in which to sleep (§49).

She preferred constructions "without excess, poor and simple without interest." In comparison to castles and ducal palaces or richly endowed royal abbeys, the convent cells were remarkably small. But comparing them to urban dwellings in which people were crammed into comfortless and cramped rooms, Colette's monasteries seem to be of reasonable proportions. Having an individual cell was almost luxurious.

Other elements:

—Money received miraculously was used "faithfully and properly"(§52), as were donations (§51).

—She loved books "that were considered to be in the service of God" (§51). She had them purchased or received them as fine gifts from great lords; but she gave them away. When she died, she had none. Colette's love of liturgical books recalls that of Francis, as well as her generosity in giving them away. An instructive episode in the founder's life seems to have been missed by Pierre de Vaux: Francis sold a breviary in order to help the mother of one of the friars.

Chastity

She manifested her chastity by refusing to read the Old Testament and

> the early Fathers, in whose times and ages the said virtues were not ordered nor observed by these Fathers, so never did she wish to hear speak of them; ... but for the new Testament, where the said virtues were otherwise appreciated and praised by the prince of virginity and perfectly maintained and kept by him and his glorious virgin mother and many others of his true friends in this Testament, she had great pleasure and affection and singular love and devotion (§64).

For purposes of demonstration, no doubt, the biographer forces the point. In the fifteenth century, a whole strand of the Church was engaged in rediscovering the Bible as a whole. Translations into the vernacular were being made at that time; but the Colettine movement did not seem to join this immediately. It is difficult to evaluate how well Colette knew the Scriptures. She read the lessons from the office. It is highly possible that she had not read the whole of the sacred text, and the above motivation for this, ascribed to her by her biographer, is interesting.

Her attraction to chastity guides her choice of favorite saints. We have seen the episode of Saint Anne. Her favorite saint was John the Evangelist, who "was especially gifted and endowed with the precious and angelic virtue of virginity." For this reason, she made him,

> before God her advocate and special intercessor and the preserver of the very noble treasure, representing and inspiring the frail and weak vessel of her precious body (§64).

A mystical wedding ring was presented to her

> and placed on her finger [by John the Evangelist] on behalf of the sovereign king and prince of virginity and all purity (§66).

Perrine claims to have seen the ring and states that the friars recount this story. As always for Pierre de Vaux, chastity goes back to childhood. It guides the choice of vocation:

> And to fulfill the said proposal, she made so many representations to our holy father the pope, who well knew her holy desire, that she obtained a bull from him, stating that no women of any state could be received into the religion of madame Saint Clare, which she was repairing and reforming, unless she was a maiden or virgin (§65).

Benedict XIII's bull, however, has no mention of these conditions. The biographer hastens to add that God "ordered otherwise for the better": some "notable ladies" were received, but "none of them was so intimate or familiar as those who had come as virgin or maiden into the said religion."

So was this an invention by Pierre de Vaux? Or was it the remains of a preference that had to go when faced with requests from noble ladies to join as the fame of the reform increased? If this attitude was true, other reasons might have been behind Colette's hesitation. Did she perhaps fear the disparity between young, inexperienced, but easily formed girls and rather older women? Such disparity can arise in newly-founded communities. When the group is better established and of longer standing, it is easier for people to fit in.

Humility

One of the first signs of Colette's humility, let us recall, was the desire to enter the religious life as a "servant." This is also the name by which she described herself: "she named and entitled herself unworthy servant and poor speaker"

(§13). This information is accurate: her correspondence carries many such expressions (typical, incidentally, for this style of letter).

Clare wanted to refuse the title of abbess, but Francis imposed it on her. In her *Rule* and her *Testament,* Clare avoids it, using paraphrases such as: "she who will succeed me in my responsibility." Colette retained the same attitude, reacting against the style of urban abbesses of royal or princely foundations.[7]

Her humility can also be seen in her general behavior and physical attitude:

> –"Never in her life did she allow anyone to say or write anything in her honor or praise" (§13).
> –She had the book that Henry de Baume wrote about her burned (§14).
> –She took "no pleasure" in hearing a "short text" at the head of the constitutions in which she was named "mother."
> –She was merciful to sinners, as was Christ himself.
> –She cared for lepers "with no horror or abhorrence" (§17).
> –When she had to preside, "as in chapter or refectory and elsewhere, she had such great doubt and tremor," and also "in any place where she was, or in community with others, or individually, she always wished to take the lowest and most humble place. And when she was alone, commonly she was on her knees or seated on the ground. And very rarely did she choose the higher" (§17).

The physical attitude was also important in prayer, and the same in the refectory. When she was alone,

---

[7] Rather than the rule of Saint Clare and practice of the "very highest poverty," these Clarisses had adopted the rule of Pope Urban IV, allowing possession of goods and property. Cf. 2nd Part.

most often she took it [the meal] seated on the ground, crying and groaning so abundantly and piteously that she and her meat were all bedewed in tears (§17).

She called on a novice to begin the office, although according to monastic custom, only a professed sister could do it.

Obedience

From the time that she was a recluse, she encouraged others to keep, through obedience, "the commandments of God and the Holy Church." Her concept of obedience was hierarchical. Laity must obey the commandments and the Church, religious their superiors most directly. Colette refused the title of mother, but in her "ordinances" required the religious sisters to carry out the orders of their "sovereigns": "you must obey and submit to the will and determination of the one who presides" (§23). Self-will is the "broad road that leads to hell." Religious obedience is rooted in that of Christ, who was obedient "even unto his very agonizing and painful death and passion" (allusion to the letter of Saint Paul to the Philippians); or again: "there is no sacrifice in the world that pleases our Lord so much as true obedience."

Later on we will consider at a theological level the consequences of this view of obedience. For now, we note that the quotation from the *Rule* (X, 2) is incomplete, and the term, "sisters," used by Clare, is replaced by "subjects." The content of obedience in this passage from the *Rule* covers what the sisters "have promised the Lord to observe, and which is not contrary to their soul nor to their profession." It is not the abbess, but the *Rule,* that determines the purpose of the obedience that would open the way to domination of spirit and intelligence.[8]

The chapter mainly gives examples of Colette's concern to ensure that feasts and solemnities were observed by her

---

[8] The Middle Ages were very hierarchical, particularly the fifteenth century: "obedience" was a concept much favored by jurists imbued with Roman law, who related it to the attitude to be taken towards the king.

sisters and by the laity. As we have seen, this involved suspending work, business, and military activities.

THE FUNCTION OF SUFFERING

As we have already seen in the discussion on antithetical structure, suffering is very important. It involves the subjection of the body to the soul through mortification, especially related to food:

> She fasted every day, never tasting or eating any flesh, no matter what sickness or weakness she had … (P. de Vaux §114).

This exceeded the provisions of the *Rule*.[9]

As regards her various sufferings and austerities, we have, even more than before, a sense of the quantitative and qualitative totality of her undertaking. Expressions such as "for all times in her life," "from her young age" (§114) occur frequently. The example of constant fasting is typical of the extreme nature of Colette's actions. Hyperbole demonstrates sanctity from the physical point of view. The accumulation of evils is an aspect of hyperbole. One consequence of this is comparison: Colette suffered "more than" all the martyrs and desert ascetics. The comparison of equality, used most often in demonstrating childhood holiness, gives way to the comparison of superiority in respect to her adult holiness.

Natural illnesses have a supernatural meaning – they are signs of divine election. Almost all parts of her body were affected: her feet were hot, her eyes sore (recalling Francis,

---

[9] *Sainte Claire d'Assise, Documents,* rassemblés, présentés et traduits par Damien Vorreux, O.F.M. (Paris: Ed. Franciscaines, 1983), Rg III, 8-10: "At Christmas, however, she may take two meals, no matter what day of the week it is. The very young sisters, those who are weak and those who serve outside the monastery, may be dispensed from fasting at the discretion of the abbess. If there is a clear need, sisters will not be held to the corporal fast." *CA:ED*, 113.

who suffered with his eyes?), her mouth was on fire (§63a), her body was full of pain (bones cracking, etc.) (§42).

Pierre de Vaux distinguishes between sufferings that were caused by demons or men and those sent by God. To a great extent, these were physical sufferings. Austerities may also be included in this context, because of their consequences.

We have seen examples of the physical sufferings sent by God. Without going over these again, we note here that they had an educational value, purifying the senses and subordinating the body to the soul. Pierre de Vaux does not see his own contradiction – a being so pure since childhood, comparable even to the Virgin, would have no need of this kind of purification. Clearly once again the biographer is following a schema of proofs, a discourse that was taking place prior to the case under consideration.

– Suffering appears and disappears without cause.
– This suffering is primarily physical.
– Sufferings are linked, and thus accounted for in connection with the liturgical cycle or with Colette's activities: when she receives in the parlor, her sufferings cease; but when the visit is finished, they return redoubled.
– The greater the feast, the more she suffers (inversely proportional relationship).

The devil manipulates humans. For example, old friends turn abruptly against her, becoming the cause of trials (P. de Vaux §42). Religious who do not accept the reform slander her. Perrine (§71, 263) mentions the case of the fathers of Dole led by John Foucault. Pierre de Vaux is not interested in the differing point of view of her opponents. Neither author says anything about the content of these differences. Such information would be helpful today for understanding an important episode in the story of the reform.

While the demons caused countless sufferings, these fell into two main categories: extreme vexations leading to physical violence and fear increasing to terror caused by hideous apparitions (P. de Vaux §159). The vexations hinder Colette's sleep or prayer (P. de Vaux §153). Some seem comical (the demon, it might be recalled, threw the lamp to the ground several times to stop her reading). Others are terrifying, causing agonizing reactions and visions that agitate her nervous system.

All these sufferings affected her body in all its members and the use of her senses. They weakened her nerves. God placed on this person a mark exclusively and essentially painful.

Here there are signs of the *sequela Christi* [following of Christ], which underlay all religious and monastic inquiry during the preceding centuries. The imitation of Christ was the foundation of the virtues, with the classic distinction between precepts and counsels. Virtues, however, were manifested by a series of typical behaviors, as with prayer, and affected areas of activity and appearance. There was no analysis of the inner being, hence a very formal or even materialistic notion of the spiritual. All aspects of action, human relations, and behavior were saturated with this idea of the supernatural, whose essential characteristic was to be irrational.

Using the criteria for sanctity as developed by the Holy See in the fourteenth and fifteenth centuries, Pierre de Vaux had no other means of showing holiness. Other *vitae* of that time use the same procedures.[10]

There was, however, a different current in Italy somewhat later on. A companion of Catherine of Bologna wrote her biography, sketching out an analysis of her inner life. But this comes from a different cultural milieu, that of the Italian Renaissance – humanist and highly cultivated.[11]

---

[10] A. Vauchez, *La sainteté en Occident,* 2nd Part, "L'Église romaine face à la sainteté," 553 ff.

[11] I. Bembo, *Specchio di Illuminazione, vita di Santa Catarina da Bologna,* 1787, Edizione divulgata a cure delle clarisse del Corpus Domini da Ferrare, collana serafica, I (Ferrare, 1975). While giving much attention to the virtues, the account of the spiritual life is clearly important. The author evidently felt that the originality of Catherine's holiness lay in her spiritual experience. It is true that the saint herself transcribed it: we are

in the presence of foretastes of what will come later, the spiritual autobiography, brilliantly represented by *El libro de mi vida* [*The Book of My Life*] by Teresa of Avila.

CHAPTER 7

Eternity in Time

Reality Emerges

Colette's particular form of sanctity is demonstrated by a set of fixed, pre-determined evidential data. Her sanctity is heroic from the outset, rather than the slow transfiguration by grace of a free nature rooted in a specific society and period. These latter merely form a backdrop against which a conventional schema unfolds.

Sometimes, however, a breach appears in the canopy that overhangs reality as the spirit attempts to exorcise a painful, trying event. This breach reveals an unexpected emergence of reality demonstrating its rootedness in the story. In this context, what is omitted can be as telling as the identifiable facts.

The most interesting of these give indications about the how society and Church are viewed.

Social Types

These appear occasionally in relationship to Colette, indicating which social stratas were interested in the Colettine reform and in what ways.

Nobles were involved from the outset of the heavenly mission in the form of Henry de Baume, a religious brother and Burgundian nobleman.[1] Through him, the recluse received the support of Madame de Brisay.[2] A network of relationships developed then, giving Colette access to the pope and enabling her to begin the reformed life. The Countess of Geneva, whom Perrine mentions by name, received Colette and her companions at her castle and later, according to Perrine, took Colette to Besançon with her niece Mahaut, subsequently Duchess of Bavaria (Perrine §22 and P. de Vaux §42).

Noble men and women appear, from time to time, throughout the story. They provide the saint with the gold she needs or give her valuable books. An exchange system operates. They obtain financial help and support for Colette and, eventually, give a daughter or niece to the monastery. Colette puts her healing gifts or the effectiveness of her prayers for protection or cures at their disposal. The presence of nobles enhances Colette's reputation. Overall, however, the biographies remain discreet. The Bourbon king, James, known to be "a devoté of Colette," is not named, even by Perrine.

Pierre de Vaux reveals other features through elements of the story. Section 18 offers a brief account of contemporary manners, the accuracy of which is confirmed in literary accounts from a slightly later date. Marguerite de Navarre's *Heptameron* evokes the same atmosphere in her châteaux. The noble lover of a young woman whom he cannot marry

---

[1] This definitely explains Colette's work in Burgundian-owned lands. Henry's father and brother served the Duke of Burgundy. Cf. H. Lippens, "Henry de Baume, coopérateur de S. Colette: recherches sur sa vie et publications de ses statuts inédits," *Sacris Erudiri*, I (Bruges, 1948), 235.

[2] On Madame de Brisay, see Marquis de Brisay, *Histoire de la maison de Brisay depuis le IXe siècle jusqu'à nos jours*, part 1 (Maners, 1889). Madame de Brisay was Colette's loyal companion on her journeys at the start of her mission. In particular, clues to their visit to Péronne on December 3, 1406 appear in the accounts of the poor pensioners: "item to Madame de Brisay, Sister Colette recluse of Corbie when they came to Péronne the first time, they were sent a batch of wine, for this II sols." Quoted by M. Estienne: "Séjour de sainte Colette à Péronne," *Bulletin des antiquaires de Picardie*, (1937/38).

because of their different social positions has only one desire: to seduce and then abandon her.[3]

In Pierre de Vaux's uplifting account, Colette's indirect intervention shatters the process. It demonstrates the influence of religious brothers and sisters, especially the mendicants, in the life of the nobility. Marguerite de Navarre describes this in detail but in a different way. The literary work is an indictment against the mendicants, who had become a real scourge on society. It criticizes the Friars Minor and wishes to break free from their influence. Pierre de Vaux, on the contrary, less than a century earlier, brings the Order's beneficial action right into people's daily lives. Despite writing about quite similar social environments, the religious author and the secular author diverge, showing that some social classes were beginning to gain independence of judgment and action outside the context of "religion." Pierre de Vaux indirectly confirms this in his "Letter to the Inhabitants of Amiens." Some of the assurances he gives show that the townspeople did not always receive religious men and women favorably and may even have rejected them. He assures them that the reformed religious are not "false, deceitful and hypocritical." These are precisely the qualities with which the *Heptameron* reproaches religious.[4]

Pierre de Vaux fairly frequently mentions a "leading citizen" without naming him. Perrine, for her part, identifies him as Adam Mangnier. The social class of the bourgeois is less typical, but it also plays a part in the reform, though not as significant. Perrine names some individuals who give Colette financial help, create bonds of friendship with her

---

[3] In the Friar Minor's account, the nobleman sometimes also spoke "disrespectful words" about the saint and even experienced carnal desire for her. These points are confirmed by literary or historical accounts at the time: the nobleman exercised his power, gave into his instincts, and often had respect for nothing.

[4] The reluctance of the towns to welcome mendicants would continue to increase. A century later in very Catholic Spain, a character as radiant as Teresa of Avila would have serious problems being accepted in the towns as she began her Carmelite reform. She reports this herself in the *Book of the Foundations*.

to the extent that they go with her on her journeys (Perrine §41, P. de Vaux §86), or give her, with some hesitation, their daughter (Perrine §16, P. de Vaux §92). These are wealthy merchants who travel a great deal on business (Perrine §15-16). Compared to the nobility, who had no occupation other than warfare, the middle classes were seen as workers holding a certain amount of economic power. This is borne out by historical fact. These bourgeois groups were sometimes cautious about welcoming religious foundations.

Ordinary people appear rarely. Whether they live in town or countryside, they are hardly ever identified individually. There are no adversaries among them. At the heart of those who admire Colette or benefit from her miracles and prayers, there are those who put themselves out on feast days to welcome her (Perrine §44), the sick whose affection for her does not pose a danger to society, the lepers to whom Colette has been drawn since childhood, and beggars, including the young, to whom she gives her meals.

Rough soldiers, mercenaries, armed men from one party or another belong to the background of war and appear fairly often in the account (particularly in that of Pierre de Vaux, as Perrine is more concerned to remain within the religious world). During her travels, Colette meets them often. They are characterized by verbal aggression (Perrine §32) and threats of physical violence. They besiege towns and thus hinder travel plans. On one occasion, there is reference to a battle that Colette's prayers prevent.

Priests and religious are mentioned more often. The significance of the Abbot of Corbie is indicated by the role he plays in Colette's life. Perrine describes a great dinner and the scene where Colette is enclosed in her cell in the presence of the Abbot, of Father Pinet, of some religious from the abbey, and of a crowd of people. This religious ceremony is a sensation in the town.

As with other groups, their only function in the story is in terms of their relationship to Colette. Pierre de Vaux spends little time on the entourage of religious, male or female. Perrine identifies individuals by name, as she does for members of other groups. One can actually make up a list of Colette's sisters and brothers: her confessors, two of whom, Father Pinet and Brother Henry, acted as her spiritual directors; Pierre de Reims (no doubt Pierre de Vaux); Brother François Claret, a lay brother; the sisters, her first companions, and the abbesses. Among the male religious and priests, there were "enemies": e.g. a theology teacher, Brother Foucault.

Saint Vincent Ferrier's meeting with Colette during the Aragonese Dominican's missionary journeys increased her reputation.

The detailed information given by the texts, especially that of Perrine, effectively illustrates the diverse social categories that Colette met during her travels and extended stays in the various reformed convents.

Pierre de Vaux's image of the saint is somewhat different. She is never entirely alone within her monasteries, as we have seen: people watch over her, care for her, etc. Her decisions, the directions she takes, are always discussed with her confessors. She relies much on her companions, either in recalling memories or recounting apparitions.

There must have been frequent communication between monasteries. One abbess recounts her memories of Colette (Perrine §33), while another sister writes hers down. The "Memorial of Hesdin," which we will look at in the next chapter, reports more or less the same facts as the biographies, demonstrating an interchange among the monasteries.

There were close relations between the two branches of the Colettines and not just among their leaders. Under what conditions did meetings take place? The episode of the lay brother cutting out the habit deserves attention: where was he working? Colette seems to have been in the same room with him, on the other side of the grille. Otherwise, it would seem difficult for her to hold the fabric. There were, in any case, frequent exchanges in the parlor between Colette and the friars, as well as with the latter and the sisters, as Perrine often reports. We get the impression of a life of intense fraternity, based on the shared experience of a common task, of which Colette is the pivot and the driving force.

The State of Society and Church

From the few facts that can be detected, the most important (apart from continuous and widespread civil or foreign wars) is the lack of any political authority. A situation of insecurity prevailed throughout the journeys and within the towns. On one occasion, the bell for matins aroused the people, who thought it was the alarm, and they accused the community of sending signals to the enemy (Perrine §74c). Colette, despite her fame, was taken to be a spy (Perrine §74a).

Neither Pierre de Vaux nor Perrine give many details and never name the various combatant parties. The names were well known at the time, so reticence was no doubt a matter of discretion towards the great opposing families, Burgundy and Armagnac. Colette had supporters in both camps: James of Bourbon's son-in-law was an Armagnac. This anonymity however gives the impression that what the witnesses remember is not the identity of the parties in these confrontations but the almost continuous violence. The impression is strengthened by the fact that there is no mention of the king or the royal government. Political structures seem to be loose.

The pope is named by his title and surrounded by his court at the interview in October 1406. Neither Perrine nor Pierre de Vaux mentions the Great Schism. Perrine does name Felix V, however – this later schism did not last long and was less traumatizing to the Christian conscience than the first. The biographers' silence may perhaps also be explained by the need of hagiography to disengage itself from reality. When Perrine says Rome instead of Nice (§23), it may indicate that, beyond the schism, the Christian conscience is linking up to the Apostolic Church once more.[5]

Underlying a traditional account of sanctity that uses an evocative symbolism in a religious environment, it is possible

---

[5] Around 1300, Cardinal Lemoine wrote: "Where the Pope is, there is Rome." This lapse by Perrine might therefore be deliberate or perhaps "automatic."

to detect, even in Pierre de Vaux, a link to reality, possibly unintentional. There emerges, at the very heart of the saint's legend, the unexpected – History itself.

In a wartime context, there are rare economic indicators revealing a difficult situation.

Apart from the lepers, who belong to the urban landscape, the text includes references to epidemics and to plague (P. de Vaux §71). On one occasion, nearly the whole community is struck down by an epidemic. Famine is mentioned several times. As the sisters often lack the necessities of life, they are helped by the charity of people in towns. Collecting alms is a regular occupation. Some of the friars are appointed especially to this task.

The monastery is then an integral part of the life of the town. The town, being fortified, provides a safe haven for the community in times of trouble.[6]

Other indications show the exchanges that took place between the monastery and the people. In Poligny, the sisters go to look for water outside the monastery, demonstrating a certain flexibility. At Besançon, a sick woman (who seems to have been an epileptic) does not stay outside the convent. Colette brings her into the parlor in order to cure her.

More surprising, a priori, is the presence of lay people in Colette's private oratory when she attends Mass. This could happen only with the agreement of at least some of her entourage. Assuming the oratory adjoined the choir, it should have been strictly contained within the enclosure. This leads us to observe that the idea of enclosure was not as absolute then as it became in the post-tridentine period, particularly with Teresa of Avila, who struggled with the laxity she experienced in her own convent of the Incarnation.

Moreover while traveling among her foundations, Colette and her sisters in their wagon were entirely surrounded by lay people, who acted as escort. The text says twice that

---

[6] The Poligny site, for example, had been chosen for its safety. One part of the convent backed onto a steep rock. The building itself stood on the site of a very old arsenal with thick walls and an underground path that emerged into open country in case the town was besieged.

Colette and her sisters rode behind regular visitors to the convent (Perrine §86). One of the "leading bourgeois" even observed that Colette was very light.[7]

Little more than a century apart, the two reformers (Colette and Teresa) have different perceptions of enclosure. In Colette's time, there was greater integration of the monastery with the town and with people's ordinary lives. It was not entirely cut off from the urban environment; there were "bridges."

Life inside the Convent

Here too, Perrine gives more information about life inside the convents. The atmosphere evoked results from various factors, already described. There are also signs of sisterly life, manifested by their care for Colette and hers for them. She is concerned for the sick sisters and watches over their psychological health, as noted in the case of the one who was absent from the office for eight years and for whom, apparently, the reformer could do nothing all that time (§63, P. de Vaux §73).

The regular life must be followed, but not rigidly. There are distractions in the office that Colette tries to curb, chattering on leaving the choir after the saint has been in ecstasy, races through the convent chasing after a "heavenly animal," and certainly idle talk about the abbess's actions or behavior: Perrine actually mentions that the incidents she reports were told to her by one sister or another. The parlor meetings with the friars must also have contributed to the convent gossip. Perrine often writes that they have told her some fact.

Colette is, therefore, closely watched and always surrounded, both while traveling and in the convent. Her moments of solitude seem to have been during the night or in

---

[7] This would have been unthinkable for Teresa of Avila, for example, who made her daughters wear stockings (although she would have preferred bare feet, hence the term "carmelitas descalzadas") because during a journey, when a sister was boarding a cart, the driver noticed her bare heel.

her prolonged "ecstasies." There is always at least one sister near the oratory. Colette arouses affection and faithful friendships. Her "mistress," with her at the beginning of her Christian life in childhood and later on in Besançon, is present in the parlor with the friars. The group of religious sisters and brothers, along with Henry, was certainly a source of powerful and unshakeable support to her. History will forget these faces and that of Brother Henry who certainly deserves better. Pierre de Vaux is the reason for this oblivion. The criteria for sainthood at the time required that, in order to be raised to the altars, Colette must appear out of the ordinary, a "celestial" being invested with an exceptional mission, a solitary character against whose greatness others must diminish.

Perrine's ignorance of this requirement permitted her to express a communion between friars and sisters, limitless devotion to Colette, "the little handmaid," and the dynamism of renewal as they worked side by side. Along with the help and friendship of the laity, was this not the secret of the undertaking's success?

True fraternity, deeply rooted in the spirit of Francis and Clare of Assisi, which Pierre de Vaux does not mention and which only here and there emerges in Perrine's text, is certainly at the core of true reform. In terms of this endeavor, one might wonder whether such a constraint did not produce a lasting effect on the reform itself.

Shaping the Story

The story moves from childhood to death, giving a catalogue of miracles; but the whole story is itself, largely speaking, a catalogue of miracles. Basically, the biographer is interested in the religious vows and various gifts and virtues. This underlying structure follows the pattern of biographies of Francis of Assisi and a priori perhaps even more closely that of Clare by Thomas of Celano.[8] The framework is the same, but the focus is different.

---

[8] *Sainte Claire d'Assise, Documents,* traduits par Damien Vorreux, OFM (Paris: Ed. Franciscaines, 1983), *Vita*:

The *Vita* of Francis follows chronology more closely. Furthermore, it traces a spiritual journey, from a gilded youth to a naked death on the bare earth. We see Francis become a saint, grow in sanctity. Another important point is his experience of true "conversion" of heart. His commitment to follow the poor, crucified Christ takes place in stages. Francis takes a long time to find his way. He does not feel himself to be the founder of an order. No more does Clare, who wants only to live an evangelical life like Francis, with a few companions, according to the options available at the time to women. Celano describes her spiritual journey as more linear; her sanctity develops earlier. Although the *Vita* includes a number of miracles, the spiritual dimension is still dominant.

Pierre de Vaux's lesser concern for chronology goes along with an increase in accounts of marvels and a lack of interest in scriptural roots. Only the structure of Celano's *Vitae* remains, with a rather different spiritual content, most noticeable in the concept of sanctity and the spirituality that it assumes. Pierre de Vaux's saint is "disincarnated" from family and social milieu.

Ch. VI to XI, her virtues, some miracles.

Ch. XII to XX: Clare's prayer and its effectiveness, her devotion to the Eucharist and the Passion.

Ch. XXI to XXIV: her miracles, her great charity.

Ch. XXV to XXIX: sickness and death, her funeral.

For the English see *CA:ED*, 272-329.

Saint François d'Assise, Documents: Ecrits et première biographies, rassemblés et présentés par les PP. Théophile Desbonnets et Damien Vorreux, OFM (Paris: Ed. Franciscaines, 1981), *Vita Prima*:

1st part:

Ch. I to IX: conversion of Francis, its stages.

Ch. X to XV: beginnings of the Order of Friars Minor.

Ch. XVI to XXII: the virtues of Francis, his prayer and preaching.

Ch. XXIII to XXX: some miracles, his great charity.

2nd part:

Ch. I to VII: the stigmata, the virtues of the first friars, Francis's return to the Portiuncula.

Ch. VIII to X: death and funeral.

3rd part:

Canonization and miracles *post-mortem*. See 1, 171-308.

Time, in the sense of a period unfolding, is, so to speak, non-existent. The frequency of expressions such as "for her whole life" and others of the same kind assumes linear time, where, strictly speaking, nothing unexpected occurs. The idea of the development of the human person is not part of the biographer's mental plan. Predestination is always implicit.

Similarly, geographical location does not have precise features: "once in a convent," "in a region, in a country." In an indeterminate place, in a landscape tortured by war, violence, famine and plague, where the scenery has no impact on sanctity, roles seem to have been cast beforehand: the nobles, the bourgeois, the religious, the peasant, the town-dweller, the rough soldier, the highway robber, and a luminous figure, not human because holy and celestial from the time of her youth – the saint.

This is clearly not history; it is a story with a "poetic" and cathartic function. Human types are not individualized. They are characters in a drama of good versus evil involving all the invisible powers. Supernatural beings are no more amazing than human beings, the "poor weak creatures" who succumb to the traps of the "enemy from hell."

But our story is not purely one of this type. Reality does break through, especially in Perrine, as if the unexpected were erupting, cracking the structures and the backdrop used by generations of hagiographers.

Before giving her own views, Perrine reveals her material. At a time of deep crisis in a broken world that is gradually binding up its wounds, the reflections of a woman religious are seen as powerless to discern the signs of sanctity. Tried and tested schemas are applied to what may be a new phenomenon: reform of a decadent order by a woman.

It is remarkable that Pierre de Vaux does not cover the history of the reform in his *Vita*. The system of signs that he uses is defective; but in his failure even to describe reality, he reveals his anguish and disarray. Our astonishment at the absence of the history of the Colettine reform in his work lessens if we understand that definitive reform was less important than the "salvation" brought about by the saint taking on herself the punishment deserved by the people. For Pierre de Vaux, therefore, the Colettine reform meant that young people would come forward to offer themselves and to pray for sinners. The marvelous was a way of indicating the magnitude of the sacrifice and its approval by a God who was vengeful and just.

This plan for unfolding the meaning of holiness, however, stumbles against the one irreducible fact that the marvelous cannot overcome: Colette's death.

COLETTE CONFRONTS ETERNITY: THE STORY RESTORED

Chapter XIX, entitled "of the consummation of her days and her passing," consists of sections 190 to 200. Sections 190 to 194 cover the period just before her death and the death itself, while section 195 describes her burial. Sections 195 to 200 describe the visions of persons who confirm Colette's entry into heaven.

The only important differences in Perrine are details on the sources of the testimonies. There are two kinds of testimonies for the period just before the death and the death itself: direct and indirect.

Testimonies

Perrine has "heard tell" from Colette, "at the convent of Liesdin," that "she was all ready to begin to do well again, as if she were strong enough, and as if she had never done well" (§78). In addition to quotations from Colette, she adds her own testimony on the saint's zeal, repeating the words of Pierre de Vaux's text.

The indirect testimonies begin in section 79, after the announcement at Hesdin of Colette's imminent death, with the words

> I heard tell from the good Father de Rains and Sister Marie and several sisters from the convent at Gand who at her passing were in Arras.

A little later on, she states that Pierre de Rains is her confessor.

Perrine does not deviate at all from the lines of Pierre de Vaux's text that we are going to consider. His testimony is particularly valuable as he was present at Gand.

This text reverses the normal roles of Perrine and the Franciscan. Perrine is usually the direct witness, unveiling earlier material, the sources of the facts recounted by Pierre de Vaux, and adding others. Here, however, Pierre de Vaux is the eyewitness. Perrine is absent.

The four sections describing the death are striking in their general tone, different from the rest of the account. Strictly speaking, there are no marvelous components. Colette's words are reported directly, the only time this happens in the Franciscan's story. Dates are given, also a unique feature in his account.[9] The style is altered. We have here a text taking a new direction, as if her death were resistant to the shaping of the story and to the marvelous. The a priori plan for interpreting reality had no hold over the insurmountable fact of death. The favored witness leaves behind his arguments and symbolism and becomes a simple, faithful observer. This final moment provides the truest possible approach to Colette. Faced with death, with her work, with her companions, the brothers and the sisters, she reveals herself.

---

[9] According to A. Vauchez, from the fourteenth century onwards, the *Ars moriendi* influenced the "holy death," just as in the *Vitae:* it was important for death to be as similar to that of Christ as possible. Saints announce the time and date of their passing, speak edifying words, and receive the last sacraments showing their attachment to the Church. One word, one attitude could jeopardise the life of the saint, who is always uncertain of going to heaven. Some of these features are found in Pierre de Vaux, but the dominant feature is something else, in that here, the death is neither spectacular nor public Cf. *La sainteté en Occident aux derniers siècles du Moyen-Age d'après les procès de canonisation et les documents hagiographiques* (Rome, 1981), 598-99.

One Last Look

Together with Francis, who exclaims: "Let us begin, brothers, to serve the Lord, for up until now we have done little or nothing,"[10] Colette was

> all ready and prepared to start again to work properly as if she were strong, and as if she had never done anything well up to now (§190).

Nonetheless, at the final point of no return that was her death, she declares to her confessor:

> My father, what I have done through our Lord I have done despite being a great sinner and entirely flawed, and if I have more to do, I do not know how I can do it, other than just as I have done it (§192).

As death approaches, from February 26, 1447 onward, Colette will cease to think about her work at all. There is now only prayer and silence.

Colette remains in the presence of her entourage, the friars and the sisters. No lay people are mentioned as being present, but only the sisters of the community, her confessor, and her companion.

She solemnly takes leave of her sisters about three weeks before she dies (§191). Her farewell to the two friars has a different tone:

> On the Friday [before her death] at vespers, she spoke gently and comfortably to the friars, and on the Saturday after Mass she very humbly took leave of them (§193).

She foretells her death two years in advance and announces it more precisely three weeks beforehand. It is as

---

[10] Saint François d'Assise, Documents, *Vita prima*, 103, *Legenda Major*, XIV, 1. See *FA:ED* 1, 272-73; *FA:ED* 2, 640.

if space has contracted for this woman who had traveled the length and breadth of France. Her oratory is her entire world before she takes to the bed that will become her deathbed. For her biographer, time also becomes concentrated. There remains her last confession (on February 26th) and communion during Mass. For her companions, this day begins the final stage:

> She was as in a state of childhood and innocence, with no care or concern for things of the world but only to pray and to praise God aloud and in silence.

Time is measured now by daily mass, which she "hears" up to the last on that Saturday in March when she has "a greater abundance of tears ... than she has had any other day." She feels a "severe and great pain," which "will last to her final breath" (§193). After this Mass,

> she went to her bed, the final bed, and she laid herself down on the bed fully dressed in her normal attire, and the black veil on her head which our holy father the pope gave her and placed on her when he received her profession and made her abbess. Forthwith she closed her mouth and eyes, and they never opened again ... (§194).

She remains in this state to the end. Pierre de Vaux again writes:

> XLVIIIJ [49] hours was she on this bed in the pain that God had especially given to her, without seeing and without any movement or gesture, nor sign on her face nor any other part of her body ...

From such comments we conclude that her general attitude was one of peace and certainty. She found no serious errors in herself: looking back caused her no futile regret. This state of mind gave her calm inner strength.

Some elements point to a return to her origins: she wears the veil given her by Benedict XIII, symbol of the start of her mission. Sinking into silence and prayer, her eyes closed, recalls her time as a recluse. Colette wanted to be alone with death, with God. Has she always had this longing for the hermit life? Long periods alone in her personal oratory during her lifetime and the withdrawal in her final days would seem to indicate this. While her attitude to the friars is courteous, her behavior to her sisters seems more remote.

We have seen how Colette was watched, even spied on by her companions, particularly the sisters. If she could, she would have prevented all the gossip and overattentiveness around her. It was common to wish to collect the last words of a "saint" in a convent. "Nothing will I say or speak to you": Colette firmly prevents any attempt at this. Her attitude might also assume a certain weariness towards her companions, a refusal to be the subject of observation and comment, because she has had to endure it. Breaking all contact with the outside world (eyes and mouth closed, silence and prayer) would then be not just a return to the starting-point (seclusion) but also the wish to live out her death in the quiet truth of her being.

The somber account concludes with the final sections of the chapter where the marvelous is discreetly introduced once more. It appears gradually after twelve hours:

> Her whole body was transmuted into a marvelous beauty. It was white like snow, and the veins that appeared among the white were of finest azure and all her members were so beautiful, so fine, soft, tractable, scented and sweet-smelling that they seemed to be limbs that represented a state of innocence and all purity and cleanness (§195).

Pierre de Vaux reprises the characteristics of death given in the *Vitae*: a flexible body and extraordinary phenomena.

In sections 196 to 200, Colette appears in a vision to sisters in different convents, two of which are named by Perrine: Orbe and Castres. Twice she appears shining like the sun. Twice she is in a heavenly procession. In one, she is already with the blessed of the heavenly court and followed by the souls she had freed from purgatory. In the other, her soul is being borne, melodiously and joyously, to paradise "by a great multitude of angels" (§200). This final scene recalls various depictions of the assumption of the Virgin, as well as the famous painting by El Greco in Toledo, the "Burial of Count Orgaz."[11]

From the point of view of our story, the fact of death provides the pivot between the traditional account of sanctity and the emergence of reality, as we have already observed. It cannot be reduced to a mere system of signs. Colette assumes her true stature at this final moment. From here, her past can be read and her whole life assessed. Having completed her work, Colette returns to the silence of the contemplative standing before her God who, in the utter emptying that is death, is now revealed.

Summary

As we finish our study of the two biographies, what do we now know about the reform and about the saint herself?

In the modern meaning of the term, there is no history of the reform in these works. There is, moreover, no "time" in the sense of events occurring that have been prepared for by causes and that alter facts. The spatio-temporal reference is vague. We find only supernatural phenomena or those perceived as associated with the invisible world.

---

[11] While the body of the Count was carried for burial by Saint Augustine and Saint Sebastian in priestly vestments and in the presence of knights dressed all in black, his soul was carried to heaven by angels. As well as the perfection of the picture itself, the painter's genius consists in gathering up heaven and earth into a single vision at the decisive moment of burial. Pierre de Vaux separates these two elements. From one point of view, however, it might be said that this extreme spiritual vision, typical of French biography and the end of the Middle Ages, saw its culmination in El Greco's masterpiece a century later.

Properly speaking, the content of the Colettine reform is not analyzed. To a modern reader, references to the Franciscan Order and to Clare seem formal. They are in fact often non-existent, brief or taken out of context. The key concept of poverty is emptied of its spiritual content. Stress is placed exclusively on material destitution rather than on the path of inner self-emptying. The consequence of this, naturally, is a lack of investigation into Colette's interior life. Her prayer for example is reduced to a series of formulae, attitudes or paranormal phenomena.

Biblical roots are also scanty. The same can be said of facts that might indicate the enormous importance of contemporary cultural constraints or sociological and ecclesiastical experience. Colette's sanctity is perceived mainly through the criteria of the period. The typology of a saint is restricting. This is generally the case in France in the fourteenth and fifteenth centuries: a saint is unusual and always and everywhere victorious. A saint is also a Christian hero. Sanctity involves being a scapegoat for sinful people who merit only divine wrath.

In this sense, a saint has a cathartic function in the religious imagination. Rather than belonging to the historical world, a saint belongs to a "poetic" domain saturated with a kind of degraded spirituality. At this time, clerical thought manages badly the various fields of reflection and the position of saints in Church and society. Language tries to express, in spite of everything, the pain of an era all too recently torn apart. The way the story is told, however, reveals motives that are not entirely innocent. Particular gaps in the account and the arrangement of some topics indicate other agenda. No reference, for example, is made to the Great Schism. Memory conceals traumas because it cannot analyze them or picture them rationally.

From another point of view, it would have been interesting if Pierre de Vaux, wanting to raise Colette to the level of the greatest saints, had compared her to Joan of Arc – the one saved the nation, the other the Church. Subsequent ages did not fail to make the comparison and exploit it.

For Pierre de Vaux, however, Colette is the woman who brings salvation, who agrees to give birth in pain. In her, the woman no longer has a national or political dimension (as did Joan of Arc) or even an ecclesial dimension (as did Catherine of Siena). A non-historical approach to the Colettine reform, then, makes complete sense. Colette's "prophecies" and miracles take place in the people's private domain, without social, political or ecclesial dimension.

The consecrated woman, burdened with the pain of the age, remains necessary. But, as far as male religious are concerned, she remains in retirement, outside society, even though the convent retains links to the town, especially for reasons of economic dependence. She is an angelic intercessor, essential to a Christian, sinful society that places upon her the responsibility of prayer, reserved solely to "celestial" beings who, in virtue of such title, are capable of obtaining grace.

For a long time, and even more so after the hardening of attitudes during the Counter Reformation, such a woman would, after her lifetime, become increasingly isolated, enshrined in Christian consciousness as in a kind of reliquary.

CHAPTER 8

THE FIRST INQUIRIES FOR CANONIZATION

Around 1471, about twenty-five years after Colette's death, the first inquiries into the informative process for Colette's canonization began in Gand, Hesdin, Amiens and Corbie. Memories were collected from her contemporaries (or from those who knew her contemporaries) and depositions were taken about post mortem miracles.[1] The *Vitae* by Pierre de Vaux and Sister Perrine date from this period and are the best structured and most complete of these works.

The texts considered below are in the form of much shorter testimonies, covering specific points and sometimes giving direct answers to the questionnaire from the informative process.[2]

They come from Colette's immediate circle or from lay or religious individuals who knew her or who were the subject of miraculous cures.

---

[1] Looking at the documents, it doesn't seem as though the testimonies from Besançon and Poligny were attached. One likely explanation is the fire that destroyed the monastery at Poligny during the first third of the seventeenth century.

[2] Two other texts from this period are considered in Part 3, Ch. V, since they cover matters internal to the Order. They are a letter from Sister Jeanne Labeur and an indirect account from Marie de la Marche, daughter of Count James of Bourbon. These documents do not seem to have been written for the initial inquiries, but were collated during the eighteenth-century process.

Testimony of the "Old People of Corbie"

This document dates from March 6, 1471. A fifteenth-century copy was found in the Amiens archives, another in the papers from the Gand process of 1747 in the archives at Poligny.[3] The witnesses are a cleric, Jacques Guiot (76), a widow, Agnès de Baudemont (84), a certain Guillaume de Bousière (84) and his wife or sister Roberte de Bousière (78). They state that they have "known by sight, name and public reputation, from her childhood or youth, the deceased Sister Colette of blessed memory."

The names of her parents, by "legitimate marriage," were Robert and Marguerite. As a child, Colette obeyed

> her parents humbly, the teaching of her mother and the examples taken from the Passion of our Lord Jesus Christ, on which she meditated continually.

This passage may mean that her mother exhorted her to meditate on the Passion, confirming Perrine's evidence of a confidence made to her by Colette about this.

The account given by the Old People says nothing of the mother's advanced age at the time of the birth. They may have felt this to be unimportant and so did not recall it. They emphasize the young Colette's early-flowering devotion, using a stereotypical formula reminiscent of that of the scribes:

> She despised the attractions of the flesh and the deceptive pleasures of the world and devoted herself entirely to divine service and holy meditations and continual prayer.

---

[3] This testimony is published by P. Sellier, *Vie de sainte Colette,* 2 (Amiens, 1855), Book X, chap. 1. The transcription is not complete: the influences on Colette and her formation are missing. The nineteenth-century author, despite showing historical concern, erases from the testimony anything that could modify the hagiographial portrait of Colette set by Pierre de Vaux. The Bollandists reproduced the Latin text, 1, 534-35.

Of the four witnesses, only the cleric, Jacques Guiot, could have known Latin. The scribe, then, would certainly have been transcribing the vernacular into the Latin normally used for this kind of document and employing a formula that was conventional in describing the precocious devotion of candidates for beatification.

Here more details are given than in the first biographies about the year Colette spent with the beguines. It was probably during this time that her friendship began with the "mistress," mentioned by Perrine. The other periods spent in monasteries are omitted. However, seclusion seems to have been decided on by Colette and those near to her (the bourgeois are perhaps Adam Mangnier who, according to Perrine, knew Colette from childhood, and "other devout people," including the provost) and funded by them. The Lord of Corbie, her guardian (thus after the death of her parents), had only to give his consent. This is an interesting point: the priest is described here in his administrative role, while Perrine's text (§12) seems to show a more paternal, if negative, attitude towards Colette. It is her immediate, friendlier followers that act on her behalf.

She also seems better situated in the town than in Perrine's account, in which she seems rather solitary and relates directly to the priest of Corbie. This is not so likely in a medieval context with its strong sense of hierarchy and community. The place of her seclusion lies between the cemeteries of the two parish churches, one of which is named St. John the Evangelist. Was this the source of her devotion to the apostle or just a coincidence?

One of the witnesses, Jacques Guiot, states that he visited her "frequently, on the orders of monsignor Jean Guiot, his brother and the confessor of the said Sister Colette"; he taught her the psalter.

Thus it was the secular clergy who, in the first place, took responsibility on a regular basis for her spiritual well-being and gave her some space on parish church property. Local people and parish clergy surrounded and assisted the young recluse, who certainly benefited from the affectionate and devoted friendship of her fellow-citizens. The duty of being her extraordinary confessor was given to the Franciscan Jean Pinet, and her ordinary confessor was Jean Guiot. The text seems to indicate that Father Pinet already knew Colette when she was a recluse: "... and there ... Brother Jean Pinet ... visits her frequently."

Some "revelations" are mentioned during this time, along with Colette's desire to do the divine will "with the advice likewise and the consent of the venerable friars Jean Pinet and Henry de Baume." This emphasizes their role in her future direction. The visit to the pope is noted, without specifying its purpose, in the company of Madame de Brisay, who then took her to her own country of Burgundy. An attempt to return to Corbie and to Picardy is not mentioned. Perhaps the witnesses had forgotten or the memory was too recent of Colette's failed attempts to make a foundation in her birthplace, thwarted as they were by the monks. She certainly did return, as Pierre de Vaux comments, even though her reception was not as bad as he states. Indeed, the visit of Colette, accompanied by Madame de Brisay, is recorded in the Péronne town register in December 1406. There she was welcomed as a fairly important guest. A plan to establish a foundation in Péronne (Noyon diocese) is suggested, following the permission granted by Benedict XIII,[4] along with a journey to Bray and Corbie.[5] It is strange that the Corbie witnesses do not mention her return to her birthplace but have her go straight from Nice to the "land of Burgundy" for a "beneficial rest."

---

[4] Cf. Part 1, Chapter III.

[5] *Bulletin des Antiquaires de Picardie*, 1937-38. "Item to Madame de Brisay, to sister Colette, recluse of Corbie, when they came to Peronne the first time, they were sent a batch of wine, for II sols." "Item for the expenses of the II horses of the recluse of Corbie, when they were for III days at a hotel, at XVI deniers the day for each horse, came to X sols VIII deniers." "Item for straw ... peat, to place in the chapel and in front of the house of Sister Colette VIII deniers." "Item for the recluse to go to Bray and to Corbie to take leave of her friends, when she considered she was going to stay in Peronne ... horse ... Jehan Penneton for II days, II sols."

There are several interesting features about this testimony. Although it stresses the future reformer's exceptional religious qualities, there is no mention of the marvelous. The part played by Colette's fellow-citizens and the local clergy is clearly depicted. With an origin similar to that of Joan of Arc, the young woman comes from a medieval Christian people whose fervor encourages the dawning of sanctity.[6] Her religious vocation appears later, under the spiritual influence of the Franciscans.

The return from Nice, despite an attempt to settle in the district of her birth, marks her uprooting from Picardy. With a Burgundian friar as her director and accompanied and funded by a Burgundian lady, Colette soon follows her benefactors into "their own country" where she is given valuable support. Despite pontifical permissions, however, it will take four more years to find a place (Besançon) where she can live a religious life.

The beginnings, despite the support of Brother Henry, are not very easy. Might it be that the silence of witnesses about this period of her life reflects a memory of some disappointment on the part of the inhabitants of Corbie with this young woman whom they had helped so much and who was now following other, more influential people?

In any case, the part played by Brother Henry, already discussed, is indirectly confirmed. Upon the death of Father Pinet, he took into his own hands the destiny of the young recluse.

KATHERINE RUFINÉ'S LETTER[7]

It dates from after 1492, as indicated by the allusion to the opening of Colette's tomb, and is no doubt sent from Besançon to Gand. It seems to form part of the recollections

---

[6] Cf. 1 Part, Ch. II.

[7] *A.F.H., An. III*, III, 1910, 82-86. There is a copy in the Gand Records for 1747, book 14, held in the archives at Poligny. The original has been lost.

being gathered by the monastery of Gand, perhaps as part of the informative process. In this case, it also responds to problems within the Order.

This Sister Rufiné knew Colette's young companions, hence the value of this first-generation testimony. It has two aspects: one familiar, as we might say, that relates to Colette and Brother Henry; the other touches on the relations between Colettines and Observants.

Brother Henry told his niece Perrine how he came to know Colette. It is the first text we have on this subject. The writings of Pierre de Vaux and Perrine must have seemed inadequate. Memories were being sought from someone who knew Perrine. Brother Henry was living in a convent of "good observance," which Katherine identifies as being at Mirebeau, which, we will see, is on land belonging to the de Brisay family (cf. Part 3, ch. I). Desperate to lead a demanding religious life, he decides to make a pilgrimage to Jerusalem. In a "far town," a recluse he visits "prophesies" that he should retrace his steps because he has to meet a young woman with whom he will bring a work to completion. Shortly thereafter, having obeyed this instruction, Brother Henry hears about Colette and recognizes the fulfillment of the prophecy.

For the first time, Brother Henry's situation is seen in the context of tensions between Observants and Conventuals. The Provincial Minister appoints a guardian (certainly a Conventual), who causes the Observant Friars to leave, since Mirebeau was one of the centers for the Observance in France. If Katherine's memories contain elements of truth, we may deduce that Brother Henry, at odds with his community, had to find an Observant monastery able to take him in. Hesdin, led by Father Pinet, belonged to the Observance. Brother Henry's meeting with Colette at this critical time gives him the chance to develop a more consistent and structured plan, but with the nuns rather than with the Observant friars, whose initiatives were sometimes uncoordinated. It is his painful experience, no doubt, that encourages the two future reformers to begin something new and highly centralized, more independent, too, from the First Order, in order to avoid the dissensions tearing it apart and hindering the progress of the French Observance.

The text makes reference to the business at Dole, thus from the beginning of the reform. Colette would have affirmed that the pope had given Dole to her so "freely" that she would have been able to put sisters there if she had wanted to. All the sisters, old and young, confirm this to Katherine. But, Katherine adds, the "friars of the bull" had it incorporated surreptitiously by the Council of Constance.[8] Before these events, the convent of Dole had received Colette. This was where the business of Jean Foucault took place, as mentioned by the first biographers. A new factor is reported: the dispute was submitted to the court at Dijon. The people of Dole turn against the Colettines and refuse them alms, so that the abbess of Auxonne has to give them food three times a week for a whole year.

The Dole convent, alleging intrigues, submits itself once more to the authority of the Provincial Minister in 1426. This reassertion of Conventual jurisdiction perhaps indicates the decisive influence of Colette in this matter, in opposition to the Observant friars. In 1452, however, the friars in this convent will request authorization from Rome to return to the Observance. The jurisdiction of the Conventuals left Colette relatively free to have at the service of the women's monasteries "Colettine" friars, that is those formed by Brother Henry and entirely devoted to his reform, without the risk of seeing the Observants take over control of her monasteries.

Thus the "official" versions of Colette's life offered by Pierre de Vaux and Perrine, while helping to form a picture of the future saint, leave open certain questions that subse-

---

[8] *Bull. Franc.*, VII, 493, n 1362 (the decree names twelve convents); Sessevalle, *Histoire Générale de l'Ordre de saint François*, vol I, 178 ff. In fact, Katherine Rufiné is confusing the cases. It was not until 1446 that Pope Eugene IV, given the impossibility of maintaining unity between the two branches, Conventual and Reformed, promulgated this bull *Ut sacra Ordinis Minorum religio*, written by John of Capistrano. It removed from the General Minister the faculty of appointing Observant vicars and gave the Observant branch the freedom to govern itself. It is from this that the Observants became known as "friars of the bull."

quently become crucial when the informative process begins, with potential harm to the cause for her canonization. Hence the reminder, noting the meeting between the two reformers, that the pope "gave" Dole to Colette thus establishing, well before the bull was issued at Constance, the independence and legitimacy of the Colettine reform and enhancing the reputation of the "glorious mother."

THE "MEMOIR OF HESDIN"

A copy of this memoir is in the archives of the monastery of Amiens, following a text written by Sister Élisabeth de Bavière at the convent of Vieil-Hesdin, "founded and reformed" by "our mother Saint Colette." This is a curious expression. Normally she is described as "our glorious mother" or the "very devout Sister Colette." This is, no doubt, scribal license, since the text is, according to some notes written at the end, a copy dating from 1624. The author, a Capuchin, is called Brother Sylvester. He also copied out a series of post mortem miracles attributed to Colette.

In his work on Colette dedicated to the queen mother, Marie de Médici, the Capuchin Sylvère d'Abbeville says he consulted old documents in the archives at Amiens. No doubt it was he who recopied an old manuscript that was itself a copy of an original kept in the monastery of Hesdin and that later disappeared.

This group of texts – the statement by Élisabeth de Bavière and the post mortem miracles from the end of the fifteenth century – is also included in the first inquiries of the informative process, as shown by the formulae used.

The manuscript of 1624 mixes direct testimony ("I, Sister Élisabeth de Bavière ...") with that reported in folios 5, 6 and 7, which uses an oral tradition transmitted by the "good mothers."

Katherine Rufiné's letter underlines the need to gather memories, but these details show reworking and in places signs of several hands, which explains some of the rather unlikely errors in Élisabeth de Bavière's memoir. For example, in folio 2, Madame de Brisay is called "Blanche de Brisay, Countess of Geneva." Élisabeth de Bavière could not have confused her mother's aunt, Mahaut of Savoy, with Colette's first companion. Similarly, la Baume is in the Geneva region – there seems to be some confusion about places.

Sister Élisabeth de Bavière's memories, as written down, closely follow Pierre de Vaux's plan, with few new elements. Her testimony returns to the *Legenda* several times, demonstrating how much it is a reference.

The account of Colette's vision in her cell in which Francis requests that she be a reformer is a variant of Pierre de Vaux's. To Francis and Clare are added John the Baptist and Mary Magdalene, who claim her for the contemplative and solitary life. Such a transposition may have resulted from remembering Colette's eremitical preferences, stressed elsewhere by Pierre de Vaux, who compares her to the Precursor.

As in Perrine, the part played by the confessors in what is known of Colette's life is often recalled. Thanks to them, it is written, "we know many of these facts."

As required by the informative process, Élisabeth de Bavière recalls a confidence from one of the confessors to the nuns (fol. 1):

> My daughters, you know only something of the holiness of the blessed mother. If I could speak of what I know of it, I would tell you wonders. I hope God gives me the grace to live a bit longer than she, so I might say what I know of it. I am certain that if the Holy Father knew what I know of her holiness, he would hardly wait at all after her death to canonize her.

More personal elements appeared: "I often lay near her in her oratory" (fol. 3). In the night, a sister remained near Colette. These companions included Perrine, Élisabeth de Bavière and Agnès de Vaux, who served her.

As we know from elsewhere, Colette heard Mass "privately," that is, in her oratory. In addition to the celebrant, there were her companion and a sister, often Élisabeth.

Eighteen months before Colette died at Amiens (fol. 7), where she had predicted her own death within two years, she called in Brother François Claret to put her intentions in writing.

The set of folios on the post mortem miracles includes testimony from Guillemette, first abbess of Hesdin (fol. 10), who mentions some aspects of Colette's behavior: her tears during Mass, her vigilance in seeking out the sisters' distractions during the office, her knowledge of the inner life of her daughters ("the state of my conscience"). She too ends by referring to the *Vita* of Pierre de Vaux, confirming his words: she has heard it from the "venerable mothers" and from Brother Pierre himself.

A strange testimony from the monastery of Vieil-Hesdin should be noted (fol. 18). A sister who died in "prison" (so after some serious fault) appeared three times to one of the sisters to whom she entrusted her story. Colette had appeared to her several times at the hour of her death to reproach her "very bitterly" and to encourage her to repent under pain of damnation. The sister finally begged pardon, but would remain in "pain and torment" until "the day of judgment." A note adds: "The apparition is not of her, because if you knew who she is, you would give it neither faith nor credence." The testimony seems discredited even by those who are reporting it. An attempt to curb accounts of the marvelous seems to be in play here.

The miracles listed below are said to be from an old, hand-written book dating from 1461 and kept at Vieil-Hesdin (fol. 11). It gives information about Colette's sanctity and miracles collected by a Dominican investigator at the order of the bishop. The date suggested is not certain (fol. 12) since one miracle is dated twenty-five years after Colette's death. But the dating error is slight and does not invalidate the account.

Pierre de Vaux had already written down some of her miracles, and they can also be found in the Flemish process held at the monastery of Poligny in Gand.

Where dates are given, the miracles occur at intervals between 1463 and 1494, grouped mainly around these two dates. They happened at Gand or at Hesdin. Hence, various copies had to be made and sent to the different monasteries in the region. These, along with the collected oral accounts, form materials that contribute to the developing legend.

One series organizes the miracles according to how they benefited religious brothers or sisters in Colette's entourage; another series describes the cures of lay people, adults or children.

– A fragrance (fol. 9) is detected in the convent of Vieil-Hesdin, a sign that Colette has "visited," since she said that she would return after her death. The confessors said that this fragrance was a grace, but the text specifies that some could smell it and others could not.

– Some friars, one of whom had seen Colette's dead body (fol. 12), tell how once, when lost in a forest, they prayed to Colette; a young man appeared and led them out of the forest, then disappeared.

– In the monastery of Hesdin, a thirty-three-year-old sister had a vision of a procession during which Colette told her to go to confession. Another, who had been sick for months, was miraculously cured after praying to the reformer. In 1463, abbess Guillemette said that a young professed sister lost her sight, but was cured also after having prayed (fol. 15).

– The account of a certain Brother Lucas is not without interest (fol. 3). He knew Colette when he was twenty-five and in service to a lord as a groom for his horses, working even on Sunday. At the advice of a gentleman, he met Colette who, having admonished him, kept him as her servant for seven years, after which he took the habit at Dole and then returned to serve the abbess. He said that he knew Brother Henry well, and spoke of the veneration

for Colette felt by James of Bourbon who joined the Third Order[9] and died in the presence of the "holy mother."
– Men, women and children experienced cures of physical injuries (a leg, fol. 12, a child's serious fall, fol. 13), fever, madness, possession by demons; a couple infertile for twenty-six years have a child after praying to Colette.

Miracles are always obtained through praying a novena, using soil from her sepulcher, or applying the saint's head covering or water that has washed over her relics. For a mad person or one possessed, her head covering or a little of the soil is placed on the head.

Summary

There are several facts deserving of note in all these documents. The informative process provides an opportunity to revive the recollections of Colette's former companions or of the sisters. The Colettine friars take the initiative, making the nuns aware of their neglect in setting down in writing what they "heard said," to the good mothers as well as the reformer's last wishes.[10] This fixed oral tradition reflects the concerns and tensions prevalent at the time of writing, especially the differences with the Observants. The past is invoked as a guarantor of the present and of the future of the Colettine reform, which wanted to retain its own autonomy within the Order. There was continuous communication among Colette's monasteries, according to the documents that have come down to us, mainly between Gand, Amiens and Hesdin.

---

[9] Cf. Part 3, ch. I for the issue of the Count's membership in the Third Order. This note confirms the truth of the fact.
[10] Cf. Part 2, ch. I. The texts collected under the title *Intentions* and *Ordinances* of which, as we have seen, there are variants, were certainly edited at the end of the fifteenth century when the heirs made a kind of inventory of their spiritual legacy.

The archives of the "proto-monastery" of the reform (Besançon) and those of Poligny have disappeared, the latter in a fire in the seventeenth century and the former during the Revolution. Thus, we can only assume that all the reformed monasteries continued to stay in touch with each other. The friars were a valuable link in this process, as they were free to travel.

It was also they who passed on the main features of Colette's sanctity, as the study of the first two biographies has already shown. Since Pierre de Vaux arranged what sparse information there was in his *Legenda*, subsequent documents refresh only slightly the account of Colette's sanctity. Nonetheless, as Perrine's text shows, these first or secondhand memories from the nuns are less "literary." Colette's daily life can be detected from her habits and her behavior, as well as from the members of her entire religious entourage, male and female alike, who were especially devoted to her. They respected her reforming mission, which isolated her, despite all the communities she founded. The hieratic dimension of her character was attenuated for the sake of her life story.

If the miracles reported demonstrate the popular devotion of people in modest or easy circumstances, the reputation of the great abbess is strongest in vicinities around the monasteries she founded, where the memory of her is still very much alive.

Witnesses to her childhood and youth remained discreet about the place of the marvelous during the period of her seclusion, as if their account were independent of that of Pierre de Vaux's contemporary version. This makes them more valuable. The text of the "Old People of Corbie" recognizes the spiritual ascendancy of the young girl from Picardy. The memory of the part played by her fellow citizens and the local clergy in awakening her vocation reveals a Colette who is hesitant as to the path she should follow and feels the need for advice and support. The part played by her parents, especially by her mother, is also remarkable, and, very quickly, the guidance of this young, indecisive girl is taken on by a Franciscan friar with effective social relationships. Her religious entourage, especially the ordained friars, will retain and emphasize her unusual spiritual ascension in the hope of a speedy canonization. They seem to neglect Colette's actual work, which, as she soon became abbess and founder, created the conditions for a durable reform through the impact of her important writings. These reveal, in an unparelleled way, an essential aspect of her real personality.

PART TWO

COLETTE'S WRITINGS AND CONTEMPORARY WORKS

CHAPTER 1

The Letters

The extant writings of Saint Colette are few and far between. The most significant are administrative in nature (constitutions, advice, opinions, etc.,) dealing with the internal life of reformed communities. There are also letters, addressed either to religious or lay people, discussing precise situations less directly linked to the internal operation of the monasteries.

Presentation

There are actually fifteen letters[1] of varied length and significance offering a good sample of the range of Colette's correspondence. The monasteries kept old copies of these letters. Few originals exist: Le Puy and Poligny have some in a very poor state of preservation. We do not know if they are written by St. Colette's own hand. We do not even know if she

---

[1] Plus a plea to Pope Martin V, in 1418, asking him to allow her to visit convents in Besançon, Auxonne, and Poligny, – to assign a friar minor to the said convent, "either priest or layman," for the administration of the sacraments and to support them in their poverty, – not to permit a sister to be transferred to another place without the permission of the abbess and the majority of the discretorium or an explicit apostolic letter. U. D'Alençon, "Documents sur la réforme de sainte Colette en France," A.F.H., II, 1905.

could write. The archivist from Lons-Le-Suanier, M. Hours, considers the letters the work of a number of copyists.[2]

In any case, Colette's signature is considered authentic, and there is nothing to contradict the oral tradition. Her literacy is proved by the fact that she read the psalter and recited the office. She must have attended the abbey school. We know however that it was fairly rare to write personally. Letters were usually dictated and then signed by the sender. An initial reading of the *Letters* reveals a stranger's hand, if only from the use and frequency of legal expressions and turns of phrase, unlikely to feature in Colette's vocabulary.

The friars provided more than just a spiritual role. As well as collecting alms on behalf of the monastery, they also had to provide intellectual services. Other contemporary documents demonstrate this: Henry, Pierre de Vaux, and Brother Claret were all involved in the business of the order and went to Rome for the constitutions.[3]

Dates

For the fifteen extant letters, we observe the following dates:

DATES	NUMBER
1416	1
1438 (uncertain date)	1
1439	3 + 1 (uncertain date)
1442	3
1445	1
1446	4
1447?	1

Twenty-two years separate the first and the second, thirty-one years the first and the last.

---

[2] Monsieur Hours believes that the one to the people of Gand, kept in the archives of the town's monastery and considered authentic until recently, is a copy.

[3] H. Lippens, "Henry de Baume, coopérateur de Ste Colette...," *Sacris Erudiri,* I, 1948, 235-42 ff.

Most of the *Letters* cover the final ten or eleven years of her life. We must assume that many were lost or are still buried in unexplored archives, but this is not the only plausible explanation. Indeed, one might say that 1439 marked the beginning of Colette's correspondence period. That was the year that Brother Henry de Baume died. It might therefore be assumed that this first companion, faithful and efficient, her elder also, played a very important part in maintaining the many contacts made as a result of the reform. After his death, Colette did not find anyone among the younger friars to provide her with similar expertise and friendship. His role may have been even more important than the first stories would indicate. No doubt too, as Colette's fame increased, her letters took on even greater value in the eyes of their recipients. This would have been only partly true for the nuns and friars, who would naturally have valued receiving letters from their spiritual mother.

Recipients

NATURE	RECIPIENTS		DATES
-To laity:			
2 collectives	Notables of Gand	L4	1437-40
		L5	1442
3 individuals	A woman	L1	1442
	King Charles VII	L3	1445
	A man	L2	1446
-To religious:			
7 collectives	2 -Convent of Puy	R4	Aug 1439
		R6	Feb 26, 1439
	1 -Convent of Gand	R7	
	1 -Besançon	R8	
	2 -Monks of Corbie	R10	
1 circular letter	(on the occasion of Henry's death)	R5	1439
3 individuals	A religious sister	R1	1416
	P. de Vaux	R2	1439?
	A friar	R3	1447?

Setting aside the letter announcing Brother Henry's death and the one sent to Pierre de Vaux showing that this friar took on part of the role provided up to then by Henry, the assumption about Henry's work for Colette is confirmed. After he was gone, Colette felt she had to be more involved in the temporal affairs of the reform.

Colette wrote few personal letters, even to her own daughters and to the friars of the reform, which explains the relatively few documents remaining to us. Her letters are to the point and deal with precise situations. They are not very "spiritual"; they do not deal with the interior life. On a first reading, these documents do not permit us to situate her in the tradition of mystical or spiritual writers. They are interesting for other reasons. They allow us to see aspects of her personality from life, general ideas about her concerns as a reformer. Few of these facts appear in the *Vita* of Pierre de Vaux or in that of Perrine. The results of this study provide us with some interesting comparisons with the *Vitae*.

The Purpose of the *Letters*

Correspondence Addressed to Lay People

To individuals:

–Dame Marie Boen (L1): This is an entirely spiritual letter. The terms "beginners" and "perseverers" used after the introduction indicate it concerns a pious person who has experience of the interior life. Perhaps she wants to pursue a religious commitment, since Colette sketches out a "theology" of the three vows – effective weapons in the fight against the world, the flesh, and the enemy.

–Sieur Bartholomé of Dijon (L2, written in Gand on 15 October 1446. The original is in the Besançon B. M., ms. 1490-1491, t. 1; folio 67.): Because of the detail "under my seal," we conclude that this was dictated to a secretary. It is an "official" document, acknowledging services rendered by this man to the sisters and brothers at the convent of Besançon. He has been resident there a long time, working and serving. In exchange, Colette and her "congregation" undertake to ensure that he benefits fully from the spiritual blessings enjoyed by herself and her sisters. The matter of providing for his material needs until death is not raised. It seems that he personally is free from financial need. ("You were pleased, in your humility, to reside and dwell here a long time.") Bartholomé, fed and lodged with the sisters, seems to have been an intimate associate at the monastery.

–King Charles VII (L3. The Amiens Archives copy is kept at Poligny. Strangely enough, the date is not given. For such an important letter of an official nature, the copyist should have transcribed the date): Philippe de Saveuse, the governor of Amiens in the service of the Duke of Burgundy, obtained a bull from Pope Eugene IV authorizing him to establish a monastery at Corbie according to Colette's wishes. The monks at the abbey opposed the plan and appealed to the Parliament of Paris, which supported them. Colette then turned to the king to ask him to intervene. The sovereign's favorable response and the financial compensation he offered to the monks failed to overcome their objections. The former recluse, pupil of an abbot of Corbie, could not establish a foundation in the town of her birth.

The reformer gave a fairly long account of the details of the matter and indicated that Saveuse had begun to build the monastery. The monks' refusal was based on economics: they feared a reduction in their own income if a new convent was established there.

Colette referred the problem to the highest level: it was a question of "the honor of God, the augmentation of his divine service, and saving souls." The king was the "last and sovereign refuge." In fact, the letter stresses that the favor requested would not be exorbitant but simply a matter of continuing the work already begun by Saveuse. The sisters would not affect the abbey's income since they lived "purely on alms."

To collectives:

–The benefactors of Gand (L4): This is the first of two extant letters, the original of which is in the archives of the monastery of Gand. The year of writing would be between 1437 and 1440, after the foundation of Hesdin in Picardy and before the monastery in Gand was built. Although the Duke of Burgundy, Philip the Good, had agreed a separate peace with Charles VII at Arras in 1435, the situation remained tense. Colette was well known and appreciated by the leaders of both sides. The purpose of the letter is very specific. Colette apologizes for not sending her daughters who had already been selected and gathered at Hesdin. Because of the risks of the current situation, she had been advised several times not to engage upon the journey. She understood the legitimate desire of these benefactors to see the convent inhabited, since they had invested their time and money in it. So if they could not wait for better times, they should give it to another religious family. All that mattered was that God should be praised and served.

–The benefactors of Gand (L5): This letter was also written at Besançon, where Colette had just arrived to meet Saint John of Capistrano, sent there by the pope as the visitator. This would therefore certainly have been in October 1442.

The letter's purpose was to thank the benefactors, some of whom would have been the same as those in L4. They are asked to keep at all times "the commandments needed for the salvation of their souls" and to watch over the regular observance of the convent.

Letters addressed to religious sisters and brothers

Individuals:

–Sister Loyse Bassande (R1, around 1416): We know of this letter from a book written in 1717, published in the *Voyage littéraire de deux religieux bénédictins* and reproduced by

Bizouard in his *Histoire de sainte Colette et des clarisses en Bourgogne*. The original would have been burned in 1792.

The vocabulary and style seem to be Colette's. The document is fairly short: Colette reminds this sister of her commitment to the religious life. She must obey her superiors and her sisters and not preoccupy herself with her relatives and friends, except to pray for their intentions.

–Pierre de Vaux (R2): Bizouard says that the autograph of this letter was burned by the revolutionaries (84-85) along with the previous one. Gand would have possessed the original. It is not absolutely certain if it should be dated after 1439, the date when Brother Henry died. Colette could have had close relationships with other friars before Brother Henry's death, particularly the one who would become (or already was?) her confessor. It is a spiritual letter, without a particular subject. It is simply an exchange of confidences about the interior life. It assumes a similar letter from her correspondent.

–Brother Jehan Lainé (R3): This is written from Gand on the second day of Lent and perhaps dates from the final months of Colette's life, but there is no particular reason to date it in 1447. Addressed to the confessor at the monastery of Puy, it is intended to make him accept a replacement as he can no longer perform his role given "his weakness and age." The tone brooks no reply.

Collectives:

–The community at Puy (R4): Dated before 1439, the year Brother Henry died, it is preserved in the archives of the monatery and has always been considered an autograph of Colette.[4] It confirms the election of a new abbess and encour-

---

[4] The list of abbesses of Puy does not include the name of Sister Agnès de Montfaucon, appointed as abbess by Colette. Receipts and bills signed by the whole community, dating from 1447 onwards, show that she was

ages the community at Puy to obey her, as she is "approved" by Colette and Brother Henry.

–Circular letter (R5) on the occasion of Brother Henry's death, February 26, 1439 at Besançon. It was written the same day for the sisters at Vevey, according to a tradition recorded by Bizouard (208). It is also contained in the *Analectae Juris Pontificii* 1819, 28.

This may be considered a crucial text in the life and work of Colette since it begins a series of the most important letters we currently possess. After the usual greetings, Colette expresses her sorrow, describes the final days of her faithful friend and companion, and asks for prayers for him, while, at the same time, certain that he will be praying for all the sisters.

–Second letter to the community at Puy (R6, 1439): This letter was also written at the time of Brother Henry's death. It is certainly later than the previous one, because it does not report the circumstances of his death. It asks for prayers for the repose of his soul and recalls the role he played in regard to all the sisters. The advice it gives also sketches out a picture of the "good religious sister." Moreover, it introduces an important new element: Colette recommends Peter of Rheims, who, it seems, will now take on part of Brother Henry's role.

–The Clarisses in Gand (R7): The undated original is in the archives in Gand. It may date from the same period as that of the second letter to the benefactors of this town.

This letter is important in defining the religious and contemplative life from the viewpoint of an experienced, older person. The role of Brother Peter (of Rheims, no doubt) is confirmed. His name appears at the end of the letter.

---

vicar from that date. Might it be assumed she did not serve the three-year term or that the list is false?

–The Clarisses at Besançon (R8, dated 18/VII/1446): The original, written at Hesdin, is kept in the B. M. of Besançon, document 1490-1491, t. 1, folio 3; it was deciphered in 1880 in M. A. Castan, archivist and paleographer.

Another important letter, this is apparently a valedictory, giving final instructions. The reformer knows she will never again visit the "proto-monastery" of the reform and wants to emphasize to her daughters how they must keep not just the Rule but also her own legislative writings. Brother Pierre is again named, appearing more and more as Colette's right hand man, implicitly placing him as a possible "guardian" of the work.

–First letter to the monks at Corbie (R9): The manuscripts of these two letters are kept in the Amiens archives and held at the monastery of Poligny. They are generally believed to date from 1445-1446. Colette was actually at Hesdin during this time.

Uneasy at Colette's approach to the king, the monks at Corbie write directly to her, asking her to desist and stop the work that Saveuse has begun. Regretfully, Colette agrees, at the same time recalling the permissions already granted and stating that none of her monasteries has ever harmed anyone – on the contrary they have been a source of abundant spiritual blessings.

–Second letter to the monks at Corbie (R10): The previous one dates from March 2nd, this one from March 10th. Did their letters cross, or did the monks find that things were moving too slowly for their liking? Colette answers that she has already approached Saveuse twice to have him stop the work. This letter is brief, with no details, dryly concise. The reformer considers the matter closed. She soothes the monks one last time.

CHAPTER 2

THE THEMES OF THE LETTERS

The themes of the letters fall under two headings: the reformer's relationships with people in the world (or outside her order) and her relationships with the religious sisters and brothers within the reform.

RELATIONSHIPS WITH PEOPLE OUTSIDE THE ORDER

Colette's relationships with those outside the order are, nonetheless, entwined with the life of the reform. One letter discusses the founding of a monastery, another acknowledges services rendered to a convent, and the third examines the possible entry of a pious laywoman into a community.

Opponents to the Foundations

There was opposition to founding a house in Corbie. After her return from Nice in 1406, Colette wished to establish a foundation in her native town. Nearing the end of her life, acknowledged as a reformer by the Franciscan order and by her noble protectors, and with the theoretical agreement of the parish priest of Corbie, Colette tried once more to establish a reformed monastery there. Much has already been said about the rejection by Corbie Abbey. The letter to the king and the two missives to the monks highlight the essential issues, which were economic in nature. Colette asked the king "to write off the cost of the place where the said convent must be built," the building of which had already begun with authorization from the pope. Through her benefactors, she undertook to "make restitution [to the monks] for everything that will be said and found, and more besides."

She also recalled the particular characteristic of her order: "to have, at any time, neither lordship or jurisdiction nor rent nor charge nor revenue, but to live only on alms according to the counsel of the holy gospel of our Lord Jesus Christ." The monks feared the loss of property as a result of construction taking place on land that undoubtedly belonged to the abbey. They also envisioned the loss of rents and jurisdictions if, in future, the new convent attracted donations from benefactors or itself acquired new property.

Not without a frisson of pride, Colette recalled that the "poor religious sisters" lived according to different principles, those based on the Gospel,[1] stating clearly the difference in economic structure between the Benedictine order and that of the Clarisses – individual but not collective poverty on the one hand, individual and collective poverty on the other. The archives of the Clarisses in Amiens or in other monasteries demonstrate that the monks had reason to feel uneasy. Although, generally speaking, the Colettine convents were careful not to acquire property, they did, on the other hand, drain significant donations from both the upper and the middle classes. Colette was fully aware of the risk: her "legislative" *Writings* warn her daughters against accepting sizeable donations that would alter the character of their vowed poverty.

In this regard, we note one of the features of the quarrels between the mendicant religious and the monastic orders (such as the Benedictines) and secular clergy. Established in towns of medium importance, monasteries of mendicants or Clarisses diverted some of the income of the clergy and

---

[1] Note the accumulation of economic terms, preceded by the negative particle "nor": "nor lordship or jurisdiction, nor rent nor charge nor revenue," and the contrast of their lifestyle, marked by the adversative preposition "but": "but live only on alms, according to the counsel of the holy gospel of Our Lord Jesus Christ."

the monks to their own benefit. Such was the case when a town was built around an abbey, such as that of Corbie. The lay authorities soon got involved in such matters, since the convents, as poor communities requiring assistance, would claim gifts in kind or help for repairs, etc.[2] Conflict could arise when economic circumstances were unfavorable. Later on, and for the same reasons, Teresa of Avila, despite her prestige, had problems establishing Carmels in urban areas. The pope rejected Colette's desire to observe "the highest poverty" in imitation of Saint Clare (that is, without income or goods) because of issues of this kind. Monasteries had to show they had the means to meet their own needs. The letters also cast light on the monks' quibbling nature and on the politico-economic dimensions of founding a convent.

Several authorities were involved when a foundation was proposed in a town under the jurisdiction of an abbey. Agreement was required from a number of parties, including the pope and the lay authority, which in this case was the sponsor, Philippe de Saveuse, Duke of Burgundy. All gave their consent, which was agreed to by the parish priest and the prior. The refusal by the community of monks, however, was enough to block the procedure. They appealed to the parliament of Paris, which applied a legal bond to the refusal. Only the king could resolve the dispute.

Colette's appeal to the king as supreme judge foreshadowed Teresa of Avila's intercession with Philip II, even if their socio-political contexts were different. On the brink of her venture in 1406, Colette appealed to the pope, and at the completion of her work, she called on the king, thus confirming the hierarchy of values – economic interests were to give way before religious values. She stressed the particular nature of the contemplative life she had created, its ecclesial and missionary aspects. The monastery performed a service of prayer for the Church and for the good of the people. She

---

[2] H. Martin, *Les Ordres mendiants en Bretagne vers 1230-1530* (Paris, 1975), 223. Cf. also "Annales du Monastère d'Amiens," quoted in J. Desobry, *Un aspect peu connu de la Révolution française de 1789 à Amiens: le monastère des Clarisses* (Amiens, 1986), 8.

affirmed this to the monks, thus setting aside the economic and legal issues with which they were concerned in favor of religious and spiritual issues:

> I believe before God that this construction will be for God's honor and for yours, a credit to your monastery and to its benefit, as well as for the consolation of you and all the inhabitants of the town. As I have always seen and learned from experience, wherever our convents have been built, and they are in large and medium and small towns, smaller and poorer than Corbie, I have seen none that was not provided for from the goodness of God, with no injury or damage to any other. Neither the lords, nor the regular and secular inhabitants have had any dishonor or injury, but spiritually and corporally they have benefited from them and been consoled and comforted by them (R9).

This quotation is a good demonstration of Colette's position relative to the economic issue: she did not ignore it, but she relied on God's providence alone, entirely in keeping with the thought of Francis. We should note however that she does not raise the issue of the sisters' subsistence through their work. Was she refusing to justify herself? She also knew that the community would receive donations. For her, the real challenge was the spiritual one.

This demonstrates a basic aspect of the reformer's personality. Out of her action and perseverance came certainty of her mission and the particular character of her monasteries. She was aware of her personal contribution to the religious life of her time, its habits and economic choices. Like Francis and all reformers, she differentiated herself from current customs, from the expected route. She claimed the right to be different.

She did, however, have the advantage of a solid support network, as she explained in her letter to the king and to the monks. She used all available political and religious opportunities available through the social structures of her time.

In this respect, Corbie was not an isolated case. For example, the king had assisted with the foundations in le Puy and Amiens. The Corbie situation involved both the Duke of Burgundy and the King of France.

Her reform broke with religious custom in the essential aspect of personal poverty, reviving the movement first launched in the thirteenth century by Francis and Clare of Assisi. At the same time, she fitted perfectly into contemporary structures and respected them. In order to exist, her foundation had to be part of the existing, socio-religious fabric.

Colette's final, twice-confirmed rejection was the logical outcome. If she had persevered, the resulting process would have been of little value to the reform and to her reputation. She did not hide her regret, even bitterness, but she was certain that the monks would be judged by God, even if they escaped human judgment. They were guilty of hindering "such a great good." Her perspective was consistently spiritual, a constant attitude that set her apart from the monks with their exclusively material preoccupations. In the end, however, she had used every register of argument, from the most legal to the most moral, appealing finally to divine justice to chastise the recalcitrant monks.

SUPPORTERS OF THE FOUNDATIONS

The letters about the Gand foundation are also instructive. Both these letters to benefactors, like the three above, demonstrate the reformer's relationship with the laity and with her own socio-religious world, but with some new features.

As in Corbie, lay people funded the foundation. In this case, these were named members of the bourgeoisie rather than nobles. Their material support gave them several benefits:

- "The approbation and the prayers of the religious. You will not, nor can be deprived of this offering."

–A right to view the interior life of the convent. Once the house had been founded, Colette wrote to them to ask them to watch over it: "... have the convent always cordially commended, and do not allow anything to be done that is against God and against regular observance" (L5). The benefactors therefore provided an external check on the life of the convent. Was this a precaution by Colette to avoid too many donations or requests to enter the enclosure that could have led to a relaxing of the regular life, a reminder that the town must ensure that the religious authorities were warned if there were any flagrant scandals? Both of these reasons certainly had a part to play, as shown by some articles from the *Constitutions* or from the *Advice* and *Sentiments*. The order's history shows that the municipal authorities sometimes had to intervene to bring an end to abuses.

–The undertaking to pray for benefactors (cf. letter to Sieur Bartholomé de Dijon), normal practice in the Middle Ages, could have resulted in a change to the religious life, to the very concept of the contemplative life itself. Monasteries could not escape becoming dispensers of vocal prayer for benefactors, living and dead. Colette did not try to alter received belief that the efficacy of intercessory prayer was proportional to its quantity. One also perceives, from another point of view, the profound and lively interdependence of the monastery with the social fabric. Today, one might call it "ecclesial insertion," since the society of the time was Christian. The link between money and prayer was obvious. Benefactors had faith enough to feel that the prayer of the nuns was sufficient compensation for their gifts. This factor was unknown in Clare's time, and Francis of Assisi's distrust of money is well known. The friars worked with their hands and begged "for the love of God." In this respect, Colette's pragmatic attitude to money was closer to Clare's than to Francis's.

Since the order had also become part of the Church's heritage, integrated closely into the ecclesial and social body, the reformer followed normal practices making best use of them in accordance with circumstances. We should also note that convents were commonly established in towns. In her letter to them, Colette reminded the monks of Corbie that she had foundations in medium and small towns: a detail not without significance. The Franciscan Order, including the Clarisses, was becoming a firmly rooted feature of urban life, taking advantage of the inherent social structures of the town with all its consequent interchanges and interdependent links. In the following century, Teresa of Avila, inspired by the example of Clare, would also prefer her "dovecotes of the Virgin," as she liked to call her Carmels, to be small and medium-sized communities integrated into town-life.

The movement was unstoppable. The life of the cloister was no longer assumed to need a rural environment. Since the time of Clare, the monastery was part of the medieval townscape. In the fifteenth century, there was a further reason for making this choice: the town was safer for the nuns, and, in impoverished times after war, it was easier to find help there from friars or pious lay people.

Benefactors: Wisdom and the Spiritual Argument.

An urban foundation did not guarantee a tranquil life in every case, as shown by the "Letter to the bourgeois of Gand": the roads were not very safe. Colette had to justify her delay in sending her daughters to the town because the circumstances were unfavorable for a journey. Similarly, some aspects already considered for the Corbie foundation arose again, but in another guise. In addition to their right to observe the quality of the observance and the guarantee of the prayers of the community, the benefactors who reported on the progress and status of the work to Colette were now demanding that the promised sisters should come. The position was precisely the reverse of that of Corbie. In both cases the obstacle was outside Colette's control – a legal and economic issue on the one hand and that of circumstances on the other. In the latter case, the founder refused to jeopardize the lives of her daughters during a period of war. She also expressed regret at not having overseen the construction work, to satisfy her desire for a poor and austere convent. But the bourgeois had invested their capital and wanted to recover their costs in some way by ensuring a functioning place of prayer.

Further confirmation of the interdependence of the monastery and the town, together with those who financed it, appears in the reference to the "quarrels" and "divisions" caused by the absence of the sisters. This was a significant challenge for Colette, as any refusal might risk cutting off future material benefits for other foundations.

A monastery could not be founded without a support network of influential friends ensuring the goodwill of the various interested parties (local councilors, civil and religious authorities, the local people and clergy), funding the project, and giving donations to the new community. Hence, Colette had to provide a number of arguments showing that the journey was impossible:

- She had come especially to Hesdin as a preliminary step.
- She had brought the sisters together ready for the foundation.
- She mentions in passing the proximity of her powerful protector, to whom the benefactors are answerable: the duchess of Burgundy, who accepted the postponement.
- "Notable people, and merchants," used to this journey, had advised her and her sisters against it.

Colette's attitude, as shown by the letter, is all the more interesting when compared to Pierre de Vaux's description of her as unhesitating in traveling through war-torn areas, crossing and recrossing enemy lines. Her sanctity was heightened by this. After attacking her with verbal abuse, the fighting men were seduced by the authority of her words. She also understood "foreign languages," which did not fail to astonish these rough soldiers, craving pillage and even rape.[3]

---

[3] See above, Part I, Chapter 5.

Colette, in fact, adopted a position entirely opposite to that described by de Vaux. She preferred to lose the benefits of a foundation rather than expose herself and her daughters to the very real problems:

> I would place them in great risk and expose them to distress, since the way is greatly endangered and perilous, even more for women and religious sisters than others.

Further on, she expresses little hope for the future:

> ... considering the dangers and perils there are at present and even greater and more difficult problems to come.

These few sentences give the lie to Pierre de Vaux's legend of Colette crossing the war-torn areas of France to establish places of prayer. Claudel's beautiful vision must be seen in a more spiritual sense.

> So then, like a diligent needle, in and out of the torn
>   and ravelled realm of France
> Glides she, and mends from beneath; and whatever
>   the lance
> Has left agape, with charity sweet she bindeth in
>   one.[4]

Solid common sense and clear-sighted prudence oversaw the process of foundation. From Nice to Gand, Colette advanced only after preparing the ground well through her contacts and a firm infrastructure. She surrounded herself with advisers, specialists in their own fields: religious, local worthies, lawyers, and travelers.

---

[4] "Sans cesse en route comme une aiguille diligente à travers la France déchirée, Colette en recoud par dessous les morceaux avec la charité." P. Claudel, *Oeuvre poétique* (Paris, 1985) (Coll. La Pléiade), 613. English translation from http://www.poorclarestmd.org/claudels.htm (July 2008).

The spiritual argument, aimed at achieving complete acceptance of her refusal, also reveals her as reformer:

> ... consider that all religious brothers and sisters are ordered or appointed for the holy service of God in order to preserve better the said honor of God and maintain the good devotion and intent of these donors. If you and the lords of the town please, by mutual agreement, to put into the said convent good and devout religious men or any good and devout religious sisters by license and order of those who have the right to decide, in order that they live there in regular observance, serving God very exactly and devoutly, know that this would please me very well and my consent is given to it.

The argument was no doubt an answer to one of those used by the people of Gand to put pressure on Colette:

> ... I heard, she continues, that many already desire and endeavor to make it so, against whom I would not wish that you should have any disputes or divisions relating to the said convent.

Asked to make a decision one way or the other, Colette consents, given the impossibility of establishing herself there.

In itself, this response is a simple matter of common sense. It becomes significant when compared to that given to the monks of Corbie, where the Colettine foundation is

> [to] the honor of God and of you, and to the commendation of your monastery and its profit, as well as to your comfort and that of all the people of the town.

This was also the argument used in her letter to the king:

For the matter is clear and mainly concerns the honor of the souls he has created and redeemed.

Depending on the situation, the reformer either emphasized the particular nature of the contemplative vocation and of regular observance (possibly insinuating that the abbey of Corbie was inadequate from this point of view) or issued a reminder that this whole ecclesial mission was intended to "serve very correctly and devoutly."

The ease with which she handled the arguments, depending on the events and people concerned, combined well with her talent in using the skills of her friends and benefactors. She measured everything against her own mission: to establish centers of contemplative and observant life. Her strength and efficiency came from the fact that everything (whether or not external conditions were favorable) contributed to a single end. This attitude reveals an efficient and pragmatic woman of action.

SPIRITUAL ADVICE

The Official Aspect

The letter to Sieur Bartholomé de Dijon is rather official in nature. Colette is an abbess with power to grant advantages and privileges. There are several features that distinguish this letter from other correspondence, especially in the second part.

At a formal level, there are typical phrases such as "We offer and grant you for life and after death" in the final sentence. This sentence is not the usual formula of prayer or blessing, and it includes the abbess's seal: "Given in Gand, under my seal." The date comes next, with a phrase used only in this case: "The year of our Lord."

The content explains that, in compensation for the work and services provided (perhaps freely given), there would be full participation in all good works ... Masses, fasting, prayers and vigils, abstinences and disciplines or any other good deeds that will be carried out in perpetuity in our congregation (L2).

As in earlier letters under other circumstances, the specific nature of the monastic life is affirmed: prayer in return for material help. Within a social fabric impregnated with Christianity, the monastery is deeply rooted in the world around it. This kind of exchange characterized medieval religious life, especially in the mendicant orders, which, at least at first, tried to live in the strictest poverty and thus refused to have property movable or immovable. Francis and Clare of Assisi are, however, original in emphasizing the need to work for a living. Gifts and collections are not a *sine qua non*, but supplement income when work alone is inadequate for subsistence. There is nothing in Colette's *Letters* to show that she found this an important aspect of Franciscan life. In the letter to the monks of Corbie, for example, the argument that the future foundation would not harm them was not used as might have been expected. She simply reminds them that her convents had neither property nor income.

Spiritual Direction

Spiritual direction is particularly evident in L1.[5] The text will be considered below with those addressed to religious sisters. Although this letter was sent to a laywoman, it provides a religious view of life, providing a formulation and theology of the three vows as means to fight "the enemy from hell," the world and its vanities. For now we can say that Marie Boen was perhaps considering religious life, which would explain the subject discussed. We remember how life at the time was

---

[5] This letter was sent to a certain Marie Bocquiel. It is reproduced in *La Règle de l'Ordre de Sainte Claire, avec les Statuts de la Réforme de Sainte Colette, quelques lettres de cette Glorieuse Réformatrice, ses Sentiments sur la Sainte Règle, etc.* (Société de Saint Augustin: Bruges, 1892). (This work will now be known by its standard title of: *Livre de Bruges*.)

seen in very warlike terms – as an armed struggle in which only the religious vows of poverty, chastity, and humility (or "true obedience") could ensure victory over the world, the flesh, and the enemy, respectively.

This is a classic theme, found earlier in Francis of Assisi[6] and later in Teresa of Avila.[7] The formulation is also classic. Medieval society (the fifteenth century, in particular, torn apart by war and schism) was strongly marked by feudal values that still dominated western culture through the clergy. This warlike view originated, partly at least, with Saint John, who described the three vices: the lust of the flesh, the lust of the eyes and the pride of wealth (1 John 2:16). Saint Paul also frequently used images of war in a different cultural context: the helmet, the belt, the breastplate (Eph 6:14-17 etc.).

But in Colette, the theme associated with the three religious vows reflected a restrictive idea of Christian social life. Everything not governed by the three vows belonged to the "world, the flesh, and the enemy," and must be rejected as such. Colette did not seem to be aware of another kind of path, one that involved discerning the evangelical elements of poverty, chastity, and obedience in the social life of the baptized, for which religious life would then be a radical expression. This reveals the reversal of values that had taken place since Francis's "Letter to All the Faithful." The *Poverello,* going among the people, proclaimed the Kingdom already present, hidden in the Christian town. Colette, however, in an extension of the monastic *contemptus mundi,* postulated an intrinsically negative value of the "world" without the range of meanings expressed in the Johannine vocabulary:

–the world in the sense of creation wounded by sin and contrary to God,

---

[6] Cf. the vision of the knight's armory at the start of Francis's conversion, *Saint Francis of Assisi, Documents, Vita secunda,* Th de Celano, 6, 325 and Saint Bonaventure, *Legenda Major,* 1-3, 216; *FA:ED* 2, 245; *FA:ED* 2, 532-33.

[7] Teresa of Avila, *Book of Instructions,* "First Instructions," ch. II, 831.

- the material world as opposed to the spiritual and invisible universe,
- the pagan world as differentiated from the Christian world,
- the socio-cultural world that, while Christian, is seen as dangerous for religious life, which is the only authentic expression of Christianity (Colette's view).

RELATIONS WITH RELIGIOUS BROTHERS AND SISTERS OF HER CONGREGATION

The reformer's relationships with religious men and women reveal other aspects of her nature. Here we get a better idea of the extent of her power, the internal organization of the reform, and, at another level, her affective and spiritual life.

COLETTE: ABBESS AND REFORMER

Governance Documents

This study of Colette as abbess and reformer includes the letter to Sister Loyse Bassande (R1), even though its tone is not quite of the kind mentioned. Nonetheless, the text is of interest, as Colette was acting here as abbess. Later on we will study the definition of a good religious sister that this letter provides and the affective character of Colette's relations with her sisters and daughters. Our attention is held here by the affirmation of what such a sister is. Mentioning the affective break with parents and friends suggests that this was a source of suffering for Sister Loyse. She might have been asking to have more outside contacts:

> Place your heart in God, since we who have left the world must not concern ourselves with relatives or friends, except to pray to God for their salvation.

The main argument here is "theological" – "You are in Auxonne for your salvation." No other explanation is necessary.

There are two comments to make here. As Colette was writing, there is no doubt she was responding to information received either from the abbess of Auxonne or from Sister Loyse. She was acting as the superior of the congregation, whose authority was greater than that of the abbess. The style of governance expressed through this occasional letter is different from that of Francis of Assisi when consulted by Brother Leo on a choice he had to make: "If you want to come, come."[8]

Francis's third admonition applies to the relationship between superior and subject. The first point Francis makes involves the subject's doing or saying what seems good to him, "which he knows is not contrary to the will of his prelate" (Adm 3:4).

The second point covers the issue that concerns us here:

> And should a subject see that some things might be better and more useful for his soul than what a prelate commands, let him willingly offer such things to God as a sacrifice, and instead let him earnestly strive to fulfill the prelate's wishes (Adm 3:5).

We see here a vivid picture of Francis's idea of obedience. It is based on true dialogue and respect for the opinion of the subject, who knows what is "most useful for his soul." Through the superior's decision, the subject is invited to discern the will of God, to which he must try faithfully to

---

[8] "Letter to Brother Leo," *Saint Francis of Assisi, Documents*, 134: "Brother Leo, your brother Francis wishes you health and peace! I am telling you, my son, like a mother, everything we have said on the road in a few words, and one piece of advice; and you do not need to come to me later for counsel because here is what I advise, 'In whatever way seems best to you to please God and to follow his footsteps and poverty, do it with the blessings of God and with my obedience. But if you need this for your soul and your consolation, and if you want to come to me, Leo, then come.'" See *FA:ED* 1, 122.

conform his own. These are stages of psychological maturity that help one enter into a relationship of faith. Colette seems to suppress these stages in her letter, which apparently is a response to a request. Her line of argument invalidates the possible cogency of Sister Loyse's reasons. This changes the nature of obedience and the subject-superior relationship.

By eliminating the stages of the dialogue and the search for the good of the subject, the letter implicitly transforms the relationship of faith. The command is issued from "on high," overshadowing the lived reality of the subject, who then is obliged to use the interpretation applied by the superior.

Letter to Brother Jehan Lainé

Even more than the previous letter, this one to Brother Jehan Lainé reveals the extent of Colette's authority. She removed this friar from office, as he had become too old to exercise his function as confessor to the community of Puy. "I have heard that you can no longer properly perform the office." This reference suggests a complaint from the community. According to the structures of the reform, Colette provided for each monastery a number of Colettine friars, responsible for celebrating daily Mass, hearing confessions, collecting alms, and acting on behalf of the nuns with the outside world. This letter shows that the statutes were being applied and that the right to dismiss any particular friar from his position belonged to Colette and not to Henry de Baume, who was responsible for the reformed friars. The abbess would have received this right from one of the bulls issued by Benedict XIII.[9]

Once more Colette was acting as the superior of the congregation, as an "abbess general," revealing that the autonomy of the monasteries she had founded was, in fact, quite relative, at least during her lifetime. She kept firm hold of all authority, certainly with the intention of structuring the reform and imprinting it with her own lasting mark.

---

[9] *Bull. Franc.*, n° 1015, t .VII, 347.

She named Lainé's successor, Brother Jehan Frosseau, adding: "This is my pleasure and my wish, that he should do this." As before, her tone is firm, brooking no reply. There seems no possibility of a discussion that would take the friar's point of view into account. The reform was very centralized. The power to appoint and dismiss the confessor (or chaplain) of a monastery would today belong to the diocesan bishop. This gives us some sense of the measure of Colette's authority. In passing we should note that the usual expression of thanks was the shortest and most common type:

> I thank you, my dear Father, for all comfort and service you have given to my sisters, who praise you most highly. I pray Him for whom you have done it.

Elections in a Convent

The letter to the community at Puy (R4) throws light on the legal relations between Colette and the communities she founded and on the role of Brother Henry to be considered below.

An abbess had been elected at the monastery of Puy. Colette replied to letters addressed to Brother Henry and to herself:

> ... to the best of our ability we accept the election of your abbess for the honor of God and salvation of your souls, according to your votes.

The community had notified both persons responsible for the reform. This process does not seem to have been a simple matter of courtesy. It was also a "legal" action. Their agreement was required in order to validate or ratify the result of the election. Though it had been held according to the constitutions and in the presence of the canonical visitator and his assessors, this in itself was not enough. Here, too, the reformer's authority was equivalent to that of the diocesan bishop, who, although he could not himself attend conventual elections, had to be kept informed of their results and was answerable for them in the name of the Church. The next sentence gives us pause, however. Did the community simply ratify a nomination already made by Colette?

> We have appointed Sister Agnès de Montfaucon as your abbess, whom we have approved and herewith confirmed, sending and conveying her to you, beseeching you very humbly to receive her as mother and abbess of you all, loyally and peacefully, obeying her humbly and promptly and holding yourselves subject to her commands ...

We know, from other sources, that Colette placed the first companions in charge of various foundations. The text quoted here appears to confirm this practice. Colette appointed the abbess and the community's vote gave confirmation and approval. After receiving the result of the election, the reformer ratified it. The process showed that the reform remained at the same time very autonomous within the second order and very tied to the reformer, who was grafting a new branch onto the original trunk and imprinting her own mark on it by a thorough structuring resulting from the centralization of power.[10]

Colette's recommendation of the new abbess, who certainly originated from the community of Puy, leads to the assumption that this appointee, coming from another monastery, would have found problems in being accepted by everyone. The full authority of the reformer was required to ensure that this process, not in compliance with the normal

---

[10] There are two possible cases nowadays for this: a community makes a new foundation (especially in a so-called mission country). The person responsible for the foundation is appointed by the abbess of the founding monastery, with Rome's agreement, for however long it takes for the community to grow to autonomy. Elections are then held, in which, in theory, another sister may be elected. This would normally be a member of the community. The second situation would be if a monastery had problems, through lack of leadership for instance. A superior is appointed by Rome with the community's agreement for a period of two or three years, after which elections take place: the superior is then elected abbess. The monastery is once more autonomous with an elected government.

practices of the Poor Clare monasteries, would finally be accepted:

> ... and to you, mother vicar, who already know the spiritual and temporal government, I recommend her affectionately, begging you most dearly to be willing to help and advise her in every way you can, for the well-being and proper running of the whole convent, and the proper observance of all.[11]

It should be noted that never, to our knowledge, did Clare of Assisi act in this way. It appears that her Sister Agnes may have left at the request of the local community. Communities attached to the Damianites were linked by a spiritual rather than a legal bond. Clare never developed so clearly a structure for what would become an order.[12] There are a number of reasons for this. Although towards the end of her life she had some intuition of the scope of her mission, she could never have foreseen the numerical and geographical spread of her family of poor ladies. Colette took on a much-weakened heritage, and her aim was to build a durable structure, based on solid foundations. The Clarisses that she formed, when placed

---

[11] Traditionally, the monasteries jealously guarded their right to vote. In the matter of Corbie – where the parish priest in fact held real power – the community opposed the priest's decision as well as the opinion of the king, and was finally successful. At the end of her life, Teresa of Avila would have problems with the prioresses of some of her convents, who wanted to acquire real independence from Teresa, their *madre fundadora*. Cf. M. Auclair, *Vie de Thérèse d'Avila* (Paris, 1960).

[12] Thus, for example, the rule of 1253 was granted by the pope only for the monastery of San Damiano. The same applied to the privilege of "the strictest poverty," by which Clare was granted the right to live without income or property. She did not impose this on other communities as a *sine qua non* of belonging to the family she had created. The example of Agnes of Prague was significant: Agnes certainly had heard of Clare through the friars minor; she wished to live like her, but apparently did not know about Clare's wish to live in personal and collective poverty. Agnes's parents built her a wealthy convent, richly endowed with goods. Later on, when she had learned of the choice made by the Damianites, Agnes asked for the same privilege of living in "the strictest poverty." There does not seem to have been any pressure applied to the Prague abbess by Clare.

in positions of authority, would pursue her mission. At another level, we must realize that the Franciscan springtime and its early youthful enthusiasm were now past. Another way of living a spiritual life was in place, one that stressed ideas of hierarchical organization. The beginnings of a pyramidical structure, which would become the essential pattern as the years went by, were already being sketched in.

BROTHERS COLLABORATING IN THE REFORM

Two particular brothers are named in the letters: Brother Henry and Brother Pierre de Rains (also known as Pierre de Vaux). The latter, present at Colette's deathbed, would write the first *Legenda* at the order of the general minister. These two brothers are mentioned in six letters:

R4: letter of election	Brother Henry	before 1439
R2: spiritual letter	Brother P. de Vaux	about 1416
R5: circular letter	death of Brother Henry	1439
R6: letter to Puy	death of Brother Henry and recommendation of Brother Pierre de Rains	1439
R7: letter to Gand	P. de Rains	1442?
R8: letter to Besançon	P. de Rains	1446

Brother Henry is named three times: once to note his agreement for a conventual election and twice on the occasion of his death. These few references are not, it seems to us, proportional to his importance to Colette. We have already noted that, after his death, the amount of correspondence from the reformer increased. This points to Brother Henry's involvement in the business of the reform. The double mention of his death in the documents we have shows that he was a companion and colleague. Colette's description to the Clarisses at Puy also emphasizes his spiritual role:

> Keep your holy Rule perfectly, as well as the fine admonitions from your sovereign prelates, and the fine

> admonitions, commands and excellent examples that your reverend father, Brother Henry de Baume, so often showed and taught you ... he has always been a true father and good pastor to us.

Brother Pierre de Rains is named four times in the letters, three times after 1439, though the date of one is uncertain. This latter is the only one that addresses the topic of the interior life, but it is not necessarily an account of Colette's spiritual life, despite referring to it. It is more of a reply to Pierre de Rains in the form of spiritual advice:

> I beg you to make every effort you can to love Our Lord. Set your heart on fire in the blessed passion of your blessed Savior. Bear and feel his pains like true children. Follow him everywhere ... scorn every love other than his. Let all your hope be in him.

Whether it was written before or after the death of Brother Henry does not change the fact that, of the two correspondents, Colette seems to be the elder. Brother Pierre is being guided, probably after having confided in her and asking for advice. The reformer was no doubt a spiritual guide for the Colettine brothers as well as for others. If the letter dates from before 1439, this task would not have fallen to her only after the death of Brother Henry. It would indicate that she already exercised a particular and well-recognized spiritual function before his death.

The second mention of Brother Pierre is especially interesting. It appears in the letter to the Clarisses at Puy, reporting the death of Henry. At the end of the letter she writes:

> I recommend to you our reverend father, Brother Pierre de Rains, who labors continually for the love of God and the good of the religious life.

In context, this brief note presents Pierre de Rains as a successor to Brother Henry, as one who "labors ... for the good of the religious life" (that is, for the reformed branch of the Clarisses). After 1439, every letter addressed to communities of Colettines mentions Brother Pierre. In the letter to Gand, she writes: "my father, Brother Pierre humbly recommends himself to you." Here it is a simple reminder of his presence as a co-worker. On the other hand, in the letter to the monastery of Besançon, she puts him on the same level as herself, within the same syntactic unit. This letter dates from a few months before her own death, which she felt to be imminent, and casts light on her purpose. It is no longer just a brief reminder, as in the earlier letter. His name, linked with the coordinating conjunction "and" to the phrase containing the substantive "my duty," designates this faithful and sure co-worker as heir to her work and her thought:

> I beg very humbly for myself, my poor soul, my poor person, all my duty with all my pitiful intentions and our good Brother Pierre, that it please you always to remember ...

To sum up, these texts, illuminating her personality as abbess and reformer, give a clear picture of a strongly centralized reform founded on the person of Colette herself, who legislated without explicit reference to a Franciscan or Clarissan tradition.

As founder, she chose and arranged the elements in her new construction. She relied firmly on co-workers devoted to her own endeavor, but who remained in her shadow. Strangely, no other woman seems to have played the role of counselor or spiritual adviser, and none of the Clarisses seemed ready to take over leadership from Colette. She, herself, does not seem to have envisaged such a thing. Given these premises, the continuity of the reform did not seem to have been based on the moral and spiritual radiance of any great figures from among the Clarisses themselves, but rather on the very sound organization Colette had established. The long-term consequences of this, which the subsequent history of the Colettines demonstrates, would be:

–self-government for each monastery,
–emphasis on Colette's prescriptions seen as the sole guarantee of the durability of the work.

This latter reality risked giving the letter precedence over the spirit of the law – a logical consequence of fidelity to Colette, who was seen to be irreplaceable. This real risk of rigidity and fixation on a particular moment in the order's history was avoided by Clare of Assisi by reason of the flexibility of her *Rule*, quickly challenged by other rules issued by the Holy See or by the First Order.

Bonds of Affection with her Correspondents

Colette reveals herself mainly in the letters addressed to her daughters and brothers. The circular letter at the time of Brother Henry's death gives a good picture of how her affective life might have been, as well as her relations to brothers and sisters within her reform. Some personal comments appear: "… great pain and anguish and bitterness of heart and body came to me …" and later:

> which (soul) I recommend to you as much as I am able and know dearly and with as much affection as possible, begging you with all my heart, that, if you have loved him faithfully while living, after his passing this love should not be lessened but increased …

The second letter to the Clarisses of Puy, also recalling the death of the "true brother and good pastor" who was Brother Henry, does not repeat a personal expression of her affliction. As this letter was not a circular, such sentiments might naturally have been included there. Colette seems not to have been an extrovert. Moreover, the era was not characterized by affectionate effusions or self-analysis.[13] It was not until the next century that introspection would become more widespread, though it was already known in the Italy of the *Quattrocento*. Within the mystical tradition, analysis of spiritual states had begun with Catherine of Siena, Angela de Foligno, and, later on, the Clarisses Battista Varani[14] and Catherine of Bologna. Colette belonged to another cultural and religious tradition, well-established in France, which found its perfect expression in the Pascalian aphorism, "the ego is hateful." Nonetheless, the reformer's resolve does not prevent her using some expressions of affection. Colette wants to remain the "little servant" and the "affectionate mother."

A series of such terms appears in the letters addressed to the Clarisses and, to a lesser extent, to the brothers, normally as the opening and closing formulae. For example:

–very humbly and dearly (R1),
–begging you affectionately (R1),
–my dear and much loved daughter of God (twice) (R1),
–very affectionately,
–affectionately,
–my very dear and beloved father in Our Lord (letter to Pierre de Vaux),
–she signs herself "sister Colette," not "mother" and "abbess."

The use of identical terms, often in the same place in a letter, seems to indicate that they are clichés rather than truly affectionate expressions specific to a particular person. The same phrases are used whether she is writing to individuals (Sister Loyse, Brother Pierre, and Brother Jehan Lainé) or to communities (Gand, le Puy). We have no exchanges of letters with Brother Henry, her brother and friend. The com-

---

[13] Clare of Assisi and Agnes of Prague express intense affection in their letters: cf. "Fourth Letter to Agnes," *Writings,* 111, "Letter from Agnes to Clare," *Documents,* 241.

[14] B. Varani, *Istruzioni al discepolo* (Rome, 1984).

parison might have been enlightening. Within her religious family she is certainly affectionate, but does not express it distinctly. The intention of her letters is always described in detail, having a specific aim within the affairs of the reform. Personal exchanges are almost non-existent, at least in correspondence.

The biographies considered in Part I preserve other contemporary testimonies that witness to confidences by Colette, friendly exchanges, but these were spoken rather than written. Society then did not in general use letters for personal confidences and was even less willing to encourage literary outpourings. The monastic life used and would continue to use correspondence as a bond between friends as well as for spiritual direction. However, certain periods, notably the fifteenth century, favored a level of asceticism in personal expression, affective and spiritual, to the extent of despising all the values of the heart in the Pascalian sense of the word.

In a period shaken by war and religious crises, the time was ripe for mobilizing combative forces. For Colette, her reform implicitly involved rejection or ignorance of any personal expression or affective life. A century later, Teresa of Avila, mobilizing for reform, lived in a different cultural context. Despite everything, it was impregnated with a contemporary humanism still unknown in France in the first half of the fifteenth century, though it was already blossoming in the houses of the Italian Clarisses.

Comparing these formulae with those used by Colette when addressing her lay correspondents confirms the impression of a true affection towards her brothers and sisters of the reform, even though not reserved only for them:

- –to Dame Marie Boen of Gand, she says: "my dear lady and very special beloved in Jesus Christ"
- –to the loyal Bartholomé of Dijon: "our dear and much loved ..."
- –to the bourgeois and benefactors of Gand: "respectable and very honorable Lords ...," "very dear and very honorable Lords ...."

We note that the expression "dear and much loved," also used for the Clarisses and for the brothers, are less expressive than exclusive use would be. Nonetheless the context as a whole conveys a more or less affectionate stylistic effect. For lay people, the terms "lady," "master," or "lord" do not have the weight of affection carried by the terms "daughters" or "father," which indicate a close human and spiritual link rooted in a living community. The adverb "affectionately," also used in the letters to the sisters and brothers, reinforces this meaning, since it is not used in the letters to lay people.

COLETTE'S CONCEPT OF THE RELIGIOUS LIFE

Counsels and comments contained in some of the letters help discern some aspects of the kind of religious life the reformer wanted for her sisters. These will be put back into their proper contexts later, when we evaluate their import within the regulations and in her work. For the time being we can sketch in a portrait of the good religious sister and evaluate the content of the cloistered life according to Colette.

The profile of the good religious sister is drawn from Colette's letters to the communities and to sister Loyse Bassande. There seems to have been no evolution of this typology. We conclude that, from the start (if the date of 1416 applies to Sister Loyse), Colette, with the support of Brother Henry, had very clear ideas about one of the purposes of the reform. It was to create, through formation in the monastic life, a type of Clarisse who would be evaluated according to her conformity to Clare's initial project in the thirteenth century.

Morally speaking, the religious sister must be "always a good daughter" (without the slightly pejorative meaning the expression has acquired), namely "devout, humble, patient, obedient to [her] superiors and all [her] good sisters," in a "good convent," among "good religious" (R1). The frequency of the adjective rather unexpectedly emphasizes the moral rather than the spiritual domain. The qualities defining the good religious sister are moral, not theological. They give rise to a particular kind of behavior and shape attitudes. Apparently unquestioning obedience underpins behavior arising more from submission than from a freely given commitment. The text of Francis's third admonition on obedience again provides a useful comparison.[15]

The reference to Christ's obedience unto death as justifying religious obedience is not explicitly linked to the relationship of Love by the Son for the Father, to the mystery of Trinitarian Love. Christ seems submissive, even unto death, to a will outside his own. The pyramid of the religious hierarchy imitates, dare one say, the trinitarian pyramid.

The letters sent to the communities of Puy, Besançon, and Gand describe in detail and expand on these sketches. The second letter to Puy repeats, in its address to the whole community, the terms used to sister Loyse:

---

[15] *Saint Francis of Assisi, Documents*, 42: "Admonition 3. Perfect obedience and imperfect obedience":

The Lord says in the Gospel: Whoever does not renounce all that he possesses cannot be my disciple; and: whoever wishes to save his life must lose it.

That person who offers himself totally to obedience in the hands of his prelate leaves all that he possesses and loses his body. And whatever he does and says which he knows is not contrary to his will is true obedience, provided that what he does is good.

And should a subject see that some things might be better and more useful for his soul than what a prelate commands, let him willingly offer such things to God as a sacrifice; and, instead, let him earnestly strive to fulfill the prelate's wishes. For this is loving obedience because it pleases God and neighbor.

If the prelate, however, commands something contrary to his conscience, even though he may not obey him, let him not, however, abandon him. And if he then suffers persecution from others, let him love them all the more for the sake of God. For whoever chooses to suffer persecution rather than wish to be separated from his brothers truly remains in perfect obedience because he lays down his life for his brothers. In fact, there are many religious who, under the pretext of seeing things better than those which the prelate commands, look back, and return to the vomit of their own will. These people are murderers and, because of their bad example, cause many to lose their souls. [Translation from R. Armstrong, J.A.W. Hellmann, W. Short, *Francis of Assisi: Early Documents*, Vol. 1, *The Saint* (New York: New City Press, 1999), 130.]

> ... always have good patience in all things and be a humble, devout, and perfect religious.

The expression, "good patience" also appears in R7 (Gand) and R8 (Besançon) as does "perfect religious." The "perfect religious" is essentially a sister who is observant of the rules:

> Perfectly keep your holy Rule and the fine admonitions of your sovereign prelates, the fine orders and admonitions and good example that our reverend father, Brother Henry de Baume, has so often shown you and taught you (R6).

Colette's last letter to the Besançon Clarisses repeats this strong idea:

> I always recommend to you the holy Rule, the holy declarations, and all the holy commands.

A few lines further on she repeats this point, stressing the responsibility of each one to observe what she has promised, an even greater responsibility for the abbess who must

> take care that everything is done well and do whatever is necessary so that all may be done and observed ....

As for the sisters, they will keep

> faithfully all the things that by their free will they have promised to God: the holy Rule, the holy declarations, and all the holy commands.

Any stubborn offenders must eventually know that:

> faults [are] justly punished, as the holy commands say (R8).

The definition of the religious life is thus conveyed by a set of regulations giving a model for behavior. It should be noted that, in practice, Colette's "legislative" work and the teaching of Brother Henry are placed on the same footing as the "holy rule." We will come back to this, since it is of decisive importance in providing information about the founder's rule and her own personal work.

Already it may be noted, as confirmed by a study of the *Constitutions* and *Commands*, that one of the essential aspects of the reform relates to observance of the regular life, restructured from the *Writings* of Colette and Henry. "The legislative apparatus" includes coercive measures if the texts are not applied in full. One aspect of the abbess's duties is given particular emphasis – her personal responsibility for application of and respect for what can in fact be called "the corpus of the law." Although she does not create the law, she has the legal power to impose it.

The definition of the vows makes explicit the content of this overlying framework of law. It is also briefly covered in the *Letters*, curiously in the one addressed to a laywoman, Marie Boen. Her possible intention to enter the monastery is not the only reason for this. The letter ends by clearly stating that it is above all a question of "serving and loving [God] in the state most agreeable to him, fighting in his Church to reign in his glorious heavenly palace." Religious vows therefore apply to the entire Christian life, which unfolds here "in the present life," like a combat againt "perils ... to be feared" and "enemies" – the "world of the flesh that night and day makes war against us." But weapons are given to the fighter, the armor of Christ himself:

> Against the world, true and holy poverty ... until death, naked on the cross; against the flesh, pure, holy and simple chastity of heart and body; ... against the enemy, perfect humility and true obedience to death, and all in perfect charity.

Christ's armor is reserved for those whom he has called to the "evangelical state and holy apostolic life." The religious sisters belong to the holy militia, the elite body that fights as vanguard for the rest. Implicitly, then, those who do not join (as shown in the biographies of Pierre de Vaux and Perrine) are "poor defaulters," inveterate sinners who, not clad in this armor, are easy and often consenting prey for "the enemy from hell."

It is true that Francis called his brothers knights, but now this symbolism has mutated. Although drawn from the world of chivalry, his images were less warlike, evoking rather the courtly world of ladies and troubadours.

The symbology and the terminology (battle, victory, armor, adversaries) demonstrate, in Colette, a plan of the Christian life, conceived particularly from the viewpoint of the religious vows. A dichotomy appears between light and darkness, very Johannine in its use of terms (world, flesh). This transforms the Christian experience into a confined battlefield, where the forces of light and of shadow confront each other. It is hard not to see a transposition, to a spiritual and religious level, of the daily political and social reality of these tormented years:

> And as we are in the present life, there are *commonly*[16] *numerous dangers, which are much to be feared, like these enemies particularly: the world and the flesh which night and day make war in many ways and against which we must be armed and defend ourselves since of necessity, they conquer us even if we do not wish to be conquered, and as Saint Paul says, we can have no victory without a battle nor crown without victory. And as we can do nothing of ourselves without the help and grace of Our Lord Jesus Christ nor resist our adversaries, we need to turn back to our good and true patron, Our Lord Jesus Christ, and pray him to*

---

[16] Our emphasis.

be pleased to arm us with his weapons, so that we may better and more surely overcome them (L1).

Of course, John the Evangelist never set out his thought in systematic form. Certain passages of the Apocalypse describe the end of time as a battle between the children of light and the children of darkness, but there it is actually a question of the time before the parousia when Evil will confront the holy and just, those faithful to God. This ultimate battle becomes, in this letter from Colette, the daily battle of the "present life." It is the course of human existence. Those who fight beneath the banner of Christ seem to be, above all, those faithful who wish to follow him to the "worthy evangelical state and the holy apostolic life."

In conceptual terms, we have both a radicalization and a split: the religious and monastic plan is perceived as the authentic and unique expression of the Christian life and no longer as an element, a possible blossoming, within the life of a people who are "priests, prophets and kings."

We must beware, however, of too hasty a conclusion that in spiritual terms the monastery is an island lost in a sea of shadows. On the contrary, the *Letters* to lay people demonstrate the close links the reformer and her daughters had with the people of their time. What matters here is to discern the components of what we might call a "theology of the contemplative life," with a definition of religious vows.

THE INNER LIFE AND THE REPRESENTATION OF SPIRITUAL REALITIES

Colette is not very forthcoming about her inner life, even though the issues we are tackling may give some clues. The formulae used to close or open the *Letters* may indicate a certain spiritual climate, even though it is not particular to Colette. We can identify the images of God, of Christ, and of the Spirit and, within this plan, consider the individual's relationship to God, to others, and to the world.

God is "the sovereign Judge" (R2, to the monks of Corbie: "The Lord who judges"). This expression from Colette's pen is very valuable. It provides authentication of an invocation attributed to her by Pierre de Vaux: "My God, my creator, my judge." She mainly uses the term "God," in the body of the letter, in the conclusion or in the introduction (for example R7, L4 and L5), without specifying whether she is referring to the Father or to the Triune God. Typically, the religious life and the function of the monastery within the town is defined, above all, as a service to God. Colette never changes, whether addressing her sons and daughters or the king or the monks of Corbie or lay benefactors:

> ... all religious brothers and sisters are ordered or appointed in the holy service of God, the better to preserve the honor of God (L2, Gand).[17]
> ... this is a pious matter, mainly concerning the honor of God, the increase in his divine service and the salvation of the souls he created and redeemed ....
> ... so that God may be served very readily ... (Letter to the king).
> ... I believe before God that the said construction will be to the honor of God and of you ... (Letter to the monks of Corbie).
> ... that they may be true Christians, tending towards God alone, faithfully keeping all things that by their free will they have promised to God ... (Letter to Besançon).
> ... do not wish to suffer anything to be done that may be against God and against regular observance (L. Gand).

God is named here as "sovereign majesty," a common term found also in the writings of Teresa of Avila. The association of ideas with the contemporary political system is obvious,

---

[17] "The honor of God": while the devotion of the laity and the world is inconstant, the religious remain unshakeable servants of God.

though it need not be over-emphasized. This sovereign majesty sees all at all times and is also the judge:

> Wherever we are, we are present to him and he sees us clearly, within and without, and knows us better than we know ourselves, so we must be in all places and at all times on our guard so that we do not think, say or do anything that might be displeasing and detestable to him (2nd L to Gand).

This definition of the relationship between the human being and God and of her understanding of God's activity also confirms the authenticity of some passages of Pierre de Vaux. According to him, as we have seen, the brothers, in their own living places and even when traveling far away, had the feeling that she knew everything they did. She often reproached them with their actions.

Comparison of these two texts allows us to discern better one aspect of Colette's spirituality and of her concept of sanctity. Omnipotence is characterized by this faculty of seeing, by observing everywhere and always the external actions of human beings, knowing what might infringe on the divine commands. A code, therefore, is the only way of knowing for sure if the divinity is satisfied or angered by the behavior of the human being.

The human being is the one who is seen, who is constantly observed by God's watchful eye. The Psalms themselves emphasize this condition: "... where will I flee from your gaze?" (Ps 37).[18] But this gaze is benevolent, a look of love, the human marvels at this prevenient tenderness. But in Colette's world, we are in another religious climate: the gaze becomes that of a judge, an inquisitor. Hence such watchfulness, characteristic of extreme holiness, must be attributed to Colette. Pierre de Vaux's book allows us to see that Colette's divinatory gaze over others is reciprocated by their gaze over her. The walls of the cloister do not protect her from the gaze of

---

[18] And further on: "The more unworthy I am, the more Our Lord pities me."

those who want to detect in her face or hear in her words an extraordinary manifestation of the divine. The monastery is an enclosed space, in which the gaze penetrates the heart. Nothing escapes others or God. Everyone lives constantly under a searching, judging gaze, so the code of behavior must be meticulous.

The first French novel, *La Princesse de Clèves* by Madame de La Fayette, provides a perfect literary equivalent of this, reflecting the social and moral reality. Literary critics have unravelled the novel's underlying structure. One of the most famous scenes is that of the mirror, in which each sees the other in an enclosed space. From signs of behavior, the mirror reveals the inner life that by its nature should be hidden but is in fact betrayed by almost imperceptible signs, detected instantly by the vigilant gaze of others.

No doubt the novel reflects the situation at court in the seventeenth century, but would similarly reveal the climate at the start of the French Renaissance when the nobility, as it began to be harnessed by the central authority, adopted its own image and code. Transcendence, though virtually nonexistent, was implicitly laicized and transposed to the person of the king or to a moral value such as personal honor. There was still a highly religious climate, however. The very language used revealed a continuing concern for the honor of God, intolerant of any offence.

"Morality" and "Honor" provided a foundation for this omnipotent and omnipresent view. We seem to be witnessing both a process of laicization (together with a deterioration in theological and spiritual values) and a transfer of the function of religious values from a religious world to an ever more secularized world. The Renaissance would, in general, adopt from the religious or monastic life structures and motivations of particular tried and tested values, their meaning altered and eroded by a loss of spiritual dynamism and distance from their origins.

Confronted by a God understood as "sovereign majesty" or "sovereign judge," the human being feels intensely sinful.

Colette describes her own experience and inner state in a few lines to Pierre de Rains:

> I recommend to you my poor soul, the poorest in the whole world. Alas! what will I be, what will become of me before the sovereign judge? Certainly I dare not think of my horrible offenses, which I believe are the cause of all despair. I have no sense of spiritual good (R to Pierre de Vaux).

Once more, Pierre de Vaux's words in his *Vita* are confirmed: she "considered herself the vilest and most sinful of creatures," and when she is told there were greater sinners, she stated she was the vilest.

This is the classic experience of the sinful state found in the spiritual life. The contemporary *Imitation of Christ* describes this kind of experience frequently and forcefully. The Carmelite masters, following the example of the Rhenish mystics, would analyze the successive stages of the "Ascent" from their own experience. Teresa of Avila saw the place reserved for her in hell.[19] This stage of the spiritual life, however, precedes entry into peace and light – the transfiguration. John of the Cross will call it "divinization through participation" of all the powers of the soul. This is the dawn at the end of the dark night. Once freed, the soul enjoys the beatific vision, separated from it by only a thin veil.

Nothing in the extant *Letters* leads us to suppose that Colette had such an experience. The overall tone reflects that of the *Vita* but even darker. Fascinated by the Passion of Christ, the harrowing drama replayed during this period, Colette seems to remain on the threshold of Easter. In the same letter, cited above, she certainly preaches what she herself practices:

---

[19] *Saint Teresa of Avila, Complete Works*, "Autobiography," 344.

Let your heart burn in the blessed Passion of our blessed Savior. Bear and feel his pain like a true child.[20]

The medieval spiritual movement in which Colette participated was also typical of the Franciscan spirituality of the time. Clare of Assisi frequently mentions the need for the mediation of the Passion.[21] A prayer called the "Five Wounds" is attributed to her. However, the dimension of joyfulness, the certainty of love, the experience of the power of the risen Christ still dominate. There is nothing of this in Colette, though this does not mean she was ignorant of this theology. It is still legitimate to assume that she moved in the spiritual night where drama predominated. The Christ she knew was essentially the Christ of the Passion, he "who was for you obedient unto death" (R4), as she wrote to sister Loyse.

The other pole opposing God is Satan (evil), through whom human beings, caught between two opposing forces, risk going to hell. God as supreme judge keeps an account of the number of times we fall into the traps of the enemy of hell, who seems very powerful. The germ of this concept appears in Francis of Assisi, for instance in the "Letter to all the Faithful."[22] In Colette, however, the idea is more developed, as is true elsewhere in medieval spirituality. Once again we see confirmation of the spiritual climate expressed in the *Legenda,* where the devil plays a leading role.

In almost every *Letter,* the Holy Spirit is frequently invoked, especially in the closing formula. The function of the Holy Spirit seems to be "To preserve one in his holy grace and finally grant everlasting glory" (L. Gand). For religious sisters, the Holy Spirit is always: "the guide for soul and

---

[20] The expression "child" of Christ appears in Angela of Foligno. A very famous multi-colored wooden statue in Seville is called *nuestro Padre, el Jésus del gran Poder* (our Father, Jesus the all-powerful). Medieval spirituality seems to have known this kind of fatherhood of Christ, indicated in the gospels. Cf. the expression attributed to Christ: "my little children."

[21] Clare of Assisi, *Writings,* "Letters to Agnes of Prague," 83-119; CA:ED, 43-58.

[22] Saint Francis of Assisi, Documents, "Writings"; FA:ED 1, 41-51.

body, giving joy, peace, health, salvation and everlasting life" (R. Besançon).

In terms of spirituality, Colette has little that is original relative to the general trends of her period. The accent lies mainly on Christ's Passion. While the three persons of the Trinity are present, this is more as formulae rather than particular components of a spirituality. It seems that the Franciscan heritage has only partially reached her. Emphasis on the suffering Christ leads her to the idea of a God who is sovereign judge and something of an avenger. The mother of God, venerated and praised so highly by Francis and Clare, is scarcely mentioned in Colette's letters.

It is true that the purpose of her letters does not lend itself well to spiritual confidences. When corresponding with important people, including the king himself, Colette seems to be a very active nun, mainly concerned with founding new monasteries despite some unfavorable political and economic circumstances. Pragmatic by nature, she makes best use of the relationships and various circumstances available to her. She appears surrounded by devoted and efficient co-workers, despite the loss of her irreplaceable mentor and faithful friend, Brother Henry. Little inclined to express affection towards her religious companions and preoccupied with her mission as reformer and abbess general of this new branch, Colette nonetheless seems to have aroused veneration, tinged very little with fear. This confirms certain features of her contemporary biographies. There is no doubt that she showed what she was capable of in her legislative writings, the most complete expression of her true personality.

CHAPTER 3

THE HERITAGE

For a better evaluation of the place Colette holds in the renewal movement of the fifteenth century and before examining her legislative writings, it would be helpful to set out the main elements of the founding rule of St. Clare of Assisi, to which Colette makes constant reference.

THE ORIGINS OF THE RULE OF SAINT CLARE

When she retired to San Damiano in 1212, Saint Clare had no intention of founding an order. She simply wanted to lead a life of prayer with a few companions, adopting the life of evangelical poverty conceived by Saint Francis.[1]

Following the Fourth Lateran Council in 1215, however, the Church began trying to restrict the burgeoning of new communities, especially as some of them were degenerating

---

[1] "They live according to the form of the primitive Church of which it is written: 'The multitude of believers was of one heart and one soul....' They go into the cities and villages during the day, so that they convert others, giving themselves to active work; but they return to their hermitages or solitary places at night, employing themselves in contemplation. The women live near the cities in various hospices. They accept nothing, but live from the work of their hands." ("The Witness of Jacques de Vitry, 1216" in *Clare of Assisi: Early Documents,* ed and trans. Regis Armstrong (New York: New City Press, 2006), 428. (All English translations of citations from the writings of Clare and early documents in this chapter are taken from this source, as indicated by *CA:ED* plus page number, unless otherwise noted.)

into heretical sects. The council fathers banned the foundation of any new convent that was not attached to an existing approved order or to an already approved rule (canon 13). The rule of Saint Francis, verbally approved in 1208, was only just tolerated, so the San Damiano community was first attached to the Benedictine order, while retaining its own practices: a short formula for daily life and observances given by Saint Francis. Clare was named abbess in 1215.

This link to the order of Saint Benedict did not actually change the way of life at San Damiano, but it did threaten the choice of strict poverty so desired by Francis and Clare. Benedictine life relied on revenue from farmlands and the collection of income from property. Clare, therefore, sought from Pope Innocent III the privilege of "highest poverty," which he granted in 1216.[2] Pope Gregory IX confirmed this in 1228.

The life experience of Clare and her companions was not unique however. Other groups were being formed, particularly in the Rieti valley. They were largely independent of each other, but, to an observer able to read the signs of the times, they displayed a number of points in common. Cardinal Hugolino, the papal legate in Tuscany, took an interest in them and brought them under his protection. Using the rule of Benedict as a framework, he wrote a set of very austere constitutions for them, known as "Hugoline" (1218-19), establishing almost perpetual silence, continual fasting, and strict enclosure. In principle, the rule was to be applied to all new communities. The cardinal hoped that it would be definitive, but it did not cover either of Clare's two essential points – poverty and the link to the Friars Minor. Cardinal Hugolino was not initially hostile to communal poverty. When he took

---

[2] "Therefore, we confirm with our apostolic authority, as you requested, your proposal of most high poverty, granting you by the authority of this letter that no one can compel you to receive possessions. And if any woman does not wish to or cannot observe a proposal of this sort, let her not have a dwelling place among you, but let her be transferred to another place" (*CA:ED*, 86).

on the task of organizing these new communities, he sought and obtained

> the right to receive in the name of the Church and incorporate into his domain land offered to build monasteries and oratories for religious sisters who wanted to live without possessing anything under heaven except their dwelling places.[3]

These communities would be exempt from episcopal jurisdiction as long as they had no property. But little by little, the cardinal changed his mind and urged monasteries to accept some property and exempted monasteries to receive possessions.

The pope wanted to entrust the spiritual direction and material supervision of these new convents to the Friars Minor. The friars, however, were reluctant to take on extra work. Thus, each case was dealt with on its merits, with the result that the nascent order was not unified.

In 1247, Pope Innocent IV hoped to establish some uniformity by promulgating a rule based on that of Cardinal Hugolino, but relaxing some points and clarifying two issues left unresolved: the re-attachment of these monasteries to the order of Saint Francis and permission for all monasteries to hold possessions in common henceforward.

But the friars to whom government and spiritual direction of the Clarisses was entrusted considered the task too onerous. In 1250 they succeeded in being relieved of it. This was the final blow to the rule of Innocent IV. In June 1250 the pope admitted that he could not force any monastery to adopt it and allowed a return to diversity. It then became possible for Clare to write, at least for San Damiano, a rule that would be fully in line with her ideas, one that adapted the rule of the Friars Minor to a monastic situation and that clearly affirmed the principle of most high poverty. Pope In-

---

[3] P. Gratien, *Histoire de la fondation et de l'évolution de l'Ordre des frères Mineurs au XIIIe siècle* (Paris, 1928), 600.

nocent IV approved it two days before he died, on August 3, 1253 (Bull *Solet annuere*).

The order's legislative work did not stop on that date, however. This rule was binding only on the convent of San Damiano. When Isabelle of France, sister of Saint Louis, founded the convent of Longchamp in 1259, she tried to give it a personal touch. She had French theologians write a new rule, allowing possessions to be held in common and introducing the vow of perpetual enclosure.

In 1263 Pope Urban IV tried to make uniform, definitive rules governing the position of the new order. He gave it the official name of the Order of Saint Clare. He largely adopted the Longchamp rule (possessions in common, vow of enclosure), but he found a new solution to the issue of the relationship with the Friars Minor. He put the Clarisses under the jurisdiction of the Cardinal Protector of the Franciscan family, effectively placing them, for the most part, under the control of the Friars Minor. This was the so-called "Urbanist" rule, adopted by most monasteries during the fourteenth century.

Some Aspects of the Rule

Clare therefore wrote her rule after having lived for a long time at San Damiano under other rules. Clearly, the legislation imposed on the monastery, or suggested for it, did not entirely satisfy her. She felt it should reflect the reality of life there. Before she died, Clare wanted to ensure that the mission she had received from God and from Francis of Assisi would endure. In a Church in which consecrated women had always received their rule from priests or religious brothers, this simple fact is indicative of her powerful influence. From the outset of her lived experience, she was not afraid to pursue, with tenacity and gentleness, the implementation of her original inspiration. Her rule, while taking into account the juridical requirements of the Lateran Council of 1215, resulted from choices that followed mature reflection and were tested by life itself.

This rule unambiguously expresses basic elements characteristic of monasticism from the beginning: fasting, silence, poverty, enclosure, and the cenobitic life. Clare's originality therefore lies not in the invention of new elements but in their proportionality and interconnectedness. We will analyze enclosure later on in the section on relations with the outside world. Here, however, it is immediately clear that the choice of silence, fasting, communal life, and poverty takes place within what might be called a structure of retreat relative to ordinary social organization. Similarly, poverty indicates detachment from existing socio-economic conventions.

Daily Life at San Damiano

Silence

The way of life at San Damiano was immersed in continual silence: "Let a continuous silence be kept by all at all times" (Rule of Hugolino 6). The influence of the Cistercian reform, of which Hugolino was a great admirer, seems to have infiltrated the law of silence he drew up, followed later by Innocent IV:3: "Let a continuous silence be kept by all at all times."[4]

Permission to speak must be given by the abbess. Clare adds detail and clarity to this in Chapter V of her *Rule*:

> Let the sisters keep silence from the hour of Compline until Terce, except those who are serving outside the monastery. Let them also continually keep silence in the church, the dormitory, and the refectory only while they are eating. At all times, however, they may be permitted to speak with discernment in the infirmary

---

[4] *CA:ED*, 78, 92. *Silentium vero continuum sic continue ab omnibus teneatur.* (All Latin quotations from Hugolino's Rule and that of Innocent IV are from I. Omaechevarria, *Escritos de Santa Clara*, here 218 for Hugolino and 240 for Innocent IV.)

for the recreation and service of the sick. Nevertheless, they may always and everywhere communicate whatever is necessary, briefly and in a quiet voice.⁵

The rule of silence is therefore not so strict and relies not on the abbess's permission but on the sisters' own responsibility. It is always permitted to speak "with discernment" in the infirmary. Clare leans towards greater flexibility. Each sister must own her own silence, learning to discern between what is truly lacking in the recollection essential for the life of prayer and what is needed for acts of charity or essential communication among the sisters. Clare's option for choices modifies the classic framework of the cenobitic life.

Fasting

Hugolino directs that "... they should fast daily at all times"⁶ Clare, in chapter III, says: "Let the sisters fast at all times." The expression used here applies to liturgical seasons. Exceptions are made for "the Nativity of the Lord," for the young, the weak, and those serving outside the monastery, at the abbess's discretion. Clare adds: "Let the sisters not be bound to corporal fasting in time of manifest necessity." She takes this passage from the *Later Rule* of Saint Francis, III:9.

On February 9, 1237, Hugolino added a Cistercian practice forbidding the Clarisses to eat meat.⁷ Clare later followed

---

⁵ *CA:ED*, 116.

⁶ "... omni tempore ieiunent quotiodie," Hugolino 7 (Omaechevarria, 220; *CA:ED*, 79), *Sorores autem et servientes a jesto exaltationis sanctae Crucis usque ad festum Resurrectionis Dominicae continuum servent ieiunium, dominicis diebus, beati Michaelis, beati Francisci, omnium sanctorum Nativitatis Dimini cum duobus inmediate sequentibus diebus, nicnin Epiphaniae et Purificationis festis exceptis,* Innocent IV (Omaechevarria, 241-42). [Let the sisters and the servants continuously keep the fast from the feast of the Exaltation of the Holy Cross until the feast of the Resurrection of the Lord, except on Sundays and the feasts of Saint Michael, Saint Francis, All Saints, the Nativity of the Lord, and the two days following it, the Epiphany, and the Purification" (CA:ED, 93)]

⁷ *Licet velut ignis*, *CA:ED*, 354.

that directive. In the "Third Letter to Agnes of Prague," she says that Francis made exemptions to this fast *omni tempore*, but three times she insists:

> None of us who are healthy and strong should eat anything other than Lenten fare, either on ferial days or on feast days. Thus we must fast every day except Sundays and the Nativity of the Lord …(32).

And further on, she says:

> However, we who are well should fast every day except on Sundays and on Christmas (35)

and also

> We who are well and strong always eat Lenten fare (37).

Clare's attitude is unambiguous. She discards the instruction of Innocent IV as being too conciliatory and gives greater nuance to the rather brusque instruction of Hugolino, although the latter recommends a merciful freedom for the weak and the young. The letter to Agnes, confirmed by the testimony of sisters during the canonization process,[8] shows that it was Francis, in fact, who intervened to modify Clare's rule, specifying days when two meals were allowed. He made Clare herself take food, at least a little bread and water. She herself longed for a physically tough life that, according to monastic tradition, encouraged spiritual strength by mastery over the body and orientation of the spirit to prayer.

Poverty

Structurally the chapter in the rule devoted to poverty is linked to those governing the relations between abbess and

---

[8] *CA:ED*, "Process of Canonization," 1:8, 2:8, 3:5, 4:5, 6:5, 6:7, 7:4, 10:4, 11:5, 12:6, 13:1.

sisters and among the sisters (chapters VI to X). In these, Clare's personal contribution is most marked. While she follows the rules of Hugolino and Innocent IV with some modifications of which we have just seen examples, she abruptly inserts completely new or considerably modified chapters. This inclusion breaks the unity of the chapters covering the monastery's relationships with the outside world. Chapter XI (on enclosure) picks up the thread broken in chapter V (on silence, the parlor, and the grill). As the rule consists of twelve chapters, Clare's intention seems very clear. She means to put the two basic aspects of the Franciscan project at the heart of her text – poverty and sisterly love.

Clare began writing her own rule almost immediately after the promulgation of the rule of Innocent IV. Comparing the two, it is obvious that she is seeking some re-balancing. By restoring poverty and relationships to the center, Clare emphasizes her unswerving desire to bind herself to Franciscan spirituality, to the first order, and to Francis, whose "little plant" she was."[9]

Pope Innocent IV had not made allowance for the "privilege of poverty" granted to the Damianites in 1216.[10] This makes it easier to understand Clare's emphasis on poverty and her desire for her rule to be approved before she died. Chapter VI includes two texts written by Francis and added there to indicate that the second and the first orders came from one source.[11] Following Christ in poverty is essential for

---

[9] Neither Innocent IV nor Cardinal Hugolino covered relations among sisters in their rules, although they devoted one chapter to care of the sick, and they hardly mentioned the issue of the office of abbess.

[10] Cardinal Hugolino wrote in 1216: *Liceat vobis in communi redditus et possessiones recipere* et *habere ac ea libere retinere* ["It is allowed to you to receive income and possessions in common and to have and also hold them freely."] (I. Omaechevarria, 255.)

[11] "He wrote a form of life for us as follows: 'Because by divine inspiration you have made yourselves daughters and handmaids of the most High, most Exalted King, the heavenly Father, and have taken the Holy Spirit as your spouse, choosing to live according to the perfection of the holy Gospel, I resolve and promise for myself and for my brothers always to have the same loving care and special solicitude for you as for them.'" (Rule of Clare VI:3-4; *CA:ED*, 118). "Shortly before his death he repeated in writing his

the Franciscan project. It is its sign of distinction among the consecrated families within the Church. Francis had been canonized in 1228, and the Friars Minor had a rule approved by the Holy See.

After Francis's death, Clare felt even greater urgency to establish an approved text of the founder's legacy, all the more so as it was under threat. Her *Testament*, written also during these last years of her life, repeats almost word for word the beginning of chapter VI of her rule.[12]

A consequence of this communal and individual poverty, lived with integrity, was the need for the sisters to work "in such a way that, while they banish idleness, the enemy of the soul, they do not extinguish the Spirit of holy prayer and devotion to which other temporal things must contribute"(VII:2). It also made them dependent on alms. Chapter VIII repeats the favorite theme of poverty:

> Let the sisters not appropriate anything to themselves, neither a house nor a place nor anything at all (VIII:1).

This is taken directly from the *Later Rule* of Francis (VI:1-6), along with most of the subsequent sections. These lines consist of a sequence of quotations from scripture, demonstrating the biblical roots of the common project of Francis and Clare.[13] The choice of poverty, one of the bases of Clare's way of life, has its source in the poverty of Christ, who "made himself poor for us in this world" (VIII:3).

---

last will for us. He said: 'I, little brother Francis, wish to follow the life and poverty of our most high Lord Jesus Christ and of His most holy Mother and to persevere in this until the end; and I ask you, my ladies, and I give you my advice that you live always in this most holy life and poverty. And keep most careful watch that you never depart from this by reason of the teaching or advice of anyone.'" (Rule of Clare VI:6-9, *CA:ED*, 118). In the context of 1253, this sentence also covers the rule of Innocent IV.

[12] Cf. *Testament*, 33-35 (*CA:ED*, 62).

[13] See the references noted in the Christian Sources edition, 146, note to chapter 8:1-6; Ps 38:13; 1 Peter 2:11; 2 Cor 8:9; 2 Cor 8:2; Matt 5:3; Luke 6:20; Ps 141:6.

Clare joined the poor of her own time, though only as a consequence of her choice. Like them, she and her sisters worked with their hands, and, when their work was not sufficient, they turned to "the table of the Lord." In other words, they begged.

Clare introduced a new element into women's contemplative religious life, which considerably changed the face of monasticism. It has already been shown that this phenomenon flowered in a favorable social and economic environment. The nerve centers of society were moving from powerful fortified castles in rural areas to fast-growing towns. Here the dropouts, those left behind by economic expansion, were already appearing, becoming more and more dependent on a few powerful members of the bourgeoisie and of the merchant class. Near the flourishing town of Assisi, there were now some few dozen women mendicants, poor by choice, not for the sake of solidarity or philanthropy, but in the name of Christ. For the Church and for the wealthy, the Poverello and the Damianites were reminders of the urgency of building the Kingdom.

There were two other inseparable elements that were going to modify the traditional monastic framework: the concept of the abbess's responsibility and the relationship of the sisters with each other.

Interpersonal Relationships at San Damiano

This topic is covered mainly in chapters II, IV, VII, VIII, IX and X of Clare's rule, although others also mention it. We can see how interested Clare was in this subject. It was part of her original contribution, as compared to Hugolino and Innocent IV, who paid little attention to it.

As in the sections on poverty, Clare borrowed heavily from Francis's *Later Rule*. He himself quotes from Scripture, especially the Gospels.[14] This supports well the observation

---

[14] Chapters IX and X deal exclusively with relations among the sisters and between the abbess and the sisters, using the following references to Francis, according to the Christian Sources: Cap 10 § 1-3: 2 Rg 7 § 5: 2 Rg

already made on poverty as a foundation: the source of these choices and attitudes lies in the *sequela Christi* and in gospel teachings. The portrait of the abbess sketched throughout these texts also owes much to the Rule of St. Benedict, as we will see later.

Governance: Its Composition

Clare's reluctance to accept the title and responsibility of abbess is well-known.[15] She agreed to it only after the Lateran Council of 1215.

In 1253, while writing her own *Rule* (the fruit of forty years of religious and community life), she did use the term "abbess," but changed its content considerably. She enriched it with new layers of meaning. Chapter IV is devoted to the "Election and Office of the Abbess: the Chapter, and the Officials and the Discreets." The abbess is chosen by all the sisters gathered in the presence of the minister general or provincial of the first order. As in the Benedictine rule, the abbess seems to be elected for life. "At her death, let the election of another abbess take place" (IV:6). It is stipulated however that she may be dismissed:

> If at any time it should appear to the entire body of sisters that she is not competent for their service and common good, these sisters are bound as quickly as possible to elect another as abbess and mother (IV:7).

(This passage refers to Francis's *Later Rule* 8:2-4). The abbess is in some way responsible to the whole community.

7,3; § 13-14: 2 Rg 11,1-3; § 17: 2 Rg 7,2; Cap. 10 § 1-3: 2 Rg 10, 1-3; § 4-5: 2 Rg 10,5-6; § 6-8 13: 2 Rg 10, 7-12. Scripture references: Cap 9, § 7: Matt 6:15; Matt 18:35; Cap 10, § 5: Matt 20:27; § 6: Luke 12:15; Matt 13:22; Luke 21:34 § 7: Col 3, 14; § 11: Matt 5:44; § 12: Matt 5:10; § 13: Matt 10:22.

[15] In the Testament, where Clare does not use the legal vocabulary of the rule, it is interesting that the word "abbess" appears only once, replaced by the periphrastic: "the sister who shall be in office" (53) or "who will be in an office of the sisters" (61) (*CA:ED*, 63-64).

Elsewhere, Clare deals with an all too likely situation: sickness or serious incapacity of the abbess.

Another point was made about the abbess, who was no doubt the first among her sisters, but within the context of the religious life itself:

> Let her preserve the common life in everything, especially in whatever pertains to the church, the dormitory, refectory, infirmary, and clothing (IV:13).

For the Damianites, it was impossible for the abbess to have her own apartment, let alone servants, as happened in some Benedictine abbeys.[16]

In fulfilling her task, she is assisted not by a prior, as in the Benedictine monasteries, but by a "vicar," who must above all fulfill her religious duties. Governance is completed by a council around the abbess, consisting of sisters chosen by the community (IV:23). This instituted and elected council did not exist in the rules of Hugolino and Innocent IV. The Benedictine rule did have a consultative council, but it was formed of older members (Rule of Benedict III:12).

Its Function

First of all, our attention is drawn to the collegial or properly communitarian nature of decision-making:

> In order to preserve the unity of mutual love and peace, let all who hold offices in the monastery be chosen by the common agreement of all the sisters (IV:22).

In this context, such an element appears to be new. Apart from this essential but infrequent procedure, the community also had a part to play in the daily life or administration of

---

[16] The Urbanist Clarisses, or "Rich Clares" who could possess property, began, from the fourteenth century onwards, to resemble the large Benedictine monasteries; for instance, royal foundations such as Longchamp, Naples, etc.

the monastery. The weekly chapter had a dual function: it was a community meeting and a chapter for all to confess faults.

> There let her consult with all her sisters concerning whatever concerns the welfare and good of the monastery (IV:17):

Using an article from the rule of Saint Benedict for her own purposes, Clare adds the following: "Indeed, the Lord frequently reveals what is best to the least [of us]."[17] The Latin word Clare uses is *minori,* while the Benedictine rule uses *juniori*. Clare's choice of word is certainly deliberate. It refers to the *minores*, a term Francis commonly used to describe his brothers. It had, for him a spiritual connotation and indicated their form of life.[18] While Clare uses some elements of the Benedictine rule not found elsewhere, she adapts them, even changing their meaning to suit her own project, which is fundamentally that of Francis.

In the daily administration of the monastery, the community is also involved. The phrase "the abbess and her sisters" occurs frequently throughout the rule, whether referring to an attitude to hold or to a decision to be made.[19] It means that no decision belongs solely to the abbess. She appoints the novice mistress "from among the most discern-

---

[17] Rule of Benedict III:3: "For the Lord often reveals what is best to one of the least."

[18] The Benedictine rule covers the community meeting, but only for "whenever there is an important issue in the monastery" (III:1). Moreover, having once heard the advice of the friars, the abbot "deliberates alone and does what he thinks best" (III:2); "the decision will depend on the abbot: what he considers to be most appropriate, all will obey" (III:5). If there is a correction, the abbot must arrange everything "with foresight and justice," since the relationship between the friars and the abbot is that of subordinates to their superior, "it befits the disciples to obey their master" (III:6).

[19] "… let the abbess and her sisters take care that they be not concerned about her temporal affairs" [of the postulant] (II:9; *CA:ED*, 110); "… Let the abbess and her sisters, however, be careful that nothing be deposited in the monastery" (IV:20; *CA:ED*, 115); "… The abbess and her sisters, however, must beware not to become angry or disturbed on account of another's sin," (IX:5; *CA:ED,* 121).

ing sisters of the entire monastery" (II:19). She excuses the weak and the sick from fasting (III:10). She gives permission for the sisters to make their confession twelve times a year (III:12). She allocates work to each person in the presence of the whole community (VII:3) and distributes alms or donations received according to the "common good" or need, but through the council of discreets (VII:5). However, it seems that the abbess or her vicar is directly responsible for the enclosure.[20]

The establishment of this kind of government may be seen as a "democratization of the community regime," influenced by the "free towns or communes," where, in principle, all citizens had a "vote at the chapter." This development certainly had an effect on Clare, who was a child of her time. Such an observation is, no doubt, judicious, since it places the development of the rule in the context of the period. However, Clare did not invent the idea of electing the abbess (Innocent IV had already stipulated this) and the community's opinion had long been important among Benedictines, as we have already seen.[21]

It is clear, nevertheless, that Clare moved from a feudal system to a more collegial type of arrangement. She extended the scope of possible action by the community. The term "democratization" has political connotations, but here we are in the religious domain. We may need to seek elsewhere for the origin of such a novel concept without denying that the "spirit of the times" favored the blossoming of this phenomenon. It is also reasonable to suppose that contemporary churchmen were unlikely to be impressed by the politico-economic move-

---

[20] To appoint the three sisters who accompanied the sister with permission to speak at the grille (V:7; *CA:ED*, 116), to keep one of the keys of the enclosure (XI:4; *CA:ED*, 124), to place a sister at the gate responsible for opening up to workers (XI:10; *CA:ED*, 124), to allow a confessor to enter the enclosure (V:17; *CA:ED*, 117), to keep one of the keys of the enclosure (the other being kept by the portress) (XI:4; *CA:ED*, 124), to receive or send letters or other items and gifts (VIII: 7, 8, 9; *CA:ED*, 120).

[21] Two centuries later, Colette could not establish a foundation at Corbie, despite having the support of the king, the abbot, and the prior, because the community of monks opposed it. Cf. chapter 2.

ments of the time. Certainly they could not have imagined the future irreversible development of these movements.

Mutual Love

Studying the relationship between abbess and sisters provides us a better perspective and a more complete picture of the abbess and of the functioning of the community. The fundamental term that described Clare and her companions at San Damiano was *"sister"*: *"ordinis sororum pauperum"* (I:1). The expression "poor sisters" is closer to that chosen by Francis, emphasizing as it does the brotherly and sisterly dimension inherent in Clare's vocation from the outset;[22] Within the traditional monastic context, Clare operated from choice. The term "brother" can be found in the Benedictine rule, but there are other equivalent terms belonging to another register, such as "disciple" matched with "master" and "guide" corresponding to "abbot." "Poor sisters" is closer to "lesser brothers." This choice results then from personal experience following the call that is received.

Because they have the same call, the relationship between Clare and her companions is rooted in mutual trust, in an open exchange in which each is certain of being listened to, understood, and loved.[23] While the abbess has primary responsibility for the sick sisters, each serves them as she herself would wish to be served, if she too were ill.

---

[22] "After the most high heavenly Father saw fit in his mercy and grace to enlighten my heart that I might do penance according to the example and teaching of our most blessed father Francis, a short while after his conversion, I ... willingly promised him obedience," (Testament, 24-25; *CA:ED*, 61); and also: "I admonish, beg and encourage my sisters," (Rule, II:24; *CA:ED*, 112) and "I, together with my sisters, have ever been solicitous" (Rule VI:10; *CA:ED*, 118).

[23] "Therefore, if you are offering your gift at the altar and there remember that your brother has something against you, leave your gift there in front of the altar. First go and be reconciled to your brother, then come and offer your gift" (Matt 5:23); "But if you do not forgive men their sins, your Father will not forgive your sins" (Matt 6:15); "This is how my heavenly Father will treat each of you unless you forgive your brother from your heart" (Matt 18:35).

The attitude towards the sick (like that towards the youngest and weakest who, as we have seen, were excused from fasting) is one of the tests of sisterly charity. This was the context into which Clare added a new relationship for the sisters among themselves, that of mother and daughter. In addition to the equality implied by the term "sister," "mother" assumes a mutual, faithful gift of self. The relationship of love that unites the sisters, mothers, and daughters, is essentially one of faith rooted in an experience of Divine Love. Clare unambiguously avoids affectionate relationships.

But this community of sisters also experiences tensions and faults. The attitude of the abbess and the sisters also reveals the truth of the lived experience of sisterly charity. Undoubtedly, there were punishments applied that to a modern mind seem repugnant. Our values are not those of the men and women of another civilization. The rule of Saint Benedict includes corporal punishments. But, at a time when the whip, the hair shirt, and physical asceticism were normal practice, Clare does not mention any of these. The "even greater punishment" (IX:3), left to the judgment of the abbess, is difficult to identify. When the fabric of the community has been damaged by the fault of one among them, the attitude of the sisters and the abbess is to pray "that the Lord will enlighten her heart to do penance" (IX:4).

Tension may arise between sisters (IX:6-10): Clare suggests both that it may exist and that it should be exceptional. Verses seven and ten are quotations from Matthew's gospel.[24] As we have noted, the relationship between the sisters, a relationship of faith, originates in the Gospel.

Chapter X expands on the spiritual role of the abbess, already outlined. She has an essential function as guarantor of the rule, with the duty and the right to encourage her sisters along the path of evangelical perfection. But this respon-

---

[24] "Let each one confidently make her needs known to another. For if a mother loves and cares for her child according to the flesh, how much more attentively should a sister love and care for her sister according to the Spirit?" (VIII:15-16; *CA:ED*, 120-21).

sibility is exercised in humility and charity[25] as "she must render an account of the flock committed to her" (IV:8). This whole chapter borrows freely from Francis and from the gospels.[26] The relationship of trust combines with the spirit of obedience, since the sisters "have renounced their own will" (X:2,3). The abbess guarantees the rule; she does not create it, but is herself subject to it. The core of these relationships, attitudes, and choices is "the unity of mutual love which is the bond of perfection" (X:7).

For these women stripped of their material possessions and their own will, the Holy Spirit is their only, complete property:

> Let them direct their attention to what they should desire above all else: to have the Spirit of the Lord and Its holy activity (X:9).

In this context, the portrait of the abbess outlined in chapter IV takes on its full meaning:

> Let her also strive to preside over the others more by her virtues and holy behavior than by her office, so that, moved by her example, the sisters may obey her more out of love than out of fear (IV:9).

The monastic tradition was familiar with this role of the abbot as servant, one who was to be loved more than feared.[27] The abbot, *abba*, that is father of his monks, was however

---

[25] "Let the Abbess admonish and visit her sisters, and humbly and charitably correct them, not commanding them anything that is against their soul and the form of our profession" (X:1; *CA:ED*, 122; cf. *Later Rule*, X:1, *FA:ED* 1, 105).

[26] For X:5 see Matt 20:27; for X:6 see Luke 12:15, Matt 13:22, Luke 21:34, Col. 3:14; for X:11 see Matt 5:44; for X:12 see Matt 5:10; for X:13 see Matt 10:22.

[27] Rule of Benedict LXIV:7-8: "Once appointed, let the abbot always reflect on the burden he has taken on ... and let him know that he should serve rather than be the head," and also LXIV:15: "... let him try to be loved rather than feared."

seen as a spiritual guide, a master teaching his disciples.[28] Clare is aware of this essential aspect of being a spiritual teacher, but she puts it into an entirely different context. While not losing the primary quality of being sister to her sisters, the abbess becomes the mother, one capable of generating spiritual life; and more than anything else she is a servant.[29]

Clare completely reverses the abbot-brother relationship of the Benedictine role, without apparently being afraid of opening the way to excess. This familiarity arises from the intimacy of mutual love, of spiritual friendship that unites the abbess with her sisters, the freedom possessed by those who truly love each other. They manage to combine obedience and familiarity, trust and freedom to be themselves within a human and spiritual balance. One sees that Clare is very demanding as regards the quality and intensity of relationships, a rough road no doubt towards the integration of the whole personality. Some writers suggest that the "servant-mistress" coupling echoes the influence of the social upheavals of the time. Clare took an opposing view towards social relationships. As for governance, the generous use of scripture references supports the argument that her project is to follow the poor, crucified Christ.

She refers to the Gospel where Christ reminds his disciples that the first among them must be the servant of all. He calls himself servant (referring to the Suffering Servant of Isaiah) on the evening of Holy Thursday, when he washed the feet of his disciples. Clare, like Francis, thoroughly under-

---

[28] "... his commandment and his teaching are blended into the spirit of his disciples like the leaven of divine justice" (Rule of Benedict 11:5) and "In his teaching ... the abbot must always observe the rule expressed thus by the apostle: correct, appeal, reprimand" (II:2-3).

[29] "Let the abbess, on her part, be so familiar with them that they can speak and act with her as ladies do with their handmaid. For this is the way it must be: the abbess should be the handmaid of all the sisters" (X:4-5, *CA:ED*, 123).

stood the meaning of this concrete gesture. She would herself take the same attitude toward her mendicant sisters.[30]

Another meaning of the word servant emerges when we realize that Francis uses it in an identical way in the *Salutation to the Virgin*, referring to Mary, "daughter and servant of the heavenly Father."[31] The abbess is a figure of both Christ and Mary. While Saint Benedict favored the image of *abba*, Clare preferred that of Christ, the Servant of his brothers, handed over to death. She adds a feminine and maternal note, that of Mary, mother, servant, and sister.

Relationships Outside the Monastery

Although independent, the monastery was not isolated. Outside contacts were essential to the community, providing support and help. Conscious of the need to serve, the monastery had many links – with friars, with ministers of the Church, with clergy, with the surrounding country, with the laity. The paradox is that this life of relationship, in order to achieve its full potential, also required a structure of withdrawal.

The Friars

Clare wanted a very close relationship between the two orders, based on her own relationship with Francis, as solemnly stated in the first chapter of her Rule: "Clare, the little plant of the most Blessed Father Francis." Obedience to the founder and his successors flowed naturally from this. The obedience of the nuns, including the abbess, had two dimensions: they were anchored in the Church (obedient to the pope and to the Church) and in the men's order.

---

[30] "Canonization process," 3:9, *CA:ED*, 174 and T. De Celano, *Vita*, 12, 40, *CA:ED*, 123.

[31] *Saint Francis of Assisi, Documents*, 148-49. Editor's note: the reference to "daughter and servant of the heavenly Father" is actually found in the Antiphon for Compline in "The Office of the Passion," *FA:ED* 1, 141.

The various modalities of the first order's jurisdiction are described in detail throughout the chapters of the rule, as related to situations foreseen by Clare. The Rules of Innocent IV and Urban IV implicitly acknowledge the jurisdiction of the first order.[32] Hugolino's earlier rule is silent on this point, understandably enough. In 1219, both orders were of very recent foundation and the Damianites were just getting organized. In her rule, Clare still recalled (VI:4-5) how Francis was engaged with the poor ladies. This is given concrete expression in Chapter IV by directing that the minister general be present at the election of the abbess (IV:2). Similarly, the canonical visitator was to be a member of the first order (XII:1). As in the Rule of Hugolino, he had the authority to correct both "the head and the members" (XII:3). To fulfill his role as chaplain, officiating in some circumstances inside the monastery (confession, communion, the last sacraments to the sick), he had to remain in a public place where he could be seen. His companions should also remain visible at all times (XII:4-7). Lay brothers were attached to the monastery as mendicant friars.[33]

The Clergy

Clergy were, particularly, the ministers of the Church who had authority over the monastery at Clare's express wish: mainly the cardinal protector, who had the same function for the Friars Minor (XII:12). He was to authorize re-

---

[32] We know that, following Francis's example, the friars tended to give up the responsibility of care for the second order very quickly. Legally speaking, the links were fairly loose, even though membership in the same Franciscan family remained very important. In 1250 at the chapter of Genoa, Cardinal Raynaldo relieved the friars of their care for the Clarisses. The Council of Trent would place almost all monasteries under the jurisdiction of the local bishop. Sometimes the monastery would therefore have two hierarchical superiors: the local ordinary and the Franciscan Provincial Minister, when the monastery also wanted to have the jurisdiction of the first order. As regards Francis's attitude to San Damiano, note the friars' insistence on inviting him to visit the sisters, cf. T. De Celano, *Vita secunda*, 205-07; *FA:ED* 2, 379-80.

[33] Omaechevarria, 238 and 297.

ception of a young woman to the monastery (II:2) and the entry of strangers into the monastery enclosure (XI:7). Other clergy, including the bishop, might enter the enclosure in exceptional cases (blessing of an abbess, celebrating mass) and always accompanied by "as few and as virtuous companions and assistants as possible" (XI:9).

The Laity

Relationships with lay people were nurtured during visits in the parlor or at the grille, where two sisters listened to what was said (V:6). Sisters who served outside the monastery, and therefore came into contact with lay people, were not to carry back any "gossip of the world" (IX:15), nor conversely take news of the monastery to the outside world. These sisters, at the boundary between the two worlds, acted as bridges. They went out to beg for subsistence and, at the same time, acted as filters to prevent anything entering the monastery that might be perceived as "entertainment" (in the Pascalian sense of the word) or leaving the monastery that might reveal any internal tensions to the public forum. The part they played was, therefore, especially delicate. It should be noted that these sisters seemed to belong fully to the community of the nuns. There was no differentiation into two categories.

Lay people might legally enter the enclosure in order to carry out specific tasks. They were to be supervised by sisters posted to observe them and restrict their movements; no nun was to be seen by these workers (XI:10-12). The same applied to those visiting sick sisters (VIII:20): doctors, no doubt, and perhaps family members of seriously ill sisters. .

Nuanced permission was given to sisters to beg outside the monastery. These provisions of Clare's rule aligned with those of other rules given to the Damianites. Clare appears to have been a bit more flexible, perhaps, more attentive to specific situations, tried and tested as she was through forty years of religious life. But her general conception of enclosure, the need for withdrawal, was as strict as that of Hugolino, Innocent IV, and Urban IV. Although, as has recently been affirmed, these provisions were imposed on her by the Curia, it is nonetheless true that she endorsed them by incorporating them into her rule. On other issues she appears resolutely original: such as the practice of complete poverty, sisterly love, the concept of the abbess's responsibility (which she changed considerably even while retaining official terminology).

The rule of Saint Clare is short, only twelve fairly brief chapters, but it clearly expresses the main lines of her vocation. However, even during her lifetime, it stood as an hiatus between her reputation and the diffusion of her form of life. She was very much loved, and she founded a number of convents of Clarisses, but few of them lived fully what she proposed. Eventually, the papacy gave preference to the Urbanist rule.

CHAPTER 4

THE CONSTITUTIONS OF SAINT COLETTE

Saint Colette's *Constitutions* were approved and promulgated by William of Casals, General Minister of the Order, under the authority of Pope Eugene IV, on September 28, 1434 and confirmed in 1458 by Pope Pius II. The confirmation was accompanied by an introductory letter from the General Minister:[1]

> We, touched by your humble prayers and theirs, by the authority of our position and the apostolic power endowed on us for this purpose, send to each and every abbess and sister in the monasteries founded by the merits you have before God under the above-mentioned rule and to those that will be founded in the same way and under the same rule, the declarations and statutes set out herein, which have been made with mature deliberation to be observed in perpetuity. You must keep them with all the more zeal and respect as they have been studied with care and approved by our Reverend Fathers in Jesus Christ, the cardinals of Sainte-Croix and Saint-Ange, legates of the Apostolic See presiding at the present time over

---

[1] The *Rule* of Saint Clare is presented in the same way, embedded in the letter of Cardinal Raynaldo, bishop of Ostia and protector of the order of Friars Minor and of the Clarisses. It was confirmed by Pope Innocent IV on August 9, 1253. *Livre de Bruges,* 105 and 185 (pages referred to will be shown in parentheses in the text).

the holy Council, by several doctors of theology, and by venerable Fathers distinguished as much by their knowledge as by their virtue ...

It concludes:

> In order for each and every one of these declarations to have the greater force and more authority with you and be received with greater devotion and humility, we have had them supplied with and confirmed by the common formalities, such as signature, study, approval, and imposition of the seal of our office.
>
> Given in Geneva, in the province of Burgundy, in the year [of the Incarnation] of Our Lord, one thousand four hundred and thirty four, on the twenty-eighth day of September, the third year of the pontificate of the most Holy Father in Christ, the Lord Pope Eugene IV, and the third year from the opening of the Holy Council of Basel, which is happily continuing and which has met for the reformation of all the states and to achieve peace among the faithful (189).

STRUCTURE

The final text has fifteen chapters, while the *Sentiments*, a simple commentary on the *Rule*, has twelve. The new chapters develop certain points from Clare's basic text[2] and therefore indicate some of Colette's concerns. Clare's first chapter does not appear here: it gave the name of the order (the poor sisters), recalled that it was a matter of "observing the holy gospel ... living in obedience without appropriating anything to oneself, and in chastity." Above all it emphasized the link to Francis and filial obedience to the pope and the Church.

---

[2] The original text of the *Rule* of Saint Clare is not divided into chapters. The titles were added afterwards according to content: they have, however, become traditional in the order; cf. *Clare of Assisi, Writings*, 21 and note 33.

Colette doubtlessly took for granted that all accepted this. Thus her Chapter 1 covers entry into religious life, which corresponds to Chapter III of the *Rule*. The following summary table of the chapters is offered for clarity:

Rule of St. Clare	Constitutions of St. Colette
I) the form of life	
II) reception of sisters	1) entry into religious life and rite of profession
	2) quality of habits
III) divine office	3) divine office
fasting	4) abstinence
Confession	5) Confession, Communion, the confessor and his companion
Holy Communion	
	6) enclosure
IV) election of the abbess	7) election of the abbess, officers and discreets
	8) how to hold a chapter
V) silence and the way of speaking in the parlor and at the grille	9) silence and the way of speaking at the grille and in the parlor
VI) the sisters may not receive any possession or property	10) poverty, dispossession of all things and that the sisters may not receive any possession
VII) the way of working	11) occupations of the sisters
VIII) the prohibition on possessions and care of the sick	12) sick sisters
IX) penances to be imposed on the sisters	13) correction
X) admonition and correction of the sisters	
XI) the door-keeper	14) the door-keeper
XII) the visitation	15) the visitator

In chapter 2, Colette adds a directive on "quality of clothing," which Clare includes in her chapter II. Similarly, chapters 3, 4, and 5 cover the material of chapter III of the *Rule*: the office, fasting, abstinence, Confession and Communion. Colette adds the issue of the confessor and his companions: Clare covers the issue of the chaplain in one line of Chapter III and returns to it briefly in the last chapter.

Chapter 6, entitled: "enclosure," develops the subject of chapter XI, but seems badly placed, continuing, as it does, the subject introduced at the end of chapter 5 with the confessor. Clare went another direction – she stayed within the area of the internal life of the community by covering, in chapter IV, the election of the abbess and other office-holders. After chapter 6 on enclosure, Colette takes up the commentary on the *Rule* again, returning to the internal life (election of the abbess, chapter 7). But she uses chapter 8 to describe how to hold the chapter, a subject included in chapter IV of the *Rule*.

Clare devotes chapter VII to work, while Colette covers this in chapter 11, calling it: "the sisters' occupations." Clare mentions sick sisters in chapters IV and VIII in relation to the office of abbess (along with almsgiving). Colette gives chapter 12 exclusively to the sick sisters.

Chapters VI and VII in Clare are linked: poverty imposes the need to work, and almsgiving (covered in chapter VIII) is also a result of poverty, as mentioned in verse one. Almsgiving also results when work is inadequate. It appears that Colette did not really grasp this relationship or did not want to highlight it, since between chapters 10 and 12, she inserts chapter 11 on poverty and almsgiving. She mentions sick sisters here since they will be cared for and served according to available resources.[3]

Chapters IX and X cover relationships between the sisters and possible tensions (along with the issue of "extern" sisters that might create tensions). Colette calls chapter 13 "Correction." Chapters XI and XII, together with XIV and XV, cover matters relating to enclosure and relations with the outside world.

---

[3] "... providing charitably and mercifully, from the available goods" (Rg Cl. VIII, 13); *CA:ED*, 120.

In brief, it seems that Colette concentrated on issues of governance, enclosure and its various implications, and internal operations or behavior. Of the fifteen chapters:
- eight are devoted either to governance, to internal operations or to behavior (chapters 1, 2, 3, 4, 7, 8, 12 and 13).
- five are devoted to issues relating to enclosure (chapters 5, 6, 9, 14 and 15).
- two address poverty and sick sisters (chapters 10 and 11).

Chapters 6 and 9 ("enclosure" and "silence and the way of speaking at the grille and in the parlor") frame chapters 7 and 8 ("election of the abbess" and "how to hold a chapter"). These four chapters are in fact the heart of the *Constitutions*. In Clare's rule, on the other hand, the central chapters (6 to 10) are, as we have seen, the most personal, developing the dual theme of poverty and mutual love. Poverty is certainly present in Colette, but it is no longer central; and sisterly love seems to give way to "correction of the sisters" (chapter 13). This topic is also treated in the lengthy chapter 15 ("the visitator"). Clare, although she deals with the canonical visitation in chapter XII, ends her rule as she began it, with an assertion of faithfulness to the Church and a reminder of the vocation: that "we may observe in perpetuity the poverty and humility of Our Lord Jesus Christ and His most holy Mother and the holy gospel we have firmly promised" (XII:13).

These few observations allow us to situate the detailed analysis of the chapters within a proper perspective. Colette is not just commenting on Clare's rule. She imprints on it her own concerns after thirty years' experience as reformer and founder of monasteries.

ANALYSIS

The analysis proposes to emphasize in particular the similarities and differences between the *Constitutions* and the *Rule* and evaluate their significance. Allowing for the structure of the *Constitutions*, two main strands can be identified: operations and relations with the outside world.

Internal Operations of the Community

The Abbess's Role in Daily Life

This role was established in chapter 1 ("for reception of the sisters"). While Clare (II:2) points out the need for authorization from the cardinal protector, Colette states that, given the distance from Rome, the provincial ministers or their representatives

> could give and grant to abbesses permission to receive as religious sisters women who want to flee and abandon the world (chapter 1).[4]

This understandable measure did not include, however, "the agreement of the sisters," which Clare desires (II:1). We note in passing that, for Clare, the postulancy is a dynamic, positive process ("if, by divine inspiration, anyone comes to us desiring to accept this life"). With Colette, it is more a matter of *contemptus mundi*, so beloved in the Middle Ages and which Pierre de Vaux evokes in his biography of Colette.

Later, Colette slightly moderated her scorn for the world as being the primary motivation for the religious life, underlining the need for the "love of God," the desire for the soul's salvation, and the sign of the Holy Spirit.[5] On the other hand, "the abbess and her sisters" would receive no gift from the postulant.

The abbess receives a sister for profession: Clare gives no details about this. Colette, however, revives the vassalage ritual, borrowed perhaps from the Benedictines and Urbanist Poor Clares:

---

[4] *Livre de Bruges*, 115.
[5] *Livre de Bruges*, 115.

So the abbess who receives her will promise her eternal life, if she observes what she has promised.

Advised by her discreets, the abbess may provide clothing in addition to that specified. But, in order to have the clothing of a sick person or to have two black veils and several white ones, the abbess's permission or "good pleasure" must be sought (123-24). Needing to ask permission of the abbess alters relations among the sisters. Colette states:

> And we do not wish that a sister should be permitted, without the good pleasure and express permission of the abbess ... to give other sisters who may be in need or an outside person that which her parents may have given or sent to her ... (162).

Exemption or absence from the divine office, from community service, or from attending to the sick needed permission from the abbess or her vicar (126).

Exemption from fasting was at the discretion of the abbess (130). Colette insisted on the need for

> the true charity of Jesus Christ rather than love of the flesh, since such dispensations (granted without discretion) often give rise to much laxity (130-31).

These proposals were nuanced by Colette's emphasis that "a lack of sufficient shared discussion" may result in abandonment of the way of life begun (131).

Permission was given for confession twice a month and delayed communion. Confession to a different confessor would be at "the good pleasure and with the permission of the abbess and the consent of most of the discreets, for a just and reasonable motive" (133).

The title of chapter 7: "Election of the abbess, the officers and the discreets" omits the term "the office of abbess," and throughout this long chapter, the only subject covered is that of the procedures for the minutely regulated ballot.

The presence of the minister general or the provincial was desirable, although given the costs involved, the confessor or the visitator might be sufficient. The elected abbess had to be confirmed by the provincial or by a representative of the first order.

Reasons for election of a new abbess were: death, serious illness, dismissal for "well-founded and reasonable cause," a request by all the sisters. The conditions for eligibility were: thirty years of age, professed, and having "proved her ability in this regard" (144).

Colette then described at length the ceremony led by the vicar. The vote was oral, counted by the vicar; it seems there was a certain amount of secrecy about the balloting: "each sister spoke the name proposed separately" (145). If no name stood out, (although no absolute majority was required, but only "a greater number of votes"), the sisters might leave it to one or two of their number, "the most discreet and God-fearing," to appoint the abbess.

Colette envisioned (146-47) two other possibilities. In one, a secretary and two sisters to act as witnesses, might collect and write down the names. In another, the sisters might discuss, before the election, some name to be chosen among themselves and "listen to each other's good advice about the election." The atmosphere must be peaceful, "without division or trouble" (148). The eight counselors and the officers were to be elected in the same way and had the same role as they did in Clare's community. They served as an organ of counsel.

For the convent chapter (chap. 8), the ceremony was also tightly regulated. Living and dead benefactors were particularly remembered. This was followed by a series of invocations and prayers in Latin.[6] Faults were acknowledged by a gesture: "Both knees and both arms on the ground, with

---

[6] Clément Schmitt, *Un pape réformateur et un défenseur de l'unité de l'Eglise: Benoît XII et l'Ordre des frères mineurs, 1334-1342* (Quaracchi, 1959). This writer notes that the constitutions always required (for the intention of benefactors) "masses, *Paters*, psalms and other prayers at the chapter of faults" (33).

hands joined" (152). The abbess imposed a penance for each fault admitted, "as seems best to her" (153). Apart from admitting faults, no sister might speak "without the permission of the abbess." The sisters would then speak of "matters to be considered ... with the necessary gravity and honesty ... with calm reflection, abstaining completely from superfluous, injurious or impertinent speech" (154).

Clare covered the judicial aspects of these points only briefly (chapter IV). Colette retains from Clare only that the said sister must be professed and that she may be dismissed if she becomes "unable to work in the service of the sisters." About the ceremony, on which Colette placed so much importance, Clare gave no details at all.

As regards correction of the guilty and relationships among the sisters, the beginning of chapter 13 repeats some words from Clare's chapter X. However, it completely changes the meaning. The guarantee of freedom and respect made by Clare becomes:

> We order that, in each convent, the abbess or her vicar in her absence, exhort and correct the sisters in all humility and charity, for fear that by neglecting to warn and correct them, the sisters may fall into laxity and transgressions of the *Rule* (170).

The very concept of relationships was changed. Clare assumed that the sisters had taken to heart the form of life, and deep down their obedience was simply the expression of their own choice to live in relationship with their abbess. In Colette, the reverse was true. Sisters transgressed the rule and tended towards laxity if the abbess did not intervene. In her admirable chapter X, Clare set out a theological concept of the life and emphasized that the abbess was the servant of her sisters. Colette's perspective was radically different. While granting charity and humility, she immediately added:

But let them (the abbesses) ensure that, under the appearance of humility and kindness, they do not give those who are at fault an opportunity for neglect and laxity, and that, under the pretext of charity and wishing to spare the body, they are not being cruel to souls (171).

For a more serious fault or a "grave sin," a discipline room, "severe but suitable," was provided, "in which the guilty party will be held on bread and water for a period of time to be determined by the abbess and the discreets, as may be required by the fault" (171). It was no longer a matter of speaking with "familiarity" to her abbess, as a lady to her servant. It was stipulated that, if a sister rose up against the abbess or her vicar, or used "inappropriate, injurious, or outrageous words to them in front of all the sisters, she will eat bread and water on the floor for one meal."

Colette did not mention possible tensions between the sisters, requests for pardon, or peace of heart to be kept in the event of trouble or scandal. There is also a significant absence of scriptural references. The procedure for correction is similar to that described in the Rule of Saint Benedict,[7] and the Colettine abbess's attitude was closer to that of the abbot than to that of Clare.[8] Colette, therefore, seems to have introduced a new factor, typical of a reform during a troubled period.

Organization of the Interior Life

We have noted that obstacles to entering religious life arose from the *contemptus mundi*. In the early rule, they arose from the married state (if the spouse did not undertake

---

[7] Rg Ben. XXVIII: "If the brother who has often had to be rebuked for the same fault and even excommunicated, still has no compunction, a more bitter remedy must be applied to him, that is corporal punishment."

[8] Rg Ben. II: "Those who are evilly-disposed, as also shameless, insolent and disobedient characters, he [the abbot] should check them at their first offence by corporal punishment ..."

to live in continence), from advanced age, from physical or mental infirmity "which prevents the observance of this life" (II:5). This does not differ from Hugolino in any way. Colette is more precise. She includes contemporary concerns:

> Let her not be suspected of any error; let her be free of debt; let her not be under any sentence of excommunication or interdict…. Her state of life must also be free.

The habit would not be given before the age of twelve, nor would profession take place before eighteen. From the age of thirteen and before being admitted, her "life, conduct and honesty" must be fully known and examined. When the postulant appeared satisfactory on these points, then

> according to the command of our Holy Father Pope Innocent IV, let her be told of the hard and painful things through which one might reach God and that might be necessary to keep her in this religious life,[9] so that, after entering, there may be no excuse from ignorance (113).

The explicit reference to Innocent IV and not Clare is significant. Passionate attention is given again to poverty: the girl entering must accept complete poverty, the sisters "must give her to the Crucified One, entirely stripped of earthly goods," and a variant, not used by the Roman Chancellery, adds: "to our Savior Jesus Christ, stripped of everything for us on the tree of the Cross" (115).

A new element was introduced: the upper age limit for admission is forty years,

> unless she is very distinguished, so her admission may be a source of great edification for the people and the clergy, or that she is strong and fit enough to be

---

[9] This term indicates the reformed order or congregation.

able to serve God and the order according to this form of life (117).

As shown in the *Letters*, Colette had a very pragmatic understanding of how to expand the order. With solid good sense, she used the recruitment methods of the time, not losing sight of the interests of the community. If a great lady should enter, she still had to be able to serve and work. The issue of formation was scarcely mentioned, but was developed in the *Sentiments*. Here appears the possibility of learning the divine office, although before the age of twenty-five. Clare and Colette are in agreement; they are not concerned about the sisters' studies. The rule of Hugolino and that of Innocent IV suggest that it is possible to teach "the letters." Colette, who often followed both these rules, does not include this point.[10]

Clare covered the subject of habits in two verses (II:15-16). Colette followed the other rules, which dealt with this either in a separate chapter (Hugolino) or in a longer chapter. She distinguished between "the habit of the order and the undergarments." She specified the quality, length, and width of the habit and its sleeves, the shape of the mantle ("neither upright nor smoothed around the neck," 123), the way in which the headgear should hide the face.[11] She repeated the rule of Innocent IV to which the Longchamp rule added: *non enim decet sponsam Regis aeterni alteri se exponere, nec etiam in aliquo alio delectari* (II) ["indeed it is not fitting for the betrothed of the eternal King to display herself to others,

---

[10] Rule of Innocent IV, *Escritos de Santa Clara*, P. Omaechevarria, 240: *Quod si iuvenculae aliquae, vel etiam grandiores, capacis ingenii fuerint, si abbatissae visum fuerit, faciat eas litteras edoceri* ... Hugolino, ibid., 218: *Quod si iuvenculae aliquae, vel etiam grandiores, capaces ingentii et humiles fuerint, si abbatissae visum fuerit, faciat eas litteris edoceri....* [Because if any very young woman, or even those older, should be receptive, (submissive) and talented, if the abbess were to see this let them be taught their letters.] Hugolino and, even more so, Innocent IV were themselves intellectuals concerned for the instruction of the clergy.

[11] "Let the whole head, breast, and shoulders be covered, and the forehead, cheeks and chin also, for the most part, so that the face is never entirely visible" (*Livre de Bruges*, 123).

nor yet to be pleasing in any other way"]. The "veils and all head-coverings shall be of common, rough, heavy material, so that the holy poverty and austerity of their profession will shine forth" (124).

As for Clare, she ended with a sentence that reveals the source of her very brief recommendations:

> Out of love for the most holy and beloved Child wrapped in poor little swaddling clothes and place in a manger and of His most holy Mother, I admonish, beg, and encourage my sisters always to wear poor garments (II:24).

Her spiritual attitude was that all the sisters were responsible for poverty as a consequence of their imitation of Christ. Colette took a different view, with minute detail indicating rather a certain dogmatism rather than a supernatural, creative freedom.

Clare wished that the postulant's goods, as the gospel says, be given to the poor, perhaps with the advice of reliable friends of the monastery or else "as the Lord would inspire her" (I:9). Colette, doubtlessly, had the same perspective, although with some subtle and interesting differences. Constitutionally-speaking, she was more flexible than Clare on this matter. The fifteenth-century postulant may give her goods to the monastery "in small quantities, so that no one might look unfavorably on them as a result; except sometimes, if the donor (through sheer generosity) without being required to do so, should wish to give them something as she would to any other poor person, to relieve them and help support them in a time of great necessity" (114). In passing, we note once more the importance attached to the opinion of those outside the monastery and to the effect its image had on them.

Poverty, as we have seen, is the subject of Chapter 10, which Clare covered in her chapters VI and VIII. It returns as a fairly frequent leitmotiv, always in reference to the poverty of Christ and of his imitator, Francis. Colette certainly spoke of it from the outset and, in the chapter on habits (but at a technical level), related it to practical matters of organization. Starting with verse twelve of chapter VI, she recalled the absolute ban on ownership of goods, as promised "to the Lord God and blessed Francis," then made this explicit in a long list of goods that must not be owned. The tone was completely different from that of Clare, who begged and exhorted for the love of Jesus Christ (VIII:4). Colette wrote:

> We forbid them (the sisters), by virtue of obedience, ever to receive or own (158).

The forbidden goods included stores of more than a year's supply of food and drink (wheat and wine), flocks, plate, furnishings, and precious stones (159). A parallel was drawn with the first order as regards "legacies to the sisters from the last wishes of the dying" (160). The provisions made by Popes Nicholas III and Clement V applied to the Colettines: each sister and the community were to make an "act of expropriation and abdication of ownership of everything in the sight of God" (160).

Colette also seems to have been inspired by the decrees of Benedict XII[12] regulating the life of the friars. An issue specific to the mendicants is revealed here. One of the reasons behind the quarrel between religious brothers and sisters and the secular clergy was the flow of legacies by which families of the deceased were ensured of prayers or masses in perpetuity for the salvation of their relatives. This practice had not yet existed in the time of Clare.

On the other hand, it was specified that, "with a sure conscience" (160), the sisters could use anything not forbidden by the rule: those things required for the office or the mass, "for dwelling and subsistence of the human body, to fulfill duties and deal with necessary business, according to the form of life and the holy religion ..." as long as these objects were not "manifestly contrary to their state of poverty and of religion" (161).

---

[12] Cl. Schmitt, 33.

Colette introduced a new distinction between possession and use of goods. With the option of receiving alms from fortunate postulants, she allowed greater flexibility as regards poverty. While preserving the essentials desired by Clare, she seems to demonstrate a realistic approach and a certain capacity for management unknown to the Damianite.

We might note (and the history of the first friars confirms this[13]) that, in Clare's time, mendicancy could be a problem since it was not customary. For the Damianites, it must have been a sign of their "disconnection" from socio-economic life (VIII:1-3).

There is no sign of this in Colette. Mendicancy had been institutionalized. In addition, the issue of legacies showed that it was not always essential. The fifteenth-century monastery was an integral part of socio-economic life. The *Letters* fully demonstrate this. The psychological aspects of choosing poverty had changed. Clare could write in complete truth at the beginning of chapter VI:

We had no fear of poverty, hard work, trial, shame or contempt of the world.

Clare and her companions were uncompromising in their radical choice.[14] Colette received the daughters of great families. For her, the danger came from the difficulty of containing the flow of donations and of maintaining the rigor of the life as had been decided from the outset.

Clare herself foresaw the danger. Her insistence in the rule, repeated in her *Testament,* is evidence enough of her anxiety over the difficulties of maintaining poverty in its pure form. Francis's own *Testament*, around 1225-1226, was already looking back nostalgically to the origins when "we

---

[13] Also when Francis sent out his first friars to beg: T. De Celano, *Vita prima*, 42, *Vita secunda*, 44 and 47; he himself was received badly at the start, *Vita secunda*, chapters 7 and 9: *FA:ED* 1, 220, *FA:ED* 2, 276, 279, 251, 253.

[14] For example, T. De Celano mentions the violent opposition of her family to the entrance of her sister Agnes, *Vita*, chap. 15; *CA:ED,* 302-04.

were little and poor."[15] In the early rule, work had to meet the dual criteria of "honesty and mutual usefulness."

The relations between abbess and sisters, for Colette, were governed by the relationship between order and obedience. The sister "must submit her will to the one who has given the order, as befits those who are vowed to holy obedience," with this proviso: the abbess must guard against "giving an order to a sister who cannot carry it out" (168). All work must be decided, first of all, by the abbess: "in fact no work will be done without her good pleasure and her wishes, and any sister who acts otherwise will be punished" (169).

Strangely, Colette did not use the expression that "holy prayer" was to be preserved during work. She forbad "joking, clowning, and vain and worldly games," but permitted talk of "our Lord, the lives of the saints, living or dead," which seems to contradict the rule of silence mentioned in chapter 9. Here Colette seems to hesitate between the provisions imposed by Clare, which she gives only in part,[16] and those of Gregory IX, which "commanded in the first rule that the sisters should keep a perpetual silence ..." (155).

In chapter 12 (incidentally one of the longest), the tone is quite different. As we have seen in Clare, care for the sick was a sign of mutual love. It is certainly present in Colette, but practical organization takes precedence over the rest. Charity was regulated, with explicit and telling reference to Innocent IV on this matter.

"Seriously ill" sisters were provided with what they needed and were served by sisters appointed for this purpose. These were expected to be charitable and humble. The sick were visited once a day by the abbess, when she was not "legitimately occupied." Sufferers from contagious diseases and those "of long duration such as leprosy or dementia ...," who

---

[15] *Testament* of Saint Francis: "And those who came to receive the life gave all they might have to the poor and were satisfied with a single tunic, patched inside and out, with a belt and breeches. And we did not want to have more." *Writings*, 207 (§16-17); *FA:ED* 1, 125.

[16] Colette does not mention the option of "speaking always and everywhere in a low voice, using few words" (Rg Cl., V); *CA:ED,* 116.

cannot "without danger remain with the other sisters, will be placed outside the community; they must be given a small room within the enclosure, and there served and cared for" (164). Colette exhorted the sisters, "present and future, to serve them for God in all humility and devotion, in whatever way is needed."

According to Clare, all must be concerned with a sick sister. She affirmed in fine terms the superiority of spiritual love in such circumstances (VIII:16). For Colette, it was no longer simply that a sister must make her needs known to another sister. It was not enough for a sister to note the need of another sister for woolen slippers or a mattress for example. Now, a council meeting was required. Colette threatened punishment for any negligent abbess (165).

A feather bed was allowed, for practical reasons, *in articulo mortis* (for one who was "seriously and gravely ill"), and again a meeting was needed between the abbess and her discreets, who would consult "their good and strict conscience" (165).

Prayer Life and Divine Office

Prayer and the divine office were subject to regulations: "Night and day they must be fulfilled for the glory of the Lord" (124).[17] As they came into choir the sisters were to "conduct themselves humbly and observe peace and silence, without talking, murmuring, laughing, or looking about" (125). No one left the choir before the end of the office without permission. From start to finish, it was said "devoutly, entirely, precisely, and religiously." No one was exempt from office or from mass, except for serious illness or permitted work.

In addition to the divine office, the sisters also recited the office of the Virgin Mary and of the dead. The office of Saint Clare was said from her feast day to the feast of the Assump-

---

[17] Colette borrowed the term from Innocent IV and the Longchamp rule: P. Omaechevarria, 302: *tam in die quam in nocte, ad lautem Dei et gloriam celebrandum* [both day and night, celebrating to the praise and glory of God].

tion. After that, her "commemoration was included with the *Benedictus* and the *Magnificat*." At the end of the divine office "... when the sisters have said their *Pater Noster*, they [will say] in honor of the most glorious Virgin Mary, the *Salve Regina* together with certain accustomed prayers" (128).

> If there is a general interdict [allusion to the troubled state of the Church and of the times], all the sisters will conform to the mother Churches.... And then with the doors closed and the interdicts excluded, they will say the office of Our Lady as is the custom on ordinary days, standing all the time and not sitting (128).

In the event of a death it was important to "take care to omit none of the rites and prayers of funerals or of the communion (for the dying)."

As regards positions of prayer, Colette added factors not present in Clare:[18]

> As for the way in which the bell is rung for the mass and for the hours and as for the ceremonies to be observed in the holy service of God, how to stand and sit, kneel and bow, turn and face the altar, the sisters will follow the same instructions as in general use with the friars minor, except where it is not appropriate for them to do so (126).

Colette seems to be confirming a longstanding common practice here.[19] A place reserved for the office was also "appointed for sisters who are not choir sisters." It seems that these went to the church at the same time as the choir sisters in order "to fulfill their obligation for divine office" (127).

---

[18] The Damianite simply specified the number of *Paters* to be said by illiterate sisters and for the deceased. Sisters who could read said the office of the dead for the deceased. Fifty *Pater Nosters* had to be said for a deceased sister.

[19] Cf. comment by Cl. Schmitt, 9 and 10.

The importance given to the office gradually emerged within the first and second orders as they aligned themselves with other monastic orders. The divine office was supplemented by other offices or prayers. We know from the *Vita* of Pierre de Vaux[20] that Colette had her personal devotions and that she liked to recite the Psalter, but she was wise enough not to impose this in the *Constitutions*. Such offices were considerably expanded in the fifteenth century by the addition of little offices. Not until Vatican II did the divine office proper recover its privileged, unique position.

Virtually no time was allowed for individual *lectio divina* or silent prayer. It is significant that Colette did not mention it at all. During the following century, Francisco de Osuna and Teresa of Avila would rediscover such prayer. But Colette seemed to know nothing of the Rhenish mystical movement,[21] though it was contemporary with her reform and gave pride of place to dialogue with God in the silence of the heart. In this sense, Colette came at the end of an era. No new ideas were germinating in the biography of Pierre de Vaux, who effectively captured Colette's lived reality. Clare, herself, did not mention prayer in her rule, though the *Vita* of Celano and the *Process* bear witness to her intense prayer life; and her *Letters* demonstrate an authentically mystical contemplative experience. None of Colette's writings demonstrate this, and it seems she knew nothing of Angela of Foligno and the Franciscan school. This does not mean, of course, that Colette had no personal experience of prayer in the sixteenth-century sense. When Pierre de Vaux describes Colette's "prayer," however, he speaks mainly of vocal prayer, as we have seen.

---

[20] P. De Vaux, *Vita*, chapter ten on prayer.

[21] For example, T. De Celano, *Vita*: "She opened her heart wide to the torrents of divine grace," chap. 13, *CA:ED*, 298; cf. too, chap. 17, 19, 20, *CA:ED*, 304-07; *Documents*: "Fourth Letter to Agnes of Prague," 111-19, *CA:ED*, 54-58.

Enclosure and Relations with the Outside World

Enclosure of Nuns

In chapter 6, Colette repeats explicitly the words of Innocent IV about enclosure and not what Clare had to say.[22]: "Those who profess this rule must live enclosed for the whole of their lives" (137). To Colette, Clare's criteria seemed too vague, no doubt, and following Innocent's rule, she gave legitimate reasons for leaving the enclosure. For the sake of foundation, reform, government or correction of other monasteries, or "to avoid some serious problem" (137), one might leave the cloister, but the permission of the minister general or the minister provincial was required. She then added that these absences must be carried out "in haste ... in safe and trustworthy company." The sisters' behavior is described in minute detail. It must be

> edifying ... avoiding any indiscreet word and any vain or too free gaze on anyone: (the sisters) will always be modest, humble and reserved in their language, as they should be ... (138).

The fourth vow of enclosure, not used by Clare, was included in the rite of profession. Colette would have been able to use the formula from the Urbanist Clarisses or the rule of blessed Isabelle of France,[23] known as the "rule of enclosed little sisters." As in the rule of Innocent IV, immediately after the evangelical counsels of obedience, chastity, and poverty, it is stated that the sisters will remain enclosed for their entire lives. Urban IV gave a more concise and specific formula: "... living in obedience, with no possessions and in chastity, enclosed."[24]

---

[22] "... that she may not go outside the monastery without a useful, reasonable, evident and approved purpose" (Rg Cl. II, 12): *CA:ED*, 111.

[23] P. Omaechevarria, 256.

[24] P. Omaechevarria, 330.

The expression, "the sisters who serve outside the monastery," was deleted. A category of sisters had quickly been developed in connection with the Urbanist Clarisses: the sister penitents. Colette seemed to think that at the time of Clare, the rite of the vows included the fourth vow of enclosure. In fact, it may be assumed that with the papal enclosure established by Boniface VIII, the formula contained in the Longchamp rule, which includes it, spread quickly. Colette wrote:

> Nonetheless, because of many dangers and problems that it may cause to the said sisters and to the convents, our holy Father Pope Benedict XII established and ordered that from now on, no professed sister may leave the enclosure, except in certain situations stated in the form of life.

Clément Schmitt, quoted above, states that in fact, Benedict XII was repeating the rule of Boniface VIII, suppressing the sister penitents and replacing them with the "household" (58). Colette used the name "servants" (139) to indicate this category of people affiliated to the monastery but not bound by the vow of enclosure: "these women will wear the secular habit and will not in any way be admitted to the interior of the monastery."

Further controls were then imposed on letters sent or received. For Clare, the permission of the abbess required for correspondence (VIII:7) formed part of the self-emptying process, stripping bare in order to be "totally attached (to the greatest poverty) in the name of our Lord Jesus Christ and his most holy mother …" The context, once more, is entirely different in the *Constitutions*

> … to obviate and remedy most certainly the problems which may arise, we command that no sister … may … put or cause to be put in any way whatever, in the parlor, the turn, at the grille or the door or anywhere else, any letter of recommendation or missive, sealed or open, to be sent or carried out of the convent.

Passive Enclosure

Passive enclosure applied to people received into the parlor or monastery. They had to pass through the single door, where a sister appointed for the purpose was placed, or they had to enter the parlor. Colette did not hesitate to change the founder's rule, which specified that the porter "should stay during the day in an open, doorless cell." She gives her reason: "… because, although at the time of Saint Clare it was legitimate and appropriate, at the present time it could be harmful and very damaging for the sisters." The porter had to be "diligent and discreet, of mature character and a suitable age," as the rule stated. The porter was never alone: "a companion … assigned to her and a discreet, who may be changed every week …" (173). "All three will be together" and would answer when someone rang at the door, and only the main porter would reply to those wishing to speak. The other two would be present and would hear the conversation.

As for entry into the monastery, there was an existing, general interdict: "… we impose on abbesses and all other sisters a severe and rigorous instruction never to allow regular or secular individuals, whatever their position, to enter the monastery enclosure" (174). Permitted cases were regulated.[27]

The chaplain or confessor was the first with the right to enter the enclosure. As already noted, "household" servants of the monastery were excluded. Once more, Colette modifies the provisions of Clare's rule:

---

[27] Cf. the Longchamp rule, 309: … *ut nulla unquam abbatissa nullaeque eius sorores aliquam religiosam personam vel saecularem, cuiuscumque dignitatis existat, intra monasterium, sive claustrum, id est ad locum aliquem, ad quem sorores accedere possint, intrare permittant sine Sedis Apostolicae licentia speciali* [that no abbess and none of the sisters at any time should permit any religious or secular person, of whatever status they might be, to enter the monastery or the cloister, that is to any place, where they might have access to the sisters, without special license from the Apostolic See.]

... because of the many dangers and great problems, given these times, that might in future result for the sisters ... we order, under obedience, all abbesses, porters, and other sisters, now and in future, in all places and convents, never to permit or suffer any regular or secular priest to enter their enclosure to celebrate mass or to give communion or minister to healthy or sick sisters (133).

The only exception was mortal illness or leprosy (in these cases very precise) and, "for the seven times expressed in the form of life," the confessor might celebrate within the enclosure.[28] This subject is taken up again later: the confessor and his companion, as in the Longchamp rule, were clothed in "sacred vestments ...," that is alb and surplice;[29] and also "... we similarly order that, with regard to the differences between the present time and that when the rule was given, from now on, no mass will be celebrated inside the monastery, either for the living or for a funeral, except where it is unavoidable, as has been said above with respect to the sick" (178-179). Another legitimate case was burial of a sister: "once the interment is complete, let the confessor and all the others leave without delay."

If he so wished, a cardinal might be received "with great reverence and devotion," but not alone. He had to be accompanied by "two or three of the most honorable persons" (175). No sister might speak to him, not even in the infirmary, except in the specified situation, which seems to be just the abbess in the presence of two or three discreets. Colette recalled that the essential point, whoever might be authorized to enter, was "that there should be no possibility of giving rise to a just scandal."

---

[28] Christmas Day, Holy Thursday, Easter, Pentecost, the Assumption of the Most Holy Virgin, Saint Francis, and All Saints days.

[29] Cf. P. Omaechevarria, 312: ... *Confessor ipsarum, sacerdotalibus indumentis praeter casulam ingrédiatur indutus* [Their own confessor vested, with priests clothed besides, enters in], Longchamp rule, chapter VI.

Doctors, surgeons or barbers were to be "among the best and most devout catholic persons" (164) in order to be permitted to enter. They had to be accompanied by the abbess and two or three discreets. Twice (164 and 175), Colette recommends a "present need" or "urgent need" for the situation to be legitimate.

As regards workers, it was permitted to allow competent people to enter "in the event of fire, or if some building is ruined, or another danger or damage that may occur, or for some work that cannot be conveniently performed outside the monastery" (175). For delivery of important objects like wood, wine, stone, etc.,

> the porter and her companions must take great care that the door does not stay open longer than necessary; and also that the porters or carters who have brought these things do not penetrate to any part of the convent, except between the two doors mentioned above, or to other necessary places ..."

No sister, except the one appointed, might speak to them or appear in their presence. The porter might speak briefly only of the work to be done. If she had to go to the place of work, this would be with a "good and safe companion from among the discreet sisters," observing the rule of brevity of speech. No worker, or any other person besides, could eat inside (178).

Colette also forbad the blessing of abbesses. In the context, this was less from a sense of minority than from a desire not to have others enter the enclosure: "... let their holy profession suffice them ..." (178). The first order in fact seemed always vigilant in avoiding abbesses having themselves blessed.[30]

---

[30] P. Péano, "Les ministres provinciaux de la primitive province de Provence (121/-1517)," *A.F.H.*, LXXIX (1986), 57.

Relationships with the Order and the Church

Except in situations requiring courtesy, such as the visit of a cardinal, or "functional" situations involving the confessor, Colette foresaw other circumstances that might arise regarding relations with the order and the Church.

First of all, the confessor: "He must not be a simple cleric but a priest of good reputation and tried and tested discretion." Like Clare, Colette foresaw the need for mendicant friars who, with the rapid clericalisation of the order were here called "lay brothers," that is to say, penitents. The reformer picked up Clare's insistence on asking for this help and support from the first order:

> The abbess of each convent, her council and discreets must humbly and graciously ask the minister general and ministers provincial for four friars, and the said general for all the convents of the sisters or the ministers provincial for those in their provinces must mercifully grant the said request and petition for the love of God and blessed Francis, and bestow these four friars (135).

But Colette wanted these friars to come from reformed convents, that is mainly Colettines. One of the first convents to come under her influence was Dole, from 1427. Henry de Baume received jurisdiction over four Colettine convents in Burgundy: Dole, Chariez, Sellières, and Beuvray.[31] Later when John Capistrano came to France with full powers as visitator and delegate of the vicar general, Colette was careful to obtain written confirmation of the option of having friars in the service of monasteries:

> ... I ratify and confirm all the graces and privileges granted by our very reverend fathers general, to you

---

[31] U. D'Alençon, "Lettre de Pierre de Vaux aux habitants d'Amiens (1443)," *Etudes Franciscaines,* t. 23 (1910), 656, note 4.

and your confessor Pierre de Vaux,[32] as well as to confessors of convents you have founded and will found in future ...[33]

For the foundation of Amiens, she took care to prepare a convent of reformed brothers, who were able to help the Clarisses live according to the reform. Capistrano gave two brothers, including Pierre de Vaux, "letters of obedience" to try to establish the Colettine reform among the Abbeville conventuals, who would soon be providing religious service to the Colettine Clarisses in Amiens.[34]

For elections, as mentioned, Colette required the presence of a friar minor,[35] preferably the minister general or provincial, otherwise the visitator. "In his absence, the confessor" would suffice (143). The election had to be confirmed by the minister general or provincial or by their delegate. But above all, even more so than Clare, Colette described the role of the visitator and the procedure for a canonical visitation. Once more she was clearly inspired by, or even simply copying, the Longchamp rule and the provisions of Benedict XII.

The issue of the visitator was closely linked to the relationship of the sisters with the first order and, in view of cloister regulations, to their relationship with outsiders. Almost all the factors analyzed with regard to the various aspects of the enclosure reappear here.

Colette omitted reference to the cardinal protector, which she said, "in our time can no longer be observed" (180). Unlike Clare, who held onto this relationship with the Church, the reformer believed that reference to the order was enough, quoting pontifical decisions:

---

[32] As we can see, the *Letters* assume confirmation of this: Pierre de Vaux's role as collaborator after the death of Henry de Baume, cf. chap. 1 of this second part.

[33] P. Larceneux, *Vie de soeur Colette. Dédié à Madame Louise de France, 1785*, ch. 12 of volume 43 (Archives of Poligny).

[34] H. Lippens, "Saint Jean de Capistran en mission aux États Bourguignons, 1442-1443," *A.F.H.*, An. XXXV, 33.

[35] The Longchamp rule repeats these instructions from Clare giving more detail. Cf. Omaechevarria, 309-15.

... for certain legitimate reasons, the Lord Pope Innocent IV and several other sovereign pontiffs have fully and entirely handed over direction and government of their houses to the minister general and the minister provincials of the order."[36]

The visitator, then, must be a good religious, meaning reformed. He must be "faithful in observing the rule and love holy poverty and perfect honesty." The visitation may take place one or more times a year, "if necessary" (182). He may enter the enclosure only for the purposes of the visitation: "Let him stand with his companion in a common place, close enough so they can easily see each other; and, having fulfilled his duty, let him not delay in the enclosure but leave immediately" (182).[37] The estimated time required was two or three days.[38] During this time, the visitator might speak to individuals as long as two sisters stood "at a short distance, so that the good reputation of all remained intact" (185).

The procedure for the visitation strongly resembled an inquiry, the questions for which covered "the main and essential points of the rule" (186). Then came a list of thirteen points that applied mainly to the rigor of observance and to the vows. They included questions on poverty, on respect for enclosure and the vigilance of the officers, including the abbess, on the service of the sick, on the peace of the community, on the frequenting of the sacraments, and on the vitality of

---

[36] In the letter from John Capistrano mentioned in note 34, Colette also gives approval for the visitator, but this is where it is noted that P. de Vaux can name him, since he has jurisdiction over the sisters and friars in the convent being visited.

[37] P. Omaechevarria, "Longchamp Rule," 315: *Et quando monasterii claustra causa visitationis intraverit, duos religiosos socios et idoneos secum ducat; iidem vero socii, quamdiu fuerint intra claustrum, nullatenus ab invicem separentur ...* [And when he enters an enclosed monastery for a visitation, he brings two accompanying, suitable religious; these must truly accompany him as long as they are within the enclosure; by no means must they be separated from one another ...]

[38] Five days for a community of fifty sisters, according to the Longchamp rule, 317. Colette wanted from eighteen to twenty sisters, according to the *Intentions*.

the life of prayer. After reading the rule, each sister beat her breast before the assembled community and left. It was then that she could be accused of any faults. The Longchamp rule explained this practice and, intending to avoid any excesses, added some correctives: the abbess must not be accused in public without proof; the visitator listens to the accused who do not wish to recognize their faults; he may severely punish any who accuse without proof.[39]

Colette, as was her practice, regulated with minute details the various stages of what may be called an inquiry.

> ... the names of the accused and accusers will be written down, along with the faults of which they are accused, as long as they can be legally proved by two sisters of good testimony.... The names of the accusers must not be revealed, unless the accused does not wish to justify herself and prove her innocence (184).

She who accused wrongly would be punished with the same penance that the accused sister would have undergone. If the accused party "is not entirely innocent, she will be called before the chapter, where her significant faults will be legally proclaimed ... and a proper penance imposed on her." She might however try to excuse herself, wholly or partly. Thus each sister accused and called before the chapter "was punished as she deserved" in the presence of all. In chapter XXVI of his constitutions, Benedict XII also required inquiries for the Clarisses. The procedures were similar to those used for the friars minor.[40]

The abbess was to assist the work of the visitator by indicating herself the faults committed against observance or mutual charity. If she dissimulated, "this would be a serious sin and a fault worthy of severe punishment" (185).[41] After all these conditions, the conclusion of chapter 15 (which closes the *Constitutions*) recalls the need to correct and punish

---

[39] P. Omaechevarria, 316-17.
[40] Cl. Schmitt, 51 and 137.
[41] *Livre de Bruges,* 101-02.

"with discretion, through a zealous charity and love of justice, as the nature of the fault or the frequency of the lapses might require" (187).

The *Constitutions* of Saint Colette appear generally severe. William of Casals wrote to Colette: "I am afraid of imposing too heavy a burden on your sisters." Was this only because of the need to ensure that the reform worked, or was it because of Colette's own personality and her concept of the religious life? Her other writings will illuminate this question.

CHAPTER 5

Colette's Other Writings

While the *Constitutions* portray the official side of Saint Colette's legislative work, her other writings are less sophisticated or of a more circumstantial character. But they were widely distributed and much used by the Colettine community. They were largely responsible for shaping the mindset of the sisters and creating a family tradition.

The *Testament* completes the *Writings*, although, as we will see, it certainly does not belong to the first half of the fifteenth century.

The *Sentiments*: Key Ideas

The *Sentiments*, finished in Orbe in 1430, are valuable in that the text completes the *Constitutions*. The Pontifical Chancellery or the friars removed certain passages from the *Constitutions* because they were of a less legal style or related to issues considered less important. The *Sentiments*, therefore, reflecting Colette's thought more faithfully and in a less juridic manner, reveal a more personal expression.

Colette's particular concerns stand out within these commentaries. Issues relating to enclosure and poverty are more developed. Discussions around relations with the Church and the order demonstrate contemporary conflicts that the official document does not recognize. The portrayal of the abbess and the formation of the young, hardly touched in the *Constitutions,* appear to be new additions; and relations between the sisters and the abbess are discussed at length, showing how vital this subject was to the reformer.

Some aspects of her spirituality emerge more clearly. There is explicit reference to the *Rule*, while in the *Constitutions* this issue is touched on very lightly. It can be seen, however, that the founder's text underpins the *Constitutions*. The *Sentiments* actually comment on the *Rule* without modifying either the title or the sequence of the chapters. The *Constitutions*, which marked a further stage in the development of Colette's thought, were ultimately approved by the Franciscan order and the Holy See. This approval was perhaps a definitive confirmation of tendencies already present in the *Sentiments*.

Colette insisted on poverty in the buildings and in the construction methods used. She modified the ban on storing goods at the monastery (226): they might be received and kept for "some time through charity." Her dominant concern, however, was for extreme poverty, including liturgical ornamentation: Christ does not like to be richer than his servants (229).

Regarding enclosure, she took a stricter attitude. For instance, in chapter five, the black curtain in the parlor must not be removed, as Clare recommends, because, according to Colette, "it is necessary to submit to the circumstances of the present time, and impose this restriction."

Tensions inside the order and problems of reform in the Church become evident (211-12): Colette was careful to point out cases of "religious disobedience" towards prelates, meaning, in general, anything that conflicts with the law of God. The sisters must allow the fathers to lead them "for as long as they are under obedience to our holy mother the Church and to the father general of their order." The fathers must also be virtuous. There is a sharp echo here of the problems between conventuals and reformed friars and the governance of the nuns by one or other movement of the order. Colette sides with the reform, but under obedience to the conventual general of the time. This factor will be considered later when we examine the relations between Colette and John Capistrano, the vicar of the observants.

Community Life

Charity is to be exercised towards the sick, but this is always expressed in legal terms (233). It is "a commandment." Note that a sick sister may open her heart only to the abbess. Caring for a sick sister is a "duty imposed" on the sister appointed.

Colette repeats several times the obligation to obey the abbess (239): "This is a strict commandment ... a binding obligation ..." The criterion for selecting the abbess indicates a formal rather than a spiritual conception of the role: she must be "the most capable of observing and ensuring observation of our form of life" (223). If this proves not to be the case, "she must be considered unworthy, useless and the enemy of the community's good, and as such will be shamefully deposed" (224). This severe approach to the function of the abbess may no doubt be explained by the laxity in Urbanist monasteries and the behavior of certain abbesses.

We will see later, however, that another approach was being taken at this same period by Catherine of Bologna, abbess and founder. She continually emphasized the importance of offering maternal support to sisters in trouble, along the lines suggested by Clare. Elsewhere, Colette approached the issue of relationships in the terms Clare used when she wrote in her *Rule*: "Let the abbess be so familiar with them that they can speak and act with her as ladies do with their handmaid" (X). The reformer, however, removes all the evangelical power from the text, defining it in limited terms:

> It does not mean that the sisters can cause injury to their abbess, in word or gesture, or show her scorn, as sometimes ladies do to their servants ... (240).

Where Clare, like Christ, risks the evangelical paradox, responding to possible tensions with the power of charity alone, Colette installs an abbess who is entirely mistress of herself, clothed in evangelical virtues, but whose power is never affected or threatened. Other texts, including the *Little Regulations* (which we will examine later), would help to resolve the problem of tensions between a sister and an abbess.

The abbess "occupies the place of God" (238), a turn of phrase that demonstrates the change in attitude since Clare and hence the meaning that Colette applies to the term "servant." The question then arises: if Colette differentiated herself from the Benedictine-style Urbanist abbesses regarding regular observance, did she not also retain the idea of power as they practiced it and from which Francis, and even more so Clare of Assisi, had resolutely departed?

While Colette rarely mentioned interpersonal relationships, she no doubt believed that mutual love should predominate. She specifies

> that mutual charity, love and tenderness should not cool in them, but on the contrary should each day gain new vigor (236).

The impact of this fine text is reduced by the recommendation made in the *Constitutions*, as we have just seen, that a culpable sister should be denounced to the visitator. Moreover, sisters who offend others must ask pardon "in the form prescribed by the *Rule*: otherwise the abbess will punish them in an exemplary manner" (237). The adjective "exemplary" underlines the idea that the other sisters of the community are being warned. Sisterly love, then, remains in the moral domain of obligation, and behavior is governed in advance.

The *Constitutions* are actually a reworking of the *Rule*, using a particular idea of the religious life. They constitute an evaluation of the founder's document. For each chapter, Colette specifies this is a commandment, this is a counsel. When a sister was guilty, for instance (235), punishment was a "commandment," praying for her was a "counsel." We sense the difference in the use of these two terms. One prays, "according to charity and devotion, prayers ordered by the abbess ..."

Colette was perfectly aware that her approach to the *Rule* was not simply commentary. The *Sentiments* conclude with a judgment on the work as a whole, casting light on the purpose of the *Constitutions*, which, in no way, intends to change the substance of "our form of life." On the contrary,

> my intention is to assist your understanding of it, so that you can keep it more perfectly and surely, according to the circumstances of the present time. Because of the dangers of this time and to obviate them, I have been forced to speak of some matters more precisely than does our form of life. These matters, although they are not the essence of the *Rule* and hardly affect its substance since these might subsist without such matters, nonetheless might occasion ruin, and therefore I have removed and omitted some things and modified others (245-46).

She listed issues dealing with active or passive enclosure. About other issues that might seem to us decisive (such as relations between abbess and sisters), she simply said: "... and such other things contained in this present document."

We have noted that she considered it very important to strengthen the enclosure "by reason of the dangers of this time." She seemed to take a less urgent view toward significant changes in the nature of relations between the abbess and the sisters and the idea of responsibility. We must recall that this reformer who legislated on community and sisterly life had not herself experienced it. (Her time in the royal abbey of Montcel was too brief to be called experience.) From being a recluse, she became an abbess. She knew of Clare, not through the life, but through the text of the *Rule* that had been brought, no doubt, from the protomonastery of Assisi. She had not been nourished or formed in a Clarisse monastery.

This was a fundamental difference between her and the Italian Clarisses whose vocations as reformers matured in Poor Clare communities, some of them over many years. Many had first hand experience of living through the change from the Urbanist Rule to the Rule of Clare. For instance, Catherine of Bologna, abbess and founder, had first lived in a community of tertiaries under the first *Rule*. Brother Henry de Baume also lived in a convent before setting out alongside Colette on the path to reform. Colette, therefore, lacked the point of view of a simple professed sister and the experience of living for any length of time in an existing community.

The *Regulations*

In the light of the introduction (I-VI) to the text of the *Regulations*, taken from the same work as the *Constitutions* and the *Sentiments*, it is difficult to be absolutely certain of its authenticity. It appears that this text has been transcribed from old copies. Did Colette write these herself or were they dictated? It is impossible to answer that without an authentic manuscript. Nonetheless, it is probable, given the tradition of the Colettine monasteries of Gand, Poligny, and Besançon, that these *Regulations* were practiced in Colette's lifetime, even if they were not written down until slightly later.[1]

The detail of the *Regulations* is, in fact, her way of doing things. Moreover, her domination over all the communities was too strong for this to have been the result of a common effort, even with other abbesses, since these all were nuns whom she had personally recruited and formed. They could have had only a minor part to play, if any at all. The personal devotion of those around her was also too great for them to do

---

[1] H. Lippens, "Inventaire des Archives des Colettines à Bruges," *Col. Franc.*, (1956), vol 20: "The writing in this book has been taken from the hand of the Rev. Mother Abbess, Sister Catherine de Longueville, first abbess of Bruges, come from the convent of Gand to form this convent. Having lived at Gand with our holy Mother Colette, heard from her mouth and written down her regulations and the declarations of her intention on the Rule."

otherwise than scrupulously respect the basis and the form of her thought. The same would certainly apply to the *Counsels* and the *Little Regulations*.

The text of the *Regulations* deals mainly with ceremonies attached to the divine office and to the refectory. Later on it was used as the basis for a number of seventeenth- and nineteenth- century monastery manuals.

The Divine Office

Rather than produce exhaustive lists that would prolong our study, we choose just a few typical examples. The ceremonies for the office were fairly complex because of the considerable details included (199-205), no doubt adopted from monastic practices that became more elaborate as the years went by. For the canonical hours, for example, after the last bell sounds, the hebdom strikes on her stall; all the sisters then bow deeply and recite the *Pater* and *Ave*. At Prime and at Matins, they say the *Credo in Deum*. With a further rap on the stall,

> all rise at once [they were still bowing deeply] and turn towards the altar. The hebdom then begins respectfully and devoutly the *Domine labia* or *Deus in adjutorium*. All remain standing, turned towards the altar, until the *Gloria Patri,* then they turn to each other and bow low again until the *Sicut erat*.... They repeat this for all the psalms, responses, hymns, antiphons, and verses...,

except where the responses or antiphons are said at the lectern in the middle of the choir.

The frequency with which the bells were rung to assemble the sisters before the various offices may be noted:

> The large bell must first be rung briefly to give the signal. After a suitable interval ... it will be rung again longer for the second signal (191).

Behavior during the office is described in detail. The abbess and the council were personally responsible for the quality of the office, which had to edify those who attended (202). This concern shows clearly how the monastery was part of the life of the town. Nonetheless, the office was the special concern of the nuns. One "attends" the office as one "attends" mass. There was no participation, and the nuns were not seen because of the grilles and the black veil.

For the Office of the Virgin, the sisters remained standing without support. For the Office of the Dead, they remained seated,

> ... excepting those who recite the lessons, prayers, and verses of the night prayers, and the responses, and at the *Magnificat*, the *Benedictus*, the *Laudate Dominum de Coelis* and the *De profundis*, which is said for the first vespers of the feria.

One part of the choir stood, while the other remained seated for the psalms in the daytime hours and for night prayers:

> But when two or four psalms are said without an antiphon, the sisters must remain standing during these two or four psalms, and those of the other choir sit down, and so on, except during the psalms mentioned above.

These few examples show a strengthening of the so-called "monasticism" characteristic of religious life. Here and there Colette insisted on the necessity for reciting the whole office without leaving before the end and without reading another book, which seems to indicate that some decadent monasteries were neglecting and hurrying through the divine office. Nothing like this appears in Clare's *Writings*: the sisters say the office like the friars.

Here, too, it seems Colette wanted to warn against any laxity by developing and considerably intensifying her requirements for behavior, specifying every movement the sisters should make. There is a notable emphasis on the Office of the Dead, on the Office of the Virgin, and on various prayers. The duration of the office overall would therefore have been fairly long, with several offices perhaps being said (207), one after another, or after the mass. In winter, vespers were said after the meal. Personal prayer did not fit into a schedule already so filled with spoken prayer nor would time for reading or *lectio divina*. Pierre de Vaux mentioned, as already said, that Colette, like everyone else, said the penitential psalms.

The *Regulations* also specify the various types of bows to be made and the proper times for genuflections. The sisters knelt at the beginning and at the end of the office, at the *Preces*, at the *Credo*, at the suffrages, at the *Preces* for each of the hours; at the first prayer of vespers and of matins, and the same for the prayers of the Virgin, of Francis, and of Clare.

> Speaking these names, they must give an external mark of respect, particularly in the commemorations of Lauds and of Vespers, and when the priest says them at the mass.... The sisters must be kneeling while they recite the *Ave Regina Coelorum* and the *Salve Regina* after the office when it is chanted in the *Vexilla Regis* during Passiontide.

Regulation 6 (205-06) describes "how one must bow deeply": for the *Gloria Patri*, at the verse of the *Te Deum*, *Te ergo quaesumus famulis tuis subveni*, at the final strophe of hymns, at the penultimate verse of the *Benedicite*, at the first prayer of every hour, at the *Pater* for non-ferial days. On the other hand, on entering the choir, there was only one deep bow and not a genuflection or prostration, as one might expect. Just after the antiphon, the sisters turn to the altar and make a medium bow.

Behavior at Table

Table rituals are explained in regulations 3 and 4. A bell sounded to assemble the sisters, who prayed for their benefactors and for the deceased in four prayers; then a second bell sounded for them to enter the refectory. A third rang after all the sisters had entered, and they recited the *Benedicite*. Then the reader was blessed, as she bowed "very humbly" (193) and she remained "in this posture until the hebdom gives her permission to rise reverently." The graces and the other prayers were recited by the hebdom. "The abbess is in the middle of the sisters, as our Lord Jesus Christ was in the middle of his apostles, placing the younger ones and the novices in the lowest place." (The sisters each took their place according to the hierarchy and the year of their profession.) The abbess ended the reading during the meal by ringing the bell. Ringing it a second time was the signal for grace.

The midday meal was followed by nones, for which they walked in procession to the choir, saying the *Miserere*.

Silence and Other Practices

As in the *Rule*, silence was observed from compline until after tierce. At this point we find a trace of the appearance of the *Angelus* associated with the practice of indulgences (197):

> After compline, the bell is rung three times, with three rings each time, and the sisters say three *Ave Marias* in honor of the most glorious Virgin Mary, to earn one hundred days' pardon.

Prayer times seem to have been confused with times of rest:

> ... withdrawing devoutly to her cell ... to present herself before Our Lord, with the sacrifice of holy prayer.

The expression, associated with silence, indicates a period of recollection. Time for rest was also the time for temptation (198). In order to help the sisters and ensure that "all have withdrawn to their cells," the vicar and another sister would visit "all the beds in the dormitory between seven and eight o'clock, sprinkling holy water on the beds and on the sisters, saying: *Asperges me, Domine*. She [the vicar] will ensure that all the sisters are there." The role and significance of the devil reappear here, as well as the control exercised over the sisters.

In the various sections studied, frequent repetitions and even slight contradictions, especially regarding times for kneeling and bowing, show that we are dealing with texts from a number of sources. Modifications may have been made as the texts were recopied at various times, without affecting the essential meaning.

The abbess had little to do in the choir and the refectory. Sisters were appointed each week to do the readings, responses, prayers, and blessings. Although the duties were assigned in advance, with no room for creativity, it is still of interest that the sisters took on these roles. Professed sisters did have a certain amount of responsibility, even though they were not involved in governance itself. Participating in the office was important for the nuns, since most of the day was spent in the canonical hours and other offices. The need for individuals to exercise some responsibility, difficult as it was to reconcile with the total centralization of power in the hands of the abbess, was thus given expression, with the advantage of "sublimating" natural instinct.

THE *COUNSELS*, *LITTLE REGULATIONS*, AND *INTENTIONS*

The Corpus

The *Counsels* are mainly devoted to the office, demonstrating Colette's interest in this. Her emphasis on the divine office could have a variety of causes. Since childhood she had been immersed in the Benedictine liturgy at the abbey of Corbie, and she longed to combat the neglect of the office in the monastic environment. It was also a pedagogical tool for structuring the life of the nuns around public prayer, in default of initiating them into personal prayer. We will look at the *Counsels* along with the *Little Regulations*, since the corpus we have shows that they are the same text (although, in the *Counsels*, the passages on penances to be imposed in the event of faults have been removed). Comparison of these different but unedited texts shows clearly that, even more so than the *Regulations*, this is a series of oral "traditions," written down after Colette's death. Some copies that come from Gand allude specifically to her death:

> Feeling her end approaching, Saint Colette wished to assemble her daughters once more to give them her final instructions.

The author's style of writing shows it is a posthumous text, given the use of the word "Saint." (Without anticipating Rome's decision, her companions normally used the words "blessed" or "our glorious mother.")

> She said to them, "Oh my dear daughters, how despondency has seized your hearts because I am telling you these things!" (Poligny archives).

This re-transcription certainly dates from the nineteenth century: Poligny was re-opened around 1820 after the expulsion of the sisters in 1792, and the monastery does not have any copies older than the text quoted.

The expression of devotion to the Virgin is also anachronistic:

> Is it necessary for me to ask of you devotion and trust towards the most Holy Virgin? This is too deeply engraved on your hearts to be ever erased or even altered. Mary is the mother of God and our mother. She is the guardian of the reform. Therefore, serve her constantly. She will support you in your weaknesses.

The essence of the life of a "Clarisse [is] the holy fire of divine love." The terms "Clarisse" and "holy fire" are not part of the religious vocabulary of either the fifteenth or the sixteenth centuries.

Although devotion to the Virgin was real in the fifteenth century, it focused mainly on the Pietà or the Virgin with child. The writer, clearly having the religious sensitivity of his or her own time (which we may assume to be the nineteenth century), is transposing onto the fifteenth what is perceived to be lacking in Colette.

The text as a whole brings together on common ground issues with regard to the religious life, awareness of personal fault, and the need for mercy on appearing before the judgment seat of God. These things belonged to the kind of Middle Ages that the nineteenth century rediscovered and "recreated." Pierre de Vaux and François Claret are named, however. The end of the text shows signs of a dramatization very much in the edifying style of the literary and pictorial genre of Chateaubriand's *Genius of Christianity*:

> After speaking thus, Saint Colette withdrew to her cell, appearing no more at the common exercises and devoting all her time to prayer. For their part, the sisters withdrew in silence, seeking solitude to allow their tears to flow freely.

If the author of this piece had ever read Pierre de Vaux, it was with little attention. De Vaux reports Colette as already on her deathbed when she summoned her daughters (P. de Vaux, § 191 to 193).

If, as we believe, this text dates from the nineteenth century, it seems to be an attempt, after the disruption of the Revolution and the dispersal of the sisters, to reconnect to the tradition by putting some oral memories down in writing. The author reveals concern that the reform endure: "I do not need to remind you of the consoling words spoken to me by the Queen of Heaven, knowing that the reform of the convents would endure until the end of time," and the certainty that much-feared "alteration" to the observance will take place. The underlying stylistic device in the whole text is that of apophecy, i.e., putting into the mouth of an historical person something that will happen after his or her lifetime and which, for the narrator, has already occurred.

Analysis of this text is outside the scope of a study of Colette's *Writings;* but it is a good example, a borderline case of what makes it difficult to determine the *corpus.*

The *Little Regulations* are found in book two of the canonization process of 1747, a copy of which is at the monastery of Poligny. They are a version of the *Counsels* published in the above-mentioned work (251-56). The *Intentions*, along with a copy of a letter in the Poligny archives, cover the same subjects: an oral tradition from a number of sources was written down, the essence of which seems to come from Gand, Colette's last home. Some trace of Colette's own words is apparent.

The Counsels

The content of the *Counsels* is similar to that of the *Little Regulations*, unedited in the canonization process. We will therefore consider only material in the second text that does not appear in the first. This mainly covers subjects already contained in the *Sentiments* but formulated differently. Above all, a balance appears between the legal and the spiritual, which gives this text its interest.

The importance of the divine office is restated. The vocabulary used remains legal ("institute the president"), moral ("we are bound and obliged by the condition of our holy profession" to say the office), and hierarchical (the office is said "before the sovereign King; it is the "holy service of the King and Savior of the whole world"). Nevertheless, more spiritual formulae define the office or the religious life. The function of the religious orders is to "adore, serve, and praise God" (247). The sisters have left the world to "praise, serve (God) fully, with heart and body, humbly and devoutly." At all times, they must "have at least a warm remembrance and recollection of him."

Demons also played their part during the office (248). Colette fought distractions and unforeseen sleepiness during the office, which was "great irreverence ... to the holy service ... attended by the angels."

One paragraph (249) discusses the interior disposition needed to receive the Eucharist. These lines seem inspired by manuals of the period on this subject, covering the moral dimension of communion[2]: "cast aside any fault ... correct any sins," and first one must "purify the conscience by confession beforehand." Communion and confession were inseparable, hence the monthly rhythm of communion. A properly spiritual dimension does appear: "unite with God through love and fervent charity ..." But the expression is coupled by the coordinating conjunction "and" to the phrase "virtuously resisting temptation." This suggests the presence of the other character inseparable from God: the devil.

For the first time a spousal dimension appears. The nuns are "spouses of Jesus Christ and temples of the Holy Spirit." Saint Bernard, originator of this spousal dimension, covered it at length in his *Homilies on the Song of Songs*.[3] But he remained close to the spirituality of the Greek fathers, never losing sight of the subsistence in the soul of "a mark of its divine origin, so that it retains a perpetual memory of the Word which engages to remain with it or return if the soul should have strayed."[4] God invites everyone to his mystical nuptials with the Son. Saint Bernard based his address to his monks on this essential truth.

We can observe the contraction of the theology of the contemplative life in the text we are studying. It lacks the ecclesial dimension. The consecrated soul is espoused by virtue of displaying the spousal and virginal dimensions of the Church as Bride: Saint John in the Apocalypse and Saint Paul in his letters strongly underline this. In her *Letters* Clare followed the spiritual tradition of Saint Bernard, but she preserved the ecclesial dimensions as an essential component of the re-

---

[2] *D. S.*, article "Communion."

[3] *Le Cantique des Cantiques par Origène, Grégoire d'Elvire, saint Bernard*, homilies trans. R. Winling, intro. R. Winling and A.G. Hamman, (Paris, 1983). DDB, Coll. *Les Pères dans la foi*.

[4] Saint Bernard, (Winling), 154.

ligious life, while clearly favoring the spousal element of the contemplative soul's relationship with Christ.[5] Colette had none of this.

The actual presence of this expression in a text by Colette gives rise to further comment. Compared to terms used in her *Letters*, it seems alien to her thought. The relationship with God, we recall, is that of fear, service, love, and praise. We must fight the enemy. There is no sign of this mystical and spousal dimension. Must we conclude that this is a later expression? While we cannot be certain, we can at least raise the critical question. Book II of the canonization process includes, in the same passage, Colette's frequent use of the term "the blessed Holy Spirit," a possible example of an early core expression, developed over the ages.

The chapter on formation contains what seemed essential to Colette (250). The novice mistress was responsible for "diligently forming the novice by holy conversation and honesty of manners." She helped her "preserve every good commandment ... in order to persevere in regular observance." The reformer stressed the decisive importance of these years. Formation consisted of applying a technique that ensured good order, rather than initiation into the spiritual life, as was the case with Catherine of Bologna.[6] While the spiritual life was not entirely absent (it was to be found in the *Letters*), nevertheless it mainly involved

> keeping [consciences] pure and clean, resisting the temptations of the enemy, keeping holy fear before the eyes in every ... thought, word, and deed ... rooting novices in humility, enflaming them in the fervor of devotion and teaching them to bear with patience all

---

[5] Clare's discussion contains a wealth of images: the nun is the daughter of the Father, spouse, mother and sister of Christ; she supports "the yielding members of his ineffable body" [cf. all the "First Letter," "Second Letter" (3-5), "Third Letter" (8) and "Fourth Letter" (4), *CA:ED*, 43-58].

[6] Catherine was constantly concerned to teach novices the ways of God's love. Cf. Part Three below.

adversities, austerities, and other burdens found in the holy state of Religion (250-51).

Even more so than in the *Constitutions*, the admission of young women at the minimum age of twelve was considered with reluctance, since reception of such children often led to the "destruction of good order in the religious life." Moreover, they had neither "discretion nor knowledge to understand the perfection of the religious state" (251). Implicit is the issue of children vowed to "the state of religion" from an early age. Colette was caught between the exigencies of preserving the seriousness of religious life and the difficulty of dealing with "kings, dukes, counts, queens, duchesses or countesses or other people whose requests to promise them [these children] to God cannot well be refused."

We find another aspect of the monastery's relations with society that had been discussed in the *Letters*. Benefactors wishing to ensure their future in the next life founded monasteries with rich endowments or vowed their daughters to God, even if it meant demanding special arrangements for them. Colette tried to reduce the risks of laxity caused by such forced vocations. Parents "were required to feed and instruct these children until they had reached an age where they understood the state of life they wished to embrace." Colette avoided making monasteries into boarding schools or junior novitiates, which would have meant additional expenses for the community. Those in poor health were also sent away, as prescribed by the *Rule*. She also tried to protect the young postulant's freedom of choice, not for the sake of the freedom of the individual but to avoid the risk of the monastery's decadence if vocations were not authentic.

The Little Regulations

The following passages do not appear in the book edited in Bruges in the nineteenth century, but they are in Book II of the canonization process of 1747. They deal mainly with the punishments imposed on guilty sisters. The other original elements are not important and treat of subjects already covered elsewhere: prayers to be recited if unable to receive communion, recommendations on the poverty of the habit, on the vigilance of the door-keepers, on the minimum age of entry, on formation of novices. There is one interesting point to note, however. Colette wanted small communities, from eighteen to twenty sisters, explicitly referring to the *Constitutions* of Benedict XII: "so that the sisters could better preserve their strict poverty."

This gives an echo, already found in the *Letters*, of the economic factors involved in establishing convents in towns. Colette added that the foundation would actually be made "according to the size and generosity of the town and of the countryside."

The text mentions possible sanctions: missing preparation for the office meant going without a meal and admitting guilt by kneeling before the whole community. The abbess was to rebuke the culprit in public.

Colette's restrictive explanation of the "mistress-servant" image in Clare has already been noted. It reappears here with regard to necessary punishment:

> Let the guilty sister tell her fault in chapter, before all the professed, before whom the said mother, by saving obedience, is required to give her discipline of ten strokes, well and severely imposed.

The punishment that Clare imposed on the sisters, in cases of mortal sin against the form of the profession, was to eat bread and water in the refectory. The abbess could impose a more severe punishment, according to her own judgment, although Clare did not feel the need to specify this.[7] In this text, however, for an offence to a sister (injurious words), the possibility of punishment if the culprit did not ask forgiveness

---

[7] The sin is not said to be against the abbess, a matter that Clare deals with in the next chapter without mentioning any punishment. She simply writes: "I admonish and exhort the sisters in our Lord Jesus Christ to beware of all pride, vainglory, envy, avarice, care and anxiety about this world, detraction and murmuring, dissension and division" (ch. X).

before compline was seven strokes of the discipline. If she remained obstinate, she would receive "twice seven strokes" on the second day and three times on the third day. Then came prison "until such time as she was humbled." Clare's tone is quite different. The guilty sister requests pardon, and the offended sister generously gives it.

Obedience is the foundation of the other vows, and "its transgression (is) serious and mortal before God and creatures." For this reason, the culprit, having beaten her breast at the chapter, would receive "XII severe and heavy strokes by the one who, in the judgment of the mother abbess, would be best disposed to give them." If, through "diabolic temptation," the sister should continue, "for as many days as she is rebellious and disobedient, she would be disciplined as many times as said, and the IInd day put in the discipline chamber on bread and water, and every Friday disciplined with V strokes until she is humbled." The text does not specify if these five strokes were to be added to those received daily or if, on the contrary, the bread and water punishment in the discipline chamber replaced the "XII strokes" of the first three days.

For Catherine of Bologna, diabolic temptation removed some of the guilt from the sister. Here, however, it appears to deserve punishment, as if the devil and the sister are seen to have connived. For the Italian Clarisse, the pedagogical and spiritual contribution relates to being freed from temptation.[8]

Without anticipating development within the Colettines, it is still necessary to discuss the passages missing from later editions of the customary (for instance, that of Poligny, 1632) or from editions of the works of Colette. The Poligny *Annals* state that the 1632 customary was composed after consulting customaries of other Colettine monasteries. There are three possible hypotheses:

---

[8] Cf. Part Three, chap. 3.

–these passages were considered embarrassing and were not published, remaining in manuscript form,
–they no longer applied and therefore lost their meaning,
–they were not authentic and were not accepted by the Colettines who explained the traditions in the customaries.

We may dismiss the third argument, since these texts were used for the canonization process and were therefore not seen as alien to Colette's thought. The 1632 customary of Poligny seems to show that these customs were not in force after the beginning of the seventeenth century, although this cannot be stated with certainty.[9] Consideration of the later texts attributed to Colette will clarify this.

The Intentions, the Letter Discussing the Intentions, and Other Counsels

The *Intentions* and the *Letter Discussing the Intentions* are late manuscript copies of texts from Gand, archived at the Poligny monastery. The *Other Counsels* is a collection of memories and words attributed to Colette, also mainly held at Gand. These texts repeat each other frequently, but with variants.

The importance of the divine office returns as a leitmotiv, with a neat formula, used elsewhere for the office of Saint Colette:

> Any work must be left aside for the office, because serving God and singing his praises is the most important action we have to do, since it is for this that we have left the world (*Counsels*, 252).

---

[9] In 1571, Saint Charles Borromeo, reformer of the Urbanist Clarisses in Milan, would be particularly severe towards guilty sisters and would use coercive methods. Cf. P. Sevesi, "Il monastero delle clarisse in S. Apolinare di Milano," *A.F.H.*, 1925-1926: "Punishments were imposed for failure to observe silence and enclosure: a sister found guilty would have to make the sign of the cross with her tongue in the refectory" (121-23). After the Council of Trent, reforms often included return to strict enclosure.

Sisterly love is strongly emphasized, with punishment prescribed if it is not observed (which reinforces the texts considered above). Those responsible for breaking the "bond of charity" will always have to suffer from the punishment of "Our Lord." The abbess must ensure that the "culprits are severely punished" (*Counsels*, 254).

The *Intentions* and the *Counsels* offer two different versions of a summary of so-called "spiritual recommendations." As such, they are interesting because they reflect teachings Colette left for her daughters.

The *Intentions* (Archives of Poligny)

> Saint Colette recommended four things to her religious sisters: the first, that they should be careful to have the love of God; the second, acquisition and preservation of divine grace; the third, evangelical poverty; the fourth, patience with afflictions.

The *Counsels*

> Our holy mother especially recommended to her daughters these things:
>
> 1 – The divine office.
> 2 – To receive and properly keep the graces of the Lord.
> 3 – Patience in trials.
> 4 – Evangelical poverty.
> 5 – Mental prayer.
> 6 – Devotion to the Virgin Mary" (252).

The first text can be seen to be late, because of its use of "Saint Colette" and because it does not offer the recommendations as textual. Likewise, the second text seems late. It uses "our holy mother," and its typography also does not offer these admonitions as *verba* of Colette. In addition, points five and six do not match other writings of Colette. "Mental prayer" and "devotion to the Virgin Mary" indicate a later addition. The expression "mental prayer" was commonly used in France in the Carmelite school. "Devotion to the Virgin Mary" was characteristic of the French school and Grignon de Montfort during the seventeenth and eighteenth centuries. The first points in the *Intentions* and *Counsels* texts differ. Number one of the *Counsels*, "the divine office," might be considered more authentic, since, as other texts show, it was one of Colette's major concerns.

Two other suggested new elements appear elsewhere. One has to do with relations with the first order and the sisters' renovation of Colette's prescriptions. It is said:

> If the visitator or someone else wanted to increase, reduce, or produce new regulations, the sisters shall not accept them ... (*Counsels*, 256).

The thought is certainly formulated later, but the content closely matches Colette's concern to protect the reform from external pressures, including that of the friars, whether conventuals or observants. We will see that, in this respect, the Italian Clarisses were more dependent on the first order, since they had no *Constitutions* of their own produced by a nun.

The second element, explicit in the manuscript and in the edited text, betrays certain difficulties within the reform, some unease. According to the *Counsels* (255), one of the confessors of "our glorious mother" (this term tends to authenticate the episode) at Hesdin "asked her to give her convents some little regulations that he had written" that would be used to "fortify" the saint's own writings. Colette refused, saying to her sisters: "Alas, what will happen after my death when, in my lifetime, you wish to give regulations?" She reproached them for being behind the confessor's proposal and later asked them: "Why is the way I have shown you not enough for you? Because I assure you that I never taught you anything without being certain that it was God's will" (*Counsels*, 256).

This expression, according to the evidence, is later than the fifteenth century. Certain tensions may be assumed, perhaps coming from Colette's own lifetime and from among her close companions. Both texts concerned offer the example of Saint Bernard, who had the same problems with his monks, thus indicating one common source. There is another possibility: tensions appeared fairly quickly after Colette's death, encouraged by problems within the first order between the conventuals and the observants. Tensions after Francis's death were the same, all legal matters. What did this desire for innovation (256), these "personal opinions" indicate? It is difficult to know. From the available documentation, we might recall what we have already noted: the disappearance of texts on penances in later writings such as the customary of 1632. Another trend might also be hinted at in Colette's warning (*Counsels*, 254) against sisters greedy "for new austerities, long vigils, and a multitude of prayers."

To finish we might highlight two features, apparently borrowed from Pierre de Vaux's *Vita*. Colette, though weary, went to the divine office and sang the psalms with such fervor that it seemed she had no pain (*Counsels*, 252) and her final confidence:

> Everything I have done was done through the inspiration of the Holy Spirit, and if I had to begin again before God, it would be impossible for me to do better (256).

THE *TESTAMENT* OR COLETTINE FRUITFULNESS

The Problem of Sources

A publication of 1897 in *Seraphica legislationis Textus originales* mentions an "old document of the Colettine Clarisses of Tournai."[10] It is "reproduced as it is," the text being divided into sections numbered 1 to 57.

One variant of this text was published around the same time in the *Constitutions* of Saint Colette.[11] This version is shorter and shows signs of revision. This same work includes a letter attributed to Brother Henry de Baume, which in fact is a duplicate of the *Testament*, a term attributed to the text said to be by Colette.

The manuscript of the abbey of Saint-Laurent (seventeenth century, preserved in the archives of Puy) reproduces this letter. The attribution to Brother Henry is incorrect, however. No ancient manuscript mentions such a text, which, from its form, seems to date from the seventeenth century.[12]

There remains the matter of the text attributed to Colette. The monastery of Tournai, founded by Gand in 1628, appears to have been a center for the Colettine reform. The manuscript of the *Exhortation* or *Testament* deposited in the municipal archives of Besançon[13] is a copy of a manuscript of Gand, dating from the eighteenth century, according to the scribe who wrote it:

> I the undersigned Capuchin religious brother certify that I have transcribed this copy, word for word, from an old manuscript sent by the Clarisse sisters of Gand to those of Besançon, the original being kept in the archives of the community of Gand, as witnessed by a printed ritual which I have in front of me, dated from Lyon in the year 1671.

---

[10] *Ad claras Aquas*, Quaracchi, 298-307.

[11] *Le Livre de Bruges*, 265-68.

[12] The biographers seem careless in identifying the authors of the texts: hence Bizouard in his *Histoire de sainte Colette et des clarisses en Franche-Comté* (211 ff.) attributes to Brother Henry advice given by Colette to her daughters; he copies a rite from the Besançon Clarisses without further study.

[13] *Catalogue général des manuscrits des bibliothèques publiques de France*, XLV, 1490-1491, fol. 46.

The only document the Colettines of Gand presently own is a manuscript dated 1553. Unlike the Tournai copy published by Quaracchi, it is not divided into sections. From this we can conclude that it has not been revised.

This seems the oldest manuscript we have. It is immediately followed by counsels, also attributed to Colette. Sylvère d'Abbeville, who consulted the Amiens archives in the seventeenth century, does not mention any *Testament* in the writings of Colette. The canonization process, which also listed the writings, also seems not to have known of it, nor did Wadding, the chronicler of the order in the seventeenth century (Cf. Part Three, chapter VI).

As regards internal criticism, Colette did not naturally use the term God the Father, as we know. Nor is the style hers. The lyrical tendency to praise the benefits of enclosure, for instance, is unlike the known writings of Colette and Brother Henry, and the style seems later than that of other Colettine writings at the end of the fifteenth century.

The stress on enclosure, both as the fourth vow and as a significant theme in the text, arose from the reinforcement of papal enclosure after the Council of Trent. The fifteenth-century reforms quickly resulted in a theology of enclosure in the context of the Counter Reformation.

There are many more indications that this text may be considered a product of what we might call the "Colettine school," that is, from the generations immediately after those who knew Colette. As we have seen, the historical setting of these decades was particularly important for the future of the reform. Colette's legislative efforts might have been inadequate to establish a Colettine tradition. The Franciscan saints of the Observance (Bernardine of Siena was canonized in 1460) wrote a great deal on spiritual matters that would form later generations.

The text of Colette's *Intentions*, collected and transcribed for the monastery of Gand, was necessary to complete the reformer's teaching. The *Exhortation* or *Testament*, attributing writings to Colette equivalent to those of the order's founders, should be accepted, perhaps, as an expanded and re-worked form of the primitive core of Colette's own thoughts.

Analysis of the Testament

The *Testament* begins with a trinitarian invocation unusual for Colette: "Glory, honor, fear, and reverence to the Three Divine Persons in one essence. Amen."[14] The possibility of religious life and the source of the call are in the Father. The consequence of the call is given in another gospel passage: "Whoever wishes to come after me, let him renounce himself completely and take up his cross" (§6).

Christ the Foundation of the Vows

The spirituality of the Colettine school seems to be characterized by contemplation of the crucified Christ, an essential though not the only dimension of Franciscan spirituality from the outset. Religious life is defined, first of all, by the sign of renunciation, the typical sacrifice of the *sequela Christi*.

Gospel perfection, the end pursued by those who are called, may be lived through the religious vows. During the Counter-reformation period and the following decades, as structures were reinforced, the vows were stressed as a means to ensure the solidity and permanence of regular life. This emphasis was accompanied by continuous references to the traditional *contemptus mundi*: "My dearly beloved sisters, chosen from the perilous valley ... to embrace the holy and evangelical state of Jesus" (§4).

The Three Vows

A review of the *corpus* allows us to make some useful observations regarding all three vows, before considering each in turn:

---

[14] For ease of reference, we are using the Quaracchi text for this study, textually identical to the Gand manuscript of 1553.

–Obedience:

(§12) You are called by grace to perfect obedience, to obey in all things where there is no offence. Jesus Christ did this unto death.
(§16) May we die in this virtue with Jesus on the cross.

–Poverty:

(§17) Our Lord wants us to carry our cross daily, and it is our vow of holy poverty.
(§26) Live and die truly poor, as our sweet Savior did for us on the cross.
(§21) Following the example of Jesus Christ, our glorious father Saint Francis, and our mother Saint Clare, be very content with the form of your poor habit.

–Chastity:

(§28) Our Lord then said *et sequitur me*. By which I understand that we must follow Jesus Christ, the Lamb without stain, virgin and son of the Virgin.

As mentioned elsewhere with regard to Francis and Clare, the theology of the vows is christocentric.[15]

Obedience seems paramount in the monastic tradition and at the beginning of Saint Clare's *Rule*. It is an immediate consequence of the call to follow Christ. In monastic language, being professed is equivalent to "being received into obedience." Christ's obedience to death (he "preferred to lose his life in the bitterness of the Passion, rather than lose the obedience due to his Father" [§12]) results in that of the religious.

Similarly, the justification for poverty is the poverty of Christ and Christ on the cross. The text does not hesitate to make surprising combinations of words: "cross of poverty"

---

[15] Francis of Assisi, Writings, 1 Rg Fr. 5, 18-19, 1-22, 2.

(§24), "heavy cross" (§17). We see once more, in section 17, a fairly powerful image of the Crucified Christ: "nails, spines, spittle, and overwhelmed with blows: his side open." These may recall some texts from Brother Henry, from Battista Varani and, later, from Clare:

> [He] became, for your salvation, the lowest of men, was despised, struck, scourged untold times throughout His entire body, and then died amid the suffering of the Cross.[16]

Concern for concrete recommendations is clearest for the vow of poverty (§21, 22, 24). These passages bear the signs of additions and express a somewhat uncalled for severity:

> Whoever is found to own the least little thing at the time of her death will be excluded from the Kingdom of heaven.

The Colettines feared the loss of intensity. There was a real danger of this from the beginning of the sixteenth century onwards, when the observants, masters of the order, themselves began to relax their original rules.[17]

As regards the vow of chastity, the stylistic and thematic register swings the other way. The *sequitur me* reappears as a leitmotiv (§28). It is the song of the Beloved. The absence of any direct reference to the Cross is striking. The concepts of endurance (until death) and authenticity ("true purity, true vow of chastity") ensure unity of thought. Chastity is "virtue, spouse, crown, garden filled with plants, enclosure, flowering trees, fence."

---

[16] Clare of Assisi, "Second letter to Agnes of Prague," (2LAg 20); *CA:ED*, 49.

[17] From 1517, the Rheims Clarisses, not reformed, were forced by the observants to change from the Rule of Clare (containing the "Privilege of the Greatest Poverty") to the Rule of Urban IV allowing possession of property and goods.

There is clear allusion to the *Song of Songs*. Lyricism springs out of this profusion of absolute superlatives (most precious virtue, most excellent garden), accumulated qualifiers (noble, precious, excellent, three times worthy, strong, handsome), redundant substantives (dignity, price, value, excellence of your victory), and countless exclamations.

The content of the vow of chastity is the love of the only Son for the Father, the Son who is "lamb without stain, virgin, and son of the Virgin." Trinitarian love is underlined by "holy baptism, complete innocence being recovered, the soul becoming the blessed temple of the Holy Spirit" (§48).

A theme familiar in this kind of spiritual literature, the mistrust of the flesh, reappears. The flesh is described as "mad and rebellious," filled with "evil intentions," the "spur to evil" (§41). It is "the particular enemy within ourselves, whose fearsome assault we must undergo" (§40).

The vows are therefore a "cross" in the sense that they are both imitation of Christ and the practice that leads to loss of self. Hence "regular discipline, correction, fasting, cold, and bare feet" are constituent of monastic life, along with prayer and the mass.

The Vow of Enclosure

The number of sections devoted to the vow of enclosure is more or less the same as that for each of the three other vows, indicating its importance. Moreover, these sections follow those on the vow of chastity, some of the terms for which can be applied to enclosure. It is described as a closed and guarded place: garden (§30); Christ is the "doorkeeper" of chastity which the nun "faithfully keeps" and "allows to enter only true messengers" of the Spouse (§31). Enclosure is thus implicitly suggested as the warranty of chastity.[18]

A well-known theme compares enclosure to the tomb of Christ:

---

[18] The Clarisses made the fourth vow of enclosure from 1263. The Bull *Periculosa* of Boniface VIII (1298) made the enclosure observed by the Clarisses general for all nuns.

He himself deigned and wished to be laid in a stone sepulcher, and just as he was pleased to be enclosed thus for forty hours, so my dear Sisters, you follow him, keeping the holy enclosure where you will live for forty years more or less, and where you will die. You are already in your stone sepulcher (§36).

This theology of enclosure as a tomb and place of exodus is typical of fifteenth-century reforms and of Tridentine theology.

At a symbolic level, the era and the epic of the crusades had passed away. The spirit that had driven the mob to liberate Christ's tomb or that had awakened in Clare the desire to leave for the Holy Land to die as a martyr has now been interiorized in the imagination.[19] Saint Francis transposed this desire of Clare's by asking her to remain at the foot of the crucified Lord in San Damiano for some forty years.

The soul plunging into interior space in this way emerges into the full light of the Kingdom. In its final reality, the sepulcher is where the soul takes flight, because it is there that *metanoia* happens:

Oh blessed captives of the cloisters, above which the soul takes flight and soars above the heavens to hear with the ears of the spirit the nine choirs of angels sweetly praising and singing and glorifying the holy and blessed Trinity, one only God in three persons (§45).

The exultant praise is like a radiant song of triumph, the song of one loosed from the shackles of death, already anticipating the beatific vision in the impassioned, impatient trembling of love (§46 to 52).

---

[19] Later still Teresa of Avila, as a child, took to the road in Spain with her little brother with the intention of dying as martyrs at the hands of the Moors. Her brother would later harness his fervor to join an expedition to the New World with the conquistadors. Teresa would transfigure hers into a Carmel.

Praise, praise at all times the most humble Virgin who bore Jesus Christ on her breast, the holy and august Soul of our Redeemer and his precious Body hanging on the cross for us; praise the holy men and women and all the angels, the good and the just who serve God night and day.

The text does not finish with this grand finale, however. From the drunken passions of love arises the terrible reminder, already noted, of possible damnation, punishment (§56), the small number of the elect even in religious life (§55). This document thus neatly finds its place within a religious and cultural context where fear of hell lingers and will persist tenaciously for a long time, never far from the highest mystical states.

The construction of the *Testament*, as well as its style, assumes a particular literary gift, affirming theological thought. In this, the Colettine school has the gift of a valuable spiritual text that supplements Colette's own writings, which are almost exclusively devoted to her concerns for reform. The heirs and disciples of the Picardy abbess, together with their efforts to safeguard the particular features of the reform, must have also included among their members major contemplative figures, capable of ensuring transmission of Colette's spiritual project.

This set of texts, of unequal historical value, forms a constellation around the central theme of the *Constitutions* and secondarily of the *Sentiments*. It clearly supports the major themes of these texts: enclosure, divine office, the notion of the abbess's responsibility and relationship to her sisters, strict control of every aspect of monastic life.

From the twelve chapters of the primitive *Rule* of Clare, Colette, inspired by later legislation, composed a consistent, well-structured whole, filling in all the gaps Clare left in terms of community responsibility. There was an imbalance, however, between the spiritual dimension that animated the *Rule* and the legal aspects that preoccupied the reformer. Furthermore, ignorance of Clare's other spiritual writings

(*Letters* and *Testament*) meant that Colette had to borrow heavily from the legislation of the popes. She thus imposed her own interpretation on the founder's *Rule*, motivated as she was by urgent issues associated with the reform and experientially ignorant of the life of Clare. While Colette was perfectly clear about the scope and limitations of her work, she nonetheless believed that the validation of her reform could be realized only over time.

The less official texts reveal, at the same time, both a severe austerity and a clear evangelical dimension evident in mutual love and constant concern for poverty. In a time of decadence and fragmentation, the reformer seemed to believe more in a combination of structures and charity than in the absolute primacy of charity alone. In this way of thinking, it is understandable that the spiritual dimension and learning the ways of God appear only at the periphery of the key ideas.

Clare gave preference to the spiritual element of monastic life. Colette seems to have left this aspect to brother Henry.[20] Her project was the formation of austere nuns, closely observant of the *Rule* and its prescriptions, perhaps soldiers in times of disaster.

In Clare and Francis, the notion of the human person and the relationship with God was different from that adopted by Colette. To the founders, monastic life appeared to be the flowering of baptismal life. Clare could be called the "Christian." Colette, on the other hand, aimed to impose a set of regulations on the Christian life that would forge, from the outside, a way of being in the world and a way of relating to God and others. This could happen because of the importance of structures during this troubled period of the Middle Ages.

The fourteenth and fifteenth centuries were periods which, in general, were strongly marked by Roman and canonical law, as well as by the spirit of organization, administration, and hierarchisation. Colette's reform was affected

---

[20] Cf. our previous study of the newly published material from Brother Henry de Baume: "Méditation sur la vie et la passion de N.S.J.C.," *Revue Mabillon*, n° 5, 1994.

by this. Its immediate heirs felt the need to complete and enhance Colettine thought with a text, the *Testament*, which would crown the legislative work and contribute to making the reformer equal to the founders.

Part Three

Colette and Her Times:
What Became of the Reform?

CHAPTER I

Witnesses of Colette

By witnesses, we mean here the contemporaries of Colette whose writings shed light on her deeds, her personality, and the kind of relationships she had in her life. The account covers her relationship with the "world" (by which we mean the laity, individuals and groups), with the Church hierarchy, and with the Franciscan Order.

Relationship with the World

The House of Bourbon

–Jacques de Bourbon

Jacques II de Bourbon (1370-1438), the eldest of a large family, was a member of the House of France and of the cadet branch of the Bourbons. His most recent biographer was keen to stress the contrasting personality of this direct descendant of Saint Louis, making him a prototype for the princes of the first half of the fifteenth century: warriors in different parts of Europe, "at the height of grandeur and drenched in disgrace." He was captured several times, once by one of his wives, Queen Jeanne of Naples. On his return to France, he ended his days as a Franciscan tertiary.[1] One of his bastard sons, Claude d'Aix, joined the First Order, and several of his daughters became Colettine Clarisses.

Genealogical Table of the House of Bourbon

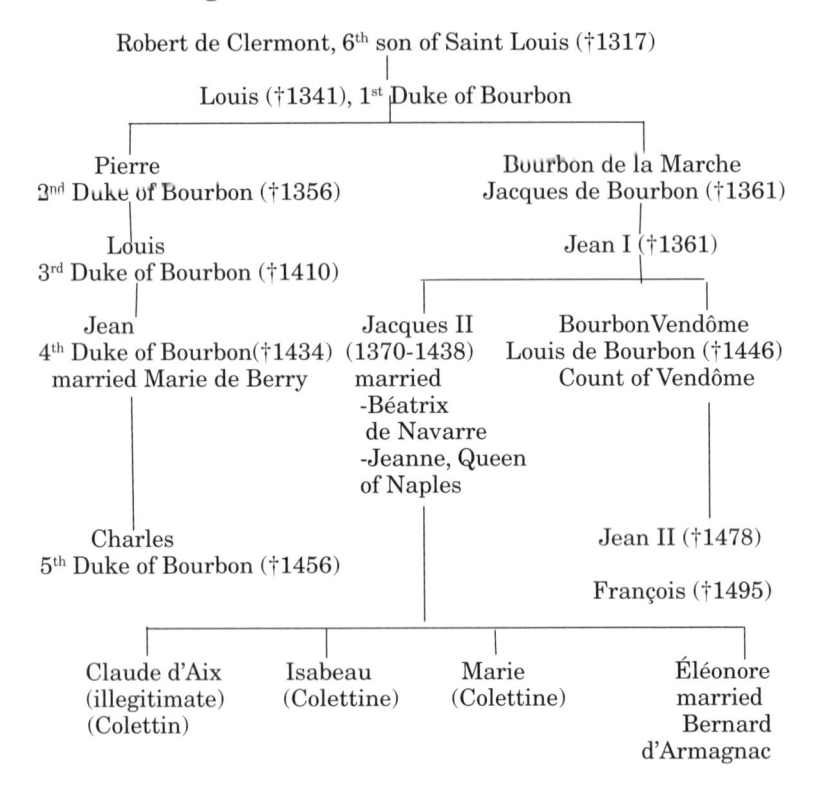

Robert de Clermont, 6th son of Saint Louis (†1317)
|
Louis (†1341), 1st Duke of Bourbon

- **Pierre**, 2nd Duke of Bourbon (†1356)
  - **Louis**, 3rd Duke of Bourbon (†1410)
    - **Jean**, 4th Duke of Bourbon (†1434), married Marie de Berry
      - **Charles**, 5th Duke of Bourbon (†1456)
        - Claude d'Aix (illegitimate) (Colettin)
        - Isabeau (Colettine)
        - Marie (Colettine)
    - **Jacques II** (1370-1438) married
      - -Béatrix de Navarre
      - -Jeanne, Queen of Naples
- **Bourbon de la Marche**, Jacques de Bourbon (†1361)
  - Jean I (†1361)
    - **Bourbon Vendôme**, Louis de Bourbon (†1446), Count of Vendôme
      - Jean II (†1478)
        - François (†1495)
          - Éléonore married Bernard d'Armagnac

After his Neapolitan adventure, Jacques II returned to religion. He had in fact already experienced moments of fervor, thanks partly to the influence of his cousin Jeanne de Maillé (1331-1414), perhaps around the time of his first marriage in 1406 to the Infanta Béatrix, his cousin and daughter of King Charles III of Navarre. A witness to Jeanne's canonization

---

[1] A misreading of an inscription on his tombstone led to it being said that he became a Franciscan friar. John Capistrano, in a treatise *De excommunicationibus,* states he was a tertiary. For a full account, see F. M. Delorme, "Jacques II de Bourbon (1370-1438): fut-il frère mineur, cordelier à Besançon," *F.F.*, t. VIII (Paris, 1925): 455-59.

process quotes the Count as among the princes of the blood who "gave (the future saint) the kiss of friendship."[2]

It appears that Jacques de Bourbon first met Brother Henry de Baume at Castres upon returning from a pilgrimage to Motte Saint-Didier. Colette's colleague came seeking permission for Jacques's eldest daughter Isabeau to enter the convent. Earlier on, Isabeau and her sisters had been received by Jacques's cousin, Marie de Berry, duchess of Bourbon.[3] It was through his daughters, then, that the Count knew Colette. A friendship sprang up between them at once. He was deeply devoted to her, and it was on his lands that the convents of Castres and Lézignan were founded. His son-in-law Bernard, Count of Armagnac, whose father had been assassinated in Paris in 1418 on the orders of John the Fearless, became the Count's executor and governor of his lands. In this role, he was also involved with the Colettine monasteries. Colette obviously had an important relationship with this family and it had an impact on the life of the reform. We will see elsewhere that the boundaries between the lay world and that of the Church were woven through with reciprocal relations and influences.[4]

Our purpose is not to analyze the witness of Jacques de Bourbon, but simply note the references to Saint Colette as being of interest. After the usual preamble to this kind of document, the testator expresses his wishes:

> Item, we wish and command that our body be placed in an ecclesiastical sepulcher, which of our certain knowledge and firm purpose we choose to be beside the monument of our reverend and blessed mother

---

[2] L. De Chérancé, *Vie de la Bienheureuse Jeanne de Maillé*, 137 and 187, as quoted in A. Huart, *Jacques de Bourbon* (Couvin, 1909), 20.

[3] Cf. next section: Colette's relations with the Duchess of Bourbon.

[4] Bernard, second son of Count Bernard d'Armagnac, husband of Éléonore, daughter of Jacques de Bourbon. Appointed by Charles VII as governor to the Dauphin, the future Louis XI, Bernard and his wife were very pious and devoted to the Colettine reform. Pope Nicholas V named him protector and defender of the reform in 1448 (archives of the monastery of Amiens).

in God, Sister Colette, mother and restorer of the order and observance of Madame Saint Clère, in some church or place where her body may rest, and because it will please God.[5]

In the event that he should die before she does, he makes provision that his body be placed in the church of the Friars Minor in "our town of Castres," waiting to be transferred to the place where "our said good mother" will rest. When he died in Besançon, on September 24, 1438, he was buried in the "Chapel of Saint Anne, part of the church of the Clarisses."[6]

It was not uncommon in the Middle Ages for great figures to be buried either in famous churches or close to the tombs of saints. In 1421, Blanche de Savoie, Countess of Geneva, realized her wish to be buried at Poligny, in the hope that Colette's tomb would one day be there. We might question the value of expressing one's wish for a place of burial – Jacques de Bourbon was not even transported to Castres as he wanted. The cost of transporting a body and of the travel required of those attending must have been prohibitive in carrying out the wishes of the deceased, all the more so as the masses required also had to be honored:

> Item, we wish and command that one mass should be celebrated daily, in perpetuity, in a church or place where our body rests.

This would have cost fifty pounds a year. The abbess of the convent was to "institute" chaplains for this purpose "at the place where the body of our mother will rest," so that the

---

[5] A. Huart, *Le Testament de Jacques de Bourbon, F.F.*, XX (1909): 10. (Other quotations also refer to this work).

[6] Huart, 11, note 3. Saint Colette is known to have died in Gand in 1447, and her body was transferred to Poligny in 1783 by the Colettines of Gand when they were driven from their convent. When they returned to their own country (1790), they left Saint Colette's reliquary at the monastery of Poligny in gratitude for their welcome.

mass will be said without interruption even in the absence of a chaplain.[7]

While there is no reason to doubt that, on this point at least, the deceased's wishes were granted, it seems that Colette herself did not escape the common tendency of the time to consider the monastery as a dispensary of prayers for the dead. The office of the dead was said by the community each time they prayed the Divine Office.

Clearly, the Count held an attitude of affectionate deference toward Colette. Nevertheless, it was not singular in the context of Count Jacques's devotion. He had masses said, as did his predecessors, at other places: Saint-Antoine de Viennois, Sainte-Cécile d'Albi, Notre-Dame des Ternes, the Chapel of Saint-Jacques founded in the church of Sainte-Clère de Lorguen.[8] The Abbey of Saint-Antoine benefited from the Count's generosity. He made a gift of a bell, weighing eighty hundredweight, to be struck daily, once for each year of his age, and a gold statue of Saint Anthony. He also founded a chapel there. In two later wills (December 1424 and January 1435), the abbey received rich grants valued at 7000 pounds. He appointed himself protector of the Antonines and, on the vigil and the feast of Saint Anthony, carried around his neck "a small pendant holding a gold bell, weighing one ounce."[9]

There was, therefore, in the religious psychology of the period, nothing exceptional about a grand personage like himself having such a devotion to Saint Colette. Considering it in context, it indicates concern for the prestige of the deceased person and a certain uneasiness as regards his eternal salva-

---

[7] In this regard, it should be noted that, although Colette unswervingly held to the "greatest poverty" (no income or goods), she had to take into account the economic system for financing masses. So once she had entered Besançon, Colette abandoned all the property owned by the former Urbanist monastery, but accepted land that provided revenue for chaplains responsible for saying masses. Cf. A. Dornier, "Clarisses de Besançon," *Sources de l'Histoire Franciscaine en Franche-Comté* (Paris, 1927), 2. "Transfer by Mahaut de Velle-le-Chatel, abbess of Montigny-lez-Chariez, to Sister Colette, everything belonging to Bussières near Chatillon (1439)."

[8] Huart sees a scribal error in this name: Lorguen for Lézignan. There is no information for Lorguen. Cf. Huart, 15, note 3.

[9] Huart, 14, note 2.

tion. Rather than trusting in divine mercy after receiving the sacraments, the Count chose to have ten thousand masses said after his death, in addition to novenas of masses following his interment.

Bonding with a woman of repute in order to raise his own prestige and perhaps ensure safe passage into the next life was also evident in the Count's relationship with Jeanne Marie de Maillé.[10] Such relationships did not in any way prevent the Count from distributing masses among other foundations of various orders. Carthusians, Benedictines, and Dominicans. The heirs also had to settle many debts. The writer of the will commented that, upon the Count's return from the "unfortunate Italian campaign," he

> ... changed only the goal of his prodigality. It was the abbeys and convents that benefited from his largesse. He spent considerable sums on pious foundations. The will shows us some of them, but we do not know of them all.[11]

King Charles VII and the States of the March helped him to overcome some of the deficit, but it was not enough. In 1427, the Count was reduced to asking his vassals for a loan.[12]

These details go some way to helping assess the character and quality of his exchanges with Colette. Thanks to him, the abbess was able to found several monasteries in the Midi. The support of a great person was indispensable. Most of the time he became protector of these foundations, and his heirs would follow suit:

---

[10] Lack of documentation means that more accurate information is not available, but it may be safely assumed that there was a relationship between the Franciscan tertiary Blessed Jeanne de Maillé and the Colettine family, perhaps through Jacques de Bourbon. Blessed Jeanne's canonization process noted that she had corresponded with Brother Henry de Baume, *AA.SS.*, ed.748.

[11] Huart, 20, note 2.

[12] In 1467, the heirs had not yet paid back the loan; the chancellor, who acted as guarantor, had to honor the deceased count's commitments.

> Item, we wish, order, charge, and require our heirs and successors in perpetuity to do all in their power to preserve, protect, and defend every one of the convents of the Observance of Saint Francis and Saint Clare, established and reformed by our said holy mother Sister Colette, from all trouble, oppression, and difficulty; and in particular to support, distinguish, and preserve those in our towns of Castres, Laiguen, d'Osillan [Azille] and also in the town of Béziers,[13] which have been founded and reformed in our time both for the salvation of our soul and to the profit of their own.

Colette was able to pursue her planned reform – founding poor monasteries without income or property – and thus maintained her authority over the Count, who respected her way of thinking. She herself, or the friars who collaborated with her, always ensured that the work was carried out according to her design. These friars, Henry and Pierre de Reims, are named at the end of the Count's will as guarantors that the testator's wishes would be effected.[14]

This text throws light on Colette's personality in the same way as the *Letters* to the leading citizens of Gand. She knew how to handle relationships with rich and sometimes importunate benefactors who were useful to her mission. She was able to keep enough distance to prevent their donations from flattering their vanity as founders and thus compromising her reform. This was done, however, at the price of some concessions, features of the contemporary mindset, such as perpetual masses and burials within the monasteries.

---

[13] Cf. Huart, 22, note 2, and 39, note 1. Castres and Lézignan were founded by Saint Colette. The Béziers monastery was reformed in 1432; the d'Azille monastery remained Urbanist, while that of the Friars Minor was reformed.

[14] We will see later that a similar arrangement was made for the daughter of Bernard d'Armagnac and Éléonore, "given" to Colette before she was born.

–The Duchess of Bourbon

Fodéré believes that the Duchess of Bourbon knew Colette through the offices of the Duchess of Burgundy,[15] who welcomed Colettine communities in Besançon, Auxonne, Poligny, and Seurre. Despite the wars between Armagnac and Burgundian rival factions, relations were never broken off.[16] As already noted, the Franciscan tertiary Jeanne de Maillé, of the family of Bourbon, was in contact with Brother Henry.

We can discern a network of relationships, influenced by princesses, either wives or mothers. Having no particular political role, they prayed and had prayers offered for their husbands and sons, living and dead. During the conflict between the two great houses of France, Marie de Berry's husband was held prisoner by the English after the battle of Agincourt, and Charles their son was held prisoner at the Louvre by John the Fearless. It was said that, if released, he (Charles) vowed to establish a second Colettine convent in his own lands. This promise was no doubt suggested by his mother, Marie de Berry, who had already founded, in 1421, a reformed monastery in Moulins, capital of her States. This second convent would be established at Aigueperse in Auvergne.

Other Houses and the Cities

–Blanche of Geneva

Blanche was well-known to Madame de Brisay and also perhaps to Brother Henry de Baume. Her noble family served the Duke of Burgundy, and she prepared the way for Colette's

---

[15] J. Fodéré, *Narration historique et topographique des convens de l'Ordre de Saint François et monastères Sainte Claire en la province de Bourgogne*, (Lyon, 1619), t. 2, 1-271.

[16] One example will be enough. In the Burgundian faction, Jacques de Bourbon was the only member of his family remaining faithful to King Charles VI, who for a time was under the influence of John the Fearless. Jacques's daughter Éléonore would marry the son of the Count of Armagnac (assassinated by John the Fearless in 1418).

audience with Pope Benedict XIII. The fourth daughter of Amadeus III, Count of Geneva, and sister to the deceased Clement VII, she had influence at the papal court in Avignon. Her niece, Mahaut de Savoie, Duchess of Bavière, followed Colette's suggestion to consecrate her first daughter, Elizabeth de Bavière, to God as a Clarisse. (Elizabeth, formed by Colette herself, would, in 1471, write a memoir of the holy abbess.) This medieval custom gave the young reformer well-born recruits, increasing the influence of her work.

–The House of Savoy

Amadeus VIII (1383-1451), first Duke of Savoy, retired to Ripaille in 1434 upon the death of his wife Marguerite of Burgundy, daughter of John the Fearless. In Ripaille, Amadeus founded the Order of Saint Maurice, while retaining control of the State, as his son Louis was still too young to manage. Amadeus enjoyed a reputation as a man of integrity and political skill. During the Western schism, he remained personally loyal to Benedict XIII, but followed France's policy in detaching from him politically. In conflict with Eugene IV, the Council of Basle elected him Pope Felix V on November 5, 1439 with a French and Savoyard majority. Duke Louis of Savoy, his son, ended up joining the King of France, Charles VII, in order to force his abdication on April 7, 1449. This occurred in exchange for France's support in Savoy's struggle against Francesco Sforza, who was disputing the inheritance of the Duke of Milan, Felix V's son-in-law. Pope Nicholas granted Amadeus many privileges – in particular the administration of the bishopric of Geneva and legation to the countries under papal obedience (Savoy, Switzerland, and the fringes of the Empire).

Colette's biographers note that Amadeus made her acquaintance very early on, receiving her at one of his castles in Bourg-en-Bresse on her way to Nice in 1406, along with her companion Blanche of Geneva. Fodéré says that the latter prepared the contacts between Colette and Amadeus in the 1420s, which resulted in the foundation of a monastery.[17] Pope Martin V, in a bull dated October 22, 1422 from Saint Mary Major, granted the Duke the necessary authorizations. Colette then met the Duke at Chambéry to select a medium-sized town, as was her custom. She chose Vevey, where construction close to the walls could guarantee safety.

The biographers follow Perrine and Pierre de Vaux in reporting Colette's prophecy of the future election of the Duke to the papacy (Perrine §53, P. de Vaux §169). Later authors even have her traveling to Ripaille to persuade Amadeus to refuse the tiara of office. While it cannot be confirmed, Colette seems to have ordered the sisters at Vevey and Orbe (founded by Jeanne de Montbéliard on Savoy lands in 1426-1430) to withhold their obedience from the antipope.

What then was Blanche of Geneva's relationship with the Duke of Savoy? In the fourteenth century, the Counts of Geneva and the Counts of Savoy were rivals over disputed possessions. On the death of Humbert of Villars in 1400, his cousin Blanche of Geneva reclaimed control of Rumilly.[18] For this reason, Colette stayed at Rumilly for awhile on her return from Nice. In August 1401, Amadeus VIII of Savoy bought the earldom of Savoy by transaction. The homage of the Genevan nobility followed, but Blanche of Geneva kept Rumilly. Some of the Franche-Comté lands belonged to the Genevan earldom until the 1401 settlement, when it passed to Amadeus VIII of Savoy.

Henry de Baume was from Franche-Comté and la Baume belonged to Blanche. Thus his pivotal role in Colette's relations with the upper social strata is understandable. Since all these families were either allied or in relationships of vassalage, to know one member was key to knowing the others.

Finally, before moving on to the House of Burgundy, we must consider Madame de Brisay, Colette's ambassador to

---

[17] Fodéré, 81.

[18] U. D'Alençon, "Introduction," *Les vies de sainte Colette Boylet de Corbie, réformatrice des frères mineurs et des clarisses, écrites par ses contemporains le P. Pierre de Reims dit de Vaux et soeur Perrine de la Roche et de Baume,* Archives Franciscaines n° 4 (Paris: Librairie Picard, 1911).

Benedict XIII. Katherine Rufiné says that Brother Henry came from the convent of Mirebeau in Poitou. Now, Mirebeau belonged to the de Brisay family,[19] and the French Observance movement began at Mirebeau. Father Pinet, guardian at Hesdin and Colette's first confessor, was part of that movement, and Brother Henry was his successor as Hesdin's guardian.

–The House of Burgundy

Most of Colette's foundations were on Burgundian lands. After the reform, these were Besançon (1410), Auxonne, Poligny, Seurre, Hesdin, Amiens, and Gand. Colette therefore enjoyed privileged relations with the House of Burgundy. Once again her first contacts must have been via Blanche of Geneva, who accompanied Colette from Rumilly to Besançon.

From there, with the intention of founding convents in Burgundy[20] where brother Henry had protection thanks to Blanche, Colette went to John the Fearless's first chamberlain to set out her wishes to begin at Auxonne. In order to obtain authorization from the Duke, who resided in Paris, she went to Dijon to ask Duchess Marguerite de Bavière to intercede with her husband. It was the start of an on-going relationship between the abbess and the duchess. Some authors date their first meeting from the journey to Nice in 1406, during which Colette would have stopped in Dijon.[21] Fodéré explains this relationship through Marguerite's concern for her husband's salvation, adding that Colette visited her often, suggesting to her that monasteries, places of prayer and penitence, could help to change the course of events. He writes:

---

[19] Brisay (Marquis de), *Histoire de la Maison de Brisay (IXe siècle à nos jours)*, première partie (Maners, 1889).

[20] Fodéré, 22.

[21] E. de Moreau, *L'Église aux Pays Bas sous les Ducs de Bourgogne et Charles Quint,* in *Histoire de l'Église en Belgique,* t. IV (Bruxelles, 1949), 326.

[She seized] the opportunity (the duchess's anxiety) and often visited the duchess, telling her that her only help would come from heaven, and to better obtain it she persuaded her to multiply religious houses ...

In any case, Colette was well able to ensure that her foundations benefited from the expansion of territory. Thus, after the treaty of Arras in 1435 when Burgundy won control of Picardy, Colette made a foundation at Hesdin (1437-1441) and at Amiens (1442-1445).

Without underestimating the influence of the Duchess of Burgundy in Colette's foundations, the policy of Burgundy towards the Church should also be considered, especially in the face of burgeoning reform movements. At one point, John the Fearless, Duke of Burgundy, joined forces with Alexander V (1401-1410) and John XXIII (1410-1415), but abandoned the latter during the conflict with the Council of Constance. Philip the Good supported Eugene IV in the struggle with the Council of Basle. In gratitude, the pope granted Philip many favors and ecclesiastical benefices.[22] At the height of his fame, the Duke seemed the safest support to the papacy. He even obtained permission, in 1442, to maintain contact with the then anti-pope Felix V, whose family was allied with his own. John the Fearless supported various religious reforms, especially the Franciscan Observants, from the beginning of the fifteenth century,[23] when, for example, the convent of Saint Omer went over to the reform.

As we have seen, Philip the Good and Isabelle continued to support Colette's work after the treaty of Arras in 1435. At the duke's request, the pope permitted the foundation at Hesdin, and, in 1440, the citizens of Gand offered the abbess a newly completed monastery. Also in 1440, the foundation at Amiens followed a written recommendation from the duke. In Corbie, which had resisted the king and where the monks were in opposition, Colette failed to establish a monastery. However, a bull from Eugene IV in 1447 (the year Colette

---

[22] E. de Moreau, 50-51.
[23] E. de Moreau, 311 ff.

died) gave Duchess Isabelle permission to make a foundation in the city.[24]

Every one of Colette's foundations, the most important of which we have described, was made through the good offices of the ruler of the region where it was established. From the very beginnings of the Order, the Clarisses enjoyed the support of notable families. They were also sometimes supported by cities, by ordinary people who might give modest funds for a small community. Colette firmly opted to create a network of influential relations, giving her access both to the money required and to members for future monasteries.

In the early period of the Order, women might group together spontaneously under the direction of the friars to live Clare's evangelical ideal. In the fifteenth century, however, the reform added more structure, taking advantage of favorable circumstances and making the best use of relationships through meetings and initiatives on the part of Colette and her collaborators. Brother Henry de Baume, because of his social position, had to have been the craftsman of this method and framework. Colette quickly became personally involved however. This founder of contemplative monasteries proved herself to be a woman of action, particularly good at forming effective relationships.

–The Cities

Pierre de Vaux's *Letter* to the inhabitants of Amiens (1443) portrays another aspect of Colette's relationship with her own society.[25] In addition to the leading citizens, great families, and monks, Colette had to consider the cities that were welcoming the foundations. Amiens had some problems agreeing to a foundation. Pierre de Vaux pleaded in its favor, reporting on the state of the reform at the time and its wide extension. (We note that a number of points in this letter are also found in Colette's *Letters* on the Corbie situation, reinforcing the view that she did not write her business letters

---

[24] Wadding, *An. Min.*, an. 1446, 306.
[25] *Études Franciscaines*, XXIII, 1910, 651-59.

alone.) The topic of finance recurs several times: a poor community does not impose a heavy burden on a city. Another recurring topic appears in this letter. Pierre de Vaux defends himself and the Clarisses from charges of hypocrisy:

> In those places (cities where monasteries are already founded), one may easily observe those who are affected or insincere; so it would seem to be greatly irreverent to God and to his church to dare and presume to say this of such a congregation called to such perfection in religious life as is this one.

Some such opposition to Colette, suggested by the same writer in his hagiography, has been authenticated.

Running through this is an echo of the scorn the townsfolk and councilors felt towards the mendicant orders with their lax lifestyle, enjoying all kinds of economic privileges in the form of exemptions and donations. Despite reforms, these abuses continued for a long time, exasperating the people. This is reflected in the literature of the time, such as Marguerite de Navarre's *Heptaméron* (1559).

By 1443 fifteen convents of women[26] and ten to twelve friaries had been founded or reformed. Pierre de Vaux listed those who supported Colette. He claimed that leading citizens, prelates, archbishops, bishops, monks of various orders, princes, lords and ladies "from both the noble house of France and of others ... succumbed with such reverence and devotion that they founded convents in their towns and cities ..." No doubt religious virtue counted, but so did many relationships that demonstrated how someone was appreciated, even sought after.

Pierre de Vaux's *Vita* of Saint Colette shows the importance of public opinion and reputation as a significant factor in sanctity. This text presents Colette from an historical per-

---

[26] A fifteenth-century manuscript lists these as Besançon, Genève, Vevey, Poligny, Chambéry, Auxonne, Seurre, Moulins, Aiguebelle, Orbe, Le Puy, and Montbrison (founded in 1496). This list is inaccurate and incomplete. Cf. *A.F.H.* (1909), 454.

spective as a reformer within a whole network of relationships. We have already seen that this author as hagiographer took a radically different point of view with hardly any historical or geographical reference point. He shows Colette as a character out of time, sent by God for a mission that is never described. The holiness it wants to prove does not come from history but from her excellence and the number of her religious virtues. This approach tended to detach her from her peers, since the saint was "more heavenly than earthly or human." Pierre de Vaux saw a clear dividing line between the world of history (that of the Colettine reform) and the world of sanctity (which has to be proved from a hagiographical account of the "glorious mother Colette"). In his eyes, the abbess's reforming work did not reveal her sanctity.

RELATIONS WITH THE CHURCH

We know that Colette visited Benedict XIII at Nice in 1406, when France was under the jurisdiction of Avignon. She received a bull from this pope, valid until 1412 (although he was deposed in 1409 by the Council of Pisa, as was the Roman pope Gregory XII). Neither of them accepted their deposal. On September 25, 1412, Colette obtained a bull for the convent of Auxonne from John XXIII, successor to Alexander V, who had been elected at Pisa. In 1414, John XXIII confirmed all the privileges granted to this monastery by his predecessors, before being himself deposed by the Council of Constance in 1415.[27] Given the lack of clarity in the situation, Colette, pragmatic as ever, chose to address herself to those who seemed to represent the Church's authority at the time and could guarantee her foundations. She ceaselessly perse-

---

[27] U. D'Alençon, "Lettres inédites de Guillaume de Casal à sainte Colette et notes pour la biographie de cette sainte," publiées par Ubald D'Alençon, *Etudes Franciscaines*, t. 19 (1908), 460-481; also *A.F.H.*, II (1909), 451; also in the archives of Doubs, *Histoire des clarisses de Besançon*, box n°1, copy of Saint Colette's renunciation of property, February 14, 1412, third year of the pontificate of John XXIII.

vered in her work through the circumstances and people she encountered.

Julien Cesarini, Cardinal of Sainte-Sabine and then of Saint-Ange, was the legate for Pope Martin V at the Council of Basle and thus one of its presidents. Upon Martin V's death in 1431, he briefly opposed Eugene IV as successor. Eugene dissolved the Council, but faced with the participants' opposition, gave in, and work resumed in 1432-1433.

The bold arguments of the Fathers about the Council's prerogatives made the pope decide to transfer it to Ferrara in 1437. In the face of the confrontation between the pope and the hardcore members of the Council, Julien Cesarini abandoned it and withdrew. This context gives a better appreciation of the two letters we have from him.[28] The first, dated February 25, 1436, addresses the "Venerable and religious lady" and does not indicate long-standing, friendly relations.

Cesarini continues: "Since I learn that, as a Catholic lady ..." (perhaps from William of Casals who wrote to Jacques de Bourbon from Basle) and then asks Colette to intervene with the Count of the March, "... with whom, we know you can do much." He asks help for "Lord Bernard, Bishop of Albi" in recovering the episcopal seat of this town, since "certain people ... scorning the Universal Church, intend to oppose vigorously this declaration" (nomination of the bishop). He concludes:

> ... we would feel very great pleasure if we learned that through your action the said recommended bishop was favorably welcomed by the lord king, mentioned above, and by his son in this matter, and we recommend this to you most urgently.

Certainly, on reading such a well-supported request from the legate of the legitimate pope, Colette would have intervened with Jacques de Bourbon, whose dearest wish was to be buried beside his "good mother."

---

[28] Bizouard, *Histoire de Sainte Colette et des Clarisses ...*, 197-200.

This missive tends to prove that the famous letter from Colette to the Council, adjuring and encouraging the Fathers in their work of reform and unity, never existed, whatever some biographers of Colette might say. This would have been a perfect opportunity for the pleader (the legate in this case) to refer to it, if only as a counterpart to the favor being requested. On the contrary, the request made in the letter is an honor for Colette as the conclusion leaves one to understand. The concern to which the Council refers would seem to reveal a general truth: "as a catholic lady," she was able to ask heaven's blessing on the Council. The legate seems to be unaware of the reformer's activities.

What matters to Cesarini is an intervention with Count Jacques. In an unstable world, ascendancy, or spiritual influence at least, is more valuable than a Council decree. Hence the important part played by "intermediaries" (holy people) in overcoming the divisions arising from schism in the institutional Church. It is an admission of weakness on the part of the clergy, who, in the matter of Church affairs, bow to women consecrated to God.

The second letter, dated September 7, 1438, marks a change in relations between Colette and the cardinal and assumes a correspondence: "your very kind letters." The tone is affectionate: "well-beloved mother" (six times), "your son" (four times). In two sentences, he uses the words "consolation" (once), "supplication" (twice), "grant" (three times), "you and I" or "we" (three times). This was an intimate relationship, in which Cesarini chose to be the supplicant affectionately asking for prayers from one who had "engendered" him. This kind of warmly expressed, mother-son relationship was common among Italian religious of the fifteenth century. (Battista Varani called herself the mother of her much loved son, the Observant provincial; Catherine of Bologna was very affectionate towards her sisters and daughters.)

The intimate relationship prompted him to make her a gift of "twelve Rhine florins" for her clothes, to remind her insistently of the need to pray for him and for the "happy outcome of this holy council." But it did not cause him to confide in her his worry, which, as we have seen, must have been very real at this time – the pope's request to transfer to Ferrara was causing no end of disputes. Colette's essential role was to pray. He even taught her the best formula to use in praying for him in his preoccupation for the affairs of the Church.

He said he had seen her *"Statutes and Declarations."* A complimentary sentence follows with no reference to a theme dear to historians of Colette, in which the Council would have approved and praised the *Constitutions*. In fact, the proceedings of the Council do not mention Colette and her work.[29]

Relations with the Franciscan Order

Some documents provide a way of defining the nature of the relationship of the Colettine reform with the First Order. They involve mainly the leaders of the Order, the General Minister William of Casals and the Vicar General Jean Maubert.

The Letters of William of Casals

Father Ubald of Alençon made a critical study of the documents held at Besançon Library.[30] One letter, addressed to Count Jacques de Bourbon, provides an indirect witness to Colette. Two are texts preceding the *Constitutions*. The other documents are letters addressed directly to Colette: two written in 1437 from Toulouse and three others that are fifteenth-century copies (one written at Thonon on September 25, 1434 and the other two at Genoa in 1440).

The letter to the Count of the March (known as "King Jacques" because of his marriage to Queen Jeanne of Naples) is a copy from the beginning of the sixteenth century, so its authenticity cannot be confirmed. Written in Basle in September 1434, it has high praise for Colette. Jacques de Bourbon is congratulated for "running" after "the odor of the per-

---

[29] U. D'Alençon, "Lettres inédites," *A.F.H.*, II (1909), 23.
[30] Cf. note 27.

fumes of my most devoted daughter, Sister Colette," ... "this beautiful bee that, in admirable imitation of the seraphic Saint Francis and the glorious virgin Saint Clare, began to enlighten the world with her holiness and most praiseworthy increase in religious life." William of Casals states his wish to help her, since she seems to have "reinvigorated" his "devout family." He is not sparing in his compliments for the reformed Clarisses whom he admires.

If this text is authentic,[31] it reflects the deep esteem of a general minister for the work undertaken and his wish to help the Colettine reform. Similarly, he supports the male and female Observant movements in Italy and elsewhere in Europe.

The two letters preceding the *Constitutions* are more official – one of them is addressed to Colette, to the abbesses, and to the sisters. These letters encourage the observance of the Rule and congratulate the sisters who have "fled the reefs of the world to shelter in the saving harbor of religious life."[32] There is one item of note in the first letter. William of Casals writes:

> Your statutes [that is the *Constitutions*] although very helpful in the precise observance of your Rule, I consider at first sight difficult in some points. I hesitated about this, since on the one hand I find it painful to deny your devotion, which is so zealous for God and the salvation of souls, but on the other hand, I feared imposing too heavy a burden on our sisters and daughters.

His prayer convinced him these "statutes [are] the special work of God."

His hesitation clarifies how the general minister and John Capistrano saw these texts as "too heavy a burden" for the sisters. We have seen that the Italian female reform, helped by the Observant friars, took quite another direction

---

[31] Wadding, *An. Min.*, an. 1439, n° 33, XI, 95.
[32] *Livre de Bruges*, 102.

– the Italians chose the primacy of the individual over structures. The general minister however did not oppose a different orientation. He remained primarily concerned with the progress of religious life during this difficult period for the Order as a whole.

The two letters written from Toulouse, according to Ubald of Alençon, were originally in Latin.[33] The first, from March 28, would have been written during the general chapter of 1437 since it mentions "King Jacques"; and the second, from July 3, is from the same year, since it mentions Brother Henry. The former died in 1438, the latter in 1439.

There are fairly close links detectable in the common task of revitalizing and restoring the Order. The second letter reveals a curious feature. The general minister says to Colette:

> ... it seems to me that your daughters do not dare to obey or acquiesce to my instructions and persuasion without your particular permission. I believe they do it out of lack of habit, and from inexperience.

Comparing this rather veiled reproach with Colette's warnings previously studied on the limits of obedience owed to the superiors of the First Order, this document appears to confirm a factor noted above: Colette remains subject to the general minister, no doubt from a concern for unity, but only in so far as she is left free to create her own reform. The sisters' reaction reveals formation in an obedience subject mainly to Colette and her writings, thus corroborating the conclusions of ordinances and other texts of the same kind.

Just as the note from the Cardinal of Saint-Ange to Colette asking her to intervene with "King Jacques" reveals a weakness in an institution of the Church (the Council in this case), so too a comment like this indicates a level of disarray and powerlessness within the Order, favorable to a strong character such as Colette in her personal task of recasting

---

[33] *Livre de Bruges*, 475-76.

the structures. We have had a brief look at the tensions in the Order and the efforts made to avoid division. So it is easier to understand the desire of William of Casals to safeguard unity and the ferment of renewal even at the cost of some concessions to his authority as general minister and to the Rule revised by Colette.

Two other letters were written in Genoa in 1440.[34] The first refers to the privilege of having four friars for "temporal and spiritual affairs," but adds nothing to what Colette has already gained. The second, confirming the first, assumes opposition, perhaps from the Conventuals or unreformed friars:

> I ratify ... and confirm all the favors that I have granted and approved in the past to you and to your confessor Brother P. de Vaux, as well as to confessors of convents of sisters that you have established or will establish, wishing that no one, without my knowing, may hinder or obstruct you in such favors.[35]

In her relations with the general minister, as well as with the various popes, Colette liked to have all the documents available to her that assured the efficacy of her activity. This tendency to leave nothing to chance only increased over the years from the time of her interview with Benedict XIII, for which she had prepared in great detail.

The last letter, from September 25, 1434,[36] was written at Thonon. We consider it here because of its importance. It begins simply with a reminder of the powers granted by Benedict XIII in his bull, *Devotionis tuae sinceritas*:

---

[34] U. D'Alençon, "Lettres inédites," *A.F.H.*, t. II.

[35] Let us recall that Benedict XIII, followed by the general ministers of the order, Antoine de Massa (1424-1430) and William of Casals himself, gave Brother Henry de Baume authority as visitator to the sisters and as superior of the Colettine friars. *A.F.H.*, III, 95; *A.F.H.*, II, 455.

[36] *A.F.H.*, II, 455.

> That you might have a confessor ... and receive the most Holy Sacrament from him when it seems fit; that you might send the fathers to me and to all the provinces of your order, both beyond and before the mountains.
>
> Item, to give abbesses permission to receive women coming to join the order.
>
> Item, to visit all the convents you have made or will make, as many times as seems expedient to you.
>
> Item, to move sisters from one convent to another for a just and reasonable cause, as well as confessors and their companions, and even to send friars from your family to well regulated convents to remain there.

This broad set of powers, making Colette a general abbess, goes even further in explaining the favor granted at the end of the introductory letter to the *Constitutions*, already studied (1434):

> ... you are not obliged in any way to observe these constitutions, in order that you may accomplish the things for which you seem to have been called by Jesus Christ: since the Apostle says that those who are led by a greater spirit, who is the Spirit of God, are no longer under the law.[37]

This demonstrates Colette's concern to ensure recognition of every aspect of her prerogatives. The general minister, because of the mission he acknowledged for her, placed her above the law she herself had created, so that it might be better observed by the sisters, "these pious young women, both now and in the future." They must "receive with great respect ... (and) humbly and effectively keep" this text promulgated by the highest authority in the Order.

---

[37] *Livre de Bruges*, 103. *Études Franciscaines*, XIX, 466.

This situation is demonstrated not only by the possibility of her leaving the enclosure but also by her situation within the monasteries where she lived for several years or several months. The letter from Thonon ends by granting this final favor:

> Item, that you might have a chamber, separate from the dormitory, where you might hear the mass that will be said outside, and there receive the Body of Our Lord, and also eat, drink and spend the night there, seeing who is outside through a small barred window, meditate and speak without a companion to all the sisters and to everyone.

We note that there was no requirement, as in the *Constitutions*, for the window to have a black curtain. For the purpose of her reforming work, Colette appeared to be only loosely involved with the community life she founded. The description of this "separate" chamber is reminiscent of the cell of the recluse. As described by Pierre de Vaux, her death seemed like an entry into seclusion.[38] We may wonder if she ever left it, at least judging by the way she lived isolated within the monastery.

The Observants: John Capistrano and Jean Maubert

When John Capistrano, legate of Eugene IV, came to France in 1442,[39] he planned, we recall, to dissuade Philip the Good, Duke of Burgundy, from acknowledging the anti-pope, Felix V. He also hoped to reunite all the friars around the vicar general, Albert of Sarteano, while waiting for the election of the next general minister after the death of William of Casals. According to the tradition recorded by Perrine and Sister Marie de la Marche, John Capistrano came to order Colette to join forces with the Observants and abandon her

---

[38] Cf. first part of this study.
[39] Cf. Lippens, "Saint Jean de Capistran en mission dans les États Bourguignons, 1442-1443," *A.F.H.*, XXXV.

own reform. Lippens asserts that, until the chapter of Padua in 1443, John Capistrano, like William of Casals before him, tried to safeguard the unity of the Order by ensuring that the vicar of the observance remained subordinate to the general minister (Conventual).

Unlike the French and Spanish, the Italians did not ask for their independence at the Council of Constance (1415). It seems very likely that John Capistrano was subsequently able to encourage Colette to continue to submit to the general minister, who had already granted her the *Constitutions*. John Capistrano's visit to Colette showed that she was recognized as one of the vanguard in the French reform movement. He noted the praise for the abbess from his master, Bernardino of Siena, during a sermon at Assisi in 1425: "as it is revealed today the Orders of blessed Francis and blessed Clare reformed by Lady Nicolette of France in Burgundy."[40]

Capistrano used Colette's influence to return all the friars of Burgundy, especially the friars of Dole, to obedience to the general minister and the provincials. Lippens describes how the abbess's prestige ensured that she would "dominate the situation of all the Franciscan institutions in Burgundy." Capistrano gave letters of obedience to two friars, one of whom was Pierre de Vaux, to "try to establish the Colettine reform among the Conventuals of Abbeville, who would soon be providing religious services to the Colettine Clarisses in Amiens."[41]

After the Padua chapter of 1443, however, it seemed impossible to achieve understanding between the Conventuals and the reformed. The pope decided that the new general minister, Anthony of Rusconibus, should appoint two vicars general, one for the Italian family and the other for the ultramontanes, retaining nominal authority over them. The general thus appointed John Capistrano for Italy and Jean Péri-

---

[40] "... sicut hodie patet reformti Ordinis beati Francisci et beatae Clarae in Domina Nicolecta de Francia in Burgundia." *A.F.H.*, III, 91-92. Archives of the convent of San Cataldo of Modena, *Codex,* 35-37; *Coll. Franc.*, X, 1940, 14.

[41] Lippens, "Saint Jean de Capistran," 31-32.

oche de Maubert for France.[42] There are no direct testimonies to Colette's relations with Jean Maubert in the new context, but there are four letters from her to her collaborator, Pierre de Vaux, that throw light on the situation.[43]

How did Colette behave towards the newly elected general minister once the reformed branch in France had achieved independence? Her original impulse was to forge her own movement of friars who would serve her monasteries (similar to how Teresa of Avila would work with Saint John of the Cross and the discalced Carmelites). Thus Colette was neither materially nor spiritually dependent on the Conventuals and had no need to fear the harmful influence they might have on her daughters. William of Casals gave her many assurances, and various popes approved or supported her work. Therefore, she needed no contribution from the reformed friars. On the contrary, her direct dependence on the general minister through the Colettine vicar (Brother Henry then P. de Vaux) left her entirely free to pursue her work. Transfer to the authority of the Observant vicariate would only have restricted her range of action and the exercise of her powers as abbess general, since she would have had a direct superior. The subsequent history of the Order also shows that the Observants never stopped absorbing the Colettine friars and trying to seize control of the nuns. This resulted in an increase of their power to the detriment of that of the Conventuals

Under such conditions Colette simply made herself more friends. She drew the friars of Dole along behind her. These Burgundian friars were first attached to the French reform through Mirebeau and then transferred to the direct obedience of the ministers. An old manuscript says:

> Clinging very firmly to the judgment of mere women, preferring it to the decree of the sacred councils, from these the Burgundian Observant convent took care to

---

[42] Glassberger, *An. Franc.*, II, n° 3085. Vicars general had authority over the Observants and the Clarisses.

[43] They also give further insight into the attitude of the Colettines, following Colette's death.

depart, leading the friars after it, and they did this as I said, in order that they might have by name those called prelates of the ministers.[44]

In such a tense context, the letter from Jean Maubert to Pierre de Vaux (written in 1443) reveals Colette's position in the Order.[45] He reports that he has written to Colette and, apparently, not received a reply. The responsibility frightens him. He only wants "the reformation of our most holy Order." He is "in such great anguish." If he has accepted the responsibility, it is with the wish to see the fulfillment of "the good union of our Order, preserving regular observance, and of our brothers in particular with the brothers of our gentle mother. By my power I have always persuaded them to come." He refers to some opposition among the reformed friars towards the Colettine friars, but offers reassurance that everything has now settled down. However he reports what he heard from "my Lord of Siena": "the friars of Sister Colette no longer like us." The same thing happened at Boulogne-sur-Mer. The next sentence is less clear. It seems the friars at Saint-Omer (one of the first of the reformed convents) are in an ambiguous position and give an example of "disobedience" not to be emulated.[46]

Jean Maubert appointed commissioners in Germany, Provence, and Burgundy to bring the reformed friars under his obedience as vicar general:

---

[44] *Mere muliebri sensui propio nimium inherens et illum preferens sacri consilii decreto, ab earundem fratrum Observantium cura se subtraxit ac dictos conventus Burgundie et fratres ad se sequendum induxit et quia id fecerunt ut dixi solum ut prelatos ministrorum nomine vocatos haberent.* Cf. U. D'Alençon, "Lettres inédites," 27 and note 1 (on Colettine-Observant relations). One of the authors of the work quoted may be a bishop.

[45] *A.F.H.*, II, 449-50 and U. D'Alençon, "Lettres inédites," 23-25.

[46] Jean Maubert's position was made difficult by Nicholas V's concession (*An. Min.* XI, 290) to the Provincial Minister of Touraine allowing the Ultramontane Observants who so wished to stay under obedience to the ministers, not the vicars general. Defections followed as discontent emerged among the Observants who stayed under obedience to Jean Maubert. Cf. Sessevale, *Histoire générale de l'Ordre*, I, 203.

> And about this matter I have been to see our mother, and from her understood that you would be sent to me to tell me about and teach me the ideas of our mother on this matter; and nonetheless, up to now I have never heard anything, which amazes me.

And he continues:

> God is my witness. ... I want to know her feelings on this; and then I wrote to her and to you about it. If you please at least write to me something so that I know what is required of me.

As a postscript, the vicar said that he had seen the provincial minister "of good will." The latter agreed that the reform could come about only by the Observants, but their independence was "less pleasing" than "the first way" allowed, "since they have persecuted the friars of our most gentle mother."

Colette was in a strong position with regard to a newly appointed vicar, who was somewhat helpless in the face of the difficulties of his task. The relations between Colettine and Observant friars had never been harmonious, even though they both wanted the reform of the Order. It seems the Colettines intended to keep their independence; and it was really Colette who was responsible for the Colettine branch, not Pierre de Vaux, who seemed to be her deputy, although responsible for the friars. Colette did not respond to Jean Maubert. The reasons for her silence may be found in other letters from him.[47]

These are dated March 11, May 11, and May 13, 1446. The position had worsened, leading to a break with the Conventuals, a split in the Order:

> I received the bull from the Pope. Before Pentecost I have to convene a chapter of the friars under my obe-

---

[47] G. Goyens, *A.F.H.*, V, 1912, 85-88.

dience: the vicars and the provincial councilors. We must elect a Cisalpine vicar general.

He suggested meeting at Châteauroux:

> Bring me your advice for the best course of action. I am writing to the Burgundian vicar, so he can attend.

This bull that changed, or rather acted on, the situation, was that of Eugene IV, dated January 11, 1446: *Ut sacra ordinis minorum religio*. Written by John Capistrano himself, it removed the right of the general minister to appoint vicars for the Observants, leaving them free to govern themselves.[48] It may be that, at this point, Capistrano led Colette to understand that the situation could lead to a split.

In passing we may observe Maubert's invitation to P. de Vaux to meet with him and certainly to adopt the Observance. It seems, from the second letter, that Maubert's state of health prevented this meeting.

The third letter records the Burgundian friars' absence from the chapter: "they wish to separate themselves from us, and live under the dependence of the general minister as before." According to the general minister, they would not be required to obey Maubert but, he assured them, the pope would soon require it of them. The Burgundian friars thought this situation would apply for only three years, but in this they were mistaken; sooner or later they would be forced to rejoin. Apart from that, he is sure that it is necessary to

> praise the prudence of our mother. She does not submit her sisters to the obedience of the friars of the observance while she is unsure of the force of the instruction. This was my advice. God is my witness of my respect for her and her sisters: I will do nothing

---

[48] In writing their accounts in 1471, Perrine and Marie de la Marche may have confused this situation with that of 1442 when there was still hope the Order could be united.

against her will and the progress of her daughters. I have never acted without her consent.

Maubert thought that Colette was waiting until the position was clearer before joining the Observance ("while she is unsure"), and he believed it was preferable for her and her daughters to remain under obedience to the general minister. Colette died in 1447. How would she have reacted to the actual split in the Order and the consequent impossibility of reforming it as a whole? No one could answer that, but one thing is sure: she would certainly have chosen what was best for her reform. Insofar as the Colettine friars became absorbed by the Observants, as Maubert wished, there was no hope for the independence of the Colettine reform, since the visitators, confessors, and superiors would become Observants. This is what happened in 1517 with the decree of Leo X.[49] But at this point the Observants lost their demands regarding religious life. The nature of the danger had changed.

Conclusions

From these direct and indirect testimonies, elements of Colette's psychological and religious character can be more clearly discerned along with features of her work already seen in the study of her *Writings*.

Her contemporaries, whether involved in or witnessing to her work, saw her as a reformer devoted entirely to her mission, while revering her as a holy religious and "gentle mother." She was an untiring woman of action, maintaining a multiplicity of relationships with all those, near or far, who could help in establishing her monasteries. These were mainly men, lay or ordained, belonging to the highest social classes or to the Church or Franciscan hierarchy. This would have been normal at a time when women had little part to

---

[49] Bull *Ite et vos,* May 29, 1517, *An. Min.*, XVI, 42.

play in religious and political structures. Nonetheless when the opportunity presented itself, the wife of some duke or other was also of service to her.

Her project was not without its problems. She experienced opposition, sometimes prolonged or virulent, from the Corbie monks, from the people of Amiens, and from certain bishops. There were Conventuals who had little appreciation for a return to strict observance, and reformed friars who saw, not without bitterness, this nun take friars away from obedience to the vicar of the Observants.

Between the two trends, reformed and conventual, there was little room for Colette to maneuver in creating her own female reform with friars devoted to her service. It was vital for her to have the unconditional support of the ecclesiastical hierarchy and the political authorities. It should not be forgotten that these two ruling powers were intertwined. A new monastic foundation had to have the blessing of several kinds of representatives.

Although Colette was careful to maintain good relationships, her personal influence with men in the Church related only to spiritual things. Despite legend, it does not seem that she even tried to intervene in the business of the Council or the Church. She knew how to keep quiet when a comment would be risky or even unwise. The Observant vicar, Jean Maubert, tried in vain to obtain from her a clear position on the Observance.

The witness of Pierre de Vaux is essential in discovering her real personality. His letter to the people of Amiens in 1446, calming their fears, is the first historical document of the reform and a testimony to Colette's prestige, even though it is somewhat inflated for the purposes of the cause. Some years later, however, in his hagiographical account of her life, his attitude toward her seems entirely different. In that work, no doubt, he was deferring to a predetermined, standard format. In order to be raised to the altar, a nun must be detached from any temporal commitments and from any relationships that have given her considerable help in carrying out her work. She must be specially chosen, without a body of followers, and unsupported in order to appease the wrath of God and convert "poor sinners."

Pierre de Vaux did not depart from this classic plan. Female holiness in a being "more heavenly than earthly" can be revealed only in the extraordinary, in hyperbolic virtue. Does the problem come with thinking of holiness as incarnating itself in the reforming action of a woman? Or was it that he did not see Colette's work as the locus for the revelation of her sanctity? And was not Pierre de Vaux himself decisive in giving her the dimension that was missing according to established criteria? A woman stripped of historical reality and thus of the possibility of error, relieved of the weight of being human, becomes a heavenly and providential being, a miracle worker, a visionary and a prophet according to the categories of the time, whose sufferings would redeem the "enormous sins" of the world. Was it not simply a case of returning woman to the place reserved for her by clerics and political leaders, a place where "spiritual" meant disincarnated, an escape from this poor world of sin?

In fact Colette, by means of her communities, wanted to have a deep impact on the ecclesial and social fabric. Would recognizing the reforming action of a woman, in the shadow of whom her religious family lived, be to admit the powerlessness and perplexity of men in the face of the crises and tensions that were shaking up Society, Church and Order?

Apart from casting light on Colette's relations with the world and with the Church, the testimonies also clarify Colette's relationship with Clare, the first founder, and with her sisters. Clare of Assisi lived for about forty years in the monastery of San Damiano.[50] On her death in 1253, around 150 monasteries had adopted her way of life – in Italy, France,

---

[50] We will not cover the issue of departures from the Assisi enclosure, very controversial among the experts as they are. Although Clare left two or three times to establish foundations in the area, the fact remains the same: Clare did not travel across Italy, or even Umbria, to establish monasteries. Women (such as Agnes of Prague), groups or communities, claimed to follow her without ever having met her in person. Cf. C. A. Lainati, "La clôture de sainte Claire dans la législation canonique et dans la pratique," *Laurentianum* (1973), fasc. 2, 223-50.

and Prague.[51] By the time Colette died in 1447, she had founded and reformed seventeen monasteries, which would soon spread.

Two very different female figures were given to the Franciscan family – one at the very beginning, who "without leaving her cloister," as noted in the bull of canonization, along with Francis produced a numerous family of nuns. Her charism as founder was to remain with her sisters beside the crucifix of San Damiano, which once had said to Francis: "Go and repair my Church."

Two centuries later, in a very different ecclesial, political, and cultural context, though just as critical, Colette left her seclusion to reveal herself as a woman of action, traveling from one monastery to another to establish a firmly structured reform. For over a century, the Church encouraged and admired this *reformatio tam in capite quam in membris* [reform of both head and members], but the reforms imposed by the hierarchy had no future. The fifteenth century saw the rise of a number of different reforming movements, and the climate seemed generally favorable to this *reformatio* because of the apathy and unease in the face of repeated crises in society and Church. The time was right for a return to observance of the Rule, encouraged by the Church in every country of Europe. The character of this *reformatio* was different in France and in Italy according to the spirit of the two nations. The hierarchy supported the reforms, despite having to mitigate those that seemed "too heavy a burden" for the nuns. These latter had to live the reforms, even if it was necessary to grant the reformer herself a special statute that set her apart and above the communities she founded, unlike Clare who lived among her sisters.

Times of decadence and crisis are favorable to the idea of a leader who is essentially above the law that she or he has created for others. The relationship to God and to Christ

---

[51] Without intending to diminish in any way the influence of Saint Clare, we can explain this large number historically by the decree of Gregory X, who, in 1274, officially attached the rapidly developing communities of women to the rules of Saint Dominic and Saint Clare.

undergoes a profound change. God is the creator, the omnipresent and omnipotent judge. The abbess takes the place of God. Christ, although he gives his life, is no longer so much the servant who goes to seek the wandering sheep, but the dispenser of justice who may condemn if the sacrifice of his life is not welcomed.

Once the law is established, it operates on its own. All that is required is to ensure that orders are passed on by those who oversee proper observance. This is the purpose of canonical visitations and, on a daily basis, of the accusations before the abbess of faults observed or personal admissions of guilt in order to avoid punishment.

At this point in the history of the Church and the Order, taking control by means of refounding the structures and weakening the spirituality takes precedence over the evangelical urgency inspired by Francis and Clare.

Colette's strong personality and constant presence ensured the unity of the reform. After her death, how did the Colettines carry on her legacy, their relationship with the First Order, and their insertion into the fabric of society? What picture of Colette would posterity remember? What would the future be for a reform initiated in a time of crisis for a time of crisis?

CHAPTER 2

THE REFORM MOVEMENT

At the time of Saint Clare's death, as we have said, the Order had about one hundred and fifty monasteries. By the beginning of the fifteenth century, there were at least four hundred, with an estimated population of around fifteen thousand nuns. Most were, of course, in southern Europe, but they were also in eastern Europe, Hungary, Poland, Sweden, and Denmark. This rapid development took place in a context very different from that of thirteenth-century Umbria. Local conditions for the foundations gradually influenced the development of the Order.

Socially speaking, from the fourteenth century on, the courts of kings, princes, lords, and even the Avignon popes became known for their ostentation. Rulers were numerous and powerful, and their power grew, especially in France, as land grants and privileges were extended. Kings and great lords willingly became patrons of the arts and sciences. The generosity of nobles towards religious orders was further boosted by the ever-present sense of the imminence of death, consequent on the widespread epidemics of the time, especially the Black Death of 1348. Concerned to assure their redemption by acts of generosity, nobles supported many new monastic foundations for Poor Clares and for other orders. Similarly, the bourgeois classes, such as Italian merchants, according to their own sometimes considerable capacities, made donations or founded "chapels."

Both groups sought glory in endowing monasteries as generously as possible. In 1335 the royal abbey of Saint-Marcel, founded by Philip the Handsome, was granted lands, forests, waterways, mills, etc.[1] Some Polish monasteries owned entire villages.[2]

The size and wealth of the buildings also bore witness to the generosity of the prince. Longchamp Abbey had a church whose spire was as high as that of the Sainte Chapelle in Paris, built slightly earlier. Some monasteries were as fine and imposing as palaces and could house up to one hundred or two hundred nuns. The *Corpus Christi* convent in Naples, intended as a necropolis for the royal family, accommodated one hundred and twenty nuns and, over a thirty-year period, swallowed up considerable sums of money. In Spain, the monastery of Pedralbes near Barcelona, built by King James and Queen Elisabeth, remains a jewel of Catalan art. Its inauguration in 1326 was the occasion for solemn celebrations in the presence of the entire court. Such examples encouraged other noblemen to follow suit according to their means.

Liberality on this scale resulted in interference by these patrons in the life of the monastery. Their right of patronage was often acknowledged and, apart from the prayers of the community for their welfare, included interment in the convent chapel, sometimes even in the nuns' choir. It allowed them to enter the enclosure, to have their children educated there, even to appoint the first abbess and the founding sisters, and to offer candidates for the postulancy.

Popes became accustomed to authorizing a foundation, no matter what the standing of the founder (prince, town, group of pious women) as long as it had sufficient resources to maintain a given number of nuns. For this reason, the Longchamp rule and particularly that of Urban IV were almost universally adopted.

Few monasteries resisted such pressure. The example of the Clarisses in Santarem, Portugal, is significant. King Al-

---

[1] Fra A. Ghinato, "L'idéale de Santa Chiara attraverso i secoli," *Studi e Cronaca del VII° Centenario di Santa Chiara d'Assisi* (Assisi, 1954), 325.

[2] Cl. Schmitt, *Un pape réformateur et un défenseur de l'unité de l'Eglise: Benoît XII et l'Ordre des frères mineurs, 1334-1342* (Quaracchi, 1959), 288-89.

phonse IV built a large and fine new monastery for the Clarisses at Lamacum near the city of Santarem and granted it a very comfortable endowment. In three apostolic letters, Alexander IV dispensed the nuns from the vow of poverty in common. In a fourth directive, the sovereign pontiff, at the king's insistence, required the Clarisses, disturbed out of zeal for their poverty, to accept the king's gifts under obedience. He writes:

> Willingly giving benevolent support to the prayers of the king, we order your community, by these Apostolic letters, and by virtue of holy obedience, to accept the said revenue without further delay, notwithstanding any of the statutes of your Order.

Wadding also quotes the commentary by Dominique de Gubernatis, the historian from whom he takes this information:

> by this means and others, ownership in common was introduced to the Clarisses, and the distinctive sign of their poverty began to disappear.[3]

The monasteries therefore participated in the economic system of the time. Not all were rich, of course. Some had only a few acres of land or some small rented houses. When the misfortunes of the fourteenth century occurred, such as the Hundred Years' War, plagues and famine, harvests were lost and rents remained unpaid. This caused great hardship for some communities and long legal wranglings for others.

By the end of the fourteenth century, there were two levels of divergence from Clare's ideal. We have just examined the institutional level – the undermining of the principle of "the greatest poverty" by the widespread adoption of the Longchamp rule or that of Urban IV. Other divergences were at a more personal level: abuses and scandals proliferated,

---

[3] Wadding, *An. Min.*, an. 1260, n° 12, IV, 187.

most of these involving personal poverty and the enclosure. In many convents, individual sisters were allowed to own property. In Marseille, the sisters could inherit property from their families and manage it independently. Sister Jeanne Astoux administered forty-eight houses and seventy-seven plots of land.[4] In 1337, at least twenty nuns in Bologna owned personal property in their own name.[5]

Nor was the enclosure better observed. It was opened to pious ladies who, together with their attendants, wished to spend a day in the community. It was also opened to young noblewomen, sometimes surrounded by servants, who came to receive a careful education. Nuns went out, not only on their own personal business but also to beg for food in times of hardship[6] or to consort with princesses. Vicountess Marguerite of Lille, Queen Jeanne of Sicily, Sancha of Naples, Isabelle of Portugal all had "court Clarisses."[7]

A worldly spirit thus pervaded the monasteries. It softened the rigors of religious life, brought in gossip and dissipation, and sowed seeds of dissolution.

Fr. Agathange Bocquet summarizes the now widespread situation:

> In most cases, the abuse of the relaxing of the Franciscan ideal already started by the Rule of Urban IV led quickly in the second order to the diminishing, or even complete abandonment, of the ideal. This means that from the last third of the fourteenth century, the

---

[4] Ch. Espeut, *Les clarisses à Marseille*, copied sheet, 8.

[5] S. Gaddoni, "Inventaria clarissarum," *A.F.H.*, IX, 1916.

[6] Cf. for instance this bull to the Clarisses of Bordeaux. The pope writes: "As you are aware, you are overwhelmed by the weight of poverty, to the point you have to ask for your food from the charitable faithful. Mindful of your supplications ... we permit you for this reason, and for all your other affairs, with however permission from the provincial minister of the Friars Minor, to go out freely every year, for one month at harvest time and the same at the grape harvest, despite all constitutions, statutes, and usage to the contrary, as long as a young sister does not go out without any old sisters. ... These present are valid for thirty years...." Wadding, *An. Min.*, an. 1308, doc. 7, VI, 510.

[7] Cl. Schmitt, *Un pape réformateur*, 197.

history of the Urbanists of South West France and especially those of Toulouse cannot be written in any detail."[8]

Although corruption was not universal, many monasteries had sunk into a mediocre life, participating in the relaxation and easing of conditions allowed by the authorities. The repression of abuse therefore became urgent, along with the reinvigorating of the founders' ideals. A movement was emerging from within the Franciscan Order, however, to prepare the ground from which Colette's reform would grow.

In the fourteenth century, the Order contained from thirty to forty thousand religious in thirty-four provinces and nine vicariates. In numbers and influence it was one of the most important in the Church, but the same scandals were found there as among the Dominicans, striking at the roots of evangelical poverty and the common life, an invasion by the spirit and manners of the world. A friar was allowed to own the alms he received and, in certain cases, had the right to a servant. The minister general granted theology teachers special permissions – for example they might go where they liked without having to request authorization.[9] Following the Great Schism, the sale of dispensations aggravated abuses.

Over the years, the friars tried to fight this decline. Even after the condemnation of the Spirituals in 1317,[10] the ideal of

---

[8] A. Bocquet, "Les monastères de clarisses au XIVe siècle dans le Sud-Ouest de la France," *Etudes Franciscaines*, 9 (1958): 133.

[9] Cl. Schmitt, *Un pape réformateur*, 186.

[10] The Bull *Quorumdam exigit* of October 7, 1317 rejected all the requests of the Spirituals, while that of December 30, 1317, *Sanita romana*, condemned and suppressed all Spirituals in Italy, Sicily, the Earldoms of Toulouse, Narbonne, and Provence, whatever name they were using: Fratricelles or Brothers of the Poor Life. Since the death of Saint Francis in 1226, those advocating a life in accordance with simplicity and strict poverty (Spirituals) and those trying to compromise in order to deal with the increasing number of friars and the missions entrusted to them by the Pope (community friars or Conventuals) were clashing with ever greater violence, until the condemnation in 1317 by Pope John XXII. See on this issue P. Gratien, *Histoire de la fondation et de l'évolution de l'ordre des frères mineurs au XIIIe siècle* (Paris, 1928).

a simple, poor life remained alluring. Writings of such people as Angelo Clareno, Ubertino da Casale, and Peter Olivi were still being read from time to time in Languedoc and even in Assisi despite condemnation. Angelo Clareno in particular, who survived until 1337, retained many followers. Known under a variety of names, such as Poor Hermits, Clarennins, and Fraticelles, they gathered in a great number of Italian hermitages.

In 1334, Jean de la Vallée (†1351) obtained permission from the general minister to withdraw with four companions to a hermitage at Brogliano in Umbria, there to observe the Rule, "purely and simply, without gloss." This return to primitive simplicity attracted other friars, who revived abandoned hermitages and received permission from Pope Clement VI to accept novices. The general minister, however, made uneasy by a possible resurgence of the quarrel between Conventuals and Spirituals, which had torn the Order apart in the thirteenth century, denounced the movement as dangerous and condemned it at the general chapter of 1354, while the pope revoked his predecessor's concessions.

The need for reform was indisputable, however, and in 1368, a lay brother, Paul de Trinci, managed, with the general minister's authority, to renew the experiment. He withdrew to the same hermitage at Brogliano and was quickly joined by other friars, who opened up former hermitages. In 1373, there were twelve of them, whom Pope Gregory XI took under his protection. In 1380, Paul de Trinci became the general *custos* of the reformed friars and received permission to accept novices and make foundations. By 1390, they had spread throughout Italy. Almost at the same time, though with no direct link, other observant movements appeared in hermitages in Portugal, Aragon, and Castille. In Spain there was yet another attempt by a small group of friars around Pedro de Villacreces (†1422). In 1395, they formed a community of strict observance in Segovia. Its solitary and austere lifestyle owed a great deal to the Carthusians.

The first reformed convent in France was established in 1388 at Mirebeau in the province of Tours. Others would follow in the provinces of Aquitaine and France. In 1407, Benedict XIII appointed a vicar general for the reformed friars of these three provinces.

Reform movements occurred a bit later for the Clarisses. Until Saint Colette arrived, the nuns took little initiative in reform. The two sisters of Benedict XIII are known to have tried it in their convent at Calatayud, but it seems the experiment failed to materialize.[11] Sometimes, the authorities imposed a reform program: for instance, in 1373-74 Pope Gregory XI sent two apostolic visitators to Castille, but they met with strong resistance. Colette was, therefore, the first to achieve some real success.

As we will see, the reform in Italy took place slightly later and resulted from exhortations and the great wave of Observant preaching. Not systematically directed towards a recovery of the Rule of Saint Clare, it often took on the character of a reform that was above all spiritual. Thus, there was no single constitution: Saint John Capistrano tried hard to impose one on the Clarisses in 1446, but it was not consistently applied. Moreover, a comparison with texts intended for lay people is clarifying in evaluating the specific character of religious life in the fifteenth century.

Two documents of Eugene IV from 1431 and 1437[12] reveal the urgency of the situation and help us appreciate the commentaries that were promulgated. The first document stresses strict observance that avoids scandals and dissensions by reform that applies *tam in capite, quam in membris* [to both head and members]. It emphasizes the enclosure, divine office, and as we have seen already in this kind of text, the right to appoint and dismiss abbesses and to transfer the nuns.

The second also deals with the correction and reform of monasteries "united under the full authority of the ministers." The general minister had already tried to correct abuses by issuing orders. Reference is made to those of Benedict

---

[11] H. Lippens, "Henry de Baume, coopérateur de sainte Colette ...," *Sacris Erudiri*, I, 239.

[12] Wadding, *An. Min.*, an. 1437, 394-96.

XII. The main point is observance of enclosure above all. It raises this as a particular issue. Clergy, religious or regular, might not enter under pain of excommunication.

Legislative Texts of the Observant Friars

Writings of John Capistrano

John Capistrano (1393-1456) wrote his *Declaratio Primae Regulae S. Clarae* in 1445 at the request of the monastery of Mantua,[13] but very soon it became a charter for the Observant monasteries.

When he wrote it, John Capistrano was vicar general of the Cisalpine Observance. He had already met Colette during his travels in France and Burgundy as legate of the Pope. His charge was to persuade Philip the Good to reject the anti-pope Felix V, and, as envoy of Albert de Sarteano, Vicar General of the Order,[14] to guarantee the loyalty of all the friars to the Vicar. In some passages, he made explicit reference to the Colettine *Constitutions*. A comparison of the two texts is therefore very useful in evaluating the approach to the *Rule* as lived by the Italian Clarisses. Battista Varani took these commentaries on the founder's text to Camerino. They were the roots of the great mystical inspiration that the reformed nuns lived out in the most concrete elements of their daily life. They are addressed to fourteenth-century religious sisters who were rediscovering, beneath the Second Order's prevailing mediocrity, the fervor of their origins. In a way, they summarize the many attempts at reform in Italy.

A thorough analysis of the text would involve needless repetition, so we will consider just those issues the importance of which can be seen from their frequent occurrence

---

[13] Text published by Fr. Donatus Van Adrichem in *A.F.H.*, t. XXII, 1929, which we used as source for the introduction to this study. The references given are to this publication.

[14] Appointed by the pope before the elections that would produce a successor for the deceased general minister William of Casals.

in other similar texts. John Capistrano's plan is clear. At the request of the abbess of the Mantuan monastery, founded in 1420, he explains and clarifies the primitive *Rule*. He intends to provide a literal commentary that will faithfully reflect the *Rule*. Straightaway, we see the first basic difference with Colette's approach. She changes the number and sequence of chapters, emphasizing or discarding particular elements of each one.

His work as a whole consists of twelve chapters, a general exhortation, and an explanation of particular points. Each chapter is subdivided into precepts, one hundred and eighteen altogether. Despite the explanations added at the end of the text, the nuns were still uneasy about the extent of their obligation. Nicholas de Osimo's text, which we will consider later, also betrays these uncertainties, since he distinguishes the binding nature of the precepts from non-observance of counsels and admonitions.

Such concerns certainly persisted. On February 5, 1447, Eugene IV, in *Ordinis tui,* declared that the precepts listed in the *Declaratio* were not binding *sub gravi* except those involving the four main vows (obedience, poverty, enclosure, chastity) as well as those "involving election and removal of the abbess."[15] The pope's document gives the impression that Capistrano was being extremely severe. However, though Capistrano used the term *praeceptum* over a hundred times, did he, in fact, intend it as a serious obligation to the point where transgression meant mortal sin? He was a lawyer by profession, a good canonist. He used canon law, pontifical decrees, and earlier constitutions, particularly Colette's. In the introduction to his *Declaratio,* he refers to Nicholas III's Bull *Exiit* of 1270, which states that the provisions of the Rule of the Friars Minor were not binding. Moreover, in his constitutions for the Observant friars,[16] he repeats this opinion.

It may reasonably be concluded that Eugene IV's text, limiting the weight of the precepts, did not necessarily undermine Capistrano's interpretation, but used the authority

---

[15] *Ordinis tui* in Wadding, *An. Min.*, 1447.
[16] Cf. *Chronologie historique*, leg. I, 111.

of the Holy See to specify the limits of serious obligation. In fact the text of Nicholas de Osimo actually shows a certain fluctuation between the legal and the moral meanings of the concept of obligation. It seems the Clarisses needed a more definitive certitude; hence their appeal to the pope.

Overall, Capistrano as commentator shows great respect for the founding text. Nowhere does the expression appear, so common in Colette: "Although the rule says that ... nonetheless, we do not wish ..."[17] He seems unafraid of making a blunder because of the *Rule's* lack of precision on certain points. He gives details, but without changing perspective or rejecting particular elements. The relationship between the First and Second Orders does seem somewhat different, however.

The excesses, or at the least some of the practices, can still be detected in the background. For example, Catherine of Bologna tells how, when she was at Ferrara (which was in fact a very fervent monastery), she received a pressing invitation from a great lady who wanted Catherine in her residence.[18]

Visitators were given considerable powers. John Capistrano, more so than Colette, stresses this precisely because of the position of the Second Order with respect to the First in Italy. There the Observant Poor Clare convents were under the jurisdiction of the friars. Colette, in order to protect herself from such jurisdiction, created a male branch, whose statutes we will consider later on. This was an essential factor in the French reform. It was controlled entirely by a woman to whom the friars, such as Henry de Baume, were utterly devoted. It gave relatively few prerogatives to the friars of the First Order. While chapter 15 of the Colettine *Constitutions* on the visitator mentions the fact that the popes handed "direction and government of the houses wholly and entirely to

---

[17] *Constitutions*, chapter 14.
[18] I. Bembo, *Specchio di Illuminazione. vita di Santa Catarina da Bologna*, 1787, Edizione divulgata a cure delle clarisse del Corpus Domini da Ferrare, collana serafica, I (Ferrare, 1975).

the general minister and the provincial ministers,"[19] Colette in fact obtained Colettine friars as visitators. These friars considered the reformer as their "mother." Thus, in Colette's lifetime at least, it seems the links between visitator and abbess were those of one superior to another.

In the Colettine text, the power of the visitator is not described in the same terms as in Capistrano's commentary. According to the latter, when correcting excesses, "the sisters have to obey the visitator rather than the abbess, since by virtue of the rule, the visitator has authority over both the head and the members" (chap. 1).[20] The expression *tam in capite quam in membris*, typically used by the curia for over a century when discussing reform, recurs.

Colette's *Constitutions* were applied to monasteries that she had created and structured. Capistrano's *Declaratio* appeared twenty-two years after the founding of the monastery of Mantua by pious women or women religious converted by Bernardino of Siena. The writer knew that his text might be used by long-standing monasteries whose communities, after slow maturing guided by the Observants, chose to adopt the first Rule. Strengthening the powers of the visitator in Italy could make up for the lack of united reform, such as France experienced. The weak point here was that the Second Order was dependent on the rigor of the life of the First Order. The Italian Clarisses ran into many problems when the friars, relaxing their observance at the end of the fifteenth and beginning of the sixteenth centuries, wanted to impose property and goods on the nuns.

Capistrano was clearly inspired by Colette in some areas. As regards reception and the minimum age for profession, in particular, he quotes:

> the venerable mother Sister Colette in France who used never to receive a girl for profession until she had reached her eighteenth year.[21]

---

[19] *Constitutions*, 189.
[20] John Capistrano, ch. I.
[21] John Capistrano, ch. I, precept XI.

He himself inclined towards reception at seventeen.

The maximum age of acceptance, everywhere, was twenty-five, but, where the *Constitutions* use the expression "we command," Capistrano wrote "I advise." These expressions show the difference between the Colettine constitutions, approved by the general minister and the Holy See, and a "private" document written at the request of an abbess.

Capistrano uses the same vow formula as Colette with three expressions added, *"omnipotenti"* before *"Deo," "semper virginae"* after *"beatae Mariae,"* and *"beatis apostolis Petro et Paulo"* before *"beato Francisco."*[22]

As regards poverty and work, Capistrano simply copied the Rule, without Clare's lyrical passage on poverty, keeping to the lawyer's formula. Unlike Colette, who devotes several pages to poverty, he does not feel it necessary to describe all aspects of material poverty inside the convent.

At the beginning of precept III, chapter III, Capistrano is just as strict as Colette on fasting, but the rest of his commentary includes some important nuances, suggesting quite a different attitude towards the sisters and a more supple practice. In the tradition of the first Rule, he waives the fast in "time of manifest need" and makes the meaning of this clear – over sixty or under twenty years old and by reason of infirmity or arduous work. He also adds that in May, June, and July the sisters may take two meals a day in moderation.

John Capistrano distinguishes between *clerica,* sisters who are able to say the divine office, and *laïca,* those who are not able to say it. Like Colette and Clare, he does not specify a different status between the two types as regards the composition of the community, counter to usage that was becoming progressively established. Twice, however, the Observant vicar, product of a particularly enlightened period and country, offers the religious sisters the opportunity to deepen their own personal development, further evidence that we are dealing with a different culture. Colette does not forbid

---

[22] John Capistrano, ch. I, precept XII.

this, but for her the issue does not even arise. The illiterate sister remains *laïca*, since she has not learned Latin, which was essential for saying the divine office.

In Chapter X, precept VII, dealing with admonition, correction of the sisters, and obedience, Capistrano quotes Francis's famous admonition, repeated by Clare: "Let those who do not know their letters not worry about learning them." This means, Capistrano says, that the sisters remain available to their superiors. He places the stress on obedience, which is also poverty of spirit or freedom from the knowledge that might give a measure of power. However, the author adds in a decisively significant aside, it is not forbidden to learn if ordered by a superior because "the manifestation of the Spirit is given to each one for the common good."

Thus, in the spirit of Francis expressed in his letter to Brother Anthony of Padua,[23] the way is opened to a religious culture, to progress in knowledge that is not exclusively reserved to men or to a limited group of elite women already educated before entering the cloister. Intellectual work, like manual work, is possible as long as it does not extinguish the spirit of prayer and devotion. Hence profane study that does not assist religious life is discarded. Here we find, as for the Italian Clarisses considered above, a happy integration of civilization with the pursuit of an authentic religious life.

As regards enclosure, John Capistrano's definition refers to Clare's text, while Colette's, as we have seen, refers to Innocent IV's. Capistrano recalls that sisters with the name *"servitialium"* are not bound by the vow of enclosure, but says there must be only a few of these. As with Clare, they seem to have the same rights as the others. Colette suppresses them, referring to Benedict XII's *Constitutions*. Hence the two reformers, dealing with the issue of abuses experienced from

---

[23] "Brother Francis sends greetings to Brother Anthony, my Bishop. I am pleased that you teach sacred theology to the brothers providing that, as contained in the Rule, you 'do not extinguish the Spirit of prayer and devotion' during study of this kind." "Letter to Brother Anthony of Padua," *Francis of Assisi: Early Documents* (FA:ED), ed. Armstrong, Hellmann, Short, Vol. I (New York: New City Press, 1999), 107.

time to time by the Second Order, hold opposing attitudes. The Picardy abbess, relying on the hierarchy's attempts at reform, changed the very *Rule* that she had been the first to reintroduce in France. The Italian vicar, on the other hand, remained faithful to his fundamental choice of returning to the founder's text as a whole, thus risking the "many dangers and problems" that Colette had denounced.

On passive enclosure, Capistrano closely followed Clare's text first, and then Colette's, but with his own male perspective that recalled some of Francis's admonitions to the friars about their attitude toward women. In confession (chap. III, precept V) there must be no superfluous words, since "it is dangerous to converse with women."[24] Similarly, only sisters who are designated may see the visitators, because "... for Christ's handmaidens, the face of a man should be considered as the eye of the basilisk." Furthermore, the doorkeeper must be at least forty years old.

He recalls the decrees of excommunication issued by the popes against anyone entering the monastery other than as specified in the *Rule* (chap. 11, precept VII). He mentions cases of legitimate entry without the need to consult Rome. (We note in passing that his referring to or not referring to pontifical texts confirms how different is his reforming orientation from that of Colette on various issues.)

He is stricter than Colette in allowing the visitator to enter the monastery. She allows entry to the "legal or ordinary" visitator, taking some precautions. He must always have a companion, and they must not be separated, but the visit may last two or three days (ch. 15). Capistrano writes: "insofar as I have the right, I establish and order" that the visitation must take place at the grille, without entering the monastery. The formula "establish and order" is rare for him, showing how seriously he takes the subject.

If the visitator has to enter (to imprison a sister for example), he must wear a surplice and be accompanied by a friar. He must return to the grille as quickly as possible, and only

---

[24] *Earlier Rule*, XII, 1-4, *FA:ED* 1, 72-73.

remove the curtain in rare situations. Wearing a surplice emphasizes the para-liturgical nature of the process and the friar's sacred character (ch. 12).

Suspicion seems to attach to men rather than to women. In section D of the work, consecrated to clarifying particular points, it was not considered absolutely necessary to have councillors at the turning box – extern sisters would be enough. Similarly, simple community sisters (not councillors) could be at the gate to receive those who entered and speak to them if necessary "because of the many passages" (40), while on the other hand, it was forbidden to give keys to the enclosure to the stonemasons in order to avoid missing the divine office. It raises the issue also of workers taking meals inside the enclosure, indicating that the practice sometimes occurred.

Interpersonal relations in community are also dealt with. A certain tone is set by the fact that no mention is made about the sisters accusing one another. This does not mean it was not being done, but indicates that Capistrano, following Clare's example, did not "legislate" on this issue, unlike Colette, who established an entire "legal apparatus." Capistrano provides a different approach to intercommunity relations, confirmed by the explicit discussion in chapter eight about sick sisters. For Colette, they were the direct responsibility of the abbess, who appointed sisters to provide for their care. Capistrano, like Clare, writes: "... all are required to provide for their infirm sisters and serve them" (ch. VIII). The sisters must express their manifest needs in an atmosphere of mutual reciprocity; and each must diligently and charitably do all she can to care for her sister in both her spiritual and temporal needs.

He returned to this subject of mutual love in chapter X, precept VI, quoting scriptural references on the primacy of love over law (Rom 13:8) and on the imitation of Christ who gave himself for us (Eph 5:2). All precepts are contained in love (Rom 2:17, Eph 4:2, Gal 6:2). A single quotation neatly summarizes all these: "He who loves his neighbor has fulfilled the law" (Rom 13:8).

Evidently Capistrano confidently and enthusiastically developed Clare's thought on the sisters' capacity for love. Colette says nothing about this. She is interested in the abbess's relationship to the sisters, but not the sisters' relationships among themselves. She puts the accent more on authority.

John Capistrano, on the other hand, emphasizes familiarity, patience, discretion, and benevolence on the part of the abbess. With Mary as her model, she is "the humble handmaid" (Luke 1:47-54), both spiritually and physically. She is the servant of the other servants who serve in the house of the Lord. He is poles away from Colette.

He clearly considers this issue vitally important, returning to it frequently in his final *Exhortation,* with many quotations from Scripture. The abbess must be a shining example, as mother to the rest, "... fair in correction, balanced in her warnings, patient to listen, slow to judge." She must always study and read holy writers, thus promoting self-development and nourishing her life. John Capistrano wants her to empty herself in service to the community and insists that she listen to the sisters. She must oversee, with great simplicity, the sanctity of the flock in her care.

> To humble the insolent, let her prostrate herself, letting go some of her own rights, to win for Christ the life of those who are difficult. Let her open her heart to the little lost sheep who have returned. Let her raise up those who fall, let her recover those who wander from the path and with unfailing piety protect and care for those who have been gathered together.

Such warm tenderness is not weakness. Like Clare, Capistrano knew from experience that there was no point in dreaming of an ideal world in which failures or even sin did not exist. He stated realistically that excessive familiarity might breed contempt, that being too quick to excuse might encourage further sin. There were also cases where severity was necessary to ensure that fear of punishment might be an effective deterrent.

These restrictions, concessions to human weakness, do not alter the overall tone. In this final passage, detached from the legal framework of the *Rule*, Capistrano speaks from the fullness of his heart, revealing the depth of his convictions. He retrieves the voices of Clare and Francis in speaking of brotherly love, sign and image of God's love. The abbess's primary responsibility, then, is not so much to govern, organize, and manage, as it is to love and help her sisters fulfill their vocation, to realize the fullness of their humanity.

Frequent scriptural references show the source of his reflection.[25] More resolutely than Colette, he sought to rediscover the evangelical vigor of the Franciscan charism. Without ignoring the risks and the frailty of human nature, he believed that the *Rule* still applied, just as it was, with all its evangelical demands. As a Franciscan Renaissance man and a Christian humanist, he had faith in the human person being called to a high vocation and in divine grace acting in the heart of each. Colette, in a society torn apart by violence and drifting spiritually, seemed to choose a strengthening of structures to ensure vitality in religious communities. Capistrano, on the other hand, without rejecting structures, seemed to believe that they must always be measured against the Gospel

Contemporary Legislative Texts in Italy

Brother Nicholas de Osimo, one of the better-known members of the Italian Observance, wrote his own "commentary on the rule of Saint Clare"[26] in 1446. It is very short and relatively unknown. Although listed by Mariano of Florence,

---

[25] These are mainly taken from the *New Testament*, primarily: Matthew, Acts of the Apostles, Letters of Paul.

[26] This reference is to the summary in *Pro Monialibus*, n° 17. The passages quoted are all from page 14.

a historian of the Order,[27] it seems to have been rediscovered only at the start of the twentieth century in the archives of the monastery of Bologna.[28] Among other things, Nicholas was apparently responding to questions being raised in monasteries and very typical of the end of the Middle Ages – what is sin, what is transgression, and what is binding? Underlying these questions is a strong tendency to quantify and to name. The legal seems to stifle the spiritual.

The author tries to disengage himself by identifying the precepts that are "mortally binding." One of these is universal: "to observe the holy Gospel of our Lord Jesus Christ." Three others are of a general nature: "living in obedience, appropriating nothing and in chastity." Some are particular. The first is simply the beginning of the Rule. Those that follow are the three vows of religious life. The particular precepts are "injunctions and defenses or whatever is equivalent. These bind, but without leading to mortal sin except in the case of deliberate transgressions." We perceive here the desire to appease consciences while retaining a rigor that avoids laxity.[29] Thus for the weekly meeting of the convent chapter:

> It is not a command, but simply a warning, so that to transgress it is not mortal.... But it may become so, by virtue of the law common to all those being directed.

As regards the obligation to work, there is an admonition that is not an order:

> ... however, idleness may reach such a degree that, according to the law common to all Christians, it would lead to a state of mortal sin.

---

[27] M. da Firenze, *Libro delle dignita et excellentie del ordine della seraphica madre delle povere donne santa Chiara da Assisi 1519,* presented by G. Bocalli (Firenze, 1986) 65, note 9.

[28] L. Muriez, *A.F.H.*, t. V, 1912, 298-314.

[29] These problems of conscience were already raised for the Observant friars, especially as regards poverty and abstinence. In 1440, Saint Bernardino of Siena, with the agreement of Pope Eugene IV, had to send an encyclical letter to all friars to overcome their scruples. Cf. Wadding, *An. Min.*, 1440, XI, 101.

The spiritual perspective did not dominate, and, over the years, this tendency increased in commentaries on the *Rule*.[30]

In 1463, the Milan provincial chapter of Observant friars minor also issued a set of commandments.[31] These cover observance of the *Rule* with some modifications or further details: the renunciation of property, two hours of prayer daily, complete enclosure, monthly confession and communion, fasting from September to Easter, the discipline applied three times a week, penances imposed at the chapter, work for all according to their capacities, rigorous silence, a humble ash-colored habit, a bed of straw, election of the abbess every three years. (Clare was silent on this latter point, although Urban IV had imposed a three-year term). It seems to be a question of simply restoring structures.

Through the texts of the Observant friars, we can distinguish a spiritual plan that puts in place again all the problems involved in the *sequela Christi*. The community is the framework that carries the deeper spiritual experience and authenticates it. But the value of Poor Clare life does not lie in observing regulations. Does Colette's clearly disciplinary attitude arise from her own temperament or from the Colettine school? A comparison with Brother Henry de Baume's work may help answer this.

THE WRITINGS OF BROTHER HENRY DE BAUME

The writings of Brother Henry are particularly interesting since they include both legislative and spiritual texts. The deep understanding between Brother Henry and Colette that served the same reforming mission makes these writings even more valuable.

---

[30] Cf. Part 3.
[31] *A.F.H.*, XVIII and XIX, 80-81 and note 7.

Biography and Bibliography

Brother Henry de Baume is still not well-known. Contemporary accounts leave him in the reformer's shadow. When he is mentioned, it is mostly in relation to Colette, as we have seen in our study of the *Legendae* of Pierre de Vaux and Perrine. Sister Katherine Rufiné, in a text written around 1492, the original of which has been lost, gives an account of her memories of the first disciples of Colette.[32] The *Hesdin Memoir* also names him.[33] A *Vita* from the end of the fifteenth century[34] gives little objective information, but, within the tradition of medieval *Legendae*, it testifies to the relative renown of Brother Henry as one of the first and leading artisans of the reform.[35]

He was born in 1367 in Burgundy, to a noble family in the service of Philip the Bold.[36] After studying the "arts" and theology, he took the Franciscan habit and joined the French reform movement. Katherine Rufiné says that he came from the convent of Mirebeau in Poitou. He could have met Colette through Brother Pinet of Hesdin. When the latter died, Henry became Colette's adviser and confessor. Perrine reports that, when he was preaching in Picardy, Colette wrote to him from her cell (*Vita*, 249), calling him to her side. It was certainly Henry who involved Blanche of Geneva, niece of the deceased Clement VII, in the joint plan to visit Benedict XIII in Nice and to found a monastery. Blanche accommodated the newly professed nun and some companions in half of her castle in the outskirts of Frontenay, Franche-Comté.[37] From 1406-1407, Brother Henry's work was combined with that of Colette as reformer.

---

[32] U. D'Alençon, *A.F.H.*, III, 82-86.//
[33] Archives of Amiens monastery.
[34] U. D'Alençon, *A.F.H.*, II, 601-07.
[35] We will mention later the *Bull. Franc.*, VII (Rome, 1904) and the *Bull. Franc.*, nova series, I (1929).
[36] This largely reproduces the first part of our monograph from *Histoire des Saints et de la sainteté chrétienne*, VII, 117-25.
[37] U. D'Alençon, "Introduction," *Les Vies de Sainte Colette*, XXXVIII.

He became her man of business, responsible for building monasteries, and went with her on her journeys. He was also concerned with the spiritual formation of the sisters. After 1429, his work slowed because of health problems, though it was said that Colette cured him at Castres. Pierre de Vaux then replaced him in the business of the reform. Henry de Baume played a significant role. From within the First Order, he was appointed visitator and superior of all the monasteries of the Colettine reform.

In 1427, the general minister of the Order, Antoine de Massa,[38] made him vicar general for some Colettine convents in Burgundy. This appointment was later confirmed by Antoine's successor, William of Casals.[39] From these convents, friars were recruited to work in the service of Colette's daughters.[40] This branch of friars was relatively independent, with the right to receive novices and issue testimonial letters for ordinations or the faculty to hear confession. These friars could not, however, hold chapters. Henry died on February 23, 1439 (1440 by the present calendar) in Besançon. Contrary to monastic practice, he was buried within the enclosure in the chapter hall. H. Lippens offers the following detail:

> ... in our time, it seemed appropriate to begin a process in the court of Rome to recognize the longstanding cult of Blessed Henry.

The new office book of the Order does not, however, mention this recognition.

H. Lippens provides a very controversial critical study of the *corpus*.[41] Henry's contemporaries describe him as a prolific writer, and posterity has ascribed many works to him (from those of Saint Bonaventure to those of Thomas à Kempis and

---

[38] *A.F.H.*, III, 95.

[39] *A.F.H.*, II, 453-55.

[40] H. Lippens, "Henry de Baume, coopérateur de sainte Colette," *Sacris Erudiri*, I, 233.

[41] H. Lippens, "Henry de Baume, coopérateur de sainte Colette," 252-56.

Gerson), even confusing him with the Carthusian Hugues de Baume. Authentic writings of Henry de Baume cannot be assessed with any certainty, since original manuscripts for several of those attributed to him are not available. We are thus more cautious than H. Lippens on some items.

At the moment, we have the Statutes considered below, an autograph letter to the abbess of Besançon at Easter 1420,[42] and some prayers published by a historian of the Order in the seventeenth century.[43] There are several meditations and treatises in the *Clarisses* dossier in the Besançon municipal library, some of which are probably his. The archives of the monastery of Gand have an exhortation on the religious life very similar to that known as Colette's *Testament*, an ordinary business letter, and an exhortation. These items clearly share the same spirituality and were accepted very early as being written by Brother Henry. From this perspective, they reveal the spirituality of the Colettine world.

The Main Elements of Henry's Spirituality

We will primarily deal with texts covering religious life, more specifically fraternal life, which actually dominates the *Writings* we have at our disposal and which are believed to be by Brother Henry or accepted early on as his. These are the Letter to the Abbess of Besançon, a text called "*Exhortation on religious life,*"[44] a *Treatise on the spiritual life,* and a *Meditation on our Savior's life and death, fifteen principal sufferings.*[45]

---

[42] *A.F.H.*, II, 607 ff.

[43] J. Fodéré, *Narration historique et topographique des convens de l'Ordre de Saint François et monastères Sainte Claire en la province de Bourgogne* (Lyon, 1619), 676.

[44] J. Th. Bizouard, *Histoire de sainte Colette et des Clarisses en Franche-Comté* (Besançon, 1888).

[45] *Manuscrit du catalogue de la Bibliothèque Municipale de Besançon,* XXXII (Paris, 1897), 38 and 52-53.

The Letter to the Abbess of Besançon

This is simply a letter of thanks to the abbess after a stay at the monastery. Henry seems to be writing from Auxonne, and he says he visited the sisters around Easter. The opening formula of the letter is similar to that Colette uses in her *Letters*: "... in humility and as I may, I recommend myself to you in life and death ..." The expressions use the same stereotypical fifteenth-century religious vocabulary. The body of the letter contains some counsels on the religious life – the necessity of remembering death in order to stimulate "good works that accumulate merit":

> Never doubt that death approaches; strength and life are crushed; after death, merits cannot be recovered or increased.

He recalls the theological virtues of faith, hope, and charity and a series of monastic and religious virtues he wants to see the abbess practice. Apart from the traditional virtues of patience, humility, obedience, poverty, and meditation, it is worth noting that "zeal for perfection" is balanced by "the spirit of moderation."

These virtues are also those stressed in the *Statutes*, as we will see. The *Letter* ends on a more familiar note: Brother Henry asks for someone to send to Poligny (where he has to go, no doubt)

> the cloak and the fur jacket I left at Besançon and if you please the purse that was given to me for my needs, for the needs of our journey.

Then come greetings to the father confessor and to lay friends of the monastery, including in particular "our good friend Hanoquin," also named in the *Vita* of Pierre de Vaux.

The value of this letter lies in the fact that, according to Ubald d'Alençon, it is an autograph. It therefore provides some immediate insight into the spiritual and human personality of Colette's companion. He is primarily concerned with teaching within a typical spiritual context marked by the reminder of death and the need to gain merit before the inevitable end. The overall tone is both affectionate and familiar (my "gentle and humble daughter," "to all your beloved daughters"; the sisters of Auxonne "to whom I have warmly recommended you; those bound indissolubly by charity, I recommend you to all"). It reveals the links among reformed monasteries and gives the sense of a whole group of devoted lay people around the monastery itself.

Texts on the Religious Life:
The *Exhortation* and the *Treatise*

The *Exhortation* mainly covers community life, regulated by the "labor of the community" and divine service, that is the office (371). Silence is compulsory, but the nuns may speak of "God, the Rule, salvation of the soul, briefly." Brother Henry is chiefly concerned with rooting out "bad language" that causes "murmuring, disparagement, division, and dissension." He recommends a method quite similar to that used in the *Constitutions* to preserve peace and unity in the community, mentioning the canonical visitation. This concern he has in common with Colette demonstrates the authenticity of the text. A sister who criticizes another must be reprimanded. She who witnessed it

> ... must afterwards humbly speak to the abbess who will tell her (the guilty sister) her fault (in the refectory) ... and will command her to ask pardon of the sisters and kiss their feet, or another penance according to the severity of the offence: Thus commands and recommends Our Lord (372).

This command seems more of an inference from a particular spiritual context. A reference to Francis may be found in a statement such as:

> True charity wishes that one should say of another only what one would wish to hear of oneself (373),

but the clause changes its orientation: "take care here." The punishment accepted is a sign of humility.

It is interesting to compare John Capistrano's idea of the attitude to be taken to a sister who uses "proud or injurious words." He asks the abbess to humble herself still further to "win back the lost sheep." Brother Henry says that the guilty sister must be "accused before the mother as a duty, [and that she] should be punished according to her fault." The reason for this is that correction here below avoids "the frightful and horrible punishment from the judgment of the much-feared Jesus Christ." It is preferable, thinking of his Passion,

> ... to bear trials and sickness to avoid perpetual torments, and more certainly obtain the sovereign good of glory (373-74).

It may be alleged that Francis of Assisi had some hard words for those dying in "mortal" sin:

> Worms eat his body so body and soul perish in this brief world and they will go to hell where they will be tortured forever.[46]

Although these words are rightly addressed to "those who do not do penance," the immense patience and tenderness recommended by Francis to his friars should be recalled.[47]

---

[46] Francis of Assisi, "Earlier Exhortation to the Brothers and Sisters of Penance," *FA:ED* 1, 43-44.

[47] We cite just two examples: "I wish to know in this way if you love the Lord and me, ... that there is not any brother in the world who has sinned—however much he could have sinned—who, after he has looked into your eyes, would ever depart without your mercy, if he is looking for mercy" ("A Letter to a Minister," *FA:ED* 1, 97) and the famous text that describes "True and Perfect Joy": A friar was rejected and beaten by the convent's doorkeeper upon asking for entry. Francis concludes the parable thus: "If I had patience and did not become upset, true joy, as well as true virtue and the salvation of my soul, would consist in this" (*FA:ED* 1, 167).

It may also be noted that, in the *Statutes,* Brother Henry seems less pessimistic about the quality of fraternal relations among the friars. No punishment is specified, and a friar unsuitable to the service of the monastery is simply expelled. This is perhaps because of the nature of the *Statutes,* a set of internal rules for a limited category of friars, those serving the nuns. One might also raise the question of punishment for the women in the context of an enclosure that does not allow expulsion. The punitive system would have tried to resolve among the sisters tensions that could generate disorder within a perpetually closed environment.

As we will see, Battista Varani chose another route – to elevate oneself spiritually to a level so bathed in charity that one does not notice the faults of others, saying in all honesty: "I live among angels."

To our knowledge, the *Treatise* remains so far unpublished. It is a pivotal text between the section on religious life and the *Meditation on the Passion* that follows. It is concerned with both religious behavior and the spiritual life itself.

It is interesting in more than one respect. While Brother Henry emphasizes once again the need for a foundation of humility in the religious and spiritual life, he twice refers explicitly to Mary's *Magnificat* (fol. 60 to 70). This Marian presence is all the more notable as it is rare among these texts as a whole, though devotion to Mary is a major factor in the spirituality of Francis and Clare.[48] Mary exclaims: "He looks on his servant in her lowliness." Thus Mary becomes a model for religious humility, along with Christ who "does the will of the one who sent him" (fol. 8).

The three virtues of love, humility, and charity are true allegorical figures. During prayer, Brother Henry advises: "speak to them in your heart," saying to them "gentle, lovely and gracious ladies ... let me know your will" (fol. 9). The Franciscan origins of these allegories may be found in Fran-

---

[48] Cf. Francis of Assisi, "Salutation of the Blessed Virgin Mary," *FA:ED* 1, 163 and all of Clare's writings, especially the "Letters."

cis's *Salutation of the Virtues*.⁴⁹ This style permeated French medieval literature, especially the *Roman de la Rose*.

For the first time in these texts there are signs of a mystical theology, teachings about the ways to union with God. But this remains only embryonic, a distant memory of scholastic teaching. It is a matter (fol. 19 and 19 v) of the "understanding of the heart," allowing the "spirit's eye" to work. Then "understanding" is placed in God, "ravished in God." One has to "become the opposite of sensual." A quotation from the Beatitudes is distorted to adopt the more moralizing tone of the text: "Blessed are the pure in heart and body, for they will see God."

The incomplete manuscript proclaims the "things" needed for religious sisters, but specifies only two of them: "… return good for evil and blessings for curses, and love your enemies." These texts have undeniable references to the Gospel and describe a religious life of undoubted quality, but they show thinking that betrays a fairly ossified cultural and religious context. A study of the next text may confirm this impression.

"Meditation on our Savior's Life, Passion, Fifteen Main Sufferings, and Death"

This text, which we have published,⁵⁰ belongs to the important genre, devotion to the Passion. After the Resurrection, Mary asks her son what were his greatest sufferings. Christ answers that he has experienced "fifteen special sufferings" (fol. 38). Before summarizing the text and picking out its features, we should note that such meditations on Christ's life seem to have originated, in terms of method and style, from the book of *"Meditations on the Life of Christ,"* written around 1305 by the Franciscan Ubertino of Casals and dedicated to a Poor Clare, Cecilia of Florence. Several histo-

---

⁴⁹ "Hail, Queen Wisdom! May the Lord protect You with Your sister, holy pure Simplicity!" (*FA:ED* 1, 164) and also the allegory of Lady Poverty, dear to Francis ("The Sacred Exchange," *FA:ED* 1, 529-54.

⁵⁰ *Revue Mabillon*, n° 5, 1994.

rians, including Émile Mâle,[51] have highlighted the influence of this work on the plastic arts and the history of western culture. For our purposes and with regard to the works of the Italian Clarisses (though to a lesser extent), we notice that this treatise on contemplation stresses the legitimacy of developments arising from the imagination. The following, rather long quotation seems to clarify Brother Henry's text:

> So that things should be engraved more deeply in memory, I will describe these scenes as if they were actually happening, as they probably would have or did happen, reconstituting them in my imagination, which has its own ways of working. We can meditate, explore, and develop Holy Scripture in any way we find useful, as long as there is nothing in it contrary to the actuality of ordinary life, justice, and doctrine, nothing contrary to faith and good morals. When, in my account, expressions appear such as: "Thus spoke and acted the Lord Jesus," ... treat my text as necessary for devout meditation.[52]

This fifteenth-century text begins with the Annunciation: Brother Henry follows the main steps in the life of Jesus, as the evangelists recount it. Then comes the account of Christ's sufferings. The first (fol. 40 v) begins: "... when you poured out your precious blood, weeping bitterly."

The second is a step back in time, since it tells of the suffering before the tomb of Lazarus. Then come the tears over Jerusalem (fol. 41). From the fourth suffering on, the text follows the stories of the Passion step by step from Judas's betrayal and Peter's denials.

The meditation rests on a description of the Passion, of the agony and death on the cross. As it did for Pierre de Vaux (the similarity is extremely important for us), the process involves visualizing, "restoring through the imagination," as

---

[51] E. Mâle, *L'Art religieux de la fin du Moyen Age en France* (Paris, 1925).
[52] Quoted in *Pro Monialibus*, n° 33, 1972.

recommended above by Ubertino of Casals. It aims to provoke emotion in the person "gazing." In the tradition of Franciscan spirituality, this kind of meditation does not appeal to the intellect but to the heart, we might say to the emotions. Thus (fol 45), when Christ was nailed to the cross, his "flesh (was) torn and cut up;[53] the saints tell how he had five thousand wounds and four hundred and fifty bruises plus fifteen." The "blood streamed down" and the "Jewish felons"[54] pressed in the "crown of thorns almost to the brain," opening up, so say the saints, sixty-two wounds in his head. The effect of raising the cross was to stretch the nerves and split the veins. With his hands and feet nailed, the blood flowed in "streams" and his fingers were broken (fol. 47). Mary had first covered her son's naked body and embraced him: her face and mouth were covered with blood. Similarly, Magdalene, with tears (more precisely, "cries") and groanings, embraced his feet and had blood all over her face and mouth. The contemplative, meditating on this, wishes to "remain in (his) wounds and drink "the stream of living water"(fol. 49).[55]

There is no reference to Christ's inner sufferings, which B. Varani would say were immeasurably worse than his physical sufferings.[56] The two authors hold measurably different positions in the history of Passion meditations. Varani does not hesitate to say that anyone who remains simply at the level of Christ's physical sufferings has not yet entered into the mystery of his agony.

A disproportionate amount of the text is devoted to the Passion and death compared to other stages of Christ's life. Fol. 38 to 40 treat of his birth and his life up to the last Supper (excluding the two lamentations on the dead Lazarus and Jerusalem. Fol. 40 v to the end of 51 v treat of the fifteen

---

[53] The image recalls Colette's vision of the child cut up on a platter and presented to the Virgin, cf. Part 1, Chapter V.

[54] This expression is repeated elsewhere. The anti-semitism typical of the Middle Ages may be noted in passing.

[55] Devotion to Christ's wounds among Franciscans reached Clare, to whom a prayer to the five wounds is attributed. Let us remember that Francis received the stigmata.

[56] B. Varani, *I Dolori mentali di Gesù*.

sufferings. Fol. 52 to 53 treat of the Resurrection, the Ascension, Pentecost, and instructions for the religious life. The Passion and death form the focal point of a meditation on Christ's life.

As a corrective, however, we observe that God is called "Father" several times. The idea of divine justice applied to Christ in the place of sinners does not appear. The purpose is different, i.e., to arouse compassion in order to achieve conversion of life.

Another interesting feature should be stressed. The division into fifteen sufferings evokes what would become the sorrowful mysteries of the rosary: the agony, the crucifixion, etc., and also an initial design for the Way of the Cross, both the stations themselves and the style of the prayer. For example in the tenth suffering (fol. 46 v), when Christ meets his mother and the daughters of Jerusalem, the pain of seeing his suffering mother causes Christ to fall on the road to Calvary and the "holy women" wipe his face.

The prayers, in the style of the "stations," have a didactic purpose. Christ remains silent before Pilate: "By your silence, may I keep my mouth from all evil words" (fol. 45 v); the face of Christ on the "towel" used by the "holy ladies": "Please imprint these great sufferings on my heart and my soul" (fol. 47). For Brother Henry, devotion to the Passion remained caught in a spiritual movement that relied considerably on emotion.

Henry de Baume, not an innovator, was seemingly ignorant of the Rheno-Flemish mystical movement that stressed a heart to heart relationship with God. Nor was he situated in the purely Franciscan mystical tradition. Indeed, if devotion to the Passion became traditional after the time of Francis, it was animated by a passionate fervor towards Christ, loved as a spouse who leads to the Father, as was the case for the Italian Poor Clares.

The use of allegories would also have been a fairly common feature of the most typical schools of thought at that time.

The Statutes[57]

Text and References

The single copy of the manuscript of the *Statutes* used by Father H. Lippens, was found in the monastery of the Clarisses at Gand. The learned Franciscan dates it approximately to the end of the fifteenth century. He attributes it to Brother Henry de Baume because of the ideas, style, and the name written on the text. Its value to this work lies in the fact that it was intended for the friars who had been given the special task of serving the Colettine Poor Clares. It cannot be properly compared with the *Constitutions*, since it is, of course, for "internal regulation" only. But it is nonetheless important. How did these friars, whom Colette requested, live their life? What spirituality nourished them?

These *Statutes* are subdivided into seventy-three sections, covering the relations of the friars with the monastery and the life of the little fraternity. Henry sketches out, with a few strokes, an ideal moral and spiritual picture of the Colettine friars in the service of the nuns.

First of all, let us note the references, of which there are many. These indicate the author's orientation, what influenced him, and, by default, any originality he might have had. Quotations from the *Rule* of the Friars Minor and from the *Lives* of Saint Francis dominate thirteen sections that treat of the friars' life and spirituality.[58] Obviously, there are also references to Saint Clare and to Colette's *Constitutions*, of which an extravagant description is given.

In an arena where he could have been creative since he was dealing with particular statutes, Henry instead chose to draw mainly on the legislation of the founders and the reformer. This approach was similar to that of John Capistrano, who simply commented on the *Rule*. Also like Capist-

---

[57] It seems the *Statutes* were published for the first time by H. Lippens, 261-76. We have used this author for our overall description of the work.

[58] H. Lippens, 252 and notes on the text of the *Statutes*.

rano, Brother Henry quoted from scripture, mainly the New Testament.

Interpersonal Relations and Relations with the Sisters

There were to be four friars, as specified in Saint Clare's *Rule* (XII:5). Benedict XIII allowed for two *(Quanto personae*, October 16, 1406). These must follow a religious, moral life, be honest and of mature years. The ordained friar is the preacher and confessor. He has a *socius* alongside him. The other two are lay brothers, responsible for seeking alms for the sisters.[59]

A distinction can be made between the religious life as such and the relationships of the friars with each other, with the sisters, and with those who frequented the monastery. Brother Henry draws a picture of his ideal friar.

The religious life of the friars was governed by recitation of the divine office, including matins (§54), and had the features of conventual life – silence in the refectory, the chapter of faults (§34), and prayers for the dead (§22). The friars were to read and internalize their *Rule* and Saint Francis's *Testament*.

Once the ordained friars had completed their service to the nuns, "all were to withdraw to their appointed cell nearby,... free to devote themselves to prayers, meditations, solitude, and evangelical silence" (§17).[60] The lay brothers said their office with the *Pater*, meditating on Christ's passion, thinking of their high vocation, and praying for the salvation of the living and the dead (§18).

Benedict XII's legislation had been extended in 1316 to cover monastic practice as previously lived in the Order. Thus, Brother Henry de Baume was only adapting this practice to a smaller fraternity. The emphasis was placed on a contemplative life of silence and meditation (§38). The sub-

---

[59] In accordance with the *Rule* of Saint Clare, chap. XII.

[60] ...*omnes fratres, in locis stantes reteirant se ad eoum cellam assinatam ... vacando orationi, meditationi, solitudini ac silencio evangelico.*

ject of Christ's passion was taken up again in two other places (§33) with a false reference to the *Rule*.

The friars are to live in peace. Lay brothers must not go to the trouble of learning to read, according to the wish of Francis (§45), but rather they should strive to "possess the spirit of the Lord and his holy work." Capistrano's attitude to this subject is more open, as we have seen.

Brother Henry places a strong emphasis on brotherly love, especially towards the sick. Friars must love each other in mutual and sincere charity. As Francis recommends, lay brothers must show great reverence for ordained friars because they are ministers of the Eucharist. He recalls the *Rule*:

> If a mother loves and nourishes her daughter in the flesh, how much more should a friar love his fellow in the spirit (ch. VI).

The sick person is the image of Christ who suffered so much for us. Like Christ, he must suffer his weakness patiently (§46).

Current and future friars must help the sisters spiritually and in their "corporal and temporal" needs (§26), thus imitating Jesus Christ who "for us was obedient even to death (Phil 2:8). Entrance into the enclosure was governed by the *Constitutions*, hence the reference to Colette (§15). The ordained friar was to serve by celebrating mass and hearing confessions. The lay brother was to beg alms and, no doubt, deal with municipal authorities and benefactors.

Certain points clearly show a shared viewpoint with Colette: scrupulous observance of the Sabbath (§8) as Pierre de Vaux reports to be one of the reformer's constant concerns (cf. *Vita*, 211); confession and communion as often as required by the *Constitutions* (§9 and §10), i.e., every fortnight for the former and every Sunday for the latter, as well as when prescribed by the *Rule* (seven times a year); observing strict poverty, perhaps even more severely marked than for the reformer. The friars are to have two silver chalices, but no silver reliquary. The presence of the body of Christ is enough (§61). Under no circumstances may wax candles be sold, since Christ chased the sellers out of the temple (§62). The confessor must never allow the sisters to own cockerels, chickens, pigs, or other domestic animals, while in chapter X of the *Constitutions*, Colette permits flocks of livestock. Without going into detail, she says that the sisters may have the use of the things required for divine office and mass. Both reformers insist on obedience (§27): religious must be submissive to all creatures.

A certain relationship existed with the faithful. The Sunday sermon was to be short, simply proclaiming the truths of God and "holy mother Church" (an expression of Saint Francis), teaching about vices and virtues, about punishment and heavenly glory. When the friars spoke, their conversation was to be honest. Everywhere and always they were to set a good example.

They were to guard themselves, inside and out, against women (as in chapter XII of the *First Rule*), nurturing the fear and love of God. They were never to rely on their own strength (§53). One finds here, more concisely than in John Capistrano, a truly male expression of an attitude towards women.

The Moral and Spiritual Picture of the Friar Minor

No doubt Brother Henry recalled that, as in Matthew 7:13, the way is narrow; but several times (§68, §40, §75) he collected scattered elements from the *Statutes* to reiterate his conviction and desire. The friar minor must have deep humility and the simplicity of a dove; he must practice the strictest poverty, as Christ did, set a good example, and give encouragement; he must pray in secret and continually (Matt 6:6), observe the *Rule*, overcome temptations, never give in to natural inclination, prefer others to himself, never judge, etc.

In the last but one paragraph, he summarizes the friar's charter for life, quoting the *incipit* of the *Rule,* which contains the whole:

To observe the Holy Gospel of Our Lord Jesus Christ, living in obedience, without appropriating anything and in chastity.

While individual creativity is much less marked in Brother Henry than in Colette, his spirituality is truly Franciscan. One of the terms most frequently used is *humilitas,* constantly referring to the Gospel, as Francis himself does. However, more emphasis is placed on the monastic life, which is not so clear in the *Rule* where fraternal life, apart from what is prescribed, is almost never mentioned. His return to the *Rule* and to the spirituality of Francis was taking place within the limitations of the schema of his time. One good example is the lack of information on the work of individuals as practiced by Saint Francis and his friars. From the thirteenth century onward, the Order was quick to depart from this path laid out by the founder.

Finally, although the picture of the "true friar minor" is sketched out, that of the guardian of the friars is not. We have seen that John Capistrano was concerned to draw a detailed portrait of the abbess. Brother Henry, for his part, governed the life of a small fraternity, not a large, numerically important community.

This fraternity, as envisioned by Colette and Henry, would lead an austere and fervent life of devotion and evangelical virtue in the service of the enclosed nuns. It certainly needed Brother Henry's deep humility and self-effacement in Colette's wake to encourage the friars to leave their own community and live in the shadow of a women's monastery. This may be perhaps one of the reasons why Colette placed such importance on the independence of "her" reform within the much larger Franciscan Observance movement.

It seems that, while Brother Henry had ideas similar to Colette's as regards the practices of the women's community, his attitude towards the friars' was somewhat different. As regards the nuns, he bowed to the influence of the reformer, possibly believing that she knew better than he the mysteries of women's monastic life. In his instructions to the sisters, he followed her way without taking sufficient account of the text of Clare's *Rule*, which had quite a different tone.

WORKS INTENDED FOR THE LAITY

Gerson and His Sisters (1363-1429)

There is clear value in comparing Colette's project with various writings of Franciscan authors previously studied. This allows us to assess the demands of the monastic life while taking into account what was expected of fervent Christians in general and to evaluate the originality of monastic spirituality as compared to that of the laity.

The French theologian, Gerson, wrote letters and short pieces to his younger sisters, whom he firmly advised to remain virgins and to lead an intense Christian life, the features of which he himself described. He insisted on the "excellence of virginity" in a text with this title.[61] For them it is the state that "... will be the most profitable and most agreeable in this mortal and brief pilgrimage." As eldest brother, he used his moral authority to stress that, since the friars have chosen celibacy, "... why can you not be in a similar state?" As a consequence, all but one of his sisters remained at home unmarried, since Gerson did not approve of convents. Clearly he made the decision for his sisters. This was the medieval context in which parents could give their daughters to Saint Colette. The girl had almost no free choice.

Other texts aimed to organize the lives of his sisters and help in their spiritual progress, such as: *Nine considerations* (1399), *Eleven commandments* (1401), *Letter from Bruges* (winter 1391-1400), the *Spiritual Dialogue* (around 1406-

---

[61] *Oeuvres*, VII, 416-21, and Fledwidge, "Relations de famille dans la correspondance de Gerson," *Revue Historique*, CCLXXI, (1984), 3-23.

1407), which discusses twelve points for the seven days of the week.[62] As in Brother Henry de Baume, there are always detailed instructions.

In his writings, Gerson aimed to form his sisters in a life of prayer and a Christian life of obedience, humility, and chastity. We find the common topics of overcoming temptation and carnal pleasure, "battle" as a feature of the spiritual life, and demons who assail the soul.[63] God is a harsh judge who punishes sinners severely. The consequent salvific fear moves one to avoid sin and thus be saved from hell. The traditionally monastic theme began to penetrate the spiritual literature being written in the vernacular for women. Thus it enjoyed a wide readership:

> The dominant thought of death would remove and limit the sad and painful lust of the world and replace it with the sweet and religious pleasure of the things of the other time and of divine love, first making hateful and chasing away every sin.[64]

In this constant fight against temptation and the pleasures of the world, the sign of the cross is

> the sign of the victory of the sovereign king in the battle against vices and especially against the power of the prince of darkness.[65]

In Pierre de Vaux, the sign of the cross echoes the miracle of the bread marked with this sign in Clare's *Vita*. It also dispels demons and brings about spectacular cures. Gerson, however, stays within the limits of the spiritual life, not mentioning miracles that may be obtained through this sign.

His description of the inner life emphasizes the believer's anguish before the severity of the sovereign judge. In the face

---

[62] *Oeuvres*, respectively II, 1-3; II, 55-57; II, 14-17 and VII, 158-93.
[63] *Oeuvres*, II, 15.
[64] *Oeuvres*, VII, 162.
[65] *Oeuvres*, VII, 172.

of this "very strict judge,"⁶⁶ the dread of damnation rises up: "... can we hope for salvation when so few will be saved, and most condemned?"

There is one essential difference here, compared to the underlying spirituality of Pierre de Vaux's *Vita* of Colette: the repeated affirmation of the "very great frailty" of the human being.⁶⁷ It is not the heroic, ascetic achievements of physical penance that will stop the wrath of God, but God's mercy. Gerson's theological training means that he avoids the dolorist views found in the texts of Brother Henry de Baume and the excessive importance given to the physical sufferings of the Passion. The biblical, scholastic, and profane learning of the university chancellor shows through in many places and gives his analysis of the inner life quite another tone, a remarkable doctrinal solidity.

Although the *Spiritual Dialogue* is addressed to women, who have less learning than priests, Gerson shows how the senses are doorways to the soul and how one temptation gives rise to another yet greater⁶⁸ through a sort of cause and effect chain. He avoids abstract and overly intellectual discourse, however, by the "remedies" he offers: for instance, the word of God that "nourishes the soul" and concern for the poor:

> The outrageous amount you spend, perhaps on one dinner, would be enough to feed many poor people who have bread to eat only with great difficulty.⁶⁹

In order to avoid abstract meandering or spiritual "laziness" in prayer, Gerson structures each day by designating a precise theme (Letter to his sisters in Bruges). For example: "On Monday I consider the holy angels and the benefits they give us." Tuesday is for "prophets, patriarchs, apostles,

---

⁶⁶ *Oeuvres*, VII, 169.
⁶⁷ *Oeuvres*, VII, 171.
⁶⁸ *Oeuvres*, VII, 187.
⁶⁹ *Oeuvres*, VII, 191.

disciples, and evangelists."⁷⁰ He briefly develops this general topic, providing a concrete "exercise" affecting behavior:

> On Tuesday, I especially ask for the gift of knowledge, to know how to conquer my frailty, my end, my state, that of my friends, and so that I might come to the third beatitude which is for holy weeping and devout tears and against sinfulness in life, and ask God to pardon my faults, as I pardon those of my neighbors, which is the third request.

It seems, then, that some elements of the monastic life apply to the lay life. The pre-eminence of virginity over marriage is one. When Pierre de Vaux emphasized Colette's preference for virginity to the point of not loving Saint Anne before she is granted a special vision of her, he was transposing into a *Legend* a cultural fact that had become a "topos" for the priests, even though it could not have been a historical truth in the life of the holy woman of Picardy. Extension of monastic experience into the Christian life, a well-known feature of the Middle Ages, can also be seen in the subject of the reminder of death and in daily religious piety.

On the other hand, the *Devotio Moderna* paid much greater attention to "the inner life" than did the spirituality of the Colettine movement. The discretion of the former regarding paranormal manifestations of devotion and marvelous events and its theological grounding make it a more valuable source of teaching than the writings of Brother Henry de Baume. It tends to release the laity from a mystical straitjacket, reduced merely to a set of observances. Once having accepted a commitment to a life given fully to Christ, lay people nourished on such teaching were spiritually privileged compared to the nuns of the reform.

---

[70] *Oeuvres*, II, 15.

The Rule of Saint Antonino (1389-1459)[71]

Saint Antonino, Archbishop of Florence from 1456 to 1459, was a Dominican who exercised authority in his Order. Hence this Rule, written for a Florentine practitioner, might be expected to reflect Antonino's own experience. As a preacher, he was concerned to teach and correct morals by denouncing the vices and sins hidden in human hearts. The book is in three parts:

- Purification: this involves "rooting out vice from the heart" and separating oneself from evil. Having reached perfect peace, the penitent must protect herself from flattery and from vainglory.

- Virtue: this means persevering in good, putting a curb on the tongue, and guarding the heart. Immoderate laughter is denounced, a clear reference to the life of the court. A good spiritual father and daily examen of conscience help one achieve virtue and stay in God's grace.

- The rule of life itself: this has eighteen points, governing all aspects of the daily life of a great lady who has certain worldly obligations such as "feasts, dances, jousts, and other rejoicing." The rule transposes and adapts monastic life to lay life:

Once you have, by the grace of God, taken on the religious life in your life if not in the habit, by the obedience you have promised to God and to me as his vicar in his name, you must follow everything belonging to the religious life in spiritual things, as you do for yourself in corporal things.[72]

---

[71] *Une règle de vie au XVe siècle: la mère de Laurent le Magnifique à l'école de saint Antonin*. The original work, *Opera a ben vivere*, was written, according to the manuscripts, by Dianora Tornabuoni or her sister Lucrezia, wife of Piero the Gouty, and mother of Laurent.

[72] *Une règle de vie au XVe siècle*, 173.

Some examples will suffice to show that the proposed rule fulfills its task at all points by adding the "religious" way of being in the world.[73]

The Dominican specifies how the "offices and devotions" are said:

> ... first, the office of the Virgin every day, according to normal practice, that is with the changes made according to the seasons, nocturn to matins, for the psalms and some anthems.... Then devoutly say the seven penitential psalms with the litanies. Then the little office of the Cross with sixteen *Paters*.... I think you could also say the office of the dead in this way: every day a nocturn with lauds, beginning with vespers. But if you have the time, I would recommend you say the whole of the office.[74]

---

[73] *Une règle de vie au XVe siècle,* 173. The titles of the eighteen points are explicit: Rule – Description of the rule or mode of conduct you must follow in your life, depending on your rank, throughout the year:
1 – How and in what times you must fast.
2 – Times of the year you must go to confession.
3 – Times of the year you must receive communion.
4 – When you must take the discipline.
5 – When you must give alms.
6 – Offices you must say. Seasons and times you must say them.
7 – Reading.
8 – How you must pray.
9 – When and how you must say the office of the Madonna.
10 – What you have to do when you are in church, at your offices and at Mass.
11 – Meditations on the Passion of Christ, with sixteen Paters.
12 – What to do in Lent, on the prescribed feasts, on Saints days, and for a pardon.
13 – Feasts, dances, jousts, and other rejoicings.
14 – How you must bless the table morning and evening, and say grace after meals.
15 – What you must do after dinner. How to arrange your house.
16 – How each day you must undertake some manual work.
17 – What you must do after supper.
18 – What you must do before bed.
General conclusion to the work – To show you what you have undertaken.

[74] *Une règle de vie au XVe siècle,* 149.

A special chapter describes in detail how to begin the office, what invitatory psalm to say, and so on. Colette recommends that the nuns should also say the office of the Virgin, the penitential psalms, and the office of the dead. For this, the nuns had an associated obligation to say it in gratitude for their benefactors, who also, on their death, requested masses in perpetuity. Now Saint Antonino's "Philothea" was not bound by such obligations. The Christian Middle Ages was concerned with the salvation of souls, resulting in devotions and religious practices.

Vocal prayer took precedence in the time available, as it did for Colette. Some time was, however, devoted to mental prayer: "If you have a moment of rest, I would advise you to put yourself to prayer, seeking to pray in your mind."[75] As it may be difficult to concentrate, the author recommends turning very quickly to meditation on the life of Christ.

The mention of mental prayer should be noted as it is rare in Colette and her entourage. Saint Antonino thought that lay people were not ready to practice it, although at that time in Italy, the Italian Clarisses were beginning to explore the paths to union with God. It had to wait for Teresa of Avila to affirm vigorously that lay people, too, could have such experiences and at the very highest level. (Rheno-Flemish mysticism seemed to reserve this for religious sisters, while the *Devotio Moderna* only gradually accepted these realities).

Meditation on the Passion was to be practiced every day. Although the time available might be short because of family obligations, the Passion should "always be present in thought."[76] When time allowed, one was to meditate "on the hands" of the Crucified one, "on his side," "on the divine body," on the "Passion of the mother of God," "on the face of Christ," on the "placing in the tomb." Saint Antonino develops every point.

The discipline must be taken

---

[75] *Une règle de vie au XVe siècle,* 156.
[76] *Une règle de vie au XVe siècle,* 156.

... every Friday in Advent and Lent and on the eve of days on which there is fasting or communion. It is suggested it should be taken every Friday.[77]

The penitent could herself decide when to go to confession, as long as she observed the obligation to go once a month. General permission was given for more frequent confession, if it was felt necessary.

Communion would be received twelve times a year.[78] Antonino makes an interesting point here by hastening to add:

... if you can do it without too much ostentation. Perhaps, my daughter, you may find it is too often.... I would love you to be able to receive communion every Sunday. However, because of your rank, I dare not instruct you on this matter in any way.[79]

The archbishop aligns the practice of communion for a pious laywoman with that of the religious. The monthly frequency might risk comment from those around her even more than daily devotions in church.

We point out a feature already noted in Pierre de Vaux – the importance of the gaze, both as regards the people and the host. On the way to church and in church during mass the penitent must not look at anyone and must keep her gaze lowered. She only raises it at the moment of the elevation.[80]

The rhythm of the day, built around reciting the offices, attending mass, and engaging in devotions, must give way to household duties that have to be performed diligently in order to leave the spirit free to attend to the things of God. Almsgiving and manual work must also be practiced: "Never waste a moment, and always be busy at some useful occupation."[81]

---

[77] *Une règle de vie au XVe siècle*, 177-78.
[78] P. De Vaux, *Vita*, 102 and 113.
[79] *Saint Antonino, Rule*, 146.
[80] *Saint Antonino, Rule*, 158.
[81] *Saint Antonino, Rule*, 177.

Meals would also be consecrated to prayer, preceded by the *Benedicite*, the *Gloria Patri*, and then the *Pater* followed by a spoken prayer. Behavior at table was regulated. Since there could not be reading aloud as for religious, it was appropriate to put "nothing in [the] mouth before saying an *Ave Maria*." After the meal, rather than taking part in laughter, it would be better to withdraw to say the thanksgiving: praying "the *miserere* psalm, the *Gloria*, the *Pater* and the *Dispersit*."[82] On fast days the supper prayers were used instead.

Perhaps because he is aware of the excess of spoken prayers and the risk they might involve, Saint Antonino concludes:

> God ... does not consider the number of our prayers, but the sentiment in which we say them.... I must tell you that the perfection of prayer does not consist in the number of words, as people believe, but in saying it devoutly.[83]

The day ends by sprinkling holy water on oneself, on the bed, and around the bedroom with a suitable prayer, and finally by making the sign of the cross on oneself and over the bed.[84] Fear of the devil and of carnal thoughts is mentioned as being an unavoidable occurrence at such times. Colette, as we have seen, required the vicar to visit the cells every evening to check that the sisters were there and sprinkle them with holy water.

It is difficult, then, to separate the lay Christian life described here from the monastic model that permeated the West in the Middle Ages. Gerson, perhaps more aware of the *Devotio Moderna* movement, was in a sense its precursor, even though the main strands of monastic spirituality are present in his writings.

His experience as a priest may have helped him. His text demonstrates that, apart from the vows, the life of a pious

---

[82] *Saint Antonino, Rule*, 172-76.
[83] *Saint Antonino, Rule*, 184.
[84] *Saint Antonino, Rule*, 185.

laywoman and that of a nun were, in fact, fairly similar. From her youth, a young woman (as in the case of Colette, Catherine of Bologna, Battista Varani, and many other daughters of great houses) received intense preparation for monastic life. The severe austerity of the Colettines was not qualitatively different from the daily lives of devout laywomen. The psychological break with the ordinary environment was thus less drastic. Despite enclosure, nuns and this significant section of the pious laity lived in the same spiritual and moral world.

Conclusion

Study of the major texts of the Colettine and Italian reforms produces a number of observations. In France, the structured and cohesive reform was intended to produce religious sisters who were firmly rooted in Observant practice, virtuous, and diligent in praying the office. However, in an impoverished spiritual context, they risked fossilization and confusion between the letter and the spirit of the law. Structures took the place of the monastic life. Once they had crossed the threshold of the enclosure, the sisters seemed no longer free to own their own choices. Deeply evangelical individuals were needed to breathe mysticism into these restrictive structures.

Italy, a more cultured and humanist society, adopted more diversified structures that emphasized the primacy of the person. The relative fragility of the structures, more dependent on the vitality of the First Order, was compensated for by an intense monastic life of deep fraternal charity, giving the Italian reform a color of its own.

The two reforms complemented each other in terms of the Order as a whole. For historical and cultural reasons, each seemed to favor a different aspect of the founder's Rule: monastic structures, on the one hand, and a fervent, evangelical spirit on the other. Moreover, in France, one woman made the rules, and the friars, devoted to her, took responsibility for maintaining her monasteries and the spiritual life of the sisters. This schematic pairing was reversed in Italy. There the women gave themselves up to the *vacare ad Deum* [freedom for God] in a passionate search for Christ, and the friar minor John Capistrano (though to a lesser extent than Colette) made the rules and tried to structure the burgeoning reform movement.

Comparing texts written for the laity allows us to evaluate the significance of these reform movements in the fifteenth century Church. The reformed branches of the orders, because of their strong structures and their legal and spiritual centralization, were at the vanguard of the general reform movement. Nonetheless they were closely associated with the life of the laity in individual and demanding initiatives. If only for their own recruitment, monasteries were reliant on the lay environments being particularly committed to renewal of the Christian life and to the deepening of personal faith. As regards the exigencies of ascetic life, the religious and lay were equivalent. As for the spiritual life, Gerson's writings for his sisters raised the Christian life to the level of that of the nuns.

Colette's reform, while remarkable, formed part of a general movement, rather than being innovative in either structures or spiritual renewal.

CHAPTER 3

THE ITALIAN CLARISSES OF THE FIFTEENTH CENTURY

The character of the female reform in Italy was different from the Colettine reform. It was more extensive, geographically and temporally, and therefore slower. It lasted throughout the century, while in France, the second generation of Colettines was already spreading by 1450.

The initial impetus came from the Observant friars who had begun a reform of the First Order at the end of the fourteenth century. Their institutional or fraternal links with the Clarisses helped spread the ideal of a radical return to Clare's initial project among communities governed by the rule of Urban IV.[1] This explains the multiplicity of centers and the relatively slow spread of the reform. In France, it was unified around Colette, and expanded by means of new foundations placed immediately under the first *Rule* and the Colettine constitutions. In Italy, however, the friars did not develop a general plan. When Saint John Capistrano produced his constitutions in 1445 towards the end of his life, he was simply responding to a request from the monastery of Mantua. Bernadino of Siena (1380-1444), a great preacher throughout the peninsula, visited towns to preach against heresy. The Urbanist nuns, touched by these calls to a poorer and more fervent way of life in the footsteps of Christ, spontaneously

---

[1] The rule of Urban IV had become almost the only one followed by the Clarisses. Only half a dozen monasteries had retained the *Rule* of Saint Clare, known as the First Rule, with its privilege "of the highest poverty."

undertook to return to a stricter religious life, without immediately abandoning the rule of Urban IV.[2]

The Main Centers of Reform in Italy[3]

1   1400-1420 – SAINT URSULA of MILAN:
* Foundations   *Corpus Christi* of MANTUA 1420
                     Corpus Domini of PESARO 1439
* Reform   S. Clare of Miliarino or
                     St Joseph at MANTUA 1435.

2   1420 – CORPUS CHRISTI of MANTUA:
                     S .Jean de la Vallée at VERONA 1424
                     Corpus Christi at FERRARA 1431
* Foundations   S. Bernardino at PADUA 1439-1446
                     La Cella at TREVISO 1439
                     S. Marie des Anges at FELTRE 1492

* Reforms   S. Guillaume at FERRARA 1439
                     S. Claire of MURIANO 1441

* Adoption   S. Claire at RAVENNA 1439
 of practices   St Paul at RAVENNA 1439
                     Corpus Christi of AQUILA 1447
                     at REGGIO-EMILIA 1454
                     at PARMA 1458.

3   1425 – SAINTE LUCIE of FOLIGNO :
* Foundation   S. Marie of COLOMATA 1449
* Reforms   *Monteluce* of PERUGIA 1448
                     S. Claire of NARNI 1504

4   1431 – CORPUS CHRISTI of FERRARA:
                     at CREMONA 1449

---

[2] At Alexandria, in Piedmont, Clarisses "mended their ways so well following the reproaches of Saint Bernadino of Siena that they were then given the task of reforming the convents of Savona, Pavia, Savigliano, and Asti and of founding the monastery of Casale-Montferrato." R. Pratesi, "Le Clarisse in Italia," in *Studi e Cronaca del VII° Centenario di Santa Chiara d'Assisi* (Assise, 1954): 351.

[3] This table is reproduced with the permission of M. Colette Roussey, O.S.C., from *Regard sur l'histoire des Clarisses, pro manuscrito* (Paray-le-Monial, 1982).

* Foundations		*Corpus Domini* of BOLOGNA 1456
		S. Bernardino of FERRARA 1510-1516
5	1439 – CORPUS DOMINI of PESARO:	
* Foundation		S. Barthélemy of ANCONA 1444
6	1448 – MONTELUCE of PERUGIA:	
* Foundation		S. Claire of URBINO 1455
* Reform		SS. Cosmos and Damien at ROME 1451
		S. Chiara Novella at AREZZO 1492
		S. Claire of MONTEFALCO 1500
* Formation		S. Claire of GUBBIO 1517
		S. Pontien of SPOLETA 1520
7	1458 – MONTEVERGINE of MESSINA:	
* Foundations		at REGGIO DI CALABRIA 1472
		Montevergine of PALERMO 1498

S. Claire of URBINO founded at CAMERINO 1484 and CAMERINO founded at FERMO 1505.

Sometimes, with the help of the friars, some young women would found a monastery.[4] Other women, already living a style of religious life as tertiaries, adopted, with the support of the Observant friars, the Rule of Saint Clare. (At the end of the fourteenth and beginning of the fifteenth centuries, they had the option of taking vows and saying the office.) Thus was the ground fertile for the renewal of the nuns.

GENERAL FEATURES OF THE REFORM

The Main Centers

One of the first and most important centers of reform was the monastery of St. Ursula in Milan. Founded by the Augustinians in 1341, it adopted the Rule of Urban IV at the end of the fourteenth century. The community eagerly took up the practice of this rule and was spiritually influential,

---

[4] For instance, at Bergamo in 1422, cf. Pratesi, 353.

especially after the entry of blessed Felicia Meda (1398). At the request of Paola Malatesta, and with the advice of Saint Bernadino of Siena, some sisters left there in 1420 to found the monastery of *Corpus Christi* in Mantua.

Corpus Christi in Mantua very quickly became a new and flourishing center of reform. On their arrival in Mantua, the nuns from Milan found, in addition to two monasteries of Urbanist Clarisses, a group of pious women who would form the core of the new foundation. They lived under the Rule of Saint Clare, observed personal and collective poverty, and were guided by Observant friars. The community soon generated five other foundations, as well as the reform of the two existing monasteries.

The monastery of Saint Lucia of Foligno was founded in 1425 under the Rule of Urban IV, although there had already been three monasteries of Clarisses there since 1216, 1225, and 1252 respectively.[5] This monastery was founded initially by five religious sisters from one family, who had fled in distress from the town of Sulmona because of political disturbances.[6] They were taken in by the Bishop of Foligno. One of them, Alexandra (d. 1458), was elected abbess three times. She began to write the chronicles of the monastery, which is one of the most precious documents of the Franciscan fifteenth century. Although it was Urbanist originally, the community asked to be transferred to the jurisdiction of the Observants, and it was zealous in living Clare's ideal. It grew rapidly with strong vocations and, in turn, founded or refounded other communities.

The monastery of *Corpus Christi* in Ferrara was founded in 1431 by Mantua together with a small community of pious women from Ferrara who followed an Augustinian spirituality. This foundation became one of the most important centers in Northern Italy thanks to the quality of its spiritual life. One of its outstanding members was Saint Catherine Vigri,

---

[5] Saint Clare died in 1253. For foundation dates for these three monasteries, cf. Pratesi.

[6] Archives of monastery, A. Fantozzi, "Documenti interno alla B. Cecilia Coppoli...," *A.F.H.*, XIX, 78, note 1.

future founder of the monastery of Bologna, which also took the name, *Corpus Christi*. The Ferrara monastery would go on to found two other monasteries, including another in Ferrara itself.

The Clarisses of Saint Ursula of Milan founded the monastery of Corpus Domini Pesaro in 1439. Despite opposition from other Clarisses in the town, they formed tertiaries for their regular life, and the community quickly became influential through the sanctity of three of its members: Felicia Meda, the first abbess from Milan, Battista Malatesta, widow of the Duke of Pesaro, and Suave, daughter of the Count of Montefeltro.

When it was reformed in 1448, the monastery of Monteluce of Perugia was one of three existing in the city. It had been founded in 1218, having received the privilege of poverty in 1229 from Pope Gregory IX. But it had gradually relaxed observance of the Rule to the point that the town's authorities called on the pope to impose reform with the help of nuns from Foligno.[7] Twenty-four arrived to join the twenty-two already there. Some of these latter refused to return to observance and left to join the convent of Santa Maria degli Angeli (the third monastery having been closed down).[8] The newly formed community became one of the most vital of the reform, though no strong personalities emerged from it. It was influential in founding or reforming communities that would subsequently ask to be incorporated into the Order of Saint Clare.

The monastery of Montevergine at Messina was founded in 1458. When the first monastery of Clarisses in Messina relaxed its observance, Blessed Eustachia of Calafato (1430-1485) left with two companions to join her mother and sister, who had built the monastery of Montevergine. Despite opposition from the original monastery and the Conventual

---

[7] A. Fantozzi, "La riforma osservante dei monasteri delle clarisse nell'Italia centrale," *A.F.H.*, XXIII.

[8] Twenty years later, with no vocations and decimated by natural deaths, it was transferred to the monastery of Monteluce.

friars, the new little community adopted the Rule of Saint Clare and, in turn, made foundations in southern Italy.

The monastery of Camerino, famous for the presence of Battista Varani, is something of a separate case because of its origin. It was initially founded by a prince, Battista's father, lord of Camerino, who built it in 1484 so that his daughter, a Clarisse at Urbino, would return to the town of her birth. Battista returned, but refused the property offered by her father. She chose to live under the Rule of Saint Clare, as Saint John Capistrano reports.

At the end of the century, while the Observant friars were gaining prominence within the First Order, several communities of regular tertiaries joined the Second Order so as not to lose the benefit of the spiritual direction of these friars. This increased the number of communities living under the First Rule of Saint Clare.[9] The popes gradually put the Clarisses under the governance of the Observants or else closed down monasteries that had collapsed. Hence by the end of the fifteenth century, most nuns had returned to observance of the regular life and true fervor, although their practice of poverty varied.

The Issue of Poverty for Italian Clarisses

The issue of poverty, along with the return to observance of regular life, highlights the decisive part played by the First Order friars. Reform of the Clarisses throughout France was the work of one woman to whose service the reformed friars were devoted. However, despite many great personalities among the nuns, no one person in Italy managed or even sought to create a unified movement. Once Bernadino of Siena had started the ball rolling, the provinces of Observant friars gradually became involved with reformed

---

[9] The Observant friars of the province of Milan wrote constitutions for all Clarisses under their jurisdiction: "Ordinationi delle Monache di S. Orsola caltri Monasteri dell'Ordine de S. Clara, nella Provincia di Milano, fatte nel convento di S. Angelo l'anno 1463, e per essi dato a Monache Osservanti," quoted by P. Sevesi, "Il monastero delle clarisse in S. Apollinare di Milano," *A.F.H.,* vol. XVIII-XIX, 1925-26, 80, note 7.

or recently founded monasteries of women. These monasteries would therefore experience the effects of the fluctuations within the movement and the tensions between the return to rigor, on the one hand, and the beginnings of laxity among the friars on the other. This became all the more apparent as the Observants, initially cautious, came to see how governance of the nuns might extend their influence at the cost of that of the Conventuals.[10]

An interesting issue emerges as regards poverty for the Clarisses. Unless they adopted the strictest poverty at the time of their founding, Urbanist nuns took years to adapt to it, even when they had rediscovered their early fervor. We give two examples of this and highlight an interesting case.

Santa Lucia in Foligno[11]

Some sisters of the Monastery of Santa Lucia in Foligno (1425), influenced by Blessed Cecilia Coppoli, wanted to make their profession under the Rule of Saint Clare, meaning essentially to take a vow of poverty (without property or goods). Blessed Cecilia, the abbess, had the Clarisses of Messina, Mantua, Bologna, Ferrara, and Aquila praying for this intention for years. The Observant friars, with whom she had close links,[12] had the people pray as well.

Circumstances helped the abbess, as a need arose for the building of an infirmary. With the visitator's agreement, some of the monastery's goods were sold. A little later, the dormitory needed enlarging and the church had to be repaired. The monastery became truly poor. In 1469, with their confessor's agreement, some of the sisters took a private vow of poverty. They hoped that the whole community, linked to the Observant superiors, might profess the Rule of Saint Clare. For

---

[10] When Leo X placed the monasteries of the Second Order under their jurisdiction in 1517, he was only ratifying the almost universal situation, at least in Italy.

[11] The account is taken from A. Fantozzi, "La riforma osservante," 35ff.

[12] In 1427, Martin V put S. Lucia de Foligno under the jurisdiction of the Observants.

eight years the sisters prayed, fasted, and took the discipline for this intention.[13]

The Vicar Provincial of Perugia became alarmed, fearing that the community would not be able to survive without possessions. Sister Cecilia, to calm things down, left the monastery and went to Urbino, where she became abbess. In 1476, Pope Sixtus IV, while on a journey, visited the community. Every sister who came to kiss his feet, begged the favor of living under the First Rule. He reserved his reply, but soon sent them a bull giving his agreement. The friars, however, continued their opposition and put pressure on him to change his mind, arguing that the sisters had not been unanimous. The Roman pontiff then sent the vicar general for the Observance to question each of the sixty-two religious on the matter. In 1447 he received the profession of them all to the Rule of Saint Clare.

Saint Apollinarus of Milan

Founded around 1224-1228 by Giacoma, a companion of Agnes of Assisi, Saint Apollinarus of Milan quickly received donations and legacies and then obtained exemptions and indulgences from Gregory IX (the same pope who had supported Francis and Clare in their plans to establish the evangelical life). Over the years, it became a large, wealthy monastery, but around 1470-1472, it adopted the Observant constitutions used by other monasteries in Milan that had been founded at the instigation of Bernadino of Siena.[14] The commitments made at that time illustrate the difference between a reformed Observant monastery and an Urbanist monastery:

---

[13] A. Fantozzi, "La riforma osservante," 40: "... *per spatio de otto anni facemmo continuamente grandissime orazione, digiunii e discipline in comuno e in particulare senza numero, con molte amerissime lacrime et suspiri de cuore* [for a period of eight years, we continued the most ardent prayers, fasting and discipline together and individually, without number, with the most bitter tears and sighs of the heart]."

[14] Sevesi, "Il monastero delle clarisse in S. Apollinare di Milano," note 10.

renunciation of goods, complete enclosure, daily and nightly office, two hours of prayer a day, recitation of the penitential psalms, monthly confession and communion, fasting from the birthday of the Virgin to Easter, ... the discipline three times a week, penances imposed at the chapter, work according to capability, strict silence, humble clothing, bed of straw.

The abbess was to be re-elected every three years.[15]

But very quickly, the monastery began to receive gifts and to benefit from exemptions, kept the right of burial for pious lay people, and also received legacies for masses for the dead. It took the vigorous intervention of Saint Charles Borromeo, who promulgated ordinances in 1571, for the monastery to recover some of its influence.[16]

Blessed Illuminata Bembo (1415/18-1493)

In her biography of Saint Catherine of Bologna, *Specchio di Illuminazione*,[17] the holy abbess's companion and biographer describes Catherine's qualities, especially her charity. While still a simple nun in Ferrara, she watched over the health of her sisters. If she saw a weak or sick sister needed something, she would ask the abbess for an egg or some meat as if it was for herself. Her request was granted, but "prudently," notes the biographer, she left the shells in her place in the refectory. Throughout this period, the monastery was suffering hardship, which explains the restrictions and the embarrassment at asking something for oneself. Nonetheless, the mention of the empty shells is strange. The Rule of Saint Clare emphasizes that the sisters must be open to their fellow sisters about their needs, in complete security,

---

[15] Sevesi, "Il monastero delle clarisse in S. Apollinare di Milano," 80-81.

[16] Sevesi, "Il monastero delle clarisse in S. Apollinare di Milano," 116-20.

[17] I. Bembo, *Specchio di Illuminazione, vita di Santa Catarina da Bologna*, 1787, edizione divulgata a cure delle clarisse del Corpus Domini da Ferrare, collana serafica, I (Ferrare, 1975).

and that they must go to the abbess for what they consider is necessary. It is possible that in this monastery there was still a difference made between sisters who came from comfortable social backgrounds (like Catherine) and the rest.

This detail raises, as a secondary issue, the question of the "convent hierarchy." The Second Order monasteries, which from the end of the thirteenth century had largely become Urbanist, were very similar in appearance to Benedictine monasteries. They had possessions, and legacies to daughters from great families upon entry to the community produced different categories of sisters. The distinction Clare draws between the literate and illiterate would encourage the division of the sisters into two categories: choir sisters and others who recited *paters* for the office. These latter often did the hardest work. After the general imposition of papal enclosure and promulgation of the bull *Pericolosa* of Boniface VIII at the end of the thirteenth century, the enclosed sisters were no longer allowed to go out to beg alms, at least in theory. So another category of persons attached to the monastery was formed. These worked the land around the monastery or carried out other work and were considered *serventi* and *servitori*.[18]

The 1370 constitutions of Cardinal Philippe, the Order's protector, list these various, apparently standard, categories. It should be noted that the Cardinal specifies that the Clarisses use the Rule of Urban IV,[19] several times employing the term *sorores (sorores servitiales, sorores conversae)*. This hierarchical structure seemed to persist even after communities returned to the stricter observance of the Rule of Saint

---

[18] Including ordained friars (to celebrate mass and hear confessions) and *conversi* or lay brothers (to collect alms), there was a significant number of people living in or around a monastery, requiring considerable organisation and the necessary income. In fact, the sisters who were *conversae* continued to go out, as the 1495 constitutions of the Spanish Clarisses show *a contrario*; cf. P. Tarcisias De Azcona, "Reforma de las clarissas de Cataluña en tiempo de los Reyes católicos," *Coll. Franc.*, 27, 1957: it states that *conversae* must no longer go to dubious houses and must no longer eat meals with individuals.

[19] Wadding, *An. Min.*, VIII, 705-13, 1370.

Clare. In a document of 1439 written by William of Casals, the Order's general minister, to Felicia Meda, whom he appointed abbess of the monastery of Pesaro, we find the terms "*suore venerabili ..., familiari, serventi, conversae servitori.*" All these people owed her ready obedience as their abbess and mother.[20] We have already seen that the monastery of Saint Apollinarus of Milan adopted the Rule of Saint Clare, although somewhat late, changing its full name to include "*dell'Osservanza di santa Chiara.*" A census taken in 1501 showed that the community consisted of sixty-eight nuns, "excluding *conversae* and the infirm."[21]

One of the features of the Colettine reform was the return to a single class of sister with the removal of the extern sisters. All appear to have had a vote in elections; but because of the illiteracy still prevalent in the fifteenth century, the distinction made by Clare's Rule between sisters who recited the choral office and those who said the *paters* remained. The Italian documents quoted above seem to show clearly how the choir sisters, *moniales* and *venerabili* formed a separate category.

THE NUNS

Some Individual Clarisses

The figures of Catherine of Bologna and Battista Varani will be considered in a separate section because of the importance of their written works that enable a more accurate picture to be drawn of the spiritual movement characteristic of the Italian Clarisses. Here we will simply point out some indications of the renewal at a socio-cultural and spiritual level and highlight its richness through the number of Clarisses who illustrate it. This list of some fifteenth-century Cla-

---

[20] F. Meda, "Una insigna clarissa milanesa, la B. Felice Meda (1378-1444)," *A.F.H.*, XX, 1927, 11.

[21] Sevesi, "Il monastero delle clarisse in S. Apollinare di Milano," 81.

risses, while not claiming to be complete, includes the most notable figures of the period.

- Blessed Franceschina Guissana was an original member of the monastery of Saint Ursula, which, as we have seen, was chronologically the first to return from the Rule of Urban IV to complete Observance. She was called by Paolo Malatesta to become the first abbess of the monastery of *Corpus Christi* in Mantua, established as a convent under the Rule of Saint Clare in 1420.
- Blessed Felicia Meda (1378-1444), also an original member of Saint Ursula's in Milan, was appointed by Battista Malatesta as the first abbess of the monastery of *Corpus Christi* of Pesaro, erected in 1439.
- Battista Malatesta (1384-1448), as we saw above, withdrew to *Corpus Christi* of Pesaro. She was an outstanding figure of the Italian Renaissance, devoting herself for many years to works of piety. In 1447, she became a notable Clarisse. "She was remembered as an admirable woman in every way."[22]
- Sister Serafina entered *Corpus Christi* of Pesaro in 1457. As a young woman she had married Alessandro Sforza, when he became lord of Pesaro. He quickly abandoned her and persecuted her until she took refuge with the Clarisses. He then demanded that she should be professed to release him from the conjugal bond. Although she refused for a long time, on the grounds of the indissolubility of the marriage, she finally gave in. She was quickly elected abbess (1475) for her religious virtues and her sanctity. She died in 1478 after winning her husband to conversion. She was popularly venerated together with Felicia Meda.[23]
- Blessed Cecilia Coppoli (1426-1500), orphaned at eighteen, inherited wealth from her father, who was the senior magistrate of Perugia. She was promised in marriage to a nobleman but fled to the monastery of Saint Lucia at

---

[22] Wadding, *An. Min.*, 1447, XI, 356-57.
[23] Wadding, *An. Min.*, 1478, XIV, 241-45.

Foligno. Elected abbess there in 1449, she later served as abbess at Perugia and at Urbino. She was primarily responsible for the monastery's transfer to the First Rule, which was not without difficulty as we have seen. She is considered the soul of the reform, which she helped extend to Rome, Urbino, Favo, Pesaro, Maroni, and Perugia.[24]

–Paola Malatesta of Mantua, whom we have already met, withdrew with her two daughters to the monastery she had founded (Corpus Christi of Mantua, 1420) and was outstanding in her community for her sanctity in a life of mortification, strict asceticism, and fervent prayer.[25]

–Blessed Paola of Mantua (1443-1514) entered Corpus Christi of Mantua at the age of fifteen. Elected abbess several times, she had a deep devotion to the Eucharist.[26]

–Blessed Antonia of Florence (1400-1472) began as superior of the tertiaries, first in Foligno, then in Aquila. In 1447, assisted by Saint John Capistrano, she began to live under the Rule of Saint Clare with some companions in Aquila. She is one of the great figures of the reform.[27]

–Blessed Eustachia of Calafato (1430-1485) came from a noble Sicilian family and entered the convent in 1449 despite her father's opposition. She was notable for her austerity, long vigils at prayer, and devotion to the Passion. She later joined her mother and sister, when, in 1458, they founded the new monastery of Montevergine at Messina.

These Clarisses knew each other either because they lived in the same monastery or because they engaged in correspondence and mutual support regarding their way of life.[28] Furthermore, there was a kind of passing on of sanctity

---

[24] A. Fantozzi, "Documenti intorno alla beata Cecilia Coppoli."

[25] Wadding, *An. Min.*, 1449, XII, 41.

[26] Marie-Angèle, O.S.C., *Histoire abrégée de l'Ordre de Sainte Claire*, Vol. II (Lyon, 1906), 40.

[27] *Pro monialibus*, n° 31 and n° 34.

[28] Blessed Cecilia de Foligno corresponded with Eustachia de Calafato; cf. D. Ciccarelli, *Contributi alle recensioni degli scritti de S. Chiara*, 350 and note 11. Eustachia was canonized on June 11, 1988.

from generation to generation as can be seen by the record of dates of death and dates of entry.

Profile of Italian Observants

The Socio-cultural Environment

Most of these nuns came from illustrious families of the Italian Renaissance, as their patronymics show, and from highly cultivated backgrounds. They would have been familiar with the greatest of the humanists. The fifteenth-century Franciscans in no way discouraged the contribution made by secular literature and the recently rediscovered ancient civilization. The Franciscan way, as it encountered humanist rationalism, led to a concrete experience of the Incarnate Word that nourished sensibilities and led to a balance between intellect and heart.

These young women had often received a careful education, open to all fields of art and thought. Once they entered the monastery, they successfully synthesized their own culture with their spiritual and mystical life. It was relatively common for these nuns to write with equal fluency Latin, Greek, and Hebrew. They would have practiced, even in public, rhetoric and philosophy. Generally speaking, they all knew music and could play it and could write in prose and/or in verse. Some of them were true writers, such as Battista de Montefeltro, Battista Varani, and Catherine of Bologna, who was also a painter and musician. Nuns from less exalted social classes were also imbued with the rich cultural milieu of the Renaissance, from which the various strata of the population, especially the town-dwellers, would have benefited.

There was a real, though mainly religious, cultural life in the monasteries. The Bible was read in Latin or in the vernacular. The Fathers of the Church and Franciscan texts were well-known (though not, it seems, Clare's letters). The monastery of Monteluce of Perugia had an entire copyist's workshop with very competent teams of nuns. They produced manuscripts of the works of Blessed Angela of Foligno, Saint Bernadino of Siena *(Legenda Major)*, Cassian, Saint Gregory the Great, the canonization process of Saint Clare, and the *Treatise on Seven Spiritual Weapons*, Catherine of Bologna's major work.

Where donations allowed, monasteries embellished their chapels with works of art. In 1483, Monteluce had a tabernacle made by a master of Fiesola, and, in 1505, a huge painting by Raphaël and his school for the church altar (not that of the nuns' choir).[29] Such a refined sense of beauty was alien to Saint Colette, whose sense of poverty was embodied in a different cultural context that would have made such things unthinkable.

The return to poverty for the Observant Clarisses in Italy did not mean a break with such a rich, highly aesthetic, though Christian, culture. The reformed monastery did not live on the margins of contemporary civilization, either mentally or psychologically. This did not mean that the Clarisses were unconscious of the violence and conflicts of the time. On the contrary, because of family bonds and relationships through marriage, they suffered dearly.[30] Experiencing the rise and fall of their family lines, they must have felt the uncertainty of this world, even at the peak of its achievement. Despite withdrawing from the world, they remained firmly rooted in this brilliant and unique European society through their culture, sensitivity, and religious conviction. This feature of the monastery's insertion into its own civilization is not found in Colette – the ideals and goals are quite different.

The General Features of these Personalities

Testimonies reveal the typical features of sanctity as it was conceived in the fifteenth century. The main religious virtues were: humility, love of poverty, fasting, discipline, vigils and hair shirts, a spirit of prayer, and the fight against demons. Careful reading shows even more specific character-

---

[29] A. Fantozzi, "La riforma osservante…," 20-21; the picture is now in the Vatican museum.

[30] Cf. the family dramas in the life of Battista Varani, below.

istics of the reformed Clarisses of this period, which supplements the personality type emerging from the reform. Contemporaries of Paola and Battista Malatesta seem to have been attracted by the contrast between their initial state and their religious life. These two sisters-in-law, who kept up a correspondence, had both been married and had known the brilliant and violent life of the Italian courts. The former became very humble, eager to serve, drawing admiration from religious sisters who saw the difference between her married life ("used to pleasures and the tender marks of her husband's affections") and the austerity of the religious life.[31] The latter was "gentle, prudent, ... learned in all liberal arts, ,,, sweet and kind, with a bright intelligence ...," a poet held in "high esteem by the writers of her time, particularly Petrarch."[32]

The general minister, William of Casals, who wrote to Felicia Meda inviting her to found a monastery at Pesaro in 1439, also sketched an admiring portrait of her, interesting for the qualities of governance it indicates:

> ... I am informed by reliable witnesses of your praiseworthy life, of your humility, zeal, prudence, vigilance and application in the monastery and also of your zeal in encouraging, your diligence in warning, moderation in correction, restraint in commanding, eagerness to sympathize, discernment in the practice of silence, your maturity of speech and your wisdom for perfect government.[33]

A sister who knew Blessed Cecilia Coppoli observed similar qualities. Before becoming abbess, she was "humble, obedient ... doing the menial work without being ordered by her superiors.... She was never idle.... Although young, she was old in her prudence, wisdom, knowledge, and good sense."

---

[31] Wadding, *An. Min.* 1449, XII, 41.
[32] Wadding, *An. Min.* 1447, XI, 356-57.
[33] F. Meda, "Una insigna clarissa milanesa," 10-11.

Once elected abbess, she was first to do the tasks the other sisters must do.³⁴

And of Sister Bernardino of Foligno, it was written:

> Her charity and love were so great that it seemed she had brought all the other sisters into the light. She had the same love towards the friars, so that they called her their mother.... She showed this great charity, especially towards the sisters who begged alms, whose feet she washed with great tenderness and gentleness.... We had another Saint Clare as our mother.³⁵

The portrait of the abbess among the Clarisses of the fifteenth century closely matched that of Clare in the "Process of Canonization" or in the "Legend of Saint Clare."³⁶ It is similar to the picture of the abbess that Clare herself draws in her Rule. The dominant features of her relationship with her sisters are moderation, prudence, and humility in relationships, personally undertaking physical work, warm tenderness to all her sisters and to the friars, expressed by the term "mother" which contains strongly affective, non-hierarchical connotations. One of the consequences of adopting the First Rule at the expense of the Urbanist Rule or a return to a stricter life was the rediscovery of this unique role for the abbess. As a woman of prayer, humble and patient, she is essentially mother, not the rather remote great lady of royal or princely monasteries.

The *Constitutions* of Colette paint a significantly different picture of the abbess and of her links to the sisters. The emphasis is placed on government, on obedience by the sisters, with a certain distance between the "subjects" and the superior. There is no impression of familiarity and warm proximity. Clearly, the texts are of a different nature. Colette's are le-

---

³⁴ A. Fantozzi, "Documenti intorno alla beata Cecilia Coppoli," 60-66.
³⁵ A. Fantozzi, "La riforma osservante," 52 ff.
³⁶ *Clare of Assisi: Early Documents, CA:ED,* "The Legend of Saint Clare," 22-23; "Process of Canonization" 6:2, 3:31, 18:6.

gal documents, while the Italian texts are private documents speaking of admiration, such as that of William of Casals, or of fond memories after the departure of a beloved abbess. The reference to Clare in the latter shows a particular focus, whereas Colette specifically says that these sections of the Rule on the abbess are not to be taken entirely literally.

Spirituality

We will only outline general features here, since Catherine of Bologna and Battista Varani, considered below, are very representative of the whole picture. The spirituality of these fifteenth-century nuns was centered entirely on a passionate and exclusive attachment to Christ, the Son of God made man, in a personal relationship of love. No doubt they knew of other aspects, such as the relationship to the Trinitarian God, but it was lived with Christ and through him. The vocabulary used in the writings recalls that of marriage. The nun had an essentially spousal relationship to Christ, lived above all through the Passion and the cross. Blessed Cecilia Coppoli appeared to a sister and told her that throughout her whole life she had carried the Passion of Christ in her heart.[37] Sister Bernardino of Foligno shed many tears, caused by the almost constant recollection of Christ's Passion.[38]

The nuns encountered Christ through the sacraments, mainly the Eucharist, either in communion or in long periods of prayer before the tabernacle. Prayer was a decisive element in their life of union with God. They frequently kept vigils before or after matins; and during the day they practiced devotions centered on the various moments in Christ's life: the crib, the cross, the agony in the garden, the entombment, as often shown in paintings of the time. Some of them focused on the Sacred Heart of Christ, a devotion that had deepened following the paths opened by Francis and Clare. It was not uncommon for many to experience mystical states, with ec-

---

[37] A. Fantozzi, "Documenti intorno alla beata Cecilia Coppoli," 75.
[38] A. Fantozzi, "La riforma osservante," 52.

stasies, visions, gifts of miracles or prophecy.[39] Continuous contemplation of Christ[40] led them to practical imitation in their daily lives. We have already noted humility, great charity towards their sisters, gentleness, and hard work. This imitation went as far as wishing to suffer for him and like him. We cite a prayer of Blessed Eustachia de Calafato:

> May I follow you, she says to Christ, by the way of the cross and tribulations.... Lord, you had the crown of thorns, may I have contrition of heart; your bitter thirst was quenched with gall and vinegar, may my thirst also be quenched with anguish and pain, and may no consolation ever cause me to rejoice; you were weakened with bitterness and shame, may I spend my whole life in great pain and bitterness; never allow me to pass along any path other than that on which you walked.[41]

These sisters avoided the risk of morbidness, however, by the certainty of the Love that saves; and, although aware of their sinful state, they were sure of mercy. This fervor towards the God of goodness becomes praise, exultation, and thanksgiving for the gift of the creation of beings. In this sense, they rediscovered a strong sense of Franciscan joy and energy. The latter dimension is less clear in Colette, as we have seen, with her more exclusive devotion to the Passion.

---

[39] All these facts can be found in the works of Fantozzi and Wadding.

[40] Blessed Francesca of Assisi (†1440) remained for hours on her knees before the crucifix of San Damiano; cf. Wadding, *An. Min.*, 1440, XI, 125.

[41] Ch. A. Lainati, "La Legenda della Beata Eustachia di Calafato," *Temi spirituali dagli scritti del secondo ordine francescano*, Vol. II, Coll. Antologie del pensiero spirituale francescano (Assisi, 1970).

Two Writers of a "Spiritual Treatise" and a Biography

Saint Catherine of Bologna (1413-1463)

Biography and Bibliography

Catherine Vigri was born in Bologna[42] on September 18, 1413, daughter of a diplomat in the service of Nicholas III of Este. Her family lived in Ferrara. The young Catherine was presented at court as the companion in studies to the daughter of Nicholas III, Marguerite of Este. At that time, the court was a major center for humanist studies. The young girl learned miniature painting,[43] art,[44] the viol (which would later accompany her visions), and was introduced to poetry, which she would practice happily. Her religious development within the splendors of the court is unknown. When her father died, around 1427, she entered a community of Franciscan tertiaries led by a pious woman, Lucia Mascheroni. Such groups of pious women were gradually developing a form of vowed religious life and, around 1431, under the influence of the friars (probably Bernadino of Siena in this case), took the habit of the Clarisses. They seem not to have adopted the First Rule containing the privilege of strict poverty, since Catherine is classed as an Urbanist Clarisse.[45] She was novice mistress for many years, and her work reflects her concern for formation. In 1456, with a group of companions, she returned to Bologna to found the monastery of *Corpus Domini,* of which she became abbess, a position she held until her death on March 9, 1463.

---

[42] *D. S.*, t. 2, col. 288-290; *D.H.G.E.*, t. XI, col. 1505-1506; *Catholicisme*, II, col. 690-691; *Dalla corte estense alla corte celeste*, Monastero Corpus Domini.

[43] She was an expert in this art, as the very fine breviary kept in the monastery of Bologna shows.

[44] Some of her paintings are now in the museums of Bologna and Venice.

[45] Art. "Clarisse innocenziane e urbaniste," *Dizionario degli Istituti di Perfezione*, 2, col. 1142-1146.

Her character as abbess was notable both for her concern to teach and train her sisters in the spiritual life and for her own qualities of heart. Examples of this include her wish to wash the feet of her sisters for one last time on Holy Thursday, and, close to death, she called the community together, speaking to them in especially warm terms of prayer and mutual love:

> I am going, but I leave you with holy peace.... Love each other with warm love and be consoled.... May you all remain in peace, with Christ's blessing and mine. This is my will for you.[46]

Her biographer notes that after receiving communion "she raised her eyes to gaze at her beloved sisters one by one."[47] Colette's death, on the other hand, was more austere and seems to have marked a certain distance from those around her. She called her sisters together one last time to take her leave of them saying she had no more to say, and she closed her eyes.[48] Catherine's death is bathed in the same aura as that of Clare, dominated by the sense of sweetness, peace, and sisterly love.[49]

Canonized by Pope Clement XI in 1712, her body is still at the monastery in Bologna. She led an intensely profound mystical life, shown by the extraordinary phenomena woven around her (visions, revelations, and gifts of prophecy) and above all by her writings, which place her as one of the great mystical writers of her time.

Whether in prose or in verse, in Latin or in Italian, her work mainly discusses areas of piety or devotion. Most of her writings, manuscripts that remain unpublished, are au-

---

[46] "... *Io vado, ma vi lascio la santa pace.... Amatevi insieme di cordiale amore e consolatevi ... rimanete in pace tutte, con la benedizione di Cristo e con la mia. Questo è il testamento che io vi lascio.*"

[47] Catherine of Bologna, *Le sette armi spirituali*, "Introduction," ed. P. Puliatti (Bologna, 1981), 12. References to this work will from now on be given in brackets in the text.

[48] Cf. Part One.

[49] *CA:ED*, "Legend," 39-46.

tographs preserved in the archives of the monastery of Bologna or of the archdiocese. They include some "Warnings," a "Method for Attending the Mass," and the "Mirror of the Religious for the Three Vows." She also compiled a short set of instructions under the title *Dichiarazione sopra capitoli delle Suore Povere di santa Chiara*, translated at the end of the century by Blessed Battista Varani.

She belonged to the Umbrian school of poetry, led by Jacopone de Todi. Her poetry includes a poem in Latin of 5610 hexameters, *Rosarium metricum de mysteriis Passionis Christi Domini et de vita Mariae Virginis*, and other poems in Italian. Some of these were copied by Illuminata Bembo, her companion and first biographer, whose primary work, *Specchio di Illuminazione*, we will be studying.

Catherine's major work, *Le sette armi spirituali*, was written in Ferrara in 1438 to help young sisters in their spiritual struggle. It is a veritable source of spiritual doctrine. It became known only after her death, and several editions appeared quickly in Italy, as well as translations into Latin (1520), French (1597), Portuguese (1615), and Spanish (1560). The latest editions came out in the early twentieth century, in Bologna (1900) and Florence (1922). Recently, the monastery of *Corpus Domini* in Bologna published her complete works (1981) and Bembo's biography (1983).

We will not make a complete study of her work, but only consider points of similarity and difference with Colette's spirituality as shown in the *Writings* and the first two biographies.

The plan of Catherine's work highlights the author's educational and didactic intentions. Starting with the postulancy, where religious life is depicted as a struggle, she describes the seven weapons to use, explaining the advantages of each one. Then she recounts her own experience, to which she has already alluded in the first part. The reader is told of diabolic temptations. (This period seems to cover her earlier life when she was living in a community of devout women.) She then discusses the means to distinguish diabolical suggestions from divine inspiration, true visions from false. Catherine shows, through a daily life of self-denial, humility, prudence, intense charity, and inner trials, the mystical ways by which the soul is favored with special graces.

Similarities with Saint Colette

The religious and spiritual life is depicted as a struggle with the devil, "the enemy" (19), the identical term used by Colette and Pierre de Vaux. The nun follows Christ and, like him, will experience trials. Here again is the triad, commonly found in the French reformer's letters: "Do not fear to fight boldly and readily against the *devil, the world,* and our *flesh*." Catherine, however, adds a correction to this, using an expression from Francis and changing the tone of the text: "Our flesh ... given to us to serve the spirit" (22). Religious life quickly takes the way of the cross, but this way, on which the enemy assails us disguised as a friend, is an effect of the love of God. Through it consecrated beings come to resemble his Son. Colette does not mention this detail. For her, suffering seems to replace the punishment reserved for sinners and is intended to pacify the wrath of God.

The fact remains that the monastic life is a harsh way, on which not even spiritual consolations can be expected – a lesson to be learned early on. The miracle is to persevere in the face of the world's lack of understanding. The world knows nothing of the battle between rebellious flesh and spirit and the assaults of the "enemy" (54).

The spiritual life is founded on the cross, giving up one's own will as a continual crucifixion. There are two passages offering a definition of religious life that summarize Saint Catherine's thought on the subject. The second of these also recalls a passage from Saint Paul on the life of the apostles, showing how highly the author esteemed the mystical life:

> ... continually battling invisible enemies, that is clever and very strong devils, which never cease tempting them to turn from the way of God (55).... They bear their own cross, and with true patience toil and sweat

for the monastery; they suffer cold, heat, hunger, and thirst; they incur dishonor, shame, mortification, infamy, injuries, and persecutions; they fight hard battles against angry devils; they conquer their own flesh and fragile sex and suffer indifference and blows from those who should have helped and comforted them in every anxiety and need, such as their prelates and brothers (57).[50]

Temptations and trials of the cross detach the nun from "vain pleasures of earthly life" (26). To help in this fight, she must always keep "the memory of death," reflect on it, and prepare for it continually (25), avoiding excessive mortification and without entertaining the desire to die quickly, which is a ruse of the enemy because it can lead her to break the rule of obedience. Catherine's attitude to the "world" is similar to that of Colette, with an acute sense of her sinful state. Pierre de Vaux recounts that the Picardy reformer "considered herself the vilest in the world" and maintained there was no greater sinner than herself.

Catherine stresses the same thing, disclosing her sins before the last judgment so that they will be expiated and more easily pardoned. She is "the greatest sinner.... There is no place dark enough for me, outside myself.... I have not loved with a full heart (87-8).[51] She longed for honors and a reputation for holiness; she neglected the desire to suffer on account of evil and did not keep a good will, the gift of God; she did not embrace the cross with all her strength nor love

---

[50] "... *continuamente combattono contro nemici invisibili, cioè contro i diavoli astuti e fortissimi, che mai non cessano di tentarli a tornare indietro dalla via di Dio* [55].... *Portarono la propia croce e sostennero fatiche e sudori per il monastero, con vera pazienza ; soffrirono freddo, caldo, fame e sete ; sopportarono obbrobri, vergogne, mortificazioni, infamie, ingiurie e persecuzioni, combatterono aspre battaglie contro i diavoli furiosi, vinsero la propia carne e il propio fragile sesso e patirono l'incuria e le colpe di quanti avrebbero dovuto aiutarle e confortarle in ogni preoccupazione e necessità, cioè i loro prelati e fratelli*" [57].

[51] "*la maggior peccatrice ... non esiste luogo tanto tenebroso che mi si convenga, al di fuori di me stessa ... non ho amato con pieno cuore*" [87-88].

those who hated her; she had been hypocritical as a servant of Christ; after the initial fervor of the religious life, she had been only lukewarm; she did not respond to Christ's love and has therefore been adulterous. There is a psychological difference from Colette, since the Italian Clarisse places greater emphasis on the certain intercession of the angels on her behalf and of mercy towards her (90). She verges on the edge of the abyss of despair, but her faith and hope prevent her from sinking into morbid guilt.

Her human and spiritual experience and knowledge of the contemporary rivalries to which she refers make her anxious for the salvation of sinners. She prays for them, reflecting Colette's concern for the "poor and weak." But Colette's many physical sufferings and trials are all offered up for the sake of sinners, for whom she constantly torments herself. The monastery is also a place giving spiritual protection to the town, driving away demons. This ecclesial and apostolic dimension is less prevalent in Catherine's writing. One stage of her spiritual ascent however, a burning love for all human beings, makes her cry out:

> Give me the grace, most merciful Lord, that all sinners might be saved in exchange for my damnation.... For this, unceasingly and willingly I offer myself mentally to divine justice, praying for it to take revenge on me for the faults committed by all sinners, so that their salvation may not be denied me for the sake of justice (83).[52]

Colette's attitude does not seem to go to the extreme described by Saint Anthony the Great, the father of monasticism, who attributes to a shoemaker in Alexandria, working in front of his stall and watching the passers-by, the prayer

---

[52] *"Fatemi la grazia, pietosissimo Signore, che tutti i peccatori siano salvati, in cambio della mia dannazione.... Per questo, senza sosta e ribellione, mi offro mentalmente alla divina giustizia, pregandola di vendicarsi sopra di me delle colpe commesse da tutti i peccatori, affinché la loro salute non mi sia negata per ragione di giustizia"* [83].

that "all might be saved, and I alone damned." This comparison shows, however, that the subject is characteristic of monastic life, at least among the greatest spiritual leaders. The theme of a divine justice that takes revenge on sinners occurs in Colette, especially in the portrait drawn by Pierre de Vaux.

There is no sign here of a spiritual trend that spread through Europe in the fifteenth century. Though the Italian nun refers to the end of the world being near because of sin, this is not a recurrent theme:

> He deigns to accept the innumerable faults daily committed by human nature,... the proud ambition and wicked greed that reigns in every generation today. These are the main vices of the Christian people through which they are continually brawling and fighting; there is no longer today any true charity, and natural pleasure is lost, so that there is almost no love between father and son and among brothers. And these are infallible signs of the approaching last judgment (87).[53]

A Different Cultural and Spiritual Climate

In noticing points of similarity, we are also aware that there are certain nuances peculiar to Catherine, indicative of a different context. Religious life is certainly a continuous battle, but its aim is to rediscover the beauty of the soul in the initial state of innocence and to "enter the father's house" (18). The pilgrim nun therefore shares a paschal energy with Christ, "most pure and virginal Spouse" (17).

---

[53] "*Egli si degni di sopportare le innumerevoli colpe quotidianamente commesse dalla umana natura ... della ambiziosa superbia e della crudele avarizia che, ora, regnano in ogni generazione. Questi sono i principali vizi del popolo cristiano, per cui sta in continua rissa e battaglia; non v' è più, oggi, vere carità e anche la naturale dilezione è perduta, sichè non si trova quasi face tra padre e figlio e tra fratelli. E sono segni infallibili, questi, del vicino finale giudizio*" [87].

Neither Colette nor Pierre de Vaux has the idea of God as Father. The relationship with Christ is essentially personal and spousal. Christ is close, in his divine humanity, as a being loved with every fiber of the soul. When Catherine quotes Jesus' cry from the cross, she changes the very terms of her relationship to Christ and to God: "Father, why have you abandoned me?" (22). This reaches the center of her spirituality, as we will see later. But it already shows the interaction of various elements: the cross, the trials, the temptations allowed show the Father's plan of love for the spouse of the beloved Son (48). From this arises for the nun, in the midst of all her torments and shadows, unfaltering hope: [She] knows that the eternal Father will not allow to happen to her what he does not allow to happen to his own Son (23).[54]

Assured of salvation and glory, Catherine tells her companions:

You must desire to be tried rather than consoled, thus
to strengthen our hope, and the third weapon of trust
in God can be exercised to our advantage (23).[55]

The Passion of Christ, and after that, the life of the nun, is relocated in the plan of salvation, in the economy of the Incarnation and Redemption.

In a very lyrical poem, the Passion becomes truly a transition, the birth of humanity to the Father (24):

O most glorious passion, cure for all our wounds!
Most faithful mother, who leads your children
  to the heavenly father!
Refuge ...
  True bread ...

---

[54] "... sappia che l'eterno Padre non permetterà che accada a lei quanto non lasciò accadere al propio Figlio" [23].

[55] "... dovremmo desiderare di essere tribolate piuttosto che consolate, per rafforzare cosi la nostra speranza e la terza arma, del confidare in Dio, possa essere esercitata a nostro vantaggio" [23].

Shining mirror, that illuminates those reflected in
  you, and corrects their deformities!
Impenetrable shield ...
Delicious manna ...
Most high ladder, leading those who climb to
  the infinite good!
True home, comfort of pilgrim souls!
Everlasting fountain ...
Most abundant sea ...
Sweetest olive ...
Faithful spouse, sweet and thoughtful, always beloved
  of you![56]

Christ the Spouse who accompanies and leads the loyal spouse, supports her and gives her manna, that is, himself. Catherine frequently emphasizes Christ's sweetness and humility: he is "the sweet one and my Lord" (89) and above all "Christ Jesus the immaculate lamb" (72), who gives himself in the consecrated host. Colette, as described by Pierre de Vaux, certainly expressed some Eucharistic devotion, but this involved above all the appearances of Christ, who gave her communion directly, or her ecstasies while praying, observed also by those around her, including laity, during mass.[57] For Catherine, it involved a revelation of the mystery of the In-

---

[56] *O passione gloriosissima, rimedio di ogni nostra ferita!*
Madre fedelissima, che conduci i tuoi figli al Padre celeste!
Rifugio ...
Cibo vero ...
Specchio rilucente, che illumini chi in te si riflette e ricomponi le sue
  deformità!
Scudo impenetrabile ...
Manna saporita ...
Scala altissima, che porti al bene infinito chi anela salire!
Dimora vera e confortevole delle anime pellegrine!
Fonte perenne ...
Mare pescosissimo ...
Olivo soavissimo ...
Sposa fedele, dolce premurosa, di te sempre innamorata!
[57] Cf. above, Part I.

carnation and the Eucharist, which she had questioned (71-74).

God also "showed her how and in what way the Son of God, Christ Jesus, was incarnate by the action of the Holy Spirit and born of the Virgin Mary," and straight after: "Hardly had she received the consecrated host in her mouth, she felt and tasted the sweetness of the purest flesh of the Immaculate Lamb Christ Jesus."[58]

Such devotion to the Eucharist recalls chapters three and four of the *Imitation of Christ*, and is even more directly in line with the spiritual tradition of Francis, "Admonition I" and the expression "O sublime humility! O humble sublimity!" [of Christ] in his "Letter to the Entire Order."[59]

Catherine proceeds to study the stages and various aspects of this return to the Father, this pilgrimage littered with pitfalls, always using examples and memories that, as the reader might guess, are personal. She is not a theoretician of the mystical life, but rather seeks from her lived experience to help her sisters, especially the youngest and least experienced. Her work is thus a true composition. She retains a familiar tone, addressing herself directly to her readers, "my most beloved sisters" (75). She also has a varied style, moving from memories to describing a vision to analyzing a state of soul to using a lyrical exclamation. Often she employs a very accomplished poetic expression, with real poems written, it seems, specifically for inclusion in particular passages.

She describes spiritual weapons (diligence or applying oneself to do well, recollection of death, reminder of heavenly rewards, holy Scripture engraved in the memory), devo-

---

[58] "*Le mostrò, anche, come e in che modo il Figlio di Dio, Cristo Gesù, fosse incarnato per opera dello Spirito Santo e nato dalla Vergine Maria...*" "... *Appena ricevute l'Ostia consecrata in bocca, sentì e gustò la soavità della purissima carne dell'Agnello immacolato Cristo Gesù.*"

[59] "Admonition I" and "Letter to Entire Order," 27, *FA:ED* 1, 128 and 118. Eucharistic devotion was not a special feature of the Franciscan family, even though the Franciscans seem to have strongly encouraged the practice. It is found in the following century in almost identical terms in the writings of Teresa of Avila. *Teresa of Avila, Complete Works*, "The Way of Perfection," ch. 35, 756 ff.

tions and practices (a spirit of prayer, frequent communion, devotion to the Virgin Mary), the virtues required (religious obedience, poverty, humility, fear of God, mortification and self-denial, prudence and discretion, etc.), and discernment of spirits. All the while, she identifies the pitfalls and reveals a close analysis of religious psychology and knowledge of spiritual paths.

Constant asceticism of the will and daily practice of obedience trigger inner struggles favorable to diabolical temptations. Suffering then becomes so acute that it is only the thought of the shame involved that keeps the nun from returning to the world. She fervently regrets her entry into the monastery. The memory of her family's tenderness tortures her heart; the longing for penitence gives way to greedy and even sensual desires. The result is that sadness overwhelms her and she concludes: "I served better outside the monastery" (48 ff.).

Colette's *Letter* to Sister Loyse refers to similar problems.[60] The latter expressed the wish to go to a monastery nearer her parents. Colette's response, brooking no argument, was that she was there for her own good and the rest was temptation. There was no further analysis or effort to provide the sister with spiritual and psychological help to understand herself more clearly. Once the order was given, there was no choice but to carry it out.

For Catherine, when the trap has been sprung, temptation just moves elsewhere, into the most intimate aspect of the nun's life – her relationship with God. Subtle temptations of pride may occur, not immediately identifiable but which a faithful being may eventually discover. She believes herself to be the source of good. This was an opportunity for Catherine to develop a line of reasoning on human freedom of choice (52-54). Her monastic experience also led her to reveal that prayer itself might be an escape, in which one might seek consolation as another form of sensuality. Solitude that isolated one from the community might be a subtle devia-

---

[60] Cf. above, Part II.

tion rooted in tenacious egoism or indicate a problem dealing with interpersonal relations (55-57).

Without denying the presence of marvelous features, Catherine sketches out an ideal of balance, discernment, and moderation in all spiritual and temporal virtues, expressed in the formula "there is danger in too much and in too little" (20). Pierre de Vaux's description of Colette's religious virtues uses hyperbole to provide a dramatic and tense context. Sanctity is never conceived as this balance of faculties, this harmonious integration of human qualities and spiritual virtues.

The stress here is placed on spiritual suffering rather than physical trials. The devil does not appear to attack or howl, but rather tempts the spirit, as a spirit himself. In Pierre de Vaux, we noted how the spiritual is materialized. He attributes to Colette nervous reactions (cries, gestures) as signs of diabolic temptation. Catherine, however, links suffering to love: "and as love is, so is pain" (68). Because it is easy for us to love the gift better than the giver, God removes sensual love by suffering in order to bring us into divine love. This is what the mystics call the purgative way or the night of the senses. For Catherine, this is suffering. Pierre de Vaux, however, seems to know nothing of this internalization. On the contrary, he quantifies suffering, particularly physical suffering.

Just as spiritual trials evoke the Father's tenderness, so too temptation is an integral part of the spiritual ascent.[61] Struggles and temptations are necessary for the true religious sister (61). Suffering leads to joy and to heavenly reward:

> Being a miserable beggar brings great wealth, being despised causes great honor, being lowly in all things brings great nobility, being afflicted and troubled in

---

[61] Cf. Saint Clare's "Second Letter to Agnes of Prague," 21, *CA:ED,* 49: "If you suffer with him you will reign with him, weeping with him, you will rejoice with him; dying on the cross of tribulation with him, you will possess heavenly mansions with him among the splendor of the saints."

doing good bring great consolation, being sick for Christ brings good health, the height of knowledge is to be thought stupid for love of Him, and through the same love, to end this life in great and bitter martyrdom to rejoice for eternity (62).[62]

Her work ends with a real hymn of joy and hope, which, as we have seen, is at the source of the pilgrimage – return to the Father. Hope is so strong that she already possesses it, somewhat like John of the Cross, who will say later that, for the soul that has reached its wedding day, divinization by participation, only a thin veil separates it from seeing face to face:

Most beloved sisters, you may calmly await the great and magnificent embassy your spouse will send you, and thus adorned, receive the invitation to rise to such heights (92).[63]

There is a clear reminder of Psalm 44, the so-called royal psalm,[64] along with a reference to the description in Celano's *Legend* of Clare's vision on her deathbed: Christ, and the Virgin surrounded by the heavenly court, come to fetch her.[65]

Further on, Catherine continues:

---

[62] "*Grande ricchezza, essere misere e mendiche; grande onore, essere disprezzate; grande altezza, essere infime in tutte le cose; grande consolazione, essere afflitte e tribolate nel fare il bene; grande sanità, essere inferme per Cristo; somma scienza, essere reputate stolte per amore di Lui e, per lo stesso amore, finire la vita corporale in grande e acerbo martirio, per poi godere in eterno*" [62].

[63] "*Dilettissime sorelle potrete attendere serenamente la grande e magnifica ambascieria che il vostro sposo invierà a voi e, cosi adorne, ottenere l'invito di salire a tanta altezza*" [92].

[64] Psalms 44, 14, and 16: "Daughter of the king, she is there before his glory ... they lead her adorned to the king ... her maiden companions follow her ... they enter the palace of the king."

[65] "Legend of Saint Clare," 46, *CA:ED,* 317.

... and before my God I will sweetly sing, if I will sing psalms humbly in my heart ... and of his reign I will be made ruler, if for him I was a poor beggar (93).[66]

The so-called *Testament* of Saint Colette would have these tones of praise and exultant joy, but it seems that the part relative to this theme was added later. It appears to be missing from the reformer's own writings.

Her knowledge about the difficulties of the way and the happy outcome moves Catherine to counsel her sisters, and especially the abbesses. A certain type of relationship is thus described, permitting us to compare it with Colette's view of the intercommunitarian relationship. First of all, the constant action of the devil effectively removes blame from the sister. If the abbess is clear-sighted enough to unmask prevarication in the nun, she does not overwhelm her for that or close her off within her temptation or her sin. The sister who gives way to temptation through weakness is not the source of the evil. The abbess must watch over her flock since the wolf is ready to devour it:

> Do not wait to save the sinner until she is in the wolf's jaws, but quickly and with true compassion, help the weakness of soul and body, help of the superior given before it is asked.... Give more love to those who are tempted to disobedience and unfaithfulness than to those others (43-44).[67]

Here again is Clare's concern for the most frail, for whom the abbess is their last refuge. Colette's emphasis in the *Constitutions* lies elsewhere – the relationship between the

---

[66] "... e nel cospetto del Dio mio dolcemente canterò, se in coro umilmente salmeggerò ... e del regno suo imperatrice fatte sarò, se qui, per Lui, povera e mendica sarò...." [93].

[67] *"Non aspettare di soccorrere la pecorella quando è già in bocca al lupo, ma, con prontezza e vera pietà, sovvenire le infermità delle anime e dei corpi ... l'aiuto della superiore dato prima della domanda.... Dare piu amore a quel tentate di inobbedienza e di infedeltà che non alle altre....* [43-44].

sisters' submission and their responsibility. Remember the episode related by P. de Vaux. The infirmarian fell asleep while on watch, and the sick sister died in the night. Colette predicted that the infirmarian too would die in the same way for having committed this fault. This is an entirely different notion of relationships.

The sisters must love each other and support each other's faults and weaknesses with patience. Their relationship is not just sisterly but motherly (80). There is no impression that the sick sisters were kept separate and that duties towards them were carried out in a spirit of religious virtue, as in Colette. Rather, care was to be given by all the sisters, not just by the abbess. We must not assume that Colette did not love and practice charity. Many sections of her *Writings*, as well as contemporary accounts, show clearly that she did. But the atmosphere is different, the stress being placed on a certain austerity of relationships. The guilty sister was corrected and, even in the absence of the abbess, felt her stern gaze. Catherine recommended to the abbesses a different attitude: "I remind them to hold the littlest soul entrusted to them in the greatest esteem ..."(44).[68]

This path of faith and love was to be constantly nourished by prayer and Scripture. There are abundant quotations from the psalms to Saint Paul, as we have already seen. Catherine was soaked in the Word of God, which she recommended strongly to her sisters as the seventh weapon in the struggle of religious life. Reflection on the Word, a kind of *lectio divina,* would gradually transform their entire being: "To overcome our enemies, there is the recollection of Holy Scripture, to carry always in our hearts" (28).[69]

The daily readings in the office and the mass are letters from the Spouse, on which the nun must meditate in the cell of her heart, while she understands and "tastes" the Word. The writings of Saint Francis, Saint Bernadino of Siena

---

[68] "*Ricordo a quelle tenere in maggior stima la più piccola anima loro affidata,...*" [44].

[69] "*Per vincere i nostri nemici, è la memoria della Santa Scrittura, da portare sempre nel nostro cuore...*" [28].

(quoted several times), Saint Bernard, and Saint Augustine help one gain an understanding of Scripture and give practical advice. Saint Clare's letters do not seem to have been known, but there are references to her Rule and to her Legend. Catherine's death, mentioned above, seems to show that the process of canonization, which had been copied, was also known.

We can observe in conclusion that Catherine's spiritual world was more varied and rich than that of Colette. We have seen some aspects of the latter in her *Writings* and the biographies. Catherine's work was also more structured. It reveals a dynamic depth and a certain knowledge of joy that seems alien to Colette, who was marked more by suffering and the cross without the prospect of glory, though these would be inseparable.

Suffering and trials are also more internalized in Catherine, less spectacular. They are immersed in a calmer, less tortured atmosphere, very perceptible in the visions, even those of demons. The demon takes on the appearance of Christ, but this is not a nightmare vision that shakes the nerves and causes fear (32-33). This spiritual world is more refined. It is bathed in sweetness and light. Anguish and trial almost always lead to reassurance; hence the song of the angels heard after a difficult period:

> The melody of the angel's song was so stupendously sweet and soft ... no language can express or mind imagine the extreme sweetness of that angelic song (55).[70]

A famous vision gives a clear idea of the psychological distance between Colette and Catherine. The former saw a child's body cut in pieces offered to her by the Virgin on a platter with the words: "this is what sinners do to my Son

---

[70] "*La melodia del canto angelico era cosi stupendamente dolce e soave ... nessuna lingua puo esprimere e mente immaginare la extrema dolcezza di quel canto angelico*" [55].

every day"; the latter saw the Virgin and Child during a vigil of prayer on Christmas Eve:

> The glorious Virgin with her most beautiful little Son in her arms, swaddled just like other little newborn infants ... the Virgin places the little one on her lap; ... and the sister ... gently hugged him, face to face. ... [and she noticed,] the sweet perfume of the purest flesh of blessed Jesus (66-7).[71]

There is a profound sense of the Incarnation here, without scorn for the flesh, as well as a familiarity with maternal gestures.

Spiritual guidance, further nourished by scripture and the founding texts of the Order, is thus combined with a particular aesthetic, a sense of beauty alien to Colette's inner world. She rejected this as vain and dangerous. The vision of the Child recalls the religious art of the Quattrocento, which certainly influenced Catherine. She also has a sense of beauty in her own writings, as shown by the final lines of her work, with their balanced assonance:

> ... and in paradise I will be content, if here I have nothing that I want; and before my God I will sweetly sing, if in my heart I humbly sing the psalms; by Him I will be made immortal and invulnerable, if for Him I do not fear death and pain ... (92-93).[72]

We have already seen some examples of her many poems. The description of visions reveals a very sure, accomplished,

---

[71] "*La Vergine gloriosa col suo dilettissimo Figliolo fra le braccia, fasciato esattamente come si usa per gli altri piccoli quando nascono ... la Vergine le pose il bambinello in grembo ...; e la religiosa ... dolcemente lo strinse a sé, viso a viso.... il soave odore della purissima carne di Gesù benedetto*" [66-67].

[72] "*... e che in paradiso contenta sarò, se qui non avrò quello che io vorrò; e nel cospetto del Dio mio dolcemente canterò, se in coro umilmente salmeggerò; e che da Lui immortale e impassibile fatta sarò, se qui per Lui morte et pena non temerò ...*" [92-93].

artistic, and pictorial hand. The great vision, in the section on the last judgment, is a picture composed from the central motif of God in majesty, around whom are the Virgin "dressed in a white mantle" and, "much further down," a huge crowd of men and women, their faces lifted up to God. The visionary "found herself among the multitude on God's right hand and called out to Him" (86).[73] This fresco closely resembles Brea's paintings on the same subject, often showing the Virgin of Mercy as the main motif.

Catherine and Colette, nun and abbess, share an interest in particular points – commitment to a consecrated life given entirely to God for the salvation of all and in faithful imitation of Christ, a certain sensibility and conviction about the judgment of sinners, about the role of the ever-present devil, and about visions and extraordinary events as necessary manifestations of the spiritual life. But these similarities are integrated into different spiritual movements. For Colette and her followers, sanctity seems to culminate in the accumulation of extreme trials, lived in a tense and frightening environment. For Catherine, paschal energy and unconquerable hope in Love transfigure all torments and enable investigation into the depths of the soul; they harmonize, with light and beauty, as praise to the Father and manifestation of tenderness; and they nourish an ever attentive, warm, and mutual love.

Colette, not an introspective woman, was always focused on the urgent need for reform and the foundation of monasteries. Catherine, on the other hand, was more subjective at a spiritual level, more inclined to gain a deeper knowledge of herself and of the paths to union with God. Thus she is situated in the tradition of the women mystics of the Rheno-Flemish school, who foreshadowed the great sixteenth-century theorists of mysticism, but in a varied and brilliant cultural environment.

---

[73] "*si trovava fra la moltitudine dalla parte destra di Dio e gridava a Lui*" [86].

The "Specchio di Illuminazione" by Sister Illuminata Bembo

We do not intend to study this work of Illuminata Bembo for itself, but only for comparison with the biographies by Pierre de Vaux and Perrine. To avoid repetition, we will mention only some aspects of Catherine's spirituality, as analyzed above. The value of Illuminata's work to our study lies in its being the first biography of Catherine of Bologna written by a witness, a woman and companion of the saint. (Perrine was, of course, writing after Pierre de Vaux and drew heavily on his work.)

Illuminata also belonged to the highly cultivated period of the Italian Renaissance. She was the daughter of a Venetian senator and entered the monastery of Ferrara in 1432. She accompanied Catherine to Bologna to found the monastery where she would then remain. She was elected abbess three times and died in 1493, outliving the saint by thirty-one years. In 1463, she wrote the *Lettera per la morte di suor Caterina Vigri*, the first draft of the *Specchio*. It was addressed to other monasteries and was a bit like a circular letter. Six years later, she composed the *Specchio di Illuminazione* and, in 1476, perhaps at the request of a superior, completed it with the *Ristretto dello Specchio di Illuminazione*, a simplified version with several accounts of miracles.[74]

As other biographies of saints and as Pierre de Vaux for Colette, the nine chapters of this work were intended to demonstrate Catherine's charity and religious virtues (obedience, humility, devotion to the office, and prayer). We find here all the typical features. In addition to the canonical office, Catherine, like Colette, loved to say the office for the dead, the office of the Virgin, and the office of the cross (51-63). She prayed for souls in purgatory. (Pierre de Vaux tells how Colette's intercession released souls from purgatory, who then appeared to her to announce the news that they had entered heaven.)

---

[74] The manuscript of the *Ristretto* is in the Brussels Royal Library. That of the *Specchio* is in the archives of the monastery of Bologna. The edition used is that of the *Corpus Domini* monastery in that city, 1983.

Like Colette, Catherine led an austere life of mortifications and long vigils in the choir during which she suffered attacks from the devil (89). She was blessed with the same graces of visions and prophecy. She saw the soul of a holy bishop of Ferrara going up to heaven; the Virgin appeared to her; she saw the destruction of Constantinople; in spirit she attended the canonization of Saint Bernadino of Siena (85). As her own work indicates, Catherine did not like spiritual consolations and ecstasies (79). Her detachment from extraordinary phenomena is all the more interesting as Pierre de Vaux says nothing like this about Colette, for whom the extraordinary seemed to be the normal locus for her kind of sanctity.

Illuminata Bembo seems caught between the traditional understanding of sanctity in the Middle Ages and the influence of Catherine, whose lived experience was in some ways original. So, for instance, certain expressions are identical to those found in P. de Vaux: "more heavenly than earthly" (63) and "she did not seem a human creature, but entirely angelic and heavenly! (101).[75] Catherine, entirely wrapped up in reflection on the Passion of Christ, refused to rest; but once Saint Thomas of Canterbury appeared to her and recalled her to common sense, she agreed to rest and learned to balance her life better (75).

Although the framework and some elements of her sanctity are in the style of fifteenth-century hagiography, there are some new features, clearly belonging to Catherine herself, since they also appear in *Sette armi spirituali*. We point them out briefly, noting those on which Illuminata Bembo focuses, such as Catherine's intense charity towards her sisters, many examples of which are given. She emphasizes universal charity, by which all are saved, and immediate charity towards the weak, tempted, sick, or anguished sisters (31, 93-105). Catherine's sisters and daughters could come in to disturb her at any time (102).

The example of a sister in agony shows how different Catherine was from Colette. When a sister was agitated be-

---

[75] "...*più celestiale que terrena*" [63] and "... *non para creature umana, ma tutta angelica e celestiale!*" [101].

fore her death, Colette prayed for her to confess her fault because, if she was dying, it might be because she had committed a "gross and enormous sin." If necessary, Colette would even revive her so she could make a good confession. For Catherine, if a sister was dying in anguish and anxiety, it was because she was being tempted by the devil. Catherine, therefore, saved her with intense charity, never wanting to leave her for a moment, sprinkling holy water on her to chase away the devil. The biographer provides this beautiful definition:

> Beloved sisters and daughters, let each of you see in the other the image of your own Creator and consider that she is the Spouse of the Eternal God (115).[76]

Catherine is constantly concerned to teach the sisters and novices. One Good Friday, she gave them a three-hour lesson. The author notes her devotion to the holy cross and to the Name of Jesus, clearly influenced by Saint Bernadino of Siena.

The environment in the biography is one of peaceful beauty and light. There is lyricism both in the account of the visions and in the transcribed poems.

Catherine's doctrine is set out in a structured format that demonstrates her concern for formation in the spiritual life. The author does not simply summarize the saint's work, but identifies three levels, each divided into five stages on the path to life in union with God. Here, Illuminata Bembo was perhaps using letters that had formed her own inner life. She says that Catherine wrote "by her own hand" and at Illuminata's request, "things" that would help her. No matter what the fact, the same elements are recognizable.

The fact that this is the first biography written by a cultivated woman, a nun and abbess herself with experience of the stages of the spiritual life, gives the work a unique value. Although its plan is not very original, it does seem

---

[76] *"Dilette sorelle e figlie, ciascuna di voi veda nell'altra, l'immagine del proprio Creatore e consideri che è Sposa dell'Eterno Dio"* [115].

to describe sanctity from within, since these two women are close in background as well as in a human and spiritual experience. Through them we gain greater access to this rich world that achieved a synthesis between the sacred and profane and rediscovered the Franciscan sources through a passionate attachment to Christ as spouse, sisterly love lived intensely, and finally a spiritual dynamic rooted in joy and hope. Pierre de Vaux, if he allows an analysis of the representation of sanctity, leaves the reader standing at the threshold of Colette's own spiritual adventure.

Blessed Battista Varani

Biography and Bibliography

Although not exactly a contemporary of Colette, Battista Varani (1458-1524) is of interest as a founding Clarisse at Camerino, after being at the monastery of Urbino from 1481 to 1484. As the daughter of the founding family, she had a part to play in the direction taken by the new monastery. She refused the property offered by her father and wanted to live by work and alms, accepting only the property for the monastery. She wrote a great deal so her spiritual path and concerns can be studied and compared to those of Colette.

She belonged to a noble family that had governed the town of Camerino for two centuries and that had endured a most tormented history. Her father, Giulio, was one of only two survivors of the fratricidal war that had decimated the Varani. He surrounded himself with a sumptuous court and gave his eldest daughter a very careful education that allowed her to take part in philosophical and theological discussions. As an adolescent, Battista already had a deep spiritual life characterized by devotion to the Passion, which she had practiced from the age of eight. Every Friday she knelt before the crucifix, reading a fifteen-point treatise on the Passion. She meditated on the Passion every day, fasted on bread and water, and flagellated herself every Friday. At night, on returning from festivities at the court, she prayed.

After a very complex inner struggle, she entered the monastery at Urbino. But her father's love was satisfied only when she returned to Camerino with eight other sisters to occupy a fully refurbished monastery. Here she lived under the Rule of Clare, according to Saint John Capistrano's commentaries. When she became abbess a few years later, she was in contact with the greatest preachers of the Observance at the end of the fifteenth century.

Her spiritual life consisted mainly of trials. During 1479 and from 1488 to 1492, she endured two great spiritual crises. In 1502-1503, a real tragedy decimated the family. Cesare Borgia invaded Urbino and Camerino after a siege. Her father Giulio and three of her brothers were captured and executed on the order of the duke. Battista had to flee to Fermo, then to Atri. The youngest brother was able to reestablish his power in the town, and his sister then restored her convent. She was subsequently sent to Fermo to found a monastery, but returned to Camerino, where she was elected abbess several times. She died during an outbreak of plague. Nothing is known of her final days, perhaps because she was placed in isolation away from the community, according to the practice of the time.

Her first work, *I ricordi di Gesù,* written in 1483 two years after she entered the monastery, tells of Christ's teaching during his youth.[77] In 1488, the most important work, *I dolori mentali di Gesù nella sua Passione*, appeared, and, in the same year, she took up the subject again in a small work, *Considerazioni sulla Passione di nostro Signore*. At the request of the Observant friar Dominique de Leonessa, her confessor, she wrote her spiritual autobiography in 1491, *La Vita spirituale*. In the same year, she wrote an account of the last days of another well-known Observant, Brother Pietro di Mogliano. For the provincial minister, Brother Giovanni da Fano, her spiritual son, she composed the *Istruzioni al discepolo*. After that she wrote little more – a *Lettera a une suora vicaria* in 1513 and the *Trattato della purità del cuore*

---

[77] Transcribed by M. Ch. Peduzzi.

in 1521, also, it seems, for Giovanni da Fano. Other undated writings witness to her continued activity, including *Movena, Preghiere, Soneto alla Vergine, Preghiere Eucaristice*, some letters, some Latin and vernacular lauds.[78]

The *corpus* indicates the significance of her literary output and its main themes. It is predominantly spiritual. But, in *Istruzioni al discepolo* (no doubt because her correspondent was the provincial minister and therefore visitator), Battista gives very specific advice on fraternal relationships, demonstrating her lengthy experience of community and monastic life.

There is one chapter on canonical visitations that outlines the ideal visitator and describes the best attitude for the sisters to have during a visitation. We have seen that Colette's *Constitutions* recommend a real investigation and require that the sisters, as well as the abbess, denounce the faults committed. Battista asks precisely the opposite: "If you do not see a clear, serious fault with your own eyes, keep quiet!" She highlights whatever unacknowledged motivation or hypocrisy there might be in reporting the faults of others. The only appropriate attitude is to remain silent during the canonical visitation. She affirms that, in all conscience, it is possible to say: "To me, they all seem like angels incarnate (18)." All the rest is "rumor," that is criticism disguised as a search for good:

> One demon is on the tongue of the one muttering, another in the ear of the one who listens. In truth, there is no need to speak of people or events, *ne di bene ne di male* [neither good nor evil] (19).

While Colette encouraged canonical visitations, Battista denounced them, seeing their grievous consequences:

> And this is why in canonical visitations souls are filled with suspicion and hearts sown with discord. It elimi-

---

[78] U. Picciafuoca, *La beata Camilla Battista Da Verano* (Camerino, 1983).

nates zeal for the honor of the Fraternity because it drives people to say, to report what is not appropriate (20).[79]

She does not try to temper her language; the truth is there. She ends by insisting: "Keep quiet, keep quiet about other people's business!" (21).

Spiritual Experience

Inspiration lay mainly with the Christ of the Passion and with the cross. Christ caused her to experience his own sufferings and revealed to her what he lived through in his soul during his hours of agony. We can see what separated her from Catherine, who relocated the experience of the cross in a paschal dynamic with the aim of teaching her sisters about the stages of union with God. Battista lost herself in a unique experience, plumbing the depths of suffering, which she lived with all her being. In some ways, therefore, she was more like Colette, whom Pierre de Vaux saw, above all, as a woman crucified in a thousand ways. The basic difference lay in the fact that the hagiographer was recounting an experience that was not his own using a particular framework. Battista, while belonging to the tradition of Passion devotion, nonetheless was sharing her own experience, the spiritual adventure to which she had committed her whole being for her whole life.

The most decisive spiritual trials came after the unspeakable joys of love in which she received so many graces that they seemed almost unbearable. Christ revealed to her that he bore her name engraved on his heart; she heard him say: *Ego te diligo, Camillam, io te amo, Camilla* [I love you, Camilla].[80] Shortly after began the entry into the heart of Christ that she had desired so much.

---

[79] "*E per questo che nelle visite canoniche riempie gli animi di sospetti, semina zizzania nei cuori. Stermina lo zelo dell'onore della Fraternità, perchè spinge a dire, a riportare cio che non conviene*" [20].

[80] U. Picciafuoca, 67.

Her spirit entered the bitter ocean of her Lord's suffering. She shows here her total focus on the Passion, describing the pains and torments suffered for the damned, for the elect, for the Virgin his mother, for Mary Magdalene, for the beloved disciple. The damned are his limbs torn from him in terrible suffering.[81] At other times, she saw in a vision the Pietà holding her dead son in her arms, and she felt Mary's sorrow, as well as that of Mary Magdalene and of John; she heard their groans.[82]

The devil came to torment her in terrifying visions as a dragon rising from the open abyss. In this respect her mental and psychological world was very similar to that of Colette as described by Pierre de Vaux. It should be noted, however that her aesthetic sense remained, even in the worst state of abandonment. The vision of the Pietà and the holy personages is a true pictorial composition, even though Battista tells us she was crushed with suffering for fifteen days, so fearful was the vision.

Her affective senses were also extremely well-developed. The visionary entered into true compassion *(cum-pati)* with Christ, the Man-God, who was very near, very real to her. Thus one day, when she was in pain, he took her soul to his heart and said gently to her "do not weep so much."[83] Compassion resulted in internalization of the suffering. Where Pierre de Vaux gives quantity and detailed description, Battista has quality and spirituality. There is an intense desire to suffer with and for the Spouse, typical of Italian Clarisses of the fifteenth century, while suffering seems more controlled in Colette's spirituality, at least according to Pierre de Vaux. This impression comes mainly from the use of hyperbole to accentuate the heroic exploit. Battista desired, through love, that her whole life could be a Good Friday, (96), including Christmas (which is somewhat surprising theologically speaking). Although she is certain of future glory and joy (except in some particularly desperate moments), her life

---

[81] *I dolori mentali di Gesù* ..., 27-31.
[82] U. Picciafuoca, 70.
[83] U. Picciafuoca, 86.

is not infused with paschal light. She is the mystic of Good Friday, of the shadow side of the mystery of the Redemption. In this sense, although she lived into the sixteenth century, she belonged entirely to the fifteenth, which had pushed contemplation of the cross to the limits.

Like the horrors of war and epidemics, divisions in the Church are able to cast light on the meaning of this spiritual tendency that pushes at the limits of theological excess. Perhaps the family dramas that had wounded her also enabled her to understand, at least psychologically, the human basis of her experience. Battista, a passionate woman never doubting the Father's love, has some admirable pages about pardoning enemies:

> Oh most sweet, I am your one hundredth little lost sheep, wandering lost and straying for many years.... Gentle God, kind Lord, now with all my heart I desire to return to you, fount of true peace.... Take me, my God, from the shadows of this world.... Bring me to you, O compassionate God. Bring me to you! (97).[84]

This cry of desire to return to the Father foreshadows that of Teresa of Avila: "...because I am dying of not dying!" At the furthest point of her journey, Battista, nourished so fully by the spirituality of her own time, finally has a vision of the New Earth.

We can conclude, then, that her work does not display the same concerns as that of Colette. Battista received the observance of the Rule and its adaptation from Saint John Capistrano, who himself had met Colette as the reformer and author of the *Constitutions*. Battista, with a trembling sensitivity, explored other areas. In her passionate, loving relationship with Christ, she was deeply feminine, as she was with her

---

[84] *O dulcissimo, io so' la tua centesima pecorella smarrita, la quale per anni so' andata errando spersa e vagabunda.... Ora, dolce Dio e pietoso Segnore, con tutto il cuore desidero tornare a te, fonte di vera pace.... Cavame, Dio mio, delle tenebre di questo mondo.... Tirame a te, o Dio pietoso. Tirame a te!* [97].

sisters and her brothers, especially with Brother Giovanni Da Fano. On every page, she calls herself his "mother."

Conclusion

With Catherine of Bologna and Battista Varani, the Clarisses favored and explored more deeply the contemplation of the poor, crucified Christ, the center of Clare's life for forty years at San Damiano. She it was who asked her daughters to keep him constantly in their minds. More so than their founder, these nuns, highly cultivated products of the Renaissance, were able to analyze and recount their own spiritual journeys without the mediation of a confessor.

The influence of the socio-cultural environment can be clearly seen in the way they describe their experience and in their approach to spirituality. The artistic dimension is ever-present in the representation of Christ and the Virgin. Even the vehemence of their religious expression is different in tone from that of Colette, who was less ardent than her Italian sisters. Nonetheless, whatever her cultural context, the fifteenth-century woman demonstrated her capability in various aspects of the religious domain, whether laying the foundations for reform or exploring the pathways of the mystical life.

CHAPTER 4

IMITATING THE MODEL OF HOLINESS

In 1447, Colette still had many projects in hand that her daughters would bring to fruition over the next decades, assisted by Pierre de Vaux, their loyal collaborator.

EXTENSION OF THE COLETTINE REFORM

Colette's reform was spreading out in different directions. It was developing in new provinces, penetrating regions already receptive to her influence, and even reaching Spain through the foundation at Lézignan thanks to an unexpected chain of circumstances.

Foundations in New Provinces

Lorraine

Saint Colette had already gained a firm foothold in Lorraine after Duke Charles II and his wife, Marguerite de Bavière, asked her to found a monastery there in 1425. Preferring, as ever, the smaller, more isolated, and better-fortified towns, she chose Pont-à-Mousson rather than Nancy, where the Court was based. The project was delayed following the deaths of the ducal couple. A few years later, their successors, René I of Anjou and Isabelle, revived it. The monastery was completed in 1444, but not occupied immediately. Colette herself had chosen thirteen Clarisses from Gand, who arrived on September 21, 1447, together with Pierre de Vaux. This was six months after her death. The first abbess, Sister Méline de Sourxe, was elected according to Colette's wishes.[1] Always renowned for its holiness, the monastery attracted many vocations from the greatest families of Lorraine. In 1519, Philippa de Gueldre requested admission.[2]

Duchy of Brittany

Ten years after the establishment at Pont-à-Mousson, Brittany accepted the reform with a foundation at Nantes in 1457, then at Dinan in 1481. The great canonization ceremonies of Saint Bernardino of Siena in 1450 had enhanced the popularity of the Franciscan family. Blessed Françoise, Duchess of Brittany, asked Calixtus III to authorize a foundation in her ducal town of Nantes (1457). But the bull set the number of sisters at eighteen and the number of priests and lay brothers serving the monastery at six, rather than four.[3]

The leading figures of the Duchy attended the enclosure ceremony, at which the pope's bull was presented with great solemnity before the public notary.[4] The bull laid down a very strict enclosure:

> The abbess and the sisters will remain in perpetual enclosure, so they may not come out, and neither man nor woman, of any state, dignity, order or condition whatsoever may penetrate into the enclosure, once the abbess and the sisters have entered there, except

---

[1] *Histoire de Philippa de Gueldre* written in 1889 by a Poor Clare at Grenoble, I (Grenoble, 1889), 275 ff. (using as her main source a biography written in 1617 by Fr. Mérigot).

[2] We will later study Philippa de Gueldre's significant role in the sixteenth century.

[3] Bull published in Latin, translated by Fr. de Lanmodez, *Les Clarisses de Nantes (1457-1893)* (Vannes, 1894), 6-10.

[4] Those present included Lord Arthur of Brittany, Count of Richemont and Constable of France; Isabeau, dowager duchess; Françoise, new duchess of Brittany; Countess of Richemont, wife of Count Arthur; Guy, Count of Laval.

in case of necessity or other reasons expressly stated in their Rule and in the declarations of their Rule.

However the Duke and Duchess of Brittany were allowed to enter and stay there without permission from anyone.[5]

For a century and a half, this monastery was the only contemplative house in the town.[6] Soon, however, the community at Nantes was large enough to plan a new foundation at Dinan.

The initiative to found the Dinan monastery came from two Franciscan friars resident with the Clarisses at Nantes. One of these, himself from Dinan, obtained a bull of authorization in 1480 from Pope Sixtus IV with the help of Francis II of Brittany. The building work began fairly quickly, but it dragged on a long time because the Duchy was in crisis. Sixteen sisters from Nantes, however, were selected to found the new convent, arriving at Dinan on December 3, 1488. The leading citizens, officers, and people of the town welcomed them solemnly and conducted them, in procession, on a tour of all the churches in the town, finally bringing them to their convent. The ceremonies ended with the singing of the *Veni Creator* and celebration of High Mass. The convent was quickly completed, and the community enjoyed a preferential relationship with the founding monastery for many years.

---

[5] Fr. de Lanmodez. *Les Clarisses de Nantes*, 6-10.

[6] One of the first postulants, Catherine Dollo, who entered at only fourteen years of age, was remarkably gifted. She translated some of Saint Clare's *Writings* ("Benediction," "Testament") and the *Privilege of Poverty* into French. Her manuscript is the oldest known French translation of these texts. She also translated the Roman breviary and part of the missal. It is recorded that, "during the Revolution, this manuscript, taken to the monastery at Dinan, was given to two Franciscan nuns, Mother Aimée de Jésus who reached the Clarisses in Amiens in 1810 and her sister, Marie-Françoise. They both died in Amiens. From Amiens, the manuscript went to the Provincial Franciscan Library at Bry-sur-Marne where it is today," *R.H.F.* I, 1924, 469 ff. D. Ciccarelli mentions this manuscript in "Contributi alla recensione degli scritti di S. Chiara," which completes the reference, ms. 188 (359), *Miscellanea francescana*, 1979.

Normandy

Jean d'Estouteville, a royal officer, and his wife Françoise de la Rochefoucault founded a Colettine monastery in Rouen in 1484. We have no other information about this monastery. The Estouteville family had noble Norman lineage, even related to the royal family. Its most illustrious member was Guillaume d'Estouteville, a cardinal legate of the pope. He was responsible for reviewing the canonization process of Joan of Arc. But it seems the monastery did not benefit long from the protection of this family.

Reform in Regions already Influenced by Colette

It took about twelve years from the time of her death before new foundations began to be made in areas that had earlier been influenced by Colette.

Northern Provinces and Flanders

The Bethlehem monastery at Gand, founded by Colette in 1442, became the center for the reform in the northern provinces and in Flanders. This was the period when Colette wrote the *Intentions*,[7] collecting her sisters' memories. A study of these texts shows that the oral tradition was in fact committed to paper at Gand.

Four convents were founded over a period of twenty years: Arras in 1460, Anvers in 1461, Liège in 1474,[8] and Bruges in 1479.[9] The foundation at Arras was planned in Saint Colette's lifetime. It was built by Philippe de Saveuse,[10] governor of

---

[7] According to the Flemish manuscript at Gand: "Eene Memorie ofte Registre vaude conventen ...," ms. 1510, fol. 6 and 7. Saint Colette died at Gand in 1447.

[8] We have no accurate information on the two monasteries of Liège and Anvers.

[9] Fr. de Meyer, "Le clarisse nei Paesi Bassi," *Studi e Cronaca del VII° Centenario di Santa Chiara d'Assisi,* 468.

[10] Philippe de Saveuse had already founded the monastery at Amiens in 1442-1444.

Picardy and Artois, chamberlain of Philippe the Good, duke of Burgundy. Thirteen sisters from Gand formed the core of the first community.[11] In Bruges, the Sinai monastery was the second Clarisse convent in the city, the first being Urbanist. The community was formed by sisters from Gand and Hesdin.

In 1481, Philippe de Gueldre, lieutenant general of Picardy and governor of the town, whose sister was a Clarisse at Hesdin,[12] founded the convent of Péronne. And in 1496, the bishop of Cambrai, Henri de Berghes, whose sister was a Clarisse at Gand, founded a monastery with financial help from Margaret of Austria,[13] daughter of Emperor Maximilian. The sisters came to Cambrai from several convents: Hesdin, Gand, Amiens, Arras, and Bruges, while the abbess, Sister Louise Barvoets, came from Bruges.[14]

The same bishop of Cambrai once gave the Clarisses some rather banal advice about preserving Saint Colette's bones:

> In 1482, Archbishop Henri came to visit his sister, the vicar at the convent of Poor Clares at Gand. They wanted to refurbish the tomb of their mother Colette, and had just exhumed the holy bones. But how should they clean these venerable remains, which had lain in earth for almost half a century?
>
> The prelate told them to wash them with Rhine wine.
>
> As the sisters had recently received a small cask of Rhine wine from Margaret of York, widow of Charles

---

[11] Cf. *Chronique du monastère d'Arras*, manuscript text written in 1950 at the monastery from documents held in the archives of the convent and the region.

[12] Wadding gives a date of 1482 (*An. Min.* 1482, n° 70, t. XIV, 384).

[13] She herself became a Clarisse later on.

[14] Mother Louise Barvoets took the habit in Gand in 1474 and knew sisters who were Saint Colette's contemporaries, particularly Mother Catherine de Longueville. She was one of the founders of the monastery at Bruges in 1475 before going on to found the monastery at Cambrai.

the Bold, they used it to wash the holy bones of their founder.[15]

Savoy, Switzerland, and the Dauphiné

The relations Colette enjoyed with the house of Savoy were sufficiently firm that, after her death, the Duchess Yolande, wife of Blessed Amadeus IX and mother of Louise, founded the monasteries of Chambéry and Geneva.

Because of the opposition of the Urbanist Clarisses and the Conventuals, Colette, despite the wishes of the Duke of Savoy, had not been able to create a foundation in the capital of the Duchy of Chambéry, The Picardy abbess had turned then to the less significant towns of Orbe and Vevey. In 1471, however, after repeated requests from Duchess Yolande to Nicholas V and Paul II, founding nuns were allowed to take possession. Marie Chevalier, former companion of Colette, was elected vicar, then abbess.[16]

In 1479, Duchess Yolande also succeeded in establishing the Colettines in Geneva. The city did not belong to the house of Savoy. It was a free town of some ten thousand inhabitants and administered by municipal magistrates under the leadership of a prince-bishop. The plan for a foundation dated back to 1457. Anne of Cyprus, mother of Amadeus IX of Savoy, had obtained permission from the pope but was not able to complete the project. The pope once again gave approval to Duchess Yolande in 1473. Despite some difficulties raised by the municipal magistrates and the cathedral chapter, the sisters from Seurre, Poligny, Vevey, Orbe, and Chambéry were able to take possession of their monastery.[17]

Between 1480 and 1484, the house of Savoy finally achieved a foundation at Bourg-en-Bresse. Duke Charles and Philippe of Savoy, Lord of Bresse, completed the plan of

---

[15] Flemish manuscript, Gand, fol. 18.

[16] Marie Chevalier was the first girl to be received by Saint Colette at the monastery of Besançon in 1410.

[17] Cf. the well-documented book by E. Ganter, *Les Clarisses de Genève* (Genève, 1949), particularly 31-53.

their grandfather Amadeus VIII, who had put the proposal to Saint Colette in 1412.[18] Sisters were sent there from Chambéry.

The foundation at Grenoble (1478) was accomplished by a young woman from the Dauphiné, Jeanne Baile,[19] with no money or support. She governed the monastery until her death in 1484 and became renowned during her lifetime for her holiness. After her death, many miracles occurred near her body, and the population of the Dauphiné proclaimed her blessed.[20]

Central France

Less information is available for central France. The construction of the monastery of Bourges began in 1468 at the initiative of the Archbishop of Bourges, Jean Coeur.[21] The pope sent a bull to his representatives at Bourges asking them to investigate and, if appropriate, authorize the "construction of a monastery of Clarisse nuns of the reform of sister Colette, as the archbishop has asked."[22]

---

[18] M. Angèle du Sacré Coeur, *Les Pauvres Dames de l'Ordre de Sainte Claire ou les Clarisses dans la Cité lyonnaise*, I, 9-11.

[19] A. M. de Franclieu, *Jeanne Baile et les Clarisses de Grenoble* (Lyon, 1887).

[20] A. M. de Franclieu, 76.

[21] Wadding disagrees with another chronicler, Gonzague, who names as founder a certain Jacques Cadoit, prior of N.D. de Sales, then archbishop of Bourges. Wadding believed that archbishop Jean Coeur instigated the foundation. After Coeur's death in 1493, Jacques Cadoit was actually appointed archbishop, but it would have been Jacques Coeur (father, brother, or nephew of the previous prelate, their relationship is uncertain) who completed the convent. The name and image of St. James are everywhere in the monastery. The building work, in any case, took a long time to complete. Wadding, *An. Min.*, 1468, n° 27, XIII, 498-99.

[22] Bull *Inter universa*, Wadding, *An. Min.*, 1468, doc. 7, XIII, 646-47. It only gives the founder's first name: "our venerable brother Jean, archbishop of Bourges." This is the first occurrence in the documents of the term "father vicar" *(qui nomen patris vicarii ac visitatoris inibi obtineat* [who there held the name of father vicar and visitator]*)* or "vicar of the abbess" *(Patrem et visitatorem ac vicarium abbatissae* [Father and visitator and vicar of the abbesses]). The term "father vicar" is obscure.

The Montbrison monastery was built in 1496 on the initiative of the great lords of the region, including Pierre III of Urfé, councilor and chamberlain to the duke of Burgundy and the King of France, grand equerry of France and Brittany. The new community was formed of Clarisses from Aigueperse, Moulins, Puy, Chambéry, and Geneva.[23]

The founders of the monastery at Gien (1500) were the regents of France, Pierre and Anne de Beaujeu. Fifteen sisters, from Moulins, Aigueperse, Seurre, and Grenoble, constituted this community. From the outset, the Gien sisters were placed under the authority of Observant friars, not friars of the Colettine reform.[24]

Foundations in Spain

The reputation of the Lezignan monastery was enhanced by the short and saintly life of Blessed Bonne d'Armagnac (1434-1457).[25] Thanks to the foundation of Gandia in Spain, this convent was the source of the spread of Colette's reform throughout the Iberian peninsula. It soon crossed from there to the Spanish colonies.

As regards the renaissance of the Second Order in Spain, there is very little information, and no systematic study has yet been carried out. The few works on the subject are almost unavailable outside Spain and so we can only point out a few landmarks.

The Gandia monastery in the Valencia diocese drove the reform forward. It gave birth to two more houses dedicated to the devout life, one being the home of Urbanist Clarisses,

---

[23] *Les Moniales de Sainte Claire de Montbrison*, edited by the Montbrison monastery.

[24] Bull *Eximiae devotionis affectiis*, Wadding, *An. Min.*, 1499, doc. 57, XV, 668-69: *sub cura Generalis ultramontani, et Provincialis Provinciae Lugdunum, vicariorum Ordinis Fratrum Minorum Regularis Observantiae...* [under the charge of the Ultramontane General, and the Provincial of the Province of Lyons, of the Vicars of the Order of Observant Regular Friars Minor]. For the origin of the sisters, J. Fodéré, *Narration Historique*, 198.

[25] See below for Bonne d'Armagnac.

set up in 1429 by Yolande, duchess of Gandia, daughter of Alfonso of Aragon.[26] The monastery was destroyed following an inheritance dispute, and the sisters had to be transferred to the convent of the Holy Trinity in Valencia.[27]

A knight of the region, Louis de Vich, councilor and master of accounts for the king of Aragon, restored the old convent, with the agreement of the bishop of Barcelona. He then looked for a community to live in it. At the advice of the General Minister Iago de Sarzuela, he called on the nuns of Lézignan.[28]

From Gandia the reform then spread steadily – to Girona in 1488, to Setubal in Portugal in 1496, to Our Lady of Jerusalem in Valencia in 1497, to the monastery of Saint Clare of Castellon de Ampurias in 1505, and to the monastery of the Holy Face in Alicante in 1518. The reform persisted throughout the sixteenth century,[29] helped along by the extension of the Colettine constitutions to the Observant Clarisses by Sixtus IV in 1482.[30]

The duchy of Gandia passed to the Borgias in 1485. This family showed a special affection for the monastery of the Clarisses. During the sixteenth century, twenty-five members of the Borgia family were nuns. Isabelle, the duchess's daughter, gained permission to enter the convent at the age

---

[26] L. Amoros, *El monasterio de Santa Clara de Gandia y la familia ducal de los Borjas*. After founding it, the duchess became a Clarisse and later was elected abbess.

[27] *Bull. Franc.*, new supplement, 460-62, n° 541. This convent previously belonged to some Trinitarian sisters, but they had been evicted by pontifical order following various scandals.

[28] Bull of Paul II, *Regimini universalis Ecclesiae*, 1-65, *Bull. Franc.*, II, n° 1302, 662-63. A. Bocquet took this explanation of the presence of the Lézignan Clarisses at Gandia from a manuscript about their convent (A. Bocquet, *Étude manuscrite sur le couvent de Lézignan*, 17). It is simple and entirely plausible, based on an authentic bull. Nonetheless, chroniclers from the sixteenth to the eighteenth centuries propagated a persistent myth, echoes of which appear in an article by A. Ivars well-documented between 1924-1925: A. Ivars, "Orígen y propagación de las clarisas coletinas o descalzas en Espana," *A.I.A.*, XXI (1924): 390-410.

[29] A. Ivars, "Orígen y propagación," 390-410.

[30] A. Bocquet, "L'établissement des Clarisses de la première Règle dans le Midi de la France," *Coll. Franc.*, 354, note 10.

of twelve. As Sister Frances of Jesus, she was later elected abbess and extended the reform throughout Spain. She died in Valladolid in 1557.[31]

Reformed Monasteries

The Perpignan Reform (1461-1500)

In 1461 a bull of Pope Pius II[32] asked for an inquiry into the monastery of Urbanist Clarisses in the deanery of Barcelona. The decadence continued, however, until the sixteenth century.[33] In 1495, two visitators, Jean Daza and Miguel Fenals, found a disgraceful situation.[34] While awaiting the necessary decisions, they tried to restore the enclosure, specifying

> a penalty of three months in prison for lay sisters who go out wearing secular clothing, or who enter unworthy houses, eat and drink with the people there, or carry letters and proposals (for meetings).[35]

However, the two visitators quickly realized that the Perpignan monastery would not truly persevere in the reform without outside help. In 1500, they called on the monastery of the Colettines at Girona. This monastery, itself reformed in 1488 from Gandia, had aroused their admiration during a visit there, as they noted in their report.

---

[31] *Histoire abrégée de l'Ordre de Sainte Claire d'Assise,* II, 234-35.

[32] Bull of Pius II, Jan 1460, *Bull. Franc.*, II, n° 872.

[33] T. de Azcona, "Reforma de las clarisas de Cataluña en tiempo de los Reyes Católicos," *Coll. Franc.*, XXVII, (1957): 27.

[34] In 1494-1495, King Ferdinand, with permission from Alexander VI, ordered a major reform mission to be conducted among the Catalunya monasteries.

[35] T. de Azcona, "Reforma de las clarisas," 27.

Reforms at Aix and Marseille in 1516

The community of Aix-en-Provence, initially very fervent in the fourteenth century, had become considerably relaxed by the fifteenth century. After a failed attempt by King René in 1473 with the Colettines from Bourges, it was not until 1516 that the reform was actually established there by Clarisses from Lézignan.[36] That same year, it reached Marseille.

The Urbanists in Marseille, much attached to their considerable community and personal property,[37] rebelled against any attempts at reform, living in such decadence that Pierre Achard, provincial of the strict observance, had to impose his authority. He brought nine Clarisses from Aix-en-Provence and forced any sisters who would not accept the reform to leave the convent in exchange for a lifetime pension.

After 1447, the Colettines continued to spread even more widely. The work of the two visitators, Jean Daza and Miguel Fenals, in the Spanish monasteries, shows that the Colettines' influence extended well beyond their own convents. Example as well as the *Constitutions* provided models for other types of renewal.[38] Perhaps because of their influence, the Colettines had to defend themselves from the dominance of the Observants, whose efforts dated from Colette's lifetime.

---

[36] A. Bocquet, "L'Établissement des Clarisses de la Première Règle dans le Midi de la France," *Coll. Franc.*, 1958, 9, using F. Gonzague, *De Origine seraphicae religionis*, III (Rome, 1587), 842, 1056, 1119.

[37] A register of acknowledgement kept in the Bouches-du-Rhône archives shows, for example, that Jeanne Atoux, abbess from 1407 to 1418, administered forty-eight houses and seventy-seven estates; cf. Canon Espeut, *Les Clarisses de Marseille*, 8.

[38] The fragmentary nature of the documentation does not allow a thorough study; there are gaps, especially as regards German territories.

THE STRUGGLE WITH THE OBSERVANTS

The Testimony of Sister Marie de la Marche

Sister Marie de la Marche's Testimony, published by Ubald d'Alençon,[39] appears at the end of a manuscript version of Pierre de Vaux's *Vita* of Saint Colette currently owned by the Clarisses at Poligny.[40] Brother Claude Champion, at the time of its publication, was at the convent of Amiens and certified its authenticity. Even more than Katherine Rufiné's letter, this text acts as an argument in the struggle between Colettines and Observants. It does this primarily by its choice of witness, specified to be the "daughter of King Jacques." The mention of social status is not accidental in this context. It underlines the authority of Sister Marie, the vicar of the Amiens monastery.

Her testimony claims to be first hand, since she was at Besançon at the time of the incident she reports: John Capistrano's visit to Colette when he asked the reformer to "place herself under the bull." Without revisiting this issue, we can observe that there seems to be confusion here, as in Katherine Rufiné, between the decree of Constance in 1415, which offered no direct threat to the friars of the Colettine reform, and the bull of Eugene IV of 1446, *Ut sacra ordinis minorum*, which attempted to separate the Franciscan family into two branches, Conventuals and Observants. John Capistrano ended up abandoning his efforts to integrate the Colettine reform into the Observance:

> O sister Colette, I beg your mercy. I admit to you my fault for having hindered and disturbed you without cause, nor will I torment you with this, for I believe that you are right and just, and your reformation is

---

[39] U. d'Alençon, "Documents sur la réforme de sainte Colette en France," *A.F.H.*, II and III (1910): 91-92.

[40] An oral tradition reports that this manuscript was given by Pierre de Vaux himself to the Clarisses at Besançon, who placed it with the monastery of Poligny.

according to God and Saint Francis and everywhere perseveres as you have begun, for God is with you.

There are clear reasons for this detailed testimony about an issue vital to the independence of the Colettine reform. The members of the movement, friars and sisters alike, rallied to resist pressure from the Observants, who were encouraged by the bull of Eugene IV granting them potential jurisdiction over all the reformed monasteries. In Colette's lifetime, Jean Maubert had already tried to bring the reformed communities together under his vicariate. Demonstrating that John Capistrano, one of the pillars of the Observance, had abandoned the idea of bringing Colette under the authority of the "bull" (hence perhaps the reason for confusion over the date of the documents involved) was to invite Capistrano's heirs to respect his presumed opinion.

Sister Marie de la Marche's testimony forms part of a much larger, more complex whole, the various points of which we will consider.

The History of the Struggle

One of the aspects of the quarrel that divided Conventuals and Observants throughout the fifteenth century was the effort by the two parties to win the greatest number of members in order to obtain recognition of their rights by the Holy See on the grounds of representation alone. Loyal to Colette, who had remained under obedience to the minister general at a time when there was still hope of preserving unity in the Order, the Colettines refused to ratify the new conditions and called on the popes for support.

What would Colette's attitude have been? The letter from Jean Maubert mentioned above, dated May 11, 1446, stresses the reformer's cautious wait-and-see approach. It appears she was expecting clarification of the situation. The bull of

Eugene IV was promulgated on July 23, 1446 and confirmed by the bull *Dum praeclara* of March 9, 1447.[41]

Colette, very ill during this period of time, died on March 6, 1447. She could not have foreseen the new situation, but her loyalty and obedience to the Church left no room for doubt, whatever her personal feelings might have been. Nonetheless it is clear that the actual situation remained very confused for years, until the decline in preference for the Observants.

The Situation of the Observants

As Hugolin Lippens[42] emphasizes, papal policy here seems contradictory, arising from pressure and an incomplete grasp of the facts. For example, Eugene IV's bull gave the northern vicars of the Observance full powers "over each and every Friar of the Observance by name, even if under another authority"[43] and, in addition, gave them the option of receiving the Conventual friars who wished to transfer their obedience to embrace a more demanding life.

The papacy encouraged the reform everywhere, while trying to contain the multiplicity of congregations. The friars of the Colettine reform had never obtained legal status.[44] But Bernard d'Armagnac, protector of the Colettine reform, intervened to have the exclusive governance of the Conventual ministers confirmed by the bull *Regimini universalis* of October 28, 1448.[45]

The same caution is evident in the 1480s. Sixtus IV entrusted the Observants with control of the Colettine monas-

---

[41] *Bull. Franc.*, I, n° 1046.

[42] H. Lippens, "Deux épisodes du litige séculaire entre les clarisses-colettines et les pères observants au sujet de leurs privilèges respectifs," *A.F.H.*, XLI (1948).

[43] *super omnes et singulos Fratres de Observantia nuncupatos, etsi alio nomine quidam eorum nominentur.*

[44] We should remember that these statutes produced by Henry de Baume were for internal use by the friars of the Colettine reform and valid only for friars attached to the monastery.

[45] *Bull. Franc.*, series I, n° 1246 in the form *Ad perpetuam rei memoriam*.

teries, then issued another bull restricting their powers. The Conventuals complained to Rome, and the same pope issued the bull *Hodie dilectis* forbidding the Observants to provide spiritual direction for Colettine nuns.[46] The duchess of Burgundy, however favorable to the Colettine nuns, successfully petitioned Rome for the authority to place under the jurisdiction of the Observants the Clarisse monasteries that she intended to found.[47]

The problem of jurisdiction of Colettine monasteries is part of the much larger issue of reform of these monasteries in Europe. Such reform was becoming urgent, as the Spanish example above shows. The papacy willingly used the Colettine constitutions to reform the monasteries. As in Spain, the tendency was, however, to entrust direction of the nuns to the Observants. This was a logical step since this friars' movement marked a return to a more demanding life. It must be admitted that it was only through the intervention of a great lord, Bernard d'Armagnac, that Rome gave this mission to the friars of the Colettine reform. As numbers and influence of the Observants grew, it seemed inevitable that the friars who followed Colette's reform would be absorbed.

The Position of the Colettines

The Colettines defended themselves vigorously against the ascendancy of the Observants. The latter sometimes showed excessive zeal in taking over houses of the nuns[48] or friars in order to enhance their own status so that an Observant might become general minister of the Order.

Thus, in addition to the monastery of Amiens that called for help in 1449 from Bernard d'Armagnac,[49] the Abbeville monastery complained about the Observants to Louis XI in

---

[46] On this issue as a whole, see Lippens, 6-7.

[47] *Bull. Franc.*, série III, n° 1783.

[48] The brief *Dudum a fel. record.*, March 18, 1493, of Alexander VI indicates this, allowing the Conventual general minister François Samson to take over direction of some Observant convents by way of compensation.

[49] Archives of Amiens, bundle II, held at the monastery of Poligny.

1463.[50] A quotation from the 1482 bull of Sixtus IV, already noted, gives some idea about the confused situation:

> Some friars minor, called observants, driven by some impulse, dared and are daring to exercise jurisdiction and superiority over the nuns and sisters of the order of Saint Clare, reformed by Sister Colette. They affirm their right by virtue of some letters or privileges, which they say were given by the Apostolic See. And some sisters, said to be of the third order, at the advice and suggestion of these friars of the Observance are believed to have changed their habit and way of life, to the point of spreading schism, dissension and confusion in the said order of Saint Clare, and among reformed sisters and nuns, to the peril of their souls and the great harm and prejudice to the general and provincials of the friars minor, to the detriment of the reformed sisters and nuns themselves, giving a pernicious and scandalous example to many.

The Colettines of Castres demonstrated their resolve. In 1497, Alexander VI, in a brief *Intelleximus* addressed to the Bishop of Albi, Louis d'Amboise, allowed four Colettine convents to be removed from Conventual jurisdiction and transferred to that of the Observants. The situation in the region was very complicated. The guardians of the friaries at Castres, Rodez, and Rabastens promised Olivier Maillard, the Observant vicar provincial, that they and their communities would submit to him if he obtained a papal bull. This was the brief *Intelleximus*.

The bishop of Albi took advantage of this by trying to place the Colettine monastery at Castres under the same authority (September 23, 1496).[51] With the support of their con-

---

[50] U. d'Alençon, *A.F.H.*, II (1909), and *Bull. Franc.*, I, n° 1604.

[51] On this, see P. H. Goyens, "Documenta circa coletanas in Belgio, saeculis XV-XVIII," *A.F.H.*, VIII (1915): 106-45, and A. Bocquet "L'établissement des Clarisses de la première Règle dans le Midi de la France," *Coll. Franc.* (1958): 353-73.

fessor, Brother Pierre Rosselin, the sisters refused to open the door to Olivier Maillard, who arrived with the bishop to impose his authority over the monastery and to carry out the canonical visitation. The sisters questioned the authenticity of the pontifical document they brought. The bishop then excommunicated their confessor, and the nuns were without mass or sacraments for sixteen weeks. Father Rosselin managed to have the censure lifted by the curator of Colettine privileges at Toulouse, and the Clarisses appealed to Rome.

A letter from the Clarisses at Castres, dated October 1, 1497, sent to all the sisters and discovered in Brussels, gives an account of all this. It is very long and impossible to quote in full, but some extracts show the solidarity of the Colettines and their loyalty to what they believed was Colette's will, as well as the close bonds that linked them with one another:

> You ordered us to write to you about our troubles, telling how we resisted our opponents, so that if a similar situation happened to you, which God forbid, you could act in the same way.... There would be enough to fill a book. Praised be God who has given us the grace to suffer it, but so that we may not be ungrateful to you, and in order to obey your wishes ... we are keeping you informed about this, informally and in brief ...

The sisters did not feel reassured by a new brief from Alexander VI (March 26, 1498) and ended the letter with a call for vigilance:

> For our opponents are pursuing us closely, and we have great need of good friends, so this is why, our most dear mothers and faithful sisters, we beg you very affectionately and piteously that for the love of God and to maintain the holy and ancient observance of our rule, please write to the king once more and to lords and ladies of the court. And as you commanded us to have help and aid, we truly need it. And please

take this letter to our good sisters at Moulins and may they please write very affectionately to my lord and lady de Bourbon specially to apply for protection for the said convent of Murat. And in doing this, our very reverend and beloved mothers and faithful sisters, you will receive even more of the great reward promised to us, which is great and glorious, which God gives you from his infinite goodness.... Written on this first day of October, at the Convent of Saint Clare of Castres, by the most desolate, poor and unworthy sisters of this convent.[52]

The two monasteries of Gand and Besançon spearheaded this continuing struggle of the Colettines. One passage of a letter sent to the Colettine monasteries by the Besançon sisters is eloquent on this matter:

We would prefer to die rather than act otherwise than our glorious Sister Colette and place ourselves under this bull, since it is something she greatly feared and never wished to accept that her convents and her religious life should be placed under this bull and family ... therefore we must fear greatly what our glorious [mother] so feared in her own life. God in his mercy will deliver us and we beg you that, for your part, you should remain firm and take great care that in our time we should not be reproached for bringing the holy religion into such decline. For if we were to accept this bull, they would shortly bind us with others even more severe, and those which our mother left us [the *Instructions* no doubt?] are enough for us. If we keep them well, our Lord will reward us in his blessed paradise, as we pray to him with good heart he will give us the grace to reach it....[53]

---

[52] P. Goyens, 106-45.
[53] Copy of Letter from the Besançon Clarisses, archives of Clarisse monastery, Puy.

Gand was not to be outdone. The Colettines there, according to a procedure already seen, evoked old memories. A letter from Sister Jeanne Labeur, distributed around the monasteries, recounts Colette's unease after putting the *Intentions* into writing:[54]

> Our glorious mother complained [to Sister Odette de Chassy, abbess of Gand]. She called together the whole community of this convent of Gand and told them in quite an obscure way about several serious causes for distress, and that the main cause would be the disordered affection the sisters would have for the friars ... and that they should have greater affection for what their holy Rule and ordinances set before them than for starting new ways that the Rule had not shown them.

The sisters were to follow her instructions and not give in to excessive familiarity "nor submit to them otherwise than I have shown them." This clearly refers to the situation at the end of the fifteenth century. The text shows the Colettines' wish to block any vague desire of the sisters to render obedience to the Observants, seeing this as a betrayal of Colette.

Leo X's bull *Ite vos* (1517) sanctioned the Observant victory: all the reformed were united with the Observants, and the right to appoint the General Minister reverted to them. But the Conventuals, now in the minority and under Observant authority, still retained some independence.[55]

At their Lyon chapter in 1518, the friars of the Colettine reform obtained some concessions despite the new structure. They were permitted to form their provinces according to the historic antecedents of their communities rather than by geographic location. At the same time, the Colettines at Gand asked the pope in 1518 to preserve their privileges. Thus, the friars minor at Gand were excluded from providing spiritual direction to the nuns there. The latter, with the

---

[54] Archives of Amiens monastery.
[55] Art. "François," *D.H.G.E.*, col. 865.

intervention of leading figures such as Philippa de Gueldre, a Colettine Clarisse at Pont-à-Mousson,[56] managed to retain, for a further century, friars from the old Colettine movement of the *Provincia Franciae* (which no longer existed in law). In Puy, on the other hand, the friars of the reform managed to retain their independent fraternity in the service of the Colettines until the Revolution.[57]

The political situation in these regions would upset the position of the friars who had been following Colette's reform. With the accession of Charles V, and especially Philippe II in 1556, the friars of the *Provincia Franciae* were ordered to return to their original convents and, from that time on, the political authorities treated them like foreigners.[58]

This stubborn struggle on the part of the Colettines might be seen as hindering the progress of Colette's canonization process, since the Observants now held power in the Order. Moreover, some of the texts considered here, along with the *Intentions*, belong to this period when the Colettines were rallying their forces and gathering useful arguments and, at the same time, soliciting help from leading figures.

From the first biographies by Pierre de Vaux and Perrine, intense work was done to record Colette's legacy. At the same time new monasteries were multiplying. The need to combine these various efforts appeared all the more urgent since Colette, devoted as she was to her work as reformer and lawgiver, had left little spiritual writing to provide sustained nourishment for future generations.

From this period, with its efforts and struggles to affirm the specific Colettine character, was born, we submit, the *Testament* or *Exhortation*. In order to appreciate the importance of this dawning of sanctity among the Colettine Clarisses, we must see them within the whole context of Franciscan reformed nuns.

---

[56] See below.
[57] Note from the Archivist at Puy.
[58] H. Lippens, 12-13.

The Colettine Clarisses

Contemporaries

Sister Marie Chevalier

The life story of Sister Marie Chevalier is at the end of a manuscript written in the eighteenth century by the abbot of Saint-Laurent, devoted to Saint Colette.[59] Marie Chevalier, from a middle-class Besançon family, was the reformer's first disciple when Colette took over the former Urbanist monastery of Besançon in 1410.

The abbot of Saint-Laurent, without quoting her works, states that Marie had an extremely intense prayer life, characterized by devotion to the Passion and the Eucharist. He writes: "The saint, having given her the habit, formed her in mental prayer" (345). This expression, commonly used after the development of the Carmelite school in France in the seventeenth century, is interesting in that it shows that the model of Colettine sanctity gained new concepts later on. The abbot of Saint-Laurent continues to describe Marie's inner life along the same lines:

> She had many visions of the mysteries of the life of Jesus Christ. One day, she was given to know, in a rapture, how the Word of God was in the Father's heart before the Incarnation (345).

Her devotion to Mary and the Child Jesus was more spiritually consoling than the tortured vision granted to Colette (the Child Jesus cut in pieces on a platter and shown by his mother):

> The Mother of God appeared to her one day, holding her son, the baby Jesus, in her arms. The God-child held a book written in letters of gold (349).

---

[59] This manuscript was published in 1835, and a copy is held in the archives at Puy, from which the references are taken.

Spiritual sensitivity had developed. Colettines no longer isolated themselves from the community, claiming mystical states. One day, feeling a rapture beginning, Marie left the choir, upon which a monster appeared. Asking Jesus Christ about this occurrence, he told her it had happened because she separated herself from the community (345).

The spiritual life of this Clarisse, Colette's companion, is known only from a late account (there are none dated earlier). Its portrayal of sanctity bears the mark of the period the biographical note was written. There are some chronological clues that indicate Colette's real trust in her, demonstrating the quality of her religious life.

One tradition says that she and Perrine accompanied the reformer on her travels. Marie refused appointment as abbess of Vevey. In 1464, Duchess Yolande of France, sister of Louis XI and wife of Blessed Amadeus of Savoy, founded Chambéry. Marie Chevalier was sent there with some companions, and the new community soon elected her abbess. In 1478, the duchess founded another monastery in Geneva. Marie was made head of the new community, dying there after six months (1479).

At Chambéry, she converted a magician, who later become a friar minor and died in the odor of sanctity at Amiens. At the abbess's request, he painted a picture of Jesus Christ on the cross, bruised and disfigured. The abbot of Saint-Laurent reported this painting was still venerated in the eighteenth century, responsible for many miracles and conversions. Two works that have since disappeared, *The Treasure of the Soul* and a *Life of Jesus Christ,* are attributed to Mother Chevalier.

Although the representation of sanctity may have modified the spiritual portrait of this abbess, her religious personality was strong enough to leave a mark on the communities she founded and an enduring memory among the Colettines.

Blessed Bonne d'Armagnac (1434-1457)[60]

The Church never recognized Bonne d'Armagnac or proclaimed her blessed, but she soon received the title within the Franciscan Order. In 1587, a general minister, François de Gonzague, noted in a document that her bones were held in great honor, obtaining many graces for those invoking her name.

One of the most interesting features of her short life was the source of her vocation. In 1424, her father Bernard d'Armagnac married Eléonore, daughter of Jacques de Bourbon. They were childless for ten years, when they asked Colette to pray for the fertility of their home. She recommended they promise their first daughter to God. Two dates are given for her birth, 1434 or 1439, but the earlier one seems preferred.

She was given the name of Clare, but she was usually known by the name of her grandmother Bonne de Berry. The couple had other children – two sons and a daughter Catherine. Later, Bonne learned of her parents' promise to God. She surprised them by refusing to enter religious life, despite being brought up fervent and devout in her faith. The youngest daughter, Catherine, seeing her parents' distress, offered herself in her sister's place. Colette then took Catherine to Amiens, where she joined her aunts Marie and Isabeau de la Marche, daughters of Jacques de Bourbon.

Catherine must have been young, because the archives of the monastery of Amiens possess clothing belonging to a young princess. These archives also possess documents showing that on three occasions (1466, 1467, and 1468) the abbess opposed the departure of Catherine de la Marche against claims that her vocation had not been freely chosen.[61]

---

[60] Recent references: *D.H.G.E.*, 9, col. 1026; *Catholicisme*: I, col. 839. The latest work we know of is by Guy Daval, *La bienheureuse Bonne d'Armagnac (1434-1457)* (Paris, 1912). It refers to the primary source, Bonne's biography by Brother Louis Boyer of Saint Martha, written in 1728 using the now vanished chronicles of the monastery of Lézignan. The Capuchins of Toulouse have a copy of this *Vie* in their provincial archives.

[61] U. d'Alençon, *A.F.H.*, 1908, 686 and Amiens Archives.

We can assume that Catherine, as an adult, tried to escape from what might have felt to be a forced vocation. We will never know what really happened. In 1466, she became abbess at the monastery of Castres, perhaps moving closer to her family or away from a monastery where she had experienced tension with her superior.

As for Bonne, at one time she was approached to become the wife of Charles, Duke of Berry and son of King Charles VIII. The biographer notes the girl's hesitation, torn between the attractions of the world and the example of her sister Catherine. One day, he continues, during the elevation of the host, she heard a "strong, sweet voice" that said: "Bonnette, you will be punished unless you become a religious sister!" She recognized the voice of her grandmother, Bonne de Berry. Turning to the altar, she saw, on one side, a bleeding Christ lying over the altar and, on the other, an angel holding three golden crowns with the words: "poverty, chastity, martyrdom."

Understanding what was being asked of her, she approached the altar and promised to give herself, body and soul. Her parents at once acceded to her request to enter the cloister. She was professed at Lézignan in 1454, receiving Colette's own veil, given her by Benedict XIII. It had been sent to the Armagnac family by the Clarisses of Gand in thanks for their devotion to the Colettine reform.

Bonne's life at the monastery would be short. She was noted for her humility and devotion to the Passion. She had the sadness of losing her father without seeing him again. Dying, she had a vision of the Child Jesus, placed in her arms by the Virgin Mary. As with Marie Chevalier, this indicates a new spirituality. Contemporary with Catherine of Bologna (who also had a vision of the Child Jesus), these French Colettines seemed to enrich their reformer's spirituality with a certain sweetness.

After hearing the Passion read aloud, Bonne died about the age of twenty-three. The documents about Catherine's attempts to leave and Bonne's hesitation at entering the cloister leave us guessing about the profound suffering of this young woman, her problem accepting a vocation decided for her before birth. She did accept it, and left the record of a humble, prayerful life, perhaps cut short by an inner struggle whose bitterness we can only sense. Coming from a very devout family, Bonne seems astonishingly "modern" in her hesitation to enter a preordained social and religious framework in which a woman has little initiative or freedom of choice.

The Second Generation: Blessed Louise of Savoy (1462-1503)[62] and Philippa de Gueldre (1464-1547)[63]

These two Colettine figures of the next generation belonged to a cultural and geographical milieu situated at the turning point of two civilizations – the very end of the Middle Ages and the French Renaissance. They were contemporaries of Battista Varani, whom we have chosen to study with the Observant Clarisses, who paralleled Colette herself.

The Italian Renaissance developed earlier than its French counterpart. Like Catherine of Bologna and the other holy abbesses of the southern Observance, Battista was a child of the Quattrocento. There is both a cultural and religious continuity there.

Our study of the two Colettine Clarisses, Louise of Savoy and Philippa de Gueldre, provides us with a better idea of some of the characteristics of Colette's daughters who were responsible for passing on her legacy. They share some common features. Unlike Marie Chevalier or Bonne d'Armagnac, both entered the monastery late, after a successful family life and widowhood. Both belonged to the high nobility that had decisive political and social influence. Both had long experience of life as a Colettine Clarisse and died in the odor of sanctity. Louise of Savoy was beatified by the Church in 1839, when Gregory XVI confirmed her cult as immemorial.[64]

---

[62] *Catholicisme*, VIII, col. 1187.

[63] *Catholicisme*, X, col. 185 and 186.

[64] The decree *Caelestes Jerusalem* of Urban VIII, July 5, 1634, stated that a cult must have endured for at least one hundred years to be known as immemorial.

Louise was the daughter of Amadeus IX of Savoy and Yolande of France, sister of Louis XI.[65] Amadeus left state affairs to his wife and, when he died in 1472, Yolande became regent. During the Burgundian wars between Louis XI and Charles the Bold, she was imprisoned with her children by Duke Charles, despite being his ally. Louise was beloved by Hugues de Chalon, a member of the cadet branch of Burgundy. She and her sister Marie, orphaned, were received at the court of King Louis XI, their uncle, who had captured Hugues.

In exchange for loyalty to Louis XI, Hugues was released and allowed to marry Louise. "They loved each other," notes the biographer. The childless couple lived very devotedly at Nozeroy. Louise's life was very monastic, a little like the mother of Laurence the Magnificent.[66] The day was regulated by the hours of the offices, devotions, and the flight from worldliness. From her youth she had a Franciscan confessor, Fr. Perrin. Although fairly well educated, Louise still belonged to the Middle Ages in terms of quantifying her prayer. On the eve of Our Lady's feasts, she fasted on bread and water and said 365 *Ave Marias* while meditating on Christ's life and Passion. On the feast of 11,000 virgins, she said 11,000 *Ave Marias*.

Philippa de Gueldre, for her part, married Duke René II of Lorraine[67] in 1485, after his first marriage to Jeanne d'Harcourt was annulled after fourteen years. She studied Latin with her sister-in-law Marguerite, who, after the death of her husband the Duke of Alençon, became a Clarisse and died at the age of fifty-eight in 1521.

Of Philippa's twelve children, seven died in infancy. She managed her husband's public affairs while he was at war

---

[65] One of her ladies-in-waiting, Catherine de Saulx, who entered the monastery of Orbe with her, wrote her life in 1507; cf. *Bibl. Sanc.*, VIII, 297.

[66] Cf. Part 2, Chapter II.

[67] *La vie de la vénérable servante de Dieu, Madame Philippa de Gueldre, recueillie fidèlement par les plus anciennes religieuses dudit couvent*, ed. Monastery of Pont-à-Mousson; P. Guinet, *Addition à la vie de la vénérable servante de Dieu*, Pont-à-Mousson.

or traveling on state business. The couple, pious and devoted to Saint Francis, founded a Franciscan house at Nancy in 1486. Widowed in 1505, she finished raising her youngest son Francis while aspiring to the silence of the cloister.

Like Louise, Philippa knew from her youth the turmoil of war that decimated the finest of the great families. Her father died in the battle of Nancy in 1477. From 1473 on, she was welcomed at Gand by Margaret of York, third wife of Charles the Bold. Unlike Louise, Philippa suffered even in the cloister the effects of political events. Her youngest son Francis died at Pavia in 1525.

Thus family and political events colored the lives of these nuns with a certain austerity, even sadness, particularly that of Philippa. They expressed their feelings, however, less dramatically than did Battista Varani. Neither of the French Colettines were extroverted women. With their austerity and sufferings lived in great dignity and silence, they were more similar to Colette, being nearer to her both culturally and geographically.

We find even clearer points of similarity: the same humility (Philippa refused election as abbess) and the same desire to follow the regular life in all its strictness. But Louise was dispensed from work because of her frailty, a matter of reproach from her fellow sisters. The more robust Philippa, however, did manual work and went barefoot.

They had the same devotion to the Passion, the Eucharist, and the Virgin; and their learning meant they could use Latin books (Gregory the Great's *Dialogues* in Philippa's case) and even write. Their biographers speak of mystical states: tears while meditating on the Passion, premonitions, etc. (Philippa had a vision of the battlefield on which her son perished), pains felt on Fridays.

Louise's enclosed life and her death were more peaceful and serene, because, no doubt, of her childless widowhood. She asked the abbess to mime the Last Supper, sharing bread and wine with her beloved sisters, and said gently to them: "I am going to heaven." She died at the age of forty-one.

Philippa de Gueldre, much older, suffered in agony a long time. As dowager duchess she played a more significant role than did Louise in the Colettine reform and within the monastery. Although refusing the position of abbess, she built an oratory dedicated to the Passion and one dedicated to Calvary, and she visited them often. She wrote to her sons, who kept her in touch with Duchy affairs so she could include State concerns in her prayer.

Above all, she mediated the dispute between the Colettines and the Observants, successfully supporting the request of the Abbess of Gand to Paul III in 1526 to retain governance of the former friars of the Colettine reform (suppressed in 1517, it should be remembered). She used to say:

> I have many friends, my allies hold the highest positions in Europe, the king (of France) is my cousin, and he loves me: that says it all.[68]

Colette was able to make so many foundations because of the help of the representatives of great houses, who continued to defend the reform after her death. She received daughters of these great people in her monasteries, forming a solid framework of abbesses and guardians of the privilege of the reform, forming an independent branch within the Franciscan Order for many years.

In addition, although Colette had hesitated to accept widows[69] whose motives she suspected, the abbesses quickly received ladies from the high nobility, widows with or without children, women like Catherine de Saulx, who came with their ladies in waiting. The strict religious life was maintained thanks to the quality of the religious life of these great ladies,

---

[68] H. Lippens, 12.

[69] She accepted the Countess of Valentinois at Vevey, a widow at nineteen after a marriage arranged by Amadeus VIII of Savoy, though she had to test her vocation; cf. E. Lopez, "Amédée VIII et Colette de Corbie," *Amédée VIII-Félix V, Ier duc de Savoie et pape (1383-1451)*, Actes du colloque international de Ripaille-Lausanne, 1990, Fondation Humbert II et Marie Josée de Savoie, Coll. Bibliothèque historique vaudoise, n° 103 (1992), 317-26.

who brought a spiritual energy to the monasteries equivalent to the moral strength they had shown in the challenges of family life. The Colettine reform also benefited from the relationships and support provided by the great families.

As regarded poverty and recruitment (e.g., taking very young girls formed in the monastery after a parental vow), Colette showed adaptability between the theory of her *Constitutions* and *Commandments* and actual practice. Her disciples continued in this vein in certain areas, such as acceptance of members of the nobility to the monastery after they had completed family life.

Reformed, Non-Colettine Clarisses (Except in Italy)

The boost that Saint Colette gave to the religious life of the Clarisses was not restricted only to those who followed her reform. Shortly after her death, several groups of monasteries emerged clearly inspired by her teaching, though not directly connected with her. From the middle of the fifteenth century, in fact, the influence of these friars spread outside Italy, as circumstances demanded.

The spread of ideas and information depended on people who had links in particular regions. For instance, the followers of Colette expanded in France during the fifteenth century in a localized way to the east of a line between Rouen and Perpignan (apart from Nantes and Dinan; see map).

Non-Colettine reformed communities also originated from the combination of individual initiative and favorable local conditions. The *Ave Maria* monasteries were characterized by their observance of Colette's *Constitutions* despite not belonging to her spiritual family. The original core was constituted by the Grey Sisters of Metz. These regular tertiaries, vowed to the care of the sick, were placed under the authority of the Observants. When they learned that a wealthy widow from the town wished to found a convent of reformed

Clarisses,[70] most of them willingly supported the project and adopted the *Rule* of Saint Clare with Colette's *Constitutions*, while still governed by the Observants, who provided them with alms and looked after the servants.[71]

A 1502 document confirms the agreement between the Clarisses and the "Baudes"[72] in the presence of Nicolas Denisé, vicar provincial:

> The guardian of the "Baudes" will provide the nuns with preachers who will also be mendicants: each will have a companion appointed by the guardian, all residing in the friars' convent, except for the confessor who will have a room near the monasteries to provide daily mass and oversee the servants.[73]

The new monastic community was officially formed in 1482.

The link to the friars minor was therefore a little different from that of the Colettines. There was no fraternity to serve the Clarisses exclusively. The friars' community had its own life and apostolate and delegated friars of whom only one lived at the monastery.

Soon after, other Grey Sisters followed the example of Metz, especially in Paris. In 1471, Louis XI gave them a former beguine house. They clashed, however, with a coalition led by the Conventuals, including the Clarisses of Saint-Marcel and Longchamp, the University, the Hôtel-Dieu, and other mendicant orders, who attempted to block registration of their letters patent. The Conventuals asserted that the

---

[70] There had been a convent of Urbanist Clarisses in Metz since the thirteenth century. Pontifical authorisation for the new monastery was given in 1480, foundation bull, *Bull. Franc.* ns. III, n° 1274, Jan. 1480. Construction of the new convent by a citizen of Metz, Wadding, 1483, n° 56, XIV, 142. Pontifical authorisation to build the new convent, Wadding, 1484, suppl. n°1, XIV, 452.

[71] Cl. Schmitt, "Agreement between the 'Colettines' of Metz and the bauds, August 20, 1502," *A.F.H.*, 61 (1968): 274-75.

[72] The "Baudes" was the common name for the Observants in this region.

[73] Cl. Schmitt, "Agreement between the 'Colettines,'" 274-75.

establishment was a pretext to introduce the Observants to Paris and claimed that "their presence in the city would ruin peace and unity." The Conventuals wanted the sisters to submit to their jurisdiction or, failing that, for Colettines to be installed in the convent.[74]

When the Grey Sisters had won their case and obtained registration of the donation, the Observants suggested they imitate their sisters in Metz by adopting the *Rule* of Saint Clare with Colette's *Constitutions*. Like the Colettines, they were then free to choose chaplains for their monastery.

On June 10, 1485, in the monastery chapel, attended by several leading figures and witnesses, the *"Ave Maria"* sisters made their solemn profession according to the *First Rule* of Saint Clare. Father Nicolas Gilbert, a friar minor of the Observance, representing the vicar provincial, "took possession and superiority over the said mothers and sisters."[75]

The following month Charles VIII authorized creation of a community of six religious men for the spiritual service of the sisters, along with a "suitable number of servants, lay brothers, and *conversi*, oblates of the order of Saint Francis, as needed to provide alms and serve all their other needs, as required by the quality of the said order of Saint Clare."[76]

Another foundation was made at Albi in 1487. As Saint Colette had done on her arrival at Besançon, the nuns hastily gave up the few possessions of the monastery in order to live in the strictest poverty. The proceeds were used to establish a chaplaincy attached to the altar of the convent church, the incumbent of which would be required to celebrate two masses a week for the intention of past benefactors. The community at Albi was noted for its great fervor until the Revo-

---

[74] P. Gratien, "Fondation des Clarisses de l'*Ave Maria* et Établissement des Frères mineurs de l'Observance à Paris (1478-1485)," *Études Franciscaines*, 27-28 (1912): 272-90, 504-16, 605-21, from where this information comes.

[75] P. Gratien, "Fondation des Clarisses," 510-12. Fr Nicolas Gilbert is not the same as Fr. Gilbert Nicolas, better known as Gabriel-Maria (note in P. Gratien, 510).

[76] Act of 1492 noting Charles VIII's decision, quoted by P. Gratien, "Fondation des Clarisses," 514.

lution. It housed many holy Clarisses, including Élisabeth of Navarre and Marie de Clermont.

Élisabeth of Navarre lived at the beginning of the sixteenth century:

> Of royal birth ... she shone marvelously with the greatest virtues.... She originated from the most illustrious family of the princes of Béarn.... Her humility, poverty and other virtues were incredible.... God endowed her with power to perform many miracles *(multis miraculis a Deo exornata)*. She flourished around 1500.[77]

Marie de Clermont, novice mistress and vicar of the Albi community, was called by her uncle, Bishop Louis d'Amboise, to Avignon with five of her companions around 1515 to bring the reform to the very lax monastery of the city. She governed the community for thirty-four years, until her death around 1550, and perfectly established regular observance there. Her exceptional personality and very holy life attracted many vocations, including nine from her own family.[78]

In 1490 Margaret of York also founded, with Grey Sisters who had opted for the Clarisse way of life, a monastery at Lille "following Sister Colette's reform."[79] In addition, there were foundations between 1484 and 1501 at Bar-le-Duc, Gouda, Malines, Brussels, and Alençon. Finally, Middelbourg was founded in 1515 and Toulouse in 1516.

At Middelbourg, Count William and his wife, with the full approval of the Observants, offered property and income to provide the nuns with material security. But the nuns formally opposed this and appealed to Pope Leo X, who granted them at their request the "privilege of strictest poverty"

---

[77] A. Bocquet, *Le Monastère des Clarisses du Faubourg Saint Cyprien de Toulouse*, 15, note 5. The author quotes the Latin text from F. Huebert, *Menelogium sanctorum beatorum ... et triplici ordine fratrum minorum, clarissarum et penitentium*, 1866, n° 10 (Munich, 1698).

[78] A. Bocquet, *Étude manuscrite sur le monastère d'Albi*. For the *Ave Maria* Clarisses, the abbess was appointed for life.

[79] Bull of April 20, 1490, Département Archives.

in a brief of September 1515. Loyal to the *Constitutions* of Saint Colette, the community never had sisters on duty at the "turn." A "Martha" (a lay sister serving the convent) was housed near the entrance to the monastery and did the daily errands.

The community was noted for its strict life, its fervor, and its remarkable loyalty to Saint Clare's ideal. The sisters lived only on alms, in great poverty and austerity of life. They rarely even received foundations for masses or for tombs in their church. The monastery's location in a most insalubrious district, near a hospital for contagious diseases, made the enclosed life particularly hard. The convent was an old building, never rebuilt and always being repaired. The sisters still unfailingly observed the *Rule* with no exceptions. Their numbers quickly reached forty and always remained numerous. The community could be considered a benchmark for Observant communities with their particularly sincere, constant, and strong character.

In most cases, these foundations adopted the Colettine *Constitutions* but under Observant authority. The papacy encouraged this with a view to unifying the reform movement in order to facilitate its governance.

The influence of Colette's reform spread thanks to the coherent legislative text provided by the *Constitutions*. Life in the convents was organized more and more around the observances put into place by Colette and the first generations of her reform.

CHAPTER 5

MONASTERY LIFE OR LIVING THE HERITAGE

MONASTERIES AND SOCIETY

A study of some of the Colettine Clarisses provides insight into certain aspects of the relationship between the monastery and society.

Recruitment from Society

The founders of the various male or female monasteries had one or more members of their own families in the Colettine reform, including:

From the first generation:

- Élisabeth de Bavière, daughter of Mahaut, niece of Blanche of Geneva.
- Perrine de Baume, niece of Brother Henry de Baume and Colette's biographer.
- Isabeau and Marie, the two daughters of Jacques de Bourbon.
- Catherine and Bonne, granddaughters of Jacques de Bourbon, daughters of Bernard d'Armagnac.
- Guillemette, Countess of Valentinois.

From the second generation:

- Philippine de Chalon, sister-in-law of Louise de Chalon.
- Louise of Savoy, wife of Hugues de Chalon, daughter of Amadeus IX.
- Philippa de Gueldre, dowager duchess of Lorraine.
- Marguerite, her sister-in-law, wife of the Duke d'Alençon.

The lists of abbesses or sisters that have come down to us from this period carry their particular names. The Annals of the monasteries of Puy, Poligny, and Amiens give the family names of the provincial nobility or the upper bourgeoisie.[1] Thus, Marie Chevalier from Besançon belonged, according to her biographer, to a "family endowed with wealth and property,"[2] and Etiennette Hannequin, mentioned by Perrine, was the daughter of a rich merchant. In turn, the presence of the daughters of the aristocracy certainly attracted vocations from the nobility or the provincial middle classes, as suggested in the *Letter to the inhabitants of Amiens*.[3]

Monastery governance most frequently lay in the hands of these sisters, who either became abbesses or held other important responsibilities within the community (vicar, councilor, etc.). Even if, like Philippa de Gueldre, they refused election as abbess, they still played an important part in supporting the reform and could build oratories or commission works of art within the monastery. However, Louise of Savoy did not seem to have exercised any authority. Catherine de Saulx, her biographer and former lady-in-waiting, commented on her humility: she carried out inferior work, perhaps because of her frail health.

---

[1] At Orbe, for instance, the list of abbesses includes: Mahaut de la Baume, François d'Aubonne, Catherine de Gavid. At Amiens, the abbess who opposed Catherine de la Marche's departure was Marguerite de Belleval.

[2] Abbé De Saint-Laurent, Ms., 343.

[3] P. De Vaux, Part 2.

An interesting document reveals that, in fact, governance of a monastery might occasionally have been assigned to a particular sister just because of her parentage. It involves a bull sent to Pierre de Vaux by Pope Nicholas V[4] (October 23, 1448), permitting ten religious brothers and ten religious sisters of illegitimate birth to exercise offices in the cloister and to act as abbess. Since the original of this bull is in the Amiens archives, it is possible that one of the princesses, a daughter of Jacques de Bourbon, perhaps Isabeau, was illegitimate. In the documents, she is given the name Jeanne and was the first abbess of Amiens. Furthermore, her sister, Marie de la Marche, was vicar.

In the sixteenth and seventeenth centuries, there were still many abbesses who belonged to the nobility, but there were few if any great families represented, and just as many abbesses seemed to have come from the bourgeoisie. In Péronne, the sixteenth-century abbesses were noblewomen: Jeanne de Famechon (†1504), Jeanne de Caulincourt (†1560), and Françoise du Bourg (†1561). This does not mean that no middleclass women had responsibility at this time. At the monastery of Vieil-Hesdin,[5] besides Agnès de Vaux, there were Marie Dormon, Huguette du Tarte, and Guillemette Chrestienne. According to the historical records, there seem to be few members from the lower social classes, although this was changing by the eighteenth century.

From the second half of the seventeenth century onwards, there was a gradual change, detectable in the Annals of Poligny and the Puy archives. Fewer noble names appear, and their places are taken by the bourgeoisie. This also applies in Besançon.[6]

The case of the monastery of Amiens on the eve of the Revolution has been well-documented.[7] Following a declara-

---

[4] U. d'Alençon, "Documents sur la Réforme de Sainte Colette en France," *A.F.H.*, II (1909): 608 ff.

[5] Bibliothèque Provinciale des Capucins (Paris), ms. 351.

[6] Archives of Doubs, *Dossier des clarisses de Besançon*, 16.

[7] J. Desobry, *Un aspect peu connu de la Révolution française de 1789 à Amiens: le monastère des clarisses* (Amiens, 1986).

tion by Louis XV from 1736, the monastery records had to include the parents' occupation. Most of the sisters in the community belonged to the middle and lower classes. Two of the fathers stated that they "do not know how to write." None of the sisters belonged to the nobility.[8]

Given these few details, it is possible to plot changes in the social background of those entering from the fifteenth to the eighteenth century. Monasteries that Colette had founded attracted the elite until the beginning of the following century, partly thanks to the network of relationships. This trend continued and spread to provincial nobility until the seventeenth century, when the upper strata of the bourgeoisie were also favorable soil for a blossoming of vocations.

The figure of the contemplative, in Colette and the first generation, was certainly attractive in its austerity and heroism, its firm detachment from the life of the court or high society that these young women had known. The best of its members, on leaving the world, preferred a very demanding life rather than the tepidity of the great abbeys with their lands and properties.

The ideals of these women were met by the monastic values offered by the Colettine reform. Colette's undeniable influence caused a flourishing of sanctity in the first generations, which in turn created a dynamic that could attract membership and commitment from the elite.

In fact, from the seventeenth century onwards, new symptoms were appearing regarding the place of women in society and Church. The monasteries of Amiens or Pont-à-Mousson, for instance, where princesses lived, became places of pilgrimage. Marie de Medici went to Amiens with her retinue to pray and view items that belonged to the princesses, daughters of Jacques de Bourbon.[9] Old memoirs record that the secretary to the queen mother (Marie de Medici) was the brother of a Clarisse.[10] The queen mother recommended that the Clarisses should pray for the birth of an heir to Louis

---

[8] J. Desobry, 36.

[9] P. Sellier, *Vie de sainte Colette*, I and II (Amiens, 1855).

[10] Archives of Amiens, held at the monastery of Poligny.

XIII. The abbess asked the queen to accept the dedication of the book being written by Sylvère d'Abbeville.

Still in the seventeenth century, the Prince of Condé (according to Jean Philippe, the narrator of the chronicle) went to Pont-à-Mousson surrounded by "disrespectful, unscrupulous people, with no conscience." But he went to the tomb of Philippa de Gueldre to pay his respects to her memory: "the name of Gueldre, the duchess's authority, the close alliance between the houses of Bourbon and Lorraine, and above all Philippa's sanctity overcame the influence of these rebels." The convent was spared from the sack by Condé who took it under his protection.

The high nobility respected and visited the monasteries in memory of the sanctity of Colette as well as in memory of the princesses who had lived there. The archives do not, however, note the entrance of members of the high nobility to the cloister.

In the fifteenth century and at the beginning of the sixteenth, some noblewomen could still find, in Colettine monasteries, the ideal they sought for their rank and their aspirations. A century later there were other opportunities open to women. The author of the *Life of Colette*, in the seventeenth century, was a contemporary of the king's niece, Anne de Montpensier (la Grande Mademoiselle), who had a somewhat fleeting part to play in the Fronde revolts. The salons were also beginning to give women from the high nobility opportunities to influence their society through culture. A little later, the first French novel was written by a woman, Madame de La Fayette, dealing with the emotional states of its eponymous heroine the Princess of Clèves (1688).

In a society where the influence of religion was in decline, women were becoming self-aware and liked to see themselves as having greater independence from men's authority. Until that time, unable to access politics and culture, a woman could express her creative power and energy only in the cloister. Almost imperceptibly, however, centers of interest were changing. To the extent that the elite were discovering new areas for self-realization, the monastic life, while retaining its prestige in memory of the "great predecessors," was attracting members from lower social strata, initially provincial nobility, then the middle and even lower middle classes.

Some members of the nobility entered the cloister in the eighteenth century, but as far as we know, they no longer chose the Colettines. Madame Louise de France, daughter of Louis XV, entered the Carmelites. The character of Teresa of Avila and the renown of the Teresian Carmel in France attracted the few vocations from the elite.

The lower classes were not entirely absent from monasteries, but their members did not enter the enclosure and did not say the choral office, since these young women were illiterate. They became lay sisters, or "sisters of the mountain," as the Annals of Poligny calls them, serving the community outside the monastery. They were dependent on the abbess and belonged to the Franciscan third order.[11]

Enclosure and Society

The Issue of Enclosure

Saint Colette established a strict enclosure, and the Council of Trent solemnly restated the inviolability of the pontifical enclosure on pain of excommunication. The monastery annals, where they still exist, show how, in time of war, conflict, or social tension, the cloister was breached. For instance the annals of the monasteries of Vieil-Hesdin or Poligny report breaches of the enclosure during the wars of religion and later during the Franco-Spanish war. Poligny recalls the fear of the nuns when the armies commanded by the Prince of Condé approached the town in 1636. The region, being loyal to "our good king of Spain," was threatened with pillage, feared all the more by the nuns since Condé,

---

[11] On this important and little known issue see our article: "Frères et soeurs extérieurs des couvents mendiants au Moyen Age," *Les mouvances laïques de ordres religieux, périodes médiévale et moderne*, Proceedings of the Third International CERCOR conference, Tournus, 1992, in preparation.

although a "Catholic prince," had Huguenot soldiers in his army. A plan was made to escape to Switzerland. The annals report the panic among the young sisters, indicating how the fear of rape haunted them. Condé lifted the siege of Dole, but plague broke out. The sisters, enclosed in their monastery, were in a difficult position. Their confessor climbed the enclosure wall by ladder to hear their confessions, but mass was not celebrated for three months.

In the following year, 1637, the duke of Longueville in turn threatened Poligny. Once more the urgent matter of abandoning the monastery arose. The community was divided, with the younger nuns wanting to flee, always mindful of the threat of rape. The town officials forbade the community to leave the enclosure, undertaking to defend them and provide for their needs.

The French returned in 1638 with six thousand Huguenots among their ranks. This time, Poligny was practically emptied of inhabitants and defenders. The terrified community sent a Capuchin to the Duke of Longueville to ask for protection. The prince agreed but added that if Poligny was taken and did not surrender, he could not prevent his own soldiers exercising their right to sack and pillage the town and to kill.

In fact, the enclosure was violated. The nuns, together with the lay sisters who had been allowed to enter the enclosure, sought refuge in the choir and were saved at the last minute by two French lords. They were evacuated during the sack of the town, despite resistance from some of them. In order to impress the soldiery, the sisters walked in procession behind the Blessed Sacrament. Every nun was under the protection of a "French lord," reported the annals, who shouted to the soldiers "on your knees, rabble!" One soldier who attempted to rape a sister was killed on the spot.[12]

In 1668 and 1674, when the earldom became French, most of the people, panic-stricken as the town was burned and pillaged, took refuge in the convent, first the women and

---

[12] P. Guinal, *Additions à la vie de la vénérable servante de Dieu.*

children, then some of the town's officials, who hid weapons and goods there to keep them from the French. The abbess however gave the weapons to the officers in order to prevent the pillaging of the monastery.

The same tragic events took place at the monastery of Vieil-Hesdin, where the nuns had to endure the presence of the armies of Charles V and the Huguenots in almost the same way. The monastery finally disappeared when Spanish control ended in 1639-1640.[13]

Some of these events show not only the threats suffered by the nuns but also their close relationship to the townsfolk. Another aspect of this integration can be seen in peacetime as well. The memoirs of 1623, written by the Clarisses of Poligny for the work by Sylvère d'Abbeville, provide valuable information on the monastery's relations with the local people. The situation at Poligny may be unusual, since the monastery housed the relics of Saint Colette during this period. But it is interesting that the following events took place after the Council of Trent, when its decrees on enclosure began to be generally applied (around the beginning of the seventeenth century).

The wagon that carried Colette on her journeys stood at the site of an oratory built for the reformer within the hall of the refurbished monastery chapter. Sick children were placed inside this wagon and came out cured. The memoir states: "Innocent little children, not yet having reached the age of reason, were given dispensation (from the enclosure) by our superiors," adding, "This devotion was long-standing and is growing day by day because of the frequent cures of these innocent little children." Some examples of miracles are then given.

A child of eight, afflicted with dysentery and accompanied by his father and uncle who happened to be workers of the monastery, was hoisted into the wagon. The writer states:

---

[13] A. Fromentin, "L'histoire des clarisses du Vieil-Hesdin," *Cabinet historique de l'Artois et de la Picardie*, I (1886-87), 254-320 and II (1887-88), 1-46.

Seeing this, we sisters felt great compassion for him, and encouraged him to have recourse to the prayers and merits of our blessed mother, and before leaving the monastery they made him climb into her wagon or carriage ... and promised to make a ladder for climbing more easily into the wagon.

Another little girl of eight or nine years old, who was "possessed," was "introduced into our chapter" continues the narrator.

More examples are given. Notably there is that of a woman, seized with a "frenzy," who had the door to the convent opened and ran here and there around the monastery, shouting, until she climbed into the wagon and had the "relics of our blessed mother" placed on her.

These facts prove that theory and practice of the enclosure sometimes diverged, even after the Council of Trent. Because of the common involvement of monastery and town in popular devotion to Colette, the observant convents exercised some flexibility so the community could share with the townsfolk in the benefits of the saint's intercession.

Jurisdiction of the Bishops

In general, the bishops took very seriously the role given them by Trent to be guardians of the enclosure. The transfer to episcopal jurisdiction took place gradually. The archives of Poligny and Salins show that the archbishop of Besançon took over jurisdiction of the communities in 1629. This permitted the communities to avoid repercussions from disputes within the Order.

Salins was founded by Poligny at the beginning of the seventeenth century, when the community was forced to leave Poligny under threat from the French armies. Some sisters remained in Salins till the seventeenth century, while others restored the monastery of Poligny.

Transfer to episcopal jurisdiction sometimes caused tensions. After 1645 in Puy, the bishop, Mgr. Maupas du Tour,[14] tried to verify the enclosure of the nuns. The abbess formally opposed this, arguing that they were exempt from diocesan jurisdiction. Despite the authorities' acknowledging the monastery's rights, the community had to give way under threats from the bishop to break down the doors.

The bishop summoned the community to the chapter, and reprimanded the confessor, who had been seen in taverns and did not go "discalced."[15] Things calmed down, but in 1648, the bishop again threatened to break down the doors unless they were opened. A legal process was prepared. The bishop stipulated appointment of a secular or regular confessor "for three months at a time." In 1649, he announced another visitation, upon which the abbess and community decided to act to avoid what they saw as an abuse of power. When the bishop arrived, the doors were barricaded. He had them broken down. A legal process was prepared and a claim was sent to the King of France (1655). The case was lengthy and, though the abbess's privileges were recognized, the bishop finally won. This case, while exceptional, is symptomatic of the possible tensions that could arise between the hierarchy and monasteries that wished to remain autonomous.

This case also had implications for the choice of confessors. As well as intervening in the enclosure, the bishop tried to impose a dismissible confessor. The Council of Trent had replaced the election of an abbess for life with a three-year term of office, a measure also applied to confessors. Generally, the Colettines had chosen their confessors from former friars of the reform or, when these had disappeared after the 1517 decree, from the Capuchins (the latest reform of the Order in the sixteenth century). The Colettines tried to distance themselves from the Observants, among whom laxity

---

[14] "Le monastère des clarisses du Puy," produced by the Puy monastery, *F.F.*, 56-104.

[15] The bishop attracted a response from a sister: "The holy bishop of Geneva said that the reform should begin not from the feet but from the head."

began to appear by the seventeenth century. Sometimes the provincial imposed an Observant friar on them, as in Amiens in 1532.

In 1574, the Capuchins obtained permission to spread beyond Italy. In 1593, a request was made by Amiens, and the plan was carried out at the beginning of the seventeenth century. In 1612, the Colettine Clarisses, under the bishop's authority, asked to be placed under the Capuchins' direction. The matter was decided by the king in 1628.[16] Poligny and Salins asked the archbishop for Capuchin confessors in 1629 "so they could better and more perfectly observe the rule."

It appears that, generally speaking, the abbesses, caught between the bishop's jurisdiction and the spiritual direction of religious or secular priests, strove to keep their authority over the monastery and prevent excessive interference in the life of the community. Sometimes they played one official off against another, but, after the Council of Trent reinforced the role of the priest, monasteries had less room to maneuver.

Relations with the Towns

Normally, insertion into the towns and relationships with the townspeople were good. Nevertheless, the foundation as such was often not welcomed by the local authorities and/or the people. We saw one example in Corbie, where a foundation could not be made, and in Amiens where Pierre de Vaux intervened in 1443. This also happened in Puy, where Claude Roussillon had a great deal of trouble establishing a foundation.[17]

Later still, when the community of Poligny fled to Salins in 1629-1631, it found refuge with difficulty. The authorities refused a new foundation, and the Carmelites gave them a house that was not acknowledged as a monastery. In 1638, the community finally managed to obtain a more commodious priory, but it was secreted away since the townsfolk were vigorously opposed to any such attempt. For the sake

---

[16] J. Desobry, 16-18.
[17] "Le monastère des clarisses du Puy," 56 ff.

of discretion, the sisters could have mass only on Sundays and feast days. The accommodation was temporary and unfit for habitation. The community did not have permission to beg in the towns, only in the villages, and thus had scant resources.

Appeals to the King of Spain succeeded in his granting them a weekly collection. In 1643, as "Duke in the earldom of Burgundy," he asked the Parliament of Dole to give the community permission to establish itself in the town and to beg for alms. The parliament refused. At the same time, a magistrate's daughter was forbidden to enter the monastery to respond to her vocation. Gradually the situation settled down, and the girl was allowed to enter. At the triennial elections in 1649, however, the magistrates of Salins once more intervened to have the election of the abbess take place at the founding monastery of Poligny, thus avoiding a permanent installation at Salins. Only in 1653 did the Salins monastery become independent, and the new building was finished in 1658.

The families of the sisters assisted the monastery financially, providing a kind of support network. Sometimes it happened, however, that problems arose when a family pressured the community to keep a girl. For example, in Poligny, the abbess returned money and effects that the novice had brought with her so the parents would take their daughter back.

The archives at Puy note the community's complaints about the racket made by neighbors during family celebrations or on the feast days of Saint John. The traditional processional route passed across land on which the monastery was built. Workers breached the enclosure, performed their dances, and continued along their way. A court case was brought resulting in a simple change of route.[18]

The monastery archives, in accounts of legacies and donations and reports of feastday celebrations, show clearly how well the community was integrated into the life of the town.

---

[18] Archives of Salins, copy held in monastery of Besançon.

Financial gifts were either stipends for masses to be said by chaplains or help to the community for its own subsistence.

From 1640-1643, Gaspard Armand XVIII, Viscount of Polignac, gave to the monastery of Puy[19] "300 livres for the repose of his soul." In 1712, Antoine Ladevèse, "official procurator for the Barony of Cereix, certifies he has given one setier [150-300 liters] of wheat to the Clarisses for fourteen years on the orders of the late Duchess of Uzès." This alms was given again in 1791. In 1759, "the cardinal of Rohan, priest of the Chaise-Dieu, gave two setiers a year during the period of his incumbency."

In Besançon, the Clarisses owned vineyards, revenue from which perhaps provided payments for chaplains; but they also received income from legacies during Colette's lifetime and later.[20] In 1444 for example: "Transfer by the religious sisters to Jean Pourcelot of their vineyard at Chamuse for his in Chamers." And in 1659, again at Baux: "Farming lease of various lands in Courcheton left by Élisabeth Cabin, widow of Adrien Peclet of Pontarlier to François Retou, the income from this lease to be paid to the Clarisse sisters."

Once established then, the sisters benefited from the sympathy and support of the local people. While there were occasional tensions, their effects were limited and had no long-term consequences.[21]

Religious ceremonies encouraged the people to take part in the life of the monastery and vice versa. In the case of jubilees, for instance, one was granted to the monastery of Puy in 1589 "in order to have a most Christian and Catholic king, rather than the heretical king of Navarre." Other jubilees in 1605 and 1634 were occasions for visitations to the Saint Clare monastery and for alms-giving. In 1630, the Clarisses

---

[19] "Le monastère des clarisses du Puy," 99-100.

[20] "Dossier Clarisses de Besançon," *Franciscan history sources in Franche-Comté*, 14.

[21] Litigation, when it occurred, was usually with religious authorities (e.g., the bishop of Puy) or other religious or priests: disputes involved either neighboring property (the Jesuits at Salins) or foundation masses to be said by chaplains (the Clarisses of Besançon), "Sources," 15.

even joined a procession following a vow made by the canons to avert the plague.[22]

In 1714, Poligny was the scene of great festivities for the canonization of Catherine of Bologna.[23] The monastery chapel was lavishly decorated with flowers, tapestries, a painting of Saint Catherine, and a crimson dais. There were processions in the town with the councilors. Every day there were speeches, orchestral concerts (motets), and masses preached by the various orders.

The life of the Clarisses, then, was firmly embedded in the social and ecclesial fabric, although Colette had intended to avoid too much influence from worldly values; hence her choice of smaller towns. The monastery maintained vital links with Church and society, but its life was not defined only by this dimension. It lived out its own dynamic plan that was able, over the years, to bring together women from various backgrounds and ages.

The Regular Life

Customaries and Books of Ritual

Customaries and books of ritual regulated the various aspects of religious life from the moment of entry and established, in writing, the customs of the monastery. These began to appear in the seventeenth and eighteenth centuries.[24]

The ritual book aimed to regulate and explain attitudes to be held during the recitation of the office, on feast days, or when celebrating the sacrament of the sick. One chapter covered reception of novices. The list of chapter titles gives an accurate idea of the content:

---

[22] "Le monastère des clarisses du Puy," 73-75.
[23] Annals of monastery of Besançon.
[24] See titles of first two collections: *Rituel ou Cérémonial à l'usage du monastère des religieuses de Sainte-Claire de Besançon* (Lyon, 1671); *Coutumier et Directoire des religieuses de Sainte-Claire de Poligny* (Lyon, 1603). (The note about Salins is later.) Another *Rituel* was written in Lyon in 1732.

Book One: The Ceremonial of the Religious sisters of Saint Clare of the Convent of Besançon, containing all the orders to be observed for Divine office and other regular exercises.
– How and when to make deep, medium, or slight bows (Ch. 6).
– Application of the discipline and the days it is to be taken (Ch. 17).

Book Two: The Ceremonial of the Religious sisters of Saint Clare and ordinaries and what has to be carried out on particular days in the year.
– Prayers to be said on particular days in the year (Ch. 14).

Book Three: The Ceremonial of the Religious sisters of Saint Clare of the Convent of Besançon, containing ceremonies for reception and profession of novices with their duties: reception and profession of our lay sisters with their exercises.
– Instructions and regulations for the novitiate (Ch. 3).

Book Four: Containing the form for administering the holy sacraments to the sick and the funeral rites; prayers and the bells to be rung for them, with some copies of letters from our B. Mother Colette.
– Prayers to be said for our deceased sisters at other monasteries of our order and for many other persons (Ch. 3).

The customary regulated conventual life outside religious offices. It assumed the practical application of the four vows, including that of enclosure. It had chapters covering formation of young sisters and the various jobs in the monastery.

Part One:
- Chapter I: The end towards which Religious Sisters of Saint Clare strive.
- From Chapter II to Chapter V: The vows.
- From Chapter VI to Chapter IX: Formation.
- From Chapter X to Chapter XXI: Organization of the regular life.
- Chapter XXII: Mortifications and penances done in public.
- Chapter XXIII: Pardons, blessings, and permissions given every Saturday in the refectory.
- Chapter XXIV to Chapter XXXIII: Some practical issues: the sick, linen, archives.
- Chapter XXXIV: Visitation by the superior.

Part Two:

- From Chapter I to Chapter XIX: The responsibilities of the abbess, vicar, counselor or discreet, and the main offices (secretaries, sacristan, etc).

Both works give classified lists of the *Commandments, Intentions,* and others of Colette's recommendations. They add headings for situations or tasks not foreseen by the legislation of the reform but certainly known from experience by the communities Colette had founded.

It should be noted that physical penances remain, including a chamber of discipline or prison for serious faults, as Colette's writings require. The discipline was to be administered in the refectory by another sister, although the number of strokes was not specified. The abbess held the key to the door of the chamber of discipline where a sister was locked up.[25] Penances and mortifications done out of devotion to Christ's Passion were laid down and took place in the refectory.[26] The sister, with a rope around her neck, would kiss the

---

[25] *Coutumier* and *Directoire*, 129 ff.
[26] *Rituel* or *Cérémonial*, 49 ff.

feet of all the sisters in turn, the abbess first. The sequence to follow was specified. No sister might draw back her foot.

Another mortification was to eat off the floor with the rope around the neck. The penance of gag and blindfold required the sister to kneel in the refectory, strips of cloth around her eyes and mouth, hands joined, until the abbess ordered her back to her place. An item broken through carelessness might also be carried around the neck. "Trampling on pride" consisted of the sister lying in the doorway of the refectory so that the community would have to step over her. Another penance imposed by the abbess involved tracing crosses with the tongue on the floor, a foot long and a foot wide: "And any more than that would depend on the fervor of the one who did it."[27]

Still others mimed moments in the Passion. At the four corners of the refectory, the sister asked pardon, the rope around her neck, for giving bad example: "… this must be done while reflecting on Jesus our Savior, falsely slandered." The sisters had to "hiss" at the penitent if ordered by the abbess:

> … the reflection will be on how Jesus Christ was dragged through the streets of Jerusalem, bound and chained, hissed, mocked and scorned by all the people.

Wearing spectacles was to mortify "wandering sight," a mortification especially recommended for novices. Another variant was to stretch out on the ground, hands joined, and another sister placed her foot on the neck of the first, saying to her: "Proud dust and ashes, learn to be humble."[28] This penance came from the life of Saint Francis, who, one day, as punishment for a sinful thought, asked a friar to put his foot on his throat.[29]

---

[27] *Rituel* or *Cérémonial*, 56. Charles Borromeo imposed this penance in Milan on sisters gossiping with priests.

[28] These passages refer to the *Rituel*, 55 ff.

[29] "The Little Flowers of Saint Francis," Ch. 3, *FA:ED* 3, 571.

This group of penances, including the discipline given in the refectory, is not found in any of Colette's writings. Monastic practices developed from meditating on the life of Christ or from imitating the life of a saint. The need to set them down in writing over the years risked the regular life being perceived as a series of ritualized practices. With no room for initiative, monastic life could become a struggle to absorb and live out all these instructions and attitudes rather than a self-emptying that would lead to the perfection of charity.

Did the observant life always proceed according to this formulaic concept?

Daily Life

There are few documents extant that give a clear picture of the pattern of daily life. There are some existing annals in archives saved wholly or partly by communities from fires, wars, or the Revolution. Available documents, interesting though they are as a direct reflection of daily life, provide a partial record since only significant events are recorded, and these for the purpose of "edifying" the reader. Brief comments or marginal notes from copyists, over a long period of time, do give us some features from real life that would not normally interest pious authors.

There is a great deal of information in the annals of the monastery of Poligny about breaches of the rule and scandals. War was not the only factor upsetting convent life. Fires threatened buildings in the town fairly often. In 1679, imminent danger from a fire affected the community's routine. At the nuns' request, some men and Capuchin friars helped the sisters inside the enclosure. The danger having passed, the Capuchins and the sisters ate in the refectory and twelve men spent the night in the enclosure because of risk of further outbreaks of fire. After several nights spent in the church, the lay or extern sisters were finally allowed to sleep with the nuns, as their room had been destroyed.

Rigorous regulations could thus be relaxed in time of need. But they also were no match for implacable behavior. The death notice of one sister ingenuously comments that she had never been able to fast, except on Good Friday. She ate all the time, claiming a weak constitution, though she had a very strong voice for singing, the narrator reports, and for all other activities. It is amusing to see that even in such a strict and observant monastery as Poligny, human nature, with all its weaknesses and limitations, could not be subdued.

Two more serious incidents also demonstrate how difficult it was for communities to ensure that regulations were followed, even when punishments and coercive measures were applicable. At Poligny again, in 1660, two sisters, said to be *conversae*, caused a scandal when one of them visited a priest in suspicious circumstances. The abbess was alerted and warned the sisters, who scorned the warning. After investigation, the abbess had them placed in the monastery's chamber of discipline on bread and water, then told them to remove the habit. They refused. Later on, outside the monastery, they persisted in their behavior and were caught in the very act. The abbess then appealed to the secular authorities to remove the habit from them. The text indicates that ten of these lay sisters living together outside the enclosure did not get on with each other, and their life was not very religious. The two guilty sisters were eventually discharged from the monastery, but they took property with them on leaving and afterwards brought a claim for damages against the monastery.

A similar situation arose some years later in 1675. A young lay sister, twenty-six years old, had a suspect relationship. Her companions and the confessor kept quiet, but some lay people, friends of the monastery, warned the abbess. She, however, delayed acting for three years, no doubt because of the previous scandal, hoping the young sister would come to her senses. (She had been in the service of the monastery since the age of fourteen.) Since this did not happen, the abbess found a pretext to bring her into the enclosure in order to end the situation, without involving the laity this time. Before the assembled community, she ordered her to remove the habit, threatening to have it stripped off her if she did not comply. The lay sister obeyed; but in order to avoid any later claim, her possessions were returned to her and also the goods that she had acquired.

These two somewhat unusual cases show how the intervention of lay people in the internal affairs of the community could create problems for the monastery: court cases, scandal, etc.

Other testimonies show regular monastic life in a more peaceful guise. The death notices of sisters in the annals note the observance, the spirit of penitence, the suffering, and the charity of the deceased. Such remarks shed light on a monastic life that might appear rigid if seen only through the customaries.

The 1623 memoir of Sylvère d'Abbeville presents the figure of Colette in a clearer way than do the biographies, making her an example to abbesses in their relationship with the sisters. Indeed, the sisters often drew on recollections transmitted by their predecessors: Colette emphasized minority and simplicity in both the spiritual and the religious life. She reconciled two sisters as soon as she noticed they were in conflict. She visited sick sisters and showed "motherly gentleness." This is the first time we find this expression in the documents we have studied. The memory of Colette as mother and reconciler was passed on and certainly permeated the quality of daily life.

The spiritual practices of the sisters developed over the years, coloring their community life. In wartime or during plagues, however, the nuns added special penances to their normal austerity. Thus, in 1672, faced with the threat of the French invasion, the nuns at the monastery of Salins[30] took the discipline every day, said the office of the dead for a month, took communion more frequently, recited one thousand *Ave Marias* with their arms crossed. They prostrated themselves face down, a rope around the neck, arms crossed, to obtain special favors from God.

When there were no dramatic events, devotions were quieter. Devotion to the Blessed Sacrament exposed on the

---

[30] Annals of the Monastery of Salins, with a copy in the archives of Besançon.

altar appeared at the end of the sixteenth and the start of the seventeenth century. In 1636, when "Louis XIII ordered a general pardon throughout France," the Blessed Sacrament was exposed at the monastery of Puy for seven days.[31] The rosary and the litanies of the Holy Name of Jesus and of the Virgin also became part of the devotions of the nuns during this period.[32] Death notices of some sisters at Poligny reveal features of their spiritual life and emphasize their prayer life and the graces from their union with God. These records show the influence of the Teresian school.

Conclusion

The framework of convent life established in the fifteenth century was further refined in the next three centuries by scrupulous fidelity to the founding texts. Practices accumulated that might give the impression of a very closely regulated, even fixed way of life. In fact, however, monastic life suffered from the upheavals of events in society or Church, as well as from those caused by the very people who lived in the monastery or served it.

Colette's daughters and the friars preserved her legacy and defended it by staying faithful to her writings in the face of the dispute between Observants and Colettines. Did this response originate in a poor understanding of Colette's position at a time when the debate got off to a confused start, or did it stem from a desire to preserve autonomy within the Observant movement and the Order? In any case, the support of great families was a determining factor in maintaining this autonomy for as long as possible despite the costs, even though, as the years went by, it became illusory.

After a century, the reformed way became the norm within the Order and seemed to lose the prestige that, at the outset, had attracted the elite so powerfully. As the monasteries

---

[31] "Le monastère des clarisses du Puy," 73.
[32] Annals of the monastery of Poligny, 73.

recruited from a wider field, they moved away from the upper echelons of society, but retained their strict observance.

Convent life was seriously affected by the upheavals of political life, and the enclosure was not always able to protect the nuns. Generally speaking, although the monasteries enjoyed the sympathy and support of the local people, there were times of tension and even conflict with civil and ecclesiastical authorities. These tensions were lived out in the enclosure – whether to move more towards the outside world or to break from it.

All these factors color the perception of monastic life as defined by Colette, despite the desire for absolute loyalty among her disciples. The tensions and problems faced by the communities were caused by the outside world breaking in, forcing monasteries to adapt and thus to live in a state of lively exchange with society and Church.

CHAPTER 6

Hagiography and History
The Canonization Process

As monasteries were established with the support of the great houses, the influence of the model of sanctity represented by Colette spread beyond the circle of her own foundations and her reform was extended.

In the eighteenth century, at the request of successive groups of petitioners, the Church began to consider all the circumstances surrounding Colette's sanctity and her influence – her personal story, her work, her life through the history of her daughters, and the trust of ordinary people in her intercession.

Fifteenth and Sixteenth Centuries

The Legenda of Pierre de Vaux

The works written during the fifteenth and sixteenth centuries were either translations of the *Legenda* of Pierre de Vaux or else a summary of the text itself, evidence that the biography written by Colette's confessor had been treated from the outset as an essential document. In 1450, Étienne de Juilly (Stephano Juliaco), a Franciscan, translated it into Latin. His version was used as the basis for later translations or studies. Laurent Surius, a Carthusian, published de

Juilly's text in 1581 in the six-volume *De probatis sanctorum historiis*.[1]

This text, in turn, was used by Michel Notel, a religious brother from Frémy near Mons, in his *Vie de sainte Colette, vierge de très digne mémoire et réformatrice de l'ordre de saint François et de sainte Claire*, published in Mons in 1594.[2]

The Biography of Josse Clichtou (1472-1543)

The biography written by Josse Clichtou is the most remarkable from this period. Published in Paris in 1512, the Latin text is in fact a summary. This humanist knew the first two *Legendae* of Pierre de Vaux and Perrine and condensed them, adding a few extra details on la Baume and mentioning the review of the body in 1492.[3]

Flemish by birth, Josse Clichtou studied in Paris and was confessor to Charles V. He was a convinced humanist, a professor at the Sorbonne, a friend of Lefèvre d'Etaples. He was notable for encouraging the renewal of studies in science and history. His work *De veratione sanctorum* avoids two pitfalls: passing to the saints our responsibility to live a Christian life and denying any value to their intercession.

His *Vie de Sainte Colette* looks at Colette's youth, the revelation of her vocation, her mission confirmed by Benedict XIII, the growth of the reform, and the last foundations made before her death at Gand. His narrative follows Pierre de Vaux's plan but is more concise and has a more historical

---

[1] U. D'Alençon says that Surius published it 1618, cf. "Introduction," *Les vies de sainte Colette Boylet de Corbie, réformatrice des frères mineurs et des clarisses* (Librairie Picard, 1911), xxiv. The text we have is dated March 1581, 150-88. Pius V gave the German Carthusian (1522-1578) the task of making this collection *(Life of the Saints)* to counteract Protestant attacks in this area (pontifical brief, June 2, 1570). There are some gaps in this work, but Surius started a trend that would lead to the *Acta Sanctorum* of the Bollandists. Cf. F. Mourret, *Histoire générale de l'Église*, V, 525 and note 1.

[2] Étienne de Juilly's text was also translated into Flemish in 1451 by Olivier de Longhe. Another Flemish translation was made by Antoine Colue in 1509.

[3] This *Vie* was translated into French by F. Douillet.

framework. Several times he summarizes the first biography of Colette and his information overlaps that of Perrine.

Clichtou may have had access to some items collected for the informative proceedings, since he names the confessor who replaced Father Pinet in the seclusion period: Jean Guiot. This detail recalls the testimony of the *Vieillards de Corbie* of 1471. He also affirms that Brother Henry was Burgundian.

The chronological markers are clearer than those of Pierre de Vaux. Clichtou notes that Benedict XIII's legate in Paris, Cardinal de Challand, allowed the bishop of Amiens to dispense Colette from her vow of seclusion on July 23, 1406. Clichtou does not mention Benedict XIII's fall in front of Colette, but does say she was made mother and abbess general of the reform. From 1410, at Besançon, vocations flowed from daughters "of kings, dukes, princes, counts, barons, and bourgeois of all kinds and conditions."

He also reports that Colette governed the seven male convents and brought many lay people into the third order. Her death occurred "in the same year and month, on the same day" as the election of Nicholas V, a clear reference to the end of Felix V's schism.

Clichtou's text follows the *Legenda* of Pierre de Vaux, which he calls "major legend," as if his own was a "minor legend," referring to Saint Bonaventure's *Legenda major* and *Legenda minor* of Saint Francis.

Mariano de Florence (1477-1523)

Colette's life and work are mentioned by Mariano de Florence, a historian of the Order. We make reference to it here since it demonstrates that Colette had a certain renown in the Order outside France.[4] Mariano wrote in Italian, and the journey to Nice became a stay in Rome to obtain the bull from the pope!

---

[4] M. da Firenze, *Libro delle dignità e eccelenza del ordine della serafica madre delle povere donne santa Chiara di Assisi*, 1986, "Della beata Coleta da Francia," n° 429-34.

The Seventeenth Century

Historians of the Order

Fodéré

In Lyon in 1619, Father Jacques Fodéré, Franciscan of the "regular observance," published a *Narration historique et topographique des convens de l'ordre de saint François et monastères sainte Claire, érigez en la province appelée de Bourgogne a présent de saint Bonaventure*. His stated intention was to produce a history of the monasteries in the province of which he was the minister. He consulted monastery archives and documents as far as possible.[5]

Of the convents founded by Colette, only those within the province are included in this narrative. Fodéré lists fifteen monasteries that Sister Colette brought under "strict observance." An abbreviated version of the "holy virgin's" life prefaces the history, a "compilation, purged of some apocryphal incidents." There are some details: Isabeau de la Roche, widow of the Count de Brisay, was permitted to leave the enclosure by the pontifical legate, Antoine de Challand, in a brief of July 23, 1406.

Did Fodéré understand the precise difference between Colettines and Observants? He wrote that in 1406 Colette submitted the monastery of Besançon "to the religious of the regular observance" (16), an anachronism, since in 1410, monastery jurisdiction was not yet an issue.[6]

The history of the monasteries sometimes notes Colette's relationship with great people. For the foundation of Auxonne, for instance, Fodéré states that she asked the Duchess of Burgundy to build on her lands. She had a cell built near

---

[5] The General Minister, François Gonzague, ordered this manuscript published in an *Histoire universelle* of the Order. This could not be done, because this work was considered of only slight importance in Saint Bonaventure's province. It was published in Lyon following this rejection.

[6] Fodéré thus refers to the Observant-Conventual quarrels and the 1458 bull of Pius II releasing the Colettines from the jurisdiction of the "friars of the bull."

the door and the turn, with an oratory opening to the Blessed Sacrament, so as not to disturb the community by her frequent journeys or meetings in the parlor (23).[7] The monastery was very costly to build using Colette's plans, since there was no stone in the area. Blanche of Savoy finally paid the extra cost.

For the Moulins foundation, Fodéré (70-71) analyzes Colette's transaction with Duchess Marie de Bourbon, a delicate one since she had to avoid offending the duchess of Burgundy, given the rivalry between the two great houses. Similarly, it was Colette who wrote to Amadeus VIII of Savoy regarding Blanche's intervention.[8]

These few points are enough to give an idea of the originality and the limitations of this historical approach. For the first time, Colette was being studied as a founder, or more precisely with regard to her concrete achievements, since the legislative work is not analyzed here. Fodéré also firmly erases all elements of the marvelous, including those from the period between youth and seclusion.

The role played by the great families from the start of Colette's mission and during the period when monasteries were being founded is heavily underlined. Her initiative was supported by both Blanche of Geneva and Brother Henry and by wives uneasy about the life and salvation of their husbands. Here Colette's holiness consists of her reforming work, which sets her apart from the communities she founded.

Wadding (1588-1657)

The Irish Franciscan, Luke Wadding, another major historian of the Order, collected all the known documents of the Order together between 1625 and 1654 in his *Annales Mino-*

---

[7] In Seurre, too, Fodéré notes the provision of a parlor and bedroom for her own use. Noblemen and seculars could visit her without going through the doorkeeper (60).

[8] Analysis of the documents has already led to this conclusion (cf. Part 3, Ch. I).

*rum.*⁹ He based his life of Colette on the work of Étienne de Juilly, Surius, Mark of Lisbon (another historian of the Order from the second half of the sixteenth century), and Mariano of Florence.

For his account of 1406, he writes a life of Colette that makes little reference to Pierre de Vaux, whose manuscript was presumably unavailable. Occasionally he makes reference to a *Legenda*. The Latin documents must have been more easily accessible in Rome than the one written in the vernacular.

For the year 1435, Wadding transcribes the *Constitutions* and notes that the cardinals and other Fathers of the Council of Basle approved them. This is no doubt the source of the statement by later biographers that the *Constitutions* were presented to the Fathers of the Council of Basle and approved by them. Wadding does not give his sources.

Wadding is of interest because he identifies Colette as an important reformer of the Order and notes she was born in the same year as Bernardino of Siena.[10] She restored discipline to the sisters as Bernardino did for the friars.

Wadding also considers her blessed, whose life gave rise to biographies, a list of which he provides.[11] He calls her *beata* and provides details about devotion to her. In 1604, Clement VIII allowed the Colettines at Gand to say the office of Blessed Colette and the Mass of Virgins. In 1610, Paul V extended this privilege to all the monasteries in Belgium.[12]

The Order's historians considered Colette's life and work in the light of documents available to them, official or not. The approach they took to the reformer's sanctity no longer used hagiography as the only possible style for expression but as one element to be combined with historical facts. As for Fodéré, he eliminates hagiography altogether from his work on the history of monasteries. Two almost contemporary analyses provide two distinct responses. While not of equal value,

---

[9] T. IX, X, and XI, ed. Rome.
[10] T. IX to XII, 1380.
[11] T. XI, N° LVI, LVII, LVIII, LIX, 1447.
[12] T. XI, n° LX, 1447.

their very discrepancies indicate an emerging unease and a lack of mutuality between hagiography and history.

Biographies of Colette

Sylvère d'Abbeville, Capuchin[13]

Sylvère d'Abbeville's book, *Histoire chronologique de la bienheureuse Colette,* is dedicated to the queen mother, Marie de' Medici, who made a pilgrimage to Amiens, partly in memory of the princesses, daughters of Jacques de Bourbon. Since her secretary was the brother of a Clarisse in the monastery of Amiens, the dedication might have ensured that the work had a wider distribution.

This text is certainly the most thorough of those written about Colette. It recapitulates earlier biographies and moreover uses investigations made in Colettine monasteries. The memoir written at Poligny in 1623 was composed especially for Sylvère d'Abbeville. He quotes the testimony of the *Vieillards de Corbie* of 1471, the letter from Katherine Rufiné, and the 1406 bull for Colette's leaving seclusion. He affirms that Colette was directed by a Celestine priest from Amiens. He also consulted documents that had not yet been published, such as the *Mémoire d'Hesdin* by Élisabeth de Bavière. Elsewhere he reports on the cult of Colette, noting how the popes gradually extended permission to say her office and how people in high society promoted her canonization. He reports on miracles in various monasteries.

The title of the work indicates a chronological account. The author maintains this up to and including Book II, after which he does not seem to know what to do with the material he has available. He discusses the later foundations and organizes the miracles according to those that occurred before Colette's death and those that occurred after. He never really follows an historical plan. Hagiography is given considerable space, the author repeating all the marvelous stories

---

[13] *Histoire chronologique de la bienheureuse Colette* (Paris, 1628).

while finding some of them debatable. Colette's aversion to the married state he considers an imperfection that God corrected with the vision of Saint Anne. While suggesting that only angels are able to read consciences, not humans, he nevertheless concedes that Colette, as an exceptionally saintly person, was granted this gift (190). His response to the diabolical apparitions is most interesting:

> Another time Satan took rotting flesh of bodies exposed by justice on public scaffolds, which he placed in this same oratory to disturb and trouble the servant of our Lord, who forced him to carry away his spoils with regret (156-57).

Sylvère gives the impression of a pious writer who "believes that these things were only illusions." But, he adds: "... it seems from the manuscripts I have read that some of them were real." Hagiography, then, begins to raise the issue of discerning the authentic from the false.[14]

Generally speaking, apart from these few reservations, Sylvère d'Abbeville accepted all the elements contained in Pierre de Vaux's biography and in the contemporary writings (Katherine Rufiné, Perrine, the Hesdin memoir). However, the use of official documents such as bulls begins to modify the place of hagiography in accounts of saints' lives.

The reformer's work is recognized for what it is, though Sylvère d'Abbeville exaggerates. (She is called abbess general with full powers over the three orders.) The hagiographical element is no longer considered the only sufficient way to prove sanctity and becomes less important than the reality of sanctity. The hagiographical seems to be more a decorative device, mainly intended to lift Colette "above the ordinary" and make her inimitable. Sylvère d'Abbeville frequently points to her exceptional, peerless qualities. The temptations in her last seven years (649) are thus so strange and frightening that no sister can remain near her. The documents, as

---

[14] The first volume of the *Acta Sanctorum* dates from 1643.

Sylvère must have known, bear witness to what is false. His work, then, mixed historical research, as understood at the time, with hagiography, which played a less important role.

Since the sixteenth century, attitudes had changed among historians of the Order. Authenticity was becoming de rigeur, and hagiographical language was considered inappropriate as an indicator of truth. This accounts, at least partly, for the author's problems in dealing with his materials. For Pierre de Vaux, his *Legenda* and his *Letter to the residents of Amiens* (the first witness to the reform) belong to two different genres with two different intentions. The *Legenda* reports Colette's holiness through images and topics that draw the reader in and express something of his or her devotion and faith in the saint's power of intercession with God. The *Letter* describes the reformer's work and influence.

Another fact also affected Sylvère d'Abbeville's project. It was not simply by chance that his biography was dedicated to the queen mother and gave a large place to the role played by the great houses in Colette's reforming work. During the first two generations at least, many members of these families joined Colette's monasteries, as we have already seen. The reform created by this exceptional woman attracted the elite and set up a situation of reciprocity and mutual support. During the period when Sylvère d'Abbeville was writing, however, high-ranking women were discovering new opportunities in cultural and social life through which they could be affirmed and fulfilled.

At the start of the seventeenth century, the elite were still paying homage to Colette, but they no longer entered the cloister. This was the time when the Grande Mademoiselle threw herself for a while into the delights of the Fronde, when the salons were welcoming another kind of woman, one who inspired the *Carte du Tendre (Map of Love)*. The sanctity of Colette, as depicted by Sylvère d'Abbeville, had to meet new socio-cultural criteria. The hagiographical elements used by ecclesiastical writers were passing from a medieval culture where they had originated to a humanist culture where the preferred mythical type was the "uncommon" hero rather than the saint. It was the time when Condé, after the victory of Rocroi in 1636, became an incarnation of this type. "All Paris had, for Chimène, the eyes of Rodrigue."

Through Sylvère d'Abbeville's writings, we witness a cultural turning point. Hagiography, which two centuries earlier could inspire imitation in its readers, was losing its power to awaken the collective imagination.

The Priest of Saint-Laurent

Ubald d'Alençon, in his Introduction to the *Vitae*, identifies the priest of Saint-Laurent as a certain Father Tharin de Besançon, whose *Life of Saint Colette* was written in 1630.[15] His work shows the same problems as that of Sylvère d'Abbeville, attempting a solution that demonstrates the impossibility of transposing medieval hagiography into a different cultural context.

The introduction to the work highlights our thesis, raising the issue of the relationship between hagiography and the emerging requirement of historical truth. Does this refer to research carried out by the Order's historians? The author regrets the disappearance of the marvelous from accounts written in the seventeenth century. He blames heretics. Their arguments have influenced Catholic scholars, who now have a "spirit of revolt against anything marvelous in the life of the saints" (xxix).

He firmly equates miracles with holiness. He defines miracles as all extraordinary manifestations, wonders, and marvels. Thus Colette's life, he says, is one of "ecstasies, revelations, prophecies, miracles and extraordinary events" (xi) – precisely signs of divine choice. Though he expresses some reservation about the credulous "who have written without attention or discernment" (xliii), it is not enough to modify his basic views.

---

[15] Published in 1635 in Lyon. The original is in the archives of the monastery of Poligny.

His account of Colette's life is a long list of extraordinary phenomena, some heretofore unpublished. The reason can be deduced from statements of this kind:

> One has never seen a girl with more talent for winning over the great ones of this world, for dealing with them, converting them and binding them to her, she who was of low birth.... However, popes, cardinals and princes who had seen her, worked with her; the princesses who sought her out, the ladies who followed her, the girls of the highest rank whom she received in her Reform all admired her spirit, her behavior and good manners, as if she had been raised among the greatest, or in some court (8).

This portrays Colette as the equivalent of the "honest man" of the seventeenth century. She has such quality that she truly seems "wellborn." Her amazing miracles attract the elite and fill her monasteries with the greatest names. Great ladies "follow in the footsteps of the saint" (190).

The work is both the acme and the end of hagiographical development, the point where cultural criteria and those of an enfeebled hagiography begin to diverge. As a discourse on sanctity, it was meant to be a model for a social class deeply interested in such a representation. If it had gone no further, the model of sanctity incarnate in Colette would have disappeared in this impasse. After the clumsy attempts in the seventeenth century to combine hagiography and history, it is not surprising that the eighteenth-century lives of Colette were little valued.

When the canonization process was resumed, two Benedictines were trying to write a biography of Colette. The first attempt by Dom Michel Marion, a monk at Corbie, failed; but the second, by Dom Grenier, was published in 1879 in the *Analectae Juris Pontificii*. A certain Father Larceneux composed a *Vie* around 1784. Of the one hundred and ten sources for this manuscript, some are copies of letters by Saint Colette and Brother Henry (references 33 to 44), texts by Pierre de Vaux and Perrine (references 70 to 84), the *Rule* and *Constitutions* (reference 46).[16]

At this time, then, the Church accomplished some work on behalf of Colette. However, the biographers seemed to have reached their limits in describing an example of medieval sanctity in contemporary cultural terms.

The Canonization Process

On January 23, 1740, the congregation of rites recognized the immemorial nature of Colette's cult. On August 26 the same year, Benedict XIV confirmed this decree. A solemn process was opened in Gand in 1747. Extracts are at Poligny (thirty-one Flemish, French, and Latin texts), left to the monastery by the Gand Clarisses[17] (originals[18] at the Bibliothèque Nationale). Sections of these were published in the *Acta sanctorum*.[19]

For the sake of clarity, the following table shows the sections printed at the Bibliothèque Nationale.

---

[16] U. D'Alençon, *Les vies de sainte Colette,* "Introduction," xxvi. Fr. Larceneux's manuscript was never published; there is a copy in the Besançon archives. The library in this town has the original as ms. 819.

[17] Emperor Joseph II closed the convent of Clarisses and a number of monasteries by decree in 1782. The Colettines took refuge at Poligny until 1791, when French monasteries were suppressed during the Revolution. At the request of Louise de France, daughter of Louis XV and a Carmelite at Saint-Denis, the Gand Colettines promised to leave Colette's reliquary at Poligny. Before returning to Gand, they also left behind part of the canonization process. (The reliquary was hidden during the Revolution until 1803.)

[18] References H 827, 828, 829, 830: they were taken by Napoleon to the Vatican archives in 1810, among the 7666 files for the canonization process. Cf. *Bulletin de l'Association des Archivistes de l'Église de France*, n° 8, 1977, VIII-3 ff.

[19] Eleven miracles at Hesdin in 1493, *AA.SS.*, martii I, 598-601. Miracles at Gand: *AA.SS.*, martii I, 592-96.

N° of Sections	Year of Printing	Topics
H 827	*1827 - 1842*	The cult of Saint Colette: miracles.
H 828	*1843 - 1847*	
	p. 15 to 244	Her virtues and life: testimonies.
	p. 35 to 197	Theological and moral virtues of the supernatural.
	p. 198 to 205	Fame in her lifetime.
	p. 205 to 219	Fame, cult, and miracles after death.
	1845 - 1847 p. 244 to 264	List of illustrious people who have written about her and her virtues.
H 829	*1848 - 1853* 1 volume	Miracles.
	1855 - 1866 1 volume	On the miracles (the first half about Colette).
End of H 830		One page: decree of canonization, 1781.

The Content of the Process

The process brings together documents from various dates and sources, from the first inquiries in the information process to the last depositions by the abbesses of Gand or testimonies to miracles. The extent of the cult and Colette's biographies are also included, along with requests for canonization. The dates lie between the fifteenth and the eighteenth centuries, but are mainly concentrated in the fifteenth century and the eighteenth century (when the process was resumed in 1740). There are some documents from the seventeenth century, particularly decrees extending the office of Colette and letters from bishops, monasteries, and the gentry asking for canonization.

Witness Statements

From the oldest documents we have already studied, we retain the 1494 claim to truth in the texts of Pierre de Vaux and Sister Perrine – further proof that these works were seen as "sources" right from the start.

When the process of canonization was resumed in the eighteenth century, one account in particular expresses the position of the investigators.[20] This was the deposition of the abbess of Gand in 1744, Marie Éléonore de Vriese. She passed on an oral tradition about the place in the monastery where Colette died. She also related what she had heard about the reformer's reputation in Spain (as well known as Teresa of Avila, according to one minister) and in Gand. On being questioned about the life of Colette, the abbess quoted works of authors she knew: Abbeville, Notel, Beyl (Flemish), Pierre de Vaux, etc. (session on May 7, 1744).

The biographies became the preferred means of describing Colette's holiness. In 1623, the *Memoir* from the monastery of Poligny provided yet more facts from Colette's life, passed on by former reverend mothers. A century later, the written accounts of authors from outside the monastery were superseding the memories of the nuns, who, however, held on to a living history.

As we have seen, these biographies did not always avoid the pitfalls of "decorative" hagiography. They gradually lost the original meaning and *exempla* that were able to offer an attractive model of sainthood.

Undoubtedly, the documents of the process were devoted to a survey of the heroic nature of Colette's theological and cardinal virtues,[21] but add nothing that was not already available in the *Vitae* or the contemporary testimonies that we have already considered. The miracles, however, show Colette's enduring influence.

---

[20] Documents from the process held in the archives of the monastery of Poligny.

[21] These were prudence, justice, temperance, and fortitude.

The Miracles

The deposition of Sister Pétronelle Van de Maele of Bruges reported a recent cure.[22] Around 1737-1738, a young professed sister was afflicted with a "sad illness," perhaps epilepsy from the description given. After medical treatments had failed, an octave of prayer to Blessed Colette resulted in a gradual healing. A deposition by the convent's attendant surgeon follows the sister's testimony. Sister Antoine de Sainte Anne of Bruges also reported that she had been cured of a "nervous tension," which had lasted six or seven years. She was completely cured after an octave of prayer and taking "the water."

These examples, contemporary with the later investigations, are fairly representative of all the *post mortem* miracles collected since the fifteenth century. The cures are mainly physical, and Colette's intercession is often accompanied by various "medications," such as:

- "The washing water," i.e., the water used to wash the bones remaining from Colette's body at the time of its inspection in 1492.[23]
- Water from the "little well" in Gand. This water from a well beside Colette's tomb was collected at the place where her head had rested. Those who drank it found that it "tasted of violets."
- Colette's cloak, worn especially by pregnant women desiring a successful delivery.
- Small pieces of her habit, which were given as relics.
- Her veil, particularly used to cure mental illness. (It gave off a pleasant smell.)
- The cart at Poligny, until its destruction by fire in 1638.

---

[22] Documents from the process held in the archives of the monastery of Poligny.
[23] The bones were previously washed in Rhine wine.

Those who benefited from miracles were religious sisters and brothers in the Order, lay people, men, women, and children afflicted by accidents or by long-term illnesses. When therapies failed, Colette's intercession was sought. The sisters in the monasteries often joined with the prayers of the people, providing relics or water to swallow.

The "geography of the miracles" covers the distribution of the monasteries. Indeed, Colette's cult developed around these communities. The canonization process that resumed in the eighteenth century particularly mentions miracles at Gand and Bruges. The seventeenth-century Poligny *Memoir* relates miracles that occurred in that town and the fifteenth-century Hesdin *Memoir* those that occurred in Hesdin.

Development of the Cult

The Church gradually gave permission to say the office of Colette as well as offer the Mass of Virgins. Pope Clement VIII first gave this privilege to the monastery of Gand in 1604. In 1610, Pope Paul V gave it to the Colettines of Flanders and Artois. In 1622, Gregory XV extended it to monasteries in Amiens, Franche-Comté and Burgundy, and, in 1630, it was extended to the whole Order.

Colette had not been beatified. The process having been resumed and then abandoned, her immemorial cult had to be approved in 1740 preliminary to the resumption of the process for canonization. Urban VIII, in March 1625, had forbidden the title of "Saint" or "Blessed" to be awarded without a prior decision of the Church unless the people thus called had been known in this way from "time immemorial." On July 16, 1634, the decree *Caelestes Jerusalem* stated that the expression "time immemorial" meant a period of one hundred years. Since this was the case for Colette, the Church authorized her office.

In the seventeenth century, the historical and hagiographical work on Colette's behalf was accompanied by numerous requests to the Holy See from notable personages for her canonization. Marie de' Medici, who made the pilgrimage to Amiens, wrote several letters. The Duc de Guise of the de Gueldre family, as holder of the benefice of Corbie, also wrote. The influence of the great families continued, but also the towns and bishops of the dioceses where the monasteries were located intervened. There are lists of these in H 828 (see table above).

The Canonization Problem

The time the Church took over the canonization is surprising, since the conditions necessary seem to have been met from the seventeenth century onward. Wadding raised the question, stating that Alexander VI wanted to proceed but was prevented by war. Later authors would offer the same argument. Other canonizations, however, did take place. Within the Franciscan Order itself, there was that of Catherine of Bologna in 1724.

Without entirely ignoring the case of war, there may have been another reason – problems within the Order. The differences between the Observants and the Colettines could only delay the progress of the cause at a time when the Observants had taken over governance of the Order.

One thing that corroborates this idea is the fact that, when the reform of the Capuchins spread beyond Italy, the cause for Colette's beatification seems to have been revived. Evidence for this is found in the biography of Sylvère d'Abbeville, Capuchin, written within the framework of the 1629 enquiry and letters from members of the nobility, many of which date from this period. But the cause was not successful at that time.

There are two possible ways of looking at this, one in the process, the other in a document from 1791.[24] The investigation into the process foundered in the seventeenth century over the requirement for a fourth miracle. The Church had authenticated three, but, in 1790, a dispensation was needed

---

[24] Archives of the monastery of Gand.

for the fourth.[25] The reports recorded at different times recounted a large number of miraculous cures, but the Church wanted recent examples. Those considered for the process particularly evoked Colette's influence and her intercessory powers. She was recognized as a saint through various testimonies of the *vox populi*, hence their value in assessing her sanctity. Recognition of her immemorial cult arose from the same requirements. Through the faith of those who had recourse to her aid and through commemoration of her life in the monasteries, Colette still lived on. Her dynamic example inspired vocations to the religious life in the Church.

The 1791 document may reveal one of the determining factors in delaying canonization. The postulator of the cause, one Father Philibert Obmexer, stated that the investigation had closed, but there was not enough money to proceed to canonization. The monasteries were poor and the Gand community had taken refuge at Poligny because of the decree of expulsion of Joseph II of Austria. There were five candidates for beatification at that time, including Colette,[26] but only one had the 18,000 Roman crowns needed. The reformer's cause had only 6000.

The postulator wrote to all the Clarisses in Europe, but received few replies. The Clarisses were too poor. He then suggested some solutions. Ask the Spanish for money, because they love to have saints canonized, or suggest Colette as the patron saint of the States General of Flanders. If they accepted they would then pay the costs of canonization. The postulator hoped to see the Colettines return to Gand. They could then beg for alms to cover the costs. He ended by saying that canonization would not take place until this condition was met.

With the shortage of money slowing down the process, the impetus for canonization, revived after a long delay, faltered because of the many difficulties experienced by the monas-

---

[25] There were three cures – of two sisters and a friar (a fractured knee, a tumor in the side, a case of consumption).

[26] The other four canonized in 1807 were François Caracciolo, Benoît de Saint-Philadelphe, Angela Merici, and Hyacinthe Mariscotti.

teries. Gand had been the driving force since the fifteenth century. It had initiated the process and remained loyal to Colette's work.[27] It seems, however, that this final obstacle was overcome, since on Trinity Sunday, May 24, 1807, Colette was canonized, along with four others already beatified, as mentioned above, including Angela Merici, Franciscan tertiary and founder of the Ursulines.

The bull of canonization[28] summarizes the elements in Colette's life already transcribed by Pierre de Vaux and stresses her continuing influence among ordinary people and those in high places through her reforming work. This document is valuable because it aims to combine hagiography (marvels are described: her torment by demons, injured at their hands, etc.) and history (chronological and geographical details are given about places, date of birth, and the beginnings of the reform, for example). It also affirms the vitality of her cult among the people. After her death people of all walks of life, those of high birth, ladies, magistrates, bishops, as well as the deaf, the mute, paralytics, the sick of every kind flocked from all sides in the certain hope of being cured by the intercession of the handmaid of God, proclaiming in unison:

> Colette is worthy of being numbered among the inhabitants of heaven.

The style of the decree also tries to translate elements of medieval hagiography into the language of contemporary culture, although constrained by the need for brevity. For example, her death is described in terms different from those of Pierre de Vaux, but it conveys the sense of a life

> plunged in contemplation of the sufferings of the Passion, feet and hands stretched out like those of Jesus Christ on the cross, among the songs of the angelic

---

[27] The monastery of Amiens had, at the beginning of the seventeenth century, also been active in this regard through the efforts of the Capuchins

[28] *Bullarium Romanum*, CCCCLXXXIIII, 912-18.

choirs, she flew into the arms of her heavenly spouse at Gand, on the 6th day of March in the year 1447.

Colette's much delayed canonization culminated, then, the hagiographical effort and reconciled the popular cult with an historical evocation of the account of her life.

CHAPTER 7

THE COLETTINES IN MODERN TIMES AND TODAY

After consolidation of the Colettine reform in Europe in the sixteenth century, there were few foundations made in the seventeenth century (Gand founded Tournai in 1628). There seem to have been none in the eighteenth century, a slowdown perhaps explained by the vigor of the Capuchin, Franciscan, and Carmelite reforms as much as by the fact that the Observants absorbed the Colettine friars in the sixteenth century.

Existing monasteries nonetheless ensured that the reform endured. Colette's canonization in 1807 seems also to have reactivated the Colettine movement, with refoundations after the Revolution.

Four of the monasteries founded by Colette survived: Besançon, Poligny, Le Puy, and Gand. After expansion in the nineteenth century and the first half of the twentieth, problems arose which caused many communities to disappear or to choose other constitutions.[1] In nineteenth-century France, the Colettines focused their efforts on refounding houses

---

[1] Amiens closed in 1976. The monasteries of Poligny and Le Puy were built by Colette, although alterations were made, particularly at Poligny, which was destroyed by fire.

The monastery of Besançon closed during the Revolution, like all the others, but was refounded in 1879 in another part of the town by the community from Poligny, which itself was re-established in 1819, although the chapel could be rebuilt only in 1837.

Cambacérès intervened to secure Le Puy's authorisation by imperial decree in 1807.

that had been destroyed or closed during the Revolution. They then moved on to make new foundations that did not adopt the Colettine constitutions, but rather local or Capuchin constitutions.[2]

THE NINETEENTH CENTURY

France

The following table clearly shows how many foundations were made. This table is taken from data supplied by Goulven in *Le Rayonnement de Sainte Colette* (as are those that follow).

	Founded in	By	**Founded**
Alençon	1498	Paris (11 sisters) and Lille (2 sisters)	Rennes, 1885
Amiens	1445	St. Colette	
Arras	1456	Gand	
Azille	1891	Orthez	
Besançon	1410	St. Colette	Pégu (Birmanie), 1932
Béziers	before 1259 prob. 1240	From Assisi, but cannot be verified	Toulouse, 1858: 4th foundation; Orthez 1874
Bordeaux-Talence	1891	Grenoble	

Unlike the Clarisses at Besançon and Poligny, who were unaffected by the anti-religious laws of 1903, those of Le Puy had to seek exile in England.

Despite being twice-exiled, the monastery of Gand endured and showed great vitality in the nineteenth century.

[2] The tables and certain information for this account are drawn from: J. Goulven, *Le Rayonnement de sainte Colette*; M.C. Koester, P.C.C., *Into this land*; Anonymous, *Vie de mère Marie-Dominique*.

Cambrai	1496	Arras, Amiens, Bruges, Gand, Hesdin	
Crest	1826	Romans	
Evian	Erec. 1569	Vevey, 1536 Orbe, 1550	
Grenoble	1478	Chambéry, Aigueperse, Moulins and Le Puy	Romans, 1621, Bordeaux-Talence, 1891
Lourdes	1876	Lyon	
Nîmes	1891	Jerusalem	
Orthez	1874	Béziers	Azille, 1891
Paray-le-Monial	1878	Périgueux	Nazareth, 1884 Jerusalem, 1888
Paris	1876	Le Puy	
Poligny	1415	St. Colette	Salins, 1636 (disappeared) Versailles, 1860
Rennes	1885	Alençon	
Romans	1621	Grenoble	Valence, 1815, disappeared in 1946 by merger with Crest; Crest, 1826; Grenoble, revived, 1878
Roubaix	1876	Tournai	Renaix (Belg.), 1903; Vinh (Indo-China), 1935
Vals	1887	Le Puy	
Versailles	1860	Poligny	Evian, restored, 1875

Belgium

There was a tremendous vitality in Belgium, with foundations established in that country and elsewhere: Ireland, movement in the Franciscan Order. In addition, the papacy, despite hesitations arising from the particular situation of the French and Belgian Colettine monasteries, tended to place all reformed monasteries under the jurisdiction of the Observant friars, especially in Spain. In most cases, the constitutions were adopted or inspired by other constitutions, such as those of the Capuchin Clarisses, under the jurisdiction of the Capuchin friars minor.

Two other factors certainly played their part. Spain suffered anti-religious laws in 1868, and monasteries were closed. When they were restored, the friars minor, with the Vatican's agreement, promulgated unified constitutions for the nuns. These were inspired no doubt by the Colettine version, but without explicit reference to the French reformer's work.

Colettine monasteries were however founded from Spain – one in Mexico at Orizaba. A Colettine community from Santiago de Chile founded one in Buenos Aires, Argentina, in 1749. Most of the other monasteries in these Latin American countries were Urbanist.

The Spirituality of the Nuns

The spirituality of the Colettine Clarisses is deeply marked by the sufferings and trials that Christians experienced during the French Revolution and later revolutions of the nineteenth century. Anti-clericalism, the rise of secularism, and wars all provoked a defensive reflex among Christians, amplified among the nuns. God was perceived as outraged by such painful events. A mentality of reparation developed, tainted by Jansenism. It quickly became dominant in religious spirituality. The Colettines heard in it a resonant echo of the devotion to the Passion so beloved of Colette and her period. Daily life was weighed down with a multitude of penances and spoken prayers. At the same time, paintings invaded every corner of the monastery (Poligny, for example), along corridors in the dormitory, in the refectory, and in the choir. These depicted characters or scenes including the Virgin, the eye of Providence, and the dismembered child (this one hung in the refectory until 1958-1960). A death's head was always displayed in the refectory, with a devout sister, from time to time, placing it before each nun during the meal, saying, "My sister, you must die."

We should note that the writings of the founders were rarely if ever studied. Second-hand works of spirituality were used in formation. After the discovery of Saint Clare's body in 1853 and the discovery of her rule in a fold of one of her cloaks kept as a relic in 1893, the founding texts began gradually to be read again in Europe. This led later on to the "return to the sources" recommended by Vatican II.

Two examples, taken from the *Lives* of nuns illustrate the mind-set of this period.[4]

Sister Anathoile Thoulier (1645-1672)

The life of Sister Anathoile Thoulier, written in 1888, gives a good picture of the attitudes of the nineteenth century. It was no accident that such manuscripts were published then. "The time seemed right to reveal them; this is a treasure needed in our day," writes the author in the *Preface*. He recalls the words of Leo XIII: God raises up saints "to regenerate societies that are lost" and sees this nun from Poligny as a perfect example:

> It may be said that Our Lord united himself with her especially as a sacrifice for the expiation of the sins of the people: she reproduces every stage of the great sacrifice of the divine Victim.

Her "special nature" was to be a "restorative soul." The writer continues:

---

[4] In addition to the life of Mother Marie-Dominique (see note 2), there is Canon Chamouton's work, *Une Âme réparatrice: Vie de la Vénérable soeur Anathoile-Françoise Thoulier* (1888).

In our times, when crimes are multiplying and faithful souls feel driven to make up for offences by love and penance, our recollections give us encouragement.[5]

The author's belief in the value of suffering is revealed in the account of ecstasies as much as in that of physical illness. One day, sister Anathoile was discovered lying on the floor in her cell as if dead. The doctor, hastily summoned, declared: "Aren't you used to these misfortunes from God?" (92).

Some physical pains recalled those of the Passion:

> She seemed to feel the thorns of a crown, buried in her head ... and all these pains were not enough to quench her thirst for suffering: when she could escape from the protection of her nurse she slipped furtively into a nearby room and inflicted a fierce and bloody discipline on herself (95).

Mother Marie-Dominique Berlamont

The *Life* of the great abbess, Mother Marie-Dominique Berlamont, was also written in 1888, like the previous one. Hence its value to this study. The anonymous author discloses her spirit of penance and sacrifice: going without food, using various "means" to make it tasteless. She wore some instrument of penance almost all the time. The author notes:

> She took the discipline so many times, with so much blood, that she had to change her headgear up to three times a day, because each time it was covered in blood (45).

She loved to say:

---

[5] The author's table of contents also indicates the underlying spirituality: for example: Chapter IV, "The novitiate or the oblation of the Victim"; Chapter V, "The Consecration of the Victim"; Chapter VI, "The Victim of divine love"; Chapter VII, "The Victim of divine love (cont)"; Chapter VIII, "The Road to Calvary"; Chapter IX, "Calvary, the way of reparation"; etc.

We must give to God life for life, love for love, blood for blood.

While charitable to her daughters, she still corrected any laziness or neglect. If she saw a nun flagging during prayers recited with arms raised as a cross, she would step "quietly behind her and raise them up."

Her biography is modeled on that of Saint Colette, describing her heroic virtues, her charity, temptations of the devil, etc. Clearly the underlying pattern remains Colette, whose zeal as a founder and whose prayer recall Teresa of Avila to the point where she was known as "Teresa of the North." The influence of the great Carmel reformer, whose teaching dominated the spirituality of religious sisters from the seventeenth century onwards, was considerable. This is understandable in that the Colettine reform, as we have seen, emerged from the spiritual decline of the fifteenth century, accompanied by an emphasis on physical suffering as a sign of the observant life. Enclosure was seen primarily as a penance. The *Testament,* said to be by Colette, compares the enclosure to a sepulcher. Teresa of Avila, on the other hand, called her strictly enclosed Carmels "the Virgin's dovecotes." These expressions are indicative of two profoundly different theologies of enclosure.

Christians in the nineteenth century viewed the Clarisses as being "buried alive," indicating a change in attitude from the more flexible approach still to be found, for example, at Poligny in the seventeenth century. In the context of this reparative spirituality, the concept of enclosure cannot avoid carrying such penitential connotations.

The penitential movement continued in the twentieth century at the same time as the Colettine expansion. Before dealing with the present day and considering the issues raised at the time of the Second Vatican Council, we must evaluate this spirituality of reparation, widespread among monastic orders, but for Colettines particularly evocative of the origins of their reform.

The life of Thérèse of Lisieux, who died in 1897, is a particularly good example. She was immersed in this religious mentality. One of the most original aspects of her spirituality was her capacity for forceful detachment, but with no concomitant loss of enthusiasm. It is outside our remit to consider this, but we can point to the judgment of one who knows the Carmelite very well. Father Marie-Eugène,[6] a Carmelite himself, wrote that a Franciscan priest (a Recollect, according to the terminology of the period) set Thérèse "on the path of Love," when previously other preachers had dismissed her saying: "My daughter, be a good religious, but do not aspire to such heights!" (45).

At the right time, this son of Saint Francis was able to release Thérèse of Lisieux from her yoke of spiritual practices, but only because she was nourished on the writings of Teresa of Avila and, especially, of John of the Cross. Father Marie-Eugène, analyzing Thérèse's spirituality, continues:

> In the nineteenth century, holiness and asceticism were negative qualities, seeking purification above all and to make reparation to God.... There was something great in this, but without the same light on Love and on Mercy.

And later he says: "Thérèse's greatness comes from her discovery of Mercy" (53-54). He recalled how the ascetic practices (hair shirt, iron chains and bracelets) were still used in his own novitiate, adding:

> [Saint Thérèse] criticized such practices, common in her time, because of the pride they caused. In the past, reparation would normally be expressed within the spiritual life by extraordinary practices of self-mortification (71).

---

[6] Founder of the Carmelite Institute of Our Lady of Life, Father Marie-Eugène (1894-1967) was the Order's definitor general. The cause for his beatification has been put forward to the Vatican. The quotations are taken from talks collected with the title: *Ton amour a grandi avec moi*.

Thérèse's life was energized by her experience of God, through which she lived a radiant charity, unswervingly faithful to the duties of her state in life. Known as the greatest saint of the twentieth century, she was able to develop a way of life accessible to everyone.

Another nun, also and significantly a Carmelite, a contemporary of Thérèse, had a similar experience of God. Blessed Elisabeth of the Trinity (1880-1906), in her Carmel in Dijon, was able to break free of the spirituality typical of the end of the nineteenth century to fix her gaze on the face of Christ "through all nights, all voids, all helplessness."

These two examples, which would deeply affect the twentieth century, give a better grasp of the limitations of reparative spirituality and the risks to nuns of getting bogged down in "techniques" of religious life.

THE TWENTIETH CENTURY

For the Colettine movement, the twentieth century was characterized by a remarkable expansion, both within and beyond Europe. After Vatican II, the communities had various reactions to the draft general constitutions that would render invalid those of Colette.

Expansion

Within Europe, expansion went hand in hand with consolidation of established monasteries by new foundations.

New Foundations in Europe

Monasteries were created in France, Belgium, England, Germany, and Holland up to 1936. Four convents were also founded in Ireland during this period. (They are listed in the Genealogical Tree, located in the appendix.)

	Founded in	By
Haubourdin	1931	This was Lille (founded by Bruges in 1866, exiled to Quiévrain, Belgium, from 1901), which transferred to Haubourdin in 1931.
La Rochelle	1922	Lutterworth (England)
Lourdes	1876	Lyon Valleyfield (Canada) 1902
St. Hilaire-du-Harcouët	1919	This was Dinant (Belgium), 1903, returning to France
St. Symphorien-les-Tours	1920	This was Sclerder (England) (1914), returning to France
Val d'Ajol	1935	Nîmes
Nancy	1920	Renaix (Belgium)
Nérac	1935	Bordeaux-Talence

In 1905, the Colettines of Paray-le-Monial founded the only Colettine monastery of our time in Assisi (Italy).

Outside Europe (Africa, America, Asia)

Outside Europe, there are North Africa and Palestine with monasteries in Algiers (1932), Rabat (1933), and Casablanca (1932) founded by Azille and Bordeaux-Talence respectively. In Canada, the Valleyfield monastery was founded by Lourdes in 1902. In turn, the Canadian Colettines founded Rivière-du-Loup in 1932.

In the United States, foundations proliferated, as the following table shows.

Düsseldorf (Germany) 1859

Cleveland, Ohio (United States) 1877

Chicago	Rockford	Oakland	Campina Gde	Newport-News
(Illinois) 1893	(Illinois) 1916	(California) 1921 (transferred to Santa Cruz 1941)	(Brazil) 1950	(Virginia) 1956

Roswell	Kokomo	SantaBarbara	LosAltos
(New Mexico)	(Indiana)	(California)	(California)
1948	1959	1928	1950

Three Colettine houses were founded in Brazil, one by Chicago. Mother Marie of the Assumption from the monastery of Besançon founded Pegu in the Indies in 1932. The community had to withdraw to Alwaige and then, in 1954, founded Mwanza in Tanzania. The Colettine monastery of Algiers founded one at Lilongwe (Malawi) in 1958. Versailles and Évian founded one in Bouar (Central African Republic). In Vietnam, the Roubaix monastery founded one at Vinh in 1935, but that community withdrew to France in 1950.

Reactions to Proposed New Constitutions

The Colettines in Europe and in the United States reacted differently to the apostolic constitution *Sponsa Christi* from Pius XII (1950). This directive caused upheaval in monastic life well before Vatican II. The Colettine foundations, most of which were no longer autonomous, generally followed their parent houses.

What was the religious mindset of the Colettines in the fifty years leading up to *Sponsa Christi*? It is difficult to answer this without a more thorough study that would be beyond the scope of this book. A few examples will serve to indicate the larger picture, still poorly understood.

Some Aspects of Spirituality

Another biography of Sister Anathoile Thoulier by a Capuchin friar minor was published in 1938.[7] The value of this *Life,* written at the request of the Colettines of Poligny, lies in its underlying spirituality. The *Prologue* gives a description of the life of the nuns:

---

[7] D. des Planches, *Le Rachat des âmes: Soeur Anathoile-Françoise Thoulier, Clarisse-Colettine du couvent de Poligny, 1645-1672* (Paris, 1938).

> [They] crucify themselves, calling down blows from heaven and earth on themselves, begging for the spitting, the thorns, the nails and the iron, they live and die on this cross. The secret of the cloister is the blood that flows, blood from veins and blood from the heart (10).

And again:

> Through the action of love, the blood of Christ flows to redeem souls.... It is necessary to love in order to sacrifice oneself, and first, to be pure so the smoke of the holocaust should please divine Justice.... Chosen souls are found most often among women, less inclined to action, better gifted for suffering (12).

Here again is seen a fascination for imitating the bloody Passion, recalling the writings of Henry de Baume and Battista Varani:

> There is blood, writes the author of the biography, much blood on the face of Sister Anatholie, because there is much love in the depths of her heart (15).

The work is arranged around the idea of sacrifice as a kind of spectacular, sacred drama. (The theatre of sacrifice appears, with the altar, the "provocations of the victim and the action of the sacrificers.")

The *Epilogue,* entitled "Lessons of the Cloister," recalls this reparative dimension of the lives of the nuns:

> As the stains of vice flood the earth, the blood of these victims drowns them in its cleansing waves. As human crimes close heaven and open hell, the reparation made by these victims closes up hell again and reopens heaven. When the victims say to Justice: "Strike me!" Mercy erupts over the sinners (167).

The voice of Christ calling us to reparation brings about "an explosion of heroism as enduring as life" (166). The difference from Thérèse of Lisieux, who truly detached sanctity from heroism, is clear – she scorned what she called "the mortifications of the great saints."

The example of the saint of Lisieux, whose fame spread quickly after her death, would however result in imitation and influence over the spirituality of nuns. Spiritual directors had a decisive role in this, but, without having thoroughly studied Thérèse's writings, they were often satisfied with imitative behavior, as may be illustrated by the case of Margaret Sinclair (1900-1925), a Colettine Clarisse from the Notting Hill monastery.[8]

The biographer is concerned to show that the Scottish nun is imitating her French counterpart. She was a "little soul," to use Thérèse's expression, through her "touching humility, her childlike candor, her joyful simplicity, by which she was seen by her family and the world, as well as beneath the veil, a living replica of Thérèse Martin." The biography endeavors to show her childlike traits:

> At fifteen years and older, she obeyed her mother like a small child ... a striking manifestation of this childlike spirit through which Margaret, perhaps without realizing it, modeled herself on her beloved saint of Lisieux, beginning with the sacrifices of the religious life (46).

The account as a whole uses an understanding of the life of Margaret as a framework for illustrating that of Thérèse. Her spiritual director's questions lead her in this direction. We must note, however, that she does not seem to have lived through the trials of the dark night of the soul (151). Despite her physical suffering, described in detail (a lung disease, the same illness as that of Thérèse), the spiritual climate is somewhat bland. So, for example, one day she confided that

---

[8] Mgr Laveille, *Marguerite Sinclair (1900-1925)* (Paris, 1929).

"the Child Jesus played with her." She called him "sweet Jesus" (155). The expression she used once "Jesus was hiding" (165), reminded the spiritual director of the Carmelite:

> He saw at once a further resemblance with the young Saint of Lisieux, also sick, and sometimes so painfully deprived of the presence of the Beloved.

Her death at age twenty-five also recalled that of Thérèse, who died at twenty-four.

Teresa of Avila had been the point of reference for the spiritual life of a Mother Marie-Dominique. After 1897, however, the saint of Lisieux tended to modify the representation of sanctity, particularly for young deceased Colettines. Lung diseases decimated young people, making comparisons easy.

The case of Sister Marie-Céline, a Colettine who died at age nineteen at the house of Bordeaux-Talence, can be compared to the previous one without making explicit reference to Thérèse. She died at the very end of the nineteenth century (1897) and began to be better known during the 1920s, so it is appropriate that we should mention her here.[9] She, too, after a very poor and miserable childhood, died of a lung disease.

In the novitiate, she was trained in humility despite the resistance of her own nature, but would soon demand humiliation for herself. The key term in formation was *agendo contra,* as expressed by the novice mistress, and one of the young sister's aims was to achieve "one hundred and fifty acts of self-denial every day" (111). Her formator noted:

> She no longer made any concessions to nature.... I was often moved with pity seeing the sacrifices she made within the privacy of her heart, this heart that she tore with blows from the cross ... (115).

---

[9] *Fleur du cloître ou vie édifiante de soeur Marie-Céline de la Présentation*, by a Poor Clare (Liège, 1927). The first edition dates from 1922.

These "heroic acts" were noticed by "her mothers" (the abbess and the formator). During her retreat before taking the habit, Sister Céline recorded her faults and her practices, so for instance from October 1 to November 21: 42 faults and 3,507 practices. The affection the young sister felt within her religious environment was real and strong. The spirituality around her, directed towards expiatory suffering, seemed the same that Thérèse of Lisieux had known and from which she had detached herself. The tone here is very emotional, probably because of Sister Marie-Céline's youth, recalling the childish language of Margaret Sinclair.

One feature of this period, from the end of the nineteenth to the beginning of the twentieth century, is how emphasis placed on physical penances goes hand in hand with emotional expression, at least in religious language. It indicates a spiritual dullness, denounced by Huysmans in *À rebours* or later by Emmanuel Mounier in *L'affrontement chrétien*. During this period, Franciscan historians began to publish critical writings on Saint Francis, but formation in the monastery novitiates generally ignored the writings of the founders and Franciscan theology.

Some years before *Sponsa Christi* was published, the search for a monastic life by Sister Marie of the Trinity (1901-1942)[10] clearly showed the problems of the monasteries and the limitations of existing customs. (Her biography does not carry the name of its author.) In seeking a religious life she had some vivid religious experiences:

> The Lord made me understand that, in addition to supernatural means of sacrifice and prayer, there must be great vigilance not to neglect any natural means of predisposing souls to seek and welcome grace (44).

and also:

---

[10] *Soeur Marie de la Trinité, clarisse de Jérusalem,* anonymous.

Now I understand how important it is to take away any avoidable suffering from others, above all it is important to spread charity (54).

It is not known which monastery she entered as a Clarisse, since she did not stay there, but she deplored the "strange idea of religious life and of perfection. One spoke of God, of the holy Church, of superiors only with trembling – almost with rancor" (61).

Though sick, the abbess stayed at her post with the community collapsing. "There was a gulf between them (the sisters) and I: education, mentality, the needs of the soul" (65). She wanted to found a monastery in French-speaking Switzerland: "It will be receiving vocations at once." She dreamed of a small convent, where the "holy rule will be lived in evangelical simplicity; ... new generations matured by war ... will make sacrifices for the true religious life; they will not do it for a distorted religious life." Sister Marie of the Trinity, rejected at the point of taking final vows, finally entered the Colettine monastery in Jerusalem in 1938.

This is certainly a case limited by difficulties, but symptomatic of a change in attitudes and the anachronism of some forms of monastic life.

Creation of Federations

The monasteries were troubled in the first half of the twentieth century.[11] Resources were fewer because of the economic crisis after the First World War. Rich families who had helped fund communities were ruined or had other areas of interest. After 1918 and the return from exile, a crisis in vocations slowed down community renewal. Attitudes had

---

[11] Sr. M. Pascal, "Les clarisses de France. Les Fédérations," dans *Claire dans nos fédérations*, bulletin interfédéral des clarisses n° 1-12, *pro manuscripto* (Toulouse, 1985-1988). *Règle de Sainte Claire et Constitutions des Pauvres clarisses de la Rédemption* (Nantes, 1936). *Constitutions pour les monastères de clarisses,* for the federation of Colettine Clarisses in the United States. *Constitutions générales de l'ordre, ad experimentum* and final.

changed without the monasteries noticing, introspective as they were, and their way of life was not able to adapt.

The apostolic constitution *Sponsa Christi* (1950) was the first papal text to raise questions posed by contemplative life to the contemporary world. Pius XII asked the nuns to work for their living, to consider changes in society and in attitudes. Three important points were covered in the same document: enclosure, solemn vows, and federations. The pope asked the monasteries to confederate in order to escape their isolation and to help each other, particularly in formation of novices.

Initially, abbesses resisted, slow to follow the directives from Rome.[12] Eventually, various constitutions and practices were adopted. In 1953, most Colettines belonged to monasteries using the general constitutions (promulgated in 1933, in order to adapt legislation to the 1917 Code of Canon Law), and others belonged to monasteries that had their own constitutions. Some Colettines, including those in the monasteries of Besançon, Poligny, and Arras, grouped themselves into a federation called "Saint Colette," which stressed strict enclosure and independence. It labored under the fear that the future President of the Federation might become Abbess General. In 1957, this federation accepted some changes to the "constitutions of Saint Colette" and started a research project on the reformer.

Generally speaking, reports from federal assemblies of all monasteries, while demonstrating a real interest in new conditions, indicated fear of a common novitiate, defiance towards a male Franciscan assistant, and rejection of an abbess as visitor.

After the Second Vatican Council, the general minister, Constantin Koser, launched a draft general constitutions for the second order. All the monasteries around the world were consulted, and Clarisses from several continents gathered in Rome to analyze the responses. From these the general

---

[12] Sr. M. Pascal, "Les clarisses de France. Les Fédérations."

constitutions *ad experimentum* were drawn up in 1973. The "Saint Colette" federation had dissolved in 1969.

The federations set up in the 1950s regrouped according to the new conditions the Council had created; but, in fact, the Colettines reacted in various ways to the draft general constitutions.

Colettines after the Council

Helped by their religious advisers and sometimes by bishops, some Colettine communities responded positively to the draft general constitutions and contributed to their development, such as the Besançon and Poligny communities. Mother Marie of the Assumption, originally from Besançon and founder of Alwaige and Mwanza, reacted very differently, as her archived letters show. We can quote just two examples of her passionate resistance. In 1957, modifications made to the constitutions of "Saint Colette" had caused fundamental disagreements among Colettine abbesses. At that time, Mother Marie of the Assumption had rebelled against the possibility that these changes might be "imposed" on her and concluded, after arguing to preserve practices: "Would it not be better for there to be a small number of true Colettine monasteries than a respectable number of "semi-Colettines?"[13]

Likewise, reactions to the draft general constitutions were often negative. A letter from the same abbess, Mother Marie of the Assumption, dated July 19, 1965, noted a petition that she had distributed. Bishops were asked to add their support to resist the introduction of the general constitutions. Some assured her, she wrote, "that they will be on 'our side' when the time comes" and they had signed the petition. The letter also referred to steps taken and requests made by the Belgian Clarisses, certainly Colettines, in favor of the general constitutions. Clearly, some Colettines were afraid of losing their particular character. The situation was similar, in some

---

[13] Letter of June 20, 1957, Archives of Besançon.

ways, to the Observant-Colettine quarrel of the fifteenth and sixteenth centuries.

Consequently the Colettine federation in the United States quickly drew up constitutions inspired by the Colettine version. They stressed the risk of losing their heritage within a second order that would incorporate a number of tendencies. They offered their draft to European monasteries, some of which were won over in 1972, such as the monasteries in Arras and in Algiers. Colettine communities compared the two draft constitutions with very interesting results, clearly indicating points of difference.

The communities of Arras and Algiers highlighted the following elements:[14] emphasis on loyalty to Saint Clare, obedience to the Church, particularly the conciliar decree *Perfectae Caritatis* on renewal of religious life (1965), and the right to the pluralism that was typical of the Franciscan Order.

Following this preface, the Colettines' critique of the general constitutions mainly focused on the potential damage that might be caused by flexibility with regard to the life of silence and penance. In this view, emphasis on fulfillment of the personality could lead to the nun living at a human level, concerned with "the search for herself."

Enclosure and correspondence, they said, must remain under strict control. The expression used by the general constitutions to describe enclosure, "ascetic institution," seemed to distort the lived reality, which is "intimate union with God," not asceticism or protection. Similarly, the general constitutions also tended to diminish the abbess's authority: "The abbess's duty seems essentially to talk with and listen to the sisters." The constitutions of the Colettine federation of the Immaculate Conception, on the other hand, speak of "the service of authority."

Without claiming to offer an in-depth study, we can detect here some of the Colettines' underlying concerns. There is evidently a fear of laxity developing after the Second Vatican Council under cover of general constitutions valid for the

---

[14] The Arras monastery authorises use of these manuscripts.

second order as a whole. This might allow a kind of "consensus" to predominate that would eliminate the stricter life.

All the Italian Clarisses immediately backed the *general constitutions*, except for the Urbanists and the Capuchins (historically independent branches of the second order). The French Colettine Clarisses took separate paths: some monasteries adopted the American constitutions. The Poligny and Besançon monasteries opted for the *general constitutions*.

Why is this Colettine revival found in the United States and not in Europe? Initially, it may be explained by the vitality of these young communities. The Belgian and French monasteries have suffered a spectacular drop in vocations and therefore do not have the human resources to draw up constitutions should they so wish. The American Colettine federation also defines itself as a "branch" of the second order, while French monasteries that have adopted these constitutions normally speak of slight differences in the way of life that protect the Colettine heritage in the order. These monasteries refuse to form a federation separate from the others. So within one federation, there are monasteries with different constitutions. Their practices differ, especially on the issue of enclosure, on the level of strictness of the abbess's governance, and on her term of office. (The general constitutions reduce this term to a maximum of twelve years, while in the American constitutions it is practically for life with successive elections.)

The Italian Clarisses, despite their fears of seeing a weakening of monastic life, were comfortable with the *general constitutions*.[15] Living in the country of Saint Clare and Saint Francis, they have a centuries-old experience of tensions and even crises in the Order, periods of laxity, and times of reform. We have already looked at the fifteenth century, but there were other local or more widespread reforms before and particularly after that period (especially the Capuchin reform). A number of Italian monasteries experienced

---

[15] These general constitutions *ad experimentum* were finally promulgated in 1988 after modifications to particular points on the life of prayer, the enclosure, etc.

a gradual change from the Urbanist rule to that of Clare, choosing personal and collective poverty.

This experience led to a certain vigilance regarding potential laxity in a fast-changing society, but also greater confidence in the resources of the Clarisses. What is more, since the legal tradition in Italy is less restrictive, there is not as much need to codify. As Saint Francis himself said of his own proposal – a way of life "in a few words." The Italian humanist spirit can still be detected in Saint John Capistran's commentaries on the Rule.

The Italian Clarisses adopted the federative principle and established shared novitiates. These do not exist in France. In a less laicized society, the Italian Clarisses perceive a smaller risk of diluting the concept of the monastic life.

In the United States, however, where the Catholic Church is a minority religion, there have been profound upheavals in traditional values. Women's religious life has been shaken by serious crises, still not resolved in some areas. Contemplatives have sometimes abandoned the enclosure and the habit (as has happened in Belgium), causing an understandable reaction in a country without the benefit of a long monastic experience.

The search for deeper roots has meant that Saint Colette seems a safe haven, a necessary route to follow in the return to the origins recommended by Vatican II. Between Saint Clare, so sparing of details and regulations, and the twentieth century, when monasteries that have long been turned in on themselves discover an unknown civilization, so to speak, the strong Colettine structures, also developed during a period of crisis in Church and society, may appear to be a support and an example for an "appropriate renewal." The issue of an independent branch within the second order is still alive among American contemplatives.

The Poligny monastery, which was the high point of Colettine observance, chose the general constitutions. This could be an example of a return to the primitive Rule, with Colette simply a staging post in the rich tradition of the order. "The little handmaid" would therefore act as a reminder and a watchword for the order as a whole, in its multiple experiences across Africa, Asia, and South America. Along with other reformers, but even more than they because of the significance of her work, Colette is a reminder to the Clarisses and also the silent overseer of the absolute nature of the gift.

Conclusion

This brief account of the history of the Colettines in the nineteenth and twentieth centuries highlights elements already present in earlier times: strengthening of structures accompanies a weakening of spiritual doctrine. Unless they stay in touch with their founding texts, the Colettines, like all contemplatives, tend to incorporate minor strands from contemporary spirituality, such as that of reparation, into their daily lives. At the same time, the generosity and heroism of the religious women ensure the Colettine reform remains durable and vital. The Colettine monasteries are the source of devotion to Saint Colette, the centenaries of whose birth and death are privileged moments.

However, the limitations of spiritual vitality cause a certain fossilization of customs and practices, rejected by many monasteries at the time of the conciliar *aggiornamento*. Risking confusion between a necessary rejection of anachronisms and a loss of ideals, a revival of the Colettine constitutions seems to have resulted mainly in a restoration of structures rather than in a spiritual renewal on the importance of which, nonetheless, everyone agrees.

Despite there being some fine personalities, no Clarisse in the nineteenth or twentieth centuries achieved the caliber of the Carmelite saints, nourished by their founding texts. More than a search for an "appropriate adaptation" of monastic life to contemporary times, the emergence of sanctity among the Clarisses could be the second order's response to the new questions raised by the Council and by the crises in Western civilization.[16]

From initial inquiries into the information process for "Sister Colette's" canonization at the end of the fifteenth century to the recent revival of her constitutions in the twentieth century, the history of Colettine reform and the portrayal of Colette's sanctity reveal a wealth of new material. The first inquiries coincided with extension of the reform and the consolidation of the legacy. Monastic foundations and the increase in writings produced in order to fix the oral tradition were the task of the first generations of Colettines and friars, many of whom were formed by the reformer herself. They were given support in this by the great houses, many of whose members joined Colettine monasteries and persevered in defense of the Colettines' independence within the vast Franciscan reform movement.

However, the seventeenth and eighteenth centuries marked a downturn in expansion at a time when women of elite society were attracted either by the Carmel or by other socio-cultural areas of interest. This was a period when communities managed to control daily life, to root heroism in

---

[16] The number of Clarisses estimated in 1971 was 22,000. There are presently more monasteries in Africa and in Asia.
Second order: about 1070 Clarisses.
842 Capuchin Clarisses.
154, order of the Immaculate Conception, founder Saint Beatriz da Silva (Spain).
4, Order of the Annunciation (France) founded by St. Jeanne de Valois.
Number of Clarisse houses by language regions:
400 Spanish (Spain and Latin America).
170 Italian (Italy).
94 English (USA 32, Asia 29, United Kingdom 23, Africa 8, Canada 2).
93 French (France 52, Belgium 8, Africa 29, Canada 4).
18 Portuguese (Portugal and Brazil).
36 Flemish-Dutch (Holland, Belgium, Indonesia).
27 German (Germany, Tyrol, Austria).
25 other (Japan, Korea, Philippines, Slavic countries, etc...).

It is not easy to assess the percentage of monasteries that have adopted the American constitutions since there are no statistics.

endurance, and thus ensure the continuing practice of their customs and asceticisms. They created a system of minute observances, all the more dangerous to the vitality of the monasteries since the spirituality of the beginnings of the reform and of the subsequent years was not enough to sustain the original spiritual experience. Colette's model of sanctity was harmed by hagiography, which became repetitive, while historicity was maintained by scholars. This hagiography inevitably became incomprehensible, since its style was that of a vanished culture.

The daughters of Colette and the popular devotion that arose around the monasteries ensured that the great abbess would have a place in history. The vitality of her spirituality was recognized by the official Church in her canonization in 1807. A second period then opened, characterized by a flourishing of foundations in Belgium and France, and, from these two countries, the establishment of foundations within and outside Europe. But the religious climate dominated by the spirituality of reparation, while expressing the sufferings of Christians after the Revolution, ran the risk of driving the nuns into a spiritual dead-end, further reinforced by their anachronistic lifestyle in a society undergoing rapid change because of two world wars.

The Church, then, in the person of Pius XII and through the Second Vatican Council, invited all nuns to spiritual and material renewal. Attempting to balance "appropriate renewal" with the risks of laxity in rejecting practices and customs not all of which were anachronistic, the American Colettines developed new constitutions, different from the general constitutions valid for the second order. Whether this is a revival of Colettine independence, long the subject of struggle in the fifteenth and sixteenth centuries, or simply a minor difference intended to incorporate a particular heritage, history alone will be able to judge. However, Colette remains a model of sanctity by her resolute standards maintained in a period of crisis.

CONCLUSION

Saint Colette remains a reference point in today's world for numerous Clarisses, offering them an example through her experience. Her main contribution to history was to reintroduce the *Rule* of Saint Clare to France during a difficult period for the Church and the Franciscan Order. In bringing the original *forma vitae* up to date, she placed considerable emphasis on two points that seemed to her essential:

- personal and community poverty by which, alongside the Italian reform movement, Colette differentiated herself from the Urbanist Clarisses, and
- the establishment of strict enclosure, necessary to safeguard the nuns themselves and their contemplative life.

Despite the force of her personality, the reformer's work would not have endured without the help of devoted co-workers and the support of the great houses, whose daughters, on joining the Colettines, ensured that the monasteries were surrounded by networks of influential lay people ready to help in any way.

Unlike Saint Clare's early project, structures were further strengthened by a more marked emphasis on hierarchy arising from the social relationships of the fifteenth century. There was also greater centralization of governance. But in smaller communities, more committed to poverty, the abbess lost the status of great lady that had been characteristic of the royal abbeys of "Rich Clares." Imposition of sanctions, even corporal punishment, through a code of faults, tended to regulate the lengthy apprenticeship in interpersonal relations described by the *Rule*. Hence, by recovering its structures, Colette contributed significant changes to convent life in a time of laxity.

Has Saint Clare's project ever truly been lived out? Certainly it was during the founder's lifetime at the monastery of San Damiano. But the papacy's reluctance to grant the privilege of "the strictest poverty" to Clare and to other monasteries and the insistence even of Saint Francis to impose the title of abbess, which she was refusing to accept, show that her project was utopian, in the evangelical meaning of the word. Such a utopia was certainly necessary to the spiritual vitality of the nuns, providing a permanent reminder of the commitment to live in a radical way. The multitude of rules (those of Hugolino, Urban IV, Longchamp) and the decline noted from the end of the thirteenth century raise the question of whether, like Saint Francis for the First Order, the founder found some difficulty in organizing and putting into practice her youthful intuition.

In this sense, Colette's work, despite its limitations, was a coherent attempt to shape the legacy and ensure development of the order, in which respect she did complete her initial project. Her undertaking was similar to that of Teresa of Avila (1515-1582) with this important difference: the latter could be said to have recreated Carmel. Her *Constitutions* and her fifteen foundations in Spain gave new impetus to women's convents, which had been living according to a rule written by men three centuries earlier. The mystical writings of the Spanish saint, a doctor of the Church, and the work of St. John of the Cross gave spiritual nourishment to the legislative endeavor, which was effective in preventing too much structural influence.

As for Colette, she was exposed to a declining theological and spiritual movement, represented by Brother Henry de Baume. The durability and extent of the Colettine work therefore relied on consistency of the legislative contribution and on Colette's own sanctity. It relied as well on the sanctity of the first generations, who gathered oral traditions, developed the heritage, and encouraged support networks around the monasteries and popular devotion to the reformer.

The picture of Colette's sanctity is enhanced by development in two areas, as described in the first biographies by Pierre de Vaux and Perrine. First, she was a healer, whose intercession relieved physical ailments. She specialized in helping women in labor and curing children. Secondly, she was a reformer, not just of the Franciscan second order, but of the first and third orders as well. In fact it is the consequences of her work, rather than the work itself, that has been studied – the spread of the reform and, at another level, the relationships generated with the elite of society. Through the eyes of her biographers and through the expectations of the socio-religious environment of the time, a figure has been forged of an exceptional woman who exercised a leading role in affairs of State and Church. This was the time when the legend was born of a meeting between the great abbess and the Maid of Orleans, whose renown was growing in the national consciousness. Even after the disappearance of female prophets such as Catherine of Siena and so many others and after Joan's tragic death, the way to God remained a woman's affair in the view of certain sectors of Church and Society that did not experience the Renaissance.

Unlike Teresa of Avila later on, who was her own biographer and who affirmed her originality despite the suspicions of the Inquisition, Colette wrote little or nothing. Formed by a Franciscan friar, she depended on another, Pierre de Vaux, for the basic components of her religious personality, recalled by hagiography and posterity. This approach to Colette's life, though limited, allows each age to modify and enrich the figure of the saint according to its own hopes and fears. Those, then, who, over the years, remained loyal to the cult of Colette around the reform's historical centers were right to do so.

As scapegoat for the fears of her age, Colette survives in her daughters, who will be asked to incarnate in some way this myth forged in a period of upheaval. During the seventeenth and eighteenth centuries, society was losing its sense of Christianity, and hagiography, with its associated cultural features, was partly responsible. It was a progressive phenomenon. In so far as the monastery and society live in a give and take relationship, whether of welcome or conflict, the nuns are anchored in a historical reality that balances and limits the influence of a reparative spirituality that makes consecrated women into "victims offered to divine justice."

After the revolutionary turmoil, the foundations brought the spirit of the Colettine reform, if not its *Constitutions*, up to date. This period saw a revival of a penitential life in which the degree of difficulty was the measure of its perfection. Poor Clares in the nineteenth century lived a physically tough life. In a laicized society, the nuns were culturally and mentally isolated. This was why the spirituality of reparation could take such a hold in the cloister. The borderline case of Sister Marie of the Trinity made a Colettine into the vestal of a vanished myth.

Pius XII and Vatican II would reintegrate monastic life into contemporary culture and reinsert it, beyond its historically recent customs, into the monastic and spiritual tradition of the founders. The cloister could once more be the "desert" beloved of monks, a place of separation and communion.

Blood might still flow, no longer from the wounds of self-inflicted penances, but rather from a life sacrificed for others, such as that of the Carmelite, Edith Stein, or the Franciscan Maximilian Kolbe, in Auschwitz.

The Council took a risk with respect to people and cultures in a *sequela Christi* resembling the Franciscan springtime inaugurated by Clare and Francis. The twentieth-century Colettine revival showed that, in a period of uncertainty, structures could provide a way of overcoming the possible drift caused by a freedom that is not always that of the Spirit.

Between these two poles, the Poor Clares retain their vital commitment to devote themselves to the service of God and of others. This disposition leads them to live with and suffer alongside a people, as they do in Algiers, in Eastern countries, or in Lebanon. In such places, according to the word of Francis, they endeavor to witness humbly through their way of life, without dispute or preaching, that they are Christians.

APPENDICES

COLETTE AND HER TIMES

CHURCH AND FRANCISCAN LIFE	POPES Rome	Avig-non	FRANCE / ENGLAND / BURGUNDY *Other countries: contemporary life*	BIOGRAPHY OF SAINT COLETTE
End 14th — Groups of friends of God in Upper Germany.				
1374-84 — Teaching and condemnation of Wyclif.				
1377 — Community of Groenendaël founded by Ruysbroeke.			*Religious theatre: Passion plays*	
1378-1417 — THE GREAT SCHISM	1378			
1378 — † *Ludolph Le Chartreux*, author of Life of Jesus Christ	U R B A N VI	C L E M E N T VII	1378-1382 — Urban social problem *Revolt in Gand.*	
1380 — † St Catherine of Siena			1380 — † Charles V Accession of Charles VI as child. Effective truce.	
1380-1444 — St Bernardino of Siena (Observant)				
1380-1381 — Friars of the Common Life, founded by Gérard Groote.				

1381	† Ruysbroeke					1381	Colette Boêllet born on 13 January at Corbie, in Picardy. Her mother, Marguerite Moyon, was elderly. Her father, Robert Boêllet, a carpenter, worked for the Benedictine abbey of St. Pierre of Corbie which had polarized the activities of the little town since the time of Charlemagne.
	Development of Carthusian Order (1st half of 15th century).			1382	The royal army wipes out the Flemish at Roosebeke		
				1383	Sack of Gand by the English		
1384-1440	St. Frances of Rome						
1385-1456	St John Capistrano (Observant)			1385	Marriage of Charles VI to Isabeau de Bavière		
				1387-1455	Fra Angelico		
1388	Beginnings of the Observance in France, Convent of Mirebeau (Poitou).					1388	A pious child, she loves listening to the office sung by the nuns, and goes away by herself to pray.
		1389					
1390	Benedictine reform in Spain: Valladolid congregation.	B O N I F A C E IX	C L E M E N T VII				
	Spread of Benedictine reform from Monte-Oliveto.						
	Beginnings of Dominican observance movement						

1390	Start of Observance in Spain.						
1391-1476	St. Jacques de la Marche (Observant)			1392	Beginnings of Charles VI's illness		
1394	Futile attempts to heal the schism. Election of Benedict XIII, Pope in Avignon.		1394 B E N E D I C T XIII	1394-1460	Henry the Navigator (in Portugal)		
1395	Meeting of Clergy in Paris to try to end the schism.	B O N I F A C E IX		1396	Disaster for Christian army against the Turks at Nicopolis.	1395	Around the age of 14, distressed at being so small, Colette makes a pilgrimage to Notre-Dame de Brebières nearby, after which, according to the "Vita" she grew spectacularly.
						1397	She loved to meet with young girls and women of her own age, to talk to them about God. The bishop however forbade her to do this, since she had not completed the necessary studies. With the creation of the universities from the 13th century onwards, knowledge and teaching were gradually becoming the province of the clergy alone
1398	22 May: The Meeting of the Clergy of France decides to withdraw obedience to Benedict XIII.			1399	In England, Richard II defeated. Henry IV of Lancaster, King of England.	1399	Colette is orphaned, and the parish priest of Corbie becomes her guardian.

C. 1400	Imitation of Christ *Profession of Felicia Meda at Milan, as Observant Clarisse.*					1400	*Colette gives away her property to the poor. On the advice of Fr. Jehan Bassand, a Celestine, and prior of the monastery of St. Benedict in Amiens, she privately takes a vow of virginity. She stays a year with the Beguines of Corbie in the service of the hospital, then with the Urbanist Clarisse of Pont-Ste-Maxence near Senlis, and finally with the Benedictines, as a lay sister.*
			B E N E D I C T			1402	*During the summer, she takes Fr. Pinet, guardian of the Hesdin Cordeliers (Observants), as her spiritual guide. She adopts the Rule of the Franciscan Third Order. At a solemn ceremony on 17 September, she enters seclusion in Corbie, in a cell attached to the Church of Notre-Dame at St-Étienne. She lives there for four years, practicing great penances, supported by a fervent eucharistic devotion with intense spiritual experiences. Many people come to ask for her prayers and advice. She foresees her mission.*
1403	May: Paris Synod. Restoration of obedience to Benedict XIII.	1404 I N NO C E NT VII	XIII	1404 1404-1419	† Philippe the Bold John the Fearless Duke of Burgundy	*c. 1404*	*Fr. Pinet dies. Fr. Henry de Baume visits and encourages her, offers his support and relationships.*

1405	Heresy of John Huss in Bohemia		1405	† Tamurlane	
1406	Council of Paris to try to end the schism. Some Cistercian reforms, especially in Spain.	1406			1406	On 22 July, the cardinal legate, Antoine Chalant, sends the Bishop of Amiens the request for dispensation from seclusion, as Colette asks. The Bishop of Amiens issues the dispensation on August 1. On August 2, Colette leaves her cell in the company of Fr. Henry de Baume and the baroness of Brissay to go to Nice to meet Benedict XIII. She has her interview with Benedict XIII at the beginning of October. On October 14, Colette is professed in the Order of Saint Clare at the hands of Benedict XIII. The pope also gives her permission to found a monastery strictly observing the Rule of Saint Clare. At the end of 1406, she tries to found in Corbie, but in vain. She leaves Corbie with her two companions to take refuge in Franche-Comté, at the castle of Alard de la Baume (brother to Fr. Henry)
1406		G R E G O R Y XII	B E N E D I C T XIII		
				1407	Assassination of Louis of Orleans.
1407	The two popes both agree to abdicate. Attempt at reform by Minister General of the Dominicans in Spain.			Quarrel between Armagnacs and Burgundians.	1408	Colette temporarily resides in a wing of a castle belonging to the Countess of Geneva at Fontenay. The Community grows. Benedict XIII's bull of 27 January 1408 grants Colette the Urbanist monastery of Besançon where only two sisters were living.

1409	Council of Pisa. Hearing and condemnation of both popes. Election of Alexander V, OFM (Observant).	**1409 ALEXANDER V** (P I S A)		1409	Peace in France between the princes.		
		†1410		*1410*	*"Les Très Riches Heures" by the Duke de Berry. Defeat of Teutons at Tannenberg. The High Gothic period. Flowering of the Renaissance in Italy.*	*1410*	*Colette takes over the monastery of Besançon, which becomes the cradle of the reform. Living by the Rule of Saint Clare, she applies the strictest poverty giving the monastery's income and property to the town almshouses. This renunciation was renewed by the deed of 1412, signed by all the sisters in the community*
				1411	John the Fearless in Paris		

1412	Excommunication of John Huss.	J		B	1412	Peace again between the princes	1412	In May, Colette goes with Henry de Baume to Dole to exhort the friars to reform. She meets opposition. Colette's second visit to the friars at Dole. She also goes to Dijon to the Duchess of Burgundy. On 25 September, a brief from John XXII authorizes the foundation of a monastery at Auxonne, in accordance with her way of life. On 28 October, she takes some of her daughters to Auxonne. Frs. de Vaux and Claret put themselves at her service.
		O		E				
				N				
		H	G	E				
			R	D	1412	Birth of Joan of Arc		
		N		I				
			E	C				
		XX	G	T	1412	Beginning of overseas expeditions		
		III		XIII				
1413-1463	St Catherine of Bologna (Clarisse)		O					
			R					
			Y		1413-1422	Henry V of Lancaster, King of England		
			XII					
					1413	States General, Cabochien revolt, Henry V resumes the war.		
1414-1418	16th Ecumenical Council at Constance.						1414	2nd June, a letter from the Duke of Burgundy gives Colette the arsenal of Poligny as a convent.
1415	The Council grants autonomy to the Observants in France.		† 1415		1415	French defeat at Agincourt.	1415	Colette moves to Poligny with a few sisters to oversee the work on the monastery. She spends some time at Besançon.

1416	General chapter for the Observance in France.					
1416	Execution of John Huss.					
			1417-1418	Conquest of Normandy by the English	1417	In October, Colette returns to Poligny and establishes her sisters in the monastery of Notre-Dame de Pitié. Tradition says that Saint Vincent Ferrier visited.
1417	11 Nov.: Election of Martin V					
1417	END OF GREAT SCHISM					
1418	March: 43rd session of the Council, seven decrees for general reform in the Church. April: end of Council.	M A R T I N V	1418-1437	Paris in the hands of the Anglo-Burgundians. Duke of Bourbon, prisoner.		
1419	† St Vincent Ferrier op		1419 Sept.:	Assassination of John the Fearless at Montereau.	1419	Colette visits the Countess of Nevers, Bonne d'Artois, daughter of the duchess of Bourbon whose husband was taken prisoner at Agincourt, and sets up a foundation on her land at Decize. She also goes to the Castle of Rouvres to see the Duchess of Burgundy, whose husband was assassinated at Montereau.
			1419-1467	Philippe the Good, Duke of Burgundy		

1420-1434	Crusade against the Hussites.	1420	Treaty of Troyes, Henry V of England inherits the crown of France.		
1420	*Monastery of Corpus Christi at Mantua, founded to follow the Rule of St Clare.*			1421	*2 July, Jacob de Bourg, a leading citizen of Seurre, gives land in the town to found a monastery. Blanche of Geneva dies, a loss to Colette of one of her first protectors. She is called by Marie de Berry to Moulins where she goes after visiting Marguerite de Bavière at Rouvres. 12 September an apostolic decree authorizes the foundation at Moulins by the Duchess of Bourbon.*
1421	General Chapter of the Dominicans. Reform of convents of Dominican nuns				
		1422	† Benedict XIII at Peñiscola. † Henry V and Charles VI. Henry VI (child), King of England and France. Regency of Bedford in France. Charles VII "King of Bourges."	1422	*5 October, William of Vienna exempts land given to the convent of Seurre from all taxes. The Duchess of Burgundy gives to Seurre a foundation bull granted by Martin V, which she never used.*

			1422-1423	English victories.	1422	On 24 October 1422, William of Vienna and the Archbishop of Besançon lay the first stone of the convent of Seurre. Mahaut of Savoy arranges transfer of the body of his aunt Blanche of Geneva from Rumilly to Poligny, where she had asked to be buried.
1423-1424	Council of Pavia-Siena		1423	Defeat of Charles VII at Verneuil.	1423	Colette establishes the Clarisses at Seurre and Moulins. She stops at the castle of Rouvres on the way, to meet the Duchess of Burgundy for the last time before her death in 1424. She goes to Aigueperse with Marie de Bourbon, who wants a foundation there. On 14 November the Duke de Bourbon lays the first stone.
			1424	Truce of Chambéry between Charles VII and the Burgundians.		
		M A R T I N V				
1425	Martin V publishes three reform decrees.		1425-1431	Van Eyck: "The Mystical Lamb."	1425	On 26 June, the chapel at the monastery of Aigueperse is blessed. Colette gives the habit to Isabeau de la Marche, eldest daughter of Jacques de Bourbon, then leaves with the Countess of Polignac, who wants a convent near her castle. Colette chooses the town of Puy.

		1426	From Puy, Colette goes to Chambéry, asked by Duke Amadeus VIII. It proves impossible to found at Chambéry because of opposition from Urbanists and Conventuals. The Duke suggests she establish herself at Vevey. She sets up a community there and stays for two years. Count Jacques joins her, is converted, and enters the third order. His son Claude enters the first order. The duchess of Valentinois visits him and discovers her vocation. Colette sends her to the monastery of Besançon. The leading citizens of Gand ask for a convent of Colettines in their town. An apostolic brief of 26 June 1427 authorizes dame Hélène Sclapper to establish a foundation.
M A R T I N V			On 17 November 1426, a bull approves yet another foundation at Orbe at the request of Jeanne de Monthliard, princess of Orange. On 13 January 1426, Colette is at Orbe to lay the first stone.
		1427	Colette returns to Poligny.
	1428	Start of siege of Orléans.	
	1429	Joan of Arc liberates Orléans. Coronation of Charles VII at Rheims. Joan's defeat at Paris.	1429	Colette visits her sisters at Moulins.

1430	*Chapter of Bologna: efforts at reconciliation.* *St. John Capistrano, vicar to the minister general William of Casal.*		1430	Capture of Joan of Arc at Compiègne.	*1430*	*Colette returns to Orbe where she writes her Constitutions.*
1431-1449	Council of Basle, 17th ecumenical council.	† **1431**	1431	Trial and execution of Joan of Arc. Coronation of Henri VI at Notre-Dame de Paris.	*1431*	*Colette goes to Languedoc, summoned by Count Jacques and his son-in-law Bernard d'Armagnac. She founds at Castres and at Lézignan.*
1432	The assembly of the French clergy votes to continue the Council.				*1432*	*In May, Colette leaves for le Puy, where she establishes her sisters on 2 July. She stays there around 18 months.*
					1433	*Colette is at Castres, then Lézignan.*
			1434	*Cosimo de' Medici takes power in Florence.*	*1434*	*Colette goes to Béziers where she reforms the community. She finishes her Constitutions. William of Casal approves them on 28 September 1434. She returns north via Moulins, Decize, Aigueperse, Seurre.*
1435	† *Abbess Angelina de Marschiano, founder of third order regular enclosed.*		1435	Peace of Arras between Charles VII and Philippe the Good. † Bedford and Isabeau de Bavière.		
1437	30 December: Council transfers from Basle to Ferrara. Break with Eugene IV.	E U G E N E IV	1437	Coalition of princes against Charles VII.	*1437*	*In spring, Colette, having returned to Besançon, sets out for Heidelberg, summoned by Louis de Bavière and his wife Mahaut. She establishes a convent there. On her return, she stops in Nancy, where she makes plans for a foundation at Pont-à-Mousson. On 25 June, a bull authorizes the Duke of Burgundy to found at Hesdin.*

1438	Pragmatic Sanction of Bourges		1438		Smallpox epidemics.	1438	Jacques de Bourbon dies, then Henry de Baume.
1439	January: Council transfers from Ferrara to Florence. Election of anti-pope Amadeus VIII of Savoy as Felix V.	F E L I X V	1439		The "Praguerie" coalition of princes.	1439	The Duke of Savoy creates a new schism and becomes anti-pope, Felix V. Colette breaks all relations with him.
1440	† St Frances of Rome St John Capistrano at Besançon.					1441	In autumn, Colette leaves Besançon and sets out for Hesdin. For her last foundations, she returns to the States of the Duke of Burgundy, but this time to those of the North, which Duke Philippe the Good recovered by the treaty of Arras in 1435.
1442	Transfer of Council.		1442		Jacques Coeur, member of King's council.	1442	On 7 July, Pope Eugene IV authorizes Philippe de Saveuse to found in Amiens. On 3 August, Colette arrives in Gand, where a monastery is ready for her, having been finished two years earlier. She returns to Besançon, where she receives John Capistrano and visits Dole with him.
1443	December: final session of schismatic Council at Basle.						
1444	† St Bernardino of Siena		1444		Anglo-French truce at Tours.	1444	In January, Colette leaves Besançon again to go north.

1445	Commentaries on the Rule of St. Clare by St. John Capistrano	E U G E N E IV	F E L I X V			1445	In January Colette enters the monastery of Amiens. She tries again to establish a monastery at Corbie, but meets the same opposition from the monks of the abbey. On 19 October, Pope Eugene IV grants Philippe de Saveuse authorization to found at Corbie, but even the king's support is not enough to overcome resistance, especially that of the Benedictines. Colette remains at Hesdin.
						1446	She leaves Hesdin for Gand arriving on 6 December
		† **1447**		1447	The Dauphin Louis retires to Dauphiné.	1447	On 6th March, Colette dies in Gand.
1449	End of schismatic council of Basle. Abdication of Felix V.	N I C H O L A S V		1449	The Passion of Arnould Greban		
1450	Canonization of St Bernardino of Siena.			1450	Gutenberg: first printing of the Bible.		
				1453	End of Hundred Years War.		
				1453	Constantinople captured by the Turks. End of Byzantine Empire.		
1455	Canonization of St. Vincent Ferrier	† **1455**					
				1456	Rehabilitation of Joan of Arc		

Table of Saint Colette's Foundations

Regions	Founder	Place	First abbess
Duchy of Burgundy	With authorisation from Benedict XIII Marguerite de Bavière, wife of John the Fearless	Reform of Besançon (1410) Auxonne (1412) Poligny (1414-1417) Seurre (1421-1423)	Mother de Toulongeon (1412) Agnès de Vaux Claudine de Courcelles Marie Sénéchal
Center of France	Marie de Berry, duchess of Bourbon Bonne d'Artois, Countess of Nevers Claude de Roussillon, Viscountess of Polignac	Moulins (1421-1423) Aigueperse (1423-1425) Decize (1419-1423) Le Puy en Velay (1425-1432)	Marie Sénéchal
Duchy of Savoy	Duke Amadeus VIII with Guillemette de Gruyère, Countess of Valentinois Jeanne de Montbéliard	Vevey (1424-1426) Orbe (1426-1428)	Claire Labeur
Languedoc	Jacques II, former king of Naples -with his brother-in-law, Bernard d'Armagnac -with two sisters from Lézignan	Castres (1426-1433) Lézignan 1430-1436 Reform of Béziers (1434)	
Palatinate	Louis II of Bavière and his wife Mahaut de Savoie	Heidelberg (1437-1443)	Isabeau or Elisabeth de Bavière
Picardy	Philippe the Good, Duke of Burgundy Philippe de Saveuse, governor of Amiens	Hesdin (1437-1441) Amiens (1442-1445)	Guillemette Chrestienne Isabeau de Bourbon
Flanders	The people and the Duke of Burgundy	Gand (1441-1444)	Sister Odette
Lorraine	King René of Anjou, Duke of Lorraine	Pont-à-Mousson (1444-1447) (after Colette's death)	

TABLE OF FOUNDATIONS MADE BEFORE 1520

Names	Foundations by Colette or the Colettins	Dates of closure	Dates of refounding
Aigueperse[1]	*1423*	1792	
Aix-en-Provence (1337)	1516	1787	
Alicante	1518		
Amiens	*1445*	1792	1800-1976
Anvers	1461	1581	1834 ->
Arras	1460	1792	1815 ->
Auxonne	*1412*	1792	
Besançon (1250)	*1410*	1792	1879 ->
Béziers (1240)	*1434*	1792	1819 ->
Bourg-en-Bresse	1480	1792	
Bourges	1468	1792	
Bruges[2]	1473	1783	
Cambrai	1496	1792	1848
Castellon de Ampurias	1505		
Castres[3]	*1431*	1792	
Chambéry	1471	1793	
Decize	*1419*	1792	
Dinan	1488	1792	
Gand[4]	*1442*	1783	1835 ->
Gandia	1457		
Geneva	1479	1535	
Gerone	1488		
Gien	1500	1792	
Grenoble[5]	1478	1792	1878 ->
Heidelberg	*1437*		
Hesdin	1441	1792	
Le Puy	*1432*	1792	1807 ->
Lézignan	*1431*	1792	
Liège	1474		
Marseille (1254)	1516	1792	1803 ->
Moulins	*1421*	1792	
Montbrison	1496	1792	1823 ->
Nantes	1457	1792	1833 ->
Orbe	*1428*	1554	
Péronne	1481	1792	1800-1968
Perpignan (1260)	1500	1792	1825 ->
Poligny	*1417*	1792	1817 ->
Pont-à-Mousson	1447	1792	
Rouen	1483	1792	
Setubal (Port.)	1496	1835	
Seurre	*1423*	1792	
Valence (Spain)	1497		
Vevey	*1426*	1536	

[1] Italicized names indicate monasteries founded or reformed by Saint Colette.

[2] The Clarisses of Bruges were expelled twice from their convent: in 1783, by the laws of Joseph II, return in 1790, in 1796, by the armies of the Revolution. The community regrouped in 1806, and joined the present convent in 1841.

[3] The community of Castres was first dispersed in 1561 by the protestants. Refounded in 1632, the convent finally closed in 1792.

[4] The Clarisses of Gand were expelled three times (and re-established three times). Expelled in 1578 by the Calvinists, in 1783 by the laws of Joseph II, in 1796 by armies of the Revolution, they were refounded in 1835.

[5] In 1955, the community transferred to Voreppe, 15 kilometers from Grenoble.

556 LEARNING AND HOLINESS

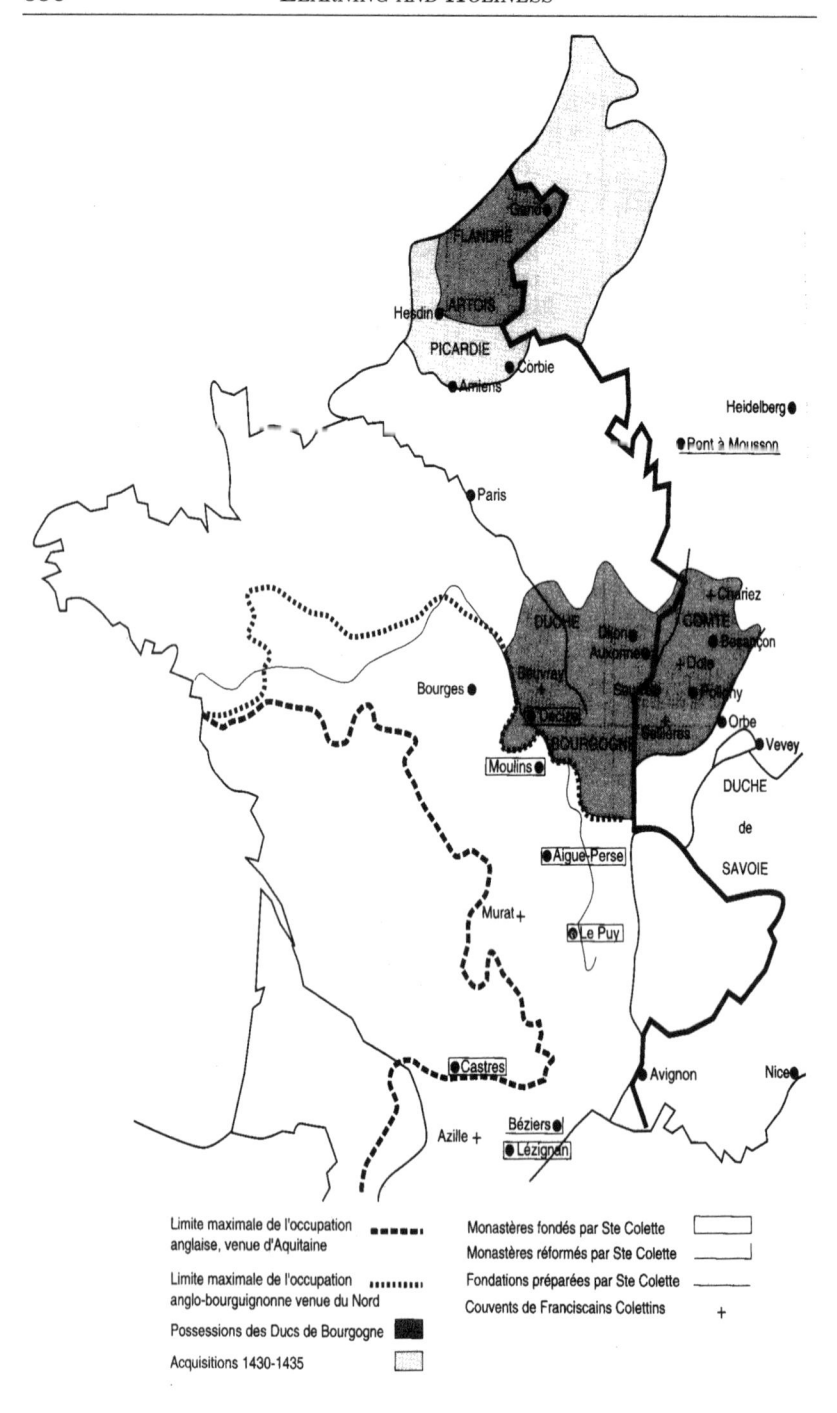

Limite maximale de l'occupation anglaise, venue d'Aquitaine	▬ ▬ ▬
Limite maximale de l'occupation anglo-bourguignonne venue du Nord	▪ ▪ ▪ ▪
Possessions des Ducs de Bourgogne	
Acquisitions 1430-1435	
Monastères fondés par Ste Colette	
Monastères réformés par Ste Colette	
Fondations préparées par Ste Colette	
Couvents de Franciscains Colettins	+

CARTE DES FONDATIONS

APPENDICES 557

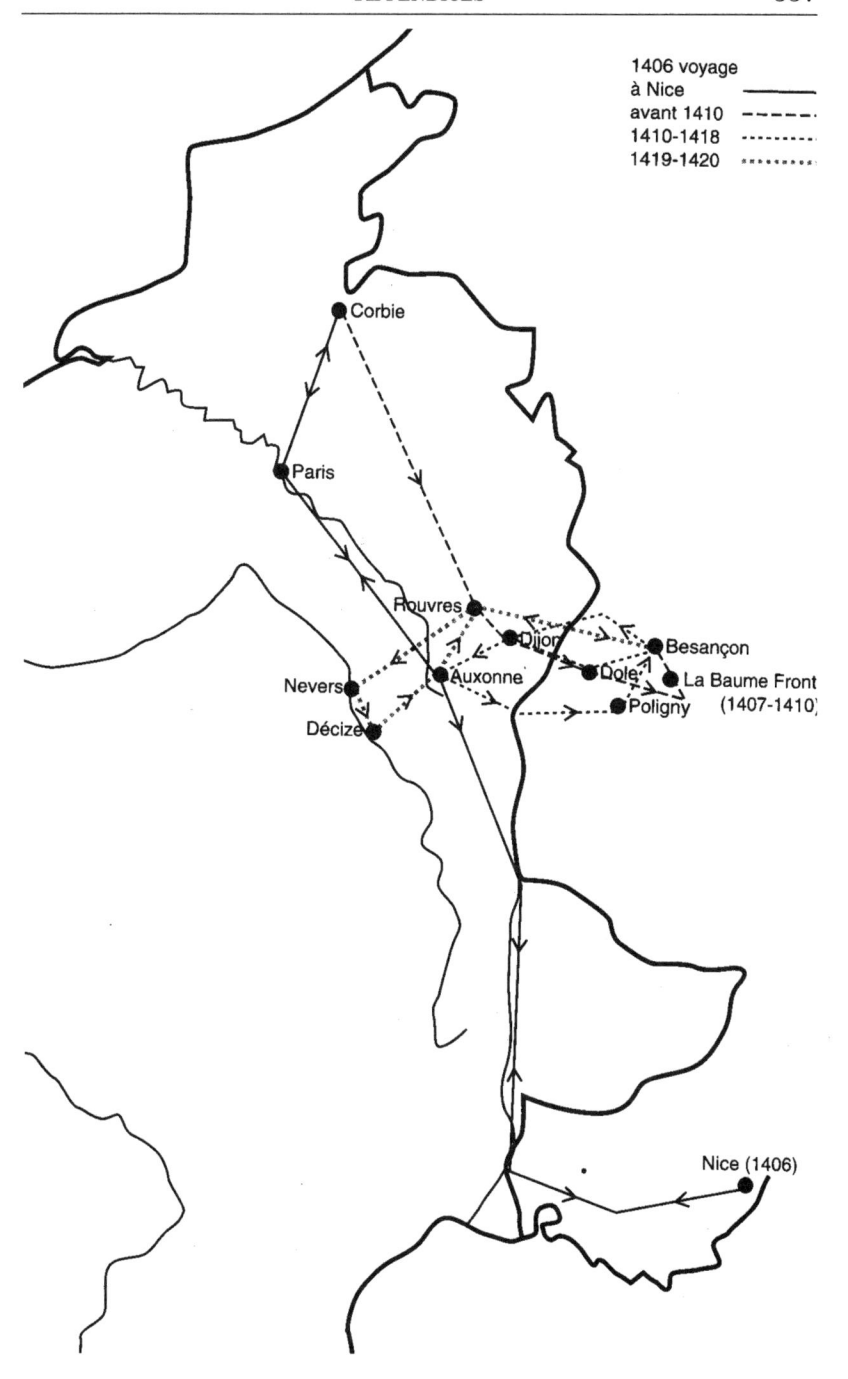

1406 voyage à Nice
avant 1410
1410-1418
1419-1420

Corbie

Paris

Rouvres
Dijon
Besançon
Nevers
Auxonne
Dole
La Baume Front
Décize
Poligny
(1407-1410)

Nice (1406)

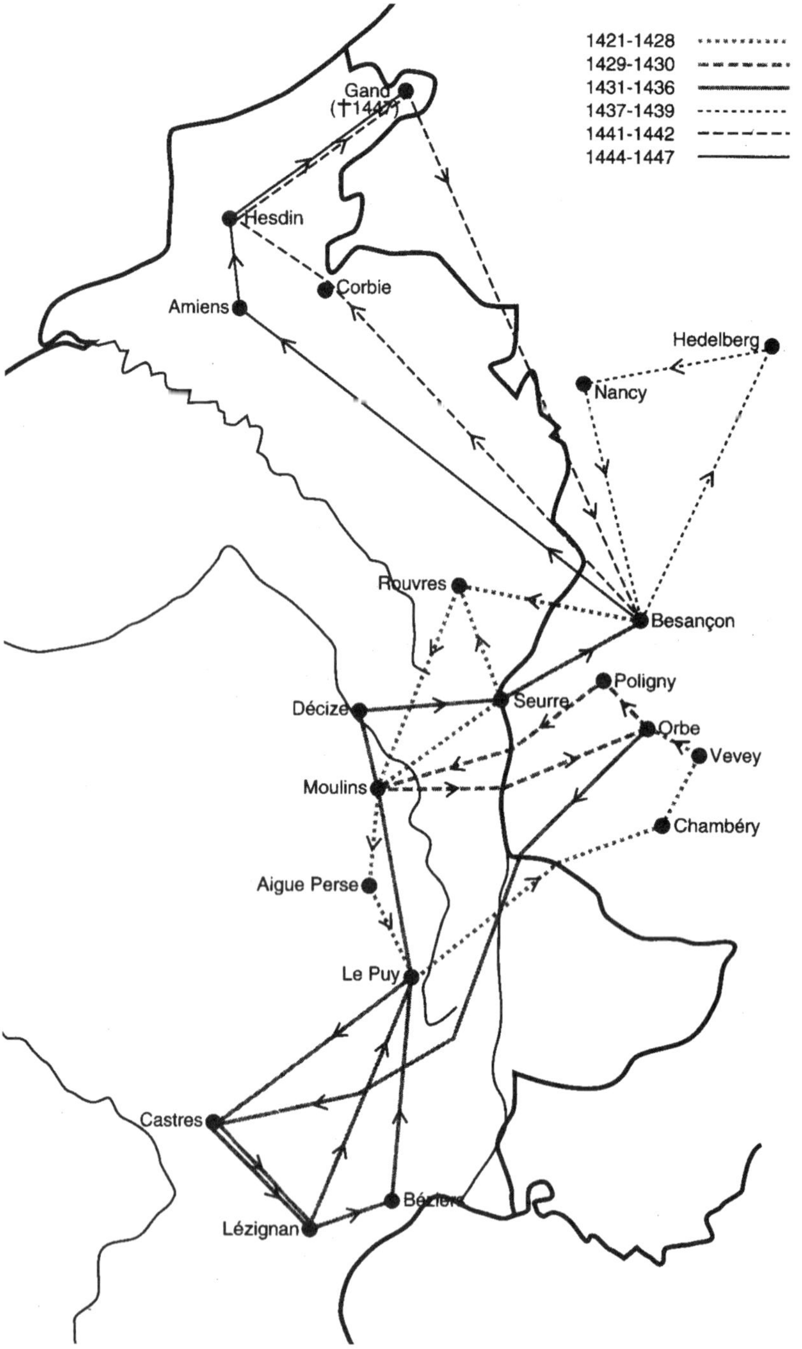
1421-1428
1429-1430
1431-1436
1437-1439
1441-1442
1444-1447
Gand
(†1447)
Hesdin
Corbie
Amiens
Hedelberg
Nancy
Rouvres
Besançon
Poligny
Seurre
Décize
Orbe
Vevey
Moulins
Chambéry
Aigue Perse
Le Puy
Castres
Béziers
Lézignan

Appendices

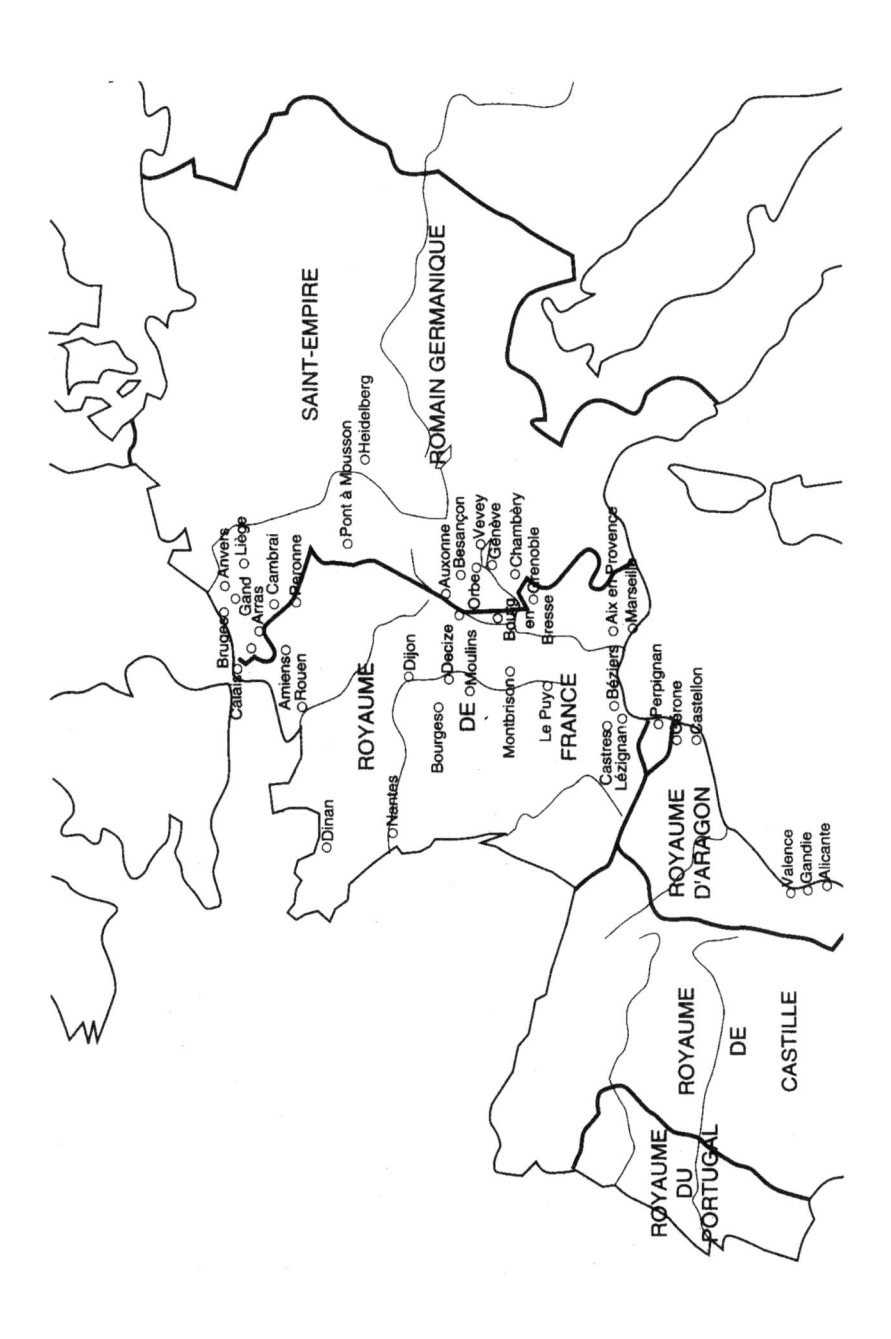

Map of Western Europe showing:

SAINT-EMPIRE ROMAIN GERMANIQUE
- Pont à Mousson
- Heidelberg
- Auxonne
- Besançon
- Orbe
- Vevey
- Genève
- Chambéry
- Grenoble

ROYAUME DE FRANCE
- Bruges, Anvers, Gand, Liège
- Calais, Arras, Cambrai
- Bayonne
- Amiens, Rouen
- Dinan, Nantes
- Dijon, Decize
- Bourges, Moulins
- Montbrison
- Le Puy
- Bourg en Bresse
- Aix en Provence
- Marseille
- Castres, Lézignan, Béziers
- Perpignan

ROYAUME D'ARAGON
- Gerone, Castellon
- Valence, Gandie, Alicante

ROYAUME DE CASTILLE

ROYAUME DU PORTUGAL

GLOSSARY

Ancelle: from the Latin *ancilla* (*Domini*), servant (of the Lord), it evokes the response of the Virgin Mary at the moment of the Annunciation.

Apophetic: a figure of speech by which one announces to another an event that one knows is past. For example: in the *Tragedies of Aubigné* (1616), the assassination de Henri IV (1610) is "announced" by the poet as a punishment.

Ars moriendi: the art of dying. In the fifteenth century, this theme was the subject of many writings and preachings.

Baudes: In the fifteenth century, the name given to the Franciscan friars in the region of Metz.

Béguinage: literally "house." A community of religious women of Belgium and the Low Countries who lived a conventual life.

Capitule: a passage of Holy Scripture read during the Divine Office.

Cardinal Protector: a cardinal designated by the pope to correct the brothers and watch over the Order with solicitude. Saint Francis had insistently asked this of the pope. (Later Rule 12: 3; Testament 33).

Chapter, conventual (monastic life): an assembly of professed religious who elect the abbot and his council or the abbess and her council and who participate in decision-making.

Cilice: A shirt or cincture made of animal hair or of rough material, worn for penance or mortification.

Confession, extraordinary: Women religious, outside of their regular times of confession (once or twice a month), confessed two or three times a year to a confessor other than their regular one.

Comtemptus mundi (latin): contempt for the world. A classic theme of religious life. Reminiscent of the Gospel of Saint John (the discourse after the Last Supper).

Conventual (Order of Friars Minor): a friar who lived community life in a convent as distinct from one who lived in a hermitage. After the end of the thirteenth century, the term designated the friars who lived a mitigated rule as opposed to the Spirituals, later known as Observants.

Counselor or "discrete": elected by the conventual chapter, a sister who formed, together with the vicaress, the council of the abbess, charged with helping her in the government of the community.

Damianite: the name given to the nuns at the Monastery of Saint Damien.

Devotio Moderna: a school of spirituality at the end of the fourteenth century that, turning away from the speculative mysticism of the scholastic period, sought God by way of adherence of the heart to God's will and by the renunciation of self. (*The Imitation of Christ,* which appeared around 1400, expresses well the spirit of this school.)

Discalced: religious of the regular observance who, for the sake of penance and in the spirit of poverty, went without shoes.

Discipline: a kind of whip, made of cords or little chains, used to flagellate oneself as a form of mortification.

Familiar: a layperson attached to a monastery who rendered material services to the community.

Forma vitae (form of life): an expression given by Saints Francis and Clare to their proposed way of life.

Guardian: in the Order of Friars Minor, the name given to the superior of a community.

Lay Brothers or "conversi": non-ordained brothers, members of a religious community. Saint Clare, in her *Rule,* asked for two lay brothers to assist the sisters who did the work and begged for alms.

Millenarianism: a doctrine of the millennium; some Christians expected the Messiah to reign on the earth for a thousand years before the day of the last judgment.

Minister General: the friar elected by the provincial ministers to be responsible for the whole Order of Friars Minor.

Minister Provincial: a friar responsible for a province, elected by the friars.

Obedience: obedience to an ecclesiastical superior. During the Great Schism, recognition by the States of the pope at Rome or of the pope at Avignon.

Observance (regular): "religious of the regular observance" designated the monk, the nun, or the religious who practiced the rule in all its integrity, without dispensation. The term also designates the reformed branch of a religious order.

Officer: a religious charged with a specific office.

Order, First: the male branch of the Franciscan Order founded by Saint Francis. Also known as the Order of Friars Minor.

Order, Third: covers laypersons who live the Franciscan spirituality. There is also the Third Order Regular made up of religious who take vows and live in community. In the fifteenth century, the extern sisters might have belonged to the Third Order Regular. After the Council of Trent, sisters of the Third Order Regular had to become cloistered.

Porter: a cloistered nun whose duties consist in dealing with persons from the outside.

Preces: fixed formulas for prayer.

Protomonastery: by comparison with the protomonastery of Assisi, the term designates the first monastery of the colettine reform at Besançon.

Sinacle: an object of devotion that preceded the rosary and with the help of which the faithful recited the *Paters*.

Sister converses: in the monasteries, other then colettine, the converses were cloistered professed sisters who, originally illiterate, did not say the office in choir and did not have a voice in the chapter. They took care of the heavy work of the monastery.

Sisters, extern (also "Sisters of the Mountain" at Poligny or, among the Colettines, "Marthas" or Sister converses): sisters, in general of the Third Order, who lived outside the cloister. They begged for alms or worked in the service of the monastery.

Sisters. Grey: a congregation of hospital sisters of the Franciscan Third Order in the north and east of France.

Visitator (canonical): a religious or secular person designated by the provincial minister (or the bishop if the monastery if not under the jurisdiction of an order) to visit a monastic community in order to assure the proper observance of the rule.

BIBLIOGRAPHY

I. MANUSCRIPT SOURCES

Writings of Saint Colette

Letters
At Besançon, municipal library:

Lettre aux clarisses de Besançon, 18 Juillet 1446. Original. Dossier 1490-1491, Tome I, folio 3.
Lettre d'affiliation à sieur Bartholomé de Dijon, 1446. Original. Dossier 1490-1491, Tome I, folio 67.

At Gand, Colettine Monastery:

Lettre à Pierre de Vaux, 1436 or 1439. Original. Section II, Réforme II.
Lettre aux bourgeois de Gand, 18 Mars 1440. Original autograph with seal. Venerated as a relic. Hors série.
Lettre à dame Marie Boën, 1442. Original. Hors série.
Lettre aux religieuses de Gand, 1442. Original. Conserved as relic. Hors série.
Lettre aux bourgeois de Gand, 1442. Original. Hors série.

At Poligny, archives of the monastery of Saint Claire:

Copies anciennes de lettres écrites par sainte Colette. Originals at Gand, series A.

At Poligny, monastery, archives of the convent of the Clarisses of Amiens (closed), deposited at Poligny:

Lettre au roi Charles VII, vers 1445. Copy.
Deux lettres aux moines de Corbie, around 1446.

At Le Puy, Monastery of Saint Claire:

Lettre aux religieuses du Puy, around 1439. Original in poor condition, under a frame.
Lettre sur le trépas de frère Henri de Baume, 1439. Original under a frame.
Lettre à frère Jehan Lanié, 1447. Original in poor condition, under a frame.

Teachings

Nothing was actually written by Saint Colette, but the documents listed here reflect her thought:

Constitutions de l'Ordre de sainte Claire données à sainte Colette par Guillaume de Casal, le 28 Septembre 1434. Original on parchment, sealed by G. de Casal. Monastery of the Clarisses of Besançon.
Les intentions ou sentiments de sainte Colette. Old copies (the original of 1430 has disappeared). Monastery of the Colettines of Gand. Manuscript copies 12 and 13 of the process of canonization of 1747, archives of the monastery of Poligny.
Les intentions de notre mère soeur Colette, exprimées avant sa mort pour les notifier à tous ses couvents pour mieux garder la Règle. Monastery of Poligny.
Les ordonnances dites de "sainte Colette." Monastery of Poligny
Les ordonnances et déclarations recueillies d'après mère Catherine de Longueville, première abbesse de Bruges. 12th-century copy. Bound in leather. Monastery of the Colettines of Bruges, document 20.
Les petites ordonnances concernant le cérémonial. Book II of process of canonization. Monastery of Poligny.

Les recommandations que notre mère soeur Colette fit à son couvent de Gand peu avant son trépassement. Monastery of Poligny, series A 14.

Lettre de soeur Agnès de Vaux à l'abbesse de Gand, au sujet de certains us et coutumes chers à la sainte réformatrice dont elle fut jadis la fidèle compagne. Original not dated. Monastery of Gand, section I, Réforme I, dossier 43.

Observations sur la vie et la discipline monastiques de sainte Colette écrites par soeur Agnès, adressées à une soeur ancienne. A writing of the 17th century. Monastery of Gand.

Copy of a letter to Jeanne Labeur, religieuse à Gand, sur les derniers avis de sainte Colette (undated). Monastery of Poligny, series A 14.

Exhortation ou Testament dit de sainte Colette: "Dévote exhortation faite par notre glorieuse mère sainte Colette à toutes nous, ses pauvres filles." Municipal library of Besançon. Monastery of Gand, an exemplary of 1553. 18th-century copy, dossier 1490-1491, Vol. I, folios 46 to 63.

Writings Directly Concerning Saint Colette

Letters

At Besançon, municipal library:

Lettre de Henry de Baume à Colette, around 1420. Original. Dossier 1490-1491, Vol. I, folio 101.

Lettre de Guillaume de Casal au "Roy" Jacques de Bourbon, 1434. Original. Dossier 1490-1491, Vol. I, folio 83.

Lettre du Cardinal Julien à sainte Colette, 25 February 1436. Original. Dossier 1490-1491, Vol. I, folio 133.

Lettre du Cardinal Julien à sainte Colette, 7 September 1436. Original. Dossier 1490-1491, Vol. I, folio 83.

Lettre de Mahaut de Savoye à sainte Colette, au sujet de sa fille Elisabeth, 15 January 1438. Original. Dossier 1490-1491, Vol. I, folio 70.

Lettre de Jean Aubert (ou Maubert) à P. de Vaux. Dossier 1490-1491, Vol. I, folio 91.

Plusieurs lettres de Guillaume de Casal, 1431-1438. Dossier 1490-1491, Vol. I, folio 74-90. Published by P. d'Alençon.

Official Documents

Permission par l'abbé de Corbie à Colette d'entrer en reclusage, 1402. Departmental Archives of the Somme.

Lettre de l'évêque d'Amiens Jean de Boissy communiquant à Colette la dispense de son voeu de reclusage accordée par le légat, 1er August 1406. Original, parchment with seal. Bibliothèque municipale of Besançon, dossier 1490-91, Vol. I, folio 64.

Sauf conduit délivré par Jean le Bon autorisant soeur Colette à se rendre à Amiens, 15 March 1443. Original parchment. Monastery of Poligny, archives of Amiens, carton 3-05.

Witnesses

Témoignages des quatre habitants de la ville de Corbie qui assurent avoir vu et connu la bienheureuse Colette, 1471. Monastery of Poligny: archives of Amiens, carton 2-05.

Lettre de Catherine Ruffiné à l'abbesse de Gand. Cahier 14 of the Process of Canonization. Poligny, monastery archives.

Le mémoire d'Hesdin, 1471. Poligny, archives of Amiens, Carton 23.

Mémoire de tout ce que nous savons et avons pu recueillir des choses particulières que notre béate mère Colette a dict et faict en ce sien monastère de Poligny, 1623. Poligny, monastery archives, série A 2.

Enquêtes et informations faites par les pères capucins pour la canonisation de sainte Colette, 1629. Poligny, archives of Amiens, carton 17.

Lettres et correspondances relatives à la béatification de sainte Colette. Poligny, archives d'Amiens, 1600-1630: carton 18; after 1630: cartons 19 and 23.

Décrets, lettres, suppliques, etc., relatifs à la canonisation de sainte Colette. Monastery of Le Puy, dossier 3 A 3.

Lettres et documents relatifs au procès de canonisation de sainte Colette. Besançon, municipal library, dossier 1490, Vol. II.

Copie du procès de canonisation de 1747. Monastery of Poligny, series A 3, 33 fascicules: the first in old French, the others in Latin or Flemish.

Mélanges historiques sur la vie et l'action de soeur Colette, l'origine et les progrès de sa réforme, 1784. Poligny, monastery archives, série A 8.

Biographies

Pierre de Vaux, *Vie de soeur Colette.* Oldest manuscript, 15th century. Poligny, monastery archives.

Manuscript of 1494. Authentic copy made at Gand. Poligny, archives of Amiens (published by Ubald d'Alençon).

Manuscript de 1468-1477, with the arms of Princesse Marguerite d'Angleterre, illustrated with miniatures (published by Van Corstanje, Y. Cazaux, J. Decavele, A. Derolez), conserved at the monastery of Gand, Tielt 1982.

Soeur Perrine, *Vie de soeur Colette* (Cahier). Authentic copy of 1494. Gand, archives of the monastère, ms 2.

Abbé de Saint Laurent, *Vie de soeur Colette,* 1630. Manuscript of the Monastery of Poligny (printed in Lyon in 1835).

Abbé Larceneux, *Vie de soeur Colette. Dédié à Madame Louise de France, 1785.* Manuscript of 110 cahiers organized into 11 files at the monastery of Poligny.

Other Documents

Bréviaire dit de sainte Colette, given, according to the traditioin, by Benedict XIII. Monastery of the Clarisses of Besançon.

Bréviaire dit de sainte Colette, manuscript of the 13th century with a letter of P. de Vaux adressed to the Clarisses d'Aigueperse. Parchement. Bound with leather on wood. Monastery of Puy.

Psautier dit de sainte Colette, manuscript, 1st quarter of the 14th century (it would have been offered to her by Benedict XIII). Vellum. Bound in leather. Monastery of Le Puy.

First Seal of the Monastery, 1432 (dim. 0.51 mm x 0.32mm). Monastery of Le Puy.

Instructions du frère Henry de Baume pour les clarisses. Original. Municipal library of Besançon, dossier 1490, Vol. I, folio 85-101.

Henry de Baume. *Recueil de traités spirituels.* Copies of the 15th century. Writings by several hands. Municipal library of Besançon, dossier 257, folio 1 à 417.

Vie de Marie Chevalier. Archives of Poligny, série A 3.

Bréviaires dits "des princesses," attributed to Marie de Bourbon and Catherine de la Marche. End of 15th century.

Mémoire rédigé en 1511 lequel rappelle la fondation en Savoie (1420) et les souvenirs jusque là transmis oralement. Cahier 23-21, archives of the monastery at Amiens.

II. PRINTED SOURCES

Writings of Saint Colette

"Lettres de sainte Colette à soeur Loyse Bassande" in Dom Durand and Dom Martène, *Voyage littéraire de deux religieux bénédictins de la Congrégation de Saint Maur.* Paris, 1717.

"Lettre circulaire de sainte Colette à l'occasion de la mort du P. Henri" 1439, in *Analecta Juris Pontificii*. 1879. P. 528.

Les lettres de sainte Colette. Ed. Clarisses of Paray-le-Monial. Pro manuscripto, 1981.

Testament attribué à sainte Colette dans *Seraphicae Legislationis Textus originales*, 1897.

Writings Directly Concerning Saint Colette

"Lettres inédites de Guillaume de Casal à sainte Colette et notes pour la biographie de cette sainte." Published by Ubald d'Alençon. *Etudes Franciscaines*, vol. 19 (1908): 460-481.

"Lettre de Pierre de Vaux aux habitants d'Amiens." Published by Ubald d'Alençon. *Etudes Franciscaines*, vol. 23 (1910).

Ubald d'Alençon, *Les vies de sainte Colette Boylet de Corbie, réformatrice des frères mineurs et des clarisses*, écrites par ses contemporains le P. Pierre de Reims dit de Vaux et soeur Perrine de la Roche et de Baume. Archives Franciscaines n° 4. Paris, Librairie Picard, 1911.

Procès de canonisation, archives of the monastery of Gand: S. Rit. Congr. Celsitudine regia Eminentissimi D. Card. Ducis Eboracensis, Ambianen, seu Gandaven. Canonizationis B. Coletae Virginis, Reformatricis Ord. S. Clarae. Positio super dubio... et ad effectum de quo agitur? Rome, 1773. Typis Rev. Camerae Apostolicae.

S. Rit. Congr... Responsio ad novas animadversiones R.P. Fidei promotoris super dubio, An et de quibus. Rome, 1778.

Procès de canonisation, Bibliothèque Nationale de Paris. 4 volumes concern the process of 1773: H 827-830 inclusive (n° 1827-1866).

Contemporary Writings

Henry de Baume. *Statuts à l'usage des frères mineurs au service des soeurs colettines*. Published by H. Lippens, article "Henry de Baume, coopérateur de S. Colette: recherches sur sa vie et publications de ses statuts inédits." *Sacris Erudiri*, I. Bruges, 1948.

Henry de Baume. "Lettres et autres écritures profitables et récréatives à l'âme devote." *A.F.H.*, II (1909).

Testament de Jacques de Bourbon. Published by Huart, Ed. Couvin, Maison St-Roch. Belgium, 1003.

Saint Jean de Capistran. "Explicatio Primae Regulae S. Clarae auctore S. Joanne Capistranensi," 1445. *A.F.H.*, XXII (1929): 336-57 and 512-28. Quaracchi, 1929.

Foundational Documents of the Franciscan Order

Saint François d'Assise, Documents: Ecrits et première biographies. rassemblés et présentés par les PP. Théophile Desbonnets et Damien Vorreux, ofm; deuxième édition revue et augmentée. Paris: Ed. Franciscaines, 1981.

François d'Assise, Ecrits. Texte latin de l'éd. K. Esser, introduction, traduction, notes et index par Th. Desbonnets, Th. Matura, J. F. Godet, D. Vorreux (frères mineurs). Paris, 1981. (Sources Chrétiennes, 285.)

Sainte Claire d'Assise, Documents. Rassemblés, présentés et traduits par Damien Vorreux, ofm. Paris: Ed. Franciscaines, 1983.

Claire d'Assise, Ecrits. Introduction, texte latin, traduction, notes et index par M. F. Becker, J. F. Godet, Th. Matura (frères et soeur mineurs). Paris: 1985. (Sources Chrétiennes, 325).

La Règle de l'Ordre de Sainte Claire, avec les Statuts de la Réforme de Sainte Colette, quelques lettres de cette Glorieuse Réformatrice, ses Sentiments sur la Sainte Règle, etc. Société de Saint Augustin. Bruges: DDB, 1892.

WADDING, L. *Annales Minorum seu Trium Ordinum a S. Francisco institutorum*. 3rd ed. Ad claras aquas (Quaracchi). Florence (33 volumes), followed by a *registrum pontificum*.

Bullarium Franciscanum, seu R. B. Pontificum constitutiones epistolae ac diplomate ordinibus minorum, clarissarum, poenitentium concessae:
First series in 7 volumes: vol 1-4, ed. J. H. Sbaralea, Rome, 1759-1768; vol 5-7, ed. C. Eubel, Rome, 1898-1904. Second or New series in 3 volumes, ed. U. Huntermann and J. M. Pou y Marti. Quaracchi, 1929-1949.

Francis of Assisi: Early Documents. Ed. Regis J. Armstrong, OFMCap., J. A. Wayne Hellmann, OFMConv., William J. Short, OFM. 4 volumes. New York: New City Press, 1999, 2000, 2001, 2002.

Clare of Assisi: Early Documents. Ed. and trans. Regis J. Armstrong, OFMCap. New York: New City Press, 2006.

Inventory of Archives

Catalogue général des manuscrits des bibliothèques publiques de France, départements. Tome XXXII. Besançon, Tome 1. Paris, 1897.

Catalogue général des manuscrits des bibliothèques publiques de France. Tome XIX. Paris, Plon, 1915, pp. 194-200, (2nd supplement).

M. Gauthier. *Inventaire des archives des clarisses de Besançon* (manuscript). 1889.

M. H. Macqueron. *Bibliographies du département de la Somme*. Tome II. Amiens, 1907.

H. Lippens, OFM. "Inventaire analytique des archives de l'abbaye des soeurs colettines à Bruges." *Franciscana*, Archives Franciscaines, St-Trond, 1960. XV-3.

H. Lippens, OFM. "Inventaire analytique des archives de l'abbaye des colettines à Gand." *Franciscana*, XI, 1956 n° 1, and XII, 1956, n° 2 and 3.

H. Lippens, OFM. "Annexe de l'inventaire analytique des archives de l'abbaye des colettines à Gand." *Franciscana*, XVII, 1962, n° 3.

J. Goyens. *Eleuchus documentorum in veteri archivo clarissarum pauperum gandavi adservatorum*. Archives de la province belge, St-Trond, section VI, cler colet Gand. *A.F.H.*, VII (1915): 143-145.

Monastère du Puy, *550 Ans d'Histoire au Monastère Sainte Claire du Puy-en-Velay*. 1982.

III. BIOGRAPHIES OF SAINT COLETTE OR STUDIES ABOUT SAINT COLETTE

Works Written before Her Canonization

ABBEVILLE (S. d'). *Histoire chronologique de la bienheureuse Colette*. Paris, 1619.

Acta Sanctorum quotquot toto orbe coluntur, 67 vols., 1643-1940. March, Vol. I. Pp. 531-626 of *Beata Coleta Virgine*.

ANNIBALI (F.). *Vita della virgine S. Coletta*. Roma, 1805.

CLICHTOU (J.). *Brevis Legenda beata virginis sacris Coletae*. Paris, 1510.

COLLET (P.). *Histoire abrégée de la bienheureuse Colette Boëllet*. Paris, 1771.

ENNTIÈRES (J. d'). *La vie de Sainte Colette*. Tournai, 1646.

FODÉRÉ (J.). *Les vies des très illustres, saintes dames, vierges et martyres de l'Eglise*. Lyon, 1638.

HAREL (E.). *Histoire de l'émigration des religieuses des Pays-Bas en France, et de la translation des reliques de Sainte Colette à Poligny*. Bruxelles, 1785.

LISBONNE (M. de). *Chroniques et institutions de l'Ordre du Père St. François*, 1557 (French translation, 1601).

MARCHE (O. de la). *Mémoires*, mis en lumière par D. Fontenaille. Lyon, 1561.

NOTEL (M.). *Vie de Sainte Colette, vierge de très digne mémoire*. Mars, 1594.

RAES (C.). *Vita della gran serva di Dio: Beata Coletta*. Foligno, 1703.

SAINT LAURENT (Abbé de). *Vie de Sainte Colette, réformatrice de l'Ordre de Sainte Claire*. Manuscript at Poligny, 1630.

SURIUS (L.). *De probatis Sanctorum historiis coloniae Agrippinae*, 1581, vol. IV, 150-88.

Works Written after Her Canonization

BASUCCI (A.). "Coletta Boylet." *Dizionario degli Istituti di Perfezione*, vol. II, col. 1210-1211 and "Clarisse colettine," col. 1132-1134.

BAUDOT (P.) OSB et CHAUSSIN, OSB. *Vie des saints*. Vol. III. Paris, 1941.

BIZOUARD (J. Th.). *Histoire de Sainte Colette et des clarisses de Bourgogne*, Besançon. 1830.

———. *Colette à Auxonne*. Lyon, 1878.

———. *Histoire de Sainte Colette et des clarisses de Franche-Comté*. Besançon, 1888.

CASOLINI (F.). "Réforme de Sainte Colette." *D.S.*, IV. Paris, 1964.

CHAMBERET (C. de). *La parfaite vie de Sainte Colette, petite ancelle de Notre Seigneur*. Paris, 1887.

CHAMOUTON. *Vie admirable de Sainte Colette*. Lons le Saulnier, 1886.

CHEVALIER (F.). *De la Réforme de Sainte Colette et du monastère Sainte Claire de Poligny. Mémoires historiques de Poligny*. Vol. II. Paris, 1956.

CLARISSES D'ENGHIEN. *L'esprit de Sainte Colette dans ses écrits*. Enghien, 1933.

CLARISSES D'ENGHIEN. *Souvenirs de famille*. Enghien, 1933.

DOMAIRON (L.). *Sainte Colette et Jacques de Bourbon*. Cabinet historique, 1864.

DOUILLET (F.). *Sainte Colette, sa vie, son oeuvre*. Translation of the work of Clichtou. Paris, 1869.

DOYON (J.). *La recluse*. Paris, 1984.

FORCEVILLE (P. de). *Sainte Colette de Corbie et son alliance avec Yolande d'Anjou*. Paris, 1958.

GAZIER (G.). *Autour de Sainte Colette de Corbie.* Besançon, 1921.
GERMAIN (A.). *Sainte Colette de Corbie.* Paris, 1903.
GOHIET (F.). *Esquisse historique sur la venue de Colette à Nice.* Paris, 1907.
GONZAGUE (L. de). *Sainte Colette, visage de sainteté.* Avignon, 1943.
GOULVEN (J.). *Le Rayonnement de Sainte Colette.* Paris, 1952.
GREMAUD (J.). *Sainte Colette à Vevey.* Romart, 1865.
GRENIER (P.N.), OSB. "Histoire de Sainte Colette." *Analecta Juris Pontificii,* 1879.
HAENENS (A.). *Spiritualité et culte de Sainte Colette de Corbie.* Archives monastery of Poligny, A. 36.
HUART (A.). *La croix miraculeuse de Sainte Colette.* Poligny, 1868.
HULPIAU (J.). *Après cinq siècles, Colette et son oeuvre.* Bruxelles, 1946.
JUMEL (E.). *Vie de Sainte Colette, réformatrice des trois Ordres de Saint François.* Tournai, 1868.
LATZARUS (M.). *Sainte Colette, qui de nonne devint grande abbesse.* Lyon, 1956.
LEBON (H.). *Vie de Sainte Colette.* Tours, 1846.
LONGPRÉ (E.), OFM. "Colette." *Catholiscisme.* Vol. II. Paris, 1949. Cols. 1298-1300.
LOPEZ (E.). "Colette de Corbie." *Histoire des saints et de la sainteté chrétienne.* Vol. VII. Paris, 1986.
LOPEZ (E.). "Amédée VIII et Colette de Corbie." *Amédée VIII-Félix V, premier duc de savoie et pape (1383-1451).* Actes du colloque international de Ripaille-Lausanne, 1990. Fondation Humbert II et Marie Josée de Savoie. Coll. Bibliothèque historique vaudoise, n° 103 (1992): 317-26.
MARY-FRANCIS (Mother), OSC. *Walled in Light: Saint Colette.* New York, 1959.
ODOARI (G.). "Colettani." *Dizionario degli Istituti di Perfezione.* Vol. II, col. 1211-1217.

PASSERIN (C.). *Un épisode de la vie du cardinal de Challant et de sa rencontre avec Sainte Colette*. Turin.
PELLETIER (H.). *Sainte Colette de Corbie*. Notes de biographies. Bulletin des antiquaires de Picardie, 1947.
PIDOUX (A.). *Sainte Colette*. Coll. "Les saints." Lyon, 1907.
POIROT (C.). *Sainte Colette, sa vie, son oeuvre, ses rencontres*. Besançon, 1947.
PORTIER (F.). *Sainte Colette de Corbie*. Opus Dei, 1968.
PROST (B.). *Documents inédits sur Sainte Colette*, archives historiques et littéraires. 1889-1890.
RAVIER (A.), SJ. *Sur les pas de François et de Claire, Colette de Corbie*. 2nd.ed. Baumes les Dames, 1988.
ROISIN (S.). "Colette." *D.H.G.E.* Vol. XIII, col. 238-46.
ROMAIN. *Sainte Colette, le jardin de Sainte Claire*. Paris, 1937.
SAINTE-MARIE PERRIN (E.). *La belle vie de Sainte Colette de Corbie*. Paris, 1921.
SCHRUNS (L. de). "Sainte Colette de Corbie." *Les Amis de St-François*. N° 42. 1947.
SELLIER (P.), SJ. *Vie de Sainte Colette*. Vol. I et II. Amiens, 1855.
SERAPHINE (Mère), OSC. *Mois de Sainte Colette*. Bordeaux, 1929.
SERENT (A. de), OFM. "Une nouvelle vie de Sainte Colette." *Etudes Franciscaines*, XVII (1907).
SERRIGNY (E.). *Sainte Colette et les cordelières de Sainte Claire à Seurre*. Gray, 1908.
SOMME (M.). "Sainte Colette de Corbie et la réforme franciscaine en Picardie au XVe siècle." *Horizons marins – itinéraires spirituels* (Ve-XVIIIe siècles). Vol. I. *Mentalités et sociétés*. Paris, 1987. 255-64.
UBALD d'ALENÇON, OFMCap. "Documents sur la Réforme de Sainte Colette en France." *A.F.H.*, II (1909): 447-56, 600-12 and III (1910): 82-97.
_____. *Miniatures et document artistiques du Moyen-Age relatifs à Sainte Colette de Corbie*. Archives franciscaines. Paris, Couvin, 1912 (tiré à part).

Van CORSTANJE (C.), CAZAUX (Y.), DECAVELE (J.), DE-ROLEZ (A.). *Vita Sanctae Coletae, 1381-1447.* Présentation de Sainte Colette et des miniatures du manuscrit de la vie de Colette par P. de Vaux, ayant appartenu à Marguerite d'York. Preserved at the monastery of Gand. Tielt, 1982.

VRÉGILLE (Ch. de). *Sainte Colette, vierge et réformatrice de l'Ordre de Sainte Claire.* Besançon, 1929.

YVER (C.). *Sainte Colette, de Corbie, la grande mystique des routes de France.* Paris, 1945.

IV. STUDIES ABOUT THE THREE FRANCISCAN ORDERS

(ANONYMOUS). *Vie de la mère Marie-Dominique dans le monde, Julie Berlemont, abbesse des pauvres claires colettines de Bruges.* Bruges, 1888.

AMBRUN (J. d'), OFM. *Méditation sur la Règle de Sainte Claire.* Annecy, 1877.

AUVERGNE (M. d'). *L'amant rendu cordelier à l'observance d'amour.* Lyon, 1881.

AZCONA (T. de), OFMCap. "Reforma de las clarisas de Cataluña en tiempo de los Reyes Católicos." *Coll. Franc.,* XXVII, 1957.

BEAUREGARD (C. de). *Madame Loyse de Savoie,* d'après un récit du XVe siècle. Paris, 1907.

BEER (F. de), OFM. *La conversion de Saint François selon Thomas de Celano.* Paris, 1963.

BEMBO (I.). *Specchio di Illuminazione, vita di Santa Catarina da Bologna,* 1787. Edizione divulgata a cure delle clarisse del Corpus Domini da Ferrare, collana serafica, I. Ferrare, 1975.

BENAC (J. M.). *La bienheureuse Bonne d'Armagnac-Fezensac, (1434-1457).* Auch, 1919.

BOCQUET (A.), OFMCap. "Les monastères de Clarisses au XIVe siècle dans le Sud-Ouest de la France." *Etudes Franciscaines,* 9 (1958): 1-34, 129-40.

_____. "L'établissement des Clarisses de la Première Règle dans le Midi de la France (1430-1516)." *Coll. Franc.,* XXVIII (1958): 353-73.

_____. "Les statuts conventuels d'un monastère de Clarisses au XIVe siècle." *Jus seraphicum*, 5 (1959): 241-88.

_____. *Les monastères de clarisses fondés au XVIIe siècle dans le Sud-Ouest de la France.* Blois, 1962.

BONAVENTURE (Saint). *La triple voie.* Trans. P. Valentin Breton. Paris, 1942.

_____. *Itinéraire de l'esprit vers Dieu.* Trans. P. Dumery. Paris, 1978.

BONAVENTURE (Saint, attributed to). *Les méditations de la vie du Christ de Jean de Caulibus.* Trans. Abbé P. Bayart. Paris, 1960.

CAPOUE (R. de). *Vie de Sainte Catherine de Sienne.* Paris, 1903.

CASOLINI (F.). *Il protomonastero di santa Chiara d'Assisi.* Milan, 1950.

CASOLINI (F.). "Sainte Claire et les clarisses." In article "Frères mineurs." *D.S.*, vol. V, col. 1401-1422.

CATAPINA da BOLOGNA. *Le sette armi spirituali.* Ed. P. Puliatti. Bologna, 1981.

CENCI (C.). "Privilegi e Costituzioni in un Codice dell'Osservanza di Siena." *A.F.H.*, LXVII (1984).

CEYSSENS (L.). "Les ducs de Bourgogne et l'introduction de l'observance à Malines, 1447-1469." *A.F.H.*, XXX (1937): 391-419.

CHAMOUTON. *Une âme réparatrice. Vie de la vénérable soeur Anathoile-Françoise Thoulier.* Lons-le Saunier, 1888.

CHANAL. *La curieuse histoire du monastère Sainte Claire du Puy.* Le Puy, 1946.

CLARISSE de BESANÇON. *D'hier à demain... les clarisses à Besançon.* Besançon, 1979.

CLARISSE de GRENOBLE. *Histoire de Philippa de Gueldre.* Grenoble, 1889.

CLARISSE de NICE. *Regard sur l'histoire des clarisses.* Vol. II, *pro manuscripto.* Paray-le-Monial, 1981.

Constitutions Générales de l'Ordre de Sainte Claire; ad experimentum, pro manuscripto.

Constitutions Générales de l'Ordre de Sainte Claire. Definitive version promulgated in Latin in 1988. Provisional translation *pro manuscripto.* Nantes, 1989.

DAVAL (G.). *La bienheureuse Bonne d'Armagnac (1434-1457).* Paris, 1912.

DANCOISNE (L.). *Monographie du couvent Sainte Claire de Lille (1453-1792).* Lille, 1866.

DELORME (F.M.), OFM. "Jacques II de BOURBON (1370-1438) fut-il frère mincur, cordelier à Besançon», *F.F.*, vol. VIII. Paris, 1925. 455-59.

DESOBRY (J.). *Un aspect peu connu de la Révolution française de 1789 à Amiens: le monastère des clarisses.* Amiens, 1986.

DORNIER (A.). *Sources de l'histoire franciscaine en Franche-Comté*, Paris, 1927.

FANTOZZI (P.), OFM. "La reforma osservante dei monasteri delle clarisse nell Italia centrale (doc. sec. XV, XVI)." *A.F.H.*, XXIII, fasc. III and IV (1930). Quaracchi 1930 (tiré à part).

FANTOZZI (P.) OFM. "Documenti intorno alla beata Cecilia Cappoli clarissa (1426-1500)." *A.F.H.*, XIX (1926) (tiré à part).

FASSBINDER (M.). *Princesse et moniale: Agnès de Bohème.* Paris, 1957.

FÉDÉRATION de la bienheureuse Vierge Marie Immaculée. *Constitutions pour les monastères de clarisses.* Modène, 1981.

FIRENZE (M. da), OFM. *Libro delle dignità e excellenza del ordine della seraphica madre delle povere donne santa Chiara da Assisi, 1519.* Presented by G. Bocalli. Firenze, 1986.

FODÉRÉ (Y.) OFM. *Narration historique et topographique des convens de l'Ordre de Saint François et monastères Sainte Claire... en la province de Bourgogne.* Vol. 2. Lyon, 1619. 1-271.

FRANCISCA-JOSEPHA (Madre) OSC. *Obras completas de la madre Francisca-Josepha de Castillo.* Bogota, 1968.

FRANCLIEU (A. M. de). *Jeanne Baile et les clarisses de Grenoble (1468-1887).* Lyon, 1887.

FRASCADORE, OFM. *Bibliografia delle bibliografie franciscane. A.F.H.*, 1964.

FROMENTIN. "Histoire des clarisses du Viel Hesdin." *Cabinet historique de l'Artois* Vol. I (1886-87), Vol. II (1887-88).

GAMON (J.), OFM. "Le monastère des clarisses du Puy." *R.H.F.*, Vol. VII. Paris, 1930.

GANTER (E.). *Les clarisses de Genève.* Genève, 1949.

GARREAU (A.). *La bienheureuse Isabelle de France.* Paris, 1955.

GEMELLI (A.), OFM. *Le message de Saint François au monde moderne.* Paris, 1948.

GIEBEN. *Francesco d'Assisi nelle storia.* Vol. I, sec. XIII, XV; Vol. II, sec. XVI, XIX. Parme, 1983.

GILLET (L.). *Histoire artistique des ordres mendiants.* Paris, 1912.

GODIN (A.). *L'homéliaire de Jean Vitrier. Spiritualité franciscaine en Flandre au XVIe siècle.* Genève, 1971.

GOYENS (J.), OFM. "Sex appelationes ad sedam apostolicam factae a clarissis coletinis gandensibus." *A.F.H.*, V (1912): 315-20.

GOYENS (J.), OFM. "Documenta circa clarissas coletanas in Belgio (XV, XVIII)." *A.F.H.*, VIII (1915): 106-45.

GRAF (T.), OFMCap. "Einleitung der Klarissenorden und seine Niederlassungen in der Schweiz." In *Die Franziskaner, die Klarissen und die regulierten Franziskaner-Terziarinnen in der Schweiz.* Helvetia Sacra. Sezione V, vol. 1. Ed. B. Degler-Spengler. (Berne, 1978).

GRATIEN (P.), OFMCap. *Histoire de la fondation et de l'évolution de l'ordre des frères mineurs au XIIIe siècle.* Paris, 1928.

_____. "La fondation des clarisses de l'*Ave Maria* et l'établissement des frères mineurs de l'observance à

_____. *Histoire abrégée de l'Ordre de Sainte Claire*. 2 vols. Lyon, 1906.

MARIE-PASCALE (Sr.), OSC. "Clarisses de France: les federations." In *Claire dans nos fédérations*, bulletin interfédéral des clarisses, n°5-11, *pro manuscripto*. Toulouse, 1985-1988.

MARLIOZ (L. de). *Les clarisses d'Evian les Bains*. Montreuil, 1885.

MARTIN (H.). *Les Ordres mendiants en Bretagne vers 1230-1530*. Paris, 1975.

_____. "Un prédicateur français du XVe siècle, Pierre-aux-Boeufs, et les réalités de son temps." *Franciscanisme et société française. R.H.E.F.*, LXX (1984):107-26.

MEDA (F.). "Una insigne clarissa milanese la beata Felice Meda (1378-1444)." *A.F.H.*, XX (1927)." Quaracchi, 1927 (tiré à part).

MUCCIOLI (M.), OFM. *Santa Catarina da Bologna, mistica del quattrocento*. Bologna, 1963.

NAVATEL (J.), SJ. *Soeur Marie-Colette du Sacré-Coeur, clarisse de Besançon (1857-1905)*. Paris, 1921.

NICOLINI (U.). "Claire d'Assise." In *Dizionario biografico degli Italia*. Vol. XXIV. Rome, 1980.

OMAECHEVARRIA (I.), OFM. *Las clarissas a traves de los siglos*. Madrid, 1972.

Osservanza francescana e Università di Bologna. Cultura laica e religiosa tra Umanesimo e Rinascimento. Bologne, 1988.

PAPASOGLI (G.). *Beata Camilla Battista da Varano*. Assisi, 1959.

PAUVRE CLARISSE (Une). *Fleur du cloître ou vie édifiante de soeur Marie-Céline de la Présentation*. Liège, 1927.

PEANO (P.), OFM. *Le Fonti francescane nel rinnovamento delle clarisse e nei movimenti femminili francescani nel 1400*. Letture delle Fonti francescana altraverso i secole. Roma, 1981. (Tiré à part.)

_____. "L'osservanza in Francia», *Il rinnovamento del Francescanesimo, l'osservanza*, Atti dell'XI Convegno internazionale di Studi Francescani. Assise, 1983. (Tiré à part.)

———. "Les ministres provinciaux de la primitive province de Provence (121/-1517)." *A.F.H.*, LXXIX (1986). (Tiré à part.)

PICCIAFUOCO (U.). *La beata Camilla Battista da Varano.* Camerino, 1983.

PLANCHES (D. des), OFMCap. *La passion renouvelée ou sainte Véronique Giuliani.* Paris, 1927.

———. *Le rachat des âmes. Soeur Anathoile-Françoise Thoulier, Clarisse-Colettine du couvent de Poligny, 1645-1672.* Paris, 1938.

PRATESI (R.). "Le Clarisse in Italia." *Studi e cronaca del VII° Centenario Santa Chiara d'Assisi.* Assisi, 1954.

———. "Nuovi documenti sul B. Alberto da Sarteano († 1450)." *A.F.H.*, LIII (1960): 78-105.

RAMBUTEAU (Ctesse de). *La bienheureuse Varani (1458-1527), comtesse de Camerino et religieuse franciscaine.* Paris, 1906.

Règle de Sainte Claire et Constitutions pour les moniales clarisses de la Réforme de Sainte Colette. Rome, 1932.

Règle de Sainte Claire et Constitutions des Pauvres clarisses de la Rédemption. Nantes, 1936.

Les Règlements et Coutumes des pauvres religieuses du monastère de Sainte Claire de Besançon. Lyon, 1670.

Il Rinnovamento del Francescanesimo: l'Osservanza, Atti dell'XI Convegno Internazionale. Assise, 1985.

Rituel ou Cérémonial à l'usage des monastères des religieuses de Sainte Claire de Besançon. Lyon, 1671.

ROGGEN (H), OFM. "Les clarisses." In article, "François (Ordre de saint). *D.H.G.E.*, vol. 18, col. 958-965.

ROUSSEY (Sr. M. C.). *Regard sur l'histoire des Clarisses.* Vols. 1 and 2, 1982-1984, *pro manuscrito*. On deposit in the monastery of Clarisses, Paray-le-Monial.

SBARALEAE, OFM. "Liste des oeuvres d'Henry de Baume." *Supplementum ad scriptores trium ordinum sancti Francisci.* Vol. I. Paris, 1978.

SCANDELLA (A.E.), OSC. *Ricordanze del monastero di Santa Lucia osc., in Foligno*. Introduction, transcription, notes, and indexes under the care of the monastery in Foligno, Assisi, 1987.

SCHMITT (Cl.), OFM. *Un pape réformateur et un défenseur de l'unité de l'Eglise: Benoît XII et l'Ordre des frères mineurs, 1334-1342*. Quaracchi, 1959.

———. "Lettres des ministres généraux." *A.F.H.*, LXIX, 1976.

SENSI (M.). *Le Osservanze francescane nell' Italia Centrale (secoli XIV-XV)*. Romo, 1945

SESSEVALE (Fr. de). *Histoire générale de l'Ordre de Saint François*. 2 vols. Paris, 1925.

SEVESI (P.), OFM. "Il monastero delle clarisse in san Apollinario di Milano, (doc. sec. XIII, XVIII)." *A.F.H.*, XVIII (1925), XIX (1926). Quaracchi (tiré à part).

THEORET (P.E.). *Claire du Canada*. Valleyfield, 1958.

UBALD d'ALENÇON, OFMCap. "Lettre de Pierre de Vaux aux habitants d'Amiens (1443)." *Etudes Franciscaines*, vol. 23 (1910).

———. "La spiritualité franciscaine XIVe- XVIe s." *Etudes Franciscaines*, vol. 34 (1927).

VAN DIJK (W.), OFMCap. *La volonté de Dieu dans la spiritualité franciscaine*. Rome, 1982.

VANNES (P.L. de), OFM. *Vie de la bienheureuse Marie-Madeleine Martinengo*. Paris, 1901.

VARANI (C.B.), OSC. *Le opere spirituale*, a cura de G. Boccanera, OFM. Jesi, 1958.

———. *Istruzioni al discepolo*. Rome, 1984.

VAUCHEZ (A.). "Influences franciscaines et réseaux aristocratiques dans le Val de Loire: autour de la bienheureuse Jeanne-Marie de Maillé (1331-1414)." *R.H.E.F.*, vol. LXX, n° 184 (1984): 95-106.

———. "La sainteté féminine dans le mouvement franciscain." *Les laïcs au Moyen Age*. Paris, 1987. Pp. 189-202.

———. *Ordini mendicanti e società italiana, XIIIe-XVe secolo*. Milan, 1990.

VEUTHEY (L.). *Jean Duns Scot: sa pensée théologique.* Paris, 1967.

VILLERMONT (Ctesse de). *Sainte Véronique Giuliani.* Paris, 1910.

VRÉGILLE (B. de). "Le bienheureux Henri de Baume (1366-1439) et les documents concernant son culte immemorial." *F.F.* Paris, 1913. (Tiré à part.)

WILMART (A.). "Le grand poème bonaventurien sur les sept paroles du Christ en Croix." *Revue bénédictine*, 47 (1935): 235-78.

ZERMATTEN (M.). *Un Lys de Savoie, la bienheureuse Loyse.* Bruges, 1960.

V. GENERAL BIBLIOGRAPHY

AIGRAIN (R.). *L'hagiographie, ses sources, ses méthodes, son histoire.* Paris, 1953.

ANCELET-HUSTACHE (J.). "Catherine de Sienne." *D.S.*, vol. II, col. 327-351.

ARONDEL (M.). *Rome et le Moyen-Age jusqu'en 1328.* Paris, 1964.

AUBENAS (R.), RICARD (R.). *L'Eglise et la Renaissance (1449-1517)*, Vol. XV. Paris, 1951. In *Histoire de l'Eglise depuis les origines jusqu'à nos jours.* Founded by Fliche (A) and Martin (V).

AUCLAIR (M.). *Vie de Thérèse d'Avila.* Paris, 1960.

BATAILLON (L.). "Le mépris du monde, de l'intérêt d'une discussion actuelle." *Revue des sciences philosophiques et théologiques*, n° 51. Paris, 1967.

BATANY (J.). "L'Eglise et le mépris du monde." *Annales E.S.C.*, n° 20 (1965).

BAUDOT et CHAUSSIN, OSB. *Vie des saints et des bienheureux.* 13 vols. Paris, 1935-1959.

BERENCE (Fr.). *La Renaissance italienne.* Paris, 1955.

BERGSON (H.). *Les deux sources de la morale et de la religion.* Paris, 1969.

BERTHEM (J.). *Sainte Françoise-Romaine et son temps (1384-1440)*. Paris, 1931.

BRAUDEL (F.). *Les structures du quotidien: le possible et l'impossible dans civilisation matérielle, économie et capitalisme, XVe-XVIIIe siècles.* Vol. I. Paris, 1955.

BREMOND (C.), LE GOFF (J.), SCHMITT (J. Cl.). *L'exemplum.* Turnhout: Brepols, 1982. Coll. Typologie des sources du Moyen-Age occidental, fasc. 40.

BRISAY (M. de). *Histoire de la maison de Brisay (IXe siècle à nos jours)*. Part One. Maners, 1889.

BUTLER (C.). *Vidas de los santos.* Vol. I. Mexico, 1967.

CAPOUE (R. de). *Vie de Sainte Catherine de Sienne.* Paris, 1903.

CARTOTTI-ODDASSO (A.). "Caterina Benincasa da Siena." *Bibl. Sanc.* vol. III, col. 996-1044.

CATHERINE DE SIENNE. *Dialogues.* Trans. E. Cartier. Paris, 1884.

_____. *Oraison.* Paris, 1919.

CECCHETTI (I.). "Brigida di Svezia." *Bibl. Sanc.* Vol. III, col. 439-533.

CERTEAU (M. de). "Historicité Mystiques." *Revue des sciences religieuses.* Strasbourg, 1985.

CHARTRES (G. de). *Sanctilogium ou miroir des légendes,* 1340.

CHELINI (J.). *Histoire religieuse de l'occident medieval.* Paris, 1968.

CHESTEL (A.). *L'humanisme italien.* Paris, 1954.

CHEVALIER (F. F.). *Mémoires historiques sur la ville et seigneurie de Poligny.* Vol. II. Lons-le-Saunier, 1769.

CHEVALIER (J.). *Histoire de la pensée.* Vol. II. Paris, 1956.

CHEVALIER (J.), GHEERBRANT (A.). *Dictionnaire des symbols.* Paris, 1982.

CLAUDEL (P.). *Oeuvre poétique.* Paris, 1985. (Coll. La Pléiade.)

COHEN (G.). *La vie littéraire au Moyen-Age.* Paris, 1953.

_____. *Scènes de la vie en France au Moyen-Age.* Ed. F. Lanore. 1964. (Coll. La Vie en France.)

COLLEDGE (E.), WALSH (J.). "Julienne de Norwich." *D.S.*, Vol. VIII, col. 1605-1611.
COMMEAUX (C.). *La vie quotidienne en Bourgogne au temps des ducs de Valois (1364-1477)*. Paris, 1979.
CONTAMINE (P.). *La vie quotidienne pendant la guerre de Cent ans en France et en Angleterre*. Paris, 1976.
DAGENS (J.). *Marguerite de Navarre*. Paris, 1963.
DEBONGNIE (P.). "La stigmatisation." *Etudes carmélitaines*. Vol. II. 1936.
———. "Brigitte de Suède." *D.S.*, vol. I, col. 719-728.
———. "Brigittins-Brigittines." *D.S.*, vol. I, col. 728-731.
———. "Devotio moderna." *D.S.*, vol. III, col. 727-742.
DELARUELLE (E.). "La spiritualité de Jeanne d'Arc." In the *Bulletin de Littérature écclésiastique*. 1964.
———. *La piété populaire au Moyen-Age*. Turin, 1975.
DELARUELLE (E.), LABANDE (E.R.), OURLIAC (P.). *L'Eglise au temps du Grand Schisme et de la crise conciliaire*, t. XIV, 2 vols. Paris, 1962. In *Histoire de l'Eglise depuis les origines jusqu'à nos jours*. Founded by Fliche (A) and Martin (V).
DELATTE (P.). *Commentaire de la Règle de saint Benoît*. Paris, 1913.
DELEHAYE (H.). *Les légendes hagiographiques*. Bruxelles, 1926.
DELORME (Y.). *Les grandes dates du Moyen-Age*. Paris, 1964.
DELORT (R.). *La vie au Moyen-Age. Paris*, 1982.
DELUMEAU (J.). *La Peur en Occident, XIVe-XVIIIe siècles*. Paris, 1978.
———. *Le monastère sainte Catherine de Sienne à Toulouse, un foyer de spiritualité dominicaine au XVIIe siècle*. Toulouse, 1976.
———. *Le péché et la peur, la culpabilisation en Occident du XIIIe au XVIIIe siècle*. Paris, 1983.
DINZELBACHER (P.). "La littérature des révélations au Moyen Age: un document historique." *Revue Historique*, n° 558 (1986): 289-305.

DOMINICAINS (The). *L'ordre des Prêcheurs, présenté par quelques-uns d'entre eux.* Paris, 1980.

DOUILLET (Abbé). *Les gloires de Corbie.* Amiens, 1890.

DUBOIS (dom J.), LEMAITRE (J. L.). *Sources et méthodes de l'hagiographie médiévale.* Paris, 1993.

DUBY (G.), MANDROU (R). *Histoire de la civilisation française (Moyen-Age et XVIe siècle).* Paris, 1958.

DUBY (G.). "L'histoire des systèmes de valeur." *History and Theory.* 1972.

———. *Histoire sociale et idéologie des sociétés.* Paris. 1974.

———. *Le temps des cathédrales: l'art et la société, 980-1420.* Paris, 1976.

———. *Les trois ordres ou l'imaginaire de féodalisme.* Paris, 1978.

———. *Le chevalier, la femme et le prêtre: Le mariage dans la France médiévale.* Paris, 1981.

DUPRONT (A.). "Anthropologie du Sacré et cultes populaires – Histoire et vie du pélerinage en Europe occidentale." *Miscellanea Historica Ecclesiasticae.* 1974.

ECKART (M.). *Oeuvres.* Paris: Aubier, 1942.

EVAGRE LE PONTIQUE. *Traité pratique ou le moine.* Paris, 1971. Sources Chrétiennes, 171.

FAGES (P.). *Histoire de saint Vincent Ferrier.* Vol. II. Paris, 1901.

FAGES (P.). *Procès de canonisation de saint Vincent Ferrier.* Paris, 1904.

———. *Notes et documents de l'histoire de saint Vincent Ferrier.* Paris-Louvain, 1905.

FAGES (P.). *Oeuvres de saint Vincent Ferrier.* Vol. I and II. Paris, 1909.

FAVIER (J.). *La guerre de Cent ans.* Paris, 1980.

FÉDOU (R.). "Jeanne d'Arc vue de Lyon." *Horizons marins, Itinéraires spirituals.* Vol. I. *Mentalités et Sociétés.* Paris, 1987.

FESTUGIERE (A.). *La sainteté.* Paris, 1942.

FIOT (R.). "Saint François de Paule." *D.S.*, vol. V, col. 1040-1051.

FLAVIGNY (Ctesse de). *Sainte Brigitte de Suède.* Paris, 1892.
FONTETTE (M. de). *Les religieuses à l'âge classique du droit canon.* Paris, 1967.
GAIFFEIR (B. de). "Etudes critiques d'hagiographie et d'iconologie." *Subsidia hagiografica,* n° 52. Bruxelles: Société des Bollandistes, 1967.
_____. "La mentalité de l'hagiographie médiévale d'après quelques travaux récents." *Analecta Bollandiana,* 86 (1968): 391-99.
GEON (H.). *Saint Vincent Ferrier.* Paris, 1939.
GERSON (J.). *Oeuvres completes.* Introduction, text and notes by Mgr Glorieux. Tournai, 1960.
GILMORE (M.P.). *Le monde de l'humanisme (1453-1517).* Paris, 1955.
GIRARD (R.). *La violence et le sacré.* Paris, 1972.
_____. *Le bouc émissaire.* Paris, 1982.
GONTHIER (N.). *Lyon, et ses pauvres au Moyen-Age (1350-1500).* Lyon, 1978. 47-50.
GORCE (M.). "Sainte Catherine de Sienne." *D.S.,* vol. II, col. 327-348.
GOUGAUD (L.), OSB. *Dévotions et pratiques ascétiques du Moyen-Age.* Paris, 1925.
GRENIER (D.). *Histoire de la ville et du comté de Corbie des origines à 1400.* Paris, 1910.
GRISWARD (J. H.). *Archéologie de l'épopée médiévale.* Paris, 1981.
GUERANGER (Dom). *Notions sur la vie religieuse des monastiques.* Solesmes, 1950.
GUIGUE (M.C.). "Recherches sur les recluseries de Lyon, leur origine, leur nombre, leur genre de vie." *Bibliothèque Historique du Lyonnais.* Lyon, 1886. 73-117.
HAUCOURT (G. d'). *La vie au Moyen-Age.* Paris, 1972.
HEERS (J.). *Le travail au Moyen-Age.* Paris. 1968.
Histoire et Sainteté, Actes de la 5e Rencontre d'histoire religieuse de Fontevraud. Angers, 1982. Centre de Recherches d'Histoire Religieuse et d'Histoire des Idées, 5.

HOURLIER (O.). *Histoire du droit et des institutions ecclésiastiques.* Vol. X (1140-1378). Paris, 1971.

HUIZINGA (J.). *Le déclin du Moyen Age.* Paris, 1932.

HUYGHE (G.). *La clôture des moniales, des origines à la fin du XIIIe siècle.* Roubaix, 1944.

HUYSMANS (J.K.). *Sainte Lydwine.*

IMBERT (P.). *Les origines de la Réforme.* Vol. II. Paris, 1946.

JANSEN (P.). "Messianisme royal et prophétisme politico-religieux en France." *Mélanges de l'Ecole Française de Rome.* Jan. 1984.

DOLHAGARAY (B.). "Clôture." *Dictionnaire de Théologie catholique*, vol. III/1, col. 244-257.

JOSSE (H.). "Canton de Corbie." *Dictionnaire d'histoire et d'archéologie de la Picardie.* V. II. Paris, Amiens, 1912.

KNOWLES (M. D.), OBOLENSKY (D.). *Le Moyen-Age. Nouvelle histoire de l'Eglise*, Vol. II. Paris, 1968.

LABANDE (E.), RAPP (F.). "France." *D.S.*, vol. V., col. 785-1004.

LE BRAS (G.). *Institutions ecclésiastiques de la Chrétienté médiévale.* vol. XII. Paris, 1959. In *Histoire de l'Eglise depuis les origines jusqu'à nos jours.* Founded by Fliche (A) and Martin (V).

LECLERQ (J.), OSB, VANDENBROUCKE (F.), OSB, BOUYER (L.). *La spiritualité au Moyen-Age.* Paris, 1961.

———. "Clausura." *Dizionario degli Istituti di Perfezione*, vol. II, col. 1166-1174.

LEDWIGE (F.). "Relations de famille dans la correspondance de Gerson." *Revue historique*, n° 549 (1984): 3-23.

LE GOFF (J.). *La civilisation de l'occident medieval.* Paris, 1964.

———. *L'imaginaire medieval.* Paris, 1964.

LEMAITRE (H.). "Les soins hospitaliers à domicile données dès le XVIe siècle par des religieuses franciscaines, les soeurs noires, les soeurs grises, leurs maisons." *R. H. F.,* vol. I (1924): 180-208.

LEMOINE (Dom). *Histoire du droit et des institutions en Occident.* Paris, 1976.

LERAT (L.). *Histoire de la Franche-Comté.* Paris: PUF, 1981.

LOYE (AB). *Histoire de l'Eglise de Besançon.* Vol. III. Besançon, 1902.

LUCE (S.). *Jeanne d'Arc à Domrémy. Recherches critiques sur les origines de la mission de la pucelle.* Paris, 1986.

MABILLE (Mgr). *Journée sanctifiée par les exercices du cloître.* 1864.

MÂLE (E.). *L'art religieux de la fin du Moyen-Age en France.* Paris, 1925.

MARIE-EUGÈNE (Père). *Ton amour a grandi avec moi, un génie spirituel, Thérèse de Lisieux.* Venasque, 1987.

MERTON (T.). *Quelles sont ces plaies? Vie d'une mystique cistercienne, Sainte Lutgarde d'Aywières.* Paris, 1953.

MOLLAT (M.). *Genèse médiévale de la France moderne.* Paris, 1970.

_____. *Etude sur l'histoire de la pauvreté.* Vol. VIII. Paris, 1974.

_____. "Amédée VIII de Savoie." *D.H.G.E.*, vol. XVI, col. 1166-1174.

MOREAU (E. de), SJ. *L'Eglise aux Pays-Bas sous les Ducs de Bourgogne et Charles Quint, 1378-1559.* Vol. IV of *Histoire de l'Eglise en Belgique.* Bruxelles, 1949.

MOULIN (L.). *La vie quotidienne des religieux au Moyen-Age (X^e, XVe siècles).* Paris, 1978.

PACAUT (M.). *Les ordres monastiques et religieux au Moyen-Age.* Paris, 1970.

PARISSE (M.). *Les nonnes au Moyen-Age.* Le Puy, 1983.

PERNOUD (R.). *Jeanne d'Arc, par elle-même et par ses témoins.* Paris, 1975.

PERNOUD (R.). *La femme au temps des cathedrals.* Paris, 1980.

_____. *Les saints au Moyen-Age. La sainteté d'hier est-elle pour aujourd'hui?* Paris, 1984.

PERRIN (J. M.). *Catherine de Sienne, contemplative dans l'action.* Paris, 1961.

PERROY (E.), J. AUBOYER, C. CAHEN, G. DUBY, M. MOLLAT. *Le Moyen-Age.* Vol. III of *Histoire générale des civilisations.* Paris: PUF, 1955.

PEYRONNET (G.). "Rumeurs autour du sacre de Charles VII." *Annales de l'Est*, 33ᵉ année, n°2. Nancy, 1981.

PIERRARD (P.). *Les papes et la France: vingt siècles d'histoire commune*. Paris, 1981.

PIETRI (L.). *Les époques médiévales*. Paris, 1971. Coll. Le Monde et son Hist. IV.

PIRENNE (H.). *Histoire de Belgique*. Vols. I-III. Bruxelles, 1922.

POURRAT (P.). "Gerson et l'appel à la contemplation mystique." *Revue d'apologétique*. Vol. 49 (1929): 427-38.

POURRAT (P.). "Gerson." *Catholicisme*, vol. IV, col. 1893-1895.

QUICHERAT (J.). *Procès de condamnation et de réhabilitation de Jeanne d'Arc*. Vol. III. Paris, 1947. 208-20.

RAPP (F.). *L'église et la vie religieuse en Occident à la fin du Moyen-Age*. Paris: PUF, 1980.

———. "Le XVᵉ siècle." In article "France." *D.S.*, vol. V, col. 880-891.

La règle de saint Benoît. Introduction, translation and notes by A. de Vogüé. Paris, 1972. Sources Chrétiennes, 181-86.

RODOCANACHI (E.). *La femme italienne à l'époque de la Renaissance, sacrée, privée et mondaine*. Paris, 1907.

ROGIER (J.). *Nouvelle histoire de l'Eglise: le Moyen-Age*. Vol. II. Paris, 1968.

SABATIER (R.). *La poésie du Moyen-Age, histoire de la poésie française*. Paris, 1975.

SAINT ANTONIN. *Une règle de vie au XVᵉ siècle*. Trans. Mme Thierard, Paris, 1921.

SAINTYVES (P.). *En marge de la Légende Dorée : songes, miracles et survivances. Essai sur la formation de quelques thèmes hagiographiques*. Paris, 1930.

SALEMBIER (L.). *Le Grand Schisme d'Occident*. Paris, 1902.

SCHELLENBERGER (B.). *Grandeur et risque de la vie monastique*. Paris, 1985.

SALVI (G.), OSB. "La regola di san Benedetto nei primordi dell'ordine di santa Chiara." *Benedictina,* VIII. Rome, 1954. 77-121.

SIGAL (P.A.). *L'homme et le miracle dans la France médiévale (XIe-XIIe siècle).* Paris, 1985.

SOYER (R.P.). *Oeuvres spirituelles.* Paris, 1674.

SUSO (B. H.). *Oeuvres completes.* Translation and notes by J. Ancelet-Hustache. Paris.

THERÈSE DE JESUS. *Oeuvres completes.* Paris, 1949.

TOULOUSE (G. de). *Terrible vision des peines de l'Enfer.* Anvers, 1522.

TOUSSAERT (J.) *Le sentiment religieux, la vie et la pratique religieuse des laïcs en Flandre maritime... aux XIVe, XVe et XVIe siècles.* Paris, 1963.

TUETEY (A.). *Journal d'un bourgeois de Paris (1405-1449).* Paris, 1881.

VAUCHEZ (A.). *La spiritualité du Moyen-Age occidental.* Paris, 1975.

_____. "Genèse et débuts du Grand Schisme d'Occident." *CNRS,* n° 586. Avignon, 1978.

_____. *Religion et société dans l'Occident medieval.* Turin, 1980.

_____. *La sainteté en Occident aux derniers siècles du Moyen-Age d'après les procès de canonisation et les documents hagiographiques.* Rome, 1981. (Bibliothèques des Ecoles Françaises d'Athènes et de Rome, 241).

_____. *Dévotion eucharistique et union mystique chez les saintes de la fin du Moyen-Age.* Sienne, 1982.

_____. "Personalità di mistiche." *Atti del Convegno su la mistica femminile del Trecento.* Todi, 1983.

_____. "Les pouvoirs informels dans l'Eglise aux derniers siècles du Moven-Age: visionnaires, prophètes et mystiques." *Mélanges de l'Ecole française de Rome,* vol. 96 (984): 281-92.

_____. "Jeanne d'Arc et le prophétisme féminin aux XIVe et XVe siècles." *Les laïcs au Moyen Age.* Paris, 1987. 277-86.

_____. "L'hagiographie entre la culture historique et la dynamique narrative." *Vie spirituelle*, Vol. 143, n° 684, 1989.

VERNET (F.). "Brigitte de Suède." *D.S.*, vol. I, col. 1943-1958.

VILLER (M.). "Communion." *D.S.*, vol. II, col. 1209-1234.

VILLON (F.). *Oeuvres poétiques*. Critical edition with notes and glossary by L. Thuasne. Paris, 1923.

VORAGINE (J. de). *La légende dorée*. Paris, 1920.

VI. DICTIONARIES, REVIEWS, AND BULLETINS

Archivo ibero americano. Madrid, 1914-1935 and 1941+.

Archivum franciscanum historicum. Revue des frères mineurs. Quaracchi: Collège Saint-Bonaventure, 1908. Grottaferrata, 1971+.

Bibliotheca Sanctorum. Rome: Istituto Giovanni XXIII, nella Pontifica Università Lateranense, 1960+.

Catholicisme, hier, aujourd'hui et demain. Encyclopedia in 7 volumes, directed by G. Jacquemet. Paris: Letouzey and Ané..

Collectanea Franciscana. Revue de l'Institut des frères capucins. Rome, 1930+.

Dictionnaire d'Histoire et de Géographie Ecclésiastiques. Published under the direction of Mgr. Baudrillart, then R. Aubert. Paris: Letouzey and Ané, 1912+.

Dictionnaire de Spiritualité ascétique et mystique. Published under the direction of M. Viller, then of A. Rayez. Paris: Beauchesne, 1937+.

Dizionario degli istituti di Perfezione. Published under the direction of G. Pelliccia, then of G. Rocca. Rome: Edizioni Paoline, 1974+.

Etudes Franciscaines. Revue mensuelle des frères mineurs capucins. Paris, 1898. Ceased publication in 1977.

Forma sororum, rivista delle clarisse d'Italia. Perugia, 1963.

La France Franciscaine. Lille, 1912; Paris, 1923. Ceased publication in 1939.

Miscellanea Franciscana di Storia, di Lettere, di Arte. Revue de la Faculté de théologie des pères conventuels. Rome.

Pro Monialibus. Bulletin for monasteries of the Order of Friars Minor. Rome, 1967+.

Revue d'histoire franciscaine. Paris. Ceased publication in 1931.

INDEX OF NAMES

A

Adam Mangnier 8, 11, 25, 131, 151
Adrien Peclet 477
Agathange Bocquet 340
Agnès de Baudemont 150
Agnès de Montfaucon 171, 192
Agnès de Vaux 37, 49, 71, 157, 467, 554, 567
Agnes of Assisi 390
Agnes of Prague 88, 193, 198, 210, 219, 253, 294, 333, 413
Alard de la Roche et de Baume 4
Albert de Sarteano xxiii, 325, 344
Alessandro Sforza 394
Alexander IV 339
Alexander V 314, 317
Alexander VI 440, 445, 446, 447, 503
Alexandra 386
Amadeus III 311
Amadeus VIII 52, 311, 312, 437, 458, 491, 554
Amadeus IX 436, 456, 466
Amadeus of Savoy 452
Anathoile Thoulier x, 513, 519
André Vauchez xiii, xx, 2, 53
Angela de Foligno 198, 210, 253, 396
Angela Merici 504, 505
Angelo Clareno 342
Anne (Saint) 71, 93, 113, 121, 306, 375, 436, 438, 469, 494, 501
Anthony of Padua 349
Anthony of Rusconibus 326
Anthony the Great 407
Antoine de Challand 490
Antoine de Massa 323, 357
Antoine de Sainte Anne of Bruges 501
Antoine Ladevèse 477
Antonia of Florence 395

Antonino viii, 376, 378, 379, 380
Augustine 7, 17, 73, 86, 145, 417

B

Baronne de Brisay 47
Bartholomé de Dijon 180, 185, 565
Bartholomé of Dijon 168, 199
Battista de Montefeltro 396
Battista Malatesta 387, 394, 398
Battista Varani ix, 198, 294, 319, 344, 362, 381, 388, 393,
 396, 397, 400, 404, 423, 429, 455, 457, 520
Benedict XII 248, 255, 262, 264, 284, 343, 349, 368
Benedict XIII 50-53, 55-57, 91, 103, 122, 144, 152, 190, 311,
 313, 317, 323, 343, 356, 368, 437, 454, 469, 485, 488-89,
 513, 554, 569, 579. 584
Benoît de Saint-Philadelphe 504
Bernardino of Siena xxiii, 4, 291, 326, 347, 354, 383, 384,
 386, 388, 390, 396, 402, 416, 421, 422, 432, 492
Bernard 17, 281, 289, 304-05, 309, 318, 417, 444-45, 453,
 465, 554
Bernardino of Foligno 399, 400
Blanche de Savoie 306
Blanche of Geneva vii, xix, 310-13, 356, 465, 491
Blanche of Savoy 491
Bonaventure ii, 6, 14, 70, 73, 77, 98, 119, 187, 357, 489, 490,
 592
Boniface VIII 255, 256, 295, 392
Bonne d'Armagnac ix, 438, 453, 455, 577, 578
Bridget of Sweden xviii, xxiii

C

Calixtus III 432
Cassian 396
Catherine de la Marche 453, 466, 570
Catherine de Longueville 272, 435, 566
Catherine de Saulx 456, 458, 466

Catherine of Bologna viii, 23, 127, 198, 269, 272, 282, 285, 319, 346, 381, 391, 393, 396-97, 400, 402-03, 420, 429, 454-55, 478, 503
Catherine of Siena xviii, xxiii, 53, 147, 198, 535
Catherine Vigri 386, 402
Cecilia Coppoli 386, 389, 394-95, 398-400
Cecilia de Foligno 395
Cecilia of Florence 363
Celano 6, 14, 15, 17, 20, 79, 80, 82, 83, 85, 137-38, 187, 231-32, 249, 253, 414, 577
Cesare Borgia 424
Charles Borromeo 286, 391, 481
Charles II 431
Charles III 304
Charles the Bold xxi, 435, 456, 457
Charles V 450, 472, 488
Charles VI 310
Charles VII xix, 62, 167, 169, 170, 305, 308, 311, 566, 590
Charles VIII 454, 461
Clare vi-xiii, xv, xvi-xvii, xix, 1, 4, 6, 15-17, 20, 23, 25-26, 28, 42-43, 46, 49, 51, 54, 56-59, 75-76, 79, 80, 82, 85, 88-90, 93, 102, 118, 122-24, 137-38, 146, 157, 177, 179, 180-81, 186, 193, 197-98, 200, 210-11, 213-28, 230-40, 242-58, 261-62, 268-72, 274-75, 281-82, 284-85, 293-94, 296-98, 309, 315, 321, 326, 333-37, 339, 343, 346, 348-53, 355, 362-63, 365-68, 372-73, 383-97, 399, 400, 403, 413-17, 424, 429, 432-33, 439, 446, 448, 453, 460-61, 463, 477, 479, 480, 513, 522, 527-29, 533-34, 536, 562, 572
Claude Champion 442
Claude d'Aix 304
Claude Roussillon 475
Clement VI 342
Clement VII 311, 356
Clement VIII 492, 502
Clement XI 403
Colette i-vii, ix-xi, xiii-xxv, 1-25, 27-30, 33-40, 42-59, 61-66, 68-73, 76-84, 87-95, 97-106, 109-16, 118-37, 140-42,

144-47, 149-63, 165-73, 175-200, 202-07, 209-11, 213, 226, 235-72, 274-75, 277-80, 282-92, 297-98, 301, 303, 305-35, 341-53, 355-60, 365, 367, 369-72, 374-75, 378, 380-84, 397, 399-401, 403-10, 412-13, 415-23, 425-29, 431-32, 434-38, 441-55, 457-63, 465-70, 472-73, 477-80, 482, 484-509, 512, 515, 517, 525-26, 529-35, 540, 554-76, 581-83

D

Dominic 41, 42, 43, 334
Dominique de Gubernatis 339
Dominique de Leonessa 424

E

Edith Stein 536
Éléonore 304-05, 309-10, 500
Élisabeth Cabin 477
Élisabeth de Bavière 42, 43, 156-57, 465, 493
Elisabeth Lopez i, xv, xvi
Élisabeth of Navarre 462
Elisabeth of the Trinity 517
Elizabeth de Bavière 311
Émile Mâle 364
Emmanuel Mounier 523
Étienne de Juilly 487-88, 492
Etiennette Hannequin 466
Eugene IV 155, 169, 235-36, 311, 314, 318, 325, 330, 343, 345, 354, 442-44
Eustachia de Calafato 387, 395, 401

F

Felicia Meda 386-87, 393-94, 398
Felix V 52, 106, 134, 311, 314, 325, 344, 489
Francesca of Assisi 401
Franceschina Guissana 394
Francesco Sforza 311
Frances of Jesus 440

Francis xii, xvii, 6, 13-14, 17, 23, 25-27, 29, 31-32, 40-43, 46, 47, 51, 56, 65, 70, 74, 79, 81-82, 85, 88-89, 93, 98, 101-02, 104, 109-10, 119-21, 123, 125, 137-38, 142, 157, 178-80, 186-87, 189, 201, 204, 210-11, 213-16, 218-23, 225, 227, 229-32, 236, 247-50, 259, 261, 270, 275, 289, 293, 296, 298, 309, 321, 326, 334-35, 341, 349, 350, 353, 360-63, 365-71, 390, 400, 405, 411, 416, 433, 443, 457, 461, 481, 489, 516, 523, 528-29, 534, 536-37, 561-63, 572

Francisco de Osuna 253
François Caracciolo 504
François Claret 39-40, 92, 133, 158, 279
François de Gonzague 453, 490
François des Maretz 4
Françoise de la Rochefoucault 434
Françoise du Bourg 467
François Retou 477

G

Gaspard Armand XVIII 477
Gerson viii, 11, 358, 372-74, 380, 382, 589, 591
Giovanni da Fano 424-25, 429
Gregory IX 214, 250, 387, 390
Gregory the Great 396, 457
Gregory XI 342, 343
Gregory XII 317
Gregory XVI 455
Guillaume de Bousière 150
Guillaume d'Estouteville 434
Guillemette 158-59, 465, 467, 554

H

Henri de Berghes 435
Henri Suso xxiii
Henry de Baume viii, xviii, 4, 39, 40, 42, 44, 48, 55, 58, 75, 81, 123, 129, 130, 152, 166-67, 190, 195, 202, 261-62, 272, 290, 298, 305, 308, 310, 312, 315, 323, 343, 346,

355-58, 366-68, 373-75, 444, 465, 520, 534, 567, 569, 570-71, 581, 583
Hugolin Lippens 444
Hugolino 214-15, 217-20, 222, 224, 232-33, 245-46, 256, 534
Hugues de Baume 358
Hugues de Chalon 456, 466
Huguette du Tarte 467
Humbert of Villars 312
Hyacinthe Mariscotti 504

I

Iago de Sarzuela 439
Illuminata Bembo viii, ix, 23, 391, 404, 420, 421, 422
Innocent III 51, 214
Innocent IV 54, 215, 217-22, 224, 226, 232, 234-35, 245-46, 250-51, 254, 263, 349
Isabeau 304-05, 432, 453, 465, 467, 490, 554
Isabelle of France 216, 254
Isabelle of Portugal 340

J

Jacopone de Todi 404
Jacques de Bourbon vii, 303-06, 308, 310, 318, 320, 453, 465, 467-68, 493, 567, 571, 574, 580
Jacques Fodéré 490
Jacques Guiot 150-51
James xxiii, 113, 130, 134, 149, 160, 338, 437
James of the Marches xxiii
Jean Coeur 437
Jean Daza 440-41
Jean de Boissy 54, 568
Jean de la Vallée 342, 384
Jean d'Estouteville 434
Jean Foucault 126, 155
Jean Guiot 151-52, 489
Jean Maubert vii, 320, 325, 327-29, 332, 443
Jeanne Astoux 340
Jeanne Baile 437, 579

Jeanne de Caulincourt 467
Jeanne de Famechon 467
Jeanne de Maillé 52, 304, 308, 310
Jeanne de Montbéliard 312, 554
Jeanne Labeur 149, 449, 567
Jeanne Marie de Maillé 308
Jeanne of Naples 303, 320
Jeanne of Sicily 340
Jean Philippe 469
Jean Pinet 152
Jean Pourcelot 477
Jehan Frosseau 191
Jehan Lainé vi, 171, 190, 198
Jehan Pinet 31
Jehan Toursiau 40
Joan of Arc xviii, 13, 46, 53, 62, 146-47, 153, 434
John Capistrano vii, viii, xxiii, 155, 170, 261, 263, 269, 303, 321, 325-26, 330, 343-49, 352, 361, 367, 370-71, 382-83, 388, 395, 424, 428, 442-43
John the Baptist 7, 8, 17-18, 20, 25, 38, 42, 45, 157
John the Evangelist 66, 93, 113, 121-22, 151, 205
John the Fearless 305, 310-11, 313-14, 554
John XXII 341
John XXIII 314, 317
Joseph Goulven xxii
Joseph II 498, 504, 555
Josse Clichtou x, 488
Julien Cesarini 318

K

Katerine de la Verdure 32
Katherine Rufiné v, 55, 153, 155-56, 313, 356, 442, 493-94

L

Laurence the Magnificent 456
Laurent Surius 487
Lefèvre d'Etaples 488
Leo X 331, 389, 449, 462

Perrine xv, xxi, 1, 4-16, 23-26, 28-31, 35-40, 43-45, 48-52, 58, 61-65, 69-73, 75, 77-79, 81-84, 86-94, 101, 103-04, 110-13, 116-17, 122, 126, 130-34, 136-37, 139-41, 144, 149-51, 154-55, 157, 161, 168, 204, 312, 325, 330, 356, 420, 450, 452, 465-66, 488-89, 494, 498, 500, 535, 569, 570
Peter of Rheims 172
Peter Olivi 342
Pétronelle Van de Maele of Bruges 501
Philibert Obmexer 504
Philip II 177, 450
Philippa de Gueldre ix, 432, 450, 455, 456, 458, 466, 469, 578, 580
Philippe de Gueldre 435
Philippe de Saveuse 169, 177, 434, 554
Philippe of Savoy 436
Philippe the Good xxi, 435, 554
Philippine de Chalon 466
Philip the Bold 356
Philip the Good 170, 314, 325, 344
Philip the Handsome 338
Pierre d'Ailly 93
Pierre de Lendresse 72
Pierre de Lyon 7, 15
Pierre de Rains 3, 7, 15, 40, 116, 141, 194, 195, 209
Pierre de Vaux x, xv, xvi, xxi, 1-7, 11-16, 18, 20, 22-24, 26, 28-30, 33-53, 55, 58-59, 61-64, 66, 68-73, 77-79, 81, 83-92, 94, 97-99, 101-02, 104-06, 109-14, 116, 121-22, 126-27, 130-35, 137-41, 143-47, 149-50, 152, 154-55, 157-59, 161, 166, 168, 171, 182-83, 194, 198, 204, 206-07, 209, 240, 253, 261-62, 275, 279, 289, 312, 315-17, 325-29, 332-33, 356-57, 359, 364, 369, 373-75, 379, 405-06, 408-10, 413, 420-21, 423, 426-27, 431-32, 442, 450, 467, 475, 487-89, 492, 494-95, 497, 500, 505, 535, 565, 569-70, 584
Pierre III 438
Pierre Rosselin 447
Pietro di Mogliano 424
Pius II 235, 440, 490

Pius XII 519, 525, 532, 536
Poor Clares xv, xvii, xix, 4, 29, 240, 337, 366, 367, 435, 536

R

Raphaël 397
René I 431
René II 456
Roberte de Bousière 150
Ruysbroek xxiii

S

Sancha of Naples 340
Serafina 394
Sixtus IV 390, 433, 439, 444, 446
Suave 387
Sylvère d'Abbeville x, 156, 291, 469, 472, 484, 493-96, 503
Sylvester 156

T

Tauler xxiii
Teresa of Avila 75, 128, 131, 135-36, 177, 181, 187, 193, 199, 206, 209, 253, 296, 327, 378, 411, 428, 470, 500, 515-16, 522, 534, 535
Tharin de Besançon 496
Thérèse of Lisieux 104, 516, 521, 523
Thomas à Kempis 357
Thomas of Canterbury 421

U

Ubald d'Alençon xv, 3, 320, 322, 359, 442, 496, 569, 570
Ubertino da Casale 342, 363
Urban IV xvi, 123, 216, 232, 234, 254, 294, 338-40, 355, 383-86, 392, 394, 534
Urban V xix
Urban VI xxii
Urban VIII 455, 502

V

Vincent Ferrier 22, 71, 133, 587, 588

W

Wadding x, xii, 41, 43, 291, 315, 321, 339-40, 343, 345, 354, 392, 394-95, 398, 401, 435, 437-38, 460, 491-92, 503
William of Casals vii, 235, 265, 318, 320-23, 325-27, 344, 357, 393, 398, 400
William of Ockham xxiv

Y

Yolande of France 452, 456

Z

Zachary 43

Index of Places

A

Abbeville x, 156, 262, 291, 326, 445, 469, 472, 484, 493, 494-96, 500, 503

Aigueperse 310, 438, 509, 554, 569

Aix-en-Provence 441, 555

Albi 307, 318, 446, 461, 462

Alençon xv, 3, 4, 14, 54-55, 65, 165, 261, 312, 317, 320, 322-23, 328, 356, 359, 442, 446, 453, 456, 462, 466-67, 488, 496, 498, 508-09, 567, 569, 570, 580

Alicante 439, 555

Amiens xiii, 3, 42, 54, 56, 65-66, 131, 149, 150, 156, 158, 160, 169, 173, 176-77, 179, 261-62, 291, 305, 313-15, 326, 332, 356, 433-35, 442, 445, 449, 452-53, 466-68, 475, 489, 493, 495, 502-03, 505, 507-09, 554-55, 565, 568-70, 572, 576, 578, 584, 587, 589

Anvers 434, 510, 555, 591

Aquila 384, 389, 395

Arras 140, 170, 314, 434-35, 508-09, 525, 527, 555

Auxonne 155, 165, 189, 310, 313, 316-17, 359, 360, 490, 554-55, 574

Avignon 55, 311, 317, 337, 462, 563, 575, 592

Azille 309, 508-09, 518

B

Bar-le-Duc 462

Basel 236, 311

Besançon viii, xiii, 22, 52, 71, 87, 90, 130, 135, 137, 149, 153, 161, 165, 167-70, 172-73, 194, 196, 201-02, 206, 211, 272, 290, 304, 306-07, 310, 313, 316-17, 320, 357-59, 436, 442, 448, 451, 461, 466-67, 473, 476-79, 484, 489-90, 496, 498, 507-08, 519, 525-26, 528, 554-55, 563, 565-70, 572, 574-76, 578, 582-83, 590

Beuvray 261

Béziers 309, 508-09, 554-55

Bologna viii, 23, 127, 198, 269, 272, 282, 285, 319, 340, 346, 354, 381, 387, 389, 391, 393, 396-97, 400, 402-04, 420, 429, 454-55, 478, 503, 577-78, 582
Bourg-en-Bresse 311, 436, 555
Bourges 437, 441, 555
Bruges 55, 130, 186, 235, 240, 246, 264, 272, 283, 290, 321-22, 324, 372, 374, 434-35, 501-02, 509-11, 518, 555, 566, 571-72, 577, 581, 584
Brussels 420, 447, 462, 510

C

Cambrai 435, 509, 555
Camerino 344, 388, 423-25, 582-83
Castres 145, 305-06, 309, 357, 446-48, 454, 554-55
Chambéry 312, 316, 436-38, 452, 509, 555
Chariez 261, 307
Châteauroux 330
Constance xxii, 155-56, 314, 317, 326, 442
Corbie i, ii, v, xix, xxi, xxiv, 8, 9, 11-13, 28-30, 34-36, 44, 48, 54, 65, 87, 106, 113, 130, 132, 149-53, 161, 167, 169, 173, 175, 177-79, 181, 184-86, 193, 206, 226, 277, 312, 314-15, 332, 458, 475, 488-89, 493, 497, 503, 566, 568, 570, 574-76, 587-89

D

Dijon 155, 168, 180, 185, 199, 313, 517, 565
Dinan 432-33, 459, 555
Dole 126, 155-56, 159, 261, 326-27, 471, 476

F

Fermo 424
Ferrara 318, 320, 346, 386-87, 389, 391, 402, 404, 420-21
Florence x, 54, 353, 363, 376, 395, 404, 489, 492, 572
Foligno viii, 198, 210, 253, 386-87, 389, 395-96, 399-400, 574, 583

G

Gand xiii, 65, 140-41, 149-50, 153-54, 159-60, 166-68, 170-72, 179, 181, 183-85, 194, 196, 198-99, 201-02, 206-07,

210, 272, 278, 280, 286, 290-92, 306, 309, 313-14, 358, 367, 431, 434-36, 448-49, 454, 457-58, 488, 492, 498-99, 500-11, 554-55, 565-70, 573, 576
Gandia 438-40, 511, 555
Geneva vii, xix, 130, 157, 236, 306, 310-13, 356, 436, 438, 452, 465, 474, 491, 555
Gien 438, 555
Girona 439, 440
Gouda 462
Grenoble 432, 437-38, 508-09, 555, 578-79

H

Hesdin v, 4, 31, 35, 37, 42, 56, 111, 133, 140, 149, 154, 156, 158-60, 170, 173, 182, 288, 313-14, 356, 435, 467, 470, 472, 493-94, 498, 502, 509, 554-55, 568, 579

L

Languedoc 34, 342, 554
Le Puy xiii, 165, 167, 171-72, 179, 190-92, 194-95, 198-98, 201, 290, 316, 438, 448, 450-51, 466-67, 474-78, 485, 507-09, 554-55, 566, 568-69, 578-79, 590
Lézignan 305, 307, 309, 431, 439-39, 441, 453, 454, 554, 555
Liège 434, 522, 555, 580, 582
Liesdin 140
Lille 340, 462, 508, 518, 578, 593
Longchamp 216, 224, 246, 251, 255-59, 262-64, 338-39, 460, 534
Lyon ii, xiii, 7, 16, 32, 46, 62, 290, 310, 358, 395, 437, 449, 478, 490, 496, 509, 518, 569, 573-75, 577, 579, 581-83, 588

M

Malines 462, 511, 578
Mantua 344, 347, 383, 386, 389, 394-95
Marseille ix, 340, 441, 555
Messina 387, 389, 395

Metz 33, 459-61, 561
Middelbourg 462, 581
Milan viii, 286, 311, 355, 385-88, 390, 393-94, 481, 578, 584
Mirebeau 55, 154, 313, 327, 342, 356
Moncel 34
Montbrison 316, 438, 555
Moulins 310, 316, 438, 448, 491, 509, 554-55
Murat 448

N

Nancy 431, 457, 518, 580, 590
Nantes 432-33, 459, 524, 555, 578, 581, 583
Naples 224, 303-04, 320, 338, 340, 554
Nice iii, 4, 5, 39, 47-48, 50, 54-56, 63, 101, 103, 134, 152-53,
    175, 183, 311-13, 317, 356, 489, 575
Noyon 56, 152

O

Orbe 145, 267, 312, 316, 436, 456, 466, 509, 554-55

P

Padua 326, 349
Paris xiii, xxii, 6, 11-13, 22, 32-33, 38, 53-54, 56-57, 62, 70,
    80, 82, 85, 93, 98, 102, 119, 125, 137-38, 169, 177, 183,
    193, 215, 281, 304-05, 307, 312-13, 338, 341, 358, 364,
    453, 460-61, 467, 488-89, 493, 496, 508-09, 519, 521,
    570-93
Pavia 384, 457
Péronne 130, 152, 435, 467, 555
Perpignan ix, 440, 459, 555
Perugia 384, 385
Pesaro 384-85, 387, 393-95, 398
Pisa 317
Poitou 55, 313, 356
Poligny xiii, 39, 49, 66, 69, 72, 99, 135, 149-50, 153, 159,
    161, 165, 169, 173, 262, 272, 278, 280, 285-87, 306, 310,
    313, 316, 359, 436, 442, 445, 466-68, 470-73, 475-76,

478, 482-83, 485, 493, 496, 498, 500-02, 504, 507-09, 512-13, 515, 519, 525-26, 528-29, 554-55, 564-70, 573-75, 583, 586
Pont-à-Mousson 431-32, 450, 456, 468-69, 554-55
Pont-Saint-Maxence 28
Prague 54, 88, 193, 198, 210, 219, 253, 294, 333-34, 413

R

Rabastens 446
Ravenna 384
Rheims 3, 172, 294
Ripaille 311-12, 458, 575
Rodez 446
Rome 2, 3, 23, 68, 112, 134, 141, 155, 166, 192, 198, 240, 278, 350, 356-57, 395, 441, 445, 447, 489, 492, 525, 563, 571-72, 581-85, 589, 591-93
Rouen 434, 459, 555
Rumilly 312-13

S

Saint Omer 314
Saint-Omer 328
Salins 473, 475-78, 484, 509
Savona 54, 384
Sellières 261
Setubal 439, 555
Seurre 71, 310, 313, 316, 436, 438, 491, 554-55, 576

T

Thonon 320, 323, 325
Tongres 510-11
Toulouse 34, 320, 322, 341, 447, 453, 462, 508, 524, 582, 587
Tournai 290-91, 507, 509-11, 573, 575, 588
Tours 342, 518, 575
Trent 232, 286, 291, 470, 472-75, 563
Treviso 384

U

Urbino 385, 388, 390, 395, 423-24

V

Valencia 438-39, 580
Valladolid 440
Verona 384
Vevey 172, 312, 316, 436, 452, 458, 509, 554-55, 575